序 言

　　「指定科目考試」開辦至今，已經有十年的歷史。這些試題內容，是命題教授們的心血結晶，每一道題目都具有代表性，非常重要。這些題目是未來考生們準備指考時，不可或缺的參考資料。

　　「指定科目考試」實施以來，考試的題型和方向大抵已有脈絡可循。就題型來說，選擇題部分沒有太大的變動；而非選擇題部分，則可能出現簡答題、中翻英、看圖說故事、書信等。至於出題方向，考生要特別注意近半年來的重大新聞議題；要應付層出不窮的新聞考題，多做最新試題是不二法門，像「劉毅英文家教班」的學生，每週都參加模擬考試，每次考試都考世界最新動態的相關文章，不管學測題目再怎麼變，「劉毅英文家教班」的學生，永遠是最後的贏家。

　　「歷屆指考英文科試題詳解」，特別將歷屆指考英文科試題全部收錄在內，且針對每一道題目，都有最完善的講解，讀者們不需另外花時間查字典。編者的目標，就是幫助考生們以最有效率的方式，研讀最重要的資料。另外，本書還附上「電腦統計歷屆指定科目考試單字和成語」，考生們只要善加利用這些資料，並在考前將常考的單字及片語背熟，就能把英文這一科，變成幫助你得高分的秘密武器。

　　本書編校製作過程嚴謹，但仍恐有疏失之處，尚祈各界先進不吝指正。

編者　謹識

CONTENTS

100 年大學入學指定科目考試試題
英文考科

第壹部分：選擇題（佔 72 分）

一、詞彙題（10 分）

說明： 第 1 題至第 10 題，每題 4 個選項，其中只有 1 個是最適當的選項，畫記在答案卡之「選擇題答案區」。各題答對得 1 分，未作答、答錯、或畫記多於 1 個選項者，該題以零分計算。

1. Many people think cotton is the most comfortable _____ to wear in hot weather.
   (A) fabric　　(B) coverage　　(C) software　　(D) wardrobe

2. Because of the engine problem in the new vans, the auto company decided to _____ them from the market.
   (A) recall　　(B) clarify　　(C) transform　　(D) polish

3. After a day's tiring work, Peter walked _____ back to his house, hungry and sleepy.
   (A) splendidly　　(B) thoroughly　　(C) wearily　　(D) vaguely

4. In team sports, how all members work as a group is more important than how they perform _____.
   (A) frequently　　(B) typically　　(C) individually　(D) completely

5. Despite her physical disability, the young blind pianist managed to overcome all _____ to win the first prize in the international contest.
   (A) privacy　　(B) ambition　　(C) fortunes　　(D) obstacles

6. Each of the planets in the solar system circles around the sun in its own _____, and this prevents them from colliding with each other.
   (A) entry　　(B) haste　　(C) orbit　　(D) range

7. Professor Wang is well known for his contributions to the field of economics. He has been _____ to help the government with its financial reform programs.

 (A) recruited   (B) contradicted (C) mediated (D) generated

8. Most earthquakes are too small to be noticed; they can only be detected by _____ instruments.

 (A) manual   (B) sensitive   (C) portable   (D) dominant

9. With Wikileaks releasing secrets about governments around the world, many countries are worried that their national security information might be _____.

 (A) relieved   (B) disclosed   (C) condensed (D) provoked

10. I'm afraid we can't take your word, for the evidence we've collected so far is not _____ with what you said.

 (A) familiar   (B) consistent   (C) durable   (D) sympathetic

二、綜合測驗（10 分）

說明：　第 11 題至第 20 題，每題 1 個空格。請依文意選出最適當的 1 個選項，畫記在答案卡之「選擇題答案區」。各題答對得 1 分，未作答、答錯、或畫記多於 1 個選項者，該題以零分計算。

第 11 至 15 題為題組

  Handling customer claims is a common task for most business firms. These claims include requests to exchange merchandise, requests for refunds, requests that work ___11___, and other requests for adjustments. Most of these claims are approved because they are legitimate. However, some requests for adjustment must be ___12___, and an adjustment refusal message must be sent. Adjustment refusals are negative messages for the customer. They are necessary when the customer is ___13___ or when the vendor has done all that can reasonably or legally be expected.

An adjustment refusal message requires your best communication skills ___14___ it is bad news to the receiver. You have to refuse the claim and retain the customer ___15___. You may refuse the request for adjustment and even try to sell the customer more merchandise or service. All this is happening when the customer is probably angry, disappointed, or inconvenienced.

11. (A) is correct　(B) to be correct　(C) is corrected　(D) be corrected
12. (A) retailed　(B) denied　(C) appreciated　(D) elaborated
13. (A) at fault　(B) on call　(C) in tears　(D) off guard
14. (A) till　(B) unless　(C) because　(D) therefore
15. (A) by and large　(B) over and over
　　(C) at the same time　(D) for the same reason

第 16 至 20 題為題組

People may express their feelings differently on different occasions. Cultures sometimes vary greatly in this regard. A group of researchers in Japan, ___16___, studied the facial reactions of students to a horror film. When the Japanese students watched the film ___17___ the teacher present, their faces showed only the slightest hints of reaction. But when they thought they were alone (though they ___18___ by a secret camera), their faces twisted into vivid mixes of anguished distress, fear, and disgust.

The study also shows that there are several unspoken rules about how feelings should be ___19___ shown on different occasions. One of the most common rules is minimizing the show of emotion. This is the Japanese norm for feelings of distress ___20___ someone in authority, which explains why the students masked their upset with a poker face in the experiment.

16. (A) as usual　(B) in some cases　(C) to be frank　(D) for example
17. (A) of　(B) as　(C) from　(D) with

18. (A) were being taped   (B) had taped
     (C) are taping   (D) have been taped
19. (A) rarely   (B) similarly   (C) properly   (D) critically
20. (A) with the help of   (B) in the presence of
     (C) on top of   (D) in place of

三、文意選填（10分）

說明： 第21題至第30題，每題1個空格。請依文意在文章後所提供的(A)到
　　　 (L)選項中分別選出最適當者，並將其英文字母代號畫記在答案卡之
　　　 「選擇題答案區」。各題答對得1分，未作答、答錯、或畫記多於1個
　　　 選項者，該題以零分計算。

第21至30題為題組

    The history of the written word goes back 6,000 years. Words express feelings, open doors into the __21__, create pictures of worlds never seen, and allow adventures never dared. Therefore, the original __22__ of words, such as storytellers, poets, and singers, were respected in all cultures in the past.

    But now the romance is __23__. Imagination is being surpassed by the instant picture. In a triumphant march, movies, TV, videos, and DVDs are __24__ storytellers and books. A visual culture is taking over the world—at the __25__ of the written word. Our literacy, and with it our verbal and communication skills, are in __26__ decline.

    The only category of novel that is __27__ ground in our increasingly visual world is the graphic novel. A growing number of adults and young people worldwide are reading graphic novels, and educators are beginning to realize the power of this __28__. The graphic novel looks like a comic book, but it is longer, more sophisticated, and may come in black and white or multiple __29__ and appear in many sizes. In fact, some of the most interesting, daring, and most heartbreaking art being created right now is being published in graphic novels. Graphic novels ___30___ the opportunity to examine the increasingly visual world of communications today while exploring serious social and literary topics. The graphic novel can be used to develop a sense of visual literacy, in much the same way that students are introduced to art appreciation.

(A) expense　　(B) fading　　(C) colors　　(D) research　　(E) replacing
(F) offer　　(G) users　　(H) rapid　　(I) gaining　　(J) medium
(K) circular　　(L) unknown

四、篇章結構（10 分）

說明：　第 31 題至第 35 題，每題 1 個空格。請依文意在文章後所提供的 (A) 到
　　　　(F) 選項中分別選出最適當者，填入空格中，使篇章結構清晰有條理，
　　　　並將其英文字母代號標示在答案卡之「選擇題答案區」。每題答對得
　　　　2 分，未作答、答錯、或畫記多於 1 個選項者，該題以零分計算。

第 31 至 35 題為題組

The effect of bullying can be serious and even lead to tragedy. Unfortunately, it is still a mostly unresearched area.

___31___ That year two shotgun-wielding students, both of whom had been identified as gifted and who had been bullied for years, killed 13 people, wounded 24 and then committed suicide. A year later an analysis by the US government found that bullying played a major role in more than two-thirds of the campus violence.

___32___ Numerous dictators and invaders throughout history have tried to justify their bullying behavior by claiming that they themselves were bullied. ___33___ Although it is no justification for bullying, many of the worst humans in history have indeed been bullies and victims of bullying.

Since bullying is mostly ignored, it may provide an important clue in crowd behavior and passer-by behavior. ___34___ Many of them have suggested bullying as one of the reasons of this decline in emotional sensitivity and acceptance of violence as normal. When someone is bullied, it is not only the bully and the victim who are becoming less sensitive to violence. ____35____ In this sense, bullying affects not only the bullied but his friends and classmates and the whole society.

(A) Hitler, for example, is claimed to have been a victim of bullying in his childhood.

(B) Campus bullying is becoming a serious problem in some high schools in big cities.

(C) The friends and classmates of the bully and the victim may accept the violence as normal.

(D) Research indicates that bullying may form a chain reaction and the victim often becomes the bully.

(E) Psychologists have been puzzled by the inactivity of crowds and bystanders in urban centers when crimes occur in crowded places.

(F) The link between bullying and school violence has attracted increasing attention since the 1999 tragedy at a Colorado high school.

五、閱讀測驗（32 分）

說明： 第 36 題至第 51 題，每題請分別根據各篇文章的文意選出最適當的 1 個選項，畫記在答案卡之「選擇題答案區」。各題答對得 2 分，未作答、答錯、或畫記多於 1 個選項者，該題以零分計算。

第 36 至 39 題為題組

Since the times of the Greeks and Romans, truffles have been used in Europe as delicacies and even as medicines. They are among the most expensive of the world's natural foods, often commanding as much as US$250 to US$450 per pound. Truffles are actually mushrooms, but unusual ones. They live in close association with the roots of specific trees and their fruiting bodies grow underground. This is why they are difficult to find.

Truffles are harvested in Europe with the aid of female pigs or truffle dogs, which are able to detect the strong smell of mature truffles underneath the surface of the ground. Female pigs are especially sensitive to the odor of the truffles because it is similar to the smell given off by male pigs. The use of pigs is risky, though, because of their natural tendency to eat any remotely edible thing. For this reason, dogs have been trained to dig into the ground wherever they find this odor, and they willingly exchange their truffle for a piece of bread and a pat on the head. Some truffle merchants dig for their prizes themselves when they see truffle flies hovering around the base of a tree. Once a site has been discovered, truffles can be collected in subsequent years.

To enjoy the wonderful flavor of what has been described as an earthly jewel, you must eat fresh, uncooked specimens shortly after they have been harvested. The strength of their flavor decreases rapidly with time, and much of it is lost before some truffles reach the market. To preserve them, gourmet experts suggest putting them in closed glass jars in a refrigerator. Another recommendation is to store them whole in bland oil.

36. Why do some people prefer using dogs than pigs in search of truffles?
　　(A) Dogs have stronger paws to dig.
　　(B) Dogs usually won't eat the truffles found.
　　(C) Dogs have a better sense of smell than pigs.
　　(D) Dogs are less likely to get excited than pigs.

37. What is the best way to enjoy truffles as a delicacy?
　　(A) Eating them cooked with pork.
　　(B) Eating them uncooked with bland oil.
　　(C) Eating them fresh right after being collected.
　　(D) Eating them after being refrigerated.

38. Which of the following statements is true?
　　(A) Truffles are roots of some old trees.
　　(B) Truffles can be found only by dogs and pigs.
　　(C) Truffles send out a strong odor when they mature.
　　(D) Truffles cannot be collected at the same place repeatedly.

39. Which of the following can be inferred from the passage?
　　(A) Truffles sold in glass jars are tasteless.
　　(B) Truffles taste like fruit when eaten fresh.
　　(C) Truffles are only used for cooking nowadays.
　　(D) Truffles are expensive because they are difficult to find.

第 40 至 43 題為題組

　　In an ideal world, people would not test medicines on animals. Such experiments are stressful and sometimes painful for animals, and expensive and time-consuming for people. Yet animal experimentation is still needed to help bridge vast gaps in medical knowledge. That is why there are some 50 to 100 million animals used in research around the world each year.

　　Europe, on the whole, has the world's most restrictive laws on animal experiments. Even so, its scientists use some 12 million animals a year, most of them mice and rats, for medical research. Official statistics show that just 1.1 million animals are used in research in America each year. But that is misleading. The American authorities do not think mice and rats are worth counting and, as these are the most common laboratory animals, the true figure is much higher. Japan and China have even less comprehensive data than America.

　　Now Europe is reforming the rules governing animal experiments by restricting the number of animals used in labs. Alternatives to animal testing, such as using human tissue or computer models, are now strongly recommended. In addition, sharing all research results freely should help to reduce the number of animals for scientific use. At present, scientists often share only the results of successful experiments. If their findings do not fit the hypothesis being tested, the work never sees the light of day. This practice means wasting time, money, and animals' lives in endlessly repeating the failed experiments.

Animal experimentation has taught humanity a great deal and saved countless lives. It needs to continue, even if that means animals sometimes suffer. Europe's new measures should eventually both reduce the number of animals used in experiments and improve the way in which scientific research is conducted.

40. What is the main idea of this passage?
   (A) The success of animal experiments should be ensured.
   (B) Ban on the use of animals in the lab should be enforced.
   (C) Greater efforts need to be taken to reduce the number of lab animals.
   (D) Scientists should be required to share their research results with each other.

41. Which of the following statements is true about animals used in the lab?
   (A) America uses only about 1.1 million lab animals per year.
   (B) Europe does not use mice and rats as lab animals at all.
   (C) Britain does not use as many lab animals as China does.
   (D) Japan has limited data on the number of lab animals used each year.

42. Which of the following is mentioned as an alternative to replace animal experiments?
   (A) Statistical studies.　　　(B) Computer models.
   (C) DNA planted in animals.　(D) Tissue from dead animals.

43. What usually happens to unsuccessful animal experiments?
(A) They are not revealed to the public.
(B) They are made into teaching materials.
(C) They are collected for future publication.
(D) They are not removed from the research topic list.

第 44 至 47 題爲題組

Spider webs are one of the most fascinating examples of animal architecture. The most beautiful and structurally ordered are the orb webs. The main function of the web is to intercept and hold flying prey, such as flies, bees and other insects, long enough for the spider to catch them. In order to do **so**, the threads of the web have to withstand the impact forces from large and heavy prey as well as environmental forces from wind and rain for at least a day in most cases.

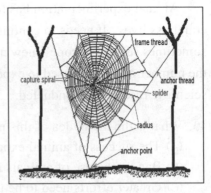

The orb web is found to have two main characteristics. The first is its geometry, which consists of an outer frame and a central part from which threads radiate outward. Enclosed in the frame are capture spirals winding round and round from the web center out to the frame. The whole web is in tension and held in place by anchor threads, which connect the frame to the surrounding vegetation or objects. The second and perhaps most important characteristic is the material with which it is built. Spider silk is a kind of natural composite that gives this lightweight fiber a tensile strength comparable to that of steel, while at the same time making it very elastic. Two types of silk threads are used in the web. One is highly elastic and can stretch to almost twice its original length before breaking and, for most types of spiders, is covered in glue. This type is used in the capture spiral for catching and holding prey. The other is stiffer and stronger, and is used for the radius, frames and anchor threads, which allows the web to withstand prey impact and to keep its structural strength through a wide range of environmental conditions.

44. What is this passage mainly about?
　(A) The food network in nature.
　(B) The construction of orb webs.
　(C) The network of geometrical studies.
　(D) The environmental challenges for spider webs.

45. What does the word "**so**" in the first paragraph refer to?
　(A) To catch and keep small creatures.
　(B) To find a good material for the web.
　(C) To observe the behavior patterns of spiders.
　(D) To present a fantastic architecture by animals.

46. Which part of the web is used for supporting the web itself ?
　(A) The center of the web.　　(B) The glue on the lines.
　(D) The anchor threads.　　(D) The capture spiral.

47. According to the passage, which statement is true about the silk threads?
　(A) They are all sticky and extendable.
　(B) They are usually strong enough to last for a day.
　(C) They remove harmful chemicals from insects.
　(D) They are made of rare plants in the environment.

第 48 至 51 題爲題組

　　Doctor of Philosophy, usually abbreviated as PhD or Ph.D., is an advanced academic degree awarded by universities. The first Doctor of Philosophy degree was awarded in Paris in 1150, but the degree did not acquire its modern status until the early 19th century. The doctorate of philosophy as it exists today originated at Humboldt University. The

German practice was later adopted by American and Canadian universities, eventually becoming common in large parts of the world in the 20th century.

For most of history, even a bachelor's degree at a university was the privilege of a rich few, and many academic staff did not hold doctorates. But as higher education expanded after the Second World War, the number of PhDs increased accordingly. American universities geared up first: By 1970, America was graduating half of the world's PhDs in science and technology. Since then, America's annual output of PhDs has doubled, to 64,000. Other countries are catching up. PhD production has sped up most dramatically in Mexico, Portugal, Italy, and Slovakia. Even Japan, where the number of young people is shrinking, has **churned out** about 46% more PhDs.

Researchers now warn that the supply of PhDs has far outstripped demand. America produced more than 100,000 doctoral degrees between 2005 and 2009, while there were just 16,000 new professorships. In research, the story is similar. Even graduates who find work outside universities may not fare all that well. Statistics show that five years after receiving their degrees, more than 60% of PhDs in Slovakia and more than 45% in Belgium, the Czech Republic, Germany, and Spain are still on temporary contracts. About one-third of Austria's PhD graduates take jobs unrelated to their degrees.

Today, top universities around the world are still picking bright students and grooming them as potential PhDs. After all, it isn't in their interests to turn the smart students away: The more bright students stay at universities, the better it is for academics. But considering the oversupply of PhDs, some people have already begun to wonder whether doing a PhD is a good choice for an individual.

48. In which country did the modern practice of granting doctoral degrees start?
    (A) France.　　　(B) Germany.　　(C) Canada.　　(D) The U.S.

49. Which of the following words is closest in meaning to "**churned out**" in the second paragraph?

　(A) Failed.　　　(B) Warned.　　　(C) Demanded.　　(D) Produced.

50. Which of the following may be inferred from the third paragraph?

　(A) PhD graduates in Austria are not encouraged to work outside university.

　(B) Most German PhDs work at permanent jobs immediately after graduation.

　(C) It is much easier for American PhD holders to find a teaching position than a research job.

　(D) It is more difficult for PhDs to get a permanent job five years after graduation in Slovakia than in Spain.

51. Which of the following best describes the author's attitude toward the increase of PhDs in recent years?

　(A) Concerned.　　(B) Supportive.　　(C) Indifferent.　　(D) Optimistic.

第貳部份：非選擇題（佔 28 分）

一、中譯英（8 分）

說明：1. 請將以下中文句子譯成正確、通順、達意的英文，並將答案寫在「答案卷」上。

　　　2. 請依序作答，並標明題號。每題 4 分，共 8 分。

1. 日本的核電廠爆炸已經引起全球對核子能源安全的疑慮。

2. 科學家正尋求安全、乾淨又不昂貴的綠色能源，以滿足我們對電的需求。

二、英文作文（20 分）

說明：1. 依提示在「答案卷」上寫一篇英文作文。

　　　2. 文長至少 120 個單詞（words）。

提示：你認為畢業典禮應該是個溫馨感人、活潑熱鬧、或是嚴肅傷感的場景？請寫一篇英文作文說明你對畢業典禮的看法，第一段寫出畢業典禮對你而言意義是什麼，第二段說明要如何安排或進行活動才能呈現出這個意義。

100年度指定科目考試英文科試題詳解

第壹部分：選擇題

一、詞彙：

1. (**A**) Many people think cotton is the most comfortable <u>fabric</u> to wear in hot weather. 許多人認為棉織品是熱天穿起來最舒服的<u>布料</u>。
    (A) *fabric*〔'fæbrɪk〕*n.* 布料
    (B) coverage〔'kʌvərɪdʒ〕*n.* 涵蓋的範圍
    (C) software〔'sɔft,wɛr〕*n.* 軟體
    (D) wardrobe〔'wɔrd,rob〕*n.* 衣櫃
    * cotton〔'katn̩〕*n.* 棉織品

2. (**A**) Because of the engine problem in the new vans, the auto company decided to <u>recall</u> them from the market. 因為這款新的廂型車引擎有問題，汽車公司決定將它們從市場中<u>召回</u>。
    (A) *recall*〔rɪ'kɔl〕*v.* 收回；召回
    (B) clarify〔'klærə,faɪ〕*v.* 清楚說明
    (C) transform〔træns'fɔrm〕*v.* 轉變　(D) polish〔'palɪʃ〕*v.* 擦亮
    * engine〔'ɛndʒən〕*n.* 引擎　　van〔væn〕*n.* 小型有蓋貨車；廂型車
    auto〔'ɔto〕*n.* 汽車　　market〔'markɪt〕*n.* 市場

3. (**C**) After a day's tiring work, Peter walked <u>wearily</u> back to his house, hungry and sleepy.
    經過一天累人的工作之後，彼得又餓又睏<u>疲倦地</u>走回家。
    (A) splendidly〔'splɛndɪdlɪ〕*adv.* 壯觀地
    (B) thoroughly〔'θɝolɪ〕*adv.* 徹底地
    (C) *wearily*〔'wɪrəlɪ〕*adv.* 疲倦地　　(D) vaguely〔'veglɪ〕*adv.* 模糊地
    * tiring〔'taɪrɪŋ〕*adj.* 累人的

4. (**C**) In team sports, how all members work as a group is more important than how they perform <u>individually</u>.
    在團隊運動中，全部成員的團隊運作比<u>個別</u>表現來的重要。
    (A) frequently〔'frikwəntlɪ〕*adv.* 經常地
    (B) typically〔'tɪpɪklɪ〕*adv.* 典型地

(C) ***individually*** 〔ˌɪndə'vɪdʒʊəlɪ〕 *adv.* 個別地

(D) completely 〔 kəm'plitlɪ 〕 *adv.* 完全地

＊member 〔'mɛmbə 〕 *n.* 成員　　perform 〔 pə'fɔrm 〕 *v.* 表現；執行

5. (**D**) Despite her physical disability, the young blind pianist managed to overcome all <u>obstacles</u> to win the first prize in the international contest. 儘管身體上有殘疾，這位失明的年輕鋼琴家設法克服所有障礙來贏得國際比賽的首獎。

(A) privacy 〔'praɪvəsɪ 〕 *n.* 隱私

(B) ambition 〔 æm'bɪʃən 〕 *n.* 野心；抱負

(C) fortune 〔 'fɔrtʃən 〕 *n.* 幸運；財富

(D) ***obstacle*** 〔'ɑbstək!〕 *n.* 障礙

＊despite 〔 dɪ'spaɪt 〕 *adj.* 儘管　　physical 〔'fɪzɪk!〕 *adj.* 身體的
disability 〔ˌdɪsə'bɪlətɪ 〕 *n.* 殘疾　　blind 〔 blaɪnd 〕 *adj.* 失明的
pianist 〔 pɪ'ænɪst 〕 *n.* 鋼琴家　　***manage to + V.*** 設法做到
overcome 〔ˌovə'kʌm 〕 *v.* 克服　　prize 〔 praɪz 〕 *n.* 獎
first prize 首獎　　contest 〔'kɑntɛst 〕 *n.* 比賽

6. (**C**) Each of the planets in the solar system circles around the sun in its own <u>orbit</u>, and this prevents them from colliding with each other. 太陽系中的每個行星都依其軌道繞著太陽運行，這樣能防止它們彼此互相碰撞。

(A) entry 〔'ɛntrɪ 〕 *n.* 進入；入口　　(B) haste 〔 hest 〕 *n.* 匆忙

(C) ***orbit*** 〔'ɔrbɪt 〕 *n.* 軌道　　(D) range 〔 rendʒ 〕 *n.* 範圍

＊planet 〔'plænɪt 〕 *n.* 行星　　solar 〔'solə 〕 *adj.* 太陽的
the solar system 太陽系　　circle 〔'sɝk!〕 *v.* 繞著…移動
prevent 〔 prɪ'vɛnt 〕 *v.* 預防；防止　　collide 〔 kə'laɪd 〕 *v.* 相撞；碰撞

7. (**A**) Professor Wang is well known for his contributions to the field of economics. He has been <u>recruited</u> to help the government with its financial reform programs.
王教授對於經濟學領域的貢獻很有名。他已經被徵召，要協助政府處理金融改革計畫。

(A) ***recruit*** 〔 rɪ'krut 〕 *v.* 徵募；招募

(B) contradict 〔ˌkɑntrə'dɪkt 〕 *v.* 反駁

(C) mediate 〔'midɪˌet 〕 *v.* 調停；仲裁

(D) generate 〔'dʒɛnəˌret 〕 *v.* 產生

* professor〔prə'fɛsə〕*n.* 教授　　***be well known for*** 以…有名
contribution〔ˌkɑntrə'bjuʃən〕*n.* 貢獻
field〔fild〕*n.* 領域　　economics〔ˌikə'nɑmɪks〕*n.* 經濟學
financial〔fə'nænʃəl〕*adj.* 財務的；金融的
reform〔rɪ'fɔrm〕*n.* 改革　　program〔'progræm〕*n.* 計畫

8. (**B**) Most earthquakes are too small to be noticed; they can only be
detected by <u>sensitive</u> instruments.
多數地震都太小了，察覺不到；它們只能由靈敏的儀器檢測出來。
(A) manual〔'mænjuəl〕*adj.* 手工的
(B) ***sensitive***〔'sɛnsətɪv〕*adj.* 靈敏的
(C) portable〔'portəbḷ〕*adj.* 可攜帶的
(D) dominant〔'dɑmənənt〕*adj.* 支配的

* earthquake〔'ɝθˌkwek〕*n.* 地震　　detect〔dɪ'tɛkt〕*v.* 檢測
instrument〔'ɪnstrəmənt〕*n.* 儀器

9. (**B**) With Wikileaks releasing secrets about governments around the
world, many countries are worried that their national security
information might be <u>disclosed</u>.
因為維基解密在全世界公開關於各國政府的秘密，許多國家都擔心
它們的國安資訊會被揭露。
(A) relieve〔rɪ'liv〕*v.* 減輕；援救　　(B) ***disclose***〔dɪs'kloz〕*v.* 揭露
(C) condense〔kən'dɛns〕*v.* 濃縮　　(D) provoke〔prə'vok〕*v.* 觸怒

* Wikileaks〔'wɪkɪ'liks〕*n.* 維基解密
release〔rɪ'lis〕*v.* 公開　　national〔'næʃənḷ〕*adj.* 國家的
security〔sɪ'kjurətɪ〕*n.* 安全

10. (**B**) I'm afriad we can't take your word, for the evidence we've
collected so far is not <u>consistent</u> with what you said.
恐怕我們不能採納你的說詞，因為我們目前收集到的證據跟你所
說的不一致。
(A) familiar〔fə'mɪljə〕*adj.* 熟悉的
(B) ***consistent***〔kən'sɪstənt〕*adj.* 一致的
(C) durable〔'djurəbḷ〕*adj.* 耐久的
(D) sympathetic〔ˌsɪmpə'θɛtɪk〕*adj.* 同情的

* take〔tek〕*v.* 採納　　evidence〔'ɛvədəns〕*n.* 證據
collect〔kə'lɛkt〕*v.* 收集　　***so far*** 目前為止

二、綜合測驗：

第 11 至 15 題為題組

　　Handling customer claims is a common task for most business firms. These claims include requests to exchange merchandise, requests for refunds, requests that work <u>be corrected</u>, and other requests for adjustments.
11
Most of these claims are approved because they are legitimate. However, some requests for adjustment must be <u>denied</u>, and an adjustment refusal
12
message must be sent. Adjustment refusals are negative messages for the customer. They are necessary when the customer is <u>at fault</u> or when the
13
vendor has done all that can reasonably or legally be expected.

　　處理顧客的要求對大部分的企業公司而言，是常見的任務。這些要求包括要求更換商品，要求退錢，要求工作正確無誤，以及其他調整的要求。大部分的要求會被同意，因為是合法的。然而，有些要求調整必須拒絕，而且要將拒絕的通知寄出。對顧客而言，拒絕調整就是否決的信函。當錯在顧客自己，或當賣家已做好所有預期到的合理且合法的事項，拒絕便是需要的。

> handle〔ˋhændḷ〕v. 處理　　customer〔ˋkʌstəmɚ〕n. 顧客
> claim〔klem〕n. 要求　　common〔ˋkɑmən〕adj. 常見的；普通的
> task〔tæsk〕n. 任務　　firm〔fɝm〕n. 公司；商行
> include〔ɪnˋklud〕v. 包括　　request〔rɪˋkwɛst〕n. 要求
> exchange〔ɪksˋtʃendʒ〕v. 更換
> merchandise〔ˋmɝtʃənˌdaɪz〕n. 商品
> refund〔ˋriˌfʌnd〕n. 退款　　adjustment〔əˋdʒʌstmənt〕n. 調整
> approve〔əˋpruv〕v. 同意　　legitimate〔lɪˋdʒɪtəmɪt〕adj. 合法的
> refusal〔rɪˋfjuzḷ〕n. 拒絕　　message〔ˋmɛsɪdʒ〕n. 訊息；通知
> negative〔ˋnɛgətɪv〕adj. 否決的　　vendor〔ˋvɛndɚ〕n. 賣家
> reasonably〔ˋriznəblɪ〕adv. 合理地　　legally〔ˋligḷɪ〕adv. 合法地
> expect〔ɪkˋspɛkt〕v. 預期

11. (**D**) request「要求」後接 that 子句，為慾望動詞的用法，也可以名詞的方式出現，that 子句中用法不變，助動詞 should 被省略，故用原形動詞，選 (D) <u>be corrected</u>。【詳見文法寶典 p.373】

12. (**B**) 由本句一開始的轉承語 However 可知，之後的文意是指「有些要求調整必須拒絕」，故選 (B)。

(A) retail〔'ritel〕*v.* 零售

(B) ***deny***〔dɪ'naɪ〕*v.* 拒絕

(C) appreciate〔ə'priʃɪ,et〕*v.* 欣賞；感激

(D) elaborate〔ɪ'læbəret〕*v.* 精心製作

13. (**A**) (A) ***at fault*** 有過錯的　　(B) on call 待用的；隨叫隨到的

(C) in tears 流淚　　(D) off guard 不設防

An adjustment refusal message requires your best communication skills <u>because</u> it is bad news to the receiver. You have to refuse the claim
14
and retain the customer <u>at the same time</u>. You may refuse the request for
15
adjustment and even try to sell the customer more merchandise or service. All this is happening when the customer is probably angry, disappointed, or inconvenienced.

　　拒絕調整的通知需要你最佳的溝通技巧，因為對接受者而言這是個壞消息。你必須拒絕他的要求，同時又要保有這個顧客。你可能拒絕他做調整的要求，甚至還試圖賣給他更多的商品或服務。這一切都是發生在顧客可能生氣、失望、或感到不便的時候。

require〔rɪ'kwaɪr〕*v.* 需要

communication〔kə,mjunə'keʃən〕*n.* 溝通　　skill〔skɪl〕*n.* 技巧

news〔njuz〕*n.* 消息；新聞　　receiver〔rɪ'sivɚ〕*n.* 接受者

retain〔rɪ'ten〕*v.* 保有　　service〔'sɝvɪs〕*n.* 服務

disappointed〔,dɪsə'pɔɪntɪd〕*adj.* 感到失望的

inconvenienced〔,ɪnkən'vinjənst〕*adj.* 感到不便的

14. (**C**) 依據文意，應選 (C) 因為。

(A) till〔tɪl〕*conj.* 直到　　(B) unless〔ʌn'lɛs〕*conj.* 除非

(D) therefore〔'ðɛr,for〕*adv.* 因此

15. (**C**) 依據文意，應選 (C)。

(A) by and large 總體而言　　(B) over and over 一再

(C) ***at the same time*** 同時　　(D) for the same reason 同樣的理由

<u>第 16 至 20 題為題組</u>

　　People may express their feelings differently on different occasions. Cultures sometimes vary greatly in this regard. A group of researchers in

Japan, <u>for example</u>, studied the facial reactions of students to a horror film.
　　　　16
When the Japanese students watched the film <u>with</u> the teacher present,
　　　　　　　　　　　　　　　　　　17
their faces showed only the slightest hints of reaction. But when they
thought they were alone (though they <u>were being taped</u> by a secret camera),
　　　　　　　　　　　　　　　　　　18
their faces twisted into vivid mixes of anguished distress, fear, and disgust.

　　人們在不同的場合表達感受的方式也不同，就這方面而言，有時文化的差
異相當大，例如，有一群日本的研究者研究學生對恐怖片的臉部反應。當日本
學生在老師在場的情況下觀賞電影時，他們的臉部只呈現出少許輕微的反應。
但是當他們認為自己是一個人的時候（不過他們被祕密攝影機拍攝下來），他們
的臉卻因極度悲痛，恐懼和厭惡而明顯扭曲在一起。

express〔ɪk'sprɛs〕v. 表達　　feeling〔'filɪŋ〕n. 感受
differently〔'dɪfərəntlɪ〕adv. 不同地　　occasion〔ə'keʒən〕n. 場合
vary〔'vɛrɪ〕v. 不同　　regard〔rɪ'gɑrd〕n. 關心；事項
in this regard 關於這方面　　researcher〔rɪ'sɜtʃɚ〕n. 研究者
facial〔'feʃəl〕adj. 臉部的　　reaction〔rɪ'ækʃən〕n. 反應
horror〔'hɔrɚ〕n. 恐怖　　film〔fɪlm〕n. 電影
present〔'prɛzn̩t〕adj. 在場的　　slight〔slaɪt〕adj. 輕微的
hint〔hɪnt〕n. 暗示　　alone〔ə'lon〕adj. 單獨的
camera〔'kæmərə〕n. 攝影機；相機　　twist〔twɪst〕v. 扭曲
vivid〔'vɪvɪd〕adj. 逼真的；清晰的　　mix〔mɪks〕n. 混合；結合
anguished〔'æŋgwɪʃt〕adj. 極度痛苦的　　distress〔dɪ'strɛs〕n. 悲痛
fear〔fɪr〕n. 恐懼　　disgust〔dɪs'gʌst〕n. 厭惡

16. (**D**) 依據文意，從之後所舉的具體實例，應選 (D)。
　　(A) as usual　如往常般　　(B) in some cases　某些例子中
　　(C) to be frank　坦白說　　(D) **for example**　例如

17. (**D**) 表示老師在場的附帶情況下，故選 (C)來形成 with + O. + O.C.的句型。

18. (**A**) 依句意，指當時的學生們正在「被攝影機拍攝著」的意思，故應用過
　　　去進行式的被動語態（was/were + being + p.p.），故選 (A)。

　　The study also shows that there are several unspoken rules about how
feelings should be <u>properly</u> shown on different occasions. One of the most
　　　　　　　　　19
common rules is minimizing the show of emotion. This is the Japanese

norm for feelings of distress <u>in the presence of</u> someone in authority,
20
which explains why the students masked their upset with a poker face in
the experiment.

　　研究也顯示出關於在不同的場合，應該如何適當表達感受，有許多不成文
的規定，其中最常見的規則就是情緒的表現降到最小，這便是日本人當有權力
者在場時，表現傷痛的準則，這也解釋了實驗中學生為何要以面無表情的方式，
來掩飾他們煩亂的情緒。

several〔'sɛvərəl〕*adj.* 數個的
unspoken〔ʌn'spokən〕*adj.* 不成文的；沒說出的
rule〔rul〕*n.* 規定　　minimize〔'mɪnəmaɪz〕*v.* 降到最小；減到最小
show〔ʃo〕*n.* 表現　　emotion〔ɪ'moʃən〕*n.* 情緒
norm〔nɔrm〕*n.* 準則；標準　　authority〔ə'θɔrətɪ〕*n.* 權力；權威
a person in authority 有權力的人；當權者
explain〔ɪk'splen〕*v.* 解釋　　mask〔mæsk〕*v.* 掩飾
upset〔ʌp'sɛt〕*n.* 煩亂　　poker〔'pokɚ〕*n.* 撲克牌遊戲
a poker face 撲克臉；面無表情　experiment〔ɪk'spɛrəmənt〕*n.* 實驗

19. (**C**) 由文意可知是指「在不同的場合，應該如何適當表達感受」，故選 (C)。
　　(A) rarely〔'rɛrlɪ〕*adv.* 很少
　　(B) similarly〔'sɪmələlɪ〕*adv.* 同樣地
　　(C) ***properly***〔'prɑpəlɪ〕*adv.* 適當地
　　(D) critically〔'krɪtɪklɪ〕*adv.* 危急地；批判性地

20. (**B**) 依據文意，應選 (B)。
　　(A) with the help of 藉由…幫助
　　(B) ***in the presence of*** 某人在場的情況；當著某人的面
　　(C) on top of 在…之上；除…之外　　(D) in place of 代替

三、文意選填：

第 21 至 30 題為題組

　　The history of the written word goes back 6,000 years. Words express
feelings, open doors into the <u>unknown</u>, create pictures of worlds never seen,
21
and allow adventures never dared. Therefore, the original <u>users</u> of words,
22
such as storytellers, poets, and singers, were respected in all cultures in the
past.

　　書寫文字的歷史可以回溯到6,000年前。文字表達感情，打開通往未知世界的大門，創造出未曾見過的世界的圖像，還有允許我們一探從不敢從事的冒險。因此，最初文字的使用者，例如：講故事的人、詩人，還有歌手，在古時候所有的文化中都是被尊重的。

> written〔ˈrɪtn̩〕*adj.* 書寫的；書面的　　***goes back*** 回溯
> express〔ɪkˈsprɛs〕*v.* 表達　　allow〔əˈlaʊ〕*v.* 允許
> dare〔dɛr〕*v.* 敢做；冒險嘗試　　original〔əˈrɪdʒənl̩〕*adj.* 最初的
> storyteller〔ˈstorɪˌtɛlɚ〕*n.* 講故事的人　　poet〔ˈpo·ɪt〕*n.* 詩人

21.(**L**) ***unknown***〔ʌnˈnon〕*adj.* 未知的　　***the unknown*** 未知的世界

22.(**G**) ***user***〔ˈjuzɚ〕*n.* 使用者

　　But now the romance is <u>fading</u>. Imagination is being surpassed by the
　　　　　　　　　　　　　23
instant picture. In a triumphant march, movies, TV, videos, and DVDs are
<u>replacing</u> storytellers and books. A visual culture is taking over the world —
　24
at the <u>expense</u> of the written word. Our literacy, and with it our verbal and
　　　　25
communication skills, are in <u>rapid</u> decline.
　　　　　　　　　　　　26

　　但現在這段羅曼史正在褪色。想像力正在被即時影像超越。電影、電視和DVD 以勝利的步調前進，他們取代了講故事的人還有書本。視覺文化正在征服這個世界－以書寫的文字爲代價。我們的讀寫能力，還有隨之的語言表達和溝通能力，都在快速衰退中。

> romance〔roˈmæns〕*n.* 羅曼史　　surpass〔sɚˈpæs〕*v.* 超越；勝過
> instant〔ˈɪnstənt〕*adj.* 立即的；即時的
> triumphant〔traɪˈʌmfənt〕*adj.* 獲得勝利的
> march〔martʃ〕*n.* 進行的步調；行進　　visual〔ˈvɪʒʊəl〕*adj.* 視覺的
> ***take over*** 征服；佔領　　literacy〔ˈlɪtərəsɪ〕*n.* 讀寫的能力
> verbal〔ˈvɝbl̩〕*adj.* 用語言表達的
> communication〔kəˌmjunəˈkeʃən〕*n.* 溝通；傳播
> decline〔dɪˈklaɪn〕*n.* 衰退；沒落　　***in decline*** 衰退中；沒落中

23.(**B**) ***fade***〔fed〕*v.* 褪色；衰退

24.(**E**) ***replace***〔rɪˈples〕*v.* 取代

25.(**A**) ***expense***〔ɪkˈspɛns〕*n.* 代價　　***at the expense of*** 以…爲代價

26.(**H**) ***rapid***〔ˈræpɪd〕*adj.* 快速的

The only category of novel that is <u>gaining</u> ground in our increasingly
                                     27
visual world is the graphic novel. A growing number of adults and young
people worldwide are reading graphic novels, and educators are beginning to
realize the power of this <u>medium</u>. The graphic novel looks like a comic book,
                            28
but it is longer, more sophisticated, and may come in black and white or
multiple <u>colors</u> and appear in many sizes.
           29

唯一一種，還能在這個逐漸視覺化的世界中壯大的，就是圖像小說。全世
界有越來越多的成人和年輕人開始閱讀圖像小說，而且教育家們也開始理解這
種媒體的力量。圖像小說看起來就像是漫畫，但比較長，更為精緻，而且可能
有空開黑白兩色，或是多重的色彩，以及有不同的尺寸。

category〔'kætə,gorɪ〕n. 種類   novel〔'nɑvḷ〕n. 小說
ground〔graʊnd〕n. 地面   increasingly〔ɪn'krisɪŋlɪ〕adv. 逐漸地
graphic〔'græfɪk〕adj. 用圖表示的
worldwide〔'wɜld'waɪd〕adv. 全世界地   adj. 全世界的
educator〔'ɛdʒə,ketə〕n. 教育家
sophisticated〔sə'fɪstɪ,ketɪd〕adj. 精緻的
come in 有…（顏色、數量、尺寸）
multiple〔'mʌltəpḷ〕adj. 多重的   appear〔ə'pɪr〕v. 出現

27. (I) *gain*〔gen〕v. 增加   ***gain ground*** 壯大；獲得進展

28. (J) *medium*〔'midɪəm〕n. 媒體

29. (C) *color*〔'kʌlə〕n. 色彩

In fact, some of the most interesting, daring, and most heartbreaking art
being created right now is being published in graphic novels. Graphic
novels <u>offer</u> the opportunity to examine the increasingly visual world of
         30
communications today while exploring serious social and literary topics.
The graphic novel can be used to develop a sense of visual literacy, in
much the same way that students are introduced to art appreciation.
事實上，一些最有趣、最大膽和最令人心碎，且正在創造中的藝術，都被出版
成圖像小說。圖像小說提供機會，來檢驗今日這個逐漸視覺化的傳播世界，同
時探索嚴肅的社會和文學主題。圖像小說能被用來培養視覺素養，幾乎就和學
生認識藝術欣賞的方式一樣。

daring〔'dɛrɪŋ〕*adj.* 大膽的；勇敢的
heartbreaking〔'hɑrt,brekɪŋ〕*adj.* 令人心碎的
explore〔ɪk'splor〕*v.* 探索　　social〔'soʃəl〕*adj.* 社會的
literary〔'lɪtə,rɛrɪ〕*adj.* 文學的　　sense〔sɛns〕*n.* 感覺
visual literacy 視覺素養【又稱圖像識讀能力，指個人對視覺影像的理解及
　運用能力，特別是對藝術品、電視及電影，擁有分析及鑑賞的能力】
be introduced to 認識　　appreciation〔ə,priʃɪ'eʃən〕*n.* 欣賞

30.(**F**) ***offer***〔'ɔfə〕*v.* 提供

四、篇章結構：

第 31 至 35 題為題組

The effect of bullying can be serious and even lead to tragedy.
Unfortunately, it is still a mostly unresearched area.

霸凌的影響可能很嚴重，甚至會造成悲劇。遺憾的是，這仍然是個大部分
尚未被研究的領域。

effect〔ɪ'fɛkt〕*n.* 影響　　bully〔'bulɪ〕*v.* 霸凌　*n.* 惡霸
lead to 導致；造成　　tragedy〔'trædʒədɪ〕*n.* 悲劇
unfortunately〔ʌn'fɔrtʃənɪtlɪ〕*adv.* 不幸的是；遺憾的是
mostly〔'mostlɪ〕*adv.* 大多
unresearched〔ʌnrɪ'sɜtʃd〕*adj.* 未被研究的
area〔'ɛrɪə〕*n.* 領域

[31] (F) The link between bullying and school violence has attracted
increasing attention since the 1999 tragedy at a Colorado high school. That
year two shotgun-wielding students, both of whom had been identified as
gifted and who had been bullied for years, killed 13 people, wounded 24
and then committed suicide. A year later an analysis by the US government
found that bullying played a major role in more than two-thirds of the
campus violence.

自 1999 年科羅拉多州的一所高中發生悲劇以來，霸凌和校園暴力之間的關
連就日益受到注意。那年有兩個手持霰彈槍的學生，這兩名學生都被認定是資
優生，他們遭受霸凌許多年，當時造成 13 人死亡，24 人受傷後自殺。一年後，
美國政府所做的一項分析發現，在三分之二的校園暴力事件中，霸凌扮演著很
重要的角色。

link〔lɪŋk〕n. 關連　　violence〔'vaɪələns〕n. 暴力
attract〔ə'trækt〕v. 吸引　　increasing〔ɪn'krisɪŋ〕adj. 越來越多的
attention〔ə'tɛnʃən〕n. 注意（力）
Colorado〔ˌkɑlə'rædo〕n. 科羅拉多州
shotgun〔'ʃɑtˌgʌn〕n. 霰彈槍；獵槍　　wield〔wild〕v. 揮舞；使用
identify〔aɪ'dɛntəˌfaɪ〕v. 確認　　gifted〔'gɪftɪd〕adj. 有天賦的
wound〔wund〕v. 使受傷　　commit〔kə'mɪt〕v. 犯（罪）
suicide〔'suəˌsaɪd〕n. 自殺　　*commit suicide* 自殺
analysis〔ə'næləsɪs〕n. 分析
major〔'medʒɚ〕adj. 主要的；較重要的　　role〔rol〕n. 角色
two-thirds n. 三分之二　　campus〔'kæmpəs〕n. 校園

---

[32] **(D)** Research indicates that bullying may form a chain reaction and the victim often becomes the bully. Numerous dictators and invaders throughout history have tried to justify their bullying behavior by claiming that they themselves were bullied. [33] **(A)** Hitler, for example, is claimed to have been a victim of bullying in his childhood. Although it is no justification for bullying, many of the worst humans in history have indeed been bullies and victims of bullying.

研究指出，霸凌可能會形成連鎖反應，受害者往往會變成惡霸。自古以來，有無數的獨裁者和入侵者，都藉由宣稱自己遭受過霸凌，使自己的霸凌行為正當化。例如，希特勒就被聲稱在童年時期遭受過霸凌。雖然這絕不是霸凌的正當理由，但是歷史上有很多壞人，的確是惡霸，而且也是霸凌的受害者。

research〔'risɚtʃ〕n. 研究　　indicate〔'ɪndəˌket〕v. 指出；顯示
form〔fɔrm〕v. 形成　　*chain reaction* 連鎖反應
victim〔'vɪktɪm〕n. 受害者
numerous〔'njumərəs〕adj. 無數的
dictator〔'dɪktetɚ〕n. 獨裁者　　invader〔ɪn'vedɚ〕n. 入侵者
throughout〔θru'aʊt〕prep. 遍及
throughout history 自古以來；有史以來
justify〔'dʒʌstəˌfaɪ〕v. 證明…為正當；為…辯護
claim〔klem〕v. 宣稱　　Hitler〔'hɪtlɚ〕n. 希特勒
childhood〔'tʃaɪldˌhud〕n. 童年時期
justification〔ˌdʒʌstəfə'keʃən〕n.（行為的）正當化；（正當化的）理由
indeed〔ɪn'did〕adv. 的確；真正地

Since bullying is mostly ignored, it may provide an important clue in crowd behavior and passer-by behavior. [34] (E) Psychologists have been puzzled by the inactivity of crowds and bystanders in urban centers when crimes occur in crowded places. Many of them have suggested bullying as one of the reasons of this decline in emotional sensitivity and acceptance of violence as normal.

由於霸凌大多被忽視，所以就可能提供有關群眾行為和路人行為的重要線索。心理學家一直很困惑，不知道為什麼在市中心人潮擁擠的地方，發生犯罪行為時，群眾和路人都不會採取行動。許多心理學家指出，大家越來越麻木不仁，並且認為暴力是正常的，霸凌就是原因之一。

ignore〔ɪgˋnor〕v. 忽視　　　provide〔prəˋvaɪd〕v. 提供
clue〔klu〕n. 線索　　　crowd〔kraʊd〕n. 群眾
passer-by〔ˋpæsəˏbaɪ〕n. 過路人；行人　　　result〔rɪˋzʌlt〕n. 結果
psychologist〔saɪˋkɑlədʒɪst〕n. 心理學家　　　puzzle〔ˋpʌzḷ〕v. 使困惑
inactivity〔ˏɪnækˋtɪvətɪ〕n. 不活動；不活躍；無活動力
bystander〔ˋbaɪˏstændɚ〕n. 旁觀者；路人　　urban〔ˋɝbən〕adj. 都市的
urban center 市中心　　　crime〔kraɪm〕n. 罪
crowded〔ˋkraʊdɪd〕adj. 擁擠的　　　suggest〔səgˋdʒɛst〕v. 指出
decline〔dɪˋklaɪn〕n. 衰退；降低
emotional〔ɪˋmoʃənḷ〕adj. 感情的；情緒的
sensitivity〔ˏsɛnsəˋtɪvətɪ〕n. 敏感（度）
acceptance〔ækˋsɛptəns〕n. 接受；認可
normal〔ˋnɔrmḷ〕adj. 正常的

When someone is bullied, it is not only the bully and the victim who are becoming less sensitive to violence. [35] (C) The friends and classmates of the bully and the victim may accept the violence as normal. In this sense, bullying affects not only the bullied but his friends and classmates and the whole society.

當有人被霸凌，不只是惡霸和受害者對暴力變得較不敏感。惡霸和受害者的朋友和同學，可能會認為暴力是常態。這樣看來，霸凌影響的不只是被霸凌者，還有他的朋友、同學，以及整個社會。

sensitive〔ˋsɛnsətɪv〕adj. 敏感的　　　**accept A as B** 認為 A 是 B
sense〔sɛns〕n. 意義　　　**in this sense** 從這種意義上來說；在這方面
affect〔əˋfɛkt〕v. 影響　　　whole〔hol〕adj. 全部的；整個的

五、閱讀測驗：

第 36 至 39 題為題組

Since the times of the Greeks and Romans, truffles have been used in Europe as delicacies and even as medicines. They are among the most expensive of the world's natural foods, often commanding as much as US$250 to US$450 per pound. Truffles are actually mushrooms, but unusual ones. They live in close association with the roots of specific trees and their fruiting bodies grow underground. This is why they are difficult to find.

從希臘羅馬時代開始，松露在歐洲就一直被當成佳餚，甚至當成藥。它們是世上最昂貴的自然食品之一，通常一磅索價二百五十到四百五十美元。松露其實就是蘑菇，不過是特殊種類。它們與特定的樹根緊密生長在一起，它們的子實體則長在地下。這是它們之所以那麼難找的原因。

Greek〔grik〕*n.* 希臘人　　Roman〔ˋromən〕*n.* 羅馬人
truffle〔ˋtrʌfḷ〕*n.* 松露　　delicacy〔ˋdɛləkəsɪ〕*n.* 佳餚
command〔kəˋmænd〕*v.*（商品）可賣（價錢）
pound〔paʊnd〕*n.* 磅【重量單位，1 磅等於 0.454 公斤】
mushroom〔ˋmʌʃrum〕*n.* 蘑菇　　close〔klos〕*adj.* 緊密的
association〔ə͵sosɪˋeʃən〕*n.* 聯結　　roots〔ruts〕*n. pl.*（植物的）根
specific〔spɪˋsɪfɪk〕*adj.* 特定的　　fruit〔frut〕*v.*（植物）結果實
fruiting body 子實體【菌類產生孢子的器官】
underground〔ˋʌndəˋgraʊnd〕*adv.* 在地下

Truffles are harvested in Europe with the aid of female pigs or truffle dogs, which are able to detect the strong smell of mature truffles underneath the surface of the ground. Female pigs are especially sensitive to the odor of the truffles because it is similar to the smell given off by male pigs. The use of pigs is risky, though, because of their natural tendency to eat any remotely edible thing. For this reason, dogs have been trained to dig into the ground wherever they find this odor, and they willingly exchange their truffle for a piece of bread and a pat on the head. Some truffle merchants dig for their prizes themselves when they see truffle flies hovering around the base of a tree. Once a site has been discovered, truffles can be collected in subsequent years.

　　在歐洲，松露的收成是藉由母豬或松露犬的協助，牠們能探查地表下成熟松露散發的強烈味道。母豬對松露的味道特別敏感，因爲那跟公豬釋放出來的味道很接近。但是用豬來找松露風險很高，牠們天性會吃掉任何可以吃的東西。因此，狗才被訓練來挖掘有松露味道的地方，而且狗會願意用松露換一塊麵包，或輕拍頭一下。有些松露商看到有松露蠅在一棵樹的樹基上盤旋時，會自己把松露挖出來。發現一個挖掘地點後，接下來的幾年都能採收松露。

harvest〔ˋhɑrvɪst〕v. 收成　　　aid〔ed〕n. 協助
female〔ˋfimel〕adj. 雌性的　　***truffle dog*** 尋松露犬
detect〔dɪˋtɛkt〕v. 探查　　mature〔məˋtjʊr〕adj. 成熟的
underneath〔ˌʌndəˋniθ〕prep. 在…之下　　surface〔ˋsɝfɪs〕n. 表面
especially〔əˋspɛʃəlɪ〕adv. 特別　　sensitive〔ˋsɛnsətɪv〕adj. 敏感的
odor〔ˋodə〕n. 味道　　similar〔ˋsɪmələ〕adj. 類似的
give off 釋放（味道、光、熱等）　　male〔mel〕adj. 雄性的
risky〔ˋrɪskɪ〕adj. 有風險的　　tendency〔ˋtɛndənsɪ〕n. 傾向
remotely〔rɪˋmotlɪ〕adv. 程度極低地
edible〔ˋɛdəbḷ〕adj. 可以食用的　　train〔tren〕v. 訓練
dig〔dɪg〕v. 挖掘　　willingly〔ˋwɪlɪŋlɪ〕adv. 願意地
exchange〔ɪksˋtʃɛndʒ〕v. 交換　　pat〔pæt〕n. 拍
merchant〔ˋmɝtʃənt〕n. 商人　　prize〔praɪz〕n. 努力獲得之物
truffle fly 松露蠅　　hover〔ˋhʌvə〕v. 盤旋（於空中）
base〔bes〕n. 底部　　site〔saɪt〕n. （特定的）地點
collect〔kəˋlɛkt〕v. 探收　　subsequent〔ˋsʌbsɪˌkwɛnt〕adj. 隨後的

To enjoy the wonderful flavor of what has been described as an earthly jewel, you must eat fresh, uncooked specimens shortly after they have been harvested. The strength of their flavor decreases rapidly with time, and much of it is lost before some truffles reach the market. To preserve them, gourmet experts suggest putting them in closed glass jars in a refrigerator. Another recommendation is to store them whole in bland oil.

　　要享受被描述爲人間瑰寶的美味，您必須在松露採收後立即生吃。它們的濃度會隨著時間快速減少，大部份的味道在抵達市場以前就不見了。爲了保存它們，美食家建議將它們裝進密封的玻璃瓶並放入冰箱。其他也有人建議要貯存在無刺激性的油之中。

flavor〔ˋflevə〕n. 滋味　　describe〔dɪˋskraɪb〕v. 描述
earthly〔ˋɝθlɪ〕adj. 人間的　　jewel〔ˋdʒuəl〕n. 瑰寶
uncooked〔ʌnˋkʊkt〕adj. 未烹調的　　specimen〔ˋspɛsəmən〕n. 樣品

shortly〔ˋʃɔrtlɪ〕*adv.* 不久　　***shortly after*** 在…不久後
strength〔strɛŋkθ〕*n.* 濃度　　decrease〔dɪˋkris〕*v.* 減少
rapidly〔ˋræpɪdlɪ〕*adv.* 迅速地　　preserve〔prɪˋzɝv〕*v.* 保存
gourmet〔ˋgurme〕*n.* 美食家　　closed〔klozd〕*adj.* 密封的
jar〔dʒɑr〕*n.* 瓶子　　recommendation〔͵rɛkəmɛnˋdeʃən〕*n.* 建議
store〔stor〕*v.* 貯存　　bland〔blænd〕*adj.* (食物) 無刺激性的

36.(**B**) 比起用豬，為什麼有些人偏好用狗來找松露？

　　(A) 狗的爪子用在挖掘比較強壯。

　　(B) 狗通常不會把找到的松露吃掉。

　　(C) 狗的嗅覺比豬還好。

　　(D) 比起豬，狗比較不容易興奮。

　　paw〔pɔ〕*n.* (貓、狗的) 腳爪　　***sense of smell*** 嗅覺

37.(**C**) 將松露當作佳餚享受的最佳方式是？

　　(A) 加入豬肉一起煮再吃。　　(B) 搭配無刺激性的油生吃。

　　(C) 採收之後立刻吃。　　(D) 冷藏之後再吃。

　　refrigerate〔rɪˋfrɪdʒə͵ret〕*v.* 冷藏

38.(**C**) 下列敘述何者為真？

　　(A) 松露是某些老樹的根部。　　(B) 松露只能透過狗跟豬來找。

　　(C) 松露成熟時會散發強烈的味道。

　　(D) 松露不能在同一個地方反覆地收成。

　　repeatedly〔rɪˋpitɪdlɪ〕*adv.* 反覆地

39.(**D**) 由本文可以推論出下列何者？

　　(A) 裝在玻璃罐裡賣的松露沒有味道。

　　(B) 現採現吃的松露吃起來像水果一樣。

　　(C) 松露現今只用來烹調。

　　(D) 因為難找，所以松露很貴。

　　infer〔ɪnˋfɝ〕*v.* 推論　　tasteless〔ˋtestlɪs〕*adj.* 沒有味道的

第 40 至 43 題為題組

　　In an ideal world, people would not test medicines on animals. Such
experiments are stressful and sometimes painful for animals, and expensive

and time-consuming for people.　Yet animal experimentation is still needed to help bridge vast gaps in medical knowledge.　That is why there are some 50 to 100 million animals used in research around the world each year.

在理想的世界裡，人們不會把藥測試在動物身上。這樣的實驗對動物來說會有壓力，而且很痛苦，對人類來說也花錢、花時間。但是，要協助彌補醫療知識的廣大漏洞，還是需要動物試驗。這也是全球每年有大約五千萬到一億隻動物被用於研究的原因。

> ideal〔aɪˈdiəl〕adj. 理想的　　test〔tɛst〕v. 測試
> experiment〔ɪkˈspɛrəmənt〕n. 實驗
> stressful〔ˈstrɛsfəl〕adj. 壓力重的　　painful〔ˈpenfəl〕adj. 痛苦的
> time-consuming〔ˈtaɪm kənˈsjumɪŋ〕adj. 費時的
> yet〔jɛt〕adv. 但是　　experimentation〔ɪkˌspɛrəmɛnˈteʃən〕n. 實驗法
> **animal experimentation** 動物試驗　　bridge〔brɪdʒ〕v. 彌補（漏洞）
> vast〔væst〕adj. 廣大的　　gap〔gæp〕n. 漏洞
> medical〔ˈmɛdɪkl̩〕adj. 醫學的　　some〔sʌm〕adv. 大約

Europe, on the whole, has the world's most restrictive laws on animal experiments.　Even so, its scientists use some 12 million animals a year, most of them mice and rats, for medical research.　Official statistics show that just 1.1 million animals are used in research in America each year. But that is misleading.　The American authorities do not think mice and rats are worth counting and, as these are the most common laboratory animals, the true figure is much higher.　Japan and China have even less comprehensive data than America.

整體上，歐洲對動物實驗的法律是最嚴格的。儘管如此，每年歐洲科學家還是使用約一千兩百萬隻動物在醫學研究上，其中大部份是老鼠。官方數據顯示美國每年的研究只使用一百一十萬隻。不過這個數據容易引起誤解。美國官方認爲老鼠不值得納入計算；而因爲老鼠是實驗室中最常見的動物，眞正的數字高得多。比起美國，日本與中國更缺乏全面性的資料。

> **on the whole** 整體上　　restrictive〔rɪˈstrɪktɪv〕adj. 限制的
> official〔əˈfɪʃəl〕adj. 官方的
> statistics〔stəˈtɪstɪks〕n. pl. 統計數字
> misleading〔mɪsˈlidɪŋ〕adj. 誤導的
> authorities〔əˈθɔrətɪz〕n. pl. 官方　　worth〔wɜθ〕adj. 值得…的
> comprehensive〔ˌkɑmprɪˈhɛnsɪv〕adj. 總括性的；全面性的

Now Europe is reforming the rules governing animal experiments by restricting the number of animals used in labs. Alternatives to animal testing, such as using human tissue or computer models, are now strongly recommended. In addition, sharing all research results freely should help to reduce the number of animals for scientific use. At present, scientists often share only the results of successful experiments. If their findings do not fit the hypothesis being tested, the work never sees the light of day. This practice means wasting time, money, and animals' lives in endlessly repeating the failed experiments.

現在歐洲正限制實驗室可使用的動物數，藉此改革動物試驗的管理規定。動物試驗的替代方案，諸如使用人體組織、電腦模組等，都被強烈建議。此外，大方地分享實驗結果，應該也能幫助減少科學使用的動物數。現在，科學家只分享成功的實驗結果。如果他們的發現不符合實驗的假設，其成果就永遠不會公諸於世。這種做法意味著在無止境的失敗實驗中浪費時間、金錢及動物的生命。

reform〔rɪˋfɔrm〕v. 改革　　govern〔ˋgʌvɚn〕v. 管理
restrict〔rɪˋstrɪkt〕v. 限制　　lab〔læb〕n. 實驗室
alternative〔ɔlˋtɝnətɪv〕n. 替代方案　　***animal testing*** 動物試驗
tissue〔ˋtɪʃu〕n. 組織　　recommend〔͵rɛkəˋmɛnd〕v. 推薦
reduce〔rɪˋdjus〕v. 減少
present〔ˋprɛznt〕n. 現在　　findings〔ˋfaɪndɪŋz〕n. pl. 發現
fit〔fɪt〕v. 符合　　hypothesis〔haɪˋpɑθəsɪs〕n. 假設
see the light (of day) 公諸於世　　practice〔ˋpræktɪs〕n. 習慣；做法
endlessly〔ˋɛndlɪslɪ〕adv. 無止境地　　repeat〔rɪˋpit〕v. 重覆
failed〔feld〕adj. 失敗的

Animal experimentation has taught humanity a great deal and saved countless lives. It needs to continue, even if that means animals sometimes suffer. Europe's new measures should eventually both reduce the number of animals used in experiments and improve the way in which scientific research is conducted.

動物試驗教導人類很多，也拯救了無數生命。儘管這代表有時候動物得受苦，動物試驗還是需要繼續下去。歐洲的新標準最終將減少實驗使用的動物，也改善科學研究的進行方式。

humanity〔hju'mænətɪ〕*n.* 人類　***a great deal*** 許多
countless〔'kaʊntlɪs〕*adj.* 數不清的　　suffer〔'sʌfə〕*v.* 受苦
measures〔'mɛʒəz〕*n. pl.* 標準
eventually〔ɪ'vɛntʃʊəlɪ〕*adv.* 最後
improve〔ɪm'pruv〕*v.* 改良　　conduct〔kən'dʌkt〕*v.* 進行

40.(**C**) 本文的主旨是什麼？
(A) 應該確保動物試驗要成功。
(B) 應該禁止在實驗室裡使用動物。
(C) <u>應該更努力減少實驗室使用的動物。</u>
(D) 應該要求科學家彼此分享實驗的結果。

ensure〔ɪn'ʃʊr〕*v.* 確保　　ban〔bæn〕*n.* 禁止
enforce〔ɪn'fors〕*v.* 實施（法律）　　effort〔'ɛfət〕*n.* 努力
require〔rɪ'kwaɪr〕*v.* 需要

41.(**D**) 關於實驗室裡使用的動物，下面敘述何者為真？
(A) 每年美國實驗室只使用一百一十萬隻動物。
(B) 歐洲完全不使用老鼠當作實驗動物。
(C) 英國使用的實驗動物沒中國多。
(D) <u>日本每年使用多少實驗動物，資料很有限。</u>

Britain〔'brɪtn̩〕*n.* 英國　　limited〔'lɪmɪtɪd〕*adj.* 有限的

42.(**B**) 下列何者是文中提及的實驗動物提代方案？
(A) 數據研究。　　　　　(B) <u>電腦模型。</u>
(C) 在動物體內植入 DNA。　(D) 死去動物的組織。

plant〔plænt〕*v.* 植入

43.(**A**) 失敗的動物試驗通常會如何？
(A) <u>不揭露給大眾知道。</u>
(B) 被做成教學材料。
(C) 收集起來將來再發表。
(D) 它們不會從研究主題列表中移除。

reveal〔rɪ'vil〕*v.* 揭露　　***the public*** 大眾
material〔mə'tɪrɪəl〕*n.* 材料　　publication〔ˌpʌblɪ'keʃən〕*n.* 發表
remove〔rɪ'muv〕*v.* 移除

第 44 至 47 題爲題組

　　Spider webs are one of the most fascinating examples of animal architecture. The most beautiful and structurally ordered are the orb webs. The main function of the web is to intercept and hold flying prey, such as flies, bees and other insects, long enough for the spider to catch them. In order to do **so**, the threads of the web have to withstand the impact forces from large and heavy prey as well as environmental forces from wind and rain for at least a day in most cases.

　　在動物建築術當中，蜘蛛網是最吸引人的範例之一。球體（圓形）蜘蛛網是最迷人也是結構最有條理的。蜘蛛網最主要的功能，就是攔截並且困住飛行的獵物，像是蒼蠅，蜜蜂和其他的昆蟲。困住獵物的時間，足夠讓蜘蛛去抓住他們。爲了要達到這個目的，蜘蛛網的線必須要能夠抵擋大型獵物的衝撞力道，以及風雨等的大自然力量，在多數情形中至少要能撐一天。

web〔wɛb〕*n.* 網　　fascinating〔ˈfæsn̩ˌetɪŋ〕*adj.* 迷人的
architecture〔ˈɑrkəˌtɛktʃɚ〕*n.* 建築
structurally〔ˈstrʌktʃərəlɪ〕*adv.* 結構地
ordered〔ˈɔrdəd〕*adj.* 井然有序的　　orb〔ɔrb〕*n.* 球體；眼球
function〔ˈfʌŋkʃən〕*n.* 功能
intercept〔ˌɪntəˈsɛpt〕*v.* 中途攔截　　prey〔pre〕*n.* 獵物
insect〔ˈɪnsɛkt〕*n.* 昆蟲　　thread〔θrɛd〕*n.* 線
withstand〔wɪθˈstænd〕*v.* 抵抗　　impact〔ˈɪmpækt〕*n.* 衝擊

　　The orb web is found to have two main characteristics. The first is its geometry, which consists of an outer frame and a central part from which threads radiate outward. Enclosed in the frame are capture spirals winding round and round from the web center out to the frame. The whole web is in tension and held in place by anchor threads, which connect the frame to the surrounding vegetation or objects.

　　圓形蜘蛛網有兩大特色。第一個特色就是幾何學，它是由外部的框架，加上由中心點往外放射的線所組成。在外框裡面的是，由中心點一圈一圈向外捕捉獵物的螺旋絲。整張蜘蛛網結構緊密，並由連結周圍的植物或物體的支撐線，固定在固定位置上。

characteristic〔ˌkærɪktə'rɪstɪk〕*n.* 特色
geometry〔dʒɪ'ɑmətrɪ〕*n.* 幾何學　　***consist of*** 由～組成
outer〔'autɚ〕*adj.* 外部的　　　frame〔frem〕*n.* 框架
radiate〔'redɪˌet〕*v.* 放射　　　outward〔'autwɚd〕*adv.* 向外地
enclosed〔ɪn'klozd〕*adj.* 包含在內的　　capture〔'kæptʃɚ〕*v.,n.* 捕捉
spiral〔'spaɪrəl〕*n.* 螺旋形的東西　　wind〔waɪnd〕*v.* 蜿蜒；纏繞
tension〔'tɛnʃən〕*n.* 緊張；張力　　***in place*** 在適當的位置
anchor〔'æŋkɚ〕*n.* 支撐物　　surrounding〔sə'raundɪŋ〕*adj.* 周圍的
vegetation〔ˌvɛdʒə'teʃən〕*n.* 植物

The second and perhaps most important characteristic is the material
with which it is built. Spider silk is a kind of natural composite that gives
this lightweight fiber a tensile strength comparable to that of steel, while at
the same time making it very elastic. Two types of silk threads are used in
the web. One is highly elastic and can stretch to almost twice its original
length before breaking and, for most types of spiders, is covered in glue.
This type is used in the capture spiral for catching and holding prey. The
other is stiffer and stronger, and is used for the radius, frames and anchor
threads, which allows the web to withstand prey impact and to keep its
structural strength through a wide range of environmental conditions.

　　第二，也可能是最重要的特色就是建造的材質。這種輕量的纖維抗張強度
和鋼不相上下，同時它的彈性也很強。蜘蛛網裡面有兩種材質的絲。其中一種
很有彈性，甚至可以拉長到原來的兩倍才斷，大多數的蜘蛛絲表層都有黏性，
捕捉獵物的螺旋絲就是用這種絲來困住獵物。另一種絲質比較堅硬，強度也比
較高，用來製成半徑活動範圍，外框以及抵擋獵物的掙脫力量，以及各種氣候
狀況的支撐線。

silk〔sɪlk〕*n.* 絲　　composite〔kəm'pɑzɪt〕*n.* 合成物
lightweight〔'laɪtˌwet〕*adj.* 輕量的　　fiber〔'faɪbɚ〕*n.* 纖維
tensile〔'tɛnsl̩〕*adj.* 可拉長的；有張力的
tensile strength 張力；抗張強度
comparable〔'kɑmpərəbl̩〕*adj.* 可匹敵的＜*to*＞
steel〔stil〕*n.* 鋼　　elastic〔ɪ'læstɪk〕*adj.* 有彈性的
stretch〔strɛtʃ〕*v.* 拉長　　glue〔glu〕*n.* 膠水；黏著劑
stiff〔stɪf〕*adj.* 堅硬的　　radius〔'redɪəs〕*n.* 半徑範圍

44. (**B**) 這篇文章的主旨為何？
(A) 自然界的食物網路。　(B) <u>圓形蜘蛛網的構造。</u>
(C) 幾何學研究網。　(D) 蜘蛛網的大自然挑戰。

network〔ˈnɛtwɚk〕*n.* 網路　construction〔kənˈstrʌkʃən〕*n.* 構造

45. (**A**) 第一段中的 *so* 指的是什麼？
(A) <u>捕捉和困住小動物。</u>　(B) 找到蜘蛛網的好材質。
(C) 觀察蜘蛛的行為模式。　(D) 表現出動物的驚人建築藝術。

refer to 指　creature〔ˈkritʃɚ〕*n.* 生物；動物
observe〔əbˈzɝv〕*v.* 觀察　present〔prɪˈzɛnt〕*v.* 表現

46. (**C**) 蜘蛛網的哪一部分是用來支撐的？
(A) 蜘蛛網的中心位置。　(B) 線上的膠。
(C) <u>支撐線。</u>　(D) 捕捉獵物的螺旋絲。

47. (**B**) 根據本文，關於蜘蛛網的絲線下列敘述何者正確？
(A) 他們全部都有黏性而且可以拉長。
(B) <u>他們的強度通常足以持續一天。</u>
(C) 他們可以去除昆蟲的有害化學物質。
(D) 他們是由自然界中稀有的植物製成的。

sticky〔ˈstɪkɪ〕*adj.* 有黏性的　harmful〔ˈhɑrmfəl〕*adj.* 有害的
chemical〔ˈkɛmɪkl̩〕*n.* 化學物質
extendable〔ɪkˈstɛnəbl̩〕*adj.* 可伸展的

第 48 至 51 題為題組

　　Doctor of Philosophy, usually abbreviated as PhD or Ph.D., is an advanced academic degree awarded by universities. The first Doctor of Philosophy degree was awarded in Paris in 1150, but the degree did not acquire its modern status until the early 19th century. The doctorate of philosophy as it exists today originated at Humboldt University. The German practice was later adopted by American and Canadian universities, eventually becoming common in large parts of the world in the 20th century.

　　Doctor of Philosophy（博士），通常縮寫成 PhD 或 Ph.D.，是一項由大學頒發的高等學位。第一個博士學位是一一五〇年在巴黎頒發的，不過這個學位要到十九世紀初期才奠定它現代的地位。現今的博士學位是起源於漢堡德大學。這項德國的做法之後被美國、加拿大的大學採用，最後於二十世紀在世界大多數地區普及。

philosophy〔fəˈlɑsəfɪ〕n. 哲學　　abbreviate〔əˈbrivɪˌet〕v. 縮寫
advanced〔ədˈvænst〕adj. 高等的
academic〔ˌækəˈdɛmɪk〕adj. 學術的　　degree〔dɪˈgri〕n. 學位
award〔əˈwɔrd〕v. 頒發　　acquire〔əˈkwaɪr〕v. 獲得
status〔ˈstetəs〕n. 地位　　doctorate〔ˈdɑktərɪt〕n. 博士學位
exist〔ɪgˈzɪst〕v. 存在　　originate〔əˈrɪdʒəˌnet〕v. 源於
Humboldt University 漢堡德大學【位於德國柏林，成立於 1809 年】
German〔ˈdʒɜmən〕adj. 德國的　　later〔ˈletɚ〕adv. 之後
adopt〔əˈdɑpt〕v. 採用　　Canadian〔kəˈnedɪən〕adj. 加拿大的
common〔ˈkɑmən〕adj. 普遍的

For most of history, even a bachelor's degree at a university was the privilege of a rich few, and many academic staff did not hold doctorates. But as higher education expanded after the Second World War, the number of PhDs increased accordingly. American universities geared up first: By 1970, America was graduating half of the world's PhDs in science and technology. Since then, America's annual output of PhDs has doubled, to 64,000. Other countries are catching up. PhD production has sped up most dramatically in Mexico, Portugal, Italy, and Slovakia. Even Japan, where the number of young people is shrinking, has **churned out** about 46% more PhDs.

　　歷史上大多數的時間，在大學裡拿到學士學位也算是少數有錢人才有的特權，大多數教職員都沒有博士學位。但在第二次世界大戰之後，高等教育開始擴展，博士的數量也因此增加。美國大學率先加速：到了一九七〇年，美國在科技方面產出世界半數的博士。從那之後，美國每年畢業的博士倍增到六萬四千人。其他國家也慢慢跟上，在墨西哥、葡萄牙、義大利跟斯洛伐克的博士產量增加最快。甚至在年輕人口縮減的日本也增加了百分之四十六的博士。

bachelor〔ˈbætʃələ〕n. 學士
privilege〔ˈprɪvlɪdʒ〕n. 特權　　staff〔stæf〕n. 職員
hold〔hold〕v. 擁有　　expand〔ɪkˈspænd〕v. 擴張
increase〔ɪnˈkris〕v. 增加　　accordingly〔əˈkɔrdɪŋlɪ〕adv. 因此

gear up 加速　　technology〔tɛk'nɑlədʒɪ〕n. 科技
annual〔'ænjʊəl〕adj. 年度的　　output〔'aʊtˌpʊt〕n. 產量
double〔'dʌbḷ〕v. 變爲兩倍　　**catch up** 追上
production〔prə'dʌkʃən〕n. 生產　　**speed up** 加速
dramatically〔drə'mætɪkəlɪ〕adv. 大幅地
Portugal〔'pɔrtʃəgḷ〕n. 葡萄牙
Slovakia〔slo'vɑkɪə〕n. 斯洛伐克
shrink〔ʃrɪŋk〕v. 縮水　　**churn out** 大量製作

Researchers now warn that the supply of PhDs has far outstripped
demand. America produced more than 100,000 doctoral degrees between
2005 and 2009, while there were just 16,000 new professorships. In
research, the story is similar. Even graduates who find work outside
universities may not fare all that well. Statistics show that five years after
receiving their degrees, more than 60% of PhDs in Slovakia and more than
45% in Belgium, the Czech Republic, Germany, and Spain are still on
temporary contracts. About one-third of Austria's PhD graduates take
jobs unrelated to their degrees.

　　研究者警告，博士的供給已遠超過需求。美國在二〇〇五年到二〇〇九年
間生產超過十萬名博士，但教授的職缺卻只有一萬六千個。在研究領域，狀況
也很類似。即使在校外找到工作的畢業生也不一定一帆風順。數據顯示在取得
學位後五年，在斯洛伐克有超過百分之六十的博士，在比利時、捷克共和國、
德國、西班牙有超過百分之四十五的博士，都只簽了短期的工作合約。奧地利
大約有三分之一的博士畢業生從事跟自己學位無關的工作。

warn〔wɔrn〕v. 警告　　supply〔sə'plaɪ〕n. 供給
outstrip〔aʊt'strɪp〕v. 超過　　demand〔dɪ'mænd〕n. 需求
doctoral〔'dɑktərəl〕adj. 博士的
professorship〔prə'fɛsəˌʃɪp〕n. 教授的職位
graduate〔'grædʒʊɪt〕n. 畢業生　　**fare well** 進展順利
Belgium〔'bɛldʒɪəm〕n. 比利時　　Czech〔tʃɛk〕adj. 捷克的
Germany〔'dʒɝmənɪ〕n. 德國　　Spain〔spen〕n. 西班牙
temporary〔'tɛmpəˌrɛrɪ〕adj. 暫時的　　contract〔'kɑntrækt〕n. 合約
Austria〔'ɔstrɪə〕n. 奧地利
unrelated〔ˌʌnrɪ'letɪd〕adj. 與…無關的

Today, top universities around the world are still picking bright students and grooming them as potential PhDs. After all, it isn't in their interests to turn the smart students away: The more bright students stay at universities, the better it is for academics. But considering the oversupply of PhDs, some people have already begun to wonder whether doing a PhD is a good choice for an individual.

現今，全球的頂尖大學仍然在挑選聰明的學生，並培訓他們成為有潛力的博士。畢竟，將聰明的學生拒於門外不符合他們的利益。愈多聰明的學生留在大學裡，對學術就愈好。但考量到博士的過量供應，有些人已經開始納悶，究竟攻讀博士學位對個人而言是否是個好選擇。

bright〔braɪt〕*adj.* 聰明的　　groom〔grum〕*v.* 培訓
potential〔pəˈtɛnʃəl〕*adj.* 有潛力的
turn sb. away 拒某人於門外　　academics〔͵ækəˈdɛmɪks〕*n.* 學術
oversupply〔ˈovɚsəˈplaɪ〕*n.* 過量供應
wonder〔ˈwʌndɚ〕*v.* 納悶
individual〔͵ɪndəˈvɪdʒuəl〕*n.* 個人

48.（**B**）現代授與博士學位的做法是從哪個國家開始的？
　　(A) 法國。　　　　　　　(B) 德國。
　　(C) 加拿大。　　　　　　(D) 美國。
　　grant〔grænt〕*v.* 授與

49.（**D**）下列哪個字跟第二段的"**churned out**"意思最接近？
　　(A) 失敗。　　　　　　　(B) 警告。
　　(C) 需求。　　　　　　　(D) 生產。

50.（**D**）從第三段可以推論出下列何者？
　　(A) 奧地利的博士畢業生不被鼓勵到大學以外的地方工作。
　　(B) 大多德國的博士都在畢業後立即找到持久的工作。
　　(C) 對美國的博士而言，找教職比找研究工作還容易。
　　(D) 對博士而言，畢業五年後要在斯洛伐克找到持久的工作比西班牙難。
　　permanent〔ˈpɝmənənt〕*adj.* 持久的
　　holder〔ˈholdɚ〕*n.* 持有人　　position〔pəˈzɪʃən〕*n.* 職位

51. (**A**) 下列何者最能描述作者對近年來博士增加的態度？

    (A) 擔心的。   (B) 支持的

    (C) 冷漠的。   (D) 樂觀的。

    attitude〔'ætə,tjud〕*n.* 態度

    concerned〔kən'sɜnd〕*adj.* 擔心的

    supportive〔sə'portɪv〕*adj.* 支持的

    indifferent〔ɪn'dɪfrənt〕*adj.* 冷漠的

    optimistic〔,ɑptə'mɪstɪk〕*adj.* 樂觀的

第貳部分：非選擇題

一、中譯英：

1. 日本的核電廠爆炸已經引起全球對核子能源安全的疑慮。

The explosion at the Japanese nuclear power $\begin{Bmatrix} \text{plant} \\ \text{station} \end{Bmatrix}$ has

$\begin{Bmatrix} \text{raised} \\ \text{triggered} \\ \text{sparked} \end{Bmatrix}$ global $\begin{Bmatrix} \text{concern} \\ \text{anxiety} \\ \text{worry} \\ \text{doubt} \\ \text{suspicion} \\ \text{fear} \\ \text{uncertainty} \end{Bmatrix}$ about the safety of nuclear energy.

2. 科學家正尋求安全、乾淨又不昂貴的綠色能源，以滿足我們對電的需求。

Scientists are $\begin{Bmatrix} \text{looking for} \\ \text{searching for} \\ \text{seeking} \end{Bmatrix}$ safe, clean, and inexpensive green

energy to satisfy our demand for electricity.

二、英文作文：

【範例】

A graduation ceremony is an event that symbolizes a sense of accomplishment. You have spent a number of years working toward a singular goal: a diploma. With that diploma, you can take the next step in your education, or perhaps, seek employment. Though the ceremony indicates a type of closure, that is, the end of one period of your life, it marks the beginning of another. Therefore, while there may be some sadness in saying goodbye to old friends, it is quickly erased by the excitement of moving forward. No matter which grade level you graduate from, the moment marks the beginning of greater personal independence.

Following the ceremony, we should have a big party and invite our friends, family and former teachers to share the achievement. There should be food and drinks, music and dancing, and everybody should be encouraged to enjoy themselves. There shouldn't be any speeches or presentations. The party should carry the spirit of excitement; celebrating the fact that we are taking the next step forward in the journey of life.

symbolize〔'sɪmbḷ͵aɪz〕v. 象徵　　sense〔sɛns〕n. 感受
accomplishment〔ə'kɑmplɪʃmənt〕n. 成就
singular〔'sɪŋgjələ〕adj. 單一的
diploma〔dɪ'plomə〕n. 文憑　　seek〔sik〕v. 尋找
employment〔ɪm'plɔɪmənt〕n. 就業
indicate〔'ɪndə͵ket〕v. 表示　　closure〔'kloʒə〕n. 終止
that is 也就是說　　mark〔mɑrk〕v. 標記
erase〔ɪ'res〕v. 拭去　　former〔'fɔrmə〕adj. 先前的
enjoy *oneself* 玩得愉快　　speech〔spitʃ〕n. 演講
presentation〔͵prɛzn̩'teʃən〕n. 報告
spirit〔'spɪrɪt〕n. 精神　　journey〔'dʒɝnɪ〕n. 旅程

100年指定科目考試英文科試題修正意見

題　　號	出　　　　處
一、詞彙 第 6 題	Each of the planets…colliding with *each other*. → Each of the planets…colliding with **one another**. ＊太陽系有九大行星，強調「整體之間」的彼此，應用 one another； 　強調「各個之間」，才用 each other。（詳見「文法寶典」p.142）
四、篇章結構 第四段 第 2 行 選項 (F)	Many of them…one of *the reasons of* this decline…. → Many of them…one of **the reasons for** this decline…. ＊reason 後應接介系詞 for，cause 後面才用 of。 The link…since *the* 1999 tragedy…. → The link…since **a** 1999 tragedy…. ＊未指定，應用不定冠詞 a，如再次提到才用定冠詞 the。 　（詳見「文法寶典」p.217）
第 36 題	Why do some people *prefer using dogs than pigs* in search of truffles? → Why do some people **prefer using dogs to pigs**…. 或→ …**prefer using dogs rather than pigs**…. ＊prefer A to B　喜歡 A 甚於 B 　= prefer A rather than B …*in search of* truffles? → …**when in search of** truffles? ＊加上 when 後句意才清楚。
第 37 題	(C) Eating them fresh right after *being* collected. → Eating them fresh right after **they are** collected. (D) Eating them after *being* refrigerated. → Eating them after **they are** refrigerated. ＊如果不改，則句意不清楚。
第 40 至 43 題 第三段 第 4 行	…number of *animals* for scientific use. → …number of **animals needed** for scientific use. ＊為了使句意清楚，須加 needed。
第 42 題	…an alternative *to replace animal experiments?* → …an alternative **to animal experiments?** ＊alternative（替代方案）後的 to 是介系詞，須接動名詞或名詞。
第 50 題 (A)	PhD graduates in Austria…*outside university*. → PhD graduates in Austria…**outside a university**. 或→ …**outside the university**. 或→ …**outside of a university**.

100 年指定科目考試英文科出題來源

題　　號	出　　　　　　處
一、詞彙 第 1～10 題	今年所有的詞彙題，除了第九題題幹 Wikileaks (維基洩密)外，對錯選項均出自「新版高中常用 7000 字」。
二、綜合測驗 第 11～15 題	改編自 Business Communication 的書第 216 頁的一文，作者為 A. C. Krizan, Patricia Merrier, Joyce P. Logan, Karen Schneiter Williams，關於處理客戶要求的文章。
三、文意選填 第 21～30 題	出自於 squidoo 網站 （http://www.squidoo.com/the-chosen-word），有關 The History of the Written Word 寫作歷史的文章。
四、篇章結構 第 31～35 題	出自於韓國 daum（http://blog.daum.net/galleriasoonsoo/200）網站，一篇作者評論（Bullying）關於霸凌看法的文章。
五、閱讀測驗 第 36～39 題	取材自 mssf（http://www.mssf.org/cookbook/truffles.html）網站裡的食譜，敘述有關松露的從希臘羅馬時代開始，松露在歐洲就一直被當成佳餚，甚至當成藥。它們是世上最昂貴的自然食品之一，通常一磅索價二百五十到四百五十美元。松露其實就是蘑菇，不過是特殊種類。它們與特定的植物根部緊密生長在一起，它們的子實體則長在地下。這是它們之所以那麼難找的原因起源及調理方法的文章。
第 40～43 題	改寫自中國海詞（http://dict.cn/kuaile/00/n-1800.html）網站 2009 年 5 月 19 日的一文，作著 webmaster 的論點為人們不會把藥測試在動物身上。但這樣的實驗對動物來說很痛苦。人們為了要協助彌補醫療知識的廣大漏洞，還是需要動物做試驗，引申至如何改善科學研究。
第 44～47 題	出自英國沃爾森學院 www.wolfson.ox.ac.uk（Wolfson College）的研究紀錄第 111 頁，關於蜘蛛絲功用的文章。
第 48～51 題	改寫自 Doctor of philosophy（http://doctor-of-philosophy.co.tv/）介紹博士 Ph.D 這個詞的起源及必備條件的文章。

※ 今年題目出得很嚴謹，只有一個地方需要修正：

題　　號	修　　正　　意　　見
三、文意選填 第一段 第 4 行	…, including e-mail and instant messaging. → including *in* e-mail and instant messaging. ＊ 依句意，須加上 in 才合理。

【100 年指考】綜合測驗：11-15 出題來源

Adjustment refusals

Handling customer is a common task for most business firms. These claims include requests to exchange merchandise, requests for refunds, requests that work be corrected.

Most of these claims are approved because they are legitimate. However, some requests for adjustment must be denied. Although the customer expects a positive response , the company must send an adjustment refusal message.

Adjustment refusals are negative messages for the customer. They are necessary when the customer is at fault or when the vendor has already done what can reasonably or legally be expected.

An adjustment refusal message requires your best communication skills because it is bad news to the receiver. You goal is refuse to the claim and, at the same time, retain the customer. You may refuse the request the adjustment request and even try to sell merchandise or service.
All this is happening when the customer is probably angry, disappointed, or inconvenienced.

【100 年指考】文意選填：21-30 出題來源

The History of the Written Word

I researched online about the history of writing to try to understand how one persons interpretation of a piece of text can be so different. We know that language existed for a long time before writing. We have probably been talking for between 50,000 and 100,000 years. But archaeology suggests that the first writing emerged around 6,000 years ago.

Pictograms (pictures whose meaning is directly related to the image: eg. a snake means a snake) were first in use in Ancient Egypt and Mesopotamia. These pictograms evolved into Hieroglyphics when the meanings came to include verbs (image of an eye might now also mean 'to see something') and phonetics, (the snake image could mean an 'ess' sound)

The spoken word has nearly all but disappeared as we find ourselves surrounded by technology, email, and internet. We even stay in touch with our families and friends through Social Networking sites, where we have shortened conversations, where we send our co-workers an email in the next cubicle, instead of standing up and walking over to talk to them.

【100 年指考】篇章結構：31-35 出題來源

Bullying

November 19, 2007

The effects of bullying can be serious and even fatal. Unfortunately, it is still a greatly unresearched area. The link between bullying and school violence has attracted increasing attention since the 1999 Columbine High School massacre. That year, two shotgun-wielding students, both of whom had been identified as gifted and who had been bullied for years, killed 13 people, wounded 24 and then committed suicide. A year later an analysis by officials at the U.S. Secret Service of 37 premeditated school shootings found that bullying, which some of the shooters described "in terms that approached torment," played a major role in more than two-thirds of the attacks. It is estimated that about 60-80% of children are bullied at school.

Since bullying is mostly ignored; it may provide an important clue in crowd behaviour and passer-by behaviour. Numerous psychologists have been puzzled by the inactivity of crowds in urban centres when crimes occur in crowded places. Many have suggested bullying as one of the reason of this decline in emotional sensitivity and acceptance of violence as normal. When someone is bullied, it is not only the bully and victim who are becoming less sensitive to iolence. In most cases, the friends and classmates of the bully and the victim accept the violence as normal.

【100 年指考】閱讀測驗：36-39 出題來源

Truffles

Since the times of the Greeks and Romans these fungi have been used in Europe as delicacies, as aphrodisiacs, and as medicines. They are among the most expensive of the world's natural foods, often commanding as much as $250 to $450 per pound. Truffles are harvested in Europe with the aid of female pigs or truffle dogs, which are able to detect the strong smell of mature truffles underneath the surface of the ground. The female pig becomes excited when she sniffs a chemical that is similar to the male swine sex attractant. The use of pigs is risky, though, because of their natural tendency to eat any remotely edible thing.

For this reason, dogs have been trained to dig into the ground wherever they find these odors, and they willingly exchange their truffle for a piece of bread and a pat on the head. Not a bad trade for the truffle hunter! Some truffle merchants dig for their prizes themselves when they see truffle flies hovering around the base of a tree. Once discovered, truffles can be collected in subsequent years at the same site.

⋮

【100 年指考】閱讀測驗：40-43 出題來源

People would not test medicines on animals

In an ideal world, people would not test medicines on animals. Such experiments are stressful and sometimes painful for animals, and expensive and time-consuming for people. Yet there are vast gaps in medical knowledge which animal experimentation can help close. People have power over animals, so they use animals to help their own species. Yet the notion that animal suffering is pitted against human welfare — animal pain against human gain — is too stark. After all, it is in scientists interests to treat animals well. If laboratory animals are properly looked after, differences in experimental results are more likely to be down to the science than to the guinea-pigs health. Sometimes, numbing animals pain makes sense, too. Research has shown that giving pain-relieving drugs to animals that are undergoing experimental surgery may enhance the results, by making the animal's experience more like a person's. And some changes in the regulation of scientific research, proposed by the European Commission on May 5th, should further reduce animal suffering and at the same time produce better science.

Murine morals Between 50m and 100m animals are used in research each year around the world ，says the Nuffield Council on Bioethics ，a British think-tank. Europe has the world's most restrictive laws on animal experiments. Even so its scientists use some 12m animals a year，most of them mice and rats，for medical research. That number has been creeping up ，mainly because scientists can now plant foreign genes into creatures so that they better mimic human responses to disease.

【100 年指考】閱讀測驗：44-47 出題來源

The wind in the webs: orb-weavers and their silk constructions

　　Spider webs are one of the most fascinating examples of animal architecture, especially the small size …

【100 年指考】閱讀測驗：48-51 出題來源

Doctor of Philosophy

　　Doctor of Philosophy, abbreviated to PhD, or Ph.D. in English-speaking countries for the Latin , meaning "teacher in philosophy", is an advanced academic degree awarded by universities. In most English-speaking countries, the PhD is the highest degree one can earn (although in some countries like the UK, Ireland, and the Commonwealth nations higher doctorates are awarded). The PhD or equivalent has become a requirement for a career as a university professor or researcher in most fields. The academic level of degrees known as doctorates of philosophy varies according to the country and time period.

　　The doctorate was extended to philosophy in the European universities in the Middle Ages. At that time all academic disciplines outside the professional fields of theology, medicine and law came under the broad heading of "philosophy" (or "natural philosophy" when referring to science). According to Wellington, Bathmaker, Hunt, McCullough and Sikes (2005), the first Doctor of Philosophy degree was awarded in Paris in 1150, but the degree did not acquire its modern status as an advanced research degree until the early nineteenth century, following the practice in Germany. Prior to the nineteenth century, professional doctoral degrees could only be awarded in theology, law, or medicine. In 1861, Yale University adopted the German practice (first introduced in the 19th century at the Berlin University) of granting the degree, abbreviated as Dr. phil., to younger students who had completed a prescribed course of graduate study and successfully defended a thesis/dissertation containing original research in science or in the humanities.

From the United states, the degree spread to Canada in 1900, and then to the United Kingdom in 1917. This displaced the existing Doctor of Philosophy degree in some universities; for instance, the DPhil (higher doctorate in the faculty of philosophy) at the University of st Andrews was discontinued and replaced with the Ph.D., (research doctorate). Oxford retained the DPhil abbreviation for their research degrees. Some newer UK universities, for example Buckingham (est. 1976), Sussex (est. 1961), and, until a few years ago, York (est. 1963), chose to adopt the DPhil, as did some universities in New Zealand.

100 學年度指定科目考試（英文）

大考中心公佈答案

題號	答案	題號	答案	題號	答案
1	A	21	L	41	D
2	A	22	G	42	B
3	C	23	B	43	A
4	C	24	E	44	B
5	D	25	A	45	A
6	C	26	H	46	C
7	A	27	I	47	B
8	B	28	J	48	B
9	B	29	C	49	D
10	B	30	F	50	D
11	D	31	F	51	A
12	B	32	D		
13	A	33	A		
14	C	34	E		
15	C	35	C		
16	D	36	B		
17	D	37	C		
18	A	38	C		
19	C	39	D		
20	B	40	C		

100學年度指定科目考試
各科成績標準一覽表

科　目	頂　標	前　標	均　標	後　標	底　標
國　文	71	66	59	50	42
英　文	79	69	51	33	23
數學甲	82	71	51	32	20
數學乙	86	75	55	34	22
化　學	75	66	51	37	29
物　理	73	73	53	34	25
生　物	77	69	54	41	32
歷　史	77	70	59	48	39
地　理	71	66	58	48	40
公民與社會	77	72	64	55	48

※ 以上五項標準均取為整數（小數只捨不入），且其計算均不含缺考生之成績，
計算方式如下：

頂標：成績位於第88百分位數之考生成績。
前標：成績位於第75百分位數之考生成績。
均標：成績位於第50百分位數之考生成績。
後標：成績位於第25百分位數之考生成績。
底標：成績位於第12百分位數之考生成績。

例：　某科之到考考生為99982人，則該科五項標準為

頂標：成績由低至高排序，取第87985名（99982×88%=87984.16，取整數，
小數無條件進位）考生的成績，再取整數(小數只捨不入)。

前標：成績由低至高排序，取第74987名（99982×75%=74986.5，取整數，
小數無條件進位）考生的成績，再取整數(小數只捨不入)。

均標：成績由低至高排序，取第49991名（99982×50%=49991）考生的成績，
再取整數(小數只捨不入)。

後標：成績由低至高排序，取第24996名（99982×25%=24995.5，取整數，
小數無條件進位）考生的成績，再取整數(小數只捨不入)。

底標：成績由低至高排序，取第11998名（99982×12%=11997.84，取整數，
小數無條件進位）考生的成績，再取整數(小數只捨不入)。

九十九年大學入學指定科目考試試題
英文考科

第壹部分：選擇題（佔72分）

一、詞彙（10分）

說明：　第1題至第10題，每題選出一個最適當的選項，標示在答案卡之「選擇題答案區」。每題答對得1分，答錯或劃記多於一個選項者倒扣1/3分，倒扣到本大題之實得分數爲零爲止。未作答者，不給分亦不扣分。

1. Chinese is a language with many _____ differences. People living in different areas often speak different dialects.
   (A) sociable　　(B) legendary　　(C) regional　　(D) superior

2. A menu serves to _____ customers about the varieties and prices of the dishes offered by the restaurant.
   (A) appeal　　(B) convey　　(C) inform　　(D) demand

3. Mary and Jane often fight over which radio station to listen to. Their _____ arises mainly from their different tastes in music.
   (A) venture　　(B) consent　　(C) dispute　　(D) temptation

4. The baby polar bear is being _____ studied by the scientists. Every move he makes is carefully observed and documented.
   (A) prosperously　(B) intensively　(C) honorably　(D) originally

5. At twelve, Catherine has won several first prizes in international art competitions. Her talent and skills are _____ for her age.
   (A) comparable　(B) exceptional　(C) indifferent　(D) unconvincing

6. After his superb performance, the musician received a big round of _____ from the appreciative audience.
   (A) vacuum　　(B) overflow　　(C) applause　　(D) spotlight

7. The water company inspects the pipelines and _____ the water supply regularly to ensure the safety of our drinking water.

   (A) exhibits   (B) monitors   (C) interprets   (D) converts

8. This year's East Asia Summit meetings will focus on critical _____ such as energy conservation, food shortages, and global warming.

   (A) issues   (B) remarks   (C) conducts   (D) faculties

9. Having fully recognized Mei-ling's academic ability, Mr. Lin strongly _____ her for admission to the university.

   (A) assured   (B) promoted   (C) estimated   (D) recommended

10. The weatherman has warned about drastic temperature change in the next few days, and suggested that we check the weather on a daily basis and dress _____.

    (A) necessarily   (B) significantly   (C) specifically   (D) accordingly

二、綜合測驗（10分）

說明： 第11題至第20題，每題一個空格。請依文意選出一個最適當的選項，標示在答案卡之「選擇題答案區」。每題答對得1分，答錯或劃記多於一個選項者倒扣1/3分，倒扣到本大題之實得分數爲零爲止。未作答者，不給分亦不扣分。

第11至15題爲題組

The sun is an extraordinarily powerful source of energy. In fact, the Earth ___11___ 20,000 times more energy from the sun than we currently use. If we used more of this source of heat and light, it ___12___ all the power needed throughout the world.

We can harness energy from the sun, or solar energy, in many ways. For instance, many satellites in space are equipped with large panels whose solar cells transform sunlight directly ___13___ electric power. These panels are covered with glass and are painted black inside to absorb as much heat as possible.

Solar energy has a lot to offer. To begin with, it is a clean fuel. In contrast, fossil fuels, such as oil or coal, release ___14___ substances into the air when they are burned. ___15___, fossil fuels will run out, but solar energy will continue to reach the Earth long after the last coal has been mined and the last oil well has run dry.

11. (A) repeats   (B) receives   (C) rejects   (D) reduces
12. (A) supplies   (B) has supplied   (C) was supplying   (D) could supply
13. (A) into   (B) from   (C) with   (D) off
14. (A) diligent   (B) harmful   (C) usable   (D) changeable
15. (A) Otherwise   (B) Therefore
    (C) What's more   (D) In comparison

第 16 至 20 題為題組

Signs asking visitors to keep their hands off the art are everywhere in the Louvre Museum, Paris. But one special sculpture gallery invites art lovers to allow their hands to ___16___ the works. The Louvre's Tactile Gallery, targeted at the blind and visually ___17___, is the only space in the museum where visitors can touch the sculptures, with no guards or alarms to stop them. Its latest exhibit is a ___18___ of sculpted lions, snakes, horses and eagles. The 15 animals exhibited are reproductions of famous works found elsewhere in the Louvre. Called "Animals, Symbols of Power," the exhibit ___19___ animals that were used by kings and emperors throughout history to symbolize the greatness of their reigns. The exhibit, opened in December 2008, ___20___ scheduled to run for about three years. During guided tours on the weekends, children can explore the art with blindfolds on.

16. (A) fix up   (B) run over   (C) take away   (D) knock off
17. (A) impair   (B) impairs   (C) impaired   (D) impairing
18. (A) collection   (B) cooperation   (C) completion   (D) contribution
19. (A) examines   (B) protects   (C) represents   (D) features
20. (A) is   (B) being   (C) has   (D) having

三、文意選填（10 分）

說明： 第 21 題至第 30 題，每題一個空格。請依文意在文章後所提供的 (A) 到
(J) 選項中分別選出最適當者，並將其字母代號標示在答案卡之「選擇
題答案區」。每題答對得 1 分，答錯或劃記多於一個選項者倒扣 1/9 分，
倒扣到本大題之實得分數爲零爲止。未作答者，不給分亦不扣分。

第 21 至 30 題爲題組

　　Textese (also known as chatspeak, texting language, or txt talk) is a
term for the abbreviations and slang most commonly used among young
people today. The ___21___ of textese is largely due to the necessary
brevity of mobile phone text messaging, though its use is also very
common on the Internet, including e-mail and instant messaging.

　　There are no ___22___ rules for writing textese. However, the
common practice is to use single letters, pictures, or numbers to represent
whole words. For example, "i <3 u" uses the picture ___23___ of a heart
"<3" for "love," and the letter "u" to ___24___ "you." For words which
have no common abbreviation, textese users often ___25___ the vowels
from a word, and the reader is forced to interpret a string of consonants
by re-adding the vowels. Thus, "dictionary" becomes "dctnry," and
"keyboard" becomes "kybrd." The reader must interpret the ___26___
words depending on the context in which it is used, as there are many
examples of words or phrases which use the same abbreviations. So if
someone says "ttyl, lol" they probably mean "talk to you later, lots of
love" not "talk to you later, laugh out loud," and if someone says "omg,
lol" they most ___27___ mean "oh my god, laugh out loud" not "oh my god,
lots of love."

　　The emergence of textese is clearly due to a desire to type less and
to communicate more ___28___ than one can manage without such
shortcuts. Yet it has been severely ___29___ as "wrecking our language."
Some scholars even consider the use of textese as "irritating" and

essentially lazy behavior. They're worried that "sloppy" habits gained while using textese will result in students' growing ___30___ of proper spelling, grammar and punctuation.

(A) quickly　(B) criticized　(C) likely　(D) abbreviated　(E) replace
(F) remove　(G) standard　(H) ignorance　(I) popularity　(J) symbol

四、篇章結構（10分）

說明：　第 31 題至第 35 題，每題一個空格。請依文意在文章後所提供的 (A) 到 (E) 選項中分別選出最適當者，填入空格中，使篇章結構清晰有條理，並將其英文字母代號標示在答案卡之「選擇題答案區」。每題答對得 2 分，答錯或劃記多於一個選項者倒扣 1/2 分，倒扣到本大題之實得分數為零為止。未作答者，不給分亦不扣分。

第 31 至 35 題為題組

　　Do you have trouble getting started in the morning? Do you have problems learning early in the day? If you do, you are not alone. ___31___ They learn better at night than they do in the morning.

　　To investigate when cockroaches learn best, researchers at Vanderbilt University tested the insects for which odor (peppermint or vanilla) they preferred. Most cockroaches preferred the smell of vanilla to that of peppermint at all times. ___32___ Therefore, the scientists trained the cockroaches to prefer the peppermint smell by rewarding the insects with a taste of sugar water when they approached a peppermint smell. ___33___

　　When the cockroaches were trained at night, they remembered the new associations (peppermint = sugar water; vanilla = salt water) for up to 48 hours. However, if the cockroaches were trained in the morning, they quickly forgot which smell went with which water. ___34___

So, cockroaches learn better at night than they do in the morning. ___35___ Because of this, it is likely that information they gather at night will be more useful to them. These experiments provide some clues about the interactions between body rhythms, learning and memory.

(A) When these insects moved toward a vanilla smell, on the other hand, they were punished with a taste of salt.

(B) This result thus shows that the time when they were trained decided the effect of their learning.

(C) They are often more active and tend to search for food during the night.

(D) They were also found to like sugar water, but not salt water.

(E) Cockroaches have the same problem!

五、閱讀測驗（32 分）

說明：　第 36 題至第 51 題，每題請分別根據各篇文章的文意選出一個最適當的選項，標示在答案卡之「選擇題答案區」。每題答對得 2 分，答錯或劃記多於一個選項者倒扣 2/3 分，倒扣到本大題之實得分數為零為止。未作答者，不給分亦不扣分。

第 36 至 39 題為題組

The following report appeared in a newspaper in February 2007.

On February 15, 2007, hundreds of people came to New York City's famous railroad station—Grand Central Terminal—to trade in old dollar bills for the new George Washington presidential US $1 coins. The gold-colored coin is the first in a new series by the U.S. Mint to honor former U.S. presidents. The Mint will issue four presidential US $1 coins a year through 2016. These coins will come out in the order in which each president served. The George Washington coin is the first to be released. John Adams, Thomas Jefferson and James Madison coins will come out later this year.

The presidential US $1 coins have a special design. For the first time since the 1930s, there are words carved into the edge of each coin, including the year in which the coin was issued and traditional mottos. Each coin will show a different president on its face, or heads side. It will also show the president's name. The other side of the coin will show the Statue of Liberty and the inscriptions "United States of America" and "$1."

There are some interesting facts about the coins. First, there will be one presidential US $1 coin for each president, except Grover Cleveland. He will have two! Cleveland is the only U.S. president to have served two nonconsecutive terms. The last president now scheduled to get a coin is Gerald Ford. That's because a president cannot appear on a coin when he is still alive. In addition, a president must have been deceased for two years before he can be on a coin.

36. According to the report, how many presidential US $1 coins were scheduled to be released by the end of 2007 altogether?
    (A) One.　　　(B) Two.　　　(C) Three.　　　(D) Four.

37. Why did the Mint issue the US $1 coins?
    (A) In response to U.S. citizens' requests.
    (B) In memory of the late U.S. presidents.
    (C) To attract more train commuters.
    (D) To promote the trading of dollar bills.

38. What may you find on the heads side of the new US $1 coin?
    (A) The name of a U.S. president.
    (B) The year when the coin was made.
    (C) The Statue of Liberty.　　　(D) English proverbs.

39. Which of the following can be inferred about the presidential coins?
    (A) President Gerald Ford's coin was issued in 2008.
    (B) The U.S. Mint has issued all the presidential coins by now.

(C) No presidential coin has been released for President Barack Obama.

(D) Every U.S. president had his coin made two years after his term was over.

第 40 至 43 題為題組

Newspapers have tried many things to stop a seemingly nonstop decline in readers. Now France is pushing forward with a novel approach: giving away papers to young readers in an effort to turn them into regular customers. The French government recently detailed plans of a project called "My Free Newspaper," under which 18- to 24-year-olds will be offered a free, year-long subscription to a newspaper of their choice.

Newspaper readership in France has been especially low among young people. According to a government study, only 10 percent of those aged 15 to 24 read a paid-for newspaper daily in 2007, down from 20 percent a decade earlier.

Emmanuel Schwartzenberg, a former media editor of *Le Figaro*, the oldest and second-largest national newspaper in France, said he had strong reservations about the government project. At a time when advertising is in steep decline, he said, newspapers should instead be looking at ways to raise more profits from readers, rather than giving papers away. "This just reinforces the belief that newspapers should be free, which is a very bad idea," Mr. Schwartzenberg said.

French readers, young and old, already have plenty of free options from which to choose, including newspaper websites and the free papers handed out daily in many city centers. Some bloggers said the new program might hold the most appeal to the few young people who do already read, and buy, newspapers.

The French government plans to promote the program with an advertising campaign aimed at young readers and their parents. However, when asked how to attract young readers to the printed press, the government said the primary channel for the ads would be the Internet.

40. Why did the French government decide to launch the free newspaper program?
    (A) To fight economic recession.
    (B) To win approval from youngsters.
    (C) To promote newspaper readership.
    (D) To improve the literacy rate in France.

41. Which of the following can be concluded from the passage?
    (A) Everyone considers the government project creative.
    (B) Newspaper readership is much higher in other countries.
    (C) Research shows young people have no interest in current affairs.
    (D) Giving away free papers is not a strong enough incentive to attract readers.

42. What is Mr. Schwartzenberg's attitude toward this program?
    (A) Skeptical.　　(B) Devoted.　　(C) Optimistic.　　(D) Indifferent.

43. According to the passage, where would the information about the free newspaper program in France most likely be seen?
    (A) In magazines.　　　　　　(B) On blogs.
    (C) In newspapers.　　　　　　(D) On the Internet.

第 44 至 47 題爲題組

Coffee experts are willing to pay large sums of money for high-quality coffee beans. The high-end beans, such as Kona or Blue Mountain, are known to cost extraordinary sums of money. Then there is Kopi Lowak (translated as "Civet Coffee"), the world's most expensive coffee, which sells for as much as US $50 per quarter-pound.

This isn't particularly surprising, given that approximately 500 pounds a year of Kopi Lowak constitute the entire world supply. What is surprising is why this particular coffee is so rare. In fact, it's not the plants that are rare. It's the civet droppings. That's right, the civet droppings—the body waste of the palm civet. Coffee beans aren't Kopi Lowak until they've been digested and come out in the body waste of the palm civet.

Palm civets are tree-dwelling, raccoon-like little animals, native to Southeast Asia and the Indonesian islands. They also have a love for coffee cherries. According to Kopi Lowak suppliers, palm civets eat the fruit whole, but only digest the outer fruit, leaving the beans intact. While the beans are not destroyed, they undergo a transformation in the animal's body. A chemical substance in the digestive system of the palm civet causes some changes to the beans to give them a unique flavor. However, this is not the only explanation why coffee beans retrieved from civet droppings have a special flavor all their own. Another possible reason is that palm civets have an unfailing instinct for picking the coffee cherries at the peak of their ripeness.

Kopi Lowak is reported to have a character in taste unlike any other coffee, complex with caramel undertones and an earthy or gamey flavor. Currently, most of the world's supply of Kopi Lowak is sold in Japan, though a few US markets are also starting to stock up on Kopi Lowak.

44. What does "**This**" in the second paragraph refer to?
    (A) Civet Coffee.　　　　　　　　(B) Blue Mountain coffee.
    (C) The high price of Kopi Lowak.　(D) The unique taste of Kona.

45. Why is Kopi Lowak expensive?
    (A) There is a very limited supply of the beans.
    (B) The coffee trees that grow the beans are scarce.
    (C) It takes a long time for the coffee beans to ripen.
    (D) Only a few experts know how to produce the beans.

46. What is the main point discussed in the third paragraph?

(A) Why palm civets like the coffee beans.

(B) Where Kopi Lowak is mainly harvested.

(C) What chemicals are found in the civet's digestive system.

(D) How palm civets change coffee fruit to Kopi Lowak beans.

47. Which of the following statements is true, according to the passage?

(A) Little palm civets eat only the outer layer of the coffee cherries.

(B) Palm civets somehow know the right time when the coffee fruit ripens.

(C) Kopi Lowak is most popular in Southeast Asia and the Indonesian islands.

(D) Kona and Blue Mountain are the most expensive coffees but only of average quality.

第 48 至 51 題爲題組

Gunter Grass was the winner of the 1999 Nobel Prize in Literature. His talents are revealed in a variety of disciplines: He is not only a novelist, poet and playwright, but also a renowned painter and sculptor. As he himself stresses, his creations are closely related to his unique personal history. His father was a German who joined the Nazi party in World War II, while his mother was Polish. As a result, he constantly suffered contradictory feelings: as a Pole who had been victimized, and as someone guilty of harming the Poles. The torment in his heart led him to denounce the Nazis and his political activism has continued throughout his career. His commitment to the peace movement and the environmental movement as well as his unfailing quest for justice has won him praise as "the conscience of the nation."

In the spring of 1996, he was inspired during a trip to Italy to write a poem with his watercolor brush directly on one of his paintings. Before long, a collection of his "water poems" was born. Painting and literature have become his major forms of creativity. For him, painting is a form of creation with concrete, sensual elements, while writing is a hard and abstract process. When he cannot find words to convey his thoughts, painting helps him find the words to express himself. In this way, Grass not only creates simple depictions of the objects he is fond of in life, such as melons, vegetables, fish, and mushrooms, but also uses them as symbols for mental associations of various kinds. For example, to express the complexity of reality, he sometimes places unrelated objects in the same painting, such as a bird and a housefly, or a mushroom and a nail. Grass has depicted a wide variety of natural scenes, animals and plants, and even human artifacts of the German countryside, portraying them in poems, and allowing words to make the paintings rich in literary value.

48. What caused Grass to feel confused and troubled when he was young?
    (A) He was the son of a Nazi and a victimized Pole.
    (B) He found himself fighting two opposing political parties.
    (C) He was trained to be an artist though he wanted to be a poet.
    (D) He was born with so many talents that he couldn't choose a direction.

49. Why has Grass been praised as "the conscience of the nation"?
    (A) He victimized the Poles and criticized the Nazis.
    (B) He has been a strong advocate of peace and justice.
    (C) He has shown great sympathy for the Poles through his poems.
    (D) He joined the Nazi party and showed great loyalty to his country.

50. Why was Grass's trip to Italy important to him?
    (A) He was inspired by a fine arts master in Italy.
    (B) He formed a new interest in painting simple objects there.
    (C) He developed a new form for creating his poems during the trip.
    (D) He found a new way to solve the conflict between the Nazis and the Poles.

51. Which of the following correctly characterizes Grass's poems, according to the passage?
(A) Most of his poems depict the cruelty of the Nazis.
(B) The theme of his poems won him the Nobel Peace Prize.
(C) The poems on his paintings are often not related to objects in the real world.
(D) The ideas in his poems are expressed more thoroughly with the help of his paintings.

第貳部份：非選擇題（佔 28 分）

一、中譯英（8 分）

說明：　1. 請將以下中文句子譯成正確、通順、達意的英文，並將答案寫在「答案卷」上。
　　　　2. 請依序作答，並標明題號。每題 4 分，共 8 分。

1. 近二十年來我國的出生率快速下滑。
2. 這可能導致我們未來人力資源的嚴重不足。

二、英文作文（20 分）

說明：　1. 依提示在「答案卷」上寫一篇英文作文。
　　　　2. 文長至少 120 個單詞（words）。

提示：　在你的記憶中，哪一種氣味（smell）最讓你難忘？請寫一篇英文作文，文長至少 120 字，文分兩段，第一段描述你在何種情境中聞到這種氣味，以及你初聞這種氣味時的感受，第二段描述這個氣味至今仍令你難忘的理由。

九十九年度指定科目考試英文科試題詳解

第壹部分：選擇題

一、詞彙：

1. (**C**) Chinese is a language with many <u>regional</u> differences. People living in different areas often speak different dialects.
   中文是一個有許多<u>區域</u>差異的語言。住在不同地區的人通常說不同的方言。
   - (A) sociable〔'soʃəbḷ〕*adj.* 善交際的
   - (B) legendary〔'lɛdʒənd,ɛrı〕*adj.* 傳說的
   - (C) *regional*〔'ridʒənḷ〕*adj.* 區域性的
   - (D) superior〔sə'pırıɚ〕*adj.* 較優秀的

   * dialect〔'daɪə,lɛkt〕*n.* 方言

2. (**C**) A menu serves to <u>inform</u> customers about the varieties and prices of the dishes offered by the restaurant.
   菜單用於<u>告知</u>顧客關於餐廳所提供的各種菜餚和價格。
   - (A) appeal〔ə'pil〕*v.* 懇求
   - (B) convey〔kən've〕*v.* 傳達
   - (C) *inform*〔ın'fɔrm〕*v.* 告知
   - (D) demand〔dɪ'mænd〕*v.* 要求

   * menu〔'mɛnju〕*n.* 菜單　　serve〔sɝv〕*v.* 有用；足夠 < to + V >
   variety〔və'raɪətı〕*n.* 多樣性　　dish〔dɪʃ〕*n.* 菜餚

3. (**C**) Mary and Jane often fight over which radio station to listen to. Their <u>dispute</u> arises mainly from their different tastes in music.
   瑪莉和珍常常為了要聽哪一個廣播電台而爭論。他們的<u>爭吵</u>主要起因於他們對音樂的愛好不同。
   - (A) venture〔'vɛntʃɚ〕*n.* 冒險的事業
   - (B) consent〔kən'sɛnt〕*n.* 同意
   - (C) *dispute*〔dɪ'spjut〕*n.* 爭論；爭吵
   - (D) temptation〔tɛmp'teʃən〕*n.* 誘惑

   * fight〔faɪt〕*v.* 打架；爭論　　*radio station* 廣播電台
   arise〔ə'raɪz〕*v.* 發生；起源
   mainly〔'menlı〕*adv.* 主要地　　taste〔test〕*n.* 愛好

4. (**B**) The baby polar bear is being <u>intensively</u> studied by the scientists. Every move he makes is carefully observed and documented.

這隻北極熊寶寶被科學家<u>徹底地</u>研究。牠的每個動作都被仔細地觀察並詳細記錄下來。

(A) prosperously〔'prɑspərəslɪ〕*adv.* 繁榮地

(B) *intensively*〔ɪn'tɛnsɪvlɪ〕*adv.* 徹底地

(C) honorably〔'ɑnərəblɪ〕*adv.* 光榮地

(D) originally〔ə'rɪdʒənlɪ〕*adv.* 原本

* *polar bear* 北極熊　　observe〔əb'zɝv〕*v.* 觀察

　document〔'dɑkjə,mɛnt〕*v.* 詳細記錄

5. (**B**) At twelve, Catherine has won several first prizes in international art competitions. Her talent and skills are <u>exceptional</u> for her age.

凱薩琳十二歲就已經在國際藝術比賽中贏得好幾個第一名。以她的年齡而言，她的才能和技巧是很<u>優秀的</u>。

(A) comparable〔'kɑmpərəbl̩〕*adj.* 可比較的

(B) *exceptional*〔ɪk'sɛpʃənl̩〕*adj.* 優秀的

(C) indifferent〔ɪn'dɪfrənt〕*adj.* 漠不關心的

(D) unconvincing〔ˌʌnkən'vɪnsɪŋ〕*adj.* 不令人信服的

* *first prize* 第一名　　competition〔ˌkɑmpə'tɪʃən〕*n.* 比賽

　talent〔'tælənt〕*n.* 才能　　skill〔skɪl〕*n.* 技巧

6. (**C**) After his superb performance, the musician received a big round of <u>applause</u> from the appreciative audience.

在音樂家精湛的表演後，他獲得有鑑賞力的觀眾的一陣熱烈<u>鼓掌</u>。

(A) vacuum〔'vækjuəm〕*n.* 真空；吸塵器

(B) overflow〔'ovɚ,flo〕*n.* 氾濫

(C) *applause*〔ə'plɔz〕*n.* 鼓掌喝采

(D) spotlight〔'spɑt,laɪt〕*n.* 聚光燈

* superb〔su'pɝb〕*adj.* 卓越的；精湛的

performance〔pɚ'fɔrməns〕*n.* 表演

musician〔mju'zɪʃən〕*n.* 音樂家

round〔raʊnd〕*n.* 一陣（歡呼聲）

appreciative〔ə'priʃɪ,etɪv〕*adj.* 有欣賞能力的

audience〔'ɔdɪəns〕*n.* 觀眾

7. (**B**) The water company inspects the pipelines and <u>monitors</u> the water supply regularly to ensure the safety of our drinking water.

水公司定期檢查管線以及檢測供水系統，來確保我們飲用水的安全。

(A) exhibit〔ɪgˈzɪbɪt〕v. 展示

(B) **monitor**〔ˈmɑnətə〕v. 監測；檢測

(C) interpret〔ɪnˈtɜprɪt〕v. 解釋　(D) convert〔kənˈvɜt〕v. 轉換

* inspect〔ɪnˈspɛkt〕v. 檢查；檢驗

pipeline〔ˈpaɪpˌlaɪn〕n.（石油、瓦斯等的）管線

supply〔səˈplaɪ〕n. 供給　　***water supply*** 供水系統

regularly〔ˈrɛgjələ‧lɪ〕adv. 定期地　　ensure〔ɪnˈʃʊr〕v. 確保；保證

safety〔ˈsɛftɪ〕n. 安全　　***drinking water*** 飲用水

8. (**A**) This year's East Asia Summit meetings will focus on critical <u>issues</u> such as energy conservation, food shortages, and global warming.

今年的東亞高峰會議將會著重於像是節能、食物短缺，以及全球暖化的重大議題上。

(A) ***issue***〔ˈɪʃʊ〕n. 議題　　　　(B) remark〔rɪˈmark〕n. 意見；評論

(C) conduct〔ˈkandʌkt〕n. 行為；品行

(D) faculty〔ˈfækḷtɪ〕n. 教職員；能力

* summit〔ˈsʌmɪt〕n. 高峰；高階層會議

East Asia Summit meeting 東亞高峰會議　　***focus on*** 集中；關心

critical〔ˈkrɪtɪkḷ〕adj. 重大的　　energy〔ˈɛnədʒɪ〕n. 能源；能量

conservation〔ˌkansəˈveʃən〕n. 保存；節約

shortage〔ˈʃɔrtɪdʒ〕n. 短缺　　***global warming*** 全球暖化

9. (**D**) Having fully recognized Mei-ling's academic ability, Mr. Lin strongly <u>recommended</u> her for admission to the university.

在完全認可美琳的學術能力後，林先生大力推薦她進入該所大學。

(A) assure〔əˈʃʊr〕v. 向～保證　　(B) promote〔prəˈmot〕v. 升遷

(C) estimate〔ˈɛstəˌmet〕v. 估計　　(D) ***recommend***〔ˌrɛkəˈmɛnd〕v. 推薦

* fully〔ˈfʊlɪ〕adv. 完全地；充分地

recognize〔ˈrɛkəgˌnaɪz〕v. 認識；認可

academic〔ˌækəˈdɛmɪk〕adj. 學術的　　ability〔əˈbɪlətɪ〕n. 能力

strongly〔ˈstrɔŋlɪ〕adv. 強烈地

admission〔ədˈmɪʃən〕n.（入學）許可；允許進入

university〔ˌjunəˈvɜsətɪ〕n. 大學

10. (**D**) The weatherman has warned about drastic temperature change in the next few days, and suggested that we check the weather on a daily basis and dress <u>accordingly</u>.

氣象播報員提醒大家，接下來的幾天，氣溫會有劇烈的變化，建議每天都要查看氣候，<u>並照</u>氣候穿衣。

(A) necessarily〔'nɛsə,sɛrəlɪ〕*adv.* 必要地

(B) significantly〔sɪg'nɪfəkəntlɪ〕*adv.* 顯著地

(C) specifically〔spɪ'sɪfɪkḷɪ〕*adv.* 明確地；清楚地

(D) ***accordingly***〔ə'kɔrdɪŋlɪ〕*adv.* 照著

　＊weatherman〔'wɛðə,mæn〕*n.* 氣象播報員

　warn〔wɔrn〕*v.* 警告；提醒　　drastic〔'dræstɪk〕*adj.* 劇烈的

　temperature〔'tɛmpərətʃə〕*n.* 氣溫　　suggest〔səg'dʒɛst〕*v.* 建議

　check〔tʃɛk〕*v.* 確認；查看　　***on a daily basis*** 每天

二、綜合測驗：

第 11 至 15 題為題組

The sun is an extraordinarily powerful source of energy. In fact, the Earth <u>receives</u> 20,000 times more energy from the sun than we currently
　　　　　　11
use. If we used more of this source of heat and light, it <u>could supply</u> all the power needed throughout the world.
　　　　　　　　　　　　　　　　　　　　　　　12

　　太陽是非常強大的能源。事實上，地球所接收的太陽能，是我們目前所使用的能源的兩萬倍。如果我們能多使用這種熱源和光源，它就能提供全世界所需要的所有能源。

　　extraordinarily〔ɪk'strɔrdṇ,ɜrəlɪ〕*adv.* 格外地；非常地

　　powerful〔'pauəfəl〕*adj.* 強有力的　　source〔sors〕*n.* 來源

　　energy〔'ɛnədʒɪ〕*n.* 能量　　***source of energy*** 能源

　　time〔taɪm〕*n.* 倍　　currently〔'kɜəntlɪ〕*adv.* 現在；目前

　　power〔'pauə〕*n.* 力量；能量

　　throughout〔θru'aut〕*prep.* 遍及；在⋯各處

　　throughout the world 在全世界

11. (**B**) (A) repeat〔rɪ'pit〕*v.* 重複　　(B) ***receive***〔rɪ'siv〕*v.* 收到；得到

　　　　　(C) reject〔rɪ'dʒɛkt〕*v.* 拒絕　　(D) reduce〔rɪ'djus〕*v.* 減少

12. (**D**) 由過去式動詞 used 可知，本句為「與現在事實相反」的假設，所以主要子句中，須用 should, would, could, 或 might 接原形動詞，故選 (D) *could supply*。【「與現在事實相反」的假設，87 年學測也考過。請參照「文法寶典」p.361】

We can harness energy from the sun, or solar energy, in many ways. For instance, many satellites in space are equipped with large panels whose solar cells transform sunlight directly <u>into</u> electric power.　These panels are
13
covered with glass and are painted black inside to absorb as much heat as possible.

　　我們可以將來自太陽的能源，也就是太陽能，用在很多方面。例如，在太空中有很多人造衛星，都配備有大型鑲板，它們的太陽能電池，能直接將陽光轉變為電力。這些鑲板都被玻璃所覆蓋，並且裡面都漆成黑色，以儘量多吸收陽光。

> harness〔'hɑrnɪs〕v. 支配利用　　or〔ɔr〕conj. 也就是
> solar〔'solɚ〕adj. 太陽的　　*solar energy* 太陽能
> *for instance* 例如　　satellite〔'sætḷ,aɪt〕n. 衛星；人造衛星
> space〔spes〕n. 太空　　equip〔ɪ'kwɪp〕v. 使配備
> *be equipped with* 配備有；具有　　panel〔'pænḷ〕n. 鑲板；嵌板
> cell〔sɛl〕n. 電池　　*solar cell* 太陽能電池
> transform〔træns'fɔrm〕v. 使轉變　　sunlight〔'sʌn,laɪt〕n. 陽光
> directly〔də'rɛktlɪ〕adv. 直接地　　electric〔ɪ'lɛktrɪk〕adj. 電的
> *electric power* 電力　　*be covered with* 被…所覆蓋
> inside〔'ɪn'saɪd〕adv. 在裡面　　absorb〔əb'sɔrb〕v. 吸收
> *as…as possible* 儘可能…

13. (**A**) *transform A into B* 把 A 轉變為 B
　　【93 年指考則考過 turn A *into* B「把 A 轉變為 B」。】

Solar energy has a lot to offer.　To begin with, it is a clean fuel.　In contrast, fossil fuels, such as oil or coal, release <u>harmful</u> substances into the
14
air when they are burned.　<u>What's more</u>, fossil fuels will run out, but solar
15
energy will continue to reach the Earth long after the last coal has been mined and the last oil well has run dry.

　　太陽能有許多吸引人之處。首先，它是種乾淨的能源。對比之下，像是石油或煤這種化石燃料，當它們被燃燒時，就會釋放出有害的物質到空中。此外，石化燃料會用完，但是太陽能卻能在最後的煤被開採完，和最後一口油井乾枯之後，長時間持續供應地球。

> offer〔ˈɔfɚ〕v. 提供
> ***have a lot to offer*** 有許多吸引人之處（= *have many attractive features*)
> ***to begin with*** 首先　　　fuel〔ˈfjuəl〕n. 燃料
> ***in contrast*** 對比之下；相形之下　　fossil〔ˈfɑsḷ〕adj. 化石的
> ***fossil fuel*** 石化燃料【煤、石油、天然氣等礦物燃料】
> coal〔kol〕n. 煤　　　release〔rɪˈlis〕v. 釋放
> substance〔ˈsʌbstəns〕n. 物質　　***the air*** 空中
> ***run out*** 用光；耗盡　　reach〔ritʃ〕v. 抵達；到達
> mine〔maɪn〕v. 開採　　well〔wɛl〕n. 井
> ***oil well*** 油井　　run〔rʌn〕v. 成為（某種狀態）；變成
> ***run dry*** 變乾；乾涸

14. (**B**) (A) diligent〔ˈdɪlədʒənt〕adj. 勤勉的
　　　　　(B) ***harmful***〔ˈhɑrmfəl〕adj. 有害的
　　　　　(C) usable〔ˈjuzəbḷ〕adj. 可用的
　　　　　(D) changeable〔ˈtʃendʒəbḷ〕adj. 易變的；可改變的

15. (**C**) 依句意，選 (C) ***What's more***「此外；而且」(= *Besides*)。
　　　　 而 (A) otherwise「否則」，(B) therefore「因此」，(D) in comparison
　　　　　「相比之下；比較起來」，則不合句意。【本題屬「轉承語」的考型，可
　　　　　說是每年學測、指考的必考題，請同學務必注意老師的上課補充。】

<u>第 16 至 20 題為題組</u>

　　Signs asking visitors to keep their hands off the art are everywhere in the Louvre Museum, Paris.　But one special sculpture gallery invites art lovers to allow their hands to <u>run over</u> the works.　The Louvre's Tactile
16
Gallery, targeted at the blind and visually <u>impaired</u>, is the only space in
17
the museum where visitors can touch the sculptures, with no guards or alarm to stop them.

　　在巴黎的羅浮宮博物館，到處都是標誌要求觀光客不要用手觸碰藝術品。但是有一個特別的雕刻展覽館，卻邀請藝術愛好者，准許他們用手來碰觸藝術作品。羅浮宮的觸覺展示廳，目標鎖定盲人或視障人士，是博物館中唯一可以讓觀光客觸摸雕刻品的場所，而不會有警衛或是警報器制止他們。

> ***keep...off...*** 不讓…接近；不讓…觸碰
> ***the Louvre Museum*** （巴黎）羅浮宮博物館
> sculpture〔'skʌlptʃɚ〕*n.* 雕刻（品）　　　gallery〔'gælərɪ〕*n.* 展覽館
> invite〔ɪn'vaɪt〕*v.* 邀請　　tactile〔'tæktḷ〕*adj.* 觸覺的
> target〔'tɑrgɪt〕*v.* 以…為目標　　blind〔blaɪnd〕*adj.* 盲的
> ***the blind*** 盲人　　visually〔'vɪʒʊəlɪ〕*adv.* 視覺上
> space〔spes〕*n.* 場所　　guard〔gɑrd〕*n.* 警衛
> alarm〔ə'lɑrm〕*n.* 警報器

16. (**B**)（A) fix up　安裝；安排　　　　(B) ***run over***　（用手）到處移動；碰觸
　　　　　　　 (C) take away　拿去　　　　　(D) knock off　敲掉　【87年學測也考過。】

17. (**C**) 依句意，為「視力障礙的」意思，故選 (C) ***impaired***〔ɪm'pɛrd〕
　　　　adj. 有…障礙的；受損的。【「過去分詞」表「被動」，以及「現在分詞」表
　　　　「主動」，是學測、指考的「綜合測驗」的重要文法題型，請同學一定要弄懂，
　　　　並參考「文法寶典」p.447】

Its latest exhibit is a <u>collection</u> of sculpted lions, snakes, horses and eagles.
　　　　　　　　　　　　 18
The 15 animals exhibited are reproductions of famous works found
elsewhere in the Louvre.　Called "Animals, Symbols of Power," the exhibit
<u>features</u> animals that were used by kings and emperors throughout history to
　 19
symbolize the greatness of their reigns.　The exhibit, opened in December
2008, <u>is</u> scheduled to run for about three years.　During guided tours on the
　　　 20
weekends, children can explore the art with blindfolds on.

最近展出的收藏品是雕刻的獅子、蛇、馬和老鷹。被展示的十五隻動物，是可以在羅浮宮其他地方看得到的著名作品的複製。這次展覽被稱為「動物，權力的象徵」，是以歷史上國王和皇帝所使用的動物為特色，來象徵他們統治勢力的偉大。這次展覽，在二○○八年十二月開幕，預定持續展出大約三年。周末導覽期間，小朋友們可以帶上眼罩來探索這些藝術品。

latest〔'letɪst〕*adj.* 最近的；最新的　　exhibit〔ɪg'zɪbɪt〕*n.* 展覽品
sculpt〔skʌlpt〕*v.* 雕刻　　reproduction〔,riprə'dʌkʃən〕*n.* 複製（品）
elsewhere〔'ɛls,hwɛr〕*adv.* 在其他地方
symbol〔'sɪmbl̩〕*n.* 象徵　　emperor〔'ɛmpərɚ〕*n.* 皇帝
symbolize〔'sɪmbl̩,aɪz〕*v.* 象徵　　greatness〔'gretnɪs〕*n.* 偉大
reign〔ren〕*n.* 統治；勢力　　schedule〔'skɛdʒul〕*v.* 預定
run〔rʌn〕*v.* 持續　　guided〔'gaɪdɪd〕*adj.* 有嚮導的
explore〔ɪk'splor〕*v.* 探索　　blindfold〔'blaɪnd,fold〕*n.* 蒙眼布

18.（ **A** ）(A) *collection*〔kə'lɛkʃən〕*n.* 收藏（品）
　　　　(B) cooperation〔ko,ɑpə'reʃən〕*n.* 合作
　　　　(C) completion〔kəm'pliʃən〕*n.* 完成
　　　　(D) contribution〔,kɑntrə'bjuʃən〕*n.* 貢獻

19.（ **D** ）(A) examine〔ɪg'zæmɪn〕*v.* 測驗；檢查
　　　　(B) protect〔prə'tɛkt〕*v.* 保護
　　　　(C) represent〔,rɛprɪ'zɛnt〕*v.* 代表；表示
　　　　(D) *feature*〔'fitʃɚ〕*v.* 以…為特色

20.（ **A** ）此題中的主詞為 The exhibit，其後的 opened in December 2008 為分詞構句，原句為 which was opened in December 2008，用來補充說明主詞 The exhibit，空格應為主要動詞，而 schedule 應用被動用法，故選 (A) *is*。【先找出主詞，再判斷所需要的動詞，83 年學測、91 年指考也考過。】

三、文意選填：

第 21 至 30 題為題組

　　Textese (also known as chatspeak, texting language, or txt talk) is a term for the abbreviations and slang most commonly used among young people today.　The popularity of textese is largely due to the necessary
　　　　　　　　　　　　21
brevity of mobile phone text messaging, though its use is also very common on the Internet, including e-mail and instant messaging.

　　簡訊語言，又被稱為 chatspeak，texting language 或是 txt talk，這個名詞指的是現代年輕人常用的簡略語或俚語。簡訊語言的流行，主要是因為行動電話的簡訊必須簡潔。不過，在網路上也很常使用，其中包括電子郵件和即時通訊。

textese〔tɛks'tis〕n. 簡訊語言

abbreviation〔əˌbriviˈeʃən〕n. 縮寫；簡略語

slang〔slæŋ〕n. 俚語

commonly〔ˈkɑmənlɪ〕adv. 通常　　*be due to*　是因為～

largely〔ˈlɑrdʒlɪ〕adv. 主要　　brevity〔ˈbrɛvətɪ〕n. 簡潔

mobile〔ˈmobḷ〕adj. 行動的　　*mobile phone*　行動電話

instant〔ˈɪnstənt〕adj. 即時的　　*instant messaging*　即時通訊

21.（ I ）*popularity*〔ˌpɑpjəˈlærətɪ〕n. 受歡迎；流行

There are no <u>standard</u> rules for writing textese. However, the common
$\qquad$ 22

practice is to use single letters, pictures, or numbers to represent whole

words. For example, "i <3 u" uses the picture <u>symbol</u> of a heart "<3" for
$\qquad$ 23

"love," and the letter "u" to <u>replace</u> "you." For words which have no
$\qquad$ 24

common abbreviation, textese users often <u>remove</u> the vowels from a word,
$\qquad$ 25

and the reader is forced to interpret a string of consonants by re-adding the

vowels. Thus, "dictionary" becomes "dctnry," and "keyboard" becomes

"kybrd." The reader must interpret the <u>abbreviated</u> words depending on the
$\qquad$ 26

context in which it is used, as there are many examples of words or phrases

which use the same abbreviations. So if someone says "ttyl, lol" they

probably mean "talk to you later, lots of love" not "talk to you later, laugh

out loud," and if someone says "omg, lol" they most <u>likely</u> mean "oh my
$\qquad$ 27

god, laugh out loud" not "oh my god, lots of love."

寫簡訊沒有標準規則。不過，常見的用法是使用單一的字母、圖案或數字來代
表整個單文字。舉例來說，在「i <3 u」中，用心的圖案「<3」來表示「愛」，
字母 u 則是代替 you。如果沒有常見略語的文字，傳簡訊的人經常會把字裡面的
母音去掉，接著讀者只好被迫把母音重新填入一連串的子音中，然後再進行解
讀。因此，「dictionary」字典這個字就會變成「dctnry」，「keyboard」鍵盤則是
變成「kybrd」。讀者解讀這些被縮短的字時，要依文字的上下文而定，因為有

很多單字或片語使用相同的縮寫。因此，如果有人說「ttyl, lol」，他們可能是指「晚點聊，愛你喔」，而不是「晚點聊，笑出聲音」。如果有人說「omg, lol」，他們最有可能是指「我的天啊，笑出聲音」，而不是「我的天啊，愛你喔」。

> practice〔'præktɪs〕*n.* 實行；用法　　letter〔'lɛtɚ〕*n.* 字母
> represent〔,rɛprɪ'zɛnt〕*v.* 代表　　whole〔hol〕*adj.* 完整的
> vowel〔'vaʊəl〕*n.* 母音　　force〔fors〕*v.* 強迫
> interpret〔ɪn'tɝprɪt〕*v.* 解讀　　string〔strɪŋ〕*n.* 線；一串
> ***a string of*** 一串　　consonant〔'kɑnsənənt〕*n.* 子音
> keyboard〔'ki,bord〕*n.* 鍵盤　　***depend on*** 視～而定；取決於
> context〔'kɑntɛkst〕*n.* 內容；上下文　　phrase〔frez〕*n.* 片語
> ***out loud*** 出聲地（= *aloud*）

22. (**G**) ***standard***〔'stændɚd〕*adj.* 標準的

23. (**J**) ***symbol***〔'sɪmbḷ〕*n.* 象徵；符號

24. (**E**) ***replace***〔rɪ'ples〕*v.* 代替

25. (**F**) ***remove***〔rɪ'muv〕*v.* 除去

26. (**D**) ***abbreviated***〔ə'brivɪ,etɪd〕*adj.* 被縮短的

27. (**C**) ***likely***〔'laɪklɪ〕*adv.* 可能地

　　The emergence of textese is clearly due to a desire to type less and to communicate more <u>quickly</u> than one can manage without such shortcuts.
28

Yet it has been severely <u>criticized</u> as "wrecking our language." Some
29

scholars even consider the use of textese as "irritating" and essentially lazy behavior. They're worried that "sloppy" habits gained while using textese will result in students' growing <u>ignorance</u> of proper spelling, grammar and punctuation.
30

　　簡訊語言的出現，顯然是因為使用者希望少打一點字，但溝通可以更快，沒有這些快捷的方法就做不到。不過，簡訊語言一直受到嚴厲批評，認為它「破壞我們的語言」。有些學者甚至認為，使用簡訊語言令人憤怒，而且基本上是懶惰的行為。他們擔心這些在使用簡訊語言時所養成的「隨隨便便的」習慣，會導致學生們越來越不知道正確的拼字、文法及標點符號。

emergence〔ɪˋmɝdʒəns〕*n.* 出現　　desire〔dɪˋzaɪr〕*n.* 渴望；希望
communicate〔kəˋmjunəˏket〕*v.* 溝通
manage〔ˋmænɪdʒ〕*v.* 應付　　shortcut〔ˋʃɔrtˏkʌt〕*n.* 捷徑
yet〔jɛt〕*adv.* 然而　　severely〔səˋvɪrlɪ〕*adv.* 嚴厲地
wreck〔rɛk〕*v.* 破壞　　irritating〔ˋɪrəˏtetɪŋ〕*adj.* 令人生氣的
essentially〔əˋsɛnʃəlɪ〕*adv.* 本質上　　sloppy〔ˋslɑpɪ〕*adj.* 隨便的
result in 導致　　growing〔ˋgroɪŋ〕*adj.* 漸增的
proper〔ˋprɑpɚ〕*adj.* 正確的　　spelling〔ˋspɛlɪŋ〕*n.* 拼字
grammar〔ˋgræmɚ〕*n.* 文法
punctuation〔ˏpʌŋktʃʊˋeʃən〕*n.* 標點符號

28.(**A**) ***quickly***　快速地

29.(**B**) ***criticized***　被批評的

30.(**H**) ***ignorance***〔ˋɪgnərəns〕*n.* 不知；無知

四、篇章結構：

第 31 至 35 題為題組

　　Do you have trouble getting started in the morning? Do you have problems learning early in the day? If you do, you are not alone. <u>[31] (E) Cockroaches have the same problem!</u> They learn better at night than they do in the morning.

　　早上要開始工作會有困難嗎？一大早起來學習會有障礙嗎？如果你會的話，你並不孤獨。蟑螂也跟你一樣有這種問題！牠們在夜間，會比在白天學習得更好。

　　　have trouble + V-ing 做…事情有困難（= *have problems + V-ing*）
　　　alone〔əˋlon〕*adj.* 孤獨的　　cockroach〔ˋkɑkˏrotʃ〕*n.* 蟑螂

　　To investigate when cockroaches learn best, researchers at Vanderbilt University tested the insects for which odor (peppermint or vanilla) they preferred. Most cockroaches preferred the smell of vanilla to that of peppermint at all times. <u>[32] (D) They were also found to like sugar water, but not salt water.</u> Therefore, the scientists trained the cockroaches to prefer the peppermint smell by rewarding the insects with a taste of sugar water when they approached a peppermint smell. <u>[33] (A) When these insects moved toward a vanilla smell, on the other hand, they were punished with a taste of salt.</u>

　　為了調查蟑螂在哪個時間學得最好，范德比爾特大學的研究人員，測試蟑螂比較喜歡哪種味道（薄荷或香草）。大部分的蟑螂，不管在什麼時間，都是比較喜歡香草味勝過薄荷味。蟑螂也被發現喜歡糖水，不喜歡鹽水。因此，科學家訓練蟑螂喜歡薄荷味，方法是當牠們接近薄荷的味道時，就獎賞牠們一口糖水。而另一方面，當蟑螂往香草味的方向走的時候，就讓牠們嚐嚐鹽水的滋味，來處罰牠們。

investigate〔ɪnˈvɛstəˌget〕v. 調查
researcher〔rɪˈsɝtʃɚ〕n. 研究人員
Vanderbilt University 范德比爾特大學【創立於 1873 年，是美國排名
　前二十的著名私立大學，位於田納西州】　　test〔tɛst〕v. 測試
insect〔ˈɪnsɛkt〕n. 昆蟲　　odor〔ˈodɚ〕n. 氣味
peppermint〔ˈpɛpɚˌmɪnt〕n. 薄荷【又稱胡椒薄荷，香料的一種】
vanilla〔vəˈnɪlə〕n. 香草【美洲產的攀藤植物，果莢可以提取香精，
　多用於烹飪甜點】　　prefer〔prɪˈfɝ〕v. 偏愛
smell〔smɛl〕n. 氣味　　***at all times*** 一直
therefore〔ˈðɛrˌfor〕adv. 因此；所以
train〔tren〕v. 訓練　　reward〔rɪˈword〕v. 獎賞
taste〔test〕n. 一口；少量　　approach〔əˈprotʃ〕v. 接近
on the other hand 在另一方面　　punish〔ˈpʌnɪʃ〕v. 處罰

　　When the cockroaches were trained at night, they remembered the new associations (peppermint = sugar water; vanilla = salt water) for up to 48 hours. However, if the cockroaches were trained in the morning, they quickly forgot which smell went with which water. [34] **(B) This result thus shows that the time when they were trained decided the effect of their learning.**

　　當蟑螂在晚上受訓時，牠們記得這種新的聯想（薄荷等於糖水；香草等於鹽水）的時間，長達四十八個小時。然而，如果蟑螂在早上受訓，牠們馬上就忘掉哪種味道配哪一種水。因此，這樣的結果顯示，牠們接受訓練的時間，決定了學習的效果。

association〔əˌsosɪˈeʃən〕n. 聯想　　***up to*** 高達；多達
go with 搭配　　result〔rɪˈzʌlt〕n. 結果；結論
thus〔ðʌs〕adv. 因此；如此
effect〔ɪˈfɛkt〕n. 效果　　learning〔ˈlɝnɪŋ〕n. 學習

So, cockroaches learn better at night than they do in the morning. [35](C)
<u>They are often more active and tend to search for food during the night.</u>
Because of this, it is likely that information they gather at night will be more
useful to them. These experiments provide some clues about the interactions
between body rhythms, learning and memory.

因此，蟑螂在晚上會比在早上學得更好。在夜間，牠們也比較活躍，而且
比較會去找尋食物。因為如此，牠們在晚上蒐集的資訊，可能對牠們來說比較
有用。這項實驗提供了一些線索，關於身體的節奏、學習、以及記憶力之間的
交互影響。

active〔'æktɪv〕adj. 活躍的　　**tend to + V** 傾向於～；較容易～
search for 尋找　　likely〔'laɪklɪ〕adj. 可能的
information〔͵ɪnfɚ'meʃən〕n. 資訊；情報
gather〔'gæðɚ〕v. 蒐集；整合　　useful〔'jusfəl〕adj. 有用的
experiment〔ɪk'spɛrəmənt〕n. 實驗　　provide〔prə'vaɪd〕v. 提供
clue〔klu〕n. 線索　　interaction〔͵ɪntɚ'ækʃən〕n. 互動；互相影響
rhythm〔'rɪðəm〕n. 節奏；有規律的變動
memory〔'mɛmərɪ〕n. 記憶（力）

五、閱讀測驗：

第 36 至 39 題為題組

The following report appeared in a newspaper in February 2007.

On February 15, 2007, hundreds of people came to New York City's
famous railroad station—Grand Central Terminal—to trade in old dollar
bills for the new George Washington presidential US $1 coins. The
gold-colored coin is the first in a new series by the U.S. Mint to honor
former U.S. presidents. The Mint will issue four presidential US $1 coins
a year through 2016. These coins will come out in the order in which each
president served. The George Washington coin is the first to be released.
John Adams, Thomas Jefferson and James Madison coins will come out
later this year.

下列報導刊登於 2007 年二月份的報紙上。

2007 年 2 月 15 日，數以百計的人到了紐約市最著名的火車站——大中央車
站——要用舊的一元紙鈔兌換新的喬治華盛頓總統的一元紀念幣。這枚金色的硬
幣是美國國家鑄幣局的最新系列的第一枚，用來向美國前任總統們表示敬意。

美國國家鑄幣局每年都會發行四枚美國總統一元紀念幣，一直到 2016 年止。這些硬幣會依照每位總統就任的順序來發行。喬治華盛頓紀念幣是最先發行的硬幣。約翰亞當斯、湯姆斯傑弗遜，和詹姆斯麥迪遜紀念幣，則會在今年稍後會陸續發行。

appear〔ə'pɪr〕v. 出現；刊登　　*hundreds of* 數以百計的

railroad〔'rel,rod〕n. 鐵路　　*railroad station* 火車站

grand〔grænd〕adj. 偉大的　　terminal〔'tɝmənḷ〕n. 終點站

Grand Central Terminal 大中央車站

trade in 以（舊貨）抵購（新貨）　　bill〔bɪl〕n. 紙鈔

presidential〔,prɛzə'dɛnʃəl〕adj. 總統的

series〔'sɪrɪz,'siris〕n. 系列　　mint〔mɪnt〕n. 鑄幣廠

honor〔'ɑnɚ〕v. 向～表示敬意　　former〔'fɔrmɚ〕adj. 前任的

issue〔'ɪʃju〕v. 發行　　through〔θru〕prep. 到…

come out 出現；出版　　order〔'ɔrdɚ〕n. 順序

serve〔sɝv〕v. 任職　　release〔rɪ'lis〕v. 發行

The presidential US $1 coins have a special design. For the first time since the 1930s, there are words carved into the edge of each coin, including the year in which the coin was issued and traditional mottos. Each coin will show a different president on its face, or heads side. It will also show the president's name. The other side of the coin will show the Statue of Liberty and the inscriptions "United States of America" and "$1."

美國總統一元紀念幣有個特別的設計。自從 1930 年代第一次發行以來，每一枚紀念幣的邊緣上都有刻字，包括發行的年度及傳統格言。每一枚紀念幣的正面會刻有不同的總統圖像。上面也會有總統的名字。紀念幣的另一面會刻印自由女神像，以及「美利堅合眾國」和「$1」的文字。

design〔dɪ'zaɪn〕n. 設計　　carve〔kɑrv〕v. 雕刻

edge〔ɛdʒ〕n. 邊緣　　motto〔'mɑto〕n. 格言；座右銘

face〔fes〕n. 表面；正面　　or〔ɔr〕conj. 也就是

heads side （硬幣的）正面　　statue〔'stætʃu〕n. 雕像

liberty〔'lɪbɚtɪ〕n. 自由　　*Statue of Liberty* 自由女神像

inscription〔ɪn'skrɪpʃən〕n. 銘刻；刻印（文字）

There are some interesting facts about the coins. First, there will be one presidential US $1 coin for each president, except Grover Cleveland. He will have two! Cleveland is the only U.S. president to have served two nonconsecutive terms. The last president now scheduled to get a coin is Gerald Ford. That's because a president cannot appear on a coin when he is still alive. In addition, a president must have been deceased for two years before he can be on a coin.

關於這些紀念幣，有一些有趣的事實。首先，每一位總統都會有一枚總統一元紀念幣，除了格羅弗克利夫蘭外。他會有兩枚！克利夫蘭是唯一一位擔任兩任美國總統但任期不連續的人。目前排定的最後一位總統，是福特總統。因為仍然在世的總統不能出現在紀念幣上。此外，總統還必須過世兩年以上，才可以刻印在紀念幣上。

except〔ɪk'sɛpt〕*prep.* 除了～之外
nonconsecutive〔͵nɑnkən'sɛkjətɪv〕*adj.* 非連續的
term〔tɝm〕*n.* 任期　　alive〔ə'laɪv〕*adj.* 活著的
in addition 此外　　deceased〔dɪ'sist〕*adj.* 死亡的；已故的

36. (**D**) 根據這篇報導，至 2007 年底，總共將發行幾枚美國總統一元紀念幣？
　　(A) 一枚。　　　(B) 二枚。　　(C) 三枚。　　(D) 四枚。
　　altogether〔͵ɔltə'gɛðɚ〕*adv.* 總共

37. (**B**) 為何美國國家鑄幣局要發行美國總統一元紀念幣？
　　(A) 為了回應美國人民的要求。　　(B) 為了紀念已故的美國總統。
　　(C) 為了吸引更多的火車通勤者。　　(D) 為了提倡美國紙鈔交易。
　　in response to 為了回應　　citizen〔'sɪtəzn̩〕*n.* 人民
　　in memory of 為了紀念　　late〔let〕*adj.* 已故的
　　commuter〔kə'mjutɚ〕*n.* 通勤者　　promote〔prə'mot〕*v.* 提倡

38. (**A**) 在新的一元紀念幣正面可以發現什麼？
　　(A) 美國總統的名字。　　　(B) 鑄幣的年份。
　　(C) 自由女神像。　　　　　(D) 英文諺語。
　　proverb〔'prɑvɝb〕*n.* 諺語

39. (**C**) 關於美國總統紀念幣，下列何者可以被推論出來？
　　(A) 福特總統的紀念幣在 2008 年發行。
　　(B) 到目前為止，美國國家鑄幣局已經發行了所有總統的紀念幣。
　　(C) 巴拉克歐巴馬總統紀念幣沒有發行。
　　(D) 每一位美國總統的紀念幣都會在其任期結束後兩年鑄造。
　　infer〔ɪn'fɝ〕*v.* 推論

第 40 至 43 題為題組

　　Newspapers have tried many things to stop a seemingly nonstop decline in readers. Now France is pushing forward with a novel approach: giving away papers to young readers in an effort to turn them into regular customers. The French government recently detailed plans of a project called "My Free Newspaper," under which 18- to 24-year-olds will be offered a free, year-long subscription to a newspaper of their choice.

　　報社已試過許多方法，來阻止表面上不斷減少的讀者人數。現在法國正計劃推行一項全新的辦法：免費贈送報紙給年輕的讀者，目的為了將他們變成固定的客戶。法國政府最近詳細敘述了這個名為「我的免費報」的計畫，18 至 24 歲的讀者免費訂閱一年份他們自己所選的報紙。

> newspaper〔'njuz,pepɚ〕*n.* 報紙；報社
> seemingly〔'simɪŋlɪ〕*adv.* 表面上　　nonstop〔'nɑnstɑp〕*adj.* 不停的
> decline〔dɪ'klaɪn〕*n.* 減少　　***push forward*** 計劃推行
> novel〔'nɑvl̩〕*adj.* 新的　　approach〔ə'protʃ〕*n.* 方法
> ***give away*** 分送；贈送　　***in an effort to V*** 為了…
> ***turn…into*** 把…變成　　regular〔'rɛgjəlɚ〕*adj.* 規律的；定期的
> ***regular customer*** 常客；固定客戶　　detail〔'ditel〕*v.* 詳細敘述
> project〔'prɑdʒɛkt〕*n.* 計劃
> subscription〔səb'skrɪpʃən〕*n.* 訂閱＜*to*＞
> ***of one's choice*** 自己挑選的

　　Newspaper readership in France has been especially low among young people. According to a government study, only 10 percent of those aged 15 to 24 read a paid-for newspaper daily in 2007, down from 20 percent a decade earlier.

　　在法國，年輕族群中的閱報人數一直都特別地少。根據一項政府調查顯示，2007 年時，15 到 24 歲的讀者中，只有百分之十，每天閱讀付費的報紙，跟十年前相比，比例下滑了百分之二十。

> readership〔'ridɚʃɪp〕*n.* 讀者人數　　aged〔edʒd〕*adj.* 有…歲數的
> paid-for〔'ped'fɔr〕*adj.* 已付費的　　daily〔'delɪ〕*adv.* 每天
> decade〔'dɛked〕*n.* 十年

　　Emmanuel Schwartzenberg, a former media editor of *Le Figaro*, the oldest and second-largest national newspaper in France, said he had strong reservations about the government project.　At a time when advertising is in steep decline, he said, newspapers should instead be looking at ways to raise more profits from readers, rather than giving papers away.　"This just reinforces the belief that newspapers should be free, which is a very bad idea," Mr. Schwartzenberg said.

　　法國國內最悠久，也是第二大的費加羅報前任媒體編輯，以馬內利・施瓦曾伯格表示，他強烈質疑政府的這項計畫。他說，在廣告量急遽減少的時候，報社應該研究一些方法，從讀者身上提高利潤，而不是贈閱報紙。施瓦曾伯格先生說：「這麼做只會讓大眾更加相信，報紙應該是免費的，這是個很糟的想法。」

　　Emmanuel Schwartzenberg〔ɪˈmænjuəl ˈʃvɑrtsənbɛrk〕*n.*
　　　以馬內利・施瓦曾伯格
　　media〔ˈmidɪə〕*n. pl.* 媒體　　　editor〔ˈɛdɪtə〕*n.* 編輯
　　Le Figaro〔ləˈfɪgəro〕*n.* 費加羅報【法國國內日報】
　　national〔ˈnæʃənḷ〕*adj.* 全國的
　　reservation〔ˌrɛzəˈveʃən〕*n.* 保留；疑慮
　　have reservations about 對…有疑慮
　　advertising〔ˈædvəˌtaɪzɪŋ〕*n.* 廣告
　　steep〔stip〕*adj.*（數量上升或下降）急劇的
　　instead〔ɪnˈstɛd〕*adv.* 代替地　　　*look at* 研究；思考
　　raise〔rez〕*v.* 提高　　　profit〔ˈprɑfɪt〕*n.* 利潤
　　rather than 而不是　　　reinforce〔ˌriɪnˈfors〕*v.* 增強；強化
　　belief〔bəˈlif〕*n.* 信念；看法

French readers, young and old, already have plenty of free options from which to choose, including newspaper websites and the free papers handed out daily in many city centers.　Some bloggers said the new program might hold the most appeal to the few young people who do already read, and buy, newspapers.

　　無論老少，法國的讀者已經有很多免費的選擇，包含了新聞網站和每天在許多市中心分送的免費報紙。一些部落客表示，此項新計畫也許會對少數已經有閱讀，或是購買報紙的年輕人最具吸引力。

　　plenty of 很多　　　option〔ˈɑpʃən〕*n.* 選擇
　　website〔ˈwɛbˌsaɪt〕*n.* 網站　　　*hand out* 分發；分送
　　blogger〔ˈblɑgə〕*n.* 部落客【部落格使用者】
　　appeal〔əˈpil〕*n.* 吸引力

The French government plans to promote the program with an advertising campaign aimed at young readers and their parents. However, when asked how to attract young readers to the printed press, the government said the primary channel for the ads would be the Internet.

法國政府打算以廣告活動來宣傳此計劃，目標族群鎖定年輕讀者及其父母。然而，當被問及要如何吸引年輕讀者注意平面媒體時，法國政府表示，廣告主要的管道應該會是網路。

> promote〔prə'mot〕v. 宣傳　　campaign〔kæm'pen〕n. 宣傳活動
> aim〔em〕v. 對準；瞄準　　***aim at*** 針對…；對象為…
> attract〔ə'trækt〕v. 吸引　　print〔prɪnt〕v. 印刷
> press〔prɛs〕n. 出版物　　***printed press*** 平面媒體
> primary〔'praɪˌmɛrɪ〕adj. 主要的　　channel〔'tʃænl̩〕n. 管道；方式

40.（ **C** ）法國政府為何決定展開提供免費報紙的活動？
　　(A) 為了對抗經濟不景氣。　　(B) 為贏得年輕人的贊成。
　　(C) 為了提高閱報人數。　　(D) 為了增進法國的識字率。
　　launch〔lɔntʃ〕v. 開始；展開　　recession〔rɪ'sɛʃən〕n. 蕭條；不景氣
　　economic recession 經濟不景氣
　　approval〔ə'pruvl̩〕n. 贊成　　literacy〔'lɪtərəsɪ〕n. 讀寫能力

41.（ **D** ）從本文可以得到以下哪一個結論？
　　(A) 每個人都認為政府的計畫很有創意。
　　(B) 閱報人數比其他國家高很多。
　　(C) 研究顯示年輕人對時事沒有興趣。
　　(D) 贈送報紙不是一個足夠吸引讀者的強烈誘因。
　　conclude〔kən'klud〕v. 結論　　creative〔krɪ'etɪv〕adj. 有創意的
　　current〔'kɝənt〕adj. 現今的　　affair〔ə'fɛr〕n. 事物
　　current affairs 時事　　incentive〔ɪn'sɛntɪv〕n. 誘因；動機

42.（ **A** ）施瓦曾伯格先生對於此項計畫的態度是什麼？
　　(A) 懷疑的。　　(B) 熱中的。　　(C) 樂觀的。　　(D) 漠不關心的。
　　skeptical〔'skɛptɪkl̩〕adj. 懷疑的　　devoted〔dɪ'votɪd〕adj. 熱中的
　　optimistic〔ˌɑptə'mɪstɪk〕adj. 樂觀的
　　indifferent〔ɪn'dɪfrənt〕adj. 冷淡的；漠不關心的

43.（ **D** ）根據本文，最有可能在哪裡看到有關法國免費報紙的資訊？
　　(A) 雜誌上。　　(B) 部落格上。　　(C) 報紙上。　　(D) 網路上。

第 44 至 47 題爲題組

Coffee experts are willing to pay large sums of money for high-quality coffee beans. The high-end beans, such as Kona or Blue Mountain, are known to cost extraordinary sums of money. Then there is Kopi Lowak (translated as "Civet Coffee"), the world's most expensive coffee, which sells for as much as US $50 per quarter-pound.

咖啡專家們願意付大筆的錢來購買高品質的咖啡豆。像科納、藍山等高品質的咖啡豆，都以格外昂貴著稱。而全世界最貴的魯瓦克咖啡（意爲「麝香貓咖啡」），每四分之一磅要賣到五十元美金。

willing〔ˈwɪlɪŋ〕*adj.* 願意的　　sum〔sʌm〕*n.* 一筆
bean〔bin〕*n.* 豆子　　high-end〔ˈhaɪˌɛnd〕*adj.* 高檔的
Kona〔ˈkonə〕*n.* 柯納【位於夏威夷，著名咖啡豆產地】
Blue Mountain 藍山【位於牙買加，著名咖啡豆產地】
extraordinary〔ɪkˈstrɔdṇˌɛrɪ〕*adj.* 格外的
Kopi Lowak 魯瓦克咖啡【產於印尼，又稱麝香貓咖啡】
translate〔trænsˈlet〕*v.* 翻譯　　civet〔ˈsɪvɪt〕*n.* 麝香貓
as much as 多達　　quarter〔ˈkwɔrtɚ〕*n.* 四分之一
pound〔paʊnd〕*n.* 磅【重量單位，一磅約等於 0.454 公斤】

This isn't particularly surprising, given that approximately 500 pounds a year of Kopi Lowak constitute the entire world supply. What is surprising is why this particular coffee is so rare. In fact, it's not the plants that are rare. It's the civet droppings. That's right, the civet droppings—the body waste of the palm civet. Coffee beans aren't Kopi Lowak until they've been digested and come out in the body waste of the palm civet.

鑒於魯瓦克咖啡每年全世界產量僅大約五百磅，這昂貴的價錢並不特別令人驚訝。眞正令人驚訝的是，爲什麼這種特殊的咖啡如此稀有。事實上，並非是這種植物很稀有，而是貓屎不多。沒錯，就是貓屎——棕櫚貓的糞便。魯瓦克咖啡要等到棕櫚貓將咖啡豆消化並排出體外之後，才算完成。

particularly〔pɚˈtɪkjələ·lɪ〕*adv.* 特別地；尤其
given that 有鑒於　　approximately〔əˈprɑksəmɪtlɪ〕*adv.* 大約
constitute〔ˈkɑnstəˌtjut〕*v.* 構成　　entire〔ɪnˈtaɪr〕*adj.* 全部的
supply〔səˈplaɪ〕*n.* 供應量　　rare〔rɛr〕*adj.* 稀有的
dropping〔ˈdrɑpɪŋ〕*n.* (鳥獸的) 糞便　　waste〔west〕*n.* 排泄物
palm〔pɑm〕*n.* 棕櫚　　***palm civet*** 棕櫚貓【樹棲野生動物，生長於印尼】
digest〔daɪˈdʒɛst〕*v.* 消化

　　Palm civets are tree-dwelling, raccoon-like little animals, native to Southeast Asia and the Indonesian islands.　They also have a love for coffee cherries.　According to Kopi Lowak suppliers, palm civets eat the fruit whole, but only digest the outer fruit, leaving the beans intact.　While the beans are not destroyed, they undergo a transformation in the animal's body.　A chemical substance in the digestive system of the palm civet causes some changes to the beans to give them a unique flavor.　However, this is not the only explanation why coffee beans retrieved from civet droppings have a special flavor all their own.　Another possible reason is that palm civets have an unfailing instinct for picking the coffee cherries at the peak of their ripeness.

　　棕櫚貓是樹棲動物，外觀接近浣熊，體型不大，生長於東南亞及印尼群島，愛吃咖啡的果實。據魯瓦克咖啡的供應商表示，棕櫚貓會將果實整個吞下去，但只會消化外面的果肉，裡頭的咖啡豆則完好無缺。雖然咖啡豆沒有被破壞，不過它們會在棕櫚貓的身體中變化。棕櫚貓的消化系統中有某種化學物質，會導致咖啡豆產生變化，因此出現一種獨特的風味。然而，這並非是這種咖啡之所以擁有獨特香味的唯一解釋。另外一種可能的原因是，棕櫚貓擁有可信賴的本能，能夠挑選最成熟的咖啡果實。

dwell〔dwɛl〕v. 居住　　　racoon〔rəˋkun〕n. 浣熊
native〔ˋnetɪv〕adj. 原產的＜to＞　　Indonesian Islands 印尼群島
coffee cherry 咖啡果【製作咖啡豆的原料，成熟時呈紅色】
outer fruit 果肉　　　intact〔ɪnˋtækt〕adj. 完整無缺的
undergo〔͵ʌndɚˋgo〕v. 經歷
transformation〔͵trænsfɚˋmeʃən〕n. 變質；變化
digestive〔daɪˋdʒɛstɪv〕adj. 消化的　　　flavor〔ˋflevɚ〕n. 風味
retrieve〔rɪˋtriv〕v. 收回　　　unfailing〔ʌnˋfelɪŋ〕adj. 確實的；可信賴的
instinct〔ˋɪnstɪŋkt〕n. 本能　　　peak〔pik〕n. 高峰；巔峰
ripeness〔ˋraɪpnɪs〕n. 成熟

　　Kopi Lowak is reported to have a character in taste unlike any other coffee, complex with caramel undertones and an earthy or gamey flavor. Currently, most of the world's supply of Kopi Lowak is sold in Japan, though a few US markets are also starting to stock up on Kopi Lowak.

　　魯瓦克咖啡據說口味獨特，混雜著淡淡的焦糖的色調及樸實、野性的味道，與其他咖啡都不同。現在，魯瓦克咖啡全世界的供應大部分銷往日本，不過，美國部分市場也開始買進。

　　be reported to* + *V 據稱　　character〔'kærɪktɚ〕*n.* 特色
　　complex〔kəm'plɛks〕*adj.* 複雜的；複合的
　　caramel〔'kærəml̩〕*n.* 焦糖　　undertone〔'ʌndɚˌton〕*n.* 淡色
　　earthy〔'ɝθɪ〕*adj.* 樸實的　　gamey〔'gemɪ〕*adj.* 野性的；原始的
　　though〔ðo〕*conj.* 不過　　***stock up*** 進貨；囤積

44.(**C**) 第二段的 **This** 指的是什麼？
　　(A) 麝香貓咖啡。　　　　　　(B) 藍山咖啡。
　　(C) 魯瓦克咖啡的高價。　　　(D) 科納咖啡的獨特風味。
　　refer to 指

45.(**A**) 爲什麼魯瓦克咖啡很貴？
　　(A) 咖啡豆的供應量很有限。　(B) 生長這種咖啡豆的咖啡樹很稀少。
　　(C) 這種咖啡豆成熟的時間很久。
　　(D) 只有少數專家知道如何製造這種咖啡豆。
　　scarce〔skɛrs〕*adj.* 稀少的　　ripen〔'raɪpən〕*v.* 成熟

46.(**D**) 第三段討論的重點是什麼？
　　(A) 爲什麼棕櫚貓喜歡咖啡豆。　(B) 魯瓦克咖啡主要在哪裡收成。
　　(C) 在棕櫚貓的消化系統中可以找到什麼化學物質。
　　(D) 棕櫚貓如何把咖啡的果實變成魯瓦克咖啡豆。
　　harvest〔'hɑrvɪst〕*v.* 收成　　chemical〔'kɛmɪkl̩〕*n.* 化學物質

47.(**B**) 根據本文，下列敘述何者正確？
　　(A) 棕櫚貓只吃咖啡果實的外層。
　　(B) 棕櫚貓不知怎地，就是知道咖啡的果實什麼時候成熟。
　　(C) 魯瓦克咖啡在東南亞跟印尼群島最受歡迎。
　　(D) 科納咖啡跟藍山咖啡最貴，但品質普通。
　　layer〔'leɚ〕*n.* 層　　somehow〔'sʌmˌhaʊ〕*adv.* 不知怎地
　　average〔'ævərɪdʒ〕*adj.* 一般的；普通的

第 48 至 51 題爲題組

　　Gunter Grass was the winner of the 1999 Nobel Prize in Literature.
His talents are revealed in a variety of disciplines: He is not only a novelist,
poet and playwright, but also a renowned painter and sculptor. As he
himself stresses, his creations are closely related to his unique personal
history. His father was a German who joined the Nazi party in World War

II, while his mother was Polish. As a result, he constantly suffered contradictory feelings: as a Pole who had been victimized, and as someone guilty of harming the Poles. The torment in his heart led him to denounce the Nazis and his political activism has continued throughout his career. His commitment to the peace movement and the environmental movement as well as his unfailing quest for justice has won him praise as "the conscience of the nation."

　　鈞特‧葛拉斯是一九九九年諾貝爾文學獎的得主。他的才華展露在各種不同的領域中：他不僅是小說家、詩人及劇作家，也是知名的畫家及雕刻家。如同他自己所強調的，他的作品跟他獨特的個人背景密切相關。他的父親是在二次大戰加入納粹黨的德國人，而他的母親是波蘭人。因此，他不斷地受到矛盾的衝突感侵擾：身為一個曾受迫害的波蘭人，卻也同時是一個迫害波蘭人的人。他心中的苦痛使他公然譴責納粹，而他政治上的激進主義也在他生涯中裡持續不斷。他對於和平及環境運動的獻身，以及他對正義無止盡的追尋，使他贏得了「國家的良心」如此的美譽。

Nobel Price〔noˈbɛl ˈpraɪz〕n. 諾貝爾獎

literature〔ˈlɪtərətʃɚ〕n. 文學　　　talent〔ˈtælənt〕n. 天分；才能

reveal〔rɪˈvil〕v. 顯露　　*a variety of* 各種

discipline〔ˈdɪsəplɪn〕n.（學問的）領域

novelist〔ˈnɑvl̩ɪst〕n. 小說家　　　playwright〔ˈpleˌraɪt〕n. 劇作家

renowned〔rɪˈnaʊnd〕adj. 著名的　　　sculptor〔ˈskʌlptɚ〕n. 雕刻家

stress〔strɛs〕v. 強調　　　creation〔krɪˈeʃən〕n. 創作

be closely related to 與～密切相關　　　Nazi〔ˈnɑtzɪ〕n. 納粹

Polish〔ˈpolɪʃ〕adj. 波蘭（人、語）的

constantly〔ˈkɑnstəntlɪ〕adv. 不斷地；一直

contradictory〔ˌkɑntrəˈdɪktərɪ〕adj. 矛盾的　　　Pole〔pol〕n. 波蘭人

victimize〔ˈvɪktɪmˌaɪz〕v. 使…受害

guilty〔ˈgɪltɪ〕adj. 有罪的＜ of ＞　　　torment〔ˈtɔrmɛnt〕n. 苦痛

denounce〔dɪˈnaʊns〕v. 譴責　　　political〔pəˈlɪtɪkl̩〕adj. 政治的

activism〔ˈæktɪvˌɪzəm〕n. 激進主義；行動主義

commitment〔kəˈmɪtmənt〕n. 獻身；投入

unfailing〔ʌnˈfelɪŋ〕adj. 無盡的；不絕的

quest〔kwɛst〕n. 探求；尋求　　　justice〔ˈdʒʌstɪs〕n. 正義

conscience〔ˈkɑnʃəns〕n. 良心

In the spring of 1996, he was inspired during a trip to Italy to write a poem with his watercolor brush directly on one of his paintings. Before long, a collection of his "water poems" was born. Painting and literature have become his major forms of creativity. For him, painting is a form of creation with concrete, sensual elements, while writing is a hard and abstract process. When he cannot find words to convey his thoughts, painting helps him find the words to express himself. In this way, Grass not only creates simple depictions of the objects he is fond of in life, such as melons, vegetables, fish, and mushrooms, but also uses them as symbols for mental associations of various kinds. For example, to express the complexity of reality, he sometimes places unrelated objects in the same painting, such as a bird and a housefly, or a mushroom and a nail. Grass has depicted a wide variety of natural scenes, animals and plants, and even human artifacts of the German countryside, portraying them in poems, and allowing words to make the paintings rich in literary value.

一九九六年的春天，在義大利的旅途上他突然有了靈感，直接用水彩筆在一張自己的畫作上寫詩。很快的，他一系列的「水彩詩」便誕生了。繪畫和文學一直是他發揮創造力的主要方式。對他而言，繪畫這種創作方式充滿了具體的、感官的元素，然而寫作卻是一種艱難且抽象的過程。當他找不到言語來傳達他的想法，繪畫幫他表達自我。以這種方式，葛拉斯不僅簡單的描繪出生命中他喜愛的物品，例如瓜果、蔬菜、魚和蘑菇，他也用這些東西做各種心靈上的聯結。舉例來說，為了表現現實的複雜性，他有時會把毫不相干的兩樣東西放進同一張畫作裡，像是一隻鳥跟一隻家蠅，或是一根蘑菇與一根釘子。葛拉斯描繪了十分多樣的自然景觀、動物和植物，甚至還有一些工藝品和德國的鄉間景色，他用詩來描寫這些事物，再透過文字讓他的圖畫更富有文學價值。

inspire〔ɪnˈspaɪr〕v. 啟發　　watercolor〔ˈwɑtəˌkʌlə〕n. 水彩
brush〔brʌʃ〕n. 畫筆　　*before long* 不久以後
form〔fɔrm〕n. 方式；型態　　creativity〔ˌkrieˈtɪvətɪ〕n. 創造力
concrete〔ˈkɑnkrit〕adj. 具體的　　sensual〔ˈsɛnʃʊəl〕adj. 感官的
element〔ˈɛləmənt〕n. 要素　　abstract〔ˈæbstrækt〕adj. 抽象的
convey〔kənˈve〕v. 傳達；傳遞
depiction〔dɪˈpɪkʃən〕n. 描繪；敘述　　*be fond of* 喜歡
melon〔ˈmɛlən〕n. 瓜　　mushroom〔ˈmʌʃrum〕n. 蘑菇
various〔ˈvɛrɪəs〕adj. 各種的　　complexity〔kəmˈplɛksətɪ〕n. 複雜
unrelated〔ˌʌnrɪˈletɪd〕adj. 沒有關聯的

housefly〔'haʊs,flaɪ〕n. 家蠅　　nail〔nel〕n. 釘子
artifact〔'ɑrtɪ,fækt〕n. 工藝品　　portray〔pɔr'tre〕v. 描寫
literary〔'lɪtə,rɛrɪ〕n. 文學的

48.(**A**) 小時候什麼事情讓葛拉斯感到又困惑又煩擾？
(A) 他是納粹跟受害的波蘭人之子。
(B) 他發現自己對抗兩個相對的政黨。
(C) 縱使他想成為一名詩人，他還是受訓成為藝術家。
(D) 他天生有太多才華，所以無法決定方向。

opposing〔ə'pozɪŋ〕adj. 相對的

49.(**B**) 為什麼葛拉斯被譽為「國家的良心」？
(A) 他迫害波蘭人並且批評納粹。
(B) 他一直是和平及正義強力的提倡者。
(C) 他透過他的詩對波蘭人表達同情。
(D) 他加入納粹並對其國家非常忠誠。

advocate〔'ædvəkɪt〕n. 提倡者　　sympathy〔'sɪmpəθɪ〕n. 同情
loyalty〔'lɔɪəltɪ〕n. 忠誠；忠心

50.(**C**) 為什麼葛拉斯的義大利之行對他很重要？
(A) 他在義大利受到一個美術大師的啟發。
(B) 他在那裡培養出一個畫簡單物品的興趣。
(C) 他在旅途中發展出一套創作詩的新方式。
(D) 他發現新方法，來解決納粹跟波蘭人之間的衝突。

fine arts 美術　　master〔'mæstɚ〕n. 大師
conflict〔'kɑnflɪkt〕n. 爭鬥；衝突

51.(**D**) 根據本文，下列何者是葛拉斯詩作的特色？
(A) 他大部分的詩作描寫納粹的殘酷。
(B) 他詩作的主題幫他贏得諾貝爾和平獎。
(C) 他圖畫上的詩作常常跟真實世界的物品無關。
(D) 他詩作的思想因為畫作的協助被更完全地表達出來。

characterize〔'kærɪktə,raɪz〕v. 說明～特色
depict〔dɪ'pɪkt〕v. 描述；敘述　　cruelty〔'kruəltɪ〕n. 殘酷
theme〔θim〕n. 主題　　thoroughly〔'θɝolɪ〕adv. 徹底地；完全地

第貳部分：非選擇題

一、中譯英：

1. 近二十年來我國的出生率快速下滑。

$$\left\{ \begin{array}{l} \text{During} \\ \text{Over} \end{array} \right\} \text{ the } \left\{ \begin{array}{l} \text{past} \\ \text{last} \end{array} \right\} \text{ twenty years, our nation's birthrate has}$$

$$\left\{ \begin{array}{l} \text{been falling quickly / rapidly.} \\ \text{declined rapidly.} \\ \text{rapidly declined.} \end{array} \right.$$

2. 這可能導致我們未來人力資源的嚴重不足。

$$\text{This may } \left\{ \begin{array}{l} \text{result in} \\ \text{cause} \\ \text{lead to} \\ \text{bring about} \end{array} \right\} \text{a} \left\{ \begin{array}{l} \text{severe} \\ \text{serious} \end{array} \right\} \left\{ \begin{array}{l} \text{deficiency} \\ \text{shortage} \end{array} \right\} \text{in human}$$

resources in our future.

$$= \text{This may cause our future human resources to be } \left\{ \begin{array}{l} \text{severely} \\ \text{seriously} \end{array} \right\} \text{deficient.}$$

rapidly〔'ræpɪdlɪ〕*adv.* 快速地　　decline〔dɪ'klaɪn〕*v.* 下滑；下跌
severe〔sə'vɪr〕*adj.* 嚴重的　　shortage〔'ʃɔrtɪdʒ〕*n.* 不足
deficient〔dɪ'fɪʃənt〕*adj.* 不足的；缺乏的

二、英文作文：

【範例】

An Unforgettable Smell

　　The sense of smell is one of the most important attributes in life. Many of our precious memories are shaped by the scents attached to them. To me, the most unforgettable smell is the aroma of my grandmother's cooking. When I was young, I especially looked forward to visiting my grandmother's place during holidays. Whenever we stopped by, she always cooked my favorite chicken soup. I can still remember the cozy feeling that embraced me when I first smelled it. The warmth and gratification it brought me was simply indescribable.

　　Growing up in a single-parent family, I saw home-cooked food as a luxury. Since my mother worked two jobs, we always ate separately. Eating alone on a regular basis, I felt lonely and isolated from time to time. Grandmother's chicken soup reminded me that I still belonged to a family. Through smelling and tasting her soup, I felt loved and treasured again. ***Although*** she is no longer with us, the memory of her fragrant chicken soup will stay with me for the rest of my life. It will surely serve as the reminder of how lucky I was.

attribute〔ˈætrəˌbjut〕*n.* 特質
precious〔ˈprɛʃəs〕*adj.* 寶貴的　　shape〔ʃep〕*v.* 塑造
scent〔sɛnt〕*n.* 氣味　　***be attached to*** 附屬於
unforgettable〔ˌʌnfəˈgɛtəbḷ〕*adj.* 難忘的
aroma〔əˈromə〕*n.* 香味　　cozy〔ˈkozɪ〕*adj.* 舒適愜意的
embrace〔ɪmˈbres〕*v.* 環繞
gratification〔ˌgrætəfəˈkeʃən〕*n.* 滿足
indescribable〔ˌɪndɪˈskraɪbəbḷ〕*adj.* 難以形容的
single-parent *adj.* 單親的　　luxury〔ˈlʌkʃərɪ〕*n.* 奢侈品
separately〔ˈsɛpərɪtlɪ〕*adv.* 個別地
on a regular basis 經常地（＝*regularly*）
isolated〔ˈaɪsḷˌetɪd〕*adj.*（被）孤立的
fragrant〔ˈfregrənt〕*adj.* 芳香的　　***serve as*** 充當；當作
reminder〔rɪˈmaɪndə〕*n.* 提醒物

99年指定科目考試英文科出題來源

題　　號	出　　　　　處
一、詞彙 第 1～10 題	今年所有的詞彙題，對錯選項均出自「新版高中常用 7000 字」。
二、綜合測驗 第 16～20 題	改編自 Lubbock Online 網站 2008 年 2 月 22 日的 Don't touch the art？ Louvre exhibit lets visitors break the rule 一文，關於羅浮宮博物館展示品的文章。
三、文意選填 第 21～30 題	改寫自維基百科有關行動電話所用之 SMS 簡訊的文章。
四、篇章結構 第 31～35 題	出自 Neuroscience For Kids 網站，一篇關於蟑螂 （Cockroaches Don't Learn in the Morning）的文章。
五、閱讀測驗 第 36～39 題	取材自美國財務部（U.S. Department of the Treasury） 2007 年 2 月 15 日所發布有關美國總統紀念幣的文章。
第 40～43 題	改寫自時代雜誌 2009 年 10 月 28 日的 In France, Free Subscriptions To Young Newspaper Readers 一文，關於法國報社如何阻止讀者減少的文章。
第 44～47 題	出自 DamnInteresting.com 網站，關於咖啡豆的文章。
第 48～51 題	改寫自台北市立美術館於 2007 年 11 月 28 日到 2008 年 2 月 24 日所展出的作品：A Writer's Vision: The Poetry and Paintings of Günter Grass 當中介紹 Günter Grass 的文章。

※ 今年題目出得很嚴謹，只有一個地方需要修正：

題　　號	修　　正　　意　　見
三、文意選填 第一段 第 4 行	…, including e-mail and instant messaging. → including *in* e-mail and instant messaging. * 依句意，須加上 in 才合理。

【99 年指考】綜合測驗：16-20 出題來源

Don't touch the art?　Louvre exhibit lets visitors break the rules

PARIS—Signs ask visitors to keep their hands off the art in the Louvre Museum.　But one special sculpture gallery invites art lovers to indulge.

The Louvre's Tactile Gallery, targeted to the blind and visually impaired, is the only space in the Paris museum where visitors can touch the sculptures, with no guards or alarms to stop them.

Its latest exhibit is a crowd-pleaser: a menagerie of sculpted lions, snakes, horses and eagles.

The 15 bronze, plaster and terra-cotta animals are reproductions of famous works found elsewhere in the Louvre. Called "Animals, Symbols of Power," the exhibit focuses on animals that were used by kings, emperors and pharaohs throughout history to symbolize the greatness of their reigns. Though the gallery was conceived for the blind and visually impaired, children and other visitors also enjoy it.　During guided tours on the weekends, children can explore the art with blindfolds on.

The Louvre opened the Tactile Gallery in 1995.　Though other French cultural exhibits offer periodic events and programs for the blind, the Louvre says it is the only museum in France with a gallery specifically set up for the visually impaired.　Elsewhere in Europe, Ancona, Italy, and Athens, Greece, have entire tactile museums.

⋮

【99 年指考】文意選填：21-30 出題來源

SMS language

　　SMS language or Textese (also known as txtese, chatspeak, txt, txtspk, txtk, txto, texting language, or txt talk) is a term for the abbreviations and slang most commonly used due to the necessary brevity of mobile phone text messaging, in particular the widespread SMS (short message standard) communication protocol.　SMS language is also common on the Internet, including in e-mail and instant messaging.　It can be likened to a rebus, which uses pictures and single letters or numbers to represent whole words (e.g. "i <3 u" which uses the pictogram of a heart for love, and the letter u replaces you).

　　For words which have no common abbreviation, users most commonly remove the vowels from a word, and the reader is required to interpret a string of consonants by re-adding the vowels (e.g. dictionary becomes dctnry and keyboard becomes kybrd).　The reader must interpret the abbreviated words depending on the context in which it is used, as there are many examples of words or phrases which use the same abbreviations (e.g., lol could mean laugh out loud or lots of love, and cryn could mean crayon or cryin(g)).　So if someone says ttyl, lol they probably mean talk to you later, lots of love not talk to you later, laugh out loud, and if someone says omg, lol they probably mean oh my god, laugh out loud not oh my god, lots of love.　Context is key when interpreting txtese, and it is precisely this shortfall which critics cite as a reason not to use it (although the English language in general, like most other languages, has many words that have different meanings in different contexts).　SMS language does not always obey or follow standard grammar, and additionally the words used are not usually found in standard dictionaries or recognized by language academies.

　　The advent of predictive text input and smartphones featuring full QWERTY keyboards may contribute to a reduction in the use of SMS language, although this has not yet been noted.

【99 年指考】篇章結構：31-35 出題來源

Cockroaches Don't Learn in the Morning

November 19, 2007

Do you have trouble getting started in the morning? Do you have problems learning early in the day? If you do, you are not alone. Cockroaches have the same problem! They learn better at night than they do in the morning.

To investigate when cockroaches learn best, researchers at Vanderbilt University (Nashville, TN) tested the insects for which odor (peppermint or vanilla) they preferred. Most cockroaches preferred the smell of vanilla to the smell of peppermint at all times. The scientists then trained the cockroaches to prefer the peppermint smell by rewarding the insects with a taste of sugar water when they approached a peppermint smell and punishing them with a taste of salt water when they approached a vanilla smell. (Cockroaches like sugar water, but they don't like salt water.)

When the cockroaches were trained in the early night, they remembered the new associations (peppermint = sugar water; vanilla = salt water) for up to 48 hours. However, if the cockroaches were trained in the early morning, they quickly forgot which smell went with which water. The effect was dependent on when the cockroaches were trained, not when they were tested.

So, cockroaches learn better at night than they do in the morning. Because these animals are more active and search for food during the night (nocturnal), it is likely that information they gather at night will be more useful to them. These experiments provide some clues about the interactions between body rhythms, learning and memory, but the brain pathways involved with these functions are still unknown.

【99 年指考】閱讀測驗：36-39 出題來源

United States Mint Puts First Presidential $1 Coin Into Circulation

George Washington to be First in Historic Presidential $1 Coin Series

WASHINGTON—The United States Mint today released into circulation the new George Washington $1 Coin, the first in a series of $1 coins honoring former United States Presidents.

⋮

Modeled after the United States Mint's successful 50 State Quarters® Program, the Presidential $1 Coin Program will feature systematically rotating designs of former United States Presidents. The George Washington $1 Coin marks the first of four Presidential $1 Coins to be released this year, with John Adams, Thomas Jefferson and James Madison to roll out later in 2007.

⋮

Traditional Subjects, Unique Design

The designs of the coins are bold and dramatic. The traditional inscriptions of "E Pluribus Unum," "In God We Trust," the date and the mint mark are featured on the edge of the coins making the Presidential $1 Coins unique among today's circulating coins.

The new Presidential $1 Coins are identical in color and size to the Golden Dollar featuring Sacagawea, and have the same distinctive rim and tactile features to assist the visually impaired. The face of each coin will feature an original image of a former President and the years of his term of office. The reverse of the coin shows an image of the Statue of Liberty and the inscriptions "United States of America" and "$1."

⋮

Presidential $1 Coin Release Schedule

Each President will be honored with a single $1 coin, regardless of the number of consecutive terms he served, except for Grover Cleveland, the only United States President to serve non-consecutive terms. He will be honored on two coins. No living former or current President can be honored on a coin.

【99年指考】閱讀測驗：40-43 出題來源

In France, Free Subscriptions To Young Newspaper Readers

Newspapers have tried many things to stave off a seemingly relentless decline in readers. Now France is pushing forward with a novel approach: giving away papers to young readers in an effort to turn them into regular customers.

The government on Tuesday detailed plans of a project called "My Free Newspaper," under which 18- to 24-year-olds will be offered a free, yearlong subscription to a newspaper of their choice.

⋮

Readership in France is especially low among young people. According to a government study, only 10 percent of those aged 15 to 24 read a paid-for newspaper daily in 2007, down from 20 percent a decade earlier.

About 60 publications are participating in the new project. In addition to papers like Le Monde and Le Figaro, they include a variety of local publications, as well as the Paris-based International Herald Tribune, the global edition of The New York Times. Even L'Équipe, a popular sports daily, is taking part.

Costs of the project are being shared by the newspapers and the state, with the government allocating 15 million euros, or $22.5 million, over three years.

Emmanuel Schwartzenberg, a former media editor of Le Figaro who has written a book about the problems of the French press, said he was skeptical about the project.

"This just reinforces the belief that newspapers should be free, which is a very bad idea," Mr. Schwartzenberg said.

French readers young and old already have plenty of free options from which to choose, including newspaper Web sites and the free papers handed out daily in many city centers.

Some bloggers said the new program might hold the most appeal to the few young people who already read, and buy, newspapers.

The government plans to promote the program with an advertising campaign aimed at young readers and their parents. But, in a sign of the possible challenges involved in attracting young readers to print, the government said the primary outlet for the ads would be the Internet.

A Coffee For When You Feel Like Crap

Coffee connoisseurs are known to be willing to shell out large sums of money for a high-quality bean. The high-end beans, such as Kona or Blue Mountain, are known to go for extraordinary sums of money. Then there is Kopi Lowak, reputed to be the most expensive coffee in the world. While price can vary, Kopi Lowak (which translates as "Civet coffee") can sell for as much as $50 per quarter-pound.

This isn't particularly surprising, given that approximately 500 pounds a year of Kopi Lowak constitutes the entire world supply.

What is surprising is why this particular coffee is so rare. It's not the plants that are rare. It's the civet droppings. That's right, the civet droppings. Coffee beans aren't Kopi Lowak until they've been passed through the digestive tract of paradoxurus hermaphroditus, otherwise known as the palm civet.

Palm civets are nocturnal, tree-dwelling raccoon-like little critters, native to SE Asia and the Indonesian islands. They also have a love of coffee cherries. They eat the fruit whole, but only digest the outer fruit, leaving the bean intact. Suppliers of Kopi Lowak opine that while the beans have not been destroyed, or even visibly changed, they have undergone a transformation while in the civet's digestive tract. Regardless of whether the digestive enzymes have wrought some changes in the beans, or whether it's the unfailing instinct that palm civets have for coffee cherries at the peak of ripeness, the beans retrieved from civet droppings have a unique flavor all their own.

Right now most of the world's supply is sold in Japan, though a very few US markets are starting to stock it. It's strictly limited availability would virtually guarantee a high price, even if the coffee were unremarkable. As it is, Kopi Lowak is reported to have a character unlike any other coffee, complex with caramel undertones and an earthy or gamey flavor.

【99 年指考】閱讀測驗：48-51 出題來源

Program A Writer's Vision: The Poetry and Paintings of Günter Grass

　　Günter Grass (1927-), winner of the 1999 Nobel Prize in Literature, has already firmly established his position as a grand master of the German-language literary world. His talents are revealed in a spectrum of disciplines: He is not only a novelist, poet and playwright, but also a painter and sculptor with a background of professional training at academies of fine arts. He is also enthusiastically active in politics.

⋮

　　In awarding Günter Grass the Nobel Prize in Literature, the Swedish Academy praised him thusly: "He is a fabulist and a scholarly lecturer, recorder of voices and presumptuous monologist, pasticheur and at the same time creator of an ironic idiom that he alone commands." This year, Mr. Grass celebrates his 80th birthday, and in recognition of this occasion, the Taipei Fine Arts Museum has specially organized this exhibition. We are particularly thankful to the Würth Museum for generously lending works from their collection; to the German Institute Taipei and the German Cultural Center, Taipei, for their diligent contributions; to Dr. Liu Hwei-ann, professor of German language and literature at Fu Jen Catholic University, for her wholehearted assistance; and to Würth Taiwan Co., Ltd., for its generous sponsorship. The 117 watercolor paintings and 10 sculptures by Günter Grass that ultimately appear here before our eyes can be described as works rich in literary value that hold a unique place in Mr. Grass's creative life. Using the translucent, clear quality of watercolor, Günter Grass has depicted a wide variety of natural scenes, animals and plants, and even human artifacts of the German countryside, one after another, while also portraying them in verse, allowing words to serve as the content of his paintings, the two conversing, engaging in dialogue, and conveying rich imaginative color, while revealing dark, deep allegorical meaning.

99 年指定科目考試英文科大考中心意見回覆

※ 題號：40

【題目】

第40至43題為題組

Newspapers have tried many things to stop a seemingly nonstop decline in readers. Now France is pushing forward with a novel approach: giving away papers to young readers in an effort to turn them into regular customers. The French government recently detailed plans of a project called "My Free Newspaper," under which 18- to 24-year-olds will be offered a free, year-long subscription to a newspaper of their choice.

Newspaper readership in France has been especially low among young people. According to a government study, only 10 percent of those aged 15 to 24 read a paid-for newspaper daily in 2007, down from 20 percent a decade earlier.

Emmanuel Schwartzenberg, a former media editor of *Le Figaro*, the oldest and second-largest national newspaper in France, said he had strong reservations about the government project. At a time when advertising is in steep decline, he said, newspapers should instead be looking at ways to raise more profits from readers, rather than giving papers away. "This just reinforces the belief that newspapers should be free, which is a very bad idea," Mr. Schwartzenberg said.

French readers, young and old, already have plenty of free options from which to choose, including newspaper websites and the free papers handed out daily in many city centers. Some bloggers said the new program might hold the most appeal to the few young people who do already read, and buy, newspapers.

The French government plans to promote the program with an advertising campaign aimed at young readers and their parents. However, when asked how to attract young readers to the printed press, the government said the primary channel for the ads would be the Internet.

40. Why did the French government decide to launch the free newspaper program?

(A) To fight economic recession.

(B) To win approval from youngsters.

(C) To promote newspaper readership.

(D) To improve the literacy rate in France.

【意見內容】

根據文章 "Newspapers have tried many things to stop a seemingly nonstop decline in readers."，因此法國政府決定推動「免費報紙」，使 young readers（18–24 歲）成為 regular customers。考生推斷此 project 是為挽救經濟蕭條之故（reader → customers），故參考答案應選 (A) 亦可。

【大考中心意見回覆】

選文內容介紹法國政府為提昇閱報率而提供報紙免費贈閱措施，本題題意為法國政府推出免費報紙計畫的原因，評量考生是否能掌握全文主旨目的之能力，作答線索為第一段第一句文意及全文之主旨大意，報業已多方嘗試阻止閱報率下降，法國政府針對 18 到 24 歲讀者推出報紙免費贈閱計畫。選項 (A) 對抗經濟蕭條，文中未提及經濟蕭條，因此選項 (C) 提升閱報率為最適當答案。

※ 題號：45

【題目】

第 44 至 47 題為題組

　　Coffee experts are willing to pay large sums of money for high-quality coffee beans. The high-end beans, such as Kona or Blue Mountain, are known to cost extraordinary sums of money. Then there is Kopi Lowak (translated as "Civet Coffee"), the world's most expensive coffee, which sells for as much as US $50 per quarter-pound.

　　This isn't particularly surprising, given that approximately 500 pounds a year of Kopi Lowak constitute the entire world supply. What is surprising is why this particular coffee is so rare. In fact, it's not the plants that are rare. It's the civet droppings. That's right, the civet droppings—the body waste of the palm civet. Coffee beans aren't Kopi Lowak until they've been digested and come out in the body waste of the palm civet.

　　Palm civets are tree-dwelling, raccoon-like little animals, native to Southeast Asia and the Indonesian islands. They also have a love for coffee cherries. According to Kopi Lowak suppliers, palm civets eat the fruit whole, but only digest the outer fruit, leaving the beans intact. While the beans are not destroyed, they undergo a transformation in the animal's body. A chemical substance in the digestive system of the palm civet causes some changes to the beans to give them a unique flavor. However, this is not the only explanation why coffee beans retrieved from civet droppings have a special flavor all their own. Another possible reason is that palm civets have an unfailing instinct for picking the coffee cherries at the peak of their ripeness.

Kopi Lowak is reported to have a character in taste unlike any other coffee, complex with caramel undertones and an earthy or gamey flavor. Currently, most of the world's supply of Kopi Lowak is sold in Japan, though a few US markets are also starting to stock up on Kopi Lowak.

45. Why is Kopi Lowak expensive?
(A) There is a very limited supply of the beans.
(B) The coffee trees that grow the beans are scarce.
(C) It takes a long time for the coffee beans to ripen.
(D) Only a few experts know how to produce the beans.

【意見內容】

根據第三段，"Another possible reason is that palm civets have an unfailing instinct for picking the coffee cherries at the peak of their ripeness." 以及第二段 "What is surprising is why this particular coffee is so rare. In fact, it's not the plants that are rare. It's the civet droppings."，考生認為參考答案 (C) 亦可。

【大考中心意見回覆】

選文內容介紹全世界最稀有、最昂貴的 Civet 咖啡的獨特生出產過程及氣味，本題題意 Kopi Lowak 昂貴原因，評量考生掌握文章內容細節之因果關係，作答線索為第一段文意及第二段第一句，全世界一年產量大約 500 磅，因此選項(A)該咖啡豆很有限為最適當答案，而選項 (C) 咖啡豆成熟的時間長，並非 Kopi Lowak 昂貴之因。

99 年指考英文科非選擇題評分標準說明

閱卷召集人：張武昌【台灣師範大學英語系教授】

　　99 學年度指定科目考試英文考科的非選擇題題型與去年一樣，分兩大題，第一大題是中譯英，試題內容與我國近年來出生率下降的現象相關，分兩小題共八分；第二大題是引導式的作文，考生需寫一篇至少 120 個單詞（words）的作文，說明那種氣味（smell）最讓考生難忘？文分兩段，第一段描述考生在何種情境中聞到這種氣味，以及初聞這種氣味時的感受，第二段描述這個氣味至今仍令考生難忘的理由。作文滿分為二十分。

　　關於閱卷籌備工作，在正式閱卷前，7 月 4 日先召開評分標準訂定會議，由正副召集人、學科專家及協同主持人共十四人，參閱了近一百本約 3000～4000 份的試卷，經過一天的討論，訂定評分標準，選出合適的樣本，編製了閱卷參考手冊，供閱卷委員共同參閱。

　　7 月 5 日上午 9：00 到 11：00，一百三十多位大學教授，分組進行試閱會議，根據閱卷參考手冊的樣卷，分別評分，並討論評分準則，務求評分標準一致，確保閱卷品質。為求慎重，試閱會議之後，並再召開評分標準確定會議，才開始正式閱卷。

　　關於評分標準，在中譯英部分，原則上是每個錯誤扣 0.5 分。作文的評分標準是依據內容、組織、文法句構、字彙拼字、體例五個項目給分，字數明顯不足或未分段皆扣 1 分。

　　依慣例，每份答案卷皆會經過兩位委員分別評分，最後以二人平均分數計算。如果第一閱與第二閱分數差距不符合標準，再找第三位委員主閱（正副召集人或協同主持人）評分。

　　由試閱樣本看來，由於這次的翻譯題句型不難，但一些關鍵字如「出生率」、「人力資源」等較容易譯錯，但整體而言得分不難。

　　作文題目為「考生最難忘的氣味」，考生可依自身經驗，發揮想像空間，作文主要內容有「阿嬤身上的花露水味道」，也有「同學體育課後的汗味」，考生只要有中上的英文程度，應可寫出一篇切題且文意連貫的英文作文。

九十九學年度指定科目考試（英文）
大考中心公佈答案

題號	答案	題號	答案	題號	答案
1	C	21	I	41	D
2	C	22	G	42	A
3	C	23	J	43	D
4	B	24	E	44	C
5	B	25	F	45	A
6	C	26	D	46	D
7	B	27	C	47	B
8	A	28	A	48	A
9	D	29	B	49	B
10	D	30	H	50	C
11	B	31	E	51	D
12	D	32	D		
13	A	33	A		
14	B	34	B		
15	C	35	C		
16	B	36	D		
17	C	37	B		
18	A	38	A		
19	D	39	C		
20	A	40	C		

九十九學年度指定科目考試
各科成績標準一覽表

科　目	頂　標	前　標	均　標	後　標	底　標
國　　文	67	62	54	44	36
英　　文	79	69	48	26	13
數學甲	79	65	45	25	14
數學乙	88	78	60	40	22
化　　學	68	57	38	21	12
物　　理	57	43	24	12	6
生　　物	81	73	58	40	28
歷　　史	75	68	57	43	31
地　　理	63	56	46	34	26
公民與社會	52	44	34	23	16

※ 以上五項標準均取為整數（小數只捨不入），且其計算均不含缺考生之成績，
　計算方式如下：

　頂標：成績位於第 88 百分位數之考生成績。
　前標：成績位於第 75 百分位數之考生成績。
　均標：成績位於第 50 百分位數之考生成績。
　後標：成績位於第 25 百分位數之考生成績。
　底標：成績位於第 12 百分位數之考生成績。

例：　某科之到考考生為 99982 人，則該科五項標準為

　　頂標：成績由低至高排序，取第 87985 名（99982×88%=87984.16，取整數，
　　　　　小數無條件進位）考生的成績，再取整數(小數只捨不入)。

　　前標：成績由低至高排序，取第 74987 名（99982×75%=74986.5，取整數，
　　　　　小數無條件進位）考生的成績，再取整數(小數只捨不入)。

　　均標：成績由低至高排序，取第 49991 名（99982×50%=49991）考生的成績，
　　　　　再取整數(小數只捨不入)。

　　後標：成績由低至高排序，取第 24996 名（99982×25%=24995.5，取整數，
　　　　　小數無條件進位）考生的成績，再取整數(小數只捨不入)。

　　底標：成績由低至高排序，取第 11998 名（99982×12%=11997.84，取整數，
　　　　　小數無條件進位）考生的成績，再取整數(小數只捨不入)。

九十八年大學入學指定科目考試試題
英文考科

第壹部份：選擇題（佔 72 分）

一、詞彙（10 分）

說明：　第 1 至 10 題，每題選出一個最適當的選項，標示在答案卡之「選擇題答案區」。每題答對得 1 分，答錯或劃記多於一個選項者倒扣 1/3 分，倒扣到本大題之實得分數為零為止。未作答者，不給分亦不扣分。

1. You'll need the store _____ to show proof of purchase if you want to return any items you bought.
   (A) credit　　　　(B) guide　　　　(C) license　　　　(D) receipt

2. Spending most of his childhood in Spain, John, a native speaker of English, is also _____ in Spanish.
   (A) promising　　(B) grateful　　(C) fluent　　　(D) definite

3. The mirror slipped out of the little girl's hand, and the broken pieces _____ all over the floor.
   (A) scattered　　(B) circulated　　(C) featured　　(D) released

4. No one knows how the fire broke out. The police have started an _____ into the cause of it.
   (A) appreciation　(B) extension　(C) operation　(D) investigation

5. When there is a heavy rain, you have to drive very _____ so as to avoid traffic accidents.
   (A) cautiously　(B) recklessly　(C) smoothly　(D) passively

6. We decided to buy some _____ for our new apartment, including a refrigerator, a vacuum cleaner, and a dishwasher.
   (A) utensils　　(B) facilities　　(C) appliances　(D) extensions

7. This math class is very _____; I have to spend at least two hours every day doing the assignments.
   (A) confidential   (B) logical   (C) demanding   (D) resistant

8. One can generally judge the quality of eggs with the naked eye. _____, good eggs must be clean, free of cracks, and smooth-shelled.
   (A) Agriculturally (B) Externally   (C) Influentially   (D) Occasionally

9. The scientist _____ his speech to make it easier for children to understand the threat of global warming.
   (A) estimated   (B) documented (C) abolished   (D) modified

10. The Internet has _____ newspapers as a medium of mass communication. It has become the main source for national and international news for people.
    (A) reformed   (B) surpassed   (C) promoted   (D) convinced

二、綜合測驗（10 分）

說明： 第 11 至 20 題，每題一個空格。請依文意選出一個最適當的選項，標示在答案卡之「選擇題答案區」。每題答對得 1 分，答錯或劃記多於一個選項者倒扣 1/3 分，倒扣到本大題之實得分數爲零爲止。未作答者，不給分亦不扣分。

第 11 至 15 題爲題組

　　Keele University in the United Kingdom has developed a "virtual patient," created by a computer, to help train the pharmacists of the future. Students in the university's School of ___11___ work with the "patient" to gain experience in effective communication and decision-making.

　　Students talk with the "patient" directly or by typing questions into a computer. The "patient" responds verbally or with gestures to indicate

____12____ such as pain, stress or anxiety. As a result, students are forced to communicate clearly ____13____ that the "patient" understands them completely. The Virtual Patient can also be used to explore various medical situations. For example, the "patient" can be programmed to be allergic to certain medicine and can ____14____ serious reactions if student learners are not aware of the situation. This kind of practice allows students to learn from mistakes in a safe environment that would not be ____15____ with textbooks alone. The unique system can both be used in a classroom setting or for distance learning.

11. (A) Education　　(B) Business　　(C) Pharmacy　　(D) Humanities
12. (A) expressions　(B) emotions　　(C) elements　　(D) events
13. (A) in order　　　(B) in return　　(C) in case　　　(D) in addition
14. (A) adapt to　　　(B) break into　　(C) provide with　(D) suffer from
15. (A) exciting　　　(B) necessary　　(C) possible　　　(D) important

第 16 至 20 題為題組

　　In spite of modernization and the increasing role of women in all walks of life, the practice of the dowry in India is still widespread. The dowry system, money or property brought by a bride to her husband at marriage, was started centuries ago with the intention of providing security for a girl ____16____ difficulties and unexpected circumstances after marriage. For this purpose, the parents gave ____17____ they could to their daughter, which consequently went to the groom's family. By the beginning of the 21st century, however, the custom had deteriorated to a point whereby the groom and his family had become very ____18____. When demands for dowry are not met, the bride is ____19____ torture, and often even killed. The more educated a man is, the ____20____ is the expectation for dowry at the time of marriage. Girls who are highly educated are required to have larger dowries because they usually marry more educated men.

16. (A) due to (B) apart from (C) in case of (D) with reference to
17. (A) whoever (B) whenever (C) whatever (D) whichever
18. (A) greedy (B) pleasant (C) regretful (D) sympathetic
19. (A) aware of (B) required by (C) furious with (D) subject to
20. (A) lower (B) higher (C) better (D) worse

三、文意選填（10 分）

說明： 第 21 至 30 題，每題一個空格。請依文意在文章後所提供的 (A) 到 (J)
選項中分別選出最適當者，並將其字母代號標示在答案卡之「選擇題
答案區」。每題答對得 1 分，答錯或劃記多於一個選項者倒扣 1/9 分，
倒扣到本大題之實得分數爲零爲止。未作答者，不給分亦不扣分。

第 21 至 30 題爲題組

Oniomania is the technical term for the compulsive desire to shop,
more commonly referred to as compulsive shopping or shopping
addiction. Victims often experience feelings of ___21___ when they are
in the process of purchasing, which seems to give their life meaning while
letting them forget about their sorrows. Once ___22___ the environment
where the purchasing occurred, the feeling of a personal reward would
be gone. To compensate, the addicted person would go shopping again.
Eventually a feeling of suppression will overcome the person. For
example, cases have shown that the bought goods will be hidden or
destroyed, because the person concerned feels ___23___ of their addiction
and tries to conceal it. He or she is either regretful or depressed. In order
to cope with the feelings, the addicted person is prompted to ___24___
another purchase.

Compulsive shopping often begins at an early age. Children who
experienced parental neglect often grew up with low ___25___ because
throughout much of their childhood they felt that they were not important
as a person. As a result, they used toys to ___26___ their feelings of
loneliness. Because of the ongoing sentiment of deprivation they

endured as children, adults that have depended on materials for emotional
____27____ when they were much younger are more likely to become
addicted to shopping. During adulthood, the purchase, instead of the toy,
is substituted for ____28____. The victims are unable to deal with their
everyday problems, especially those that alter their self-esteem.
Important issues in their lives are repressed by ____29____ something.
According to studies, as many as 8.9 percent of the American population
____30____ as compulsive buyers. Research has also found that men and
women suffer from this problem at about the same rate.

(A) support   (B) qualify   (C) affection   (D) ashamed
(E) make up for   (F) leaving   (G) turn to   (H) buying
(I) self-esteem   (J) contentment

四、篇章結構（10 分）

說明：　第 31 至 35 題，每題一個空格。請依文意在文章後所提供的 (A) 到 (E)
　　　　選項中分別選出最適當者，填入空格中，使篇章結構清晰有條理，並將
　　　　其英文字母代號標示在答案卡之「選擇題答案區」。每題答對得 2 分，
　　　　答錯或劃記多於一個選項者倒扣 1/2 分，倒扣到本大題之實得分數爲零
　　　　爲止。未作答者，不給分亦不扣分。

第 31 至 35 題爲題組

　　There was a time when Whitney didn't have a lot of friends. She
was a bit shy and reserved. ____31____ All through high school, though,
she wasn't able to make good friends or find companionship.

　　When it was time to go to college, Whitney was quite nervous. She
was going to be rooming with someone she didn't know and living in a
town 300 miles away from home. There wouldn't be a single person she
knew in town. ____32____

　　The first week of classes, something happened that changed
Whitney's life forever. ____33____ She told everyone where she came from

and all of the other ordinary details that students share in such situations. The final question for each student to answer was, "what is your goal for this class?" Most of the students said that they would like to get a good grade, pass the class or something similar. ＿＿34＿＿ She said that her goal was to make just one good friend.

While most of the students sat in silence, one student came to Whitney and held out her hand and introduced herself. She asked if they could be friends. The whole room was silent. All eyes focused on Whitney and the hand extended just in front of her. ＿＿35＿＿

Whitney learned the power of asking for what she wanted and taking action on that day.

(A) For some reason, Whitney said something entirely different.
(B) Whitney smiled and stretched her hand out and a friendship was formed.
(C) She had no idea how she was going to make friends in this new environment.
(D) In her English Composition class, she was asked to share a little about herself.
(E) She never really wanted to be popular, but she did want to have someone to share secrets and laughs with.

五、閱讀測驗（32 分）

說明：　第 36 至 51 題，每題請分別根據各篇文章的文意選出一個最適當的選項，標示在答案卡之「選擇題答案區」。每題答對得 2 分，答錯或劃記多於一個選項者倒扣 2/3 分，倒扣到本大題之實得分數爲零爲止。未作答者，不給分亦不扣分。

第 36 至 39 題爲題組

April 22, 2010 will be the 18th celebration of the annual *Take Our Daughters to Work Day* (*TOD*), a project the National Ms. Foundation for Women of America (NFW) developed to expose girls to expanding opportunities for women in the workplace.

The program offers millions of girls a first-hand view of the many career opportunities available in their futures. Now that women make up 46 percent of the U.S. workforce, girls can find role models in every occupational field—from politics to molecular biology to professional athletics, to name just a few. *TOD* encourages girls to focus on their abilities and opportunities, not just their appearance.

The NFW developed the project more than a decade ago to address the self-esteem problems that many girls experience when they enter adolescence. At school, boys often receive more encouragement in the classroom, especially in math, science and computer science, the academic fields that tend to lead to the highest salaries. Women receive on average only 73 cents for every dollar that men are paid, and remain vastly underrepresented in top executive positions and technology fields. *TOD* aims to give girls the confidence and inspiration they need to develop successful careers, particularly in non-traditional fields.

Perhaps because the program had become so widespread and successful, *TOD* had been criticized for excluding boys, and it was expanded in 2003 to include boys. The program's official website states that the program was changed in order to provide both boys and girls with opportunities to explore careers at an age when they are more flexible in terms of gender stereotyped roles. "We should also show boys that becoming a child care provider is as acceptable a choice as becoming a police officer or CEO," added Sara K. Gould, executive director of the NFW.

36. The purpose for having a *Take Our Daughters to Work Day* is _____.

    (A) to encourage girls to pursue top paying jobs
    (B) to let girls spend more time with their mothers
    (C) to show girls possibilities for work and careers
    (D) to give girls a chance to visit their mothers' offices

37. *TOD* was criticized because some people _____.

    (A) thought it was not fair to boys
    (B) did not like having children at work
    (C) did not have daughters to take to work
    (D) would rather have their daughters stay at home

38. Which of the following is true according to the passage?

    (A) Boys are now included on *Take Our Daughters to Work Day*.
    (B) Women and men have always been treated equally at work.
    (C) Homemaking and rearing children are jobs for girls only.
    (D) Girls grow up receiving more attention than boys.

39. Why are women underrepresented in some fields such as technology?

    (A) They are not interested in these fields.
    (B) They are not encouraged to work in these fields.
    (C) They are not paid the same as men in these fields.
    (D) They are not allowed to be educated in these fields.

第 40 至 43 題為題組

In all cultures and throughout history hair has had a special significance. In ancient Egypt, as long ago as 1500 BC, the outward appearance expressed the person's status, role in society and political position. Wigs played an important role in this: they were crafted with great artistry and often sprinkled with powdered gold.

In the 8th century BC, the pre-Roman Celts in Northern Europe wore their hair long. In a man it was the expression of his strength, in a woman of her fertility. The idea of long hair as a symbol of male strength is even mentioned in the Bible, in the story of Samson and Delilah. Samson was a leader of the Israelites. His long hair, which he never cut, gave him superhuman powers. The only person who knew his secret was Delilah. However, she spied for the enemy and betrayed him. One night she cut off his hair and thus robbed him of his strength.

In the classical Greek period, curly hair was not only the fashion, but it also represented an attitude towards life. Curls or locks were the metaphor for change, freedom and the joy of living. The ancient Greek word for curls and locks is related to intriguing and tempting someone.

Hair is also used as a symbol of opposition. The punk protest movement today uses hair as a symbol of disapproval of the "middle-class, conventional lifestyle" by wearing provocative haircuts and shockingly colored hair. A different form of objection could be seen in the women's hairstyles in the 1960s. Women's liberation was expressed in a short-cut, straight and simple hairstyle which underlined equality with men without neglecting female attributes. To this day hair has kept its importance as a symbol of power, youth, vitality and health.

40. The topic of this passage could best be described as _____.
    (A) the scientific study of hairstyles
    (B) the symbolic meanings of hairstyles
    (C) the art of designing different hairstyles
    (D) the contemporary development of hairstyles

41. Why did ancient Greeks like to wear curls and locks?
    (A) To attract others.　　　　(B) To show off their artistry.
    (C) To hide their real identity.　(D) To represent power and status.

42. How did women in the 1960s use hair to show objection?
    (A) They grew long hair.　　(B) They dyed their hair.
    (C) They cut their hair short.　(D) They shaved their heads.

43. What can be inferred from the passage?
    (A) Long curly hair has always been popular since ancient times.
    (B) Ancient Egyptians did not pay much attention to their hairstyles.
    (C) The punk movement is one of the most successful movements in history.
    (D) Samson might never have been defeated if he had kept the secret to himself.

第 44 至 47 題為題組

Camille Mahlknecht, 9, has some big fun planned for this weekend. She and other residents of Agoura Hills, California, plan to pick up trash during their city's annual cleanup. At the same time, Wissam Raed, 12, will be busy volunteering too. Thousands of miles away in Lebanon, Wissam plans to put on a play at an orphanage and bring potted plants to elderly people at a senior citizen center.

Some other children like Nathan White, 10, have personal reasons for volunteering. Nathan's grandmother died of a heart attack. To help raise money for medical research, Nathan participated in Jump Rope for Heart. He and five other boys took turns jumping rope for two and half hours and collected more than US$1,200 in donations for the American Heart Association.

Millions of children around the globe lend a hand to their communities every year. Schools and parents also contribute to the rise in youth service. For example, many schools offer community service activities for students to join. Teachers either combine volunteer work with classroom lessons or make service work a requirement. Parents, on the other hand, encourage their kids to volunteer and do it with them.

Community service is particularly important in this recession time. As the need for monetary support and other aid has increased, many charitable organizations have experienced a significant drop in donations. Camille and other children who volunteer thousands of hours annually can fill in some of the gaps.

According to research, kids who start volunteering are twice as likely to continue doing good deeds when they are adults. So, grab a paintbrush, a trash bag, or whatever you need to help your community. You'll love how you feel after helping others. Even dirty work can be lots of fun, if it's for a good cause.

44. What's the writer's purpose of writing this passage?
    (A) To recommend youth service programs to schools.
    (B) To ask charity organizations to serve the community.
    (C) To urge children to take part in volunteering activities.
    (D) To propose alternatives for doing community services.

45. What is the main idea of the 3rd paragraph?
    (A) Community service is gaining popularity among children.
    (B) Families and schools help to make community service popular.
    (C) Children now depend more on their teachers than on their parents.
    (D) Nathan White had a special reason to raise money for medical research.

46. Why is community service important in a time of recession?
    (A) It raises money for school activities.
    (B) It teaches children to take care of the sick.
    (C) It gives charity organizations some needed help.
    (D) It encourages parents and teachers to work together.

47. What can be inferred from the passage?
    (A) Community service can help prevent juvenile delinquency.
    (B) Children will probably leave school and work as volunteers.
    (C) Organizing sports events for the school is a kind of community service.
    (D) Children who do volunteer work are more likely to grow up to be caring adults.

第 48 至 51 題為題組

Downloading music over the Internet is pretty common among high school and college students. However, when students download and share copyrighted music without permission, they are violating the law.

A survey of young people's music ownership has found that teenagers and college students have an average of more than 800 illegally copied songs each on their digital music players. Half of those surveyed share all the music on their hard drive, enabling others to copy hundreds of songs at any one time. Some students were found to have randomly linked their personal blogs to music sites, so as to allow free trial listening of copyrighted songs for blog visitors, or adopted some of the songs as the background music for their blogs. Such practices may be easy and free, but there are consequences.

Sandra Dowd, a student of Central Michigan University, was fined US$7,500 for downloading 501 files from LimeWire, a peer-to-peer file sharing program. Sandra claimed that she was unaware that her downloads were illegal until she was contacted by authorities. Similarly, Mike Lewinski paid US$4,000 to settle a lawsuit against him for copyright violation. Mike expressed shock and couldn't believe that this was happening to him. "I just wanted to save some money and I always thought **the threat was just a scare tactic**." "You know, everyone does it," added Mike.

The RIAA (Recording Industry Association of America), the organization that files lawsuits against illegal downloaders, states that suing students was by no means their first choice. Unfortunately, without the threat of consequences, students are just not changing their behavior. Education alone is not enough to stop the extraordinary growth of the illegal downloading practice.

48. Why is it common for students to download copyrighted music?
　(A) They don't think that they will be caught.
　(B) They want their friends to know that they are smart.
　(C) They think it is a good way to make some extra money.
　(D) They are against copyright protection over Internet music.

49. What does Mike mean by saying that "**the threat was just a scare tactic**"?
　(A) One should not be afraid of threats.
　(B) A lawsuit will result from the threat.
　(C) It is unfair to scare people with a threat.
　(D) No serious consequence will follow the threat.

50. What is RIAA's attitude towards students' illegal downloading behavior?
　(A) They believe that education will help greatly in protecting copyrights.
　(B) They profit from the fines illegal downloaders pay for copyright violations.
　(C) They like to sue students for downloading music illegally from the Internet.
　(D) They think that illegal downloading behavior needs tough measures to correct.

51. What's the best title for this passage?
　(A) Copyright Violators, Beware!
　(B) How to Get Free Music Online!
　(C) A Survey of Students' Downloading Habits
　(D) Eliminate Illegal Music Download? Impossible!

第貳部份：非選擇題（佔 28 分）

一、中譯英（8 分）

說明： 1. 將下列兩句中文翻譯成適當之英文，並將答案寫在「答案卷」上。
　　　 2. 請依序作答，並標明題號。每題 4 分，共 8 分。

1. 玉山是東亞第一高峰，以生態多樣聞名。

2. 大家在網路上投票給它，要讓它成為世界七大奇觀之一。

二、英文作文（20 分）

說明： 1. 依提示在「答案卷」上寫一篇英文作文。
　　　 2. 文長約 120 至 150 個單詞（words）。

提示： 如果你可以不用擔心預算，隨心所欲的度過一天，你會怎麼過？請寫一
　　　 篇短文，第一段說明你會邀請誰和你一起度過這一天？為什麼？第二段
　　　 描述你會去哪裡？做些什麼事？為什麼？

九十八年度指定科目考試英文科試題詳解

第壹部分：選擇題

一、詞彙：

1. (**D**) You'll need the store <u>receipt</u> to show proof of purchase if you want to return any items you bought. 如果你想要退回任何你買的東西，你需要出示商店的<u>收據</u>作爲購買證明。

   (A) credit〔'krɛdɪt〕*n.* 信用　　　(B) guide〔gaɪd〕*n.* 導遊；指南
   (C) license〔'laɪsn̩s〕*n.* 執照　　(D) ***receipt***〔rɪ'sit〕*n.* 收據

   * show〔ʃo〕*v.* 出示　　　proof〔pruf〕*n.* 證據；證明
   purchase〔'pɝtʃəs〕*n.* 購買　　return〔rɪ'tɝn〕*v.* 退回
   item〔'aɪtəm〕*n.* 項目；物品

2. (**C**) Spending most of his childhood in Spain, John, a native speaker of English, is also <u>fluent</u> in Spanish.
   約翰的母語是英語。他在西班牙度過大部分的童年，所以西班牙語也很<u>流利</u>。

   (A) promising〔'pramɪsɪŋ〕*adj.* 有希望的；有可能的
   (B) grateful〔'gretfəl〕*adj.* 感激的　(C) ***fluent***〔'fluənt〕*adj.* 流利的
   (D) definite〔'dɛfənɪt〕*adj.* 明確的

   * childhood〔'tʃaɪld,hʊd〕*n.* 童年　　Spain〔spen〕*n.* 西班牙
   native〔'netɪv〕*adj.* 本地的
   a native speaker of English 以英語爲母語的人
   Spanish〔'spænɪʃ〕*n.* 西班牙語

3. (**A**) The mirror slipped out of the little girl's hand, and the broken pieces <u>scattered</u> all over the floor.
   鏡子從小女孩的手中滑落，碎片<u>散落</u>一地。

   (A) ***scatter***〔'skætɚ〕*v.* 四散　　(B) circulate〔'sɝkjə,let〕*v.* 循環
   (C) feature〔'fitʃɚ〕*v.* 以…爲特色　(D) release〔rɪ'lis〕*v.* 釋放

   * mirror〔'mɪrɚ〕*n.* 鏡子　　slip〔slɪp〕*v.* 滑落
   broken〔'brokən〕*adj.* 破碎的　　***all over*** 在…到處

4. (**D**) No one knows how the fire broke out. The police have started an
<u>investigation</u> into the cause of it.
沒有人知道火災是如何發生的。警方已經開始<u>調查</u>它的起因。
(A) appreciation〔ə͵priʃɪ'eʃən〕*n.* 欣賞；感激
(B) extension〔ɪk'stɛnʃən〕*n.* 擴大；延長；(電話)分機
(C) operation〔͵ɑpə'reʃən〕*n.* 手術
(D) *investigation*〔ɪn͵vɛstə'geʃən〕*n.* 調查
＊*break out* 爆發；突然發生　　cause〔kɔz〕*n.* 原因

5. (**A**) When there is a heavy rain, you have to drive very <u>cautiously</u> so
as to avoid traffic accidents.
下大雨的時候，你必須非常<u>謹慎</u>開車，以免發生車禍。
(A) *cautiously*〔'kɔʃəslɪ〕*adv.* 謹慎地
(B) recklessly〔'rɛklɪslɪ〕*adv.* 魯莽地
(C) smoothly〔'smuðlɪ〕*adv.* 平滑地；平穩地
(D) passively〔'pæsɪvlɪ〕*adv.* 消極地
＊*heavy rain* 大雨　　*so as to V.* 以便於～　　avoid〔ə'vɔɪd〕*v.* 避免

6. (**C**) We decided to buy some <u>appliances</u> for our new apartment,
including a refrigerator, a vacuum cleaner, and a dishwasher.
我們決定要為我們的新公寓買一些<u>電器用品</u>，包括冰箱、吸塵器、
和洗碗機。
(A) utensil〔ju'tɛnsḷ〕*n.* 家庭用具（如用手操作的像刷子、掃把、
　　鍋、碗、瓢、盆等）
(B) facility〔fə'sɪlətɪ〕*n.* 設備（多是指固定住的整體設備）
(C) *appliance*〔ə'plaɪəns〕*n.* 電器用品（= *electrical appliance*）
(D) extension〔ɪk'stɛnʃən〕*n.* 擴大；延長；(電話)分機
＊*vacuum cleaner* 吸塵器　　dishwasher〔'dɪʃ͵waʃɚ〕*n.* 洗碗機

7. (**C**) This math class is very <u>demanding</u>; I have to spend at least two
hours every day doing the assignments.
這門數學課<u>要求</u>得很<u>嚴格</u>；我每天必須花至少兩個小時寫作業。
(A) confidential〔͵kɑnfə'dɛnʃəl〕*adj.* 機密的
(B) logical〔'lɑdʒɪkḷ〕*adj.* 合邏輯的
(C) *demanding*〔dɪ'mændɪŋ〕*adj.* 要求高的；嚴格的
(D) resistant〔rɪ'zɪstənt〕*adj.* 有抵抗力的
＊*at least* 至少　　assignment〔ə'saɪnmənt〕*n.* 作業

8. (**B**) One can generally judge the quality of eggs with the naked eye.
Externally, good eggs must be clean, free of cracks, and
smooth-shelled.

通常可以用肉眼來判斷蛋的品質。好的蛋外表上必須要乾淨、沒有
裂縫，而且蛋殼要平滑。

(A) agriculturally〔,ægrɪ'kʌltʃərəlɪ〕 adv. 農業上
(B) ***externally***〔ɪk'stɝnḷɪ〕 adv. 外表上（↔ internally）
(C) influentially〔,ɪnflʊ'ɛnʃəlɪ〕 adv. 有影響力地
(D) occasionally〔ə'keʒənḷɪ〕 adv. 偶爾

* generally〔'dʒɛnərəlɪ〕 adv. 通常　　judge〔dʒʌdʒ〕 v. 判斷
the naked eye 肉眼　　***free of*** 沒有　　crack〔kræk〕 n. 裂縫
shell〔ʃɛl〕 n. 蛋殼　　***smooth-shelled*** 蛋殼平滑的

9. (**D**) The scientist modified his speech to make it easier for children to
understand the threat of global warming.

科學家修改了他的演說，好讓兒童更容易了解全球暖化的威脅。

(A) estimate〔'ɛstə,met〕 v. 估計
(B) document〔'dɑkjə,mɛnt〕 v. 以文件證明
(C) abolish〔ə'bɑlɪʃ〕 v. 廢除
(D) ***modify***〔'mɑdə,faɪ〕 v. 修正

* speech〔spitʃ〕 n. 演說　　threat〔θrɛt〕 n. 威脅
global warming 全球暖化

10. (**B**) The Internet has surpassed newspapers as a medium of mass
communication. It has become the main source for national and
international news for people.

網路已經成為超越報紙的大眾傳播媒體。它已經變成人們獲得國內
外新聞的主要來源。

(A) reform〔rɪ'fɔrm〕 v. 改革
(B) ***surpass***〔sɚ'pæs〕 v. 超越；勝過（= excel）
(C) promote〔prə'mot〕 v. 使升遷；提倡
(D) convince〔kən'vɪns〕 v. 使確信

* medium〔'midɪəm〕 n. 媒體　　***mass communication*** 大眾傳播
source〔sors〕 n. 來源　　national〔'næʃənḷ〕 adj. 國家的
international〔,ɪntɚ'næʃənḷ〕 adj. 國際的

二、綜合測驗：

第 11 至 15 題為題組

Keele University in the United Kingdom has developed a "virtual patient," created by a computer, to help train the pharmacists of the future. Students in the university's School of <u>Pharmacy</u> work with the "patient"
11
to gain experience in effective communication and decision-making.

英國的基爾大學已經研發出一個由電腦創造出來的「虛擬病患」，可以幫助訓練未來的藥劑師。這所大學藥學系的學生和這位「病患」合作，以獲得在有效的溝通及做決策方面的經驗。

> ***the United Kingdom*** 英國
> virtual〔ˋvɝtʃʊəl〕*adj.* 虛擬的
> patient〔ˋpeʃənt〕*n.* 病人　　create〔krɪˋet〕*v.* 創造
> pharmacist〔ˋfɑrməsɪst〕*n.* 藥劑師
> school〔skul〕*n.*（大學的）院；系　　***work with*** 和…合作
> gain〔gen〕*v.* 獲得　　effective〔əˋfɛktɪv〕*adj.* 有效的
> decision-making〔dɪˋsɪʒən ˋmekɪŋ〕*n.* 做決策

11. (**C**)　(A) education〔ˌɛdʒəˋkeʃən〕*n.* 教育
　　　　　　(B) business〔ˋbɪznɪs〕*n.* 商業
　　　　　　(C) ***pharmacy***〔ˋfɑrməsɪ〕*n.* 藥學
　　　　　　(D) humanities〔hjuˋmænətɪz〕*n. pl.* 人文科學

Students talk with the "patient" directly or by typing questions into a computer. The "patient" responds verbally or with gestures to indicate <u>emotions</u> such as pain, stress or anxiety. As a result, students are forced to
12
communicate clearly <u>in order</u> that the "patient" understands them completely.
13

學生可以和這位「病患」直接談話，或是將問題輸入電腦。這位「病患」會用言語回應，或是用手勢來表示像是痛苦、壓力，或是焦慮這些情緒。因此，學生不得不清楚地溝通，以便讓這位「病患」完全了解他們。

directly〔dəˈrɛktlɪ〕*adv.* 直接地　　type〔taɪp〕*v.* 打（字）
respond〔rɪˈspɑnd〕*v.* 回應；回答
verbally〔ˈvɝblɪ〕*adv.* 用言語；言詞上　　gesture〔ˈdʒɛstʃɚ〕*n.* 手勢
indicate〔ˈɪndəˌket〕*v.* 表示　　pain〔pen〕*n.* 痛苦
stress〔strɛs〕*n.* 壓力　　anxiety〔æŋˈzaɪətɪ〕*n.* 焦慮
as a result 因此　　force〔fɔrs〕*v.* 強迫；使不得不
completely〔kəmˈplɪtlɪ〕*adv.* 完全地

12. (**B**) (A) expression〔ɪkˈsprɛʃən〕*n.* 表情；說法
　　　(B) *emotion*〔ɪˈmoʃən〕*n.* 情緒
　　　(C) element〔ˈɛləmənt〕*n.* 要素　　(D) event〔ɪˈvɛnt〕*n.* 事件
　　＊本句後面所提到的 pain、stress，以及 anxiety，嚴格說來，只有 anxiety
　　　（焦慮）才是一種情緒，其他 pain（痛苦）及 stress（壓力），應是構成
　　　情緒的要素。若以此角度來考量，則 (C) element「要素」亦可視爲可選
　　　的答案之一。

13. (**A**) 依句意，學生不得不清楚地溝通，「以便於」讓「病患」能完全了解，
　　　故選 (A) *in order*「以便於；爲了」，後用 that 引導子句，表示目的。
　　　而 (B) in return「作爲回報」，(C) in case「如果」，(D) in addition
　　　「此外」，則不合句意。

The Virtual Patient can also be used to explore various medical situations.
For example, the "patient" can be programmed to be allergic to certain
medicine and can <u>suffer from</u> serious reactions if student learners are not
　　　　　　　　　　　14
aware of the situation.　This kind of practice allows students to learn from
mistakes in a safe environment that would not be <u>possible</u> with textbooks
　　　　　　　　　　　　　　　15
alone.　The unique system can both be used in a classroom setting or for
distance learning.
虛擬病患也可以被用來研究各種不同的醫療情況。例如，我們可以用程式設定
這位「病患」，讓它對某種藥物過敏，而且如果初學者沒有注意到這個情況，它
就可能會有嚴重的過敏反應。這種練習，可以讓學生在安全的環境裡，從錯誤
中學習，這是不可能只用教科書就可以做得到。這種獨特的系統可以在教室裡
使用，也可以用於遠距離學習。

explore〔ɪk'splor〕v. 探討；研究　　various〔'vɛrɪəs〕adj. 各種不同的

medical〔'mɛdɪkḷ〕adj. 醫療的　　situation〔ˌsɪtʃu'eʃən〕n. 情況

program〔'progræm〕v. 把程式輸入；把…設計成

allergic〔ə'lɝdʒɪk〕adj. 過敏的　　certain〔'sɝtn̩〕adj. 某；某一

reaction〔rɪ'ækʃən〕n. 反應　　aware〔ə'wɛr〕adj. 知道的；察覺到的

be aware of 知道；察覺到　　textbook〔'tɛkstˌbʊk〕n. 教科書；課本

alone〔ə'lon〕adv. 單單；僅　　unique〔ju'nik〕adj. 獨特的

setting〔'sɛtɪŋ〕n. 環境　　distance〔'dɪstəns〕adj. 長距離的

14.(**D**) (A) adapt to　適應 (= *adjust to*)

   (B) break into　侵入 (= *invade*)

   (C) provide *sb.* with *sth.*　提供某人某物

   (D) *suffer from*　遭受；因…而痛苦

15.(**C**) (A) exciting〔ɪk'saɪtɪŋ〕adj. 令人興奮的

   (B) necessary〔'nɛsəˌsɛrɪ〕adj. 必須的

   (C) *possible*〔'pɑsəbḷ〕adj. 可能的

   (D) important〔ɪm'pɔtn̩t〕adj. 重要的

第 16 至 20 題為題組

 In spite of modernization and the increasing role of women in all walks of life, the practice of the dowry in India is still widespread. The dowry system, money or property brought by a bride to her husband at marriage, was started centuries ago with the intention of providing security for a girl <u>in case of</u> difficulties and unexpected circumstances after marriage. For this
  16
purpose, the parents gave <u>whatever</u> they could to their daughter, which
   17
consequently went to the groom's family.

 儘管現代化以及女性在各行各業的角色日益增多，在印度，新娘結婚送嫁妝的習俗依然十分普遍。嫁妝可以是錢或房地產，結婚的時候由新娘這邊帶過去夫家，好幾百年前就有這樣的習俗，嫁妝的用意，是為了讓女性在婚後遇到困難，或其他不可預知的狀況時的一種保障。因此，父母會盡全力提供女兒嫁妝，這些嫁妝最後是歸夫家所有。

in spite of 儘管　　modernization〔͵mɑdənəˈzeʃən〕*n.* 現代化

all walks of life 各行各業　　practice〔ˈpræktɪs〕*n.* 習俗；慣例

dowry〔ˈdaʊrɪ〕*n.* 嫁妝　　widespread〔ˈwaɪdˈsprɛd〕*adj.* 普遍的

property〔ˈprɑpətɪ〕*n.* 房地產　　bride〔braɪd〕*n.* 新娘

intention〔ɪnˈtɛnʃən〕*n.* 意圖　　security〔sɪˈkjʊrətɪ〕*n.* 安全感；保障

unexpected〔͵ʌnɪkˈspɛktɪd〕*adj.* 出乎意料的

circumstance〔ˈsɝkəm͵stæns〕*n.* 情況

consequently〔ˈkɑnsə͵kwɛntlɪ〕*adv.* 因此　　groom〔grum〕*n.* 新郎

16. (**C**)　(A) due to 由於　　　　　(B) apart from 除了～以外

　　　　　(C) *in case of* 如果發生　　(D) with reference to 關於

17. (**C**)　依句意，父母會把「任何能給的東西」都給女兒，故選 (C) *whatever*

　　　　　「任何東西」(= *anything that*)。

By the beginning of the 21st century, however, the custom had deteriorated to
a point whereby the groom and his family had become very greedy.　When
　　　　　　　　　　　　　　　　　　　　　　　　　　　　　　　　18
demands for dowry are not met, the bride is subject to torture, and often
　　　　　　　　　　　　　　　　　　　　　19
even killed.　The more educated a man is, the higher is the expectation for
　　　　　　　　　　　　　　　　　　　　　　20
dowry at the time of marriage.　Girls who are highly educated are required to
have larger dowries because they usually marry more educated men.

然而，到了二十一世紀初，這樣的習俗已經惡化到讓新郎和他的家人，都變得很
貪婪的程度。當嫁妝不如預期的時候，新娘會受到折磨，甚至常常遭到殺害。男
方的教育程度越高，結婚的時候對嫁妝的期待也跟著越高。教育程度高的女性，
需要準備更多的嫁妝，因為她們結婚的對象，通常都是教育程度較高的男性。

　　　deteriorate〔dɪˈtɪrɪə͵ret〕*v.* 惡化

　　　point〔pɔɪnt〕*n.* 程度

　　　whereby〔hwɛrˈbaɪ〕*adv.* 憑藉 (= *by which*)；根據那個

　　　　(= *according to which*)

　　　demand〔dɪˈmænd〕*n.* 需求　　meet〔mit〕*v.* 符合

　　　torture〔ˈtɔrtʃə〕*n.* 折磨

　　　educated〔ˈɛdʒə͵ketɪd〕*adj.* 受過教育的；有教養的

18. (**A**)　(A) ***greedy*** 〔ˋgridɪ〕 *adj.* 貪婪的
　　　　(B) pleasant 〔ˋplɛznt〕 *adj.* 令人愉快的
　　　　(C) regretful 〔rɪˋgrɛtfəl〕 *adj.* 後悔的
　　　　(D) sympathetic 〔͵sɪmpəˋθɛtɪk〕 *adj.* 同情的

19. (**D**)　(A) be aware of　知道；察覺到
　　　　(B) be required by　被～需要　　require 〔rɪˋkwaɪr〕 *v.* 要求
　　　　(C) be furious with　對～很生氣　　furious 〔ˋfjʊrɪəs〕 *adj.* 狂怒的
　　　　(D) ***be subject to*** 容易受到

20. (**B**)　依句意，教育程度越高，結婚的時候對嫁妝的期待也「越高」，故選
　　　　(B) ***higher***。　　　「the + 比較級…the + 比較級」表「越…就越…」

三、文意選填：

第 21 至 30 題為題組

　　Oniomania is the technical term for the compulsive desire to shop, more commonly referred to as compulsive shopping or shopping addiction. Victims often experience feelings of <u>contentment</u> when they are in the
　　　　　　　　　　　　　　　　　　　　　21
process of purchasing, which seems to give their life meaning while letting them forget about their sorrows.　Once <u>leaving</u> the environment where the
　　　　　　　　　　　　　　　　　　　22
purchasing occurred, the feeling of a personal reward would be gone.　To compensate, the addicted person would go shopping again.　Eventually a feeling of suppression will overcome the person.

　　「強迫性購物症」是個專有名詞，用來表示對購物有難以克制的慾望，更常被稱為購物狂，或是購物癮。患者在購物時，通常會有滿足感，這似乎能讓他們的生活更有意義，同時讓他們忘卻悲傷。一旦離開了購物的環境，自我犒賞的感覺就會消失。為了彌補這種感覺，購物成癮的人會再去購物。最後，這個人會壓抑這種想購物的感覺。

　　　　oniomania 強迫性購物症；購買癖（源自希臘文：onios = for sale；
　　　　　mania = insanity）　　technical 〔ˋtɛknɪkḷ〕 *adj.* 專門的
　　　　term 〔tɝm〕 *n.* 名詞；用語　　***technical term*** 專有名詞；專門用語
　　　　compulsive 〔kəmˋpʌlsɪv〕 *adj.* 強迫性的；難以抑制的
　　　　commonly 〔ˋkɑmənlɪ〕 *adv.* 通常　　***be referred to as*** 被稱為
　　　　compulsive shopping 強迫性購物；購物狂

addiction〔ə'dɪkʃən〕n. 上癮

shopping addiction 沈溺性購物；購物癮

victim〔'vɪktɪm〕n. 受害者；患者　　***in the process of*** 在～的過程中

purchasing〔'pɝtʃəsɪŋ〕n. 購買　　sorrow〔'saro〕n. 悲傷

personal〔'pɝsn̩ḷ〕adj. 個人的；自身的　　reward〔rɪ'word〕n. 獎賞

compensate〔'kɑmpən,set〕v. 彌補　　addicted〔ə'dɪktɪd〕adj. 上癮的

eventually〔ɪ'vɛntʃʊəlɪ〕adv. 最後　　suppression〔sə'prɛʃən〕n. 壓抑

overcome〔,ovɚ'kʌm〕v. 打敗；征服；使無法承受

21.(**J**)　依句意，選 (J) ***contentment***〔kən'tɛntmənt〕n. 滿足。

22.(**F**)　依句意，選 (F) ***leaving***「離開」。

For example, cases have shown that the bought goods will be hidden or
destroyed, because the person concerned feels <u>ashamed</u> of their addiction
　　　　　　　　　　　　　　　　　　　　　　　　　　　　23
and tries to conceal it.　He or she is either regretful or depressed.　In order
to cope with the feelings, the addicted person is prompted to <u>turn to</u> another
　　　　　　　　　　　　　　　　　　　　　　　　　　　　24
purchase.

舉例來說，有實例顯示，買來的商品會被藏起來或摧毀，因爲當事人對於他們
上癮的行爲感到羞恥，並且想隱瞞。患者不是覺得後悔，就是覺得沮喪。爲了
要應付這樣的感覺，購物成癮的人，會受到驅使，想要再次購物。

case〔kes〕n. 病症；例子；情況　　goods〔gʊdz〕n. pl. 商品

destroy〔dɪ'strɔɪ〕v. 毀壞

concerned〔kən'sɝnd〕adj. 有關的；相關的

conceal〔kən'sil〕v. 隱瞞　　***either～or***… 不是～就是…

regretful〔rɪ'grɛtfəl〕adj. 後悔的　　depressed〔dɪ'prɛst〕adj. 沮喪的

cope with 應付；處理　　prompt〔prɑmpt〕v. 促使

purchase〔'pɝtʃəs〕n. 購買

23.(**D**)　依句意，選 (D) ***ashamed***〔ə'ʃemd〕adj. 感到羞恥的。

24.(**G**)　依句意，選 (G) ***turn to***「求助於；仰賴」。

Compulsive shopping often begins at an early age.　Children who
experienced parental neglect often grew up with low <u>self-esteem</u> because

throughout much of their childhood they felt that they were not important as a person. As a result, they used toys to <u>make up for</u> their feelings of
26
loneliness. Because of the ongoing sentiment of deprivation they endured as children, adults that have depended on materials for emotional <u>support</u> when
27
they were much younger are more likely to become addicted to shopping.

強迫性購物通常在幼年時期就開始了。受到父母忽視的小孩，在成長的過程中，通常會自卑，因爲在童年時期大部分的時間裡，他們會覺得自己不是個重要的人。因此，他們用玩具來彌補寂寞的感覺。由於在孩童時期，他們不斷地承受這樣被剝奪的情緒，年幼時依賴物質作爲情感支持的那些成年人，就更容易對購物上癮。

> *early age* 早年；幼年時期　　parental〔pəˋrɛntl〕*adj.* 父母親的
> neglect〔nɪˋglɛkt〕*n.* 忽視
> throughout〔θruˋaut〕*prep.* 遍及；在…期間
> childhood〔ˋtʃaɪld͵hud〕*n.* 童年時期　　*as a result* 因此
> loneliness〔ˋlonlɪnɪs〕*n.* 寂寞　　*because of* 由於
> ongoing〔ˋɑn͵goɪŋ〕*adj.* 不間斷的
> sentiment〔ˋsɛntəmənt〕*n.* 心情；感傷情緒
> deprivation〔͵dɛprəˋveʃən〕*n.* 缺乏；剝奪
> endure〔ɪnˋdjur〕*v.* 忍受　　material〔məˋtɪrɪəl〕*n.* 物質
> emotional〔ɪˋmoʃənl〕*adj.* 感情的；情緒的
> *become addicted to* 對～上癮

25. (**I**) 依句意，選 (I) *self-esteem*〔͵sɛlfəˋstim〕*n.* 自尊心；自尊。
　　　low self-esteem 自尊心不強；自卑

26. (**E**) 依句意，選 (E) *make up for*「彌補；補償」。

27. (**A**) 依句意，選 (A) *support*〔səˋport〕*n.* 支持；鼓勵。
　　　emotional support 情感支持；情緒支持

During adulthood, the purchase, instead of the toy, is substituted for <u>affection</u>. The victims are unable to deal with their everyday problems,
28
especially those that alter their self-esteem. Important issues in their lives

are repressed by <u>buying</u> something. According to studies, as many as 8.9
　　　　　　　　　29
percent of the American population <u>qualify</u> as compulsive buyers. Research
　　　　　　　　　　　　　　　　　　　　30
has also found that men and women suffer from this problem at about the
same rate.

成年以後，購物取代了玩具，成為感情的替代品。患者無法處理每天發生的問題，特別是那些會讓他們的自尊心產生變化的問題。他們生活中重要的問題，被買東西給平息掉。根據研究顯示，美國的人口當中，有多達百分之八點九的人可以稱得上是購物狂。研究也發現，男人和女人受這個問題所苦的比例大約相同。

> adulthood〔əˋdʌlthʊd〕n. 成年時期　　**instead of** 而不是
> substitute〔ˋsʌbstəˏtjut〕v. 用…替代　　**deal with** 應付；處理
> alter〔ˋɔltɚ〕v. 改變（= *change*）
> issue〔ˋɪʃʊ〕n. 議題；問題
> repress〔rɪˋprɛs〕v. 壓抑；平息　　population〔ˏpɑpjəˋleʃən〕n. 人口
> **suffer from** 受～之苦　　rate〔ret〕n. 比例

28.（**C**）依句意，選 (C) **affection**〔əˋfɛkʃən〕n. 愛；感情。

29.（**H**）依句意，選 (H) **buying**。

30.（**B**）依句意，選 (B) **qualify**〔ˋkwɑləˏfaɪ〕v. 適合當～；符合～的資格。

四、篇章結構：

<u>第 31 至 35 題為題組</u>

　　There was a time when Whitney didn't have a lot of friends. She was
a bit shy and reserved. **31 (E) She never really wanted to be popular, but
she did want to have someone to share secrets and laughs with.** All
through high school, though, she wasn't able to make good friends or
find companionship.

　　曾經一度，惠特妮沒有很多朋友。她有一點害羞而且拘謹。她其實從沒有想要受歡迎，但她的確想要有人可以分享秘密和歡笑。不過，在整個高中時期，她都沒能交到好朋友，或找到友誼。

a bit 有一點（＝ _a little_） shy〔ʃaɪ〕_adj._ 害羞的

reserved〔rɪ'zɝvd〕_adj._ 拘謹的；保守的

through〔θru〕_prep._ 整個～期間

though〔ðo〕_adv._ 不過；但是【置於句中或句尾】

companionship〔kəm'pænjən,ʃɪp〕_n._ 友誼

When it was time to go to college, Whitney was quite nervous. She was going to be rooming with someone she didn't know and living in a town 300 miles away from home. There wouldn't be a single person she knew in town. <u>³²(C) She had no idea how she was going to make friends in this new environment.</u>

　　當上大學的時候來臨時，惠特妮相當緊張。她即將要和不認識的人同住一房，而且要住在一個離家三百哩的城鎮。在那個鎮上她一個人都不認識。她不知道在這個新環境裡，她要如何交到朋友。

it is time to + _V._ 是該～的時候了 quite〔kwaɪt〕_adv._ 相當地

nervous〔'nɝvəs〕_adj._ 緊張的 room〔rum〕_v._ 同住

single〔'sɪŋgl〕_adj._ 單一的【與否定詞連用】；連一個…（也沒有）的

have no idea 不知道（＝ _do not know_） **_make friends_** 交朋友

The first week of classes, something happened that changed Whitney's life forever. <u>³³(D) In her English Composition class, she was asked to share a little about herself.</u> She told everyone where she came from and all of the other ordinary details that students share in such situations. The final question for each student to answer was, "what is your goal for this class?" Most of the students said that they would like to get a good grade, pass the class or something similar. <u>³⁴(A) For some reason, Whitney said something entirely different.</u> She said that her goal was to make just one good friend.

　　開課第一週，發生一件永遠改變了惠特妮一生的事情。在她的英文作文課上，她被要求分享一些有關她自己的事情。她告訴大家她來自哪裡，還有在這種情況下，學生們會互相分享的其他一般的細節。最後一個每個學生都要回答的問題是：「你對於這堂課的目標為何？」大部分的學生說，他們想要得高分、

通過這門課，或是類似的事情。由於某種原因，惠特妮說了完全不同的事情。
她說，她的目標是只要結交一位好朋友。

forever〔fə'ɛvə〕adv. 永遠　　composition〔,kɑmpə'zɪʃən〕n. 作文
ordinary〔'ɔrdn̩,ɛrɪ〕adj. 一般的；普通的　　detail〔'ditel〕n. 細節
situation〔,sɪtʃu'eʃən〕n. 情況　　similar〔'sɪmələ〕adj. 類似的
for some reason 由於某種原因　　entirely〔ɪn'taɪrlɪ〕adv. 完全地

While most of the students sat in silence, one student came to Whitney and held out her hand and introduced herself. She asked if they could be friends. The whole room was silent. All eyes focused on Whitney and the hand extended just in front of her. [35] **(B)** Whitney smiled and stretched her hand out and a friendship was formed.

當大部分學生都沈默地坐著時，有個學生走向惠特妮，伸出她的手，並做自我介紹。她問她們是否能成為朋友。全班都很沈默。所有目光都集中在惠特妮和伸出去在她前方的那隻手。惠特妮微笑，也伸出她的手，一段友誼就形成了。

in silence 沈默地　　**hold out** 伸出（= extend = stretch out）
whole〔hol〕adj. 整個的　　silent〔'saɪlənt〕adj. 沈默的
focus〔'fokəs〕v. 集中 < on >

Whitney learned the power of asking for what she wanted and taking action on that day.

惠特妮在那一天學會了，要求自己想要的，並且採取行動，是極具力量的。

power〔'pauə〕n. 力量　　**ask for** 要求
take action 採取行動

五、閱讀測驗：

第 36 至 39 題為題組

April 22, 2010 will be the 18th celebration of the annual *Take Our Daughters to Work Day* (*TOD*), a project the National Ms. Foundation for Women of America (NFW) developed to expose girls to expanding opportunities for women in the workplace.

　　2010 年 4 月 22 日將舉行一年一度的「帶女兒上班日」(TOD) 第 18 屆的慶祝活動，這是由「美國婦女基金會」研發的計劃，目的是讓小女孩們了解，女性在職場上的機會越來越多了。

celebration (ˌsɛləˈbreʃən) *n.* 慶祝活動
annual (ˈænjuəl) *adj.* 一年一度的
foundation (faʊnˈdeʃən) *n.* 基金會
expose (ɪkˈspoz) *v.* 暴露；使接觸
expand (ɪkˈspænd) *v.* 擴大
opportunity (ˌɑpɚˈtjunəntɪ) *n.* 機會
workplace (ˈwɝkˌples) *n.* 工作場所

The program offers millions of girls a first-hand view of the many career opportunities available in their futures. Now that women make up 46 percent of the U.S. workforce, girls can find role models in every occupational field—from politics to molecular biology to professional athletics, to name just a few. *TOD* encourages girls to focus on their abilities and opportunities, not just their appearance.

　　這項活動提供了數以百萬計的女孩，直接看到未來會有很多工作機會。既然女性占了美國勞動力的 46%，女孩們可以在每個工作領域中找到典範——從政壇到分子生物界，到職業運動等。「帶女兒上班日」(TOD) 鼓勵女孩專注於自己的能力與機會，而非只是外貌。

program (ˈprogræm) *n.* 計劃；活動
first-hand (ˈfɝstˌhænd) *adj.* 直接的　　view (vju) *n.* 觀看
first-hand view 直接看到；親眼看到　　career (kəˈrɪr) *n.* 職業
available (əˈveləb!) *adj.* 可獲得的　　*role model* 典範
occupational (ˌɑkjəˈpeʃən!) *adj.* 職業的　　field (fild) *n.* 領域
molecular (məˈlɛkjələ) *adj.* 分子的
biology (baɪˈɑlədʒɪ) *n.* 生物學
professional (prəˈfɛʃən!) *adj.* 專業的；職業的
athletics (æθˈlɛtɪks) *n.* 體育運動
to name just a few 等等 (= *and so on*)
encourage (ɪnˈkɝɪdʒ) *v.* 鼓舞　　*focus on* 專注於
appearance (əˈpɪrəns) *n.* 外表

The NFW developed the project more than a decade ago to address the self-esteem problems that many girls experience when they enter adolescence. At school, boys often receive more encouragement in the classroom, especially in math, science and computer science, the academic fields that tend to lead to the highest salaries. Women receive on average only 73 cents for every dollar that men are paid, and remain vastly underrepresented in top executive positions and technology fields. *TOD* aims to give girls the confidence and inspiration they need to develop successful careers, particularly in non-traditional fields.

「美國婦女基金會」（NFW）十幾年前便研發了這項計畫，以處理許多女孩在進入青春期時，都會面臨的自尊心問題。在學校，男孩們通常在課堂上獲得較多鼓勵，尤其是數學、科學，與電腦科學，而這些學術領域往往能有最高的薪酬。女性平均而言只領取男性73%的薪資，並且在高階主管與科技領域任職的比例，仍然遠遠落後男性。「帶女兒上班日」的目標，是要給女孩發展成功的專業所需要的信心與鼓勵，特別是在非傳統的領域。

decade〔ˈdɛked〕 *n.* 十年　　address〔əˈdrɛs〕 *v.* 處理（問題）
self-esteem〔ˌsɛlfəˈstim〕 *n.* 自尊（心）
adolescence〔ˌædḷˈɛsns〕 *n.* 青春期
academic〔ˌækəˈdɛmɪk〕 *adj.* 學術的　　*tend to* 易於；傾向於
lead to 導致　　salary〔ˈsælərɪ〕 *n.* 薪水　　*on average* 平均而言
remain〔rɪˈmen〕 *v.* 保持　　vastly〔ˈvæstlɪ〕 *adv.* 巨大地
underrepresent〔ˌʌndɚˌrɛprɪˈzɛntɪd〕 *adj.* 代表人數不足的；未充分派
　遣代表的　　top〔tɑp〕 *adj.* 最高的
executive〔ɪgˈzɛkjʊtɪv〕 *adj.* 執行的　　*n.* 高階主管
position〔pəˈzɪʃən〕 *n.* 職位　　*aim to V.* 打算…；企圖…
confidence〔ˈkɑnfədəns〕 *n.* 自信
inspiration〔ˌɪnspəˈreʃən〕 *n.* 激勵
particularly〔pɚˈtɪkjələlɪ〕 *adv.* 尤其

Perhaps because the program had become so widespread and successful, *TOD* had been criticized for excluding boys, and it was expanded in 2003 to include boys. The program's official website states that the program was changed in order to provide both boys and girls with opportunities to explore careers at an age when they are more flexible in terms of gender stereotyped roles. "We should also show boys that becoming a child care provider is as acceptable a choice as becoming a police officer or CEO," added Sara K. Gould, executive director of the NFW.

　　或許是因為這項活動變得非常普遍而且成功，所以「帶女兒上班日」受到批評，因為將男孩排除在外，因此於 2003 年擴大辦理，將男孩納入其中。這項活動的官方網站說，這項活動的變革，是為了提供男孩與女孩探索職業的機會，因為他們現在這個年紀，對性別較不會有角色的刻板印象。「我們應該也讓男孩了解，成為一位兒童照顧者，與成為警官或總裁，都是可以接受的選擇。」「美國婦女基金會」的執行長莎拉‧古德又說。

criticize〔'krɪtɪ,saɪz〕*v.* 批評　　　exclude〔ɪk'sklud〕*v.* 排除
official〔ə'fɪʃəl〕*adj.* 官方的　　　website〔'wɛb,saɪt〕*n.* 網站
state〔stet〕*v.* 說明　　explore〔ɪk'splor〕*v.* 探索
flexible〔'flɛksəbḷ〕*adj.* 有彈性的　　***in terms of*** 就…而言
gender〔'dʒɛndɚ〕*n.* 性別
stereotyped〔'stɛrɪə,taɪpt〕*adj.* 刻版印象的
child care provider 兒童照顧者
acceptable〔ək'sɛptəbḷ〕*adj.* 可接受的
add〔æd〕*v.* 補充說明；又說
director〔də'rɛktɚ〕*n.* 主任；董事
executive director 執行董事

36.（**C**）舉行「帶女兒上班日」的目的是 _____。
　　（A）為了鼓勵女孩追求高薪的工作
　　（B）為了讓女孩與母親有更多時間相處
　　（C）為了讓女孩知道可能的工作與職業
　　（D）為了給女孩參觀母親的辦公室的機會

37.（**A**）「帶女兒上班日」被批評，是因為有些人 _____。
　　（A）認為它對男孩不公平
　　（B）不喜歡帶小孩去上班
　　（C）沒有女兒能讓他們帶去上班
　　（D）寧願讓他們的女兒待在家裡

38.（**A**）根據內文，下列何者為眞？
　　(A) 目前男孩也被納入「帶女兒上班日」。
　　(B) 男女在職場上一直被平等對待。
　　(C) 料理家務與撫養小孩是女孩專屬的工作。
　　(D) 女孩在成長過程中，一直較男孩受到更多關注。

　　equally〔ˋikwəlɪ〕*adv.* 相等地
　　homemaking〔ˋhom͵mekɪŋ〕*n.* 持家；料理家務
　　rear〔rɪr〕*v.* 撫養

39.（**B**）爲何女性在某些領域，例如科技業，任職的人數仍落後男性？
　　(A) 她們對這些領域不感興趣。
　　(B) 她們沒有被鼓勵在這些領域工作。
　　(C) 她們在這些領域的薪資和男性不同。
　　(D) 她們被禁止接受這些領域的教育。

第 40 至 43 題爲題組

　　In all cultures and throughout history hair has had a special significance. In ancient Egypt, as long ago as 1500 BC, the outward appearance expressed the person's status, role in society and political position. Wigs played an important role in this: they were crafted with great artistry and often sprinkled with powdered gold.

　　在所有文化及歷史中，頭髮都有著特殊的意義。在古埃及，早在西元前一千五百年，外表就能表達一個人的地位、社會角色，和政治地位。假髮在其中扮演重要的角色：它們是用精湛的手藝來製造，而且上面常會灑上金粉。

　　throughout history 自古以來　　significance〔sɪgˋnɪfəkəns〕*n.* 意義
　　ancient〔ˋenʃənt〕*adj.* 古代的　　Egypt〔ˋidʒəpt〕*n.* 埃及
　　BC 西元前（ = B.C. = *before Christ*)
　　outward〔ˋaʊtwɚd〕*adj.* 外在的　　express〔ɪkˋsprɛs〕*v.* 表達
　　status〔ˋstetəs〕*n.* 地位　　wig〔wɪg〕*n.* 假髮
　　play a(n) ~ role 扮演～的角色　　craft〔kræft〕*v.* 精美地製作
　　artistry〔ˋɑrtɪstrɪ〕*n.* 手藝
　　sprinkle〔ˋsprɪŋkl̩〕*v.* 灑（粉末）於…之上
　　powdered〔ˋpaʊdɚd〕*adj.* 粉狀的

In the 8th century BC, the pre-Roman Celts in Northern Europe wore
their hair long.　In a man it was the expression of his strength, in a woman
of her fertility.　The idea of long hair as a symbol of male strength is even
mentioned in the Bible, in the story of Samson and Delilah.　Samson was
a leader of the Israelites.　His long hair, which he never cut, gave him
superhuman powers.　The only person who knew his secret was Delilah.
However, she spied for the enemy and betrayed him.　One night she cut off
his hair and thus robbed him of his strength.

西元前八世紀的時候，在北歐的前羅馬帝國時期的塞爾特族，都留著長髮。
這在男人身上是力量的表現，在女人身上則代表她的生育能力。長髮是男人力
量象徵的這種想法，連聖經裡面參孫跟黛利拉的故事中也提到過。參孫是以色
列人的領導者，他從未修剪的長髮，賦予他超越凡人的力量。唯一知道這個祕
密的人就是黛利拉。然而，黛利拉是敵人的間諜，她背叛了參孫。有天晚上，
黛利拉剪去參孫的長髮，也因此奪走他的力量。

pre-Roman〔 prɪˋromən〕*adj.* 羅馬時代前的
Celt〔 sɛlt〕*n.* 塞爾特人　　***the Celts*** 塞爾特族【現散居於英國的民族】
wear〔 wɛr〕*v.* 留（長髮）　　expression〔 ɪkˋsprɛʃən〕*n.* 表現
fertility〔 fɝˋtɪlətɪ〕*n.* 生育力　　symbol〔ˋsɪmbl̩〕*n.* 象徵
mention〔ˋmɛnʃən〕*v.* 提到　　Bible〔ˋbaɪbl̩〕*n.* 聖經
Samson〔ˋsæmsn̩〕*n.* 參孫【聖經中一位猶太人領導者，是力大無比的勇士】
Delilah〔 dɪˋlaɪlə〕*n.* 黛利拉【聖經中誘惑參孫，使他失去力量的女子】
Israelite〔ˋɪzrɪəl͵aɪt〕*n.* 以色列人；猶太人
superhuman〔͵supɚˋhjumən〕*adj.* 非一般人的；超人的
spy for 做⋯的間諜　　betray〔 bɪˋtre〕*v.* 背叛
cut off 剪去　　***rob*** *sb.* ***of*** *sth.* 奪走某人的某物

In the classical Greek period, curly hair was not only the fashion, but it
also represented an attitude towards life.　Curls or locks were the metaphor
for change, freedom and the joy of living.　The ancient Greek word for
curls and locks is related to intriguing and tempting someone.

在古典希臘時期，鬈髮不僅是流行時尚，也代表一種生活態度。鬈髮跟髮
辮隱含改變、自由、歡喜生活的意義。古希臘文中，代表鬈髮跟髮辮的字辭，
跟激發他人興趣，或是打動他人有關聯。

classicl〔'klæsɪkḷ〕adj. 古典的　　Greek〔grik〕adj. 希臘的　　n. 希臘人
curly〔'kɜlɪ〕adj. 鬈髮的　　fashion〔'fæʃən〕n. 流行；時尚
represent〔͵rɛprɪ'zɛnt〕v. 代表；象徵
attitude〔'ætə͵tjud〕n. 態度；看法　　curls〔kɜlz〕n. pl. 鬈髮
lock〔lɑk〕n. 一絡頭髮；髮辮　　metaphor〔'mɛtəfɚ〕n. 隱喻
be related to　和…有關
intrigue〔ɪn'trig〕v. 引起（他人）興趣；激發（人的）好奇心
tempt〔tɛmpt〕v. 吸引

Hair is also used as a symbol of opposition. The punk protest movement today uses hair as a symbol of disapproval of the "middle-class, conventional lifestyle" by wearing provocative haircuts and shockingly colored hair. A different form of objection could be seen in the women's hairstyles in the 1960s. Women's liberation was expressed in a short-cut, straight and simple hairstyle which underlined equality with men without neglecting female attributes. To this day hair has kept its importance as a symbol of power, youth, vitality and health.

頭髮也被用來當作反抗的象徵。現在龐克族的反抗運動，留著引發輿論爭議的髮型，以及染上駭人顏色的頭髮，作為反對「中產階級、傳統生活方式」的象徵。在 1960 年代時，還能在女人的髮型上，看到不同的反抗形式。婦女解放運動表現在剪既短、又直，而且簡單的髮型上，強調男女不等，但同時又不忽視女性特質。直到今日，短髮在權力、青春、生命力和健康方面，仍然是重要的象徵。

opposition〔͵ɑpə'zɪʃən〕n. 抵抗　　punk〔pʌŋk〕adj. 龐克風格的
the punk 龐克族【1970 年代流行於英國，以音樂以及服裝髮型表示對當時
　現況之反感的年輕族群】
protest〔'protɛst〕n. 抗議　　disapproval〔͵dɪsə'pruvḷ〕n. 不贊成
middle-class〔'mɪdḷ'klæs〕adj. 中產階級的
conventional〔kən'vɛnʃənḷ〕adj. 傳統的
lifestyle〔'laɪf͵staɪl〕n. 生活方式
provocative〔prə'vɑkətɪv〕adj. 挑釁的；引發議論的
haircut〔'hɛr͵kʌt〕n. 髮型　　shockingly〔'ʃɑkɪŋlɪ〕adv. 嚇人地
colored〔'kʌlɚd〕adj. 有顏色的　　objection〔əb'dʒɛkʃən〕n. 異議
liberation〔͵lɪbə'reʃən〕n. 解放運動　　short-cut〔'ʃɔt'kʌt〕adj. 剪短的
underline〔ʌndɚ'laɪn〕v. 強調　　equality〔ɪ'kwɑlətɪ〕n. 平等
neglect〔nɪ'glɛkt〕v. 忽視　　attribute〔'ætrə͵bjut〕n. 特質
to this day 直到今天為止　　vitality〔vaɪ'tælətɪ〕n. 生命力

40. (**B**) 最能說明本文主題的是 ＿＿＿＿＿＿。

　　(A) 髮型的科學研究　　　　　(B) 髮型的象徵意義

　　(C) 設計不同髮型的藝術　　　(D) 當代髮型的演變

describe〔dɪˈskraɪb〕 *v.* 描述；用言語說明

symbolic〔sɪmˈbɑlɪk〕 *adj.* 象徵性的

contemporary〔kənˈtɛmpəˌrɛrɪ〕 *adj.* 當代的

41. (**A**) 爲什麼古希臘人喜歡留鬈髮跟髮辮？

　　(A) 爲了吸引他人。　　　　　(B) 爲了炫燿手藝。

　　(C) 爲了隱藏眞實的身分。　　(D) 爲了展現權力跟地位。

show off 炫燿　　　identity〔aɪˈdɛntətɪ〕 *n.* 身份

42. (**C**) 1960 年代的女性如何用髮型來表示反對？

　　(A) 她們留長髮。　　　　　　(B) 她們染頭髮。

　　(C) 她們把頭髮剪短。　　　　(D) 她們把頭髮剃掉。

shave〔ʃev〕 *v.* 剃掉…的毛髮

43. (**D**) 從本文可推論出什麼？

　　(A) 自古以來長鬈髮一直都很流行。

　　(B) 古埃及人不太在意自己的髮型。

　　(C) 龐克運動是史上最成功的運動之一。

　　(D) 參孫如果不把祕密告訴別人，可能就永遠不會被打敗。

Egyptian〔ɪˈdʒɪpʃən〕 *n.* 埃及人

pay attention to 注意　　　defeat〔dɪˈfit〕 *v.* 打敗

keep a secret (***to*** *oneself*) 保密

第 44 至 47 題爲題組

　　Camille Mahlknecht, 9, has some big fun planned for this weekend. She and other residents of Agoura Hills, California, plan to pick up trash during their city's annual cleanup. At the same time, Wissam Raed, 12, will be busy volunteering too. Thousands of miles away in Lebanon, Wissam plans to put on a play at an orphanage and bring potted plants to elderly people at a senior citizen center.

九歲的卡米爾‧馬格奈特，這個週末打算要做一件非常有趣的事。她和加州亞歌拉山市的其他居民，計劃在全市一年一度的大掃除中撿垃圾。同時，十二歲的威薩‧瑞德也忙著當義工。在數千哩以外的黎巴嫩，威薩計劃要在一所孤兒院中，上演一齣戲劇，並且要送盆栽植物，給一所老人院裡的老人。

　　resident〔'rɛzədənt〕*n.* 居民　　***pick up*** 撿起
　　trash〔træʃ〕*n.* 垃圾　　cleanup〔'klin,ʌp〕*n.* 大掃除
　　volunteer〔,vɑlən'tɪr〕*v.* 當義工　*n.* 義工　*adj.* 自願的
　　Lebanon〔'lɛbənən〕*n.* 黎巴嫩【位於亞洲西南部、地中海東岸的
　　　共和國，首都貝魯特（Beirut）】　　***put on*** 上演（戲劇）
　　orphanage〔'ɔrfənɪdʒ〕*n.* 孤兒院
　　potted〔'pɑtɪd〕*adj.* 盆栽的
　　elderly〔'ɛldəlɪ〕*adj.* 年老的　　***senior citizen*** 老人

Some other children like Nathan White, 10, have personal reasons for volunteering. Nathan's grandmother died of a heart attack. To help raise money for medical research, Nathan participated in Jump Rope for Heart. He and five other boys took turns jumping rope for two and half hours and collected more than US$1,200 in donations for the American Heart Association.

　　其他一些孩童，像十歲的納森‧懷特，當義工是為了個人因素。納森的祖母死於心臟病發作。為了幫助籌募醫學研究的經費，納森參加了「跳繩強心」的活動。他和其他五個男孩輪流跳繩，長達兩個半小時，為「美國心臟協會」籌募到超過 1,200 元美金的捐款。

　　die of 死於（某種疾病）　　***heart attack*** 心臟病發作
　　raise〔rez〕*v.* 籌募　　medical〔'mɛdɪkl̩〕*adj.* 醫學的
　　research〔'risɜtʃ,rɪ'sɜtʃ〕*n.* 研究
　　participate〔pə'tɪsə,pet,pɑr-〕*v.* 參加 < *in* >
　　jump rope 跳繩
　　Jump Roap for Heart 跳繩強心【透過教授跳繩花式，鼓勵青少年勤做
　　　運動，並傳遞心臟健康的訊息。】
　　take turns + V-ing 輪流～　　donation〔do'neʃən〕*n.* 捐贈
　　association〔ə,soʃɪ'eʃən〕*n.* 協會；學會
　　American Heart Association 美國心臟協會

Millions of children around the globe lend a hand to their communities every year. Schools and parents also contribute to the rise in youth service. For example, many schools offer community service activities for students to join. Teachers either combine volunteer work with classroom lessons or make service work a requirement. Parents, on the other hand, encourage their kids to volunteer and do it with them.

全球有數百萬名兒童，每年對他們的社區伸出援手。學校和父母也是年輕人服務增加的助因之一。例如，許多學校提供社區服務的活動，讓學生來參加。老師們不是將志工活動和教室課程結合起來，就是將服務工作變成必須做的事。另一方面，父母會鼓勵他們的小孩當義工，也和他們一起做。

globe〔glob〕*n.* 地球　　**lend a hand to** 對～伸出援手
community〔kə'mjunətɪ〕*n.* 社區；社會
contribute〔kən'trɪbjut〕*v.* 貢獻；促成 < *to* >
rise〔raɪz〕*n.* 增加 (= *increase*)　　youth〔juθ〕*n.* 年輕人
combine〔kəm'baɪn〕*v.* 結合
requirement〔rɪ'kwaɪrmənt〕*n.* 需要的事物；要求的事物
on the other hand 另一方面　　encourage〔ɪn'kɝɪdʒ〕*v.* 鼓勵

Community service is particularly important in this recession time. As the need for monetary support and other aid has increased, many charitable organizations have experienced a significant drop in donations. Camille and other children who volunteer thousands of hours annually can fill in some of the gaps.

社區服務在這個不景氣的時候尤其重要。隨著對金錢資助和其他援助的需求增加，許多慈善團體都歷經捐贈物資明顯減少的困境。卡米爾以及其他兒童，每年提供數千小時的義工服務，正可以彌補部分的差距。

particularly〔pə'tɪkjələlɪ〕*adv.* 尤其；特別地
recession〔rɪ'sɛʃən〕*n.* 不景氣　　monetary〔'mʌnə,tɛrɪ〕*adj.* 金錢的
aid〔ed〕*n.* 幫助；援助　　charitable〔'tʃærətəbḷ〕*adj.* 慈善的
organization〔,ɔrgənə'zeʃən〕*n.* 組織
significant〔sɪg'nɪfəkənt〕*adj.* 顯著的；相當大的
drop〔drɑp〕*n.* 下降
annually〔'ænjʊəlɪ〕*adv.* 每年地 (= *every year*)
fill in 填滿；填補　　gap〔gæp〕*n.* 空隙；差距

According to research, kids who start volunteering are twice as likely to continue doing good deeds when they are adults. So, grab a paintbrush, a trash bag, or whatever you need to help your community. You'll love how you feel after helping others. Even dirty work can be lots of fun, if it's for a good cause.

根據研究，小時候就開始當義工的人，長大繼續做好事的可能性，是別人的兩倍。所以，拿起油漆刷、垃圾袋，或任何你需要的東西，去幫助你的社區吧。你會愛上幫助別人之後的感覺。如果是爲了好的目的的話，即使是骯髒的工作，也可能非常有趣。

deed〔did〕*n.* 行爲　　***do good deeds*** 做好事
grab〔græb〕*v.* 抓住　　paintbrush〔'pent,brʌʃ〕*n.* 油漆刷子
dirty work 骯髒的工作；打雜的工作　　cause〔kɔz〕*n.* 原因；目的

44. (**C**) 作者寫這段文章目的爲何？
　　(A) 爲了向學校推薦青年服務計劃。
　　(B) 爲了要求慈善團體爲社區服務。
　　(C) 爲了激勵兒童們參加義工活動。
　　(D) 爲了提出社區服務的替代方案。

recommend〔,rɛkə'mɛnd〕*v.* 推薦；建議
charity〔'tʃærətɪ〕*n.* 慈善（團體）　　urge〔ɝdʒ〕*v.* 力勸；激勵
take part in 參加　　propose〔prə'poz〕*v.* 提議；提出
alternative〔ɔl'tɝnətɪv〕*n.* 另一個選擇；替代方案

45. (**B**) 第三段的主旨爲何？
　　(A) 社區服務越來越受到兒童的歡迎。
　　(B) 家庭和學校有助於使社區服務更加流行。
　　(C) 兒童現在依賴老師比依賴父母多。
　　(D) 納森・懷特籌募醫學研究的經費，是有特別的理由。

popularity〔,pɑpjə'lærətɪ〕*n.* 受歡迎　　***depend on*** 依賴

46. (**C**) 爲什麼社區服務在不景氣的時候很重要？
　　(A) 它能爲學校活動募款。　　　(B) 它教導孩童照顧病人。
　　(C) 它給慈善團體一些必要的幫助。
　　(D) 它鼓勵父母和老師合作。

take care of 照顧　　***the sick*** 病人　　***work together*** 合作

47.(**D**) 從本文可以推論出什麼？

    (A) 社區服務可以幫助預防青少年犯罪。

    (B) 兒童可能會離開學校去擔任義工。

    (C) 為學校主辦運動競賽是一種社區服務。

    (D) 從事義工工作的兒童，長大之後比較有可能成為有愛心的成年人。

infer〔ɪn'fɝ〕*v.* 推論   juvenile〔'dʒuvən̩ , -,naɪl〕*adj.* 青少年的

delinquency〔dɪ'lɪŋkwənsɪ〕*n.* 罪行   ***work as*** 擔任

organize〔'ɔrgən,aɪz〕*v.* 主辦

event〔ɪ'vɛnt〕*n.*（運動）項目；大型活動

sports events 運動競賽   caring〔'kɛrɪŋ〕*adj.* 有愛心的

第 48 至 51 題為題組

    Downloading music over the Internet is pretty common among high school and college students. However, when students download and share copyrighted music without permission, they are violating the law.

    從網路上下載音樂，是高中生與大學生之間常見的行為。然而，當學生們沒有獲得許可，便下載並且分享有版權保護的音樂時，他們就是在犯法。

    download〔'daʊn,lod〕*v. n.* 下載

    copyrighted〔'kɑpɪ,raɪtɪd〕*adj.* 受版權保護的

    permisson〔pə'mɪʃən〕*n.* 允許；許可   violate〔'vaɪə,let〕*v.* 違犯

    A survey of young people's music ownership has found that teenagers and college students have an average of more than 800 illegally copied songs each on their digital music players. Half of those surveyed share all the music on their hard drive, enabling others to copy hundreds of songs at any one time. Some students were found to have randomly linked their personal blogs to music sites, so as to allow free trial listening of copyrighted songs for blog visitors, or adopted some of the songs as the background music for their blogs. Such practices may be easy and free, but there are consequences.

    有項關於年輕人所擁有的音樂的調查顯示，在青少年及大學生的數位音樂播放器裡，平均有超過八百首非法複製的歌曲。半數的受訪者會分享所有在他們硬碟裡的音樂，使其他人可以隨時複製好幾百首歌曲。研究更發現，有些學

生會任意將個人部落格連結到音樂網站，以讓部落格的訪客，可以免費試聽有版權的歌曲，或是將一些歌曲當作他們部落格的背景樂。這種做法或許很容易而且免費，但是這麼做是有後果的。

survey〔səˈve〕n. v. 調查　　ownership〔ˈonɚˌʃɪp〕n. 所有權

average〔ˈævərɪdʒ〕n. 平均　　illegally〔ɪˈligl̩〕adv. 非法地

digital〔ˈdɪdʒɪtl̩〕adj. 數位的　　player〔ˈpleɚ〕n. 播放器

hard drive 電腦硬碟　　enable〔ɪnˈebl̩〕v. 使能夠

randomly〔ˈrændəmlɪ〕adv. 任意地　　**at any one time** 隨時

link〔lɪŋk〕v. 連結　　blog〔blɑg〕n. 部落格　　site〔saɪt〕n. 網站

so as to V. 以便於　　allow〔əˈlaʊ〕n. 給予　　trial〔ˈtraɪəl〕n. 試用

adopt〔əˈdɑpt〕v. 採用　　practice〔ˈpræktɪs〕n. 做法；習俗；慣例

consequence〔ˈkɑnsəˌkwɛns〕n. 後果

Sandra Dowd, a student of Central Michigan University, was fined US$7,500 for downloading 501 files from LimeWire, a peer-to-peer file sharing program. Sandra claimed that she was unaware that her downloads were illegal until she was contacted by authorities. Similarly, Mike Lewinski paid US$4,000 to settle a lawsuit against him for copyright violation. Mike expressed shock and couldn't believe that this was happening to him. "I just wanted to save some money and I always thought **the threat was just a scare tactic**." "You know, everyone does it," added Mike.

珊桌拉·多德，一名中央密西根大學的學生，因為從 LimeWire，一個 P2P 的檔案分享程式，下載了 501 個檔案，而被罰了 7,500 元美金。珊桌拉聲稱，直到她被當局聯繫時，她才知道下載那些檔案是非法的。同樣地，麥克·路文斯基因為侵犯版權而被告，所以必須以 4,000 元美金達成和解。麥克表示他很震驚，並且無法相信這種事情會發生在他身上。「我只是想省點錢，而且我一直以為那些威脅只是個恐嚇戰術。」「你也知道啊，大家都是這麼做的，」麥克又說。

central〔ˈsɛntrəl〕adj. 中央的　　fine〔faɪn〕v. 罰款

peer〔pɪr〕n. 同輩　　**peer-to-peer (p2p)** 點對點連結

program〔proˈgræm〕v. 程式　　unaware〔ˌʌnəˈwɛr〕adj. 不知道的

authorities〔əˈθɔrətɪz〕n. pl. 當局　　similarly〔ˈsɪmələ⋅lɪ〕adv. 同樣地

settle〔ˈsɛtl̩〕v. 解決；和解　　lawsuit〔ˈlɔˌsut〕n. 訴訟

scare tactic 恐嚇戰術

The RIAA (Recording Industry Association of America), the organization that files lawsuits against illegal downloaders, states that suing students was by no means their first choice. Unfortunately, without the threat of consequences, students are just not changing their behavior. Education alone is not enough to stop the extraordinary growth of the illegal downloading practice.

對非法下載者提出告訴的組織，是「美國唱片業協會」(RIAA)。他們表示，控告這些學生絕不是他們最優先的選擇。很遺憾的是，如果沒有後果的威嚇，學生就是不會改變他們的行為。光透過教育，是不足以阻止非法下載音樂這個惡習的驚人成長。

industry〔'ɪndəstrɪ〕*n.* 行業　　file〔faɪl〕*v.* 提出（訴訟）
sue〔su〕*v.* 控告　***by no means*** 絕不
alone〔ə'lon〕*adv.* 單單；僅僅
extraordinary〔ɪk'strɔrdṇ‚ɛrɪ〕*adj.* 異常的；驚人的

48. (**A**) 為什麼學生下載有版權的音樂很普遍？
　　(A) 他們認為自己不會被抓到。
　　(B) 他們想要自己的朋友知道他們很聰明。
　　(C) 他們認為這是個賺點外快的好方法。
　　(D) 他們反對網路音樂的版權保護。

49. (**D**) 麥克說「那些威脅只是個恐嚇戰術」的意思是什麼？
　　(A) 人不應該害怕威脅。　　　　(B) 威脅會導致訴訟。
　　(C) 以威脅來嚇人是不公平的。　(D) 威脅之後不會有嚴重的後果。
result from 起因於　　unfair〔ʌn'fɛr〕*adj.* 不公平的

50. (**D**)「美國唱片業協會」對於學生非法下載行為的態度如何？
　　(A) 他們相信教育對版權的保護，有非常大的幫助。
　　(B) 他們能從非法下載者違反版權所付的罰金獲利。
　　(C) 他們喜歡控告從網路非法下載音樂的學生。
　　(D) 他們認為非法下載的行為，需要強硬的措施來改正。
profit〔'prɑfɪt〕*v.* 獲利　　tough〔tʌf〕*adj.* 強硬的；嚴屬的
measure〔'mɛʒ˞〕*n.* 措施　　correct〔kə'rɛkt〕*v.* 改正

51. (**A**) 最適合本文的標題是什麼？

　　(A) 違反版權者，要小心！

　　(B) 如何在網路上拿到免費的音樂！

　　(C) 學生下載習慣的調查

　　(D) 消滅非法音樂下載？不可能的！

　　beware〔bɪ'wɛr〕*v.* 當心；小心　　　eliminate〔ɪ'lɪmə,net〕*v.* 消除

第貳部分：非選擇題

一、英文翻譯：

1. 玉山是東亞第一高峰，以生態多樣聞名。

　Yu-shan / Mt. Jade } is the highest { mountain / peak } in East Asia, and is

　{ well-known / noted / renowned / celebrated / famed / famous / known } for its { diverse ecology. / ecological diversity. }

2. 大家在網路上投票給它，要讓它成為世界七大奇觀之一。

　People are voting for it { on the Internet / online } to make it one of the Seven Wonders of the World.

　　peak〔pik〕*n.* 山頂；山峰　　　diverse〔daɪ'vɜs〕*adj.* 多樣的
　　ecology〔ɪ'kɑlədʒɪ〕*n.* 生態
　　Seven Wonders of the World 世界七大奇觀

二、英文作文：

【範例】

A Day without a Budget

　　My family isn't poor, but we aren't exactly rich, either. ***However***, my parents still give the best of everything to me and my siblings. ***Therefore***, if there comes a day when money is not an issue, I'll definitely treat my family.　No one has given me more than they have, so they deserve it.　I have made special plans for every member of my family, and I just know they're going to love it.

　　My plans include taking my mom and my sister to the mall for some shopping.　They can finally get the new dresses and shoes they've wanted.　For my dad, I'll bring him to the auto shop and give his car the best upgrade and maintenance there is.　We can even paint it red, as it's what he always wanted.　For my brother, I'll take him to a pro basketball game, and get his favorite player to talk to him and sign autographs for him.　He's probably going to faint.　When they're all done and satisfied, I'll have seats ready for them at the best steak house in town, where we can enjoy some quality family time.　What will I get?　I will get to see my family laugh and smile.

budget〔'bʌdʒɪt〕 n. 預算
siblings〔'sɪblɪŋs〕 n. pl. 兄弟姊妹
issue〔'ɪʃjʊ〕 n. 問題　　definitely〔'dɛfənɪtlɪ〕 adv. 一定
auto〔'ɔto〕 n.【口語】汽車　　*auto shop* 汽車工廠
upgrade〔'ʌp'gred〕 n. 升級
maintenance〔'mentənəns〕 n. 維修；保養
pro〔pro〕 adj. 職業的（= *professional* ）
autograph〔'ɔtə,græf〕 n. 親筆簽名
faint〔fent〕 v. 暈倒　　done〔dʌn〕 adj. 完成的；結束的
steak house 牛排餐廳
quality〔'kwɑlətɪ〕 adj. 優質的（= *excellent* ）
get to V. 得以；能夠

98 年指定科目考試英文科試題勘誤表

【劉毅英文製作】

題　　號	修　　正　　意　　見
一、詞彙 第 2 題	*Spending* most of his childhood in Spain, …. → ***Having spent*** most of his childhood in Spain, …. ＊童年時期已經過去，應該用完成式的分詞，表示比主要動詞先發生。
二、綜合測驗 第 13 題	… in order that the "patient" *understand* them completely. → in order that the "patient" ***may understand*** them completely. ＊表「目的」的 in order that 後面要用 may。【詳見「文法寶典」p.513】 　或 → … in order ***to make the "patient" understand***….
第 11 至 15 題 第 2 段倒數 第 2 行	The unique system can *both be used* in a…*or* for…. → The unique system can ***be used both*** in a…***and*** for…. 或 → The unique system can ***be used either*** in a…or for…. ＊both…and 和 either…or 連接兩個文法作用相同的片語。
三、文意選填 第 22 題 答案 (F) leaving	Once *leaving* the environment…, the feeling of…. → Once ***they have left*** the environment…, the feeling of…. 或 → Once ***they leave***…. ＊前後主詞不一致，不能省略主詞。
第 21 至 30 題 第 5 行	… *would be* gone. → … *is* gone. ＊依句意，非假設法，也非過去的未來，故不能用 would be。
第 5 行	…, the addicted person *would go* shopping again. → …, the addicted person *goes* shopping again. ＊講事實，非假設法，應用現在簡單式。
第 5 行	*Eventually a feeling of suppression will overcome the person.* → ***Eventually the person will feel a desire to suppress the addiction***. ＊原句是中式英語。
第 7 行	… feels ashamed of *their* addiction…. → … feels ashamed of *the* addiction…. ＊主詞是 the person，不能用 their。

題　　號	修　　　正　　　意　　　見
第 24 題 答案 (G) turn to	… prompted to *turn to* another purchase. → … prompted to ***resort to*** another purchase. 或 → … prompted to ***make*** another purchase. * turn to 和 resort to 都可作「求助於」解，但「訴諸」最後的手段，就要用 resort to。像 a last resort（最後的手段）。【參照出題來源】 ***make a purchase*** 購買
第二段 第 4 行	… adults that *have depended* on…. → … adults that ***depended*** on….　* 與現在無關，該用過去式。 … *materials* for…. → … ***material goods*** for…. * materials 是「物質；材料」，依句意，應改成 material goods（有形的商品）。
第二段 倒數第 4 行	*Important* issues…. → ***Feelings about important*** issues…. * 因為動詞是 repress（壓抑），所以被動式的主詞，應該是 Feelings 才合乎句意。
四、閱讀測驗 第 36 至 39 題 第 1、6 行等	… *TOD* → TOD * 縮寫字不可用斜體。
第 41 題 答案 (A)	(A) *To attract others*. → (A) ***To show their attitude toward life***. * 主要是顯示他們對生活的看法，並非要吸引他人。
第 44 題	What's the writer's purpose *of* writing this passage? → What's the writer's purpose *in* writing this passage? 或 → What's the ***purpose of this passage***? * in writing this passage 是副詞片語修飾動詞。
第 44 至 47 題 第二段 第 1 行	Some other *children like* Nathan White, …. → Some other ***children, like*** Nathan White, …. * like Nathan White 是插入語，前後都須有逗點。
第 48 至 51 題 第三段 第 1 行	…, a student *of* Central Michigan University, …. → …, a student *at* Central Michigan University, …. * 只能說 a student of business（商科學生）、a student of biology（生物系的學生），在某一所大學就讀，須用 at。【詳見「麥克米倫高級英漢辭典」p.2182】

99 年指定科目考試英文科出題來源

【劉毅英文製作】

題　　號	出　　　　　　　　　　處
一、詞彙 第 1～10 題	所有詞彙題的對錯選項全部出自「新版高中常用 7000 字」。
二、綜合測驗 第 11～15 題	改編自英國基爾大學（Keele University）新聞辦公室 （press office）網站，關於虛擬病患如何幫助訓練未來藥劑師的文章（"Virtual Patient" helps train pharmacists of the future）。
第 16～20 題	改編自婚姻與家庭百科全書（Marriage and Family Encyclopedia）網站，有關嫁妝的文章（India — Dowry System）。
三、文意選填 第 21～30 題	改寫自維基百科有關強迫性購物症（Oniomania）的文章。
四、篇章結構 第 31～35 題	出自 Best-Friends-Forever.com 網站，一篇關於友誼的故事 （Whitney's Story）。
五、閱讀測驗 第 36～39 題	出自 National Organization for Women 網站，Take Our Daughters to Work Day is April 25 一文，介紹美國婦女基金會所提出的活動。
第 40～43 題	改寫自 Pantogar 網站中，關於頭髮的文章（Hair & History）。
第 44～47 題	出自 Time for Kids 網站，Teachers 版中的 Building a Better World 一文。
第 48～51 題	改寫自英文郵報網站，關於違法下載音樂的文章。
作文題	類似「英語演講寶典」第 78 篇的 "The Best Day I Ever Spent with a Special Friend"（我和一個特別的朋友度過最美好的一天）

"Virtual Patient" helps train pharmacists of the future

Keele University has developed a "virtual patient" to help train the pharmacists of the future.

Students in the Staffordshire-based university's School of Pharmacy interact with the computer-generated characters to gain experience in effective communication and decision-making.

Learners talk with the "patient" via voice recognition technology or by typing questions into a standard computer interface and the "patient" responds verbally or with a range of non-verbal gestures to indicate emotions such as pain, stress or anxiety. At the end of the session the "patient" gives feedback to the trainee about their performance.

The Virtual Patient can be used to explore a number of different conditions, including dyspepsia and hypertension. When ethnicity, age or gender are relevant to the treatment of the patient, the case can be designed to demonstrate to the learner how such factors are clinically significant.

The Keele team are now working on a £50,000 project for Monash University in Melbourne, Australia, developing a new set of four avatars for their new undergraduate pharmacy programme.

They have also developed a "virtual doctor" to help with the training of pharmaceutical sales representatives. The system can be used in a classroom setting or for distance learning via the internet.

⋮

【98 年指考】綜合測驗：16-20 出題來源

India – Dowry System

An important consideration in the mate selection process is the giving of the dowry by the girl's parents to the boy's family. According to Leela Mullatti (1992), "the custom of dowry has taken the form of a market transition in all classes and castes irrespective of the level of education" (p. 99). The dowry system was initiated with the intention of providing security for a girl in case of adversity and unexpected circumstances after marriage. The parents gave whatever they could to their daughter (consequently to the groom's family) for this purpose. By the beginning of the twenty-first century, however, the custom had deteriorated to a point whereby the prospective groom and his family had become very greedy. They made tremendous demands, which if not met after marriage result in dowry deaths—burning girls alive if the dowry is insufficient, so that the boy can remarry another girl for a higher or better dowry (Mullatti 1995). The more educated a man is, the higher the family is in the caste and social hierarchy, the better his employment prospects, the higher is the expectation for dowry at the time of marriage. This makes A Hindu bride dressed in a red wedding sari, wearing traditional gold jewelry. NILUFER MEDORA it difficult for families with daughters who are highly educated to arrange marriages because the girls are required to have even more educated husbands (Seymour 1999).

【98年指考】文意選填：21-30 出題來源

Oniomania

⋮

Symptoms

Similar to other compulsive behaviors, sufferers often experience the highs and lows associated with addiction. Victims often experience moods of satisfaction when they are in the process of purchasing, which seems to give their life meaning while letting them forget about their sorrows. Once leaving the environment where the purchasing occurred, the feeling of a personal reward has already gone. To compensate, the addicted person goes shopping again. Eventually a feeling of suppression will overcome the person. For example, cases have shown that the bought goods will be hidden or destroyed, because the person concerned feels ashamed of their addiction and tries to conceal it.

⋮

Causes

The addicted person gets into a vicious circle that consists of negative emotions like anger and stress, which lead to purchasing something. After the buying is over, the person is either regretful or depressed. In order to cope with the feelings, the addicted person resorts to another purchase.

Shopaholism often begins at an early age. Children who experience parental neglect often grow up with low self-esteem because throughout much of their childhood they experienced that they were not important as a person. As a result, they used toys to compensate for their feelings of loneliness. Adults that have depended on materials for emotional support when they were much younger are more likely to become addicted to shopping because of the ongoing sentiment of deprivation they endured as children. During adulthood, the purchase instead of the toy is substituted for affection. Shopaholics are unable to deal with their everyday problems, especially those that alter their self-esteem. Most of the issues in their lives are repressed by buying something.

⋮

【98 年指考】篇章結構：31-35 出題來源

Whitney's Story

There was a time when Whitney didn't have a lot of friends. She was a bit shy and reserved. She never really wanted to be popular, but she did want to have someone to share secrets and laughs with. All through high school, though, she just slipped in and out of "light" friendships where she didn't find a lot of comfort or companionship.

When it came time to go to college, Whitney was quite nervous. She was going to be rooming with someone she didn't know and living in a town 300 miles away from home. There wouldn't be a single person she knew in town. She had no idea how she was going to make friends in this new environment.

The first week of classes, something happened that changed Whitney's life forever. In her English Composition class, she was asked (as were all the students) to share a little about herself. She told everyone where she called home and all of the other ordinary details that students share in such situations. The final question for each student was always the same: "What is your goal for this class?" Now, most of the students said it was to get a good grade, pass the class or something similar, but for some reason, Whitney said something entirely different. She said that her goal was to make just one good friend.

While most of the students sat in silence, one student came to Whitney and held out his hand and introduced himself. He asked if she would be his friend. The whole room was silent – all eyes focused on the Whitney and the hand extended just in front of her. She smiled and stretched her hand out to take his and a friendship was formed. It was a friendship that lasted all through college. It was a friendship that turned into a romance. It was a friendship that brought two people together in marriage.

Whitney learned the power of asking for what she wanted, being honest and taking action.

【98 年指考】閱讀測驗：36-39 出題來源

Take Our Daughters to Work Day is April 25

April 25 is the tenth celebration of the annual Take Our Daughters to Work Day, a project the Ms. Foundation for Women developed to expose girls to expanding opportunities for women in the workplace.

⋮

The program offers millions of girls a first-hand view of the many career opportunities available in their futures. Now that women make up 46 percent of the U.S. work force, girls can find role models in every occupational field — from politics to molecular biology to professional athletics, to name just a few. Take Our Daughters to Work Day encourages girls to focus on their abilities and opportunities, not just their appearance.

The Ms. Foundation for Women developed the project more than a decade ago to address the self-esteem problems that many girls experience when they enter adolescence. At school, boys often receive more encouragement in the classroom, especially in math, science and computers, the academic fields that tend to lead to the highest salaries.

Women receive on average only 73 cents for every dollar that men are paid, and remain vastly underrepresented in top executive positions and technology fields. The fastest-growing occupations require advanced computer skills that many girls are not acquiring. Take Our Daughters to Work Day aims to give girls the confidence and inspiration they need to develop successful careers, particularly in non-traditional fields.

⋮

"Through Take Our Daughters To Work Day, millions of girls have witnessed women in non-traditional occupations — drafting legislation, managing small and large businesses, and training to go to the moon," said Sara K. Gould, executive director of the Ms. Foundation. She added that we should also show boys "that becoming a child care provider is as acceptable a choice as becoming a police officer or CEO."

【98 年指考】閱讀測驗：40-43 出題來源

Hair & history

⋮

The Egyptians - Hair as a symbol of status

In ancient Egypt, as long ago as 1500 BC, the outward appearance expressed the person's status, role in society and political position. Wigs played an important role in this: they were crafted with great artistry and often sprinkled with powdered gold.

The Bible - The story of Samson and Delilah

The idea of long hair as a symbol of male strength is even mentioned in the Bible, in the story of Samson and Delilah. Samson was a leader of the Israelites and had been chosen by God. His long hair, which he never cut, gave him superhuman powers. The only person who knew his secret was Delilah. However, she spied for the enemy and betrayed him. One night she cut off his hair and thus robbed him of his strength. This was the only way in which he could be caught by his enemies.

The Greek - Hair as an expression of attitude

In the classical Greek period (from 500 - 400 BC) curly hair was not only the fashion of the day, but it also represented an attitude towards life. Curls were the metaphor for turbulence, change, freedom and the joy of living. The ancient Greek word "oulos" is related to intrigue, and the German word "locken" still has two meanings: to curl and to tempt someone.

Medusa - Hair as an expression of danger

⋮

Punk - Hair as a symbol of opposition

The punk protest movement today uses hair as a symbol of disapproval of the "bourgeois lifestyle" by wearing a provocative haircut and shockingly coloured hair.

The 1960ies - Hair as a sign of liberation

A different form of objection could be seen in the women's hairstyles in the 1960's. Women's liberation was expressed in a short-cut, straight and simple hairstyle which underlined equality with men without neglecting female attributes.

⋮

【98 年指考】閱讀測驗：44-47 出題來源

Building a Better World

Camille Mahlknecht, 9, has some big fun planned for this weekend. She and other residents of Agoura Hills, California, plan to pick up trash during their city's annual cleanup. Okay, gathering garbage may not sound like a good time to you--but it does to Camille. "It makes me feel terrific inside to help out and make the community clean," she says.

At the same time, Wissam Raed, 12, will be busy volunteering too. Thousands of miles away in Hasbaya, Lebanon, Wissam plans to help put on a play at an orphanage and bring potted plants to elderly people at a senior citizen center.

⋮

Some kids like Nathan W., 10, of Lake Zurich, Illinois, have personal reasons for volunteering. Nate's grandmother died of a heart attack. To help raise awareness of heart disease and money for medical research, Nate participated in Jump Rope for Heart last month. He and five other boys took turns jumping rope for 2 1/2 hours. He collected more than $1,200 in donations for the American Heart Association.

LIFELONG LESSONS

According to a report issued last November by YSA and a research group called Independent Sector, kids who start volunteering are twice as likely to continue doing good deeds when they are adults. It's never too early to start. "Volunteers can be any age," says Camille, who has done community service since she was 5.

So grab a paintbrush, trash bag, shovel or whatever you need to help your community. If you're like Camille, Wissam and Nate, you'll love how you feel after helping others. Even dirty work can be lots of fun, if it's for a good cause.

【98 年指考】閱讀測驗：48-51 出題來源

40% of illegal music download cases by college students: NPA

The intellectual property protection task force under the National
Police Agency cracked down a total of 243 cases of copyright
infringement via illegal transmission of music works for use on
personal blogs in the first six months of the year, with some 40
percent of them being committed by university students, according
to statistics released by the NPA.

The statistics showed that up to 97 out of the 243 violations
were conducted by university or graduate school students aged
between 18 and 25, indicating the students had little compulsion to
uphold the current intellectual property protection laws, NPA officials
said. According to Article 92 of the Copyright Law, any public oral
citation, broadcasting or transmission of copyrighted works without
prior permission from owners of the works is a violation of the law.

The IP protection task force has been regularly surfing websites
to see if there are copyrighted works being used illegally, and
sometimes based on clues offered by the International Federation
of the Phonograph Industry (IFPI).

Some students were found to have randomly linked their personal
blogs to music sites, so as to allow free trial listening of copyrighted
songs for blog visitors, or adopted some of the songs as the
background music for their blogs. Such practices, in fact, have
already violated the Copyright Law, and violators can be fined
NT$750,000 or face a jail term of under three years.

98 年指定科目考試英文科大考中心意見回覆

※ 題號：**12 及 14**

【題目】

　　Keele University in the United Kingdom has developed a "virtual patient," created by a computer, to help train the pharmacists of the future. Students in the university's School of ___11___ work with the "patient" to gain experience in effective communication and decision-making.

　　Students talk with the "patient" directly or by typing questions into a computer. The "patient" responds verbally or with gestures to indicate ___12___ such as pain, stress or anxiety. As a result, students are forced to communicate clearly ___13___ that the "patient" understands them completely. The Virtual Patient can also be used to explore various medical situations. For example, the "patient" can be programmed to be allergic to certain medicine and can ___14___ serious reactions if student learners are not aware of the situation. This kind of practice allows students to learn from mistakes in a safe environment that would not be ___15___ with textbooks alone. The unique system can both be used in a classroom setting or for distance learning.

12. (A) expressions　　　　(B) emotions
　　(C) elements　　　　　(D) events

14. (A) adapt to　　　　　(B) break into
　　(C) provide with　　　(D) suffer from

【12 題意見內容】

　　選項 (C)應為合理答案，因為 pain 和 stress 不是 emotions，句中的 pain（痛苦），stress（壓力）or anxiety（焦慮），都是人類的情感「成份」(elements)，Pain, stress or anxiety are elements of human feelings.

【12 題大考中心意見回覆】

　　emotion 的定義並非僅於情緒或情感，也是一種心理意識的反應及藉由生理反應的行為，因此選項 (B) emotions 為最適當答案。更何況選項 (C) 的語意範疇太廣，無法視為合理答案。

　　請參考 Merriam-Webster OnLine Search（http://www.merriam-webster.com/dictionary/pain）對於 emotion 的相關定義：

emotion：

a：the affective aspect of consciousness : feeling

b：a state of feeling

c：a conscious mental reaction (as anger or fear) subjectively experienced as strong feeling usually directed toward a specific object and typically accompanied by physiological and behavioral changes in the body

請參考以下示例

　　The limbic system is responsible for not only regulating some of the basic emotions such as pain and pleasure, but also the creation of memories (Grabowski, 2000)[1]
(http://www.yale.edu/ynhti/curriculum/units/2006/6/06.06.05.x.html)

　　These *emotions*, *such as stress* and perceived test accuracy, ... (http://www.upenn.edu/ldi/issuebrief8_5.pdf)

* 1. Grabowski, S.R., & Tortora, G.J. (2000). Principles of Anatomy and Physiology.
　　New York: John Wiley & Sons, Inc. College level anatomy and physiology textbook

【14 題意見內容】

　　選項 (B) 作「突然…起來」解，亦應為合理答案。

【14 題大考中心意見回覆】

　　本題評量考生是否能參酌上下文意，掌握段落文意的發展，本句語意為此模擬病人可被設計對特定藥物過敏而可能引發嚴重的反應。選項 (B) break into 雖譯為「突然…起來」，與本文因藥物過敏所引發的反應文意不符，而且涉及主語（主詞）與賓語（動詞）能否建立關係之問題（一個 patient 不可能 break into 什麼情況的），因此選項 (D) 為最適當答案。

※ 題號：22

【題目】

　　Oniomania is the technical term for the compulsive desire to shop, more commonly referred to as compulsive shopping or shopping addiction. Victims often experience feelings of ___21___ when they are in the process of purchasing, which seems to give their life meaning while letting them forget about their sorrows. Once ___22___ the environment where the purchasing occurred, the feeling of a personal reward would be gone. To compensate, the addicted person would go shopping again. Eventually a feeling of suppression will overcome the person. For example, cases have shown that the bought goods will be hidden or destroyed, because the person concerned feels ___23___ of their addiction and tries to conceal it. He or she is either regretful or depressed. In order to cope with the feelings, the addicted person is prompted to ___24___ another purchase.

Compulsive shopping often begins at an early age. Children who experienced parental neglect often grew up with low __25__ because throughout much of their childhood they felt that they were not important as a person. As a result, they used toys to __26__ their feelings of loneliness. Because of the ongoing sentiment of deprivation they endured as children, adults that have depended on materials for emotional __27__ when they were much younger are more likely to become addicted to shopping. During adulthood, the purchase, instead of the toy, is substituted for __28__. The victims are unable to deal with their everyday problems, especially those that alter their self-esteem. Important issues in their lives are repressed by __29__ something. According to studies, as many as 8.9 percent of the American population __30__ as compulsive buyers. Research has also found that men and women suffer from this problem at about the same rate.

(A) support　　　(B) qualify　　　(C) affection　　(D) ashamed
(E) make up for　(F) leaving　　　(G) turn to　　　(H) buying
(I) self-esteem　(J) contentment

【意見內容】

　　本題句法結構有瑕疵，應無答案。

　　因為 Once leaving (F) the environment where the purchasing occurred, the feeling of a personal reward would be gone.的主要子句的主詞不同，形成文法上錯誤的句子叫做 "dangling sentence"，本題主要子句的主詞 "the feeling"不會 "leaving" the environment；做 "leaving" 動作的主詞是購物者，而非 "the feeling"。

【大考中心意見回覆】

　　本題評量考生是否能依據篇章段落之上下文意，掌握實詞詞彙的運用。本句之語意主詞並未佔據句法主詞的位置，整句句法仍按照語意主詞，亦即句法主詞的方式來安排，本試題下一句馬上又回到 the addicted person，所以整個篇章的脈絡並沒有因此散掉，因此應不致影響考生作答。

　　下列示例提供參考：

After having made the point that models of governance were culturally based, the following pictorial representation was made in the sand of the symbolic difference, and a potential compromise. (http://www.nrhsn.org.au/client_images/789293.pdf)

※ 題號：**39**

【題目】

April 22, 2010 will be the 18th celebration of the annual *Take Our Daughters to Work Day* (*TOD*), a project the National Ms. Foundation for Women of America (NFW) developed to expose girls to expanding opportunities for women in the workplace.

The program offers millions of girls a first-hand view of the many career opportunities available in their futures. Now that women make up 46 percent of the U.S. workforce, girls can find role models in every occupational field—from politics to molecular biology to professional athletics, to name just a few. *TOD* encourages girls to focus on their abilities and opportunities, not just their appearance.

The NFW developed the project more than a decade ago to address the self-esteem problems that many girls experience when they enter adolescence. At school, boys often receive more encouragement in the classroom, especially in math, science and computer science, the academic fields that tend to lead to the highest salaries. Women receive on average only 73 cents for every dollar that men are paid, and remain vastly underrepresented in top executive positions and technology fields. *TOD* aims to give girls the confidence and inspiration they need to develop successful careers, particularly in non-traditional fields.

Perhaps because the program had become so widespread and successful, *TOD* had been criticized for excluding boys, and it was expanded in 2003 to include boys. The program's official website states that the program was changed in order to provide both boys and girls with opportunities to explore careers at an age when they are more flexible in terms of gender stereotyped roles. "We should also show boys that becoming a child care provider is as acceptable a choice as becoming a police officer or CEO," added Sara K. Gould, executive director of the NFW.

39. Why are women underrepresented in some fields such as technology?
    (A) They are not interested in these fields.
    (B) They are not encouraged to work in these fields.
    (C) They are not paid the same as men in these fields.
    (D) They are not allowed to be educated in these fields.

【意見內容】

選項 (C)亦應為合理答案。

【大考中心意見回覆】

本題語意為為何女性於科技領域低於適當比例？雖然第三段第三句提及男女薪資的差異並指出女性目前仍極少擔任主管職務與從事於科技領域，但該句之語意為描述就業婦女目前所處之現狀，「男女薪資差異」以及「婦女極少擔任主管職務與從事於科技領域」二者於該句中地位相等，均為目前之事實，就語意而言，二者並不具因果關係。

本題之題幹內容涉及因果問題，試題問的是 Why are women underrepresented? 由前文得知此一狀況的發生很清楚是因為「在學校裡，男孩通常受到更多的鼓勵，尤其在數理以及電腦等相關領域」，此一原因導致了後來薪資的差異，因為那些領域的工作通常薪資較高。是故，薪水較少很可能同樣也是此一因素所導致之結果，但並不是造成女性極少擔任主管職務與從事於科技領域之原因，兩者均為結果，而非具有能相互解釋之因果關係。

選項 (C) 指出因為女性於此領域的薪資與男性不同；此乃本文內容已提及之現象，並未解釋女性為何於科技領域低於適當比例，因此選項 (B) 女性於此領域未被鼓勵，為最適當答案。

※ 題號：47

【題目】

Camille Mahlknecht, 9, has some big fun planned for this weekend. She and other residents of Agoura Hills, California, plan to pick up trash during their city's annual cleanup. At the same time, Wissam Raed, 12, will be busy volunteering too. Thousands of miles away in Lebanon, Wissam plans to put on a play at an orphanage and bring potted plants to elderly people at a senior citizen center.

Some other children like Nathan White, 10, have personal reasons for volunteering. Nathan's grandmother died of a heart attack. To help raise money for medical research, Nathan participated in Jump Rope for Heart. He and five other boys took turns jumping rope for two and half hours and collected more than US$1,200 in donations for the American Heart Association.

Millions of children around the globe lend a hand to their communities every year. Schools and parents also contribute to the rise in youth service. For example, many schools offer community service activities for students to join. Teachers either combine volunteer work with classroom lessons or make service work a requirement. Parents, on the other hand, encourage their kids to volunteer and do it with them.

Community service is particularly important in this recession time. As the need for monetary support and other aid has increased, many charitable organizations have experienced a significant drop in donations. Camille and other children who volunteer thousands of hours annually can fill in some of the gaps.

According to research, kids who start volunteering are twice as likely to continue doing good deeds when they are adults. So, grab a paintbrush, a trash bag, or whatever you need to help your community. You'll love how you feel after helping others. Even dirty work can be lots of fun, if it's for a good cause.

47. What can be inferred from the passage?

(A) Community service can help prevent juvenile delinquency.

(B) Children will probably leave school and work as volunteers.

(C) Organizing sports events for the school is a kind of community service.

(D) Children who do volunteer work are more likely to grow up to be caring adults.

【意見內容】

選項 (A) 亦應為合理答案。

【大考中心意見回覆】

選文內容說明社區服務的重要性，本題評量考生的閱讀推理能力，作答線索為選文最後一段文意，社區服務的工作內容，並從中所帶來的感受與樂趣。選項 (A) 指出社區服務有助於防範少年犯罪，然而整篇選文並未提及少年犯罪內容，因此選項 (D) 為最適當答案。

※ 題號：50 及 51

【題目】

Downloading music over the Internet is pretty common among high school and college students. However, when students download and share copyrighted music without permission, they are violating the law.

A survey of young people's music ownership has found that teenagers and college students have an average of more than 800 illegally copied songs each on their digital music players. Half of those surveyed share all the music on their hard drive, enabling others to copy hundreds of songs at any one time. Some students were found to have randomly linked their personal blogs to music sites, so as to allow free trial istening of copyrighted songs for blog visitors, or adopted some of the songs as the background music for their blogs. Such practices may be easy and free, but there are consequences.

Sandra Dowd, a student of Central Michigan University, was fined US$7,500 for downloading 501 files from LimeWire, a peer-to-peer file sharing program. Sandra claimed that she was unaware that her downloads were illegal until she was contacted by authorities. Similarly, Mike Lewinski paid US$4,000 to settle a lawsuit against him for copyright violation. Mike expressed shock and couldn't believe that this was happening to him. "I just wanted to save some money and I always thought **the threat was just a scare tactic**." "You know, everyone does it," added Mike.

The RIAA (Recording Industry Association of America), the organization that files lawsuits against illegal downloaders, states that suing students was by no means their first choice. Unfortunately, without the threat of consequences, students are just not changing their behavior. Education alone is not enough to stop the extraordinary growth of the illegal downloading practice.

50. What is RIAA's attitude towards students' illegal downloading behavior?
　　(A) They believe that education will help greatly in protecting copyrights.

(B) They profit from the fines illegal downloaders pay for copyright violations.

(C) They like to sue students for downloading music illegally from the Internet.

(D) They think that illegal downloading behavior needs tough measures to correct.

51. What's the best title for this passage?

(A) Copyright Violators, Beware!

(B) How to Get Free Music Online!

(C) A Survey of Students' Downloading Habits

(D) Eliminate Illegal Music Download? Impossible!

【50 題意見內容】

選項 (A) 應為合理答案。

【50 題大考中心意見回覆】

選文內容關於青少年盜用網路音樂的問題，並舉例因為非法下載所引發法律訴訟。本題作答線索為全文內容及第四段內容，RIAA 認為對學生提出訴訟原本不是第一選擇，然而教育已無法有效阻止盜用網路音樂行為。選項 (A) RIAA 相信教育將對於保護著作權有極大助益，與第四段選文內容不符。選項 (D) RIAA 認為非法下載音樂行為需藉由強硬的手段來指正，才是最適當答案。

【51 題意見內容】

選項 (D) 亦應為合理答案。

【51 題大考中心意見回覆】

選文內容關於青少年盜用網路音樂的問題，並舉例因非法下載所引發法律訴訟案例，RIAA 認為唯有採取法律途徑才能有效遏止網路非法下載。選項 (D) 語意為不可能消滅非法音樂下載，與全文內容不符。選項 (A) 為最適當答案。

九十八學年度指定科目考試（英文）

大考中心公佈答案

題號	答案	題號	答案	題號	答案
1	D	21	J	41	A
2	C	22	F	42	C
3	A	23	D	43	D
4	D	24	G	44	C
5	A	25	I	45	B
6	C	26	E	46	C
7	C	27	A	47	D
8	B	28	C	48	A
9	D	29	H	49	D
10	B	30	B	50	D
11	C	31	E	51	A
12	B	32	C		
13	A	33	D		
14	D	34	A		
15	C	35	B		
16	C	36	C		
17	C	37	A		
18	A	38	A		
19	D	39	B		
20	B	40	B		

九十八學年度指定科目考試
各科成績標準一覽表

科　　目	頂　標	前　標	均　標	後　標	底　標
國　　文	65	60	51	42	34
英　　文	74	63	44	24	12
數學甲	74	59	38	20	10
數學乙	66	55	39	24	15
化　　學	73	62	44	26	16
物　　理	72	59	40	22	12
生　　物	79	70	56	42	32
歷　　史	68	61	52	39	29
地　　理	67	62	52	41	30
公民與社會	73	65	52	39	30

※ 以上五項標準均取為整數（小數只捨不入），且其計算均不含缺考生之成績，
計算方式如下：

頂標：成績位於第 88 百分位數之考生成績。
前標：成績位於第 75 百分位數之考生成績。
均標：成績位於第 50 百分位數之考生成績。
後標：成績位於第 25 百分位數之考生成績。
底標：成績位於第 12 百分位數之考生成績。

例：　某科之到考考生為 99982 人，則該科五項標準為

頂標：成績由低至高排序，取第 87985 名（99982×88%=87984.16，取整數，
小數無條件進位）考生的成績，再取整數(小數只捨不入)。

前標：成績由低至高排序，取第 74987 名（99982×75%=74986.5，取整數，
小數無條件進位）考生的成績，再取整數(小數只捨不入)。

均標：成績由低至高排序，取第 49991 名（99982×50%=49991）考生的成績，
再取整數(小數只捨不入)。

後標：成績由低至高排序，取第 24996 名（99982×25%=24995.5，取整數，
小數無條件進位）考生的成績，再取整數(小數只捨不入)。

底標：成績由低至高排序，取第 11998 名（99982×12%=11997.84，取整數，
小數無條件進位）考生的成績，再取整數(小數只捨不入)。

九十七年大學入學指定科目考試試題 英文考科

第壹部份：選擇題（佔72分）

一、詞彙（10分）

說明：　第1至10題，每題選出一個最適當的選項，標示在答案卡之「選擇題答案區」。每題答對得1分，答錯或劃記多於一個選項者倒扣1/3分，倒扣到本大題之實得分數為零為止。未作答者，不給分亦不扣分。

1. The new stadium was built at a convenient _____, close to an MRT station and within walking distance to a popular shopping center.
   (A) vacancy　　　(B) procedure　　　(C) residence　　　(D) location

2. The young Taiwanese pianist performed _____ well and won the first prize in the music contest.
   (A) intimately　　(B) remarkably　　(C) potentially　(D) efficiently

3. As thousands of new _____ from Southeastern Asia have moved to Taiwan for work or marriage, we should try our best to help them adjust to our society.
   (A) immigrants　　(B) messengers　　(C) possessors　(D) agencies

4. Although the manager apologized many times for his poor decision, there was nothing he could do to _____ his mistake.
   (A) resign　　　　(B) retain　　　　(C) refresh　　　(D) remedy

5. Last winter's snowstorms and freezing temperatures were quite _____ for this region where warm and short winters are typical.
   (A) fundamental　(B) extraordinary　(C) statistical　(D) individual

6. To overcome budget shortages, some small schools in rural areas have set up _____ programs to share their teaching and library resources.

   (A) cooperative   (B) objective   (C) relative   (D) infinitive

7. After spending much time carefully studying the patient's _____, the doctor finally made his diagnosis.

   (A) confessions   (B) symptoms   (C) protests   (D) qualifications

8. The universe is full of wonders. Throughout history, people have been _____ by the mystery of what lies beyond our planet.

   (A) notified   (B) complicated   (C) fascinated   (D) suspended

9. The president's speech will be broadcast _____ on television and radio so that more people can listen to it at the time when it is delivered.

   (A) comparatively   (B) temporarily
   (C) simultaneously   (D) permanently

10. In order to expand its foreign market, the company decided to _____ its products and provide more varieties to the customer.

   (A) exceed   (B) dismiss   (C) retrieve   (D) diversify

二、綜合測驗（20 分）

說明： 第 11 至 30 題，每題一個空格。請依文意選出一個最適當的選項，標示在答案卡之「選擇題答案區」。每題答對得 1 分，答錯或劃記多於一個選項者倒扣 1/3 分，倒扣到本大題之實得分數為零為止。未作答者，不給分亦不扣分。

第 11 至 15 題為題組

The telephone is widely considered as the most rapidly evolving technological device today. Many experts in the field believe that future

phones will not only look very different—they may not even be ___11___.
They may be hidden in jewelry or accessories, or even embedded in the
body. They will undoubtedly have a lot of additional features and
___12___ functions, and users may interact with them in new ways, too.
___13___ they are still called "phones"—a word meaning "voice" in
Greek—making voice calls may no longer be their primary function.
With advances in contemporary design and technology, the phones may
___14___ remote controls, house keys, Game Boys, maps, flashlights,
health monitors, recorders, handguns, and so on. ___15___, they will be
"the remote-control for life."

11. (A) heard	(B) sold	(C) changed	(D) seen
12. (A) remote	(B) scarce	(C) novel	(D) accidental
13. (A) As long as	(B) Even if	(C) Just as	(D) Only when
14. (A) call for	(B) get over	(C) relate to	(D) serve as
15. (A) In short	(B) As yet	(C) By the way	(D) On the contrary

第 16 至 20 題為題組

The fruits and vegetables we eat often come in distinctive colors.
The rich colors, ___16___, are not there only to attract attention. They
perform another important function for the plants.

Research shows that the substances ___17___ these colors actually
protect plants from chemical damage. The colors come mainly from
chemicals known as antioxidants. Plants make antioxidants to protect
themselves from the sun's ultraviolet (UV) light, ___18___ may cause
harmful elements to form within the plant cells.

When we eat colorful fruits and vegetables, the coloring chemicals
protect us, too. Typically, an intensely colored plant has ___19___ of
these protective chemicals than a paler one does. Research on how
chemicals in blueberries affect brain function even suggests that these

chemicals may help our own brains work more ___20___. In other words, eating richly colored fruits and vegetables makes us both healthier and smarter.

16. (A) almost　　(B) rarely　　(C) however　(D) relatively
17. (A) capable of　(B) different from　(C) inferior to　(D) responsible for
18. (A) which　　(B) that　　(C) what　　(D) such
19. (A) more　　(B) less　　(C) most　　(D) least
20. (A) obviously　(B) diligently　　(C) efficiently　(D) superficially

第 21 至 25 題為題組

　　Recent studies have shown that alcohol is the leading gateway drug for teenagers. Gateway drugs are substances people take that ___21___ them to take more drugs. Alcohol works directly on the central nervous system and alters one's moods and limits judgment. Since its way of altering moods (changing one's state of mind) is generally expected and socially acceptable, oftentimes it ___22___ over drinking. Habitual drinkers may find alcohol not stimulating enough ___23___ and want to seek other more stimulating substances. ___24___ a circumstance often preconditions teenagers to the possibility of taking other drugs such as marijuana, cocaine or heroin. Another reason why alcohol is the main gateway drug is that the ___25___ of teenagers it can affect is very wide. It is easily accessible in most societies and common in popular events such as sports gatherings and dinner parties.

21. (A) lead　　(B) leads　　(C) leading　　(D) led
22. (A) applies to　(B) arrives at　　(C) results in　(D) plans on
23. (A) in advance　(B) after a while　　(C) in the least　(D) at most
24. (A) Since　　(B) As　　(C) All　　(D) Such
25. (A) population　(B) popularity　　(C) pollution　(D) possibility

第 26 至 30 題為題組

A new year means a new beginning for most of us. On December 28ᵗʰ last year, the New York City sanitation department offered people a new way ___26___ farewell to 2007. For one hour on that day, a huge paper-cutting machine was set up in Times Square so people could ___27___ their lingering bad memories. Everything from photos of ex-lovers to lousy report cards could be cut into small pieces, as the organizers had announced ___28___ the event. Recycling cans were also provided for items such as ___29___ CDs and regrettable fashion mistakes. Former schoolteacher Eileen Lawrence won the event's $250 award for the most creative memory destined for ___30___. She had created a painting from a photo of her ex-boyfriend, who Lawrence was happy to say goodbye to.

26. (A) bid　　　　(B) to bid　　　　(C) bidding　　　(D) bidden
27. (A) destroy　　(B) maintain　　 (C) dislike　　　(D) create
28. (A) until　　　 (B) prior to　　　(C) above all　　(D) beforehand
29. (A) available　 (B) amusing　　　(C) annoying　　 (D) artificial
30. (A) machine　　(B) machines　　 (C) a machine　 (D) the machine

三、文意選填（10 分）

說明：　第 31 至 40 題，每題一個空格。請依文意在文章後所提供的 (A) 到 (J) 選項中分別選出最適當者，並將其字母代號標示在答案卡之「選擇題答案區」。每題答對得 1 分，答錯或劃記多於一個選項者倒扣 1/9 分，倒扣到本大題之實得分數為零為止。未作答者，不給分亦不扣分。

第 31 至 40 題為題組

Athletes and sports competitors compete in organized, officiated sports events to entertain spectators. When playing a game, athletes are required to understand the strategies of their game and ___31___ the rules and regulations of the sport. The events in which they compete include both ___32___ sports, such as baseball, basketball, and soccer, and individual sports, such as golf, tennis, and bowling. The level of play varies from unpaid high school athletics to ___33___ sports, in which the best from around the world compete in events broadcast on international television.

Being an athlete involves more than competing in athletic events. Athletes spend many hours each day practicing skills and improving teamwork under the ___34___ of a coach or a sports instructor. They view videotapes not only to critique their own performances and ___35___ but also to learn their opponents' tendencies and weaknesses to gain a competitive advantage. Some athletes work regularly with strength trainers to gain muscle and to ___36___ injury. Many athletes push their bodies ___37___ during both practice and play, so career-ending injury always is a risk. Even minor injuries may put a player ___38___ of replacement. Because competition at all levels is extremely intense and job security is always unstable, many athletes train year round to maintain ___39___ form and technique and peak physical condition. Athletes also must ___40___ to strictly controlled diets during their sports season to supplement any physical training program.

(A) conform　　　(B) prevent　　　(C) obey　　　　(D) guidance

(E) excellent　　　(F) techniques　　(G) professional　(H) team

(I) at risk　　　　(J) to the limit

四、篇章結構（10 分）

說明：　第 41 至 45 題，每題一個空格。請依文意在文章後所提供的 (A) 到 (E) 選項中分別選出最適當者，填入空格中，使篇章結構清晰有條理，並將其英文字母代號標示在答案卡之「選擇題答案區」。每題答對得 2 分，答錯或劃記多於一個選項者倒扣 1/2 分，倒扣到本大題之實得分數為零為止。未作答者，不給分亦不扣分。

第 41 至 45 題為題組

It is impossible to imagine Paris without its cafés. The city has some 12,000 cafés varying in size, grandeur, and significance. The cafés are like an extension of the French living room, a place to start and end the day, to gossip and debate.

____41____ The oldest café in Paris is Le Procope. It was opened in 1686 by Francesco Procopio dei Coltelli, the man who turned France into a coffee-drinking society. ____42____ By the end of the 18th century, all of Paris was intoxicated with coffee and the city supported some 700 cafés. ____43____ By the 1840s the number of cafés had grown to 3,000. The men who gathered in these cafés and set the theme of the times included journalists, playwrights and writers. Around the turn of the 20th century, the sidewalk cafés became the meeting halls for artists and literary figures.

____44____ The artists gathered at the café may not be as great as those of the past, but faces worth watching are just the same. ____45____ You'll see the old men in navy berets; ultra-thin, bronzed women with hair dyed bright orange; and schoolchildren sharing an afternoon chocolate with their mothers. The café in Paris has always been a place for seeing and being seen.

(A) When did the cafés in France start?

(B) Linger a bit and you will see that the Parisian stereotypes are still alive and well.

(C) Nowadays in Paris cafés still play the role of picture windows for observing contemporary life.

(D) These were like all-male clubs, with many functioning as centers of political life and discussion.

(E) Le Procope attracted Paris's political and literary elite, and thus played an important part among the upper class.

五、閱讀測驗（22分）

說明： 第46至56題，每題請分別根據各篇文章的文意選出一個最適當的選
項，標示在答案卡之「選擇題答案區」。每題答對得2分，答錯或劃
記多於一個選項者倒扣2/3分，倒扣到本大題之實得分數爲零爲止。
未作答者，不給分亦不扣分。

第46至49題爲題組

The Lego Group had a very humble beginning in the workshop of
Ole Kirk Christiansen, a carpenter from Denmark. Christiansen began
creating wooden toys in 1932. Two years later, he stumbled on the
Lego name by putting together the first two letters of the Danish words
Leg and *Godt*, which mean "play well." The name could be interpreted
as "I put together" in Latin; it also corresponds to the Greek verb
meaning "gather" or "pick up."

In 1947, the company expanded to making plastic toys. At first,
the use of plastic for toy manufacture was not highly regarded by
retailers and consumers of the time. Many of the Lego Group's
shipments were returned, following poor sales. However, Christiansen's
son, Godtfred Kirk Christiansen, saw the immense potential in Lego
bricks to become a system for creative play. As the junior managing
director of the Lego Group, he spent years trying to improve the
"locking" ability of the bricks and made the bricks more versatile. In
1958, the modern interlocking brick design was finally developed and
patented.

Today Lego is sold in more than 130 countries. Every minute
33,824 Lego bricks are made, and kids around the world spend 5 billion
hours a year playing with Lego. There will be more than 400 million
people playing with Lego bricks this year. On average, every person in

the world owns 62 Lego bricks, and about seven Lego sets are sold every second.

This year Lego fans all over the world are celebrating the 50th anniversary of the tiny building blocks. Though already 50 years old, Lego is still the same product it was in the 1950s. Bricks bought then are still compatible with current bricks and that is probably the reason the toy has never fallen out of favor.

46. Which of the following is true about the name *Lego*?
    (A) It is a combination of Greek and Latin words.
    (B) It was created by Ole Kirk Christiansen's son.
    (C) It was created in 1947 for naming the plastic toys.
    (D) It came from Danish words meaning "play" and "well."

47. When did the Lego brick become as a creative form of toy?
    (A) 1958　　　(B) 1947　　　(C) 1934　　　(D) 1932

48. Which of the following is true in describing the popularity of Lego?
    (A) More than 5 billion people in the world own Lego sets.
    (B) Children spend an average of 62 dollars on Lego bricks each year.
    (C) People in the world spend 400 million hours playing with Lego every year.
    (D) The Lego Group now produces more than 30 thousand toy bricks every minute.

49. What is most likely the reason why Lego still remains popular?
    (A) Old Lego bricks may still be connected to new ones.
    (B) The company hasn't changed its name since 1947.
    (C) The material for the bricks has proved to be safe.
    (D) The price of the toy is relatively reasonable.

第 50 至 53 題為題組

During my ninth-grade year, I suffered from **anorexia nervosa**. It was not enough to be thin. I had to be the thinnest. Now, however, fully recovered, I can reflect back and realize that my wishes were more complex than fitting into size five pants. Many of my subconscious emotions were related to my relationship with my father. As I was growing up, his work always came first. Sometimes I would not see him for up to two weeks. Not only did he devote his whole self to his work, but he expected me to do the same ("You cannot get anywhere unless you go to the best universities!"). Though, consciously, I never felt pressure to please him, I began dieting after the first time he told me I looked fat.

At the time, all I knew was that I had to be skinny—skinnier than anyone else. Every month my father went to Europe for a week or so and on the days he left, sorrow and emptiness consumed me: Daddy was leaving. Then, I turned to focus on a mysterious weakness—a helpless childlike emotion that came from starving. I liked to know that I needed to be taken care of; maybe Daddy would take care of me.

Now, two years later and thirty-eight pounds heavier, I have come to realize that I cannot alter my father's inability to express his feelings. Instead, I must accept myself. I know that I am a valuable person who strives to achieve and accomplish. But I cannot strive solely for others. By starving, I attempted to gain pride in myself by obtaining my father's approval or acknowledgment of my value as a person. But the primary approval must come from me, and I feel secure now that I can live with that knowledge safely locked in my mind.

50. What is **"anorexia nervosa"** as mentioned in the first paragraph?
    (A) It is an inability to express one's feelings.
    (B) It describes a situation of feeling insecure.
    (C) It refers to people who are emotionally unstable.
    (D) It is an illness that makes one want to stop eating.

51. Why did the writer suffer from anorexia nervosa?
    (A) She was told by her father to take care of herself.
    (B) She wanted to go to the best university.
    (C) She wanted her father's attention.
    (D) She grew up in a poor family.

52. Which of the following statements is true about the writer?
    (A) She has problems controlling her tempers.
    (B) She is proud of herself for working hard to succeed.
    (C) She has had great confidence in herself since childhood.
    (D) She has changed her father's way of expressing himself.

53. What's the writer's purpose of writing this passage?
    (A) To blame her father.
    (B) To report a case of child abuse.
    (C) To reflect on a stage of growing up.
    (D) To teach people how to lose weight.

第 54 至 56 題爲題組

　　Africa is a land of many ethnic groups, but when Europeans carved Africa into colonies, they gave no consideration to the territories of African ethnic groups. Some borderlines were drawn that split same groups into different colonies. Other borders threw different groups together. Sometimes the groups thrown together were enemies.

When the colonies became independent nations, these same borderlines were often maintained. Today, the Somali people remain split among Ethiopia, Kenya, Somalia, and Djibouti. On the other hand, almost every African nation is home to more than one ethnic group. In Nigeria, for example, live the Hausa, the Fulani, the Yoruba, the Ibo, and many smaller groups.

Conflicts have arisen over the way in which ethnic groups were split apart and thrown together. For example, a war between Somalia and Ethiopia was fought because Somalis wanted all their people to be a part of one nation. A civil war in Nigeria, on the other hand, was triggered partly by conflicts between ethnic groups within that nation. Similar conflicts between ethnic groups arose in Chad, Zaire, and Burundi as well. One principal goal among African nations today, therefore, is to help make it possible for their many ethnic groups to live together in peace.

54. What happened to the territorial lines drawn in Africa by the Europeans?
 (A) They disappeared as the Europeans no longer ruled the colonies.
 (B) They were respected by different ethnic groups.
 (C) They became borders between countries.
 (D) They became war memorials.

55. What does the author think to be a reason for conflicts among the Africans?
 (A) Most ethnic groups have established their own countries.
 (B) One ethnic group is broken up among different countries.
 (C) Some Europeans invaded Africa to increase their colonies.
 (D) African nations fought the Europeans to expand their territories.

56. What is the best title for the passage?
    (A) War and Peace in Africa
    (B) Africa: Borderlines Misplaced
    (C) European Colonization of Africa
    (D) Africa Recovered and Reconstructed

第貳部份：非選擇題（佔 28 分）

一、英文翻譯（8 分）

說明： 1. 將下列兩句中文翻譯成適當之英文，並將答案寫在「答案卷」上。
　　　 2. 未按題意翻譯者，不予計分。

1. 全球糧食危機已經在世界許多地區造成嚴重的社會問題。

2. 專家警告我們不應該再將食物價格低廉視為理所當然。

二、英文作文（20 分）

說明： 1. 依提示在「答案卷」上寫一篇英文作文。
　　　 2. 文長至少 120 個單詞。

提示： 廣告在我們生活中隨處可見。請寫一篇大約 120-150 字的短文，介紹
　　　 一則令你印象深刻的電視或平面廣告。第一段描述該廣告的內容（如：
　　　 主題、故事情節、音樂、畫面等），第二段說明該廣告令你印象深刻
　　　 的原因。

九十七年度指定科目考試英文科試題詳解

第壹部分：選擇題

一、詞彙：

1. (**D**) The new stadium was built at a convenient <u>location</u>, close to an MRT station and within walking distance to a popular shopping center.

這座新的體育館蓋在一個很方便的<u>地點</u>，很靠近捷運站，而且在走路就可到的距離內，有一間很受歡迎的購物中心。

(A) vacancy（'vekənsɪ）n.（職位的）空缺；空房間
(B) procedure（prə'sidʒɚ）n. 程序
(C) residence（'rɛzədəns）n. 住宅
(D) ***location***（lo'keʃən）n. 地點；位置

stadium（'stedɪəm）n. 運動場　　***close to*** 靠近
MRT 捷運（ = *Mass Rapid Transit* ）
distance（'dɪstəns）n. 距離

2. (**B**) The young Taiwanese pianist performed <u>remarkably</u> well and won the first prize in the music contest. 在音樂比賽中，這位台灣的年輕鋼琴家彈得<u>非常</u>好，於是贏得第一名。

(A) intimately（'ɪntəmɪtlɪ）adv. 親密地
(B) ***remarkably***（rɪ'mɑrkəblɪ）adv. 非常地；格外地
(C) potentially（pə'tɛnʃəlɪ）adv. 潛在地；可能地
(D) efficiently（ə'fɪʃəntlɪ）adv. 有效率地

perform（pɚ'fɔrm）v. 表演；彈奏　　prize（praɪz）n. 獎
first prize 第一名　　contest（'kɑntɛst）n. 比賽

3. (**A**) As thousands of new <u>immigrants</u> from Southeastern Asia have moved to Taiwan for work or marriage, we should try our best to help them adjust to our society.

因為有數千名來自東南亞的<u>新移民</u>，為了工作或結婚搬到台灣，我們應該盡力幫他們適應我們的社會。

(A) *immigrant*〔ˈɪməɡrənt〕*n.*（從外國來的）移民

(B) messenger〔ˈmɛsn̩dʒɚ〕*n.* 送信的人

(C) possessor〔pəˈzɛsɚ〕*n.* 所有人

(D) agency〔ˈedʒənsɪ〕*n.* 代辦處

Southeastern Asia 東南亞　　　move〔muv〕*v.* 搬家

try one's best 盡力　　　adjust〔əˈdʒʌst〕*v.* 適應＜*to*＞

4.(**D**) Although the manager apologized many times for his poor decision, there was nothing he could do to <u>remedy</u> his mistake.
雖然經理為自己不好的決定道歉了很多次，但他無法做什麼來<u>補救</u>自己的錯誤。

(A) resign〔rɪˈzaɪn〕*v.* 辭職

(B) retain〔rɪˈten〕*v.* 保留

(C) refresh〔rɪˈfrɛʃ〕*v.* 使提神

(D) *remedy*〔ˈrɛmədɪ〕*v.* 補救

apologize〔əˈpalə͵dʒaɪz〕*v.* 道歉　　　poor〔pur〕*adj.* 不好的

5.(**B**) Last winter's snowstorms and freezing temperatures were quite <u>extraordinary</u> for this region where warm and short winters are typical.
去年冬天的暴風雪和極冷的溫度對這個地區來說是相當<u>異常的</u>，因為這裡典型的冬天是溫暖且短暫的。

(A) fundamental〔͵fʌndəˈmɛntl̩〕*adj.* 基本的

(B) *extraordinary*〔ɪkˈstrɔrdn͵ɛrɪ〕*adj.* 不尋常的；異常的

(C) statistical〔stəˈtɪstɪkl̩〕*adj.* 統計的

(D) individual〔͵ɪndəˈvɪdʒuəl〕*adj.* 個別的

snowstorm〔ˈsno͵stɔrm〕*n.* 暴風雪

freezing〔ˈfrizɪŋ〕*adj.* 極冷的

temperature〔ˈtɛmprətʃɚ〕*n.* 溫度

region〔ˈridʒən〕*n.* 地區　　　typical〔ˈtɪpɪkl̩〕*adj.* 典型的

6. (**A**) To overcome budget shortages, some small schools in rural areas have set up <u>cooperative</u> programs to share their teaching and library resources.

為了克服經費的不足，一些在鄉下地區的小學校已經提出了<u>合作</u>計畫，要一同分享它們的教學及圖書資源。

(A) ***cooperative*** 〔koˋɑpə͵retɪv〕 *adj.* 合作的

(B) objective 〔əbˋdʒɛktɪv〕 *adj.* 客觀的

(C) relative 〔ˋrɛlətɪv〕 *adj.* 相對的

(D) infinitive 〔ɪnˋfɪnətɪv〕 *adj.* 不定詞的

overcome 〔͵ovəˋkʌm〕 *v.* 克服　　budget 〔ˋbʌdʒɪt〕 *n.* 經費

shortage 〔ˋʃɔrtɪdʒ〕 *n.* 不足；短缺　　rural 〔ˋrʊrəl〕 *adj.* 鄉下的

set up 提出　　program 〔ˋprogræm〕 *n.* 計畫

share 〔ʃɛr〕 *v.* 分享　　library 〔ˋlaɪ͵brɛrɪ〕 *n.* 圖書；藏書

resource 〔rɪˋsors〕 *n.* 資源

7. (**B**) After spending much time carefully studying the patient's <u>symptoms</u>, the doctor finally made his diagnosis.

經過長時間仔細研究病人的<u>症狀</u>後，醫生最後做出了診斷。

(A) confession 〔kənˋfɛʃən〕 *n.* 招供；承認

(B) ***symptom*** 〔ˋsɪmptəm〕 *n.* 症狀

(C) protest 〔ˋprotɛst〕 *n.* 抗議

(D) qualification 〔͵kwɑləfəˋkeʃən〕 *n.* 資格

study 〔ˋstʌdɪ〕 *v.* 研究　　patient 〔ˋpeʃənt〕 *n.* 病人

diagnosis 〔͵daɪəgˋnosɪs〕 *n.* 診斷

8. (**C**) The universe is full of wonders. Throughout history, people have been <u>fascinated</u> by the mystery of what lies beyond our planet.

宇宙充滿了奇蹟。自古以來，人們一直都為存在於地球以外的奧秘而<u>著迷</u>。

(A) notify 〔ˋnotə͵faɪ〕 *v.* 通知

(B) complicate 〔ˋkɑmplə͵ket〕 *v.* 使複雜

(C) ***fascinate*** 〔ˋfæsn͵et〕 *v.* 使著迷

(D) suspend 〔səˋspɛnd〕 *v.* 懸掛；暫停

universe〔'junə,vɜs〕*n.* 宇宙　　***be full of*** 充滿了
wonder〔'wʌndə〕*n.* 奇蹟　　throughout〔θru'aʊt〕*prep.* 遍及
throughout history 自古以來　　mystery〔'mɪstərɪ〕*n.* 奧秘；謎
lie〔laɪ〕*v.* 位於　　beyond〔bɪ'jɑnd〕*prep.* 在…之外
planet〔'plænɪt〕*n.* 行星【在此指「地球」】

9. (**C**) The president's speech will be broadcast <u>simultaneously</u> on
television and radio so that more people can listen to it at the
time when it is delivered.
總統的演說將會<u>同時</u>在電視及廣播中播送，如此一來就有更多的
人可以在演說發表時聽到。

(A) comparatively〔kəm'pærətɪvlɪ〕*adv.* 比較地
(B) temporarily〔'tɛmpə,rɛrəlɪ〕*adv.* 暫時地
(C) ***simultaneously***〔,saɪml̩'tenɪəslɪ〕*adv.* 同時地
(D) permanently〔'pɜmənəntlɪ〕*adv.* 永久地

president〔'prɛzədənt〕*n.* 總統　　speech〔spitʃ〕*n.* 演說
broadcast〔'brɔd,kæst〕*v.* 廣播；播送
deliver〔dɪ'lɪvə〕*v.* 發表（演說）

10. (**D**) In order to expand its foreign market, the company decided to
<u>diversify</u> its products and provide more varieties to the customer.
這家公司為了擴張國外的市場，所以決定<u>使它的產品更多樣化</u>，
提供顧客更多種類的產品。

(A) exceed〔ɪk'sid〕*v.* 超過
(B) dismiss〔dɪs'mɪs〕*v.* 解散；下（課）
(C) retrieve〔rɪ'triv〕*v.* 收回
(D) ***diversify***〔daɪ'vɜsə,faɪ〕*v.* 使～多樣化

in order to 為了　　expand〔ɪk'spænd〕*v.* 擴張
foreign〔'fɔrɪn〕*adj.* 外國的　　market〔'mɑrkɪt〕*n.* 市場
provide〔prə'vaɪd〕*v.* 提供
variety〔və'raɪətɪ〕*n.* 種類；多樣性
customer〔'kʌstəmə〕*n.* 顧客

二、綜合測驗：

第 11 至 15 題為題組

　　The telephone is widely considered as the most rapidly evolving technological device today. Many experts in the field believe that future phones will not only look very different—they may not even be <u>seen</u>.
11

They may be hidden in jewelry or accessories, or even embedded in the body. They will undoubtedly have a lot of additional features and <u>novel</u>
12

functions, and users may interact with them in new ways, too.

　　電話普遍被認為是今日發展最快速的科技裝置。許多這方面的專家相信，未來的電話不只是看起來大不相同 —— 甚至可能根本看不見。它們也許會隱藏在珠寶或配件之中，或甚至可能嵌在身體裡。無疑地，它們將有很多額外的特色和新奇的功能，而且使用者與電話之間也會有新的互動方式。

　　　widely〔'waɪdlɪ〕*adv.* 普遍地；廣泛地

　　　consider〔kən'sɪdɚ〕*v.* 認為　　　rapidly〔'ræpɪdlɪ〕*adv.* 快速地

　　　evolve〔ɪ'vɑlv〕*v.* 進化；發展

　　　technological〔ˌtɛknə'lɑdʒɪkl̩〕*adj.* 科技的

　　　device〔dɪ'vaɪs〕*n.* 裝置　　　field〔fild〕*n.* 領域；範圍

　　　jewelry〔'dʒuəlrɪ〕*n.* 珠寶

　　　accessory〔æk'sɛsərɪ〕*n.* 附屬品；配件

　　　embed〔ɪm'bɛd〕*v.* 鑲嵌

　　　undoubtedly〔ʌn'daʊtɪdlɪ〕*adv.* 無疑地

　　　additional〔ə'dɪʃənl̩〕*adj.* 額外的　　　feature〔'fitʃɚ〕*n.* 特色；特徵

　　　function〔'fʌŋkʃən〕*n.* 功能　　　interact〔ˌɪntɚ'ækt〕*v.* <u>互動</u>

11. (**D**) 根據後文「電話可能隱藏起來」，可見是不會被「看見」，故選
　　　　(D) *seen*。

12. (**C**) (B) scarce〔skɛrs〕*adj.* 稀少的
　　　　　　(C) *novel*〔'nɑvl̩〕*n.* 小說　　*adj.* 新奇的
　　　　　　(D) accidental〔ˌæksə'dɛntl̩〕*adj.* 偶然的；意外的

<u>Even if</u> they are still called "phones"—a word meaning "voice" in Greek—
　　13
making voice calls may no longer be their primary function.　With
advances in contemporary design and technology, the phones may <u>serve as</u>
　　　　　　　　　　　　　　　　　　　　　　　　　　　　　14
remote controls, house keys, Game Boys, maps, flashlights, health monitors,
recorders, handguns, and so on.　<u>In short</u>, they will be "the remote-control
　　　　　　　　　　　　　　　15
for life."
即使它們仍然被稱為「電話」──這個字在希臘文中意思是「聲音」──用聲
音打電話可能不再是它們的主要功能了。隨著現代化的設計和科技進步，電話
可以當作遙控器、住家鑰匙、掌上型遊戲機、地圖、手電筒、健康監控裝置、
錄音機、手槍等等。簡言之，電話將成為「一輩子的遙控器」。

　　primary〔'praɪ,mɛrɪ〕*adj.* 主要的
　　advance〔əd'væns〕*n.* 進步；進展
　　contemporary〔kən'tɛmpə,rɛrɪ〕*adj.* 當代的；現代的
　　design〔dɪ'zaɪn〕*n.* 設計　　remote〔rɪ'mot〕*adj.* 遙遠的
　　remote control 遙控（器）
　　Game Boy （日本任天堂公司開發的）掌上型遊戲機
　　flashlight〔'flæʃ,laɪt〕*n.* 手電筒
　　monitor〔'mɑnətɚ〕*n.* 監視器；監控裝置
　　recorder〔rɪ'kɔrdɚ〕*n.* 錄音機　　handgun〔'hænd,gʌn〕*n.* 手槍
　　and so on 等等　　*for life* 終生；一輩子

13. (**B**)　前後二句語氣有所轉折，故選 (B) ***Even if*** 「即使」。而 (A) As long
　　　　as「只要」，(C) Just as「正如」，(D) Only when「唯有～的時候」，
　　　　則不合句意。

14. (**D**)　(A) call for　要求；需要（= *require*）
　　　　(B) get over　克服（= *overcome*）；從～中恢復（= *recover from*）
　　　　(C) relate to　與～有關（= *have to do with*）
　　　　(D) ***serve as***　當作；擔任

15. (**A**)　(A) ***in short***　簡言之（= *in a word*；*in brief*）
　　　　(B) as yet　至今（= *so far*）
　　　　(C) by the way　順便一提　　(D) on the contrary　相反地

第 16 至 20 題為題組

The fruits and vegetables we eat often come in distinctive colors. The rich colors, <u>however</u>, are not there only to attract attention. They perform
　　　　　　　16
another important function for the plants.

Research shows that the substances (which are) <u>responsible for</u> these
　　　　　　　　　　　　　　　　　　　　　　　　　17
colors actually protect plants from chemical damage. The colors come mainly from chemicals (which are) known as antioxidants. Plants make antioxidants to protect themselves from the sun's ultraviolet (UV) light, <u>which</u> may cause harmful elements to form within the plant cells.
18

　　我們所吃的水果和蔬菜，常常具有獨特的顏色。然而，這些豐富顏色的存在，不只是為了吸引注意力。它們對植物而言還有另外一種重要的功能。

　　研究顯示，負責產生這些顏色的物質，事實上會保護植物免於化學物質的損害。這些顏色主要來自被稱為抗氧化物的化學物質。植物會製造抗氧化物自我保護，以防止太陽的紫外線，紫外線可能會導致植物細胞中產生有害元素。

> ***come in*** 有　　distinctive〔dɪˈstɪŋktɪv〕*adj.* 獨特的
> attract〔əˈtrækt〕*v.* 吸引　　attention〔əˈtɛnʃən〕*n.* 注意力
> perform〔pɚˈfɔrm〕*v.* 做；執行　　substance〔ˈsʌbstəns〕*n.* 物質
> ***be known as*** 被稱為　　antioxidant〔ˌæntɪˈɑksədənt〕*n.* 抗氧化物
> ultraviolet〔ˌʌltrəˈvaɪəlɪt〕*adj.* 紫外（線）的
> 【ultra = outside；violet 藍紫色】
> element〔ˈɛləmənt〕*n.* 元素；要素　　cell〔sɛl〕*n.* 細胞

16.（ **C** ）依句意，前後語氣轉折，故選 (C) ***however*** 「然而」。而 (A) almost
　　　　「幾乎」，(B) rarely〔ˈrɛrlɪ〕*adv.* 很少，(D) relatively〔ˈrɛlətɪvlɪ〕
　　　　adv. 相對地；相當地，則不合句意。

17.（ **D** ）(A) be capable of　能夠
　　　　　　(B) be different from　和～不同
　　　　　　(C) be inferior to　比～差；不如
　　　　　　(D) ***be responsible for*** 為～負責

18.（**A**）空格需要連接詞來連接前後兩句話，且需要代名詞作爲後句的主詞，由此可知，空格應爲關係代名詞，並且空格前有逗點，不能用 that，故選 (A) *which*。

When we eat colorful fruits and vegetables, the coloring chemicals protect us, too. Typically, an intensely colored plant has <u>more</u> of these
                                                       19
protective chemicals than a paler one does. Research on how chemicals in blueberries affect brain function even suggests that these chemicals may help our own brains work more <u>efficiently</u>. In other words, eating richly
                                       20
colored fruits and vegetables makes us both healthier and smarter.

　　當我們吃有顏色的水果蔬菜時，這些有色素的化學物質也會保護我們。通常，顏色強烈的植物比顏色較淡的植物，具有更多這些保護性的化學物質。有關藍莓中的化學物質如何影響大腦功能的研究甚至顯示，這些化學物質可以幫助我們的大腦運作更加有效率。換言之，攝取顏色豐富的水果蔬菜，會使我們更健康、更聰明。

      coloring〔ˈkʌlərɪŋ〕*n.* 著色；色素
      typically〔ˈtɪpɪkl̩〕*adv.* 典型地；通常
      intensely〔ɪnˈtɛnslɪ〕*adv.* 強烈地
      pale〔pel〕*adj.* 蒼白的；顏色淡的
      blueberry〔ˈbluˌbɛrɪ〕*n.* 藍莓　　affect〔əˈfɛkt〕*v.* 影響
      suggest〔səˈdʒɛst〕*v.* 暗示；顯示　　***in other words*** 換言之

19.（**A**）依句意，顏色強烈的植物，擁有「較多」保護性的化學物質，故選 (A) *more*。

20.（**C**）(A) obviously〔ˈɑbvɪəslɪ〕*adv.* 明顯地
      (B) diligently〔ˈdɪlədʒəntlɪ〕*adv.* 勤奮地
      (C) ***efficiently***〔əˈfɪʃəntlɪ〕*adv.* 有效率地
      (D) superficially〔ˌsupɚˈfɪʃəlɪ〕*adv.* 表面地；膚淺地

第 21 至 25 題為題組

Recent studies have shown that alcohol is the leading gateway drug for teenagers. Gateway drugs are substances (which) people take that <u>lead</u>
                                                                                                        21
them to take more drugs. Alcohol works directly on the central nervous system and alters one's moods and limits judgment. Since its way of altering moods (changing one's state of mind) is generally expected and socially acceptable, oftentimes it <u>results in</u> over drinking.
                                            22

　　最近的研究顯示，酒對青少年而言，是主要的誘導性毒品。誘導性毒品就是人們服用的某些會使他們再服用更多藥物的物質。酒精會直接對中樞神經系統產生作用，改變一個人的心情，並限制他的判斷力。因為酒精改變心情（改變一個人的心理狀態）的方式通常是可期待的，而且在社會上是可被接受的，所以往往會導致過度飲酒。

　　alcohol〔'ælkə,hɔl〕n. 酒精；酒　　　leading〔'lidɪŋ〕adj. 主要的

　　gateway〔'get,we〕n. 入口；入門　　　drug〔drʌg〕n. 藥物；毒品

　　gateway drug 入門毒品；誘導性毒品【一種能改變人的情緒的消遣
　　　性藥品，不會產生身體上的依賴，但長期服用會導致吸用者嘗試海洛
　　　因等烈性毒品】　　　work〔wɜk〕v. 運作；作用

　　directly〔də'rɛktlɪ〕adv. 直接地　　　nervous〔'nɜvəs〕adj. 神經的

　　central nervous system 中樞神經系統

　　alter〔'ɔltɚ〕v. 改變（= *change*）　　　mood〔mud〕n. 心情

　　judgment〔'dʒʌdʒmənt〕n. 判斷力　　***state of mind*** 心情；心態

　　socially〔'soʃəlɪ〕adv. 社會地；社交上地

　　acceptable〔æk'sɛptəbl̩〕adj. 可以接受的

　　oftentimes〔'ɔfn̩,taɪmz〕adv. 往往；常常

21.(**A**) (which) people take 和 that…take more drugs 都是形容詞子句，
　　　修飾先行詞 substances，第二個形容詞子句中，that 為關代，代替
　　　substances，為複數主詞，其後應接動詞，且依前後文為現在式，
　　　故選 (A) ***lead***「導致」。

22.(**C**) (A) apply to 適用於　　　　　(B) arrive at 到達
　　　(C) ***result in*** 導致　　　　　(D) plan on 計畫；打算

Habitual drinkers may find alcohol not stimulating enough <u>after a while</u>
23

and want to seek other more stimulating substances. <u>Such</u> a circumstance
24

often preconditions teenagers to the possibility of taking other drugs such
as marijuana, cocaine or heroin. Another reason why alcohol is the main
gateway drug is that the <u>population</u> of teenagers it can affect is very wide.
25

It is easily accessible in most societies and common in popular events such
as sports gatherings and dinner parties.

習慣飲酒的人一陣子之後，可能就會覺得酒不夠刺激了，而想要尋求其他更令
人刺激的物質。這樣的一種情況通常就會導致，青少年可能會吸食其他毒品，
如大麻、古柯鹼或海洛因。另外一個酒會成為主要誘導性毒品的原因是，酒所
能影響到的青少年人口十分廣泛。在大部分社會中，酒很容易取得，而且在一
些普遍的場合中，如運動聚會和晚宴等，酒也非常普遍。

> habitual〔həˈbɪtʃʊəl〕 *adj.* 習慣性的（= *customary* ）
> stimulating〔ˈstɪmjəˌletɪŋ〕*adj.* 刺激的；令人興奮的（= *exciting* ）
> seek〔sik〕*v.* 尋求　　circumstance〔ˈsɝkəmˌstæns〕*n.* 情況
> precondition〔ˌprikənˈdɪʃən〕*n.* 先決條件；前提（= *requirement* ）
> 　*v.* 是～的先決條件；導致
> marijuana〔ˌmɑrɪˈhwɑnə〕*n.* 大麻
> cocaine〔koˈken〕*n.* 古柯鹼　　heroin〔ˈhɛroɪn〕*n.* 海洛因
> accessible〔ækˈsɛsəbḷ〕*adj.* 容易取得的
> event〔ɪˈvɛnt〕*n.* 事件；大事　　gathering〔ˈgæðərɪŋ〕*n.* 聚會

23. (**B**) 依句意，習慣飲酒的人「一陣子之後」就覺得酒不夠刺激了，
選 (B) ***after a while*** 。(A) in advance 「事先」，(C) in the least
「至少」，(D) at most 「頂多」，均不合句意。

24. (**D**) 本句為單句，主詞是 circumstance，動詞則是 preconditions，
空格不需要連接詞，故 since 和 as 均不合。而能夠置於單數冠詞
之前的只有 ***Such*** ，故本題選 (D)。

25. (**A**) 依句意，酒所能影響到的青少年「人口」十分廣泛，選 (A) ***population*** 。
而 (B) 受歡迎程度；普遍，(C) 污染，(D) 可能性，均不合句意。

<u>第 26 至 30 題為題組</u>

A new year means a new beginning for most of us. On December 28th last year, the New York City sanitation department offered people a new way <u>to bid</u> farewell to 2007. For one hour on that day, a huge paper-cutting
26
machine was set up in Times Square so people could <u>destroy</u> their lingering
27
bad memories.

新的一年對我們大多數人而言，就意味著新的開始。在去年的 12 月 28 日，紐約市公共衛生局提供民眾一個向 2007 年告別的新方法。在那天，有台巨大的碎紙機，設置在時代廣場，為時一個小時，讓民眾可以將他們揮之不去的記憶摧毀。

> sanitation〔͵sænə'teʃən〕*n.*（公共）衛生
> department〔dɪ'pɑrtmənt〕*n.* 部門　　offer〔'ɔfɚ〕*v.* 提供
> farewell〔͵fɛr'wɛl〕*n.* 告別　　huge〔hjudʒ〕*adj.* 巨大的
> ***paper-cutting machine*** 碎紙機　　***set up*** 設立
> square〔skwɛr〕*n.* 廣場　　***Times Square*** 時代廣場
> lingering〔'lɪŋgərɪŋ〕*adj.* 留連不去的
> memory〔'mɛmərɪ〕*n.* 記憶

26. (**B**) offer sb. a new way ***to V***.「提供某人一個做⋯的新方法」，選 (B) ***to***
　　　 bid。　　bid〔bɪd〕*v.* 道（別）；說（再見）　　***bid farewell*** 道別

27. (**A**) (A) ***destroy***〔dɪ'strɔɪ〕*v.* 摧毀；破壞
　　　　 (B) maintain〔men'ten〕*v.* 維持
　　　　 (C) dislike〔dɪs'laɪk〕*v.* 不喜歡
　　　　 (D) create〔krɪ'et〕*v.* 創造

Everything from photos of ex-lovers to lousy report cards could be cut into small pieces, as the organizers had announced <u>prior to</u> the event. Recycling
28
cans were also provided for items such as <u>annoying</u> CDs and regrettable
29
fashion mistakes.

所有的東西，從前任情人的照片到差勁的成績單，都可以被切成碎片，正如同主辦者在活動進行前所說的。也提供回收桶，讓大家裝一些像是討厭的 CD，以及很後悔買錯的流行商品等物品。

photo〔'foto〕n. 照片　　　lousy〔'lauzɪ〕adj. 很糟的；差勁的
report card 成績單　　　organizer〔'ɔrgən,aɪzɚ〕n. 發起人；組織者
announce〔ə'naʊns〕v. 宣布　　　event〔ɪ'vɛnt〕n. 事件；大型活動
recycling can 回收箱（= recycling bin）
provide〔prə'vaɪd〕v. 提供　　　item〔'aɪtəm〕n. 物品
regrettable〔rɪ'grɛtəbḷ〕adj. 令人後悔的
fashion〔'fæʃən〕n. 流行；時裝

28. (**B**)　「在」活動進行「之前」所說的，選 (B) **prior to**「在～之前」
　　　　　（= before）。而 (A) until「直到」，(C) above all「最重要的是」，
　　　　　(D) beforehand〔bɪ'for,hænd〕adv. 事先；預先，均不合句意。

29. (**C**)　(A) available〔ə'veləbḷ〕adj. 可獲得的
　　　　　　(B) amusing〔ə'mjuzɪŋ〕adj. 好笑的；有趣的
　　　　　　(C) **annoying**〔ə'nɔɪɪŋ〕adj. 令人心煩的；討厭的
　　　　　　(D) artificial〔,artə'fɪʃəl〕adj. 人造的；人工的

Former schoolteacher Eileen Lawrence won the event's $250 award for the
most creative memory destined for <u>the machine</u>. She had created a painting
　　　　　　　　　　　　　　　　　　　30
from a photo of her ex-boyfriend, who Lawrence was happy to say goodbye
to.

曾當過老師的伊林‧羅倫斯，贏得這次活動中，將回憶送入碎紙機最有創意獎，得到 250 美元的獎金。她利用前男友的相片畫了一幅畫，羅倫斯很樂於和他說再見。

former〔'fɔrmɚ〕adj. 以前的；前任的
schoolteacher〔'skul,titʃɚ〕n.（小學、初中、高中的）教師
award〔ə'wɔrd〕n. 獎；獎賞　　　creative〔krɪ'etɪv〕adj. 有創造力的
destine〔'dɛstɪn〕v. 注定　　　**be destined for** 注定要到
create〔krɪ'et〕v. 創造；創作　　　painting〔'pentɪŋ〕n. 繪畫
ex-boyfriend〔ɛks'bɔɪ,frɛnd〕n. 前男友

30.（ **D** ）因有指定是那台大型碎紙機，須有定冠詞，選 (D) ***the machine***。

三、文意選填：

第 31 至 40 題爲題組

Athletes and sports competitors compete in organized, officiated sports events to entertain spectators.　When playing a game, athletes are required to understand the strategies of their game and <u>obey</u> the rules and regulations
　　　　　　　　　　　　　　　　　　　　　　　　　　31
of the sport.　The events in which they compete include both <u>team</u> sports,
　　　　　　　　　　　　　　　　　　　　　　　　　　　32
such as baseball, basketball, and soccer, and individual sports, such as golf, tennis, and bowling.　The level of play varies from unpaid high school athletics to <u>professional</u> sports, in which the best from around the world
　　　　　　　　　　33
compete in events broadcast on international television.

運動選手及參賽者，在有組織並有裁判的體育競賽中競爭，以娛樂觀眾。當運動員在比賽時，他們必須瞭解比賽的戰略，並遵守體育競賽的規定和規則。他們比賽的項目包括了團體競賽，像是棒球、籃球和足球，以及個人競賽，像是高爾夫、網球和保齡球。比賽的等級各不相同，從沒有薪水的高中校內競賽，到齊聚世界菁英於一堂，賽事還會在國際間轉播的職業性比賽都有。

athlete〔ˋæθlɪt〕*n.* 運動員　　sports〔spɔrts〕*adj.* 運動的
competitor〔kəmˋpɛtətɚ〕*n.* 競爭者
officiate〔əˋfɪʃɪ,et〕*v.* 擔任體育比賽裁判
event〔ɪˋvɛnt〕*n.*（比賽）項目　　spectator〔ˋspɛktetɚ〕*n.* 觀眾
strategy〔ˋstrætədʒɪ〕*n.* 戰略　　regulation〔,rɛgjəˋleʃən〕*n.* 規則
individual〔,ɪndəˋvɪdʒʊəl〕*adj.* 個人的　　level〔ˋlɛvḷ〕*n.* 程度；階級
play〔ple〕*n.* 競賽；比賽　　vary〔ˋvɛrɪ〕*v.* 不同；相異
unpaid〔ʌnˋped〕*adj.* 無酬勞的
athletics〔æθˋlɛtɪks〕*n.* 運動；競賽
broadcast〔ˋbrɔd,kæst〕*v.* 播送
international〔,ɪntɚˋnæʃənḷ〕*adj.* 國際的

31.（ **C** ）依句意，選 (C) ***obey***〔əˋbe〕*v.* 遵從。

32.（**H**）依句意，該空格要與後面的 individual 對比，選 (H) **team**〔 tim 〕*n.*
　　　隊。　　　***team sport*** 團隊性運動

33.（**G**）依句意，選 (G) ***professional***〔 prə'fɛʃənḷ 〕*adj.* 職業的。

Being an athlete involves more than competing in athletic events.
Athletes spend many hours each day practicing skills and improving
teamwork under the <u>guidance</u> of a coach or a sports instructor.　They view
　　　　　　　　　　　34
videotapes not only to critique their own performances and <u>techniques</u>
　　　　　　　　　　　　　　　　　　　　　　　　　　　　　35
but also to learn their opponents' tendencies and weaknesses to gain a
competitive advantage.　Some athletes work regularly with strength trainers
to gain muscle and to <u>prevent</u> injury.
　　　　　　　　　36
　　　身爲一位運動員，不只要會競賽。運動選手每天要花好幾個小時，在教練
或體育老師的指導下，練習運動技巧並增強團隊的協調性。他們會看錄影帶，
以評比自己的表現和技巧，並且瞭解對手慣用的手法及弱點，進而在競賽中佔
有優勢。有些運動選手會定期和重訓教練一起運動，以練出肌肉並避免運動傷
害。

　　　　　involve〔 ɪn'vɑlv 〕*v.* 需要…
　　　　　athletic〔 æθ'lɛtɪk 〕*adj.* 競賽的；體育的
　　　　　teamwork〔'tim,wɝk 〕*n.* 協調合作　　　coach〔 kotʃ 〕*n.* 教練
　　　　　instructor〔 ɪn'strʌktɚ 〕*n.* 指導者；教師
　　　　　not only…***but also***~ 不只…還有~　　　critique〔 krɪ'tik 〕*v.* 批評
　　　　　performance〔 pɚ'fɔrməns 〕*n.* 表現；技能
　　　　　opponent〔 ə'ponənt 〕*n.* 敵手　　　tendency〔'tɛndənsɪ 〕*n.* 傾向
　　　　　competitive〔 kəm'pɛtətɪv 〕*adj.* 競爭的
　　　　　trainer〔'trenɚ 〕*n.* 教練　　　muscle〔'mʌsḷ 〕*n.* 肌肉

34.（**D**）依句意，選 (D) ***guidance***〔'gaɪdṇs 〕*n.* 指導。

35.（**F**）依句意，選 (F) ***techniques***〔 tɛk'nik 〕*n.* 技巧。

36.（**B**）依句意，選 (B) ***prevent***〔 prɪ'vɛnt 〕*v.* 避免。

Many athletes push their bodies <u>to the limit</u> during both practice and play,
37

so career-ending injury always is a risk. Even minor injuries may put a

player <u>at risk</u> of replacement. Because competition at all levels is extremely
38

intense and job security is always unstable, many athletes train year round

to maintain <u>excellent</u> form and technique and peak physical condition.
39

Athletes also must <u>conform</u> to strictly controlled diets during their sports
40

season to supplement any physical training program.

很多運動選手在練習和比賽時，會試著超越他們身體的極限，所以，導致職業
生涯終止的運動傷害，一直是個風險。即使是輕微的傷害，也會使選手面臨被
替換的危險。因爲所有等級的比賽都十分激烈，而工作保障則永遠都不穩定，
所以許多運動選手一年到頭都在接受訓練，以保持最佳的體能狀態及技能，並
使健康狀況達到最高峰。運動選手在他們的運動季時，還必須遵循嚴格的飲食
控制，來配合體能訓練計畫。

> replacement〔rɪ'plesmənt〕n. 替換
> extremely〔ɪk'strimlɪ〕adv. 極度地　　intense〔ɪn'tɛns〕adj. 劇烈的
> security〔sɪ'kjʊrətɪ〕n. 保障　　**year round**　一年到頭
> form〔fɔrm〕n. 體能狀況　　peak〔pik〕v. 達到高峰
> **physical condition**　健康狀況　　diet〔'daɪət〕n. 飲食限制
> supplement〔'sʌplə‚mɛnt〕v. 補充

37.（ **J** ）依句意，選 (J) *to the limit*。

38.（ **I** ）依句意，選 (I) *at risk*　在危險的狀態下。

39.（ **E** ）依句意，選 (E) *excellent*〔'ɛkslənt〕*adj.* 極好的。

40.（ **A** ）依句意，選 (A) *conform*〔kən'fɔrm〕v. 遵循 < *to* >。

四、篇章結構：

<u>第 41 至 45 題爲題組</u>

　　It is impossible to imagine Paris without its cafés. The city has

some 12,000 cafés varying in size, grandeur, and significance. The cafés are like an extension of the French living room, a place to start and end the day, to gossip and debate.

很難想像沒了咖啡廳的巴黎。依照不同的大小，不同的壯觀程度和重要性來說，這個城市約有一萬兩千家咖啡廳。咖啡廳就像法國人家裡客廳的延伸，是一個開始一天的生活和結束一天生活的地方，也是個閒聊和辯論的地方。

　　imagine〔ɪˋmædʒɪn〕v. 想像　　　vary〔ˋvɛrɪ〕v. 變化
　　grandeur〔ˋɡrændʒɚ〕n. 雄偉
　　significance〔sɪɡˋnɪfəkəns〕n. 重要性
　　extension〔ɪkˋstɛnʃən〕n. 擴張　　gossip〔ˋɡɑsɪp〕v. 閒話
　　debate〔dɪˋbet〕v. 辯論

41 **(A) When did the cafés in France start?** The oldest café in Paris is Le Procope. It was opened in 1686 by Francesco Procopio dei Coltelli, the man who turned France into a coffee-drinking society. 42 **(E) Le Procope attracted Paris's political and literary elite, and thus played an important part among the upper class.** By the end of the 18th century, all of Paris was intoxicated with coffee and the city supported some 700 cafés. 43 **(D) These were like all-male clubs, with many functioning as centers of political life and discussion.** By the 1840s the number of cafés had grown to 3,000. The men who gathered in these cafés and set the theme of the times included journalists, playwrights and writers. Around the turn of the 20th century, the sidewalk cafés became the meeting halls for artists and literary figures.

　　法國的咖啡廳是何時開始的呢？巴黎最古老的咖啡廳是 Le Procope。這家咖啡廳是在 1686 年由 Francesco Procopio dei Coltelli 所開設的，這個人使得法國變成了一個喝咖啡的社會。Le Procope 咖啡館吸引了政治菁英以及文人，也因此它在上層社會扮演了一個很重要的角色。到了十八世紀末時，整個巴黎都陶醉在咖啡之中，當時巴黎約有七百家咖啡廳。這些咖啡廳就像是有著政治生活和討論中心功能的男士俱樂部。到了 1840 年代，咖啡廳的總數高達了三千家之多。聚集在咖啡廳裡討論時事主題的男士們，包含了新聞工作者、劇作家和作家。到了約二十世紀初期，人行道咖啡廳成爲了藝術家和文人雅士的聚集場所。

turn…into～　使…變成～　　literary〔ˋlɪtəˏrɛrɪ〕*adj.* 文學的
elite〔ɪˋlit〕*n.* 菁英　　upper〔ˋʌpɚ〕*adj.* 上層的
intoxicate〔ɪnˋtɑksəˏket〕*v.* 使陶醉　　male〔mel〕*n.* 男性
function〔ˋfʌŋkʃən〕*v.* 起作用　　gather〔ˋgæðɚ〕*v.* 聚集
theme〔θim〕*n.* 主題　　journalist〔ˋjɝnḷɪst〕*n.* 新聞工作者
playwright〔ˋpleˏraɪt〕*n.* 劇作家
turn〔tɝn〕*n.*（年代的）交替時期　　sidewalk〔ˋsaɪdˏwɔk〕*n.* 人行道
hall〔hɔl〕*n.* 集會處；大廳　　figure〔ˋfɪgjɚ〕*n.* 人物

44 (C) Nowadays in Paris cafés still play the role of picture windows for
observing contemporary life. The artists gathered at the café may not be
as great as those of the past, but faces worth watching are just the same.
45 (B) Linger a bit and you will see that the Parisian stereotypes are still alive
and well. You'll see the old men in navy berets; ultra-thin, bronzed women
with hair dyed bright orange; and schoolchildren sharing an afternoon
chocolate with their mothers. The café in Paris has always been a place
for seeing and being seen.

　　現在巴黎的咖啡廳還是扮演了風景窗的角色，透過這扇窗，人們可以觀察
當代的生活。現在聚集在咖啡館的藝術家也許不像以前的那麼偉大，但還是有
些臉孔是值得看的。徘徊一會兒，你就會發現，對於巴黎既有的那些印象依然
存在。你會看到上了年紀戴著海軍圓帽的男士；纖瘦黝黑染著一頭亮橙色頭髮
的女士；還有學童們和媽媽們分享著午後的巧克力點心。巴黎咖啡廳一直以來
都是個觀看和被觀看的地方。

picture window　眺望窗；大型單片玻璃窗；風景窗
observe〔əbˋzɝv〕*v.* 觀察
contemporary〔kənˋtɛmpəˏrɛrɪ〕*adj.* 當代的
linger〔ˋlɪŋgɚ〕*v.* 徘徊　　Parisian〔pəˋrɪʒən〕*adj.* 巴黎的
stereotype〔ˋstɛrɪəˏtaɪp〕*n.* 刻板印象　　alive〔əˋlaɪv〕*adj.* 存在的
well〔wɛl〕*adj.* 健康的；安好的　　navy〔ˋnevɪ〕*n.* 海軍
beret〔ˋbɛrɪt〕*n.* 小圓帽　　ultra〔ˋʌltrə〕*adj.* 過度的
bronze〔brɑnz〕*v.* 變青銅色；曬黑　　dye〔daɪ〕*v.* 染
bright〔braɪt〕*adj.* 明亮的

五、閱讀測驗：

第 46 至 49 題為題組

　　The Lego Group had a very humble beginning in the workshop of Ole Kirk Christiansen, a carpenter from Denmark. Christiansen began creating wooden toys in 1932. Two years later, he stumbled on the Lego name by putting together the first two letters of the Danish words Leg and Godt, which mean "play well." The name could be interpreted as "I put together" in Latin; it also corresponds to the Greek verb meaning "gather" or "pick up."

　　樂高集團是在一個來自丹麥的木匠，Ole Kirk Christiansen 的工作室中寒微發跡的。Christiansen 在 1932 年開始創作木製玩具。兩年後，他偶然發現 Lego 這個名字，這是把丹麥文字 Leg 和 Godt 的前二個字母結合在一起，意思是「玩得巧」。這個名字可以用拉丁文譯為「我組裝」；也相當於希臘文中的動詞「集合」或「撿拾」的意思。

> humble〔'hʌmbl〕*adj.* 謙遜的　　beginning〔bɪ'gɪnɪŋ〕*n.* 開始
> workshop〔'wɝk,ʃɑp〕*n.* 工作場合
> carpenter〔'kɑrpəntɚ〕*adj.* 木匠
> wooden〔'wʊdn〕*adj.* 木（製）的　　***stumble on*** 偶然發覺
> ***put together*** 將…組合在一起　　interpret〔ɪn'tɝprɪt〕*v.* 解釋；口譯
> correspond〔,kɔrə'spɑnd〕*v.* 一致　　meaning〔'minɪŋ〕*n.* 意義

　　In 1947, the company expanded to making plastic toys. At first, the use of plastic for toy manufacture was not highly regarded by retailers and consumers of the time. Many of the Lego Group's shipments were returned, following poor sales. However, Christiansen's son, Godtfred Kirk Christiansen, saw the immense potential in Lego bricks to become a system for creative play. As the junior managing director of the Lego Group, he spent years trying to improve the "locking" ability of the bricks and made the bricks more versatile. In 1958, the modern interlocking brick design was finally developed and patented.

　　此公司於 1947 年開始擴大生產塑膠玩具。起初，塑膠在玩具製造上的用途不被當時的批發商與消費者所高度認同。很多樂高集團的貨品在滯銷後被

退回。然而，Christiansen 的兒子，Godtfred Kirk Christiansen，看見了樂高積木成為創意遊戲方式的無限潛力。身為樂高集團的小總指揮，他花了數年努力增進積木的卡拴能力並使積木更加多功能。這個新式的連結性積木設計終於在 1958 年被開發並獲專利。

expand〔ɪkˋspænd〕v. 擴張；擴大
manufacture〔͵mænjəˋfæktʃɚ〕n. 製造；製作
retailer〔ˋritelɚ〕n. 批發商　　consumer〔kənˋsumɚ〕n. 消費者
shipment〔ˋʃɪpmənt〕n. 貨物　　return〔rɪˋtɝn〕v. 歸回
immense〔ɪˋmɛns〕adj. 廣大的　　potential〔pəˋtɛnʃəl〕n. 潛力
brick〔brɪk〕n. 積木 (= block)　　**managing director** 總指揮
locking〔ˋlɑkɪŋ〕n. 拴；鎖　　versatile〔ˋvɝsətḷ〕adj. 多功能的
interlocking〔͵ɪntɚˋlɑkɪŋ〕adj. 連結性的
patent〔ˋpætṇt〕v. 給予專利

Today Lego is sold in more than 130 countries. Every minute 33,824 Lego bricks are made, and kids around the world spend 5 billion hours a year playing with Lego. There will be more than 400 million people playing with Lego bricks this year. On average, every person in the world owns 62 Lego bricks, and about seven Lego sets are sold every second.

現今樂高在超過一百三十個國家被販賣。每分鐘有三萬三千八百二十四個樂高積木被製作，而全世界的小孩每年花五十億個小時玩樂高。今年將會有超過四億人玩樂高。平均而言，世界上每個人擁有六十二個樂高積木，而每秒鐘大約賣出七個樂高玩具組。

billion〔ˋbɪljən〕n. 十億　　million〔ˋmɪljən〕n. 百萬
on average 一般而言；平均而言

This year Lego fans all over the world are celebrating the 50th anniversary of the tiny building blocks. Though already 50 years old, Lego is still the same product it was in the 1950s. Bricks bought then are still compatible with current bricks and that is probably the reason the toy has never fallen out of favor.

　　今年全球的樂高迷要慶祝這個小型建築用木塊的五十週年紀念日。雖然已經五十歲了，樂高依然還是五〇年代當時那個相同的產品。當時所買的積木和現在的還是可以相容，而這大概也是這個玩具不曾失寵的原因。

celebrate〔ˋsɛləˏbret〕v. 慶祝
anniversary〔ˏænəˋvɝsərɪ〕n. (週年) 紀念日
tiny〔ˋtaɪnɪ〕adj. 微小的　　***building block*** 建築用的木塊
product〔ˋprɑdʌkt〕n. 產品　　current〔ˋkɝənt〕adj. 現今的
be compatible with 和…一致；與～相容
fall out of favor 失去寵愛

46. (**D**) 下面何者有關樂高的名字爲正確的？
(A) 它是希臘文和拉丁文的組合。
(B) 它是 Ole Kirk Christiansen 的兒子所創。
(C) 它是在 1947 年由於命名塑膠玩具而創。
(D) <u>它是來自於丹麥文字意爲「玩」和「巧」。</u>

47. (**A**) 樂高積木在何時成爲創意型式的玩具？
(A) <u>1958</u>　　(B) 1947　　(C) 1934　　(D) 1932

48. (**D**) 下列何者樂高的流行的描述爲眞？
(A) 全世界有超過五十億人擁有樂高玩具組。
(B) 小孩平均每年花六十二元在樂高積木上。
(C) 全世界的人每年花四億個小時在玩樂高。
(D) <u>樂高集團現在每分鐘生產超過三萬個玩具積木。</u>

49. (**A**) 何者最可能是樂高仍然維持流行的原因？
(A) <u>舊的樂高玩具還是可以和新的連結在一起。</u>
(B) 自從 1947 年公司都未改變名字。
(C) 積木的材質被證實爲安全的。
(D) 玩具的價格相當地合理。

be connected to 和…連結　　prove〔pruv〕v. 證實；證明
material〔məˋtɪrɪəl〕n. 材質；材料
relatively〔ˋrɛlətɪvlɪ〕adv. 相對地；相當地

第 50 至 53 題為題組

　　During my ninth-grade year, I suffered from **anorexia nervosa**. It was not enough to be thin. I had to be the thinnest. Now, however, fully recovered, I can reflect back and realize that my wishes were more complex than fitting into size five pants. Many of my subconscious emotions were related to my relationship with my father. As I was growing up, his work always came first. Sometimes I would not see him for up to two weeks. Not only did he devote his whole self to his work, but he expected me to do the same ("You cannot get anywhere unless you go to the best universities!"). Though, consciously, I never felt pressure to please him, I began dieting after the first time he told me I looked fat.

　　在我九年級的時候，我得了厭食症。我覺得瘦還不夠，我還必須是最瘦的。然而，現在我已經痊癒了，我可以回想當初並了解我當時的希望比想穿進五號褲子的期待還要複雜。我很多的潛意識情緒與我和我父親的關係有關。當我在成長時，他總是工作第一。有時候我會長達兩週都沒見到他的人。他不只全心全意投注於他的工作中，他也希望我可以和他一樣。（他總說：除非你進入最好的大學，不然你不可能有成就的。）雖然我從未爲了要使他高興而覺得壓力很大，但卻在他頭一次跟我說我胖時而開始節食。

suffer from 遭受；罹患　　　*anorexia* 〔͵ænəˊrɛksɪə 〕*n.* 厭食症
nervosa 是拉丁文的 nervous（緊張）（對女性用）
recover〔rɪˊkʌvɚ 〕*v.* 痊癒　　　reflect〔rɪˊflɛkt 〕*v.* 思考
realize〔ˊrɪə͵laɪz 〕*v.* 了解
complex〔kəmˊplɛks 〕*adj.* 複雜的　　*fit into* 適用於
subconscious〔sʌbˊkɑnʃəs 〕*adj.* 潛意識的
emotion〔ɪˊmoʃən 〕*n.* 情緒　　*be related to* 和～有關連
relationship〔rɪˊleʃən͵ʃɪp 〕*n.* 關係
devote〔dɪˊvot 〕*v.* 致力於　　whole〔hol 〕*adj.* 全部的
expect〔ɪkˊspɛkt 〕*v.* 期待　　university〔͵junəˊvɝsətɪ 〕*n.* 大學
consciously〔ˊkɑnʃəslɪ 〕*adv.* 有意識地
pressure〔ˊprɛʃɚ 〕*n.* 壓力　　please〔pliz 〕*v.* 取悅
diet〔ˊdaɪət 〕*v.* 節食

At the time, all I knew was that I had to be skinny—skinnier than anyone else. Every month my father went to Europe for a week or so and on the days he left, sorrow and emptiness consumed me: Daddy was leaving. Then, I turned to focus on a mysterious weakness—a helpless childlike emotion that came from starving. I liked to know that I needed to be taken care of; maybe Daddy would take care of me.

在當時，我所知道的就是我必須瘦，比任何一個人瘦。我父親每個月大約去歐洲一週，而在他離開的當天，悲傷和空虛消耗了我：父親離開了。而我又轉向專注於我那莫名的虛弱 —— 一股源於飢餓而感到孩子般無助的情緒。我知道我需要被照顧，而也許父親會照顧我。

skinny〔'skɪnɪ〕adj. 皮包骨的　　**or so** 大約
sorrow〔'saro〕n. 悲傷　　emptiness〔'ɛmptɪnɪs〕n. 空虛
consume〔kən'sum〕v. 消耗　　**focus on** 專注於
mysterious〔mɪs'tɪrɪəs〕adj. 神秘的
weakness〔'wiknɪs〕n. 虛弱　　helpless〔'hɛlplɪs〕adj. 無助的
childlike〔'tʃaɪld,laɪk〕adj. 孩子般的
starve〔starv〕v. 飢餓　　**take care of** 照顧

Now, two years later and thirty-eight pounds heavier, I have come to realize that I cannot alter my father's inability to express his feelings. Instead, I must accept myself. I know that I am a valuable person who strives to achieve and accomplish. But I cannot strive solely for others. By starving, I attempted to gain pride in myself by obtaining my father's approval or acknowledgment of my value as a person. But the primary approval must come from me, and I feel secure now that I can live with that knowledge safely locked in my mind.

兩年後的現在，我胖了三十八磅，我了解我無法改變父親不擅表達情緒的這個事實。相反地，我必須接受我自己。我知道我是個很有價值的人，我盡我所能地去追求目標並達到成就。但是我不能只是因為別人而努力。透過節食，我試著得到父親贊同並認可我身而為人的價值，進而獲得自尊。但是最重要的認可必須是來自我自己，而我現在感到很有安全感，因為我現在懂了這個牢牢鎖在我心中的事實。

come to realize 領悟；瞭解　　alter〔ˋɔltɚ〕 *v.* 改變
inability〔͵ɪnəˋbɪlətɪ〕 *n.* 無能力
valuable〔ˋvæljuəbḷ〕 *adj.* 有價值的　　strive〔straɪv〕 *v.* 努力去做
accomplish〔əˋkɑmplɪʃ〕 *v.* 達成；成就
pride〔praɪd〕 *n.* 自尊　　approval〔əˋpruvḷ〕 *n.* 贊同
acknowledgment〔əkˋnɑlɪdʒmənt〕 *n.* 認同
primary〔ˋpraɪmɛrɪ〕 *adj.* 主要的　　*now that* 既然
knowledge〔ˋnɑlɪdʒ〕 *n.* 所知之事

50.（**D**）第一段文章提到的 **anorexia nervosa** 是什麼？

　　(A) 一種無法表達個人情感的能力。

　　(B) 描述一種感到不安的情況。　　(C) 它是指情緒不穩定的人。

　　(D) <u>一種令人想要停止吃東西的疾病。</u>

insecure〔͵ɪnsɪˋkjʊr〕 *adj.* 感到不安的　　*refer to* 是指
emotionally〔ɪˋmoʃənlɪ〕 *adv.* 情緒上
unstable〔ʌnˋstebḷ〕 *adj.* 不穩定的

51.（**C**）為什麼作者會得厭食症？

　　(A) 她被父親告知要照顧自己。　　(B) 她想要進入最棒的大學。

　　(C) <u>她想得到父親的注意。</u>　　(D) 她在窮困的家庭中成長。

52.（**B**）下列哪項關於作者的敘述是對的？

　　(A) 她在情緒控制方面上有問題。

　　(B) <u>她對自己努力想要成功感到驕傲。</u>

　　(C) 她從小時候開始，就對自己有極度的自信。

　　(D) 她改變父親的表達方式。

temper〔ˋtɛmpɚ〕 *n.* 情緒　　confidence〔ˋkɑnfədəns〕 *n.* 自信

53.（**C**）作者寫這篇文章的目的為何？

　　(A) 責怪她的父親。　　　　　　(B) 報導一件虐待兒童的案例。

　　(C) <u>回想一段成長階段。</u>　　　(D) 教導人們如何減重。

purpose〔ˋpɝpəs〕 *n.* 目的　　blame〔blem〕 *v.* 責怪
case〔kes〕 *n.* 例子　　abuse〔əˋbjus〕 *n.* 虐待
reflect on 回想　　stage〔stedʒ〕 *n.* 階段

第 54 至 56 題為題組

Africa is a land of many ethnic groups, but when Europeans carved Africa into colonies, they gave no consideration to the territories of African ethnic groups. Some borderlines were drawn that split same groups into different colonies. Other borders threw different groups together. Sometimes the groups thrown together were enemies.

非洲是一塊種族多元的大地，但是當歐洲人將其劃分成為殖民地時，他們並沒有考量到非洲各族的領土範圍。有些邊界將同一種族拆散到不同殖民地。有些則將不同的種族併在一起。有時，併在一起的種族是敵對的。

> Africa〔ˈæfrɪkə〕*n.* 非洲　　ethnic〔ˈɛθnɪk〕*adj.* 種族的
> carve〔karv〕*v.* 切割　　colonies〔ˈkalənɪ〕*n.* 殖民地
> territory〔ˈtɛrəˌtorɪ〕*n.* 領土；領地
> borderline〔ˈbɔrdəˌlaɪn〕*n.* 界線　　split〔splɪt〕*v.* 切開；分離

When the colonies became independent nations, these same borderlines were often maintained. Today, the Somali people remain split among Ethiopia, Kenya, Somalia, and Djibouti. On the other hand, almost every African nation is home to more than one ethnic group. In Nigeria, for example, live the Hausa, the Fulani, the Yoruba, the Ibo, and many smaller groups.

當這些殖民地獨立成為國家時，這些邊界仍被沿用。現在，索馬利人仍被拆散於衣索比亞、肯亞、索馬利亞，以及吉布地。另一方面，幾乎每個非洲國家都不止一個種族居住。舉例來說，在奈及利亞住有豪薩族、富拉族、優魯巴族、伊布族，以及許多更小的族群。

> independent〔ˌɪndɪˈpɛndənt〕*adj.* 獨立的
> maintain〔menˈten〕*v.* 繼續；保持
> Somali〔soˈmalɪ〕*n.* 索馬利族　　Ethiopia〔ˌiθɪˈopɪə〕*n.* 伊索比亞
> Kenya〔ˈkɛnjə〕*n.* 肯亞　　Somalia〔səˈmalɪə〕*n.* 索馬利亞
> Djibouti〔dʒɪˈbutɪ〕*n.* 吉布地　　*on the other hand* 反之；另一方面
> Nigeria〔naɪˈdʒɪrɪə〕*n.* 奈及利亞　　Hausa〔ˈhausə〕*n.* 豪薩族
> Fulani〔fuˈlanɪ〕*n.* 富拉族
> Yoruba〔ˈjɔrubə〕*n.* 優魯巴族　　Ibo〔ˈibo〕*n.* 伊布族

Conflicts have arisen over the way in which ethnic groups were split apart and thrown together.　For example, a war between Somalia and Ethiopia was fought because Somalis wanted all their people to be a part of one nation.　A civil war in Nigeria, on the other hand, was triggered partly by conflicts between ethnic groups within that nation.　Similar conflicts between ethnic groups arose in Chad, Zaire, and Burundi as well. One principal goal among African nations today, therefore, is to help make it possible for their many ethnic groups to live together in peace.

這些種族分散與合併的方式，引起了許多的衝突。舉例來說，索馬利亞以及衣索比亞間發生戰爭，是因為索馬利亞人想要全部住在同一個國家。而另一方面，觸發奈及利亞內戰的原因，部分是源自其國內種族的問題。相似的種族衝突在查德、薩伊，以及蒲隆地也都有發生。因此，非洲眾國當今首要的目標，便是讓這些眾多的種族能夠和平相處。

conflict〔ˋkɑnflɪkt〕*n.* 鬥爭；衝突　　arise〔əˋraɪz〕*v.* 產生；形成
civil〔ˋsɪvḷ〕*adj.* 國內的　　　*civil war* 內戰
trigger〔ˋtrɪgɚ〕*v.* 引起；觸發　　partly〔ˋpɑrtlɪ〕*adv.* 部分地
Chad〔tʃɑd〕*n.* 查德　　Zaire〔zɑˋɪr〕*n.* 薩伊
Burundi〔bəˋrʌndɪ〕*n.* 蒲隆地
principal〔ˋprɪnsəpḷ〕*adj.* 主要的；首要的　　peace〔pis〕*n.* 和平

54.（**C**）歐洲人在非洲所劃分的領土界線發生了什麼事？
　　(A) 當歐洲人不再統治著殖民地時，它們就消失了。
　　(B) 它們獲得不同種族的尊重。
　　(C) 它們成為國家間的邊界。　　(D) 它們成為戰爭的紀念碑。
　　rule〔rul〕*v.* 統治　　border〔ˋbɔrdɚ〕*n.* 邊界
　　memorial〔məˋmorɪəl〕*n.* 紀念碑

55.（**B**）作者認為非洲人之間衝突的原因之一是
　　(A) 大多數的種族都建立了自己的國家。
　　(B) 一個種族被分散於許多不同的國家。
　　(C) 有些歐洲人入侵非洲，以擴展殖民地。
　　(D) 非洲國家與歐洲人抗戰，以擴展領土。
　　establish〔əˋstæblɪʃ〕*v.* 建立　　invade〔ɪnˋved〕*v.* 侵入
　　expand〔ɪkˋspænd〕*v.* 擴大；擴展

56.（ **B** ）這篇文章最好的題目是

    (A) 非洲的戰爭與和平　　　　　(B) 非洲：錯誤的邊界

    (C) 非洲的歐洲殖民地化　　　　(D) 非洲的復原與重建

    misplace〔mɪs'ples〕v. 誤置

    colonization〔,kɑlənə'zeʃən〕n. 殖民地化

    recover〔rɪ'kʌvɚ〕v. 恢復

    reconstruction〔,rikən'strʌkʃən〕n. 重建

第貳部分：非選擇題

一、英文翻譯：

1. 全球糧食危機已經在世界許多地區造成嚴重的社會問題。

    The global food crisis has caused serious social problems in many

    $\begin{Bmatrix} \text{parts} \\ \text{areas} \end{Bmatrix}$ of the world.

2. 專家警告我們不應該再將食物價格低廉視為理所當然。

    Experts $\begin{Bmatrix} \text{warn} \\ \text{are warning} \end{Bmatrix}$ us that we should no longer take

    $\begin{Bmatrix} \text{low} \\ \text{inexpensive} \\ \text{cheep} \end{Bmatrix}$ food prices for granted.

二、英文作文：

【範例 1】

An Impressive Commercial

    One of the commercials that I remember the most is one for Regaine, a medicine for use against hair loss. Pictures of a middle-aged man are shown from left to right, each one with less hair than the one before it. The man looks more and more depressed. However, the last picture shows the Regaine product, and the pictures now go from right to left, with the man smiling happily at the end.

I am impressed by this commercial because it looks realistic. Most hair growth product commercials show a bald man. Then after using the product, he "magically" grows hair again. However, this commercial shows the entire process of losing hair, and the gradual re-growth after using Regaine. I think it's more convincing than other hair-growth commercials, so I think it's quite impressive.

【範例 2】

An Impressive Commercial

During the recent NBA playoffs, the NBA released a series of player commercials. The commercials showed two players from competing teams, with each showing just one half of his or her face. The two faces were pieced together, and the players spoke the same lines, so it looked like one face with one voice. A total of 15 commercials were made.

These commercials were impressive because they showed how much the players wanted to win. The lines were all very dramatic and emotional, and it was easy to believe that the players meant it from the heart. No matter who you are playing against, you give your all for the chance to win. I was moved by many of these commercials, and that's why I remember them so well.

> **hair loss** 掉髮　　**middle-age** 中年
> depressed〔dɪ'prɛst〕adj. 沮喪的
> realistic〔,riə'lɪstɪk〕adj. 現實的　　bald〔bɔld〕adj. 禿頭的
> magically〔'mædʒɪklɪ〕adv. 不可思議地
> gradual〔'grædʒʊəl〕adj. 逐漸的　　growth〔groθ〕n. 生長
> playoffs〔'ple,ɔf〕n. 季後賽　　release〔rɪ'lis〕v. 發行；發表
> series〔'sɪrɪz〕n. 系列　　compete〔kəm'pit〕v. 競爭
> **one half** 一半　　piece〔pis〕v. 拼合
> line〔laɪn〕n. 臺詞　　dramatic〔drə'mætɪk〕adj. 充滿激情的
> emotional〔ɪ'moʃənḷ〕adj. 激起情感的
> **give your all** 出百分之百的力量　　move〔muv〕v. 感動

97 年指定科目考試英文科試題勘誤表

※ 今年的指考題目，出得不簡單，有很多陷阱，不小心就會寫錯。題目長
又多，沒有經過模考訓練，很難得高分。題目出得有水準，有知識性、
教育性、趣味性，也很生活化，符合大考中心的命題原則。

題　　號	修　　正　　意　　見
二、綜合測驗 第 21 至 25 題 第 4 行	... oftentimes it ___22___ *over drinking*.... → ... oftentimes it ___22___ *overdrinking*.... * overdrink 在所有字典中都是一個字。
四、篇章結構 第三段 第 1～2 行	... *but faces worth watching are just the same.* → ... *but there are still faces worth watching.* 或 → ... *but the opportunities to see the faces worth watching* 　　　*are just the same.* * 原文句意是「但值得看的臉孔都一樣」，應該是雖然咖啡廳裡坐的藝術家不像以前的那麼偉大，「但還是有些臉孔是值得看的。」不改的話，句意不合理。 選項 (E) .... *among* the upper class. → .... *in the lives of* the upper class. * 根據句意，應是「在他們的生活中扮演重要的角色」才合理。
五、閱讀測驗 第 47 題	When did *the Lego* brick *become as* a creative form of toy? → When did **the plastic Lego** brick *become accepted as* a 　　creative form of toy? * 因為 1947 年開始用塑膠製造，如果不加上 plastic，句意就不清楚。「被認為是」是 be accepted as，所以要改成 become accepted as 才對，become 是 be 動詞的變體。
第 52 題	(A) She has...*tempers*. 　　→ She has...*temper*. * temper 當「脾氣」解時，為單數，像 keep *one's* temper「忍住脾氣」，lose *one's* temper「發脾氣」等。
第 53 題	What's the writer's purpose *of writing this passage*? → What's the writer's purpose *in writing this passage*? 或 → What's the writer's purpose *of this passage*? * purpose 後面接 of 加名詞，接 in 加動名詞。

97 年指定科目考試英文科出題來源

題　　號	出　　　　　　　　　　處
一、詞彙 第 1～10 題	所有各題的對錯選項均出自「高中常用 7000 字」，只有 第 6 題選項 (D) infinitive（不定詞的），不在 7000 字中， 但它不是正確答案。
二、綜合測驗 第 11～15 題	改編自 Global Technology Forum 網站，"The Phone of the future"（未來的電話）。 （http://globaltechforum.eiu.com/index.asp? layout=rich_story&channelid=3&categoryid= 1&title=The+phone+of+the+future&doc_id=9762）
第 16～20 題	改編自 Science News for Kids 網站，關於有著鮮豔顏色的蔬 菜水果含有對人體有幫助的物質（The Color of Health）的 文章。 （http://www.sciencenewsforkids.org/articles/ 20050302/Feature1.asp）
三、文意選填 第 31～40 題	出自美國勞工局統計處網站，有關運動員、教練，裁判和 相關工作人員（Athletes, Coaches, Umpires, and Related Workers）的文章。 （http://www.bls.gov/oco/ocos251.htm）
四、篇章結構 第 41～45 題	改編自紐約時報 2005 年 6 月 17 日旅遊版，有關巴黎咖啡 店的報導。
五、閱讀測驗 第 46～49 題	改篇自維基百科（Wikipedia, the free encyclopedia）介紹樂 高（Lego）的文章

九十七學年度指定科目考試（英文）

大考中心公佈答案

題號	答案	題號	答案	題號	答案
1	D	21	A	41	A
2	B	22	C	42	E
3	A	23	B	43	D
4	D	24	D	44	C
5	B	25	A	45	B
6	A	26	B	46	D
7	B	27	A	47	A
8	C	28	B	48	D
9	C	29	C	49	A
10	D	30	D	50	D
11	D	31	C	51	C
12	C	32	H	52	B
13	B	33	G	53	C
14	D	34	D	54	C
15	A	35	F	55	B
16	C	36	B	56	B
17	D	37	J		
18	A	38	I		
19	A	39	E		
20	C	40	A		

九十七學年度指定科目考試
各科成績標準一覽表

科　　目	頂　標	前　標	均　標	後　標	底　標
國　　文	64	58	49	38	30
英　　文	76	64	41	20	9
數學甲	77	64	43	23	13
數學乙	71	58	39	21	11
化　　學	69	56	36	19	10
物　　理	63	49	29	14	7
生　　物	72	63	49	35	25
歷　　史	62	52	37	23	14
地　　理	68	62	51	38	27

※ 以上五項標準均取為整數 (小數只捨不入)，且其計算均不含缺考生之成績，
　計算方式如下：

頂標：成績位於第 88 百分位數之考生成績。

前標：成績位於第 75 百分位數之考生成績。

均標：成績位於第 50 百分位數之考生成績。

後標：成績位於第 25 百分位數之考生成績。

底標：成績位於第 12 百分位數之考生成績。

例：　某科之到考考生為 99982 人，則該科五項標準為

　　頂標：成績由低至高排序，取第 87985 名 (99982×88%=87984.16，取整數，
　　　　　小數無條件進位) 考生的成績，再取整數(小數只捨不入)。

　　前標：成績由低至高排序，取第 74987 名 (99982×75%=74986.5，取整數，
　　　　　小數無條件進位) 考生的成績，再取整數(小數只捨不入)。

　　均標：成績由低至高排序，取第 49991 名 (99982×50%=49991)考生的成績，
　　　　　再取整數(小數只捨不入)。

　　後標：成績由低至高排序，取第 24996 名 (99982×25%=24995.5，取整數，
　　　　　小數無條件進位) 考生的成績，再取整數(小數只捨不入)。

　　底標：成績由低至高排序，取第 11998 名 (99982×12%=11997.84，取整數，
　　　　　小數無條件進位) 考生的成績，再取整數(小數只捨不入)。

九十六年大學入學指定科目考試試題
英文考科

第壹部份：選擇題（佔72分）

一、詞彙（10分）

說明：　第1至10題，每題選出一個最適當的選項，標示在答案卡之「選擇題答案區」。每題答對得1分，答錯或劃記多於一個選項者倒扣1/3分，倒扣到本大題之實得分數為零為止。未作答者，不給分亦不扣分。

1. With his excellent social skills, Steven has been _____ as a great communicator by all his colleagues.
   (A) diagnosed　　(B) exploited　　(C) perceived　　(D) concerned

2. When you enter a building, be sure to look behind you and hold the door open for someone coming through the same door. It is a common _____ in many cultures.
   (A) process　　(B) courtesy　　(C) acceptance　　(D) operation

3. The telephone has changed beyond _____ in recent years. In both form and function, it has become totally different from what it was before.
   (A) recognition　　(B) possession　　(C) prevention　　(D) appreciation

4. Though Jack has moved out of his parents' house, he is _____ dependent on them still. They send him a check every month for his living expenses.
   (A) radically　　(B) physically　　(C) financially　　(D) politically

5. If you want to keep your computer from being attacked by new viruses, you need to constantly renew and _____ your anti-virus software.
   (A) confirm　　(B) overlook　　(C) esteem　　(D) update

6. Many factors may explain why people are addicted to the Internet. One factor _____ to this phenomenon is the easy access to the Net.
   (A) advancing　　(B) occurring　　(C) responding　　(D) contributing

7. We were _____ awaiting the results of the school's annual English drama contest. Our class won the first place last year, and we certainly wanted to win again this year.
   (A) consciously　(B) anxiously　　(C) fortunately　　(D) competently

8. Tropical rainforests are home to about one million plant and animal species. If the rainforests disappear, many of these species will become _____.
   (A) extinct　　　(B) hostile　　　(C) mature　　　(D) intimate

9. An honest person is faithful to his promise. Once he makes a _____, he will not go back on his own word.
   (A) prescription　(B) commitment　(C) frustration　　(D) transcript

10. The new computer game Wii provides us with an _____ way of exercising. People now may play sports in their living rooms, which was unimaginable before.
    (A) outgoing　　(B) urgent　　　(C) aggressive　　(D) innovative

二、綜合測驗（20 分）

說明：　第 11 至 30 題，每題一個空格。請依文意選出一個最適當的選項，標示在答案卡之「選擇題答案區」。每題答對得 1 分，答錯或劃記多於一個選項者倒扣 1/3 分，倒扣到本大題之實得分數為零為止。未作答者，不給分亦不扣分。

第 11 至 15 題為題組

Recent studies show that levels of happiness for most people change throughout their lives. In a British study between 1991 and 2003, people

were asked how satisfied they are ____11____ their lives. The resulting
statistics graph shows a smile-shaped curve. Most of the people ____12____
happy and become progressively less happy as they grow older. For
many of them, the most miserable period in their life is their 40s.
____13____, their levels of happiness climb. Furthermore, it seems that
men are slightly happier on average than women in their teens, but
women bounce back and overtake men ____14____ in life. The low point
seems to last longer for women—throughout their 30s and 40s, only
climbing ____15____ women reach 50. Men, on the other hand, have the
lowest point in their 40s, going up again when they reach 50.

11. (A) for　　　　(B) with　　　　(C) at　　　　(D) of
12. (A) end up　　(B) pass by　　　(C) start off　　(D) go on
13. (A) After that　(B) By that time　(C) Not for long　(D) Before now
14. (A) sooner　　(B) later　　　　(C) earlier　　　(D) slower
15. (A) once　　　(B) unless　　　　(C) before　　　(D) since

第 16 至 20 題為題組

The northern lights, known as the aurora borealis, is one of nature's
most dazzling spectacles. Science is still not certain ____16____ exactly
what these lights are and what causes them. Sometimes, the brilliant
rays of light spread upward in the shape of a fan. ____17____, they flash
here and there like giant searchlights. Farther north, the aurora
frequently looks like fiery draperies which hang from the sky and sway
____18____ while flames of red, orange, green, and blue play up and
down the moving folds.

According to scientific measurements, this discharge of light
____19____ from 50 to 100 miles above the earth. It is seen ____20____ around
the Hudson Bay region in Canada, in northern Scotland, and in southern
Norway and Sweden.

16. (A) due to   (B) instead of
    (C) as to   (D) in spite of
17. (A) At one time   (B) At other times
    (C) At all times   (D) At the same time
18. (A) here and now   (B) by and large
    (C) to and fro   (D) more and more
19. (A) takes place   (B) was taking place
    (C) had taken place   (D) took place
20. (A) in the least   (B) on the whole
    (C) for its sake   (D) at its best

第 21 至 25 題為題組

Average global temperature has increased by almost 1° F over the past century. Scientists expect it to increase an ___21___ 2° to 6° F over the next one hundred years. This may not sound like much, but it could change the Earth's climate as ___22___ before.

Climate change may affect people's health both directly and indirectly. For instance, heat stress and other heat-related health problems are caused directly by very warm temperatures. ___23___ , human health can also be affected by ecological disturbances, changes in food and water supplies, as well as coastal flooding. How people and nature ___24___ climate change will determine how seriously it affects human health. Generally, poor people and poor countries are ___25___ probable to have the money and resources they need to cope with health problems due to climate change.

21. (A) extreme   (B) additional   (C) immediate   (D) original
22. (A) ever   (B) never   (C) always   (D) yet
23. (A) Suddenly   (B) Previously   (C) Exclusively (D) Indirectly
24. (A) result from (B) count on   (C) adapt to   (D) stand for
25. (A) less   (B) very   (C) most   (D) further

第 26 至 30 題爲題組

　　The Kingdom of Bhutan is a landlocked nation situated between India and China. The entire country is mountainous, ___26___ a small strip of subtropical plains in the extreme south. The elevation gain from the subtropical plains to the glacier-covered Himalayan heights exceeds 7,000 m. Its traditional ___27___ is based on forestry, animal husbandry and subsistence agriculture. However, these ___28___ less than 50% of the GDP now that Bhutan has become an exporter of hydroelectricity. Besides, cash crops and tourism are also ___29___.

　　Bhutan is one of the most isolated nations in the world, ___30___ foreign influences and tourism regulated by the government to preserve its traditional Tibetan Buddhist culture. It is often described as the last surviving refuge of traditional Himalayan Buddhist culture.

26. (A) in terms of　　　　　　(B) as a part of
　　(C) with the exception of　(D) in accordance with
27. (A) culture　　(B) politics　　(C) religion　　(D) economy
28. (A) figure out　(B) relate to　(C) account for　(D) conform to
29. (A) significant　(B) durable　(C) frequent　(D) expressive
30. (A) by　　　　(B) with　　　(C) for　　　(D) in

三、文意選填（10 分）

說明：　第 31 至 40 題，每題一個空格。請依文意在文章後所提供的 (A) 到 (J) 選項中分別選出最適當者，並將其字母代號標示在答案卡之「選擇題答案區」。每題答對得 1 分，答錯或劃記多於一個選項者倒扣 1/9 分，倒扣到本大題之實得分數爲零爲止。未作答者，不給分亦不扣分。

第 31 至 40 題爲題組

　　A trip to the supermarket has now become an exercise in psychological warfare. Shopkeepers know that filling a store with the smell of freshly baked bread makes people feel hungry and ___31___ them to buy more food than they intended. Stocking the most ___32___ products at eye level helps them sell faster than cheaper but less visible competitors.

Researchers on customer behavior are now investigating how "swarm intelligence" (that is, how social animals like ants or bees behave in a crowd) can be used to ___33___ what people buy. The idea is that, if a certain product is seen to be popular, shoppers are ___34___ to choose it too. With the help of modern technology, some supermarkets are now able to keep customers ___35___ about what others are buying. As a customer walks past a shelf of goods in one of these supermarkets, a screen on the shelf will tell him how many people currently in the store have chosen that particular ___36___. As it turns out, such a "swarm moves" model ___37___ sales without the need to give people discounts. The reason is simple: it gives shoppers the ___38___ of knowing that they bought the "right" product—that is, the one everyone else bought.

The psychology that works in physical stores is just as ___39___ on the Internet. Online retailers such as Amazon are good at telling shoppers which products are popular with like-minded consumers. Even in the ___40___ of your home, you can still be part of the swarm.

(A) powerful　　(B) expensive　　(C) likely　　(D) informed
(E) persuades　　(F) increases　　(G) influence　　(H) privacy
(I) product　　(J) satisfaction

四、篇章結構（10分）

說明：　第 41 至 45 題，每題一個空格。請依文意在文章後所提供的 (A) 到 (E) 選項中分別選出最適當者，填入空格中，使篇章結構清晰有條理，並將其英文字母代號標示在答案卡之「選擇題答案區」。每題答對得 2 分，答錯或劃記多於一個選項者倒扣 1/2 分，倒扣到本大題之實得分數為零為止。未作答者，不給分亦不扣分。

第 41 至 45 題爲題組

Japan is dealing with a problem that's just starting to sweep the world—an aging population combined with a shrinking work force. ___41___ By so doing, it is hoped that Japan's government will save its increasingly burdened pension (i.e., payment received after retirement) system from going bankrupt. In 2000, the Japanese could get a full pension from the government at 60. ___42___ What's more, premiums paid by workers every month are set to rise while payouts they get after retirement fall.

To help workers to cope with this, Japan passed a law last year that requires companies by 2013 to raise their retirement age from 60 to 65 or rehire their retired workers. ___43___ In a country where forced layoffs are a last resort, large companies traditionally have relied on retirement to reduce payrolls. They were just about to enjoy a big cut in personnel costs because of the mass retirement of Japan's baby boomers. ___44___ Consequently, there was much opposition from corporations to the new retirement law. Early signs suggest that large corporations will hesitate in raising their retirement ages. ___45___ Violators of the new law would face only "administrative guidance," not penalties. Such resistance is hurting the effectiveness of the policies, which may thus prolong the aging problem.

(A) The new policy could be a strain for employers.

(B) Therefore, aged Japanese are now being encouraged to work longer in life.

(C) And, unlike the U.S., Japan has no law against discrimination based on age.

(D) But by 2025, they won't get any until they are 65.

(E) These people born between 1947 and 1949 make up 5.2 million members of the work force.

五、閱讀測驗（22 分）

說明：　第 46 至 56 題，每題請分別根據各篇文章的文意選出一個最適當的選
　　　　項，標示在答案卡之「選擇題答案區」。每題答對得 2 分，答錯或劃
　　　　記多於一個選項者倒扣 2/3 分，倒扣到本大題之實得分數爲零爲止。
　　　　未作答者，不給分亦不扣分。

第 46 至 49 題爲題組

　　Andrew Carnegie, once the world's richest person, was born in
1835 to a weaver's family in Scotland. As a child, he was expected to
follow his father's profession. But the industrial revolution destroyed
the weavers' craft, and the family had to leave for new possibilities in
America.

　　In 1848 the Carnegies arrived in Pittsburgh, then the
iron-manufacturing center of the country. Young Carnegie took odd
jobs at a cotton factory and later worked as a messenger boy in the
telegraph office. He was often asked to deliver messages to the city
theater, where he would stay to watch plays by great playwrights. He
also spent most of his leisure hours in a small library that a local
benefactor made available to working boys.

　　After the Civil War, Carnegie saw great potential in the iron
industry. He devoted himself to the replacement of wooden bridges
with stronger iron ones and earned a fortune. He further introduced a
new steel refining process to convert iron into steel. By 1900, Carnegie
Steel produced more of the metal than all of Great Britain.

　　However, Carnegie often expressed his uneasiness with the
businessman's life. Wishing to spend more time receiving instruction
and reading systematically, he once wrote, "To continue much longer
overwhelmed by business cares and with most of my thoughts wholly

upon the way to make more money in the shortest time, must degrade me beyond hope of permanent recovery." The strong desire for intellectual pursuit led him to sell his company and retire at 64.

Fond of saying that "the man who dies rich dies disgraced," Carnegie then turned his attention to giving away his fortune. He abhorred charity; instead, he used his money to help others help themselves. He established over 2,500 public libraries, and sponsored numerous cultural, educational and scientific institutions. By the time he died in 1919, he had given away 350 million dollars.

46. Why did Andrew Carnegie move to the United States?
　(A) Because his father was offered a good job in Pittsburgh.
　(B) Because he did not want to follow his father's profession.
　(C) Because there were serious political problems in Scotland.
　(D) Because his family could not make a good living in their hometown.

47. When did Carnegie begin to show his interest in artistic and intellectual pursuit?
　(A) After he retired from his business.
　(B) When he was a young boy back in Scotland.
　(C) After he earned his fortune from his iron business.
　(D) When he worked as a messenger boy in Pittsburgh.

48. Which of the following best characterizes how Carnegie managed his business?
　(A) He was willing to make new changes.
　(B) He set out to beat all the other competitors.
　(C) He was happy to make more money in the shortest time.
　(D) He did not hesitate in making investments in his hometown.

49. How did Carnegie handle his fortune after his retirement?
    (A) He left it to his family and friends after he died.
    (B) He gave it to poor people and charity organizations.
    (C) He used it to support organizations of higher learning.
    (D) He invested it in developing new technology in steel refinement.

第 50 至 52 題為題組

Most parents dread a note or call from school saying that their child's behavior is "not normal." If your child's academic performance and social life is suffering because they don't pay attention, can't sit still and act without thinking, it is most likely that they have AD/HD (Attention Deficit/ Hyperactivity Disorder).

AD/HD is a neurological disorder which stems not from the home environment, but from biological and genetic causes. Its symptoms typically show up in early childhood. The main characteristics are inattention, hyperactivity and impulsivity. Inattentive children have difficulty focusing on completing a task or learning something new. Hyperactive children always seem to be restless. Often they report that they need to stay busy and may try to do several tasks at once. Impulsive children often do not think before they act. They often blurt out inappropriate comments or have difficulty taking turns in conversation.

Most children can be inattentive, hyperactive, or impulsive at times. It is when these behaviors are inappropriate for their age and affect different areas in their lives that the disorder is diagnosed. Depression, anxiety, and learning disabilities may co-exist with AD/HD. Therefore, if a child is suspected of AD/HD, it is very important that he or she be evaluated by a professional.

Once your child is diagnosed with AD/HD, it is important to let the school know so that they can provide appropriate academic and social support. Your child's school should keep this information confidential and it can usually make accommodations in the classroom to fit your child's learning needs.

50. What is the cause of AD/HD?
    (A) Gene problem.
    (B) Academic pressure.
    (C) Illness in childhood.
    (D) Inappropriate home environment.

51. Which of the following are most likely AD/HD patients?
    (A) Children who are very lazy.
    (B) Children who are very attentive.
    (C) Children who act over-cautiously.
    (D) Children who have learning difficulties.

52. What is the first thing to do if your child is suspected of AD/HD?
    (A) Report it to the school.
    (B) Consult a professional.
    (C) Wait until the child grows up.
    (D) Send the child to a special school.

第 53 至 56 題為題組

Conflict diamonds, sometimes called blood diamonds, are diamonds that are sold to fund the unlawful and illegal operations of rebel, military and terrorist groups. Countries that have been most affected by conflict diamonds are Sierra Leone, Angola, Liberia and the Democratic Republic of Congo. They are places where citizens have been terrorized or even killed by groups in control of the local diamond trade.

Wars in most of those areas have ended or at least decreased in intensity, but the problem of conflict diamonds hasn't gone away. Diamonds mined in some rebel-held areas, such as Liberia, are being smuggled into neighboring countries and exported as conflict-free diamonds.

In order to stop blood diamond sales, South African countries with a legitimate diamond trade began a campaign in 2000 to track the origins of all rough diamonds. Their efforts resulted in the Kimberley Process Certification Scheme (KPCS), an international organization to make the world free of conflict diamonds. The goals of the KPCS are to document and track all rough diamonds when they enter a participating country. Shippers are required to place those diamonds in sealed boxes and provide enough detailed information about their origins to prove they did not originate in a conflict zone.

It's difficult for most of us to imagine what life is like in countries where diamonds are the source of so much chaos and suffering. Furthermore, the connection between terror and diamonds is not something that's reported heavily in the press. The 2006 movie *Blood Diamond*, starring Leonardo DiCaprio, should help make the issue more mainstream, if only temporarily. So, take some time to learn more about the problems that conflict diamonds create, and then follow your heart the next time you shop for a diamond.

53. Why are diamonds from some areas called "blood diamonds"?
    (A) They resemble blood in color.
    (B) They cause loss of human lives.
    (C) They represent love and passion.
    (D) They are of exceptionally high quality.

54. What can be inferred from the second paragraph of this passage?
  (A) Diamonds from Liberia are mostly conflict-free.
  (B) Most diamonds from Liberia are labeled correctly.
  (C) Diamonds in Liberia are still traded to support wars.
  (D) Diamonds from Liberia have been carefully investigated by the KPCS.

55. What is the major task of the KPCS?
  (A) To promote the sales of rough diamonds.
  (B) To produce movies like *Blood Diamond*.
  (C) To penalize those who sell blood diamonds.
  (D) To document where the diamonds were mined.

56. What is the author's attitude towards blood diamonds?
  (A) Indifferent.   (B) Threatening.
  (C) Sympathetic.   (D) Disapproving.

第貳部份：非選擇題（佔28分）

一、英文翻譯（8分）

說明： 1. 將下列兩句中文翻譯成適當之英文，並將答案寫在「答案卷」上。
　　　 2. 未按題意翻譯者，不予計分。

1. 大眾運輸的快速發展已逐漸縮短了都市和鄉村的距離。

2. 有了高速鐵路，我們可以在半天內往返台灣南北兩地。

二、英文作文（20分）

說明： 1. 依提示在「答案卷」上寫一篇英文作文。
　　　 2. 文長至少120個單詞。

提示： 你能想像一個沒有電（electricity）的世界嗎？請寫一篇文章，第一段描述我們的世界沒有了電以後，會是甚麼樣子，第二段說明這樣的世界是好是壞，並舉例解釋原因。

九十六年度指定科目考試英文科試題詳解

第壹部分：選擇題

一、詞彙：

1. (**C**) With his excellent social skills, Steven has been <u>perceived</u> as a great communicator by all his colleagues.

史蒂芬有極好的交際手腕，所有同事<u>看出</u>他是位卓越的溝通者。

(A) diagnose〔ˌdaɪəgˈnoz〕*v.* 診斷
(B) exploit〔ɪkˈsplɔɪt〕*v.* 利用；剝削
(C) **perceive**〔pəˈsiv〕*v.* 察覺
(D) concern〔kənˈsɝn〕*v.* 與…有關係

social〔ˈsoʃəl〕*adj.* 善交際的　　skill〔skɪl〕*n.* 手腕
communicator〔kəˈmjunəˌketə〕*n.* 溝通者
colleague〔ˈkalig〕*n.* 同事

2. (**B**) When you enter a building, be sure to look behind you and hold the door open for someone coming through the same door. It is a common <u>courtesy</u> in many cultures.

當你進到大樓時，務必要往你的後面看一下，並且要爲通過同扇門的人把門開著。在許多文化中，這是一般的<u>禮貌</u>。

(A) process〔ˈprasɛs〕*n.* 過程　　(B) **courtesy**〔ˈkɝtəsɪ〕*n.* 禮貌
(C) acceptance〔əkˈsɛptəns〕*n.* 接受
(D) operation〔ˌapəˈreʃən〕*n.* 操作；手術
be sure to 務必　　hold〔hold〕*v.* 使…保持

3. (**A**) The telephone has changed beyond <u>recognition</u> in recent years. In both form and function, it has become totally different from what it was before.

近年來，電話的演變已經使人完全<u>認</u>不出來。在外觀和功能上，都變得和以前完全不同了。

(A) *recognition* 〔͵rɛkəg'nɪʃən〕 *n.* 認識；認得

(B) possession〔pə'zɛʃən〕 *n.* 擁有

(C) prevention〔prɪ'vɛnʃən〕 *n.* 預防

(D) appreciation〔ə͵priʃɪ'eʃən〕 *n.* 欣賞；感激

beyond recognition　使人完全認不出來

recent〔'risn̩t〕 *adj.* 近來的

form〔fɔrm〕 *n.* 外觀　　function〔'fʌŋkʃən〕 *n.* 功能

4. (**C**) Though Jack has moved out of his parents' house, he is <u>financially</u> dependent on them still. They send him a check every month for his living expenses.

雖然傑克已經從他父母的房子搬出去了，但他在<u>財務上</u>仍依賴他們。他們每個月寄給他一張支票作為他的生活費。

(A) radically〔'rædɪkl̩ɪ〕 *adv.* 完全地

(B) physically〔'fɪzɪkl̩ɪ〕 *adv.* 在肉體上

(C) *financially*〔faɪ'nænʃəlɪ〕 *adv.* 財務上

(D) politically〔pə'lɪtɪkl̩ɪ〕 *adv.* 政治上

5. (**D**) If you want to keep your computer from being attacked by new viruses, you need to constantly renew and <u>update</u> your anti-virus software. 如果你想避免你的電腦遭到新的病毒侵襲，你需要常常<u>更新</u>你的防毒軟體。

(A) confirm〔kən'fɝm〕 *v.* 確認

(B) overlook〔ovɚ'luk〕 *v.* 監視；俯瞰

(C) esteem〔ə'stim〕 *v.* 尊重

(D) *update*〔ʌp'det〕 *v.* 更新

attack〔ə'tæk〕 *v.* 侵襲　　virus〔'vaɪrəs〕 *n.* 病毒

constantly〔'kɑnstəntlɪ〕 *adv.* 常常　　renew〔rɪ'nju〕 *v.* 更新

software〔'sɔft͵wɛr〕 *n.* 軟體

6. (**D**) Many factors may explain why people are addicted to the Internet. One facter <u>contributing</u> to this phenomenon is the easy access to the Net.

有很多原因可以解釋，為什麼人們沈迷於網際網路。促成這個現象的
其中一個原因，是由於網路容易取得。

(A) advance〔əd'væns〕v. 促進；前進

(B) occur〔ə'kɝ〕v. 發生

(C) respond〔rɪ'spɑnd〕v. 回答

(D) *contribute*〔kən'trɪbjut〕v. 促成；貢獻

factor〔'fæktɚ〕n. 原因　　explain〔ɪk'splen〕v. 解釋
Internet〔'ɪntɚ,nɛt〕n. 網際網路
addicted〔ə'dɪktɪd〕adj. 沈溺於…的　　*be addicted to*… 沈溺於…
contribute to… 促成　　phenomenon〔fə'nɑmə,nɑn〕n. 現象
access〔'æksɛs〕n. 接近；取得

7. (**B**) We were <u>anxiously</u> awaiting the results of the school's annual
English drama contest. Our class won the first place last year,
and we certainly wanted to win again this year.
我們<u>焦慮地</u>等著學校年度英語戲劇比賽的結果。去年我們班得到冠
軍，今年我們當然想再贏一次。

(A) consciously〔'kɑnʃəslɪ〕adv. 有意識地

(B) *anxiously*〔'æŋkʃəslɪ〕adv. 焦慮地；不安地

(C) fortunately〔'fɔrtʃənɪtlɪ〕adv. 幸運地

(D) competently〔'kɑmpətəntlɪ〕adv. 勝任地

await〔ə'wet〕v. 等待　　result〔rɪ'zʌlt〕n. 結果；成績
annual〔'ænjʊəl〕adj. 每年的；年度的
drama〔'drɑmə〕n. 戲劇　　contest〔'kɑntɛst〕n. 比賽
the first place 冠軍　　*win the first place* 得到冠軍
certainly〔'sɝtn̩lɪ〕adv. 無疑地；必定

8. (**A**) Tropical rainforests are home to about one million plant and
animal species. If the rainforests disappear, many of these species
will become <u>extinct</u>.
熱帶雨林是將近一百萬種動植物的家。如果雨林消失了，這些物種
很多都會<u>絕種</u>。

(A) *extinct* 〔 ɪk'stɪŋkt 〕 *adj.* 絕種的

(B) hostile 〔'hɑstɪl 〕 *adj.* 敵對的

(C) mature 〔 mə'tʃʊr 〕 *adj.* 成熟的

(D) intimate 〔'ɪntəmɪt 〕 *adj.* 親密的

tropical 〔'trɑpɪkḷ 〕 *adj.* 熱帶的　　　rainforest 〔'ren,fɔrɪst 〕 *n.* 雨林

tropical rainforest 熱帶雨林　　　species 〔'spiʃɪz 〕 *n.* 物種

disappear 〔,dɪsə'pɪr 〕 *v.* 消失

9. (**B**) An honest person is faithful to his promise.　Once he makes a
<u>commitment</u>, he will not go back on his own word.

一個正直的人會信守諾言。一旦他許下<u>承諾</u>，他就不會違背他自己
的諾言。

(A) prescription 〔 prɪ'skrɪpʃən 〕 *n.* 法令；處方

(B) *commitment* 〔 kə'mɪtmənt 〕 *n.* 承諾；約定

(C) frustration 〔 frʌs'treʃən 〕 *n.* 挫折

(D) transcript 〔'træn,skrɪpt 〕 *n.* 副本；成績報告單

honest 〔'ɑnɪst 〕 *adj.* 誠實的；正直的

faithful 〔'feθfəl 〕 *adj.* 忠實的；守信的

faithful to 忠於　　　promise 〔'prɑmɪs 〕 *n.* 諾言；約定

faithful to one's *promise* 信守諾言　　　*go back on* 違背

word 〔 wɝd 〕 *n.* 諾言；約定

10. (**D**) The new computer game Wii provides us with an <u>innovative</u> way of
exercising.　People now may play sports in their living rooms,
which was unimaginable before.

Wii 這個新的電腦遊戲，給我們提供了一種<u>創</u>新的運動方式。人們現
在可以在他們的客廳裡運動，這在以前是無法想像的。

(A) outgoing 〔'aʊt,goɪŋ 〕 *adj.* 外出的；外向的

(B) urgent 〔'ɝdʒənt 〕 *adj.* 緊急的

(C) aggressive 〔 ə'grɛsɪv 〕 *adj.* 侵略的；積極的

(D) *innovative* 〔'ɪno,vetɪv 〕 *adj.* 創新的

provide 〔 prə'vaɪd 〕 *v.* 提供

unimaginable 〔,ʌnɪ'mædʒɪnəbḷ 〕 *adj.* 無法想像的

二、綜合測驗：

第 11 至 15 題為題組

Recent studies show that levels of happiness for most people change throughout their lives. In a British study between 1991 and 2003, people were asked how satisfied they are <u>with</u> their lives. The resulting statistics
11
graph shows a smile-shaped curve. Most of the people <u>start off</u> happy and
12
become progressively less happy as they grow older. For many of them, the most miserable period in their life is their 40s. <u>After that</u>, their levels of
13
happiness climb. Furthermore, it seems that men are slightly happier on average than women in their teens, but women bounce back and overtake men <u>later</u> in life. The low point seems to last longer for women — throughout
14
their 30s and 40s, only climbing <u>once</u> women reach 50. Men, on the other
15
hand, have the lowest point in their 40s, going up again when they reach 50.

最近的研究顯示，對大部分人而言，幸福的程度在人的一生當中會有轉變。在一九九一年到二零零三年的一份英國研究報告裡，當人們被問及對生活有多麼滿意時，統計圖表的結果呈現微笑的曲線。大部分的人在一開始是開心的，隨著年紀增長，他們逐漸變得較不快樂。對很多人而言，一生當中最悲慘的時期是四十幾歲的時候。在那之後，幸福程度會爬升。此外，以平均值來看，男性在十幾歲的時候似乎比女性愉快，但之後女性折返回來便超越男性。女性在最低點持續較長的時間－在她們三十到四十歲之間，一旦到了五十歲才上升。另一方面，男性在四十歲時達到最低點，當他們五十歲的時候才又再度爬升。

> satisfied〔ˈsætɪsˌfaɪd〕adj. 滿意的
> statistic〔stəˈtɪstɪk〕n. 統計值
> graph〔græf〕n. 圖表　　curve〔kɝv〕n. 曲線
> progressively〔prəˈɡrɛsɪvlɪ〕adv. 漸進地
> miserable〔ˈmɪzərəbḷ〕adj. 悲慘的
> furthermore〔ˈfɝðɚˌmor〕adv. 還有；此外
> slightly〔ˈslaɪtlɪ〕adv. 稍微地　　average〔ˈævərɪdʒ〕n. 平均
> bounce〔baʊns〕v. 反彈　　overtake〔ˌovɚˈtek〕v. 超過
> **on the other hand** 另一方面

11. (**B**) *be satisfied with* 對…感到滿意，故選 (B)。

12. (**C**) 依句意，選 (C) *start off*「一開始」。而 (A) end up「最後」；(B) pass by「經過」，(D) go on「繼續」，均不合句意。

13. (**A**) 依句意，選 (A) *After that*「在那之後」。而 (B) by that time「到了那個時候」，(C) not…for long「…不會很久」，(D) before now「以前」，則不合句意。

14. (**B**) 依句意，「後來」就趕上男人了，選 (B) *later*。而 (A) sooner「較快」，(C) earlier「較早」，(D)「較慢」，均不合句意。

15. (**A**) 依句意，「一旦」女人到了五十歲，選 (A) *once*。而 (B) unless「除非」，(C) 在…之前，(D) 自從，均不合句意。

第 16 至 20 題為題組

  The northern lights, known as the aurora borealis, is one of nature's most dazzling spectacles. Science is still not certain <u>as to</u> exactly what
16

these lights are and what causes them. Sometimes, the brilliant rays of light spread upward in the shape of a fan. <u>At other times</u>, they flash here and
17

there like giant searchlights. Farther north, the aurora frequently looks like fiery draperies which hang from the sky and sway <u>to and fro</u> while flames
18

of red, orange, green, and blue play up and down the moving folds.

  北方之光，又稱爲北極光，是大自然最耀眼的奇觀之一。科學家仍不能精準地確定這些光線是什麼，或是造成他們的原因。有時，這些絢爛奪目的光線扇狀地往空中伸展。其他時候，他們像探照燈似的閃來閃去。到了更北方，北極光常常看起來像在燃燒的窗簾布，懸掛在空中來回地搖擺，而紅色、橘色、綠色以及藍色的火焰在摺層間上下玩耍。

  aurora〔ə'rorə〕*n.* 極光 ***aurora borealis*** 北極光
  dazzling〔'dæzlɪŋ〕*adj.* 耀眼的 spectacle〔'spɛktəkl̩〕*n.* 奇觀
  certain〔'sɝtn̩〕*adj.* 確定的 exactly〔ɪg'zæktlɪ〕*adv.* 精確地
  brilliant〔'brɪljənt〕*adj.* 絢爛奪目的 ray〔re〕*n.* 光線

> spread〔sprɛd〕v. 伸展　　searchlight〔'sɝtʃˏlaɪt〕n. 探照燈的光
> fiery〔'faɪərɪ〕adj. 燃燒般的　　drapery〔'drepərɪ〕n. 窗簾布
> fold〔fold〕n. 折疊；摺層

16. (**C**) 依句意，選 (C) **as to**「關於」。而 (A) due to「由於」，(B) instead of
「而不是」，(D) in spite of「儘管」，則不合句意。

17. (**B**) 因前有 sometimes（有時候），故選 (B) **At other times**（在別的時
候）。而 (A) at one time（曾經；一度），(C) at all times（總是），
(D) at the same time（同時），則不合句意。

18. (**C**) (A) here and now　就在現在；現在此刻
(B) by and large　大體而言；一般說來
(C) **to and fro**　來回地（＝*back and forth*）
(D) more and more　越來越

　　According to scientific measurements, this discharge of light
<u>takes place</u> from 50 to 100 miles above the earth. It is seen <u>at its best</u>
　　19　　　　　　　　　　　　　　　　　　　　　　　　　　　　20
around the Hudson Bay region in Canada, in northern Scotland, and in
southern Norway and Sweden.

　　根據科學測量，這些光線的釋放在地球上方五十到一百哩的地方進行。看
的最清楚的地方是加拿大的哈德遜灣區，蘇格蘭北方，以及挪威和瑞典南方。

> measurement〔'mɛʒəmənt〕n. 測量
> discharge〔dɪs'tʃɑrdʒ〕n. 放出；流出
> **Hudson Bay**　哈得遜灣（位於加拿大東北部的海灣）
> region〔'ridʒən〕n. 地區　　Scotland〔'skɑtlənd〕n. 蘇格蘭
> Norway〔'nɔrwe〕n. 挪威　　Sweden〔'swidn̩〕n. 瑞典

19. (**A**) 空格應填動詞，且依句意為現在式，故選 (A) **takes place**「產生；
發生」。

20. (**D**) 依句意，選 (D) **at its best**「在它最佳的狀態」。而 (A) in the least
「一點也（不）」，(B) on the whole「大體而言」，(D) for its sake
「為了它的緣故」，均不合句意。

第 21 至 25 題爲題組

Average global temperature has increased by almost 1° F over the past century. Scientists expect it to increase an <u>additional</u> 2° to 6° F over
21
the next one hundred years. This may not sound like much, but it could change the Earth's climate as <u>never</u> before.
22

在過去的一世紀裡，全球平均氣溫上升了將近華氏一度。科學家預估，接下來的一百年內會再上升二到六度。這聽起來似乎不怎麼樣，但是卻可能會史無前例的改變地球的氣候。

> average〔ˋævərɪdʒ〕*adj.* 平均的　　global〔ˋglobḷ〕*adj.* 全球的
> temperature〔ˋtɛmpərətʃɚ〕*n.* 氣溫　　past〔pæst〕*adj.* 過去的
> expect〔ɪkˋspɛkt〕*v.* 預期

21. (**B**) (A) extreme〔ɪkˋstrim〕*adj.* 極端的
　　　　 (B) ***additional***〔əˋdɪʃənḷ〕*adj.* 額外的；添加的
　　　　 (C) immediate〔ɪˋmidɪɪt〕*adj.* 立即的
　　　　 (D) original〔əˋrɪdʒənḷ〕*adj.* 最初的

22. (**B**) 依句意，選 (B) ***as never before*** 「前所未有地」。而 (A) as～as ever
　　　　「像往常一樣～」，(C) as always「像平常一樣；始終」，(D) as yet
　　　　「到目前爲止；至今」，則不合句意。

Climate change may affect people's health both directly and indirectly. For instance, heat stress and other heat-related health problems are caused directly by very warm temperatures. <u>Indirectly</u>, human health can also be
23
affected by ecological disturbances, changes in food and water supplies, as well as coastal flooding. How people and nature <u>adapt to</u> climate change
24
will determine how seriously it affects human health. Generally, poor people and poor countries are <u>less</u> probable to have the money and resources
25
they need to cope with health problems due to climate change.

氣候的改變可能直接地與間接地影響人的健康。舉例來說，熱壓力以及其他與熱度有關的健康問題，都是由高溫所直接引起的。人體的健康也可能會間接地被生態的擾亂，食物與水分供給的改變，以及沿海岸的水災所影響。人類與大自然如何適應氣候變遷，將會決定它影響人體健康的程度。普遍來說，貧窮的人民與國家，比較不可能有所需的錢與資源，來對付氣候變遷所引起的健康問題。

> directly〔dəˈrɛktlɪ〕adv. 直接地
> indirectly〔ˌɪndəˈrɛktlɪ〕adv. 間接地　*for instance* 例如
> heat〔hit〕n. 熱　　　stress〔strɛs〕n. 壓力
> ecological〔ˌikəˈlɑdʒɪkḷ〕adj. 生態的
> disturbance〔dɪˈstɝbəns〕n. 擾亂
> supply〔səˈplaɪ〕n. 供給　　coastal〔ˈkostḷ〕adj. 沿海的
> flooding〔ˈflʌdɪŋ〕n. 氾濫　　cope〔kop〕v. 對付；處理

23. (**D**)　(A) suddenly〔ˈsʌdn̩lɪ〕adv. 突然地
　　　　　(B) previously〔ˈprivɪəslɪ〕adv. 以前
　　　　　(C) exclusively〔ɪkˈsklusɪvlɪ〕adv. 專門地；僅
　　　　　(D) *indirectly*〔ˌɪndəˈrɛktlɪ〕adv. 間接地

24. (**C**)　依句意，選 (C) *adapt to*「適應」。而 (A) result from「起因於」，
　　　　　(B) count on「依賴」，(D) stand for「代表」，均不合句意。

25. (**A**)　依句意，「較不」可能有所需要的錢和資源，選 (A) *less*。而 (B) 非常，
　　　　　(C) 最，(D) further〔ˈfɝðɚ〕adv. 更進一步地，均不合句意。

第 26 至 30 題為題組

The Kingdom of Bhutan is a landlocked nation situated between India and China. The entire country is mountainous, <u>with the exception of</u> a
　　　　　　　　　　　　　　　　　　　　　　　　　26
small strip of subtropical plains in the extreme south. The elevation gain from the subtropical plains to the glacier-covered Himalayan heights exceeds 7,000 m. Its traditional <u>economy</u> is based on forestry, animal
　　　　　　　　　　　　　　27
husbandry and subsistence agriculture. However, these <u>account for</u> less
　　　　　　　　　　　　　　　　　　　　　　　　　28
than 50% of the GDP now that Bhutan has become an exporter of hydroelectricity. Besides, cash crops and tourism are also <u>significant</u>.
　　　　　　　　　　　　　　　　　　　　　　　　　　　　　　　29

　　不丹王國是一個位於印度和中國之間的內陸國家。除了極南端的一片亞熱帶平原以外，整個國家都是山地。此亞熱帶平原與被冰河覆蓋的喜馬拉雅高地的高度差超過七千公尺。此國的傳統經濟活動是林業、畜牧業，以及溫飽型農業。但是，現在不丹成為了水力發電出口國，所以這些活動佔國內生產毛額不到百分之五十。除此之外，商業作物以及觀光業也十分重要。

　　kingdom〔'kɪŋdəm〕n. 王國　　Bhutan〔bu'tɑn〕n. 不丹
　　landlocked〔'lænd,lɑkt〕adj. 被陸地所包圍的
　　situate〔'sɪtʃu,et〕v. 位於　　entire〔ɪn'taɪr〕adj. 全部的
　　mountainous〔'mauntn̩əs〕adj. 多山的
　　strip〔strɪp〕n. 細長的土地
　　subtropical〔sʌb'trɑpɪkl̩〕adj. 亞熱帶的
　　plain〔plen〕n. 平原　　extreme〔ɪk'strim〕adj. 極度的
　　elevation〔,ɛlə've∫ən〕n. 高度　　gain〔gen〕v. 得到
　　glacier〔'gle∫ɚ〕n. 冰河　　Himalayan〔hɪ'mɑljən〕n. 喜馬拉雅的
　　height〔haɪt〕n. 高地　　exceed〔ɪk'sid〕v. 超過
　　foresty〔'fɔrɪstrɪ〕n. 林業　　husbandry〔'hʌzbəndrɪ〕n. 農業
　　subsistence〔səb'sɪstəns〕n.（最低限度的）生計
　　agriculture〔'ægrɪ,kʌltʃɚ〕n. 農業　　*GDP* 國內生產毛額
　　hydroelectricity〔,haɪdroɪ,lɛk'trɪsətɪ〕n. 水力發電
　　cash crop 在市場上出售的農作物；商品農作物
　　tourism〔'turɪzəm〕n. 觀光

26.（**C**）依句意，選 (C) *with the exception of*「除了」（= *except*）。而 (A) in terms of「就～而言」，(B) as a part of「身為～的一部份」，(D) in accordance with「依照；與…一致」，則不合句意。

27.（**D**）(A) culture〔'kʌltʃɚ〕n. 文化
　　　(B) politics〔'pɑlətɪks〕n. 政治學
　　　(C) religion〔rɪ'lɪdʒən〕n. 宗教
　　　(D) *economy*〔ɪ'kɑnəmɪ〕n. 經濟

28.（**C**）「佔」不到 GDP 的百分之五十，選 (C) *account for*「佔～」。而 (A) figure out「了解」，(B) relate to「與…有關」，(D) conform to「遵守」，均不合句意。

29. (**A**) (A) *significant* 〔 sɪgˋnɪfəkənt 〕 *adj.* 重要的；意義重大的

(B) durable 〔ˋdjʊrəbḷ 〕 *adj.* 持久的；耐用的

(C) frequent 〔ˋfrikwənt 〕 *adj.* 經常的

(D) expressive 〔 ɪkˋsprɛsɪv 〕 *adj.* 表達的

Bhutan is one of the most isolated nations in the world, <u>with</u> foreign
                                                                        30
influences and tourism regulated by the government to preserve its
traditional Tibetan Buddhist culture. It is often described as the last
surviving refuge of traditional Himalayan Buddhist culture.

不丹是全世界最孤立的國家之一，政府為了保存其傳統的藏傳佛教文化，
而控管外國的影響力以及觀光業。不丹往往被喻為是傳統喜馬拉雅佛教文化僅
存的避難所。

influence 〔ˋɪnflʊəns 〕 *n.* 影響　　regulate 〔ˋrɛgjəˏlet 〕 *v.* 管理
preserve 〔 prɪˋzɝv 〕 *v.* 保存　　Tibetan 〔 tɪˋbɛtn̩ 〕 *adj.* 西藏的
Buddhist 〔ˋbʊdɪst 〕 *n.* 佛教徒　　describe 〔 dɪˋskraɪb 〕 *v.* 形容
surviving 〔 səˋvaɪvɪŋ 〕 *adj.* 繼續存在的
refuge 〔ˋrɛfjudʒ 〕 *v.* 避難處

30. (**B**) 表「具有」，介系詞用 *with*，選 (B)。

三、文意選填：

第 31 至 40 題為題組

A trip to the supermarket has now become an exercise in psychological
warfare. Shopkeepers know that filling a store with the smell of freshly
baked bread makes people feel hungry and <u>persuades</u> them to buy more
                                                    31
food than they intended. Stocking the most <u>expensive</u> products at eye level
                                                      32
helps them sell faster than cheaper but less visible competitors.

現在，跑一趟超級市場已經成為一場心理戰的演習了。店家知道讓店裡充
滿現烤麵包的香味，會使人覺得飢餓，並且說服他們買比預期更多的食物。將
最貴的商品擺放在可見之處，會幫助這些產品賣的比較便宜，可見度卻較低的
競爭者要好。

trip〔trɪp〕*n.* 跑一趟　　exercise〔'ɛksə,saɪz〕*n.* 演習
psychological〔,saɪkə'lɑdʒɪkḷ〕*adj.* 心理的
warfare〔'wɔr,fɛr〕*n.* 戰爭　　shopkeeper〔'ʃɑp,kipə〕*n.* 店主
freshly〔'frɛʃlɪ〕*adv.* 最近；剛剛　　persuade〔pə'swed〕*v.* 說服
intend〔ɪn'tɛnd〕*v.* 預期　　stock〔stɑk〕*v.* 庫存
visible〔'vɪzəbḷ〕*adj.* 看的見的
competitor〔kəm'pɛtətə〕*n.* 競爭者

31.(**E**)　依句意，選 (E) ***persuade***〔pə'swed〕*v.* 說服。

32.(**B**)　依句意，該空格要與後面的 cheaper 對比，選 (B) ***expensive***
〔ɪk'spɛnsɪv〕*adj.* 昂貴的。

　　Researchers on customer behavior are now investigating how "swarm
intelligence" (that is, how social animals like ants or bees behave in a crowd)
can be used to <u>influence</u> what people buy.　The idea is that, if a certain
　　　　　　　　　33
product is seen to be popular, shoppers are <u>likely</u> to choose it too.　With
　　　　　　　　　　　　　　　　　　　　34
the help of modern technology, some supermarkets are now able to keep
customers <u>informed</u> about what others are buying.　As a customer walks
　　　　　　35
past a shelf of goods in one of these supermarkets, a screen on the shelf will
tell him how many people currently in the store have chosen that particular
<u>product</u>.　As it turns out, such a "swarm moves" model <u>increases</u> sales
36　　　　　　　　　　　　　　　　　　　　　　　　　　　37
without the need to give people discounts.　The reason is simple: it gives
shoppers the <u>satisfaction</u> of knowing that they bought the "right" product—
　　　　　　　　38
that is, the one everyone else bought.

　　消費者行為研究員現在正在研究如何利用「蟲群智慧」（也就是群居的動
物，如螞蟻和蜜蜂，在群體中的行為）來影響人們所買的東西。這個想法是，
如果某一項產品被視為受歡迎的產品，顧客很有可能會選這項產品。藉著現代
科技的幫助，現在有些超級市場可以告知顧客其他人在買些什麼。當一個顧客
在這種超級市場，走過一個裝滿商品的架子時，架子上的螢幕會告訴他此刻店

裡有多少人選了那樣產品。結果證明，這種「蟲群行為」的模型，就算不給人們折扣，也能增加商品的銷售量。其原因很簡單：這種行為使消費者滿足，因為他們知道他們買到「對」的產品──也就是其他人都在買的產品。

swarm〔swɔrm〕n. 蟲群　　intelligence〔ɪn'tɛlədʒəns〕n. 智慧
social〔'soʃəl〕adj. 群居的　　crowd〔kraʊd〕n. 群
influence〔'ɪnfluəns〕v. 影響　　shelf〔ʃɛlf〕n. 架子
screen〔skrin〕n. 螢幕　　**turn out** 結果
discount〔'dɪskaʊnt〕n. 折扣

33.(**G**) 依句意，選 (G) *influence*〔'ɪnfluəns〕v. 影響。

34.(**C**) 依句意，選 (C) *likely*〔'laɪklɪ〕adj. 很可能的。

35.(**D**) 依句意，選 (D) *informed*〔ɪn'fɔrm〕v. 告知。

36.(**I**) 依句意，選 (I) *product*〔'prɑdəkt〕n. 產品。

37.(**F**) 依句意，選 (F) *increase*〔ɪn'kris〕v. 增加。

38.(**J**) 依句意，選 (J) *satisfaction*〔ˌsætɪs'fækʃən〕n. 滿足。

The psychology that works in physical stores is just as <u>powerful</u> on
the Internet. Online retailers such as Amazon are good at telling shoppers
which products are popular with like-minded consumers. Even in the
<u>privacy</u> of your home, you can still be part of the swarm.

用於實體店面的心理學，到了網路上一樣非常有效。亞馬遜等線上零售商擅長告訴顧客，哪些產品在志趣相投的消費者間很受歡迎。就算是在家中獨處的情況之下，你仍然可以是蟲群的一部分。

psychology〔saɪ'kɑlədʒɪ〕n. 心理學
physical〔'fɪzɪkl̩〕adj. 實體的；物質的
online〔'ɑnˌlaɪn〕adj. 網路上的；線上的
retailer〔'ritelɚ〕n. 零售商
like-minded〔'laɪk'maɪndɪd〕adj. 志趣相投的；看法一致的
privacy〔'praɪvəsɪ〕n. 獨處；隱私

39. (**A**) 依句意，選 (A) *powerful* 〔'pauɚfəl 〕*adj.* 效力大的；作用大的。

40. (**H**) 依句意，選 (H) *privacy* 〔'praɪvəsɪ 〕*n.* 獨處；隱私。

四、篇章結構：

第 41 至 45 題為題組

Japan is dealing with a problem that's just starting to sweep the world— an aging population combined with a shrinking work force. ⁴¹ (B) Therefore, aged Japanese are now being encouraged to work longer in life. By so doing, it is hoped that Japan's government will save its increasingly burdened pension (i.e., payment received after retirement) system from going bankrupt. In 2000, the Japanese could get a full pension from the government at 60. ⁴² (D) But by 2025, they won't get any until they are 65. What's more, premiums paid by workers every month are set to rise while payouts they get after retirement fall.

　　日本面對著一個正在席捲全球的問題－老化的人口結構，以及縮水的勞動力。因此，政府鼓勵年老的日本人多工作幾年。透過這種行為，日本政府希望能夠拯救負擔日益沉重的退休金（即退休後的薪水）系統破產。在 2000 年，日本人在六十歲時，就可以獲得政府的全額退休金。但是到了 2025 年，直到六十五歲時，他們都無法拿到任何退休金。再者，工作人員每月所付的津貼將調漲，而退休後所獲得的支出將會減少。

sweep 〔 swip 〕*v.* 席捲	aging 〔'edʒɪŋ 〕*adj.* 老化
population 〔ˌpɑpjə'leʃən 〕*n.* 人口	shrink 〔 ʃrɪŋk 〕*v.* 縮小
work force 勞動力	burden 〔'ɪnflʊəns 〕*v.* 加負擔於
pension 〔'pɛnʃən 〕*n.* 退休金	retirement 〔 rɪ'taɪrmənt 〕*n.* 退休
bankrupt 〔'bæŋkrʌpt 〕*adj.* 破產的	premium 〔'primɪəm 〕*n.* 津貼
payout 〔'peˌaʊt 〕*n.* 支出	

To help workers to cope with this, Japan passed a law last year that requires companies by 2013 to raise their retirement age from 60 to 65 or rehire their retired workers. ⁴³ (A) The new policy could be a strain for

<u>employers.</u>　In a country where forced layoffs are a last resort, large companies traditionally have relied on retirement to reduce payrolls.　They were just about to enjoy a big cut in personnel costs because of the mass retirement of Japan's baby boomers.　[44] <u>(E) These people born between 1947 and 1949 make up 5.2 million members of the work force.</u>　Consequently, there was much opposition from corporations to the new retirement law. Early signs suggest that large corporations will hesitate in raising their retirement ages.　[45] <u>(C) And, unlike the U.S., Japan has no law against discrimination based on age.</u>　Violators of the new law would face only "administrative guidance," not penalties.　Such resistance is hurting the effectiveness of the policies, which may thus prolong the aging problem.

　　爲了讓勞動者能夠對付這種情形，日本去年通過一個法案，規定到 2013 年時，公司必須把退休的年齡從六十歲調到六十五歲，或是再雇用退休的人員。這個新的政策，對雇主可能會是一個負擔。在一個強制解雇是最後手段的國家裡，大公司傳統上都是透過退休來減少薪資支出。因爲日本嬰兒潮時代的大量退休，公司才正要享受大幅的人事支出減少。在 1947 到 1949 出生的人，構成了勞動力的五百二十萬人。因此，企業對於新的退休法，非常的反對。最初的現象顯示，大公司將不願提升退休年齡。而且，跟美國不同的是，日本並沒有防止年齡歧視的法律。新法規的觸犯者，只會面對「行政輔導」，而非處罰。這一類的抵抗，降低了政策的效果，進而可能拖延老化的問題。

cope〔kop〕v. 對付　　***cope with*** 對付；處理
rehire〔ri'haɪr〕v. 再雇用　　strain〔stren〕n. 負擔
employer〔ɪm'plɔɪɚ〕n. 雇主　　forced〔forst〕adj. 強迫的
layoff〔'le͵ɔf〕n. 解雇　　resort〔rɪ'zɔrt〕n. 憑藉的手段
last resort 最後的手段　　payroll〔'pe͵rol〕n. 薪水總額
personnel〔͵pɝsn'ɛl〕n. 人員；員工
baby boomer 嬰兒潮時代出生的人　　***make up*** 組成；構成
consequently〔'kɑnsə͵kwɛntlɪ〕adv. 因此
corporation〔͵kɔrpə'reʃən〕n. 股份有限公司
hesitate〔'hɛzə͵tet〕v. 有疑慮；不願意
discrimination〔dɪ͵skrɪmə'neʃən〕n. 歧視

　　violator〔'vaɪə,letə〕n. 違反者
　　administrative〔əd'mɪnə,stretɪv〕v. 行政的；管理的
　　guidance〔'gaɪdn̩s〕n. 輔導　　penalty〔'pɛnl̩tɪ〕n. 處罰
　　prolong〔prə'lɔŋ〕v. 拖延

五、閱讀測驗：

第 46 至 49 題爲題組

　　Andrew Carnegie, once the world's richest person, was born in 1835 to a weaver's family in Scotland. As a child, he was expected to follow his father's profession. But the industrial revolution destroyed the weavers' craft, and the family had to leave for new possibilities in America.

　　安德魯‧卡內基曾是世界上最富有的人，於 1835 年誕生在蘇格蘭一戶以編織爲業的家庭。當他還是小孩的時候，就被期望能繼承衣缽。但工業革命卻摧毀了編織這項手工業，而他們一家人也必須爲開拓嶄新的未來而前往美國。

　　weaver〔'wivə〕n. 織工
　　Scotland〔'skɑtlənd〕n. 蘇格蘭（英國的一部分，位在大不列顛島的北部）
　　expect〔ɪk'spɛkt〕v. 期望　　profession〔prə'fɛʃən〕n. 職業
　　industrial〔ɪn'dʌstrɪəl〕adj. 工業的
　　revolution〔,rɛvə'luʃən〕n. 革命
　　destroy〔dɪ'strɔɪ〕v. 破壞　　craft〔kræft〕n. 行業；手工業
　　possibility〔,pɑsə'bɪlətɪ〕n. 可能性

　　In 1848 the Carnegies arrived in Pittsburgh, then the iron-manufacturing center of the country. Young Carnegie took odd jobs at a cotton factory and later worked as a messenger boy in the telegraph office. He was often asked to deliver messages to the city theater, where he would stay to watch plays by great playwrights. He also spent most of his leisure hours in a small library that a local benefactor made available to working boys.

　　卡內基於 1848 年抵達匹茲堡，那是當時全國的鋼鐵製造中心。年輕的卡內基在一家棉花工廠打零工，之後在一家電報公司擔任信差，他常必須送信去城裡的劇院，便會留在那裡欣賞偉大劇作家的作品。他大部分有空時，會待在一間由當地捐助者，特別爲打工少年所成立的小圖書館。

Pittsburgh〔ˈpɪtsbɝg〕*n.* 匹茲堡
iron-manufacturing〔ˈaɪən͵mænjəˈfæktʃərɪŋ〕*adj.* 製造鋼鐵的
take odd jobs 打零工　　cotton〔ˈkɑtn̩〕*n.* 棉花
messenger〔ˈmɛsn̩dʒɚ〕*n.* 信差　　telegraph〔ˈtɛlə͵græf〕*n.* 電報
deliver〔dɪˈlɪvɚ〕*v.* 傳送　　message〔ˈmɛsɪdʒ〕*n.* 信息
play〔ple〕*n.* 戲劇　　playwright〔ˈple͵raɪt〕*n.* 劇作家
leisure〔ˈliʒɚ〕*n.* 空閒　　local〔ˈlokl̩〕*adj.* 當地的
benefactor〔ˈbɛnə͵fæktɚ〕*n.* 捐助者
available〔əˈveləbl̩〕*adj.* 可得到的；可用的

After the Civil War, Carnegie saw great potential in the iron industry.
He devoted himself to the replacement of wooden bridges with stronger iron
ones and earned a fortune. He further introduced a new steel refining
process to convert iron into steel. By 1900, Carnegie Steel produced more of
the metal than all of Great Britain.

南北戰爭之後，卡內基看見了鋼鐵工業的極佳潛能，便致力於將木橋替換
爲較堅固的鐵橋的工作，並因而大發利市。他更進一步採用一套新的鋼鐵提煉
過程，將鐵轉換爲鋼。到了 1900 年，卡內基鋼鐵便已製造出比全英國更多的鋼
鐵。

Civil War 南北戰爭　　potential〔pəˈtɛnʃəl〕*n.* 潛能
industry〔ˈɪndəstrɪ〕*n.* 工業　　devote〔dɪˈvot〕*v.* 致力於
replacement〔rɪˈplesmənt〕*n.* 替換　　wooden〔ˈwudn̩〕*adj.* 木製的
earn a fortune 發大財 (= *make a fortune*)
further〔ˈfɝðɚ〕*adv.* 更進一步　　introduce〔͵ɪntrəˈdjus〕*v.* 採用；引進
refine〔rɪˈfaɪn〕*v.* 提煉；精煉　　process〔ˈprɑsɛs〕*n.* 步驟；程序
convert〔kənˈvɝt〕*v.* 轉換；轉變　　produce〔prəˈdjus〕*v.* 製造；生產
metal〔ˈmɛtl̩〕*n.* 鑄鐵；金屬　　***Great Britain*** 大不列顚；英國

However, Carnegie often expressed his uneasiness with the
businessman's life. Wishing to spend more time receiving instruction and
reading systematically, he once wrote, "To continue much longer
overwhelmed by business cares and with most of my thoughts wholly upon
the way to make more money in the shortest time, must degrade me beyond
hope of permanent recovery." The strong desire for intellectual pursuit led
him to sell his company and retire at 64.

　　然而，卡內基常常表達出對商場生活的不安，他希望能花更多時間接受教導，以及能有計劃地閱讀，他曾寫道：「繼續花更長的時間，被生意上的憂慮所困擾，以及將所有心思，花在如何在最短時間賺更多錢，必定會使我變得沒格調，而且永遠毫無希望改變回來。」這股對追求知性的強烈渴望，讓他賣掉了他的公司，並於六十四歲退休。

express〔ɪkˋsprɛs〕v. 表達　　uneasiness〔ʌnˋizɪnɪs〕n. 不安
businessman〔ˋbɪzɪnɪsˏmæn〕n. 商人
instruction〔ɪnˋstrʌkʃən〕n. 教導
systematically〔ˏsɪstəˋmætɪklɪ〕adv. 有計劃地；有系統地
overwhelm〔ˏovɚˋhwɛlm〕v.（精神上）制服；使無法對抗
care〔kɛr〕n. pl. 憂慮　　wholly〔ˋholɪ〕adv. 完全地
degrade〔dɪˋgred〕v. 降低（某人的身份）；使丟臉
beyond〔bɪˋjɑnd〕prep. 超出
permanent〔ˋpɝmənənt〕adj. 永久的
recovery〔rɪˋkʌvərɪ〕n. 恢復　　desire〔dɪˋzaɪr〕n. 渴望；慾望
intellectual〔ˏɪntḷˋɛktʃʊəl〕adj. 知性的
pursuit〔pɚˋsut〕n. 追求　　retire〔rɪˋtaɪr〕v. 退休

Fond of saying that "the man who dies rich dies disgraced," Carnegie then turned his attention to giving away his fortune. He abhorred charity; instead, he used his money to help others help themselves. He established over 2,500 public libraries, and sponsored numerous cultural, educational and scientific institutions. By the time he died in 1919, he had given away 350 million dollars.

　　卡內基喜歡說「帶著大筆財富過世的人，是可恥的」，於是卡內基將他的注意力轉移到捐贈財產。他厭惡施捨；相反地，他用他的錢來幫助那些自立更生的人。他設立了超過 2,500 間的公立圖書館，贊助了無數的文化、教育以及科學機構。到 1919 年他過世前為止，他已經捐出了三億五千萬元美金。

fond〔fɑnd〕adj. 喜歡的　　saying〔ˋseˏɪŋ〕n. 格言
disgrace〔dɪsˋgres〕n. 恥辱　　***give away*** 捐贈
fortune〔ˋfɔrtʃən〕n. 財產　　abhor〔əbˋhɔr〕v. 痛恨
charity〔ˋtʃærətɪ〕n. 施捨；慈善　　sponsor〔ˋspɑnsɚ〕v. 贊助
institution〔ˏɪnstəˋtjuʃən〕n. 機構

46.(**D**)　卡內基為什麼要搬到美國？

(A) 因為他父親在匹茲堡找到好工作。

(B) 因為他不想要繼承衣缽。

(C) 因為蘇格蘭有嚴重的政治問題。

(D) 因為他的家庭在家鄉無法好好過活。

make a living 維持生計；討生活

47.(**D**)　卡內基何時開始展現他對藝術以及追求知性的興趣？

(A) 當他退休之後。

(B) 當他還是個在蘇格蘭的小男孩時。

(C) 當他在鋼鐵工業賺到大筆財富之後。

(D) 當他在匹茲堡當通信員時。

artistic〔ɑr'tɪstɪk〕*adj.* 藝術的

48.(**A**)　下列何者最貼切的描繪出卡內基經營生意的特徵？

(A) 他願意做出新的改變。

(B) 他企圖打敗所有的競爭對手。

(C) 他很樂意在最短的時間內賺多一點錢。

(D) 他對於在故鄉作投資，一點都不遲疑。

characterize〔'kærəktə,raɪz〕*v.* 具…的特徵；描繪…的特徵
set out 企圖　　　hesitate〔'hɛzə,tet〕*v.* 猶豫；遲疑
investment〔ɪn'vɛstmənt〕*n.* 投資

＊ 本題答案應參照出題來源（http://www.pbs.org/wgbh/amex/carnegie/
peopleevents/pande01.html），對卡內基一生勇於接受挑戰、大膽嘗試解
說詳細，才有充份理由選答案 (A)。但是指考文章，已大幅刪減過，難
以找到段落，證明卡內基在從商生涯上，是個勇於改變的人。

49.(**C**)　卡內基在退休之後如何處理他的財產？

(A) 他在死後將財產留給了親朋好友。

(B) 他捐給窮人以及慈善機構。

(C) 他用財產資助高等教育機構。

(D) 他把財產投資在開發煉鐵的新技術上。

organization〔,ɔrgənə'zeʃən〕*n.* 組織；機構
higher learning 高等教育　　　invest〔ɪn'vɛst〕*v.* 投資
refinement〔rɪ'faɪnmənt〕*n.* 提煉；精練

第 50 至 52 題為題組

　　Most parents dread a note or call from school saying that their child's behavior is "not normal." If your child's academic performance and social life is suffering because they don't pay attention, can't sit still and act without thinking, it is most likely that they have AD/HD (Attention Deficit/ Hyperactivity Disorder).

　　大部分的家長，都很害怕從學校收到通知單或是接到電話，說他們孩子的行爲「不正常」。如果你孩子的成績以及社交生活，因爲他們無法專心、坐不住，或是無法先思後行，而變得糟糕的話，他們很有可能患有「注意力不足過動症」。

dread〔drɛd〕v. 害怕　　note〔not〕n. 紙條；短箋；短信
call〔kɔl〕n. 電話　　behavior〔bɪˋhevjɚ〕n. 行爲
normal〔ˋnɔrml〕adj. 正常的　　academic〔͵ækəˋdɛmɪk〕adj. 學術的
performance〔pɚˋfɔrməns〕n. 表現
social〔ˋsoʃəl〕adj. 社會的；社交的
suffer〔ˋsʌfɚ〕v. 受苦；變差；變糟；處於不利地位
attention〔əˋtɛnʃən〕n. 注意；專心　　***pay attention*** 專心
still〔stɪl〕adj. 靜止的；不動的　　***sit still*** 坐著不動
act〔ækt〕v. 採取行動　　likely〔ˋlaɪklɪ〕adj. 可能的
deficit〔ˋdɛfəsɪt〕n. 不足；短缺
hyperactivity〔͵haɪpɚækˋtɪvətɪ〕n. 極度活躍；過動
disorder〔dɪsˋɔrdɚ〕n. 失調；疾病
Attention Deficit / Hyperactivity Disorder 注意力不足過動症

　　AD/HD is a neurological disorder which stems not from the home environment, but from biological and genetic causes. Its symptoms typically show up in early childhood. The main characteristics are inattention, hyperactivity and impulsivity. Inattentive children have difficulty focusing on completing a task or learning something new. Hyperactive children always seem to be restless. Often they report that they need to stay busy and may try to do several tasks at once. Impulsive children often do not think before they act. They often blurt out inappropriate comments or have difficulty taking turns in conversation.

　　「注意力不足過動症」是種神經性的疾病，不是由家庭環境造成的，而是源於生物性以及遺傳性的原因。其症狀通常在童年初期就會出現。主要的特徵包括不專注、過動，以及容易衝動。無法專心的孩子，很難專注地完成一件事，或是學習新的事物。過動的孩子似乎永遠都靜不下來。他們常常說他們需要保持忙碌，並且可能會想同時做許多事。衝動的孩子在採取行動之前，往往不會思考。他們常會脫口說出不適當的話，或著是很難在談話中輪流發言。

neurological〔͵njurə'ladʒɪk!〕adj. 神經的　　stem〔stɛm〕v. 起源
stem from 起源於　　environment〔ɪn'vaɪrənmənt〕n. 環境
biological〔͵baɪə'ladʒɪk!〕adj. 生物（學）的
genetic〔dʒə'nɛtɪk〕adj. 遺傳的；基因的
cause〔kɔz〕n. 原因　　symptom〔'sɪmptəm〕n. 症狀
typically〔'tɪpɪk!ɪ〕adv. 典型地；通常　　**show up** 出現
early〔'ɝlɪ〕adj. 初期的　　childhood〔'tʃaɪld͵hud〕n. 童年
main〔men〕adj. 主要的　　characteristic〔͵kærɪktə'rɪstɪk〕n. 特性
inattention〔͵ɪnə'tɛnʃən〕n. 不注意；漫不經心
impulsivity〔͵ɪmpʌl'sɪvətɪ〕n. 衝動
inattentive〔͵ɪnə'tɛntɪv〕adj. 不注意的；注意力不集中的
have difficulty + V-ing 很難～　　**focus on** 專注於
complete〔kəm'plit〕v. 完成　　task〔tæsk〕n. 任務；工作
hyperactive〔͵haɪpə'æktɪv〕adj. 過度活躍的；過動的
seem〔sim〕v. 似乎　　restless〔'rɛstlɪs〕adj. 坐立不安的；浮躁的
report〔rɪ'port〕v. 聲稱　　stay〔ste〕v. 保持　　**at once** 同時
impulsive〔ɪm'pʌlsɪv〕adj. 衝動的
blurt〔blɝt〕v. 突然說出；脫口說出　　**blurt out** 脫口說出
inappropriate〔͵ɪnə'proprɪɪt〕adj. 不適當的；不得體的
comment〔'kamɛnt〕n. 評論　　**take turns** 輪流
conversation〔͵kanvə'seʃən〕n. 會話；談話

　　Most children can be inattentive, hyperactive, or impulsive at times. It is when these behaviors are inappropriate for their age and affect different areas in their lives that the disorder is diagnosed. Depression, anxiety, and learning disabilities may co-exist with AD/HD. Therefore, if a child is suspected of AD/HD, it is very important that he or she be evaluated by a professional.

　　大部分的孩子都可能會偶爾不專注、過動，或是衝動。當這些行為跟他們的年齡不符，並且影響了他們生活中的其他部分，這個疾病才會被診斷出來。憂鬱、焦慮，以及學習障礙，可能會與「注意力不足過動症」並存。因此，如果孩子被懷疑患有「注意力不足過動症」，那麼接受專業人士的評估，就是非常重要的。

at times 有時候；偶爾　　affect〔əˈfɛkt〕*v.* 影響
area〔ˈɛrɪə〕*n.* 領域；範圍　　diagnose〔ˌdaɪəgˈnoz〕*v.* 診斷
depression〔dɪˈprɛʃən〕*n.* 沮喪　　anxiety〔æŋˈzaɪətɪ〕*n.* 焦慮
disability〔ˌdɪsəˈbɪlətɪ〕*n.* 無能力　　*learning disabilities* 學習障礙
co-exist〔ˌko‧ɪgˈzɪst〕*v.* 同時存在；共存
suspect〔səˈspɛkt〕*v.* 懷疑　　*be suspected of* 認為有…的嫌疑
evaluate〔ɪˈvæljuˌet〕*v.* 評估　　professional〔prəˈfɛʃənl̩〕*n.* 專家

Once your child is diagnosed with AD/HD, it is important to let the school know so that they can provide appropriate academic and social support. Your child's school should keep this information confidential and it can usually make accommodations in the classroom to fit your child's learning needs.

　　一旦你的孩子被診斷有「注意力不足過動症」時，讓學校知道，是一件非常重要的事，如此學校才能提供學業以及社交上適當的援助。校方應該將這樣的訊息保密，而通常也會在教室中做些調整，以配合孩子學習上的需要。

once〔wʌns〕*adv.* 一旦　　*so that* 以便於
provide〔prəˈvaɪd〕*v.* 提供　　appropriate〔əˈproprɪɪt〕*adj.* 適當的
support〔səˈport〕*n.* 支持；援助；支援
information〔ˌɪnfɚˈmeʃən〕*n.* 消息；情報
confidential〔ˌkɑnfəˈdɛnʃəl〕*adj.* 機密的；秘密的
accommodation〔əˌkɑməˈdeʃən〕*n.* 調節；調整
fit〔fɪt〕*v.* 適合；符合；配合　　need〔nid〕*n.* 需要；需求

50.(**A**) 什麼是造成「注意力不足過動症」的原因？
　　(A) <u>基因問題。</u>　　　　　　(B) 課業壓力。
　　(C) 童年時期的疾病。　　　　(D) 不適當的家庭環境。
　　gene〔dʒin〕*n.* 基因　　illness〔ˈɪlnɪs〕*n.* 疾病

51.（ **D** ）下列何者最有可能是「注意力不足過動症」的患者？
　　（A）非常懶惰的小孩。　　　　　（B）非常專注的小孩。
　　（C）行爲過於謹慎的小孩。　　　（D）有學習障礙的小孩。

　　lazy〔ˈlezɪ〕*adj.* 懶惰的　　attentive〔əˈtɛntɪv〕*n.* 專注的；注意的
　　cautiously〔ˈkɔʃəslɪ〕*adv.* 謹慎地；小心地

52.（ **B** ）如果你的孩子疑患有「注意力不足過動症」，最先要作的事情是？
　　（A）告知學校。　　　　　　　　（B）請教專業人士。
　　（C）等到小孩長大。　　　　　　（D）把小孩送到特殊的學校。

　　consult〔kənˈsʌlt〕*v.* 請教

第 53 至 56 題爲題組

　　Conflict diamonds, sometimes called blood diamonds, are diamonds that are sold to fund the unlawful and illegal operations of rebel, military and terrorist groups.　Countries that have been most affected by conflict diamonds are Sierra Leone, Angola, Liberia and the Democratic Republic of Congo.　They are places where citizens have been terrorized or even killed by groups in control of the local diamond trade.

　　衝突鑽石，有時又被稱爲血鑽石，販售這些鑽石的所得被用來資助反叛團體、軍事團體，和恐怖份子的非法軍事行動。受到衝突鑽石影響最深的國家是獅子山、安哥拉、賴比瑞亞，以及剛果民主共和國。這些地方的人民常受到控制當地鑽石交易的團體的恐嚇，或甚至被殺害。

　　conflict〔ˈkɑnflɪkt〕*n.* 衝突　　diamond〔ˈdaɪəmənd〕*n.* 鑽石
　　conflict diamond 衝突鑽石（又稱 blood diamond，非洲交戰團體將
　　　採自當地的鑽石，拿到國際市場銷售，以籌措戰爭經費）
　　blood〔blʌd〕*n.* 血　　fund〔fʌnd〕*v.* 提供資金
　　unlawful〔ʌnˈlɔfəl〕*adj.* 非法的　　illegal〔ɪˈligḷ〕*adj.* 非法的
　　operations〔ˌɑpəˈreʃənz〕*n. pl.* 軍事行動
　　rebel〔ˈrɛbḷ〕*adj.* 反叛的　　*n.* 叛軍　　military〔ˈmɪləˌtɛrɪ〕*adj.* 軍事的
　　terrorist〔ˈtɛrərɪst〕*adj.* 恐怖份子的　　group〔grup〕*n.* 團體
　　affect〔əˈfɛkt〕*v.* 影響　　Sierra Leone〔sɪˈɛrəlɪˈoni〕*n.* 獅子山共和國
　　Angola〔æŋˈgolə〕*n.* 安哥拉　　Liberia〔laɪˈbɪrɪə〕*n.* 賴比瑞亞
　　democratic〔ˌdɛməˈkrætɪk〕*adj.* 民主的

republic〔rɪˈpʌblɪk〕*n.* 共和國　　Congo〔ˈkaŋgo〕*n.* 剛果
citizen〔ˈsɪtəzn̩〕*n.* 人民　　terrorize〔ˈtɛrəˌraɪz〕*v.* 恐嚇
be in control of 控制；支配　　local〔ˈlokl̩〕*adj.* 當地的
trade〔tred〕*n.* 交易

Wars in most of those areas have ended or at least decreased in intensity, but the problem of conflict diamonds hasn't gone away.　Diamonds mined in some rebel-held areas, such as Liberia, are being smuggled into neighboring countries and exported as conflict-free diamonds.

那些區域大多已經停戰，或至少戰況沒那麼激烈，但是衝突鑽石的問題並未消失。在某些被判軍佔領的區域，像是賴比瑞亞，所開採出來的鑽石，會被走私到鄰國，然後再當成非衝突鑽石出口。

war〔wɔr〕*n.* 戰爭　　***at least*** 至少　　decrease〔dɪˈkris〕*v.* 下降
intensity〔ɪnˈtɛnsətɪ〕*n.* 強度；激烈　　***go away*** 消失
mine〔maɪn〕*v.* 開採　　***rebel-held*** *adj.* 被叛軍佔據的
smuggle〔ˈsmʌgl̩〕*v.* 走私運入（運出）
neighboring〔ˈnebərɪŋ〕*adj.* 鄰近的
export〔ɪksˈport〕*v.* 輸出　　***conflict-free diamond*** 非衝突鑽石

In order to stop blood diamond sales, South African countries with a legitimate diamond trade began a campaign in 2000 to track the origins of all rough diamonds.　Their efforts resulted in the Kimberley Process Certification Scheme (KPCS), an international organization to make the world free of conflict diamonds.　The goals of the KPCS are to document and track all rough diamonds when they enter a participating country.　Shippers are required to place those diamonds in sealed boxes and provide enough detailed information about their origins to prove they did not originate in a conflict zone.

為了阻止販賣血鑽石，從事合法鑽石交易的南非國家在西元二〇〇〇年開始發起一個運動，追蹤所有鑽石原石的來源。它們的努力造就了國際鑽石原石認證標準機制（KPCS），這個國際組織是要讓世界上不再存有衝突鑽石。國際鑽石原石認證標準機制的目標，是在當鑽石原石進入參與國家時，要以文件證明並追蹤其來源。鑽石託運者被要求將鑽石放在密封的盒子裡，並提供充分且詳細的來源資訊，以證明那些鑽石不是產自衝突區域。

legitimate〔lɪˋdʒɪtəmɪt〕*adj.* 合法的

campaign〔kæmˋpen〕*n.* 運動；活動

track〔træk〕*v.* 追蹤　　origin〔ˋɔrədʒɪn〕*n.* 來源

rough diamond 鑽石原石；未經琢磨的鑽石

result〔rɪˋzʌlt〕*v.* 終於造成…結果 < *in* >

Kimberley〔ˋkɪmbəlɪ〕*n.* 金伯利【*南非共和國中部一城市，以產鑽石聞名*】

process〔ˋprɑsɛs〕*n.* 過程；流程

certification〔͵sɝtəfəˋkeʃən〕*n.* 證明書　　scheme〔skim〕*n.* 計畫

Kimberley Process Certification Scheme 金伯利流程證書計畫；
　國際鑽石原石認證標準機制

international〔͵ɪntɚˋnæʃənḷ〕*adj.* 國際的

organization〔͵ɔrgənəˋzeʃən〕*n.* 組織

free〔fri〕*adj.* 沒有的；免於的

document〔ˋdɑkjə͵mɛnt〕*v.* 以文件證明

participating〔pɑrˋtɪsə͵petɪŋ〕*adj.* 參與的

shipper〔ˋʃɪpɚ〕*n.* 託運人　　require〔rɪˋkwaɪr〕*v.* 要求

place〔ples〕*v.* 放置　　sealed〔sild〕*adj.* 密封的

provide〔prəˋvaɪd〕*v.* 提供　　detailed〔ˋditeld〕*adj.* 詳細的

prove〔pruv〕*v.* 證明　　originate〔əˋrɪdʒə͵net〕*v.* 源於

zone〔zon〕*n.* 區域

　　It's difficult for most of us to imagine what life is like in countries where diamonds are the source of so much chaos and suffering.　Furthermore, the connection between terror and diamonds is not something that's reported heavily in the press.　The 2006 movie *Blood Diamond*, starring Leonardo DiCaprio, should help make the issue more mainstream, if only temporarily. So, take some time to learn more about the problems that conflict diamonds create, and then follow your heart the next time you shop for a diamond.

　　鑽石在一些國家是造成許多混亂和災難的根源，而我們大多數的人都很難想像那些國家的生活是像什麼樣子。而且，恐怖行動和鑽石之間的關聯，也不是新聞會大量報導的事件。二○○六年的電影－血鑽石，是由李奧納多‧狄卡皮歐主演，這部電影應該有助於使這個議題更趨主流化，即使只是暫時如此。所以，花一點時間多去了解衝突鑽石所造成的問題，然後下次你買鑽石的時候就跟著感覺走。

imagine〔ɪˋmædʒɪn〕v. 想像　　source〔sors〕n. 根源

chaos〔ˋkeɑs〕n. 混亂　　suffering〔ˋsʌfərɪŋ〕n. 災難

furthermore〔ˋfɝðəˏmor〕adv. 而且

connection〔kəˋnɛkʃən〕n. 關聯

terror〔ˋtɛrə〕n. 恐怖行動；恐怖份子的暴力行為

report〔rɪˋport〕v. 報導　　heavily〔ˋhɛvɪlɪ〕adv. 大量地

press〔prɛs〕n. 新聞；報刊　　star〔star〕v. 主演

issue〔ˋɪʃju〕n. 議題　　mainstream〔ˋmenˏstrim〕adj. 主流的

if only 即使只　　temporarily〔ˋtɛmpəˏrɛrəlɪ〕adv. 暫時地；一時地

create〔krɪˋet〕v. 造成

follow one's heart 跟著感覺走；做自己想做的事；憑良心

shop〔ʃɑp〕v. 購買

53.（**B**）為什麼來自某些地區的鑽石叫做「血鑽石」？

　　(A) 它們的顏色類似血的顏色。　　(B) 它們造成人命的傷亡。

　　(C) 它們象徵著愛與熱情。　　(D) 它們的品質極為良好。

resemble〔rɪˋzɛmbḷ〕v. 類似；像

represent〔ˏrɛprɪˋzɛnt〕v. 象徵

exceptionally〔ɪkˋsɛpʃənəlɪ〕adv. 特殊地；異常地

54.（**C**）我們可以從本文的第二段推論出什麼？

　　(A) 來自賴比瑞亞的鑽石，大部分都是非衝突鑽石。

　　(B) 來自賴比瑞亞的鑽石，大部分都標示正確。

　　(C) 賴比瑞亞的鑽石仍被交易來資助戰爭。

　　(D) KPCS 有謹慎的調查過來自賴比瑞亞的鑽石。

label〔ˋlebḷ〕v. 用籤條標明　　investigate〔ɪnˋvɛstəˏget〕v. 調查

55.（**D**）KPCS 的主要任務是什麼？

　　(A) 促進鑽石原石的銷售。　　(B) 製作像是「血鑽石」的電影。

　　(C) 處罰販賣血鑽石的人。　　(D) 用文件紀錄鑽石的開採地。

major〔ˋmedʒə〕adj. 主要的　　task〔tæsk〕n. 任務

promote〔prəˋmot〕v. 促進

penalize〔ˋpinḷˏaɪz〕v. 對…處刑

56. (**D**) 作者對於血鑽石的態度如何？

　　　(A) indifferent〔ɪn'dɪfərənt〕*adj.* 不關心的

　　　(B) threatening〔'θrɛtn̩ɪŋ〕*adj.* 脅迫的

　　　(C) sympathetic〔ˌsɪmpə'θɛtɪk〕*adj.* 同情的

　　　(D) *disapproving*〔ˌdɪsə'pruvɪŋ〕*adj.* 反對的

第貳部分：非選擇題

一、英文翻譯：

1. 大眾運輸的快速發展已逐漸縮短了都市和鄉村的距離。

　The rapid development of mass transportation has gradually shortened the distance between the city and the country.

2. 有了高速鐵路，我們可以在半天內往返台灣南北兩地。

　With (the) high speed rail, we can get to the north or south of Taiwan and back in half a day.

二、英文作文：

【範例 1】

A World Without Electricity

　　A world without electricity would spell the end for many people. Most forms of communication and transportation we rely so much on would be cut off. International trade would be down for good, and the whole world would be affected. Most of us wouldn't even know how to live anymore.

　　A worldwide power failure would be a disaster—and a blessing in disguise. No electricity means no modern conveniences, and the source of provisions would be a problem, not to mention the riots that would break out. ***On the other hand***, Mother Earth has suffered greatly because of technological advances, and such a power outage would certainly stop the damage. It all comes down to what we care about more—the world we live *in*, or the world we live *on*?

【範例 2】

A World Without Electricity

A world without electricity would be very different from the one we know today. We would no longer enjoy many conveniences such as computers, televisions, household appliances, or even lights at night. *In addition*, the productivity of many factories would be reduced. All kinds of goods would become scarce and expensive. We would also lose the ability to communicate instantly with others.

In my opinion, the world would be worse off without electricity. Although its production causes environmental pollution, we are too dependent on it to give it up. Electricity affects nearly every aspect of modern-day life. Without it, we would no longer enjoy any of the technological advances of the past century. We would have to give up refrigeration, satellite communications, and life-saving medical devices. *In shor*t, electricity is simply too valuable to do without.

spell〔spɛl〕*v.* 意味　　*cut off* 中斷；切斷
for good 永久地　　worldwide〔ˋwɝldˏwaɪd〕*adj.* 全球性的
power failure 斷電　　blessing〔ˋblɛsɪŋ〕*n.* 恩賜
disguise〔dɪsˋgaɪz〕*n.* 假扮　　*blessing in disguise* 因禍得福
source〔sors〕*n.* 來源　　provision〔prəˋvɪʒən〕*n.* 糧食；必需品
riot〔ˋraɪət〕*n.* 暴動；騷亂　　*break out* 爆發；突然發生
advance〔ədˋvæns〕*v.* 發展
outage〔ˋaʊtɪdʒ〕*n.* (水、電等的) 中斷供應
household〔ˋhaʊsˏhold〕*adj.* 家用的
appliance〔əˋplaɪəns〕*n.* 器具；設備
household appliance 家用電器；家電產品
productivity〔ˏprodʌkˋtɪvətɪ〕*n.* 生產力
scarce〔skɛrs〕*adj.* 稀有的；珍貴的
worse off 每況愈下的　　aspect〔ˋæspɛkt〕*n.* 方面
refrigeration〔rɪˏfrɪdʒəˋreʃən〕*n.* 冷藏；冷凍
satellite〔ˋsætlˏaɪt〕*n.* 衛星

96 年指定科目考試英文科試題勘誤表

※ 今年的指考題目，完全符合大考中心的命題原則，兼具知識性、趣味性和教育性，內容包羅萬象，是難得一見的好題目。

題　　號	修　　正　　意　　見
二、綜合測驗 第 11 至 15 題 第 2 行	... how satisfied they *are*.... → ... how satisfied they *were*.... ＊根據本句的句意，該用過去式動詞 *were* 才對。
第 11 至 15 題 第 2、3 行	*The resulting statistics graph*.... → *A graph of the results*.... ＊沒有 *a statistics graph* 的說法，因為它是指世界上任何統計數字的圖表，只能說 *a graph of the results*（這項研究結果的圖表）。
第 11 至 15 題 第 3 行	*Most of the people* start off.... → *Most people* start off.... 或 → Most of the people *started off*.... ＊Most of the people 和 Most people 句意不同，Most of the people（他們當中大多數的人）是指前面接受研究的人，研究已經結束，該用過去式 started off（一開始）；Most people（大多數的人）指常態，才可用現在式動詞 start off。
第 21 至 25 題 倒數第 4 行	... by ecological disturbances, changes in food and water supplies, *as well as* coastal flooding. ＊*as well as* 應改成 *and*。and 連接三個名詞片語，即 ecological disturbances、changes in food and water supplies，和 coastal flooding，不能用 as well as。我們只能說：A, B, *and* C（正），不能說 A, B, as well as C（誤）。【詳見「文法寶典」p.468】 如果要保留 as well as，就要改成： ... by ecological disturbances *and* changes in food and water supplies, as well as coastal flooding. ＊要將 disturbances 後的逗點去掉，加上 and。我們說：A and B, as well as C。【詳見「文法寶典」p.468】
第 21 至 25 題 倒數第 2 行	... poor people and poor countries are less *probable* to.... → ... poor people and poor countries are less *likely* to.... ＊人做主詞時，必須用 *likely*，而不能用 *probable* 或 *possible* 等非人稱形容詞做主詞補語。
三、文意選填 第 31 至 40 題 第 7 行	... are likely to choose it *too*. → ... are *more* likely to choose it. ＊由於前面沒提到誰已經選擇了它，所以 too 是多餘的，且加上 more 才合乎句意。

四、篇章結構 第 41 至 45 題 第 3 行	... pension (*i.e., payment received after retirement*) system.... → ... pension (**payment received after retirement**) system.... 或 → ... pension, *i.e.,* **payment received after retirement**, system.... * 用 ( ) 就不需要 i.e.，避免重複。
第 41 至 45 題 第 5 行	... while *payouts* they get after retirement fall. → ... while **the payouts** they get after retirement fall. * 由於 payouts 後有形容詞子句修飾，先行詞 **payouts** 前面必須加定冠詞 **the**。
第 41 至 45 題 第 6、7 行	... companies *by 2013* to raise....age from 60 to 65 or *rehire* their.... → ... companies to raise....age from 60 to 65 **by 2013** or **to rehire** their.... * 原句語意不清，or 連接兩個不定詞片語，由於距離遠，應加 to。
五、閱讀測驗 第 46 至 49 題 第 1 行	...born in 1835 *to a weaver's family*.... → ...born in 1835 **into a weaver's family**.... 或 → ...born in 1835 **to a weaver**.... * { **be born to** + 人　是某人的小孩 　 **be born into ~ family**　出生於 ~ 家庭
第 46 至 49 題 第 3 行	... *leave for* new possibilities in America. → ...**leave and search for** new possibilities in America. * leave for 是「前往」，不是「為了…而離開」。本文改編自「美國公共電視網名人介紹單元」，原文是：....leave the poverty of Scotland for the possibilities in America.
第 46 題	(D) Because his family...living in their *hometown*. → (D) Because his family...living in their **home country**. * 本題 (D) 是正確答案，因為文章中只提到他們的祖國（Scotland），沒有提到他們的故鄉在哪裡，故應改成 home country 較好。
第 47 題	When did Carnegie begin to...artistic and intellectual *pursuit*? → When did Carnegie begin to...artistic and intellectual **pursuits**? * 前面有 artistic（藝術的）和 intellectual（智力的），故 pursuit 應用複數形才對。
第 50 題	(A) *Gene* problem. → (A) **A gene** problem. 或 (A) **A genetic** problem. * 本題 (A) 是正確答案，由於 problem 是普通名詞，前應有冠詞。
第 53 至 56 題 第 11 行	... organization *to make* the world free of conflict diamonds. → ... organization **dedicated to making** the world free of conflict diamonds. * **be dedicated to** 致力於 organization 不是動詞，不能接不定詞表目的。

96 年指定科目考試英文科出題來源

題　　號	出　　　　　　　　　　　　　處	
一、詞彙 　　第 1～10 題	所有各題的對錯選項均出自「高中常用 7000 字」，只有 第 4 題 (A) radically，在 7000 字中為 radical（根本的）。	
二、綜合測驗 　　第 16～20 題	www.exploratorium.edu/auroras 葡萄牙國家常識測驗題目 （http://72.14.235.104/search?q=cache:3_QQwjJJboMJ:www. cefet-ce.br/Ensino/Vestibular/Provas/Vestibular/Prova/2003 2 Conhecimentos_Gerais.doc+%22hudson+bay+region%22+ aurora+borealis&hl=zh-TW&ct=clnk&cd=13）	
第 21～25 題	http://epa.gov/climatechange/kids/bigdeal.html 美國環境保護局給兒童看的氣候變遷網站	
第 26～30 題	http://www.internetworldstats.com/asia/bt.htm 市場研究公司對不丹的介紹	
三、文意選填 　　第 31～40 題	http://www.economist.com/science/displaystory.cfm?story id=8134691 Economist.com 網站上，科學與科技單元，關於心理學方 面的文章	
四、篇章結構 　　第 41～45 題	http://www.careerjournal.com/myc/retirement/20050617- moffett.html 華爾街線上日報的報導	
五、閱讀測驗 　　第 46～49 題	http://www.pbs.org/wgbh/amex/carnegie/peopleevents/ pande01.html 美國公共電視網的名人介紹單元	
第 53～56 題	http://jewelry.about.com/cs/diamondmining/a/diamonds.htm About.com 網站上關於珠寶的文章	

九十六學年度指定科目考試（英文）
大考中心公佈答案

題號	答案	題號	答案	題號	答案
1	C	21	B	41	B
2	B	22	B	42	D
3	A	23	D	43	A
4	C	24	C	44	E
5	D	25	A	45	C
6	D	26	C	46	D
7	B	27	D	47	D
8	A	28	C	48	A
9	B	29	A	49	C
10	D	30	B	50	A
11	B	31	E	51	D
12	C	32	B	52	B
13	A	33	G	53	B
14	B	34	C	54	C
15	A	35	D	55	D
16	C	36	I	56	D
17	B	37	F		
18	C	38	J		
19	A	39	A		
20	D	40	H		

九十六學年度指定科目考試
各科成績標準一覽表

科 目	頂 標	前 標	均 標	後 標	底 標
國　文	70	64	56	45	36
英　文	60	46	26	13	7
數學甲	62	49	33	20	11
數學乙	72	60	43	27	17
化　學	74	61	41	24	15
物　理	68	51	27	12	5
生　物	84	74	56	40	31
歷　史	75	68	55	40	28
地　理	56	50	40	30	21

※ 以上五項標準均取為整數（小數只捨不入），且其計算均不含缺考生之成績，
　計算方式如下：

頂標：成績位於第 88 百分位數之考生成績。
前標：成績位於第 75 百分位數之考生成績。
均標：成績位於第 50 百分位數之考生成績。
後標：成績位於第 25 百分位數之考生成績。
底標：成績位於第 12 百分位數之考生成績。

例：　某科之到考考生為 99982 人，則該科五項標準為

頂標：成績由低至高排序，取第 87985 名（99982×88%＝87984.16，取整數，
　　　小數無條件進位）考生的成績，再取整數（小數只捨不入）。

前標：成績由低至高排序，取第 74987 名（99982×75%＝74986.5，取整數，
　　　小數無條件進位）考生的成績，再取整數（小數只捨不入）。

均標：成績由低至高排序，取第 49991 名（99982×50%＝49991）考生的成績，
　　　再取整數（小數只捨不入）。

後標：成績由低至高排序，取第 24996 名（99982×25%＝24995.5，取整數，
　　　小數無條件進位）考生的成績，再取整數（小數只捨不入）。

底標：成績由低至高排序，取第 11998 名（99982×12%＝11997.84，取整數，
　　　小數無條件進位）考生的成績，再取整數（小數只捨不入）。

九十五年大學入學指定科目考試試題
英文考科

第壹部份：選擇題（佔72分）

一、詞彙（10％）

說明： 第1至10題，每題選出一個最適當的選項，標示在答案卡之「選擇題答案區」。每題答對得1分，答錯或劃記多於一個選項者倒扣1/3分，倒扣到本大題之實得分數為零為止，未作答者，不給分亦不扣分。

1. Mastery of English _____ us with a very important tool for acquiring knowledge and information.
   (A) accesses　　　(B) conveys　　　(C) deprives　　　(D) equips

2. Languages change all the time. Many words that were found in Shakespeare's works are no longer in _____ use.
   (A) absolute　　　(B) current　　　(C) repetitive　　　(D) valuable

3. Do not just sit and wait _____ for a good chance to come to you. You have to take the initiative and create chances for yourself.
   (A) consciously　　(B) passively　　(C) reasonably　　(D) subjectively

4. Identical twins have almost all of their genes in common, so any _____ between them is in large part due to the effects of the environment.
   (A) adoption　　　(B) familiarity　　(C) stability　　　(D) variation

5. People believed in the _____ of the judge, so they were shocked to hear that he was involved in the bribery scandal.
   (A) inferiority　　(B) integrity　　(C) intimacy　　　(D) ingenuity

6. The discovery of the new vaccine is an important _____ in the fight against avian flu.
   (A) breakthrough　　　　　　(B) commitment
   (C) demonstration　　　　　　(D) interpretation

7. To avoid being misled by news reports, we should learn to _____ between facts and opinions.

(A) distinguish   (B) complicate   (C) reinforce   (D) speculate

8. After the big flood, the area was mostly _____, with only one or two homes still clinging to their last relics.

(A) condensed   (B) deserted   (C) excluded   (D) removed

9. In his speech, Dr. Huang presented all the reports about the energy crisis to _____ the need for developing new energy resources.

(A) command   (B) formulate   (C) highlight   (D) regulate

10. Hearing the art critic's bitter and _____ comments on her new painting, Molly started a heated argument with him.

(A) outrageous   (B) unreliable   (C) urgent   (D) glorious

二、綜合測驗（20％）

說明：　第 11 至 30 題，每題一個空格。請依文意選出一個最適當的選項，標示
　　　　在答案卡之「選擇題答案區」。每題答對得 1 分，答錯或劃記多於一
　　　　個選項者倒扣 1/3 分，倒扣到本大題之實得分數為零為止。未作答者，
　　　　不給分亦不扣分。

第 11 至 15 題為題組

　　Measurements are needed in many everyday activities. In kitchens you will find measures for volume (measuring cups), mass (scales and weights), and temperature (cooking thermometers). Accurate measurements are ___11___ important for scientific experiments. In a laboratory, make sure your measure meets your needs. ___12___ using any thermometer, double check that it covers the right temperature ___13___ for your activity or experiment. A garden thermometer, ___14___, will burst if you try to use it for boiling liquids.

There are different systems of measures. Most scientists now use the International System of measures, with meters for length, kilograms for ___15___, and seconds for time. If the measures in your experiment show other units, appropriate conversion tables for different systems may prove to be very useful.

11. (A) deliberately　(B) instantly　(C) particularly　(D) scarcely
12. (A) After　(B) Before　(C) For　(D) Without
13. (A) range　(B) record　(C) system　(D) unit
14. (A) in short　(B) in turn　(C) by contrast　(D) for instance
15. (A) distance　(B) mass　(C) temperature　(D) volume

第 16 至 20 題為題組

Every year Catemaco, a small town in the south of Mexico, hosts the Annual Witch Gathering. Healers and witch doctors converge on this beautiful lakeside town in March to make their yearly trade. ___16___ since pre-Hispanic times, Lake Catemaco has been a centre for alternative medicine and strange treatments. ___17___, the area's association with witchcraft dates back to Olmec times more than 2,000 years ago. If you've ever seen the Sean Connery movie *Medicine Man*, ___18___ the annual convention of wizards and witches will be familiar to you. ___19___, get prepared for the overwhelming attack of wizards and witches here. Most witch doctors are guaranteed to be charlatans, not real doctors, who ___20___ some quick money from tourists. Yet, don't be surprised if the occasional remedy offered is effective.

16. (A) Ever　(B) Not　(C) Only　(D) Rarely
17. (A) In advance　(B) In all　(C) In fact　(D) In sum
18. (A) since　(B) so　(C) then　(D) though
19. (A) If any　(B) If not　(C) If ever　(D) If only
20. (A) go after　(B) turn down　(C) give away　(D) complain about

第 21 至 25 題為題組

Young visitors to museums often complain about having museum feet, the tired feeling one gets after spending too much time in a museum. A case of museum feet makes one feel like saying: "This is ___21___. I could have done the painting myself. When can we sit down? What time is it?"

Studies of museum behavior show that the average visitor spends about four seconds looking at one object. For young visitors, the time span can be ___22___ shorter. Children are more interested in smells, sounds, and the "feel" of a place than looking at a work of art. If they stay in a museum too long, a feeling of boredom and monotony will build up, leading ___23___ to impatience and fatigue.

To ___24___ museum feet, try not to have children look at too many things in one visit. It is reported that young visitors get more out of a visit if they focus on ___25___ nine objects. One and a half hours is the ideal time to keep their eyes and minds sharp, and their feet happy!

21. (A) boring   (B) difficult   (C) cool   (D) exciting
22. (A) almost   (B) also   (C) even   (D) meanwhile
23. (A) efficiently   (B) eventually   (C) fortunately   (D) permanently
24. (A) affect   (B) approach   (C) assure   (D) avoid
25. (A) no better than   (B) no less than
     (C) no more than   (D) no sooner than

第 26 至 30 題為題組

In the desert of southwest Peru, enormous shapes, complex patterns, and thousands of perfectly straight lines are cut into the desert's surface. They are known as the Nazca lines and they ___26___ 500 square kilometers. There are about fifty animal figures ___27___ 275 meters

long, including a monkey, a spider, and an "owl man." The last of these
lines were drawn about 1,000 years ago. More ___28___ is the fact that
they can be viewed only from the air. Some people believe the Nazca
Indians were ___29___ able to fly, perhaps in balloons. Others say the
lines were landing areas for alien spaceships. Maybe the lines were to
carry water for farming, or were used as a calendar. The only thing
certain is that the Nazca lines remain one of the world's most fascinating
___30___ mysteries.

26. (A) circle   (B) contain   (C) cover   (D) wrap
27. (A) far from   (B) such as   (C) up to   (D) as much as
28. (A) amazing   (B) hesitating   (C) interacting   (D) satisfying
29. (A) someday   (B) somehow   (C) sometime   (D) somewhere
30. (A) unchanged   (B) undetermined (C) unfolded   (D) unsolved

三、文意選填（10％）

說明： 第 31 至 40 題，每題一個空格。請依文意在文章後所提供的 (A) 到 (J)
選項中分別選出最適當者，並將其字母代號標示在答案卡之「選擇題
答案區」。每題答對得 1 分，答錯或劃記多於一個選項者倒扣 1/9 分，
倒扣到本大題之實得分數爲零爲止。未作答者，不給分亦不扣分。

第 31 至 40 題爲題組

With one out of every two American marriages ending in divorce,
custody of children has become an issue in the American society. Up
until the late 1970s, it had been common practice in the United States to
automatically ___31___ custody to the mother when a divorce occurred.

However, since the 1970s, this practice has been ___32___. Most
custody battles today are decided, in theory, on the basis of who is the
more fit parent for the child. The reality, nevertheless, is that most
women still win custody of their children in a ___33___.

This legal change was the result of the social changes that ___34___ in the United States during the 1960s and 1970s. These changes challenged many of the ___35___ roles men and women were expected to play. As a ___36___, it is not uncommon nowadays to find women working outside their homes and being very ___37___ about their careers and personal lives. It is also not ___38___ to see men accepting roles that were once considered the exclusive domain of women, such as shopping for groceries, driving their children to and from school, or cleaning their homes.

Because of the ___39___ in the divorce rate, the change in the roles that men and women are expected to play, and the changing attitude of the judicial system toward child custody, more men have started to ___40___ for and win custody of their children when divorce occurs.

(A) award   (B) challenged   (C) concerned   (D) consequence
(E) divorce   (F) fight   (G) increase   (H) took place
(I) traditional   (J) unusual

四、篇章結構（10％）

說明：　第 41 至 45 題，每題一個空格。請依文意在文章後所提供的 (A) 到 (E) 選項中分別選出最適當者，填入空格中，使篇章結構清晰有條理，並將其英文字母代號標示在答案卡之「選擇題答案區」。每題答對得 2 分，答錯或劃記多於一個選項者倒扣 1/2 分，倒扣到本大題之實得分數為零為止。未作答者，不給分亦不扣分。

第 41 至 45 題為題組

Many people say that e-mail is just a faster way to deliver letters. The fact is that letter writing and e-mail are completely different processes. Handwritten or typed, letters travel in envelopes through actual space and take time getting from one place to another. ___41___ If I am writing on paper to my brother in Kenya, I will be less likely to complain about the breakfast I had this morning. I will probably write

about my relationships and some things that I've been thinking about.
___42___ People tend to regard letters as important. My brother might
save my letter; he might read it back to me years from now.

___43___ It is instant, traveling from point to point. If you don't
print it out, the message doesn't physically exist. With e-mail,
geography is no obstacle and time is not important. ___44___ The ease
of this kind of writing and sending probably makes for a different kind
of communication. I can complain about the breakfast I had this
morning or rattle on about friends and movies. That is because I am not
so focused on style and profundity. ___45___ My brother might glance
at my mail, have a laugh, and then delete it.

(A) E-mail is different.
(B) The downside is, I might be less likely to say something deeper.
(C) The time and distance, as a matter of fact, influence the letter-writer.
(D) I can zap a message to Kenya whenever I want to, and it gets there
almost in a second.
(E) I will also take more care with my style, trying to write in a way that
is interesting and worth reading.

五、閱讀測驗（22％）

說明：　第 46 至 56 題，每題請分別根據各篇文章的文意選出一個最適當的選
項，標示在答案卡之「選擇題答案區」。每題答對得 2 分，答錯或劃
記多於一個選項者倒扣 2/3 分，倒扣到本大題之實得分數爲零爲止。
未作答者，不給分亦不扣分。

第 46 至 48 題爲題組

Rice balls with folded plastic wrappers separating the rice from the
seaweed; a dozen kinds of cold tea in a dozen different bottles—enter
any convenience store in Japan, and you're immediately struck by the
great variety and quality of the packaging!

Japanese companies have been accused of over-packaging; but within the Japanese cultural context, that's not really true. The Japanese tend to use more packaging because of a cultural emphasis on freshness and a lack of storage space at home. Moreover, they believe nice packaging adds value because it's a strong signal of quality. What's more, compared with Westerners, the Japanese are more connected with packaging as a symbol of appreciation, love and care. Packaging has, therefore, attained an important place in Japan's economy. The packaging market is worth over ￥7.4 trillion. New packaging is introduced to Japanese store shelves at a rate of 20 percent per year, the highest rate in the world. In such an environment, a product has to have more than just a nice graphic design to differentiate it from its **shelf-mates**. The product has to speak to the consumer's needs with both personality and practical value. In this changing industry, nothing is really certain except one thing. You can be sure that the goods out there on display on the shelves of the convenience store will soon be looking rather different.

46. This passage is most likely taken from a _____.
   (A) cookbook
   (B) user's manual
   (C) consumer report
   (D) fashion magazine

47. Which of the following is NOT a reason for the Japanese to use more packaging?
   (A) Packaging helps to keep food fresh.
   (B) Packaging helps the Japanese to show appreciation.
   (C) The Japanese consider packaging a symbol of quality.
   (D) Packaging is a way to compete with Westerners in economy.

48. The word **"shelf-mates"** in the second paragraph most likely refers
    to _____.
    (A) co-workers on the job
    (B) other products in the store
    (C) customers' need for other products
    (D) other graphic designs on the package

第 49 至 52 題爲題組

Native Americans could not understand the white man's war on the
wolf. The Lakota, Blackfeet, and Shoshone, among other tribes,
considered the wolf their spiritual brother. They respected the animals'
endurance and hunting ability, and warriors prayed to hunt like them.
They draped themselves in wolf skins and paws, hoping they could
acquire the wolf's hunting skills of stealth, courage, and stamina. Plains
Indians wore wolf-skin disguises on raiding parties. Elite Comanche
warriors were called wolves.

The white settlers' war on the wolf raged on. Western ranchers
continued to claim that thousands of cattle were killed every year by
wolves. In 1884, Montana created its first wolf bounty—one dollar for
every dead wolf, which increased to eight dollars in 1893. Over a
period of thirty-five years, more than eighty thousand wolf carcasses
were submitted for bounty payments in Montana. Moreover, the
government even provided free poison. Finally, in 1914, ranchers
persuaded the United States Congress to provide funds to exterminate
wolves on public lands.

The last wolves in the American West died hard. No place was safe,
not even the nation's first national park, Yellowstone. The park was
created in 1872, and from its very beginning, poisoned carcasses were

set out to kill wolves. Nearly 140 wolves were killed by park rangers in Yellowstone from 1914 to 1926. In October 1926, two wolf cubs were trapped near a bison carcass. They were the last animals killed in the park's wolf control programs.

Ranchers had won the war against the wolf. Only in the northern woods of Wisconsin, Minnesota, and Michigan could the howl of native gray wolves be heard. The vast lands of the American West fell silent. The country had lost its greatest predator.

49. The white man tried to kill the gray wolf because _____.
    (A) it attacked people
    (B) it damaged the crops
    (C) it was adored by the Indians
    (D) it threatened the life of his livestock

50. This passage was most likely written by someone who _____.
    (A) liked hunting wild animals
    (B) made laws against the gray wolf
    (C) advocated the protection of the gray wolf
    (D) appreciated the gray wolf's hunting skills

51. What was an important reason for the fast disappearance of the wolf?
    (A) The wolf could not have the cattle as food.
    (B) The Indians killed the wolves for their skins.
    (C) National park rangers killed most of the wolves.
    (D) The government encouraged the killing of wolves.

52. The Indians respected the wolf because it _____.
    (A) was good at hunting
    (B) was good at disguising
    (C) had beautiful skins and paws
    (D) was an enemy to the white man

第 53 至 56 題爲題組

Recently, Dr. Stuart Campbell of a private health center in London published some ultrasound images of unborn babies between 26 and 34 weeks. The smiles of the babies in the pictures greatly shocked the public and were widely circulated on the Internet.

For the past two years, the doctor has used the medical facility in the center and has offered state-of-the-art 3-D/4-D scanning services to expectant parents. He performs an average of 30 scans a week. His outspoken enthusiasm for this blessed technology is refreshing. "Parents love them," he said. "I hear so many couples laughing when they see the pictures—it's wonderful."

How have pro-abortion activists reacted after seeing the happy, grinning photos of these unborn babies?

Anne Carp, a commentator for the *Guardian* who bills herself as a "medical sociologist," says the photos are simply misleading, and ridicules the anti-abortion lobby for being "intoxicated with evidence of a fetus' humanity." Australian Birth Control Services medical director Geoff Brodie complained that the photos "will be picked up by those groups that use anything and everything to stop abortions but ignore the fact that women have a right to choice."

In America, the pro-abortion lobby is having the same hostile reaction. It was bad enough when conventional 2-D sonograms revealed unborn hearts beating and blurry hands waving, but the abortionists are absolutely aghast over rapidly spreading access to 3-D/4-D ultrasound technology. A writer for the liberal *American Prospect* said that the new technology "blurred the distinction between a fetus and a newborn infant."

Despite these strong reactions from the pro-abortionists, the right of life takes precedence over a woman's right to choice. After all, nothing can be more persuasive than an unborn child's beaming face.

53. What is the author's attitude toward abortion?
    (A) For it.   (B) Against it.
    (C) Neutral.   (D) Indifferent.

54. How have the pro-abortionists reacted to the photos of smiling unborn babies?
    (A) All with disbelief and scorn.
    (B) All with applause and appreciation.
    (C) Some with respect and some with scorn.
    (D) Some with applause and some with disappointment.

55. Which of the following people is most likely an anti-abortionist?
    (A) Anne Carp.
    (B) Geoff Brodie.
    (C) Stuart Campbell.
    (D) A writer for the *American Prospect*.

56. Which of the following statements can be inferred from the passage?
    (A) It is wrong for doctors to publish pictures of unborn babies.
    (B) For anti-abortionists a fetus is not the same as a living human being.
    (C) Everybody agrees that a woman can decide whether to abort or not.
    (D) Anti-abortionists are pleased with the ultrasound photos of unborn babies.

第貳部份：非選擇題（佔 28 分）

一、英文翻譯（8％）

說明：　1. 將下列兩句中文翻譯成適當之英文，並將答案寫在「答案卷」上。

　　　　2. 未按題意翻譯者，不予計分。

1. 為提供一個無煙的用餐環境，許多餐廳不允許室內抽煙。

2. 雖然遭到許多癮君子的反對，這對不抽煙的人的確是一大福音。

二、英文作文（20％）

說明：　1. 依提示在「答案卷」上寫一篇英文作文。

　　　　2. 文長至少 120 個單詞。

提示：　人的生活中，難免有遭人誤解因而感到委屈的時候。請以此為主題，
　　　　寫一篇至少 120 字的英文作文；第一段描述個人被誤解的經驗，第二
　　　　段談這段經驗對個人的影響與啓示。

✻ 九十五年度指定科目考試英文科試題詳解 ✻

第壹部分：選擇題

一、詞彙：

1. (**D**) Mastery of English <u>equips</u> us with a very important tool for acquiring knowledge and information.
   精通英文<u>使</u>我們在獲得知識和訊息時，<u>具備了</u>重要的工具。
   (A) access〔'æk`sɛs〕 *v.* 存取（資料） *n.* 接近；使用權
   (B) convey〔kən've〕 *v.* 傳達
   (C) deprive〔dɪ'praɪv〕 *v.* 剝奪
   (D) *equip*〔ɪ'kwɪp〕 *v.* 使具備　　*equip sb. with sth.* 使某人具備某事物
   mastery〔'mæstərɪ〕 *n.* 精通　　acquire〔ə'kwaɪr〕 *v.* 獲得

2. (**B**) Languages change all the time. Many words that were found in Shakespeare's works are no longer in <u>current</u> use.
   語言一直在改變，許多在莎士比亞作品裡面發現的字，<u>現在</u>都不再使用了。
   (A) absolute〔'æbsə,lut〕 *adj.* 絕對的
   (B) *current*〔'kɝənt〕 *adj.* 現今的
   (C) repetitive〔rɪ'pɛtɪtɪv〕 *adj.* 重複的
   (D) valuable〔'væljʊəbḷ〕 *adj.* 珍貴的
   all the time 一直；經常　　*Shakespeare* 莎士比亞（英國劇作家）
   work〔wɝk〕 *n.* 作品　　*no longer* 不再

3. (**B**) Do not just sit and wait <u>passively</u> for a good chance to come to you. You have to take the initiative and create chances for yourself.
   不要<u>被動地</u>坐著等好機會到來。你必須主動爲自己創造機會。
   (A) consciously〔'kɑnʃəslɪ〕 *adv.* 有意識地
   (B) *passively*〔'pæsɪvlɪ〕 *adv.* 被動地；消極地
   (C) reasonably〔'riznəblɪ〕 *adv.* 合理地
   (D) subjectively〔səb'dʒɛktɪvlɪ〕 *adv.* 主觀地
   initiative〔ɪ'nɪʃɪ,etɪv〕 *n.* 主動　　*take the initiative* 採取主動

4. (**D**) Identical twins have almost all of their genes in common, so any <u>variation</u> between them is in large part due to the effects of the environment.

同卵雙胞胎幾乎所有的基因都相同，所以他們之間的任何<u>差異</u>，大部份都是因為環境的影響。

(A) adoption〔ə'dapʃən〕n. 採用；領養
(B) familiarity〔fə,mɪlɪ'ærətɪ〕n. 熟悉
(C) stability〔stə'bɪlətɪ〕n. 穩定
(D) *variation*〔,vɛrɪ'eʃən〕n. 差異

identical〔aɪ'dɛntɪkḷ〕adj. 同卵的　　*identical twins* 同卵雙胞胎
gene〔dʒin〕n. 基因　　*in common* 共同的
due to 由於　　environment〔ɪn'vaɪrənmənt〕n. 環境

5. (**B**) People believed in the <u>integrity</u> of the judge, so they were shocked to hear that he was involved in the bribery scandal.

人們相信那位法官很<u>正直</u>，所以當他們聽到他捲入賄賂醜聞時，都非常震驚。

(A) inferiority〔ɪn,fɪrɪ'arətɪ〕n. 劣等；低劣
(B) *integrity*〔ɪn'tɛgrətɪ〕n. 正直
(C) intimacy〔'ɪntəməsɪ〕n. 親密
(D) ingenuity〔,ɪndʒə'nuətɪ〕n. 巧妙

judge〔dʒʌdʒ〕n. 法官　　shocked〔ʃakt〕adj. 震驚的
involved〔ɪn'valvd〕adj. 涉及的；捲入的
bribery〔'braɪbərɪ〕n. 賄賂　　scandal〔'skændḷ〕n. 醜聞

6. (**A**) The discovery of the new vaccine is an important <u>breakthrough</u> in the fight against avian flu.

新疫苗的發現，在防禦禽流感上是很大的<u>突破</u>。

(A) *breakthrough*〔'brek,θru〕n. 突破
(B) commitment〔kə'mɪtmənt〕n. 承諾
(C) demonstration〔,dɛmən'streʃən〕n. 示威；示範
(D) interpretation〔ɪn,tɝprɪ'teʃən〕n. 解釋；說明

vaccine〔'væksin〕n. 疫苗　　fight〔faɪt〕n. 防禦；抵抗
avian〔'evɪən〕adj. 鳥的；鳥類的　　*avian flu* 禽流感

7. (**A**) To avoid being misled by news reports, we should learn to <u>distinguish</u> between facts and opinions.

為了避免被新聞報導誤導，我們應該學習<u>分辨</u>事實與見解。

(A) ***distinguish*** 〔 dɪ'stɪŋgwɪʃ 〕 *v.* 分辨
(B) complicate 〔 'kɑmplə‚ket 〕 *v.* 使複雜
(C) reinforce 〔 ‚riɪn'fors 〕 *v.* 強化
(D) speculate 〔 'spɛkjə‚let 〕 *v.* 思索；推測

mislead 〔 mɪs'lid 〕 *v.* 誤導
opinion 〔 ə'pɪnjən 〕 *n.* 見解

8. (**B**) After the big flood, the area was mostly <u>deserted</u>, with only one or two homes still clinging to their last relics.

在大水災過後，這個地區大多<u>無人居住</u>，只有一、兩戶人家留在殘留的廢墟裡。

(A) condense 〔 kən'dɛns 〕 *v.* 濃縮
(B) ***desert*** 〔 dɪ'zɝt 〕 *v.* 拋棄；撤離（某地）
(C) exclude 〔 ɪk'sklud 〕 *v.* 排除
(D) remove 〔 rɪ'muv 〕 *v.* 除去

flood 〔 flʌd 〕 *n.* 洪水；水災　　cling 〔 klɪŋ 〕 *v.* 逗留不去
relics 〔 'rɛlɪks 〕 *n.* 廢墟

9. (**C**) In his speech, Dr. Huang presented all the reports about the energy crisis to <u>highlight</u> the need for developing new energy resources.

黃博士在他的演講當中，提出了所有關於能源危機的報告，來<u>強調</u>開發新能源的必要。

(A) command 〔 kə'mænd 〕 *v.* 命令
(B) formulate 〔 'fɔrmjə‚let 〕 *v.* 使公式化
(C) ***highlight*** 〔 'haɪ‚laɪt 〕 *v.* 強調
(D) regulate 〔 'rɛgjə‚let 〕 *v.* 管制

present 〔 prɪ'zɛnt 〕 *v.* 提出　　crisis 〔 'kraɪsɪs 〕 *n.* 危機
resource 〔 rɪ'sors 〕 *n.* 資源

10. (**A**) Hearing the art critic's bitter and <u>outrageous</u> comments on her new painting, Molly started a heated argument with him.

聽到這個藝術評論家對其新畫作既嚴厲又<u>無禮的</u>批評，茉莉開始跟他激烈地辯論。

(A) ***outrageous*** 〔 aut'redʒəs 〕 *adj.* 無禮的

(B) unreliable 〔 ˌʌnrɪ'laɪəbḷ 〕 *adj.* 不可信賴的

(C) urgent 〔 'ɝdʒənt 〕 *adj.* 緊急的　　(D) glorious 〔 'glorɪəs 〕 *adj.* 光榮的

critic 〔 'krɪtɪk 〕 *n.* 評論家　　　　bitter 〔 'bɪtɚ 〕 *adj.* 嚴厲的

comment 〔 'kamɛnt 〕 *n.* 評論　　　heated 〔 'hitɪd 〕 *adj.* 激烈的

argument 〔 'argjəmənt 〕 *n.* 辯論

二、綜合測驗：

第 11 至 15 題爲題組

　　Measurements are needed in many everyday activities. In kitchens you will find measures for volume (measuring cups), mass (scales and weights), and temperature (cooking thermometers). Accurate measurements are <u>particularly</u> important for scientific experiments. In a laboratory, make
11
sure your measure meets your needs. <u>Before</u> using any thermometer, double
12
check that it covers the right temperature <u>range</u> for your activity or
13
experiment. A garden thermometer, <u>for instance</u>, will burst if you try to
14
use it for boiling liquids.

　　在日常活動中，我們都需要用到度量。在廚房裡面，你會發現測量容積（量杯），質量（磅秤和砝碼），以及溫度（烹調溫度計）的工具。精確的度量，對於科學實驗格外地重要。在實驗室中，要確定測量工具能滿足你的需求。在使用任何溫度計之前，要再次確認它有涵蓋你的活動或實驗的正確溫度範圍。舉例來說，如果你把園藝用的溫度計放到沸騰的液體裡面，溫度計就會爆裂。

measurement 〔 'mɛʒɚmənt 〕 *n.* 度量；測量

measure 〔 'mɛʒɚ 〕 *n.* 測量（工具）

volume 〔 'valjəm 〕 *n.* 體積；容積；容量

mass 〔 mæs 〕 *n.* 質量；重量　　　scale 〔 skel 〕 *n.* 磅秤

weight 〔 wet 〕 *n.* 砝碼　　　thermometer 〔 θə'mamətɚ 〕 *n.* 溫度計

accurate 〔 'ækjərɪt 〕 *adj.* 精確的　　　meet 〔 mit 〕 *v.* 滿足

burst 〔 bɝst 〕 *v.* 爆裂　　　boiling 〔 'bɔɪlɪŋ 〕 *adj.* 煮沸的

11. (**C**) (A) deliberately〔dɪˈlɪbərɪtlɪ〕*adv.* 故意地

(B) instantly〔ˈɪnstəntlɪ〕*adv.* 立即地

(C) ***particularly***〔pəˈtɪkjələlɪ〕*adv.* 特別地；尤其

(D) scarcely〔ˈskɛrslɪ〕*adv.* 幾乎沒有

12. (**B**) (A) after 在～之後　　　(B) ***before*** 在～之前

(C) for 為了～　　　　(D) without 沒有～

13. (**A**) (A) ***range***〔rendʒ〕*n.* 範圍；幅度

(B) record〔ˈrɛkəd〕*n.* 紀錄

(C) system〔ˈsɪstəm〕*n.* 系統

(D) unit〔ˈjunɪt〕*n.* 單位

14. (**D**) (A) in short 簡言之　　(B) in turn 依序地

(C) by contrast 對照之下　(D) ***for instance*** 舉例來說

There are different systems of measures. Most scientists now use the International System of measures, with meters for length, kilograms for mass, and seconds for time. If the measures in your experiment show other units, appropriate conversion tables for different systems may prove to be very useful.

度量有很多種體系。大多數的科學家目前是使用國際測量系統，其中包括用公尺來測量長度，用公斤來測量重量，以及用秒來測量時間。如果你的實驗是以其他測量單位來顯示，那麼不同系統間的適當轉換表會對你很有幫助。

> length〔lɛŋθ〕*n.* 長度
> appropriate〔əˈproprɪɪt〕*adj.* 適當的
> conversion〔kənˈvɜʃən〕*n.* 轉變；轉換
> table〔ˈtebḷ〕*n.* 表；一覽表
> prove〔pruv〕*v.* 證明；證實

15. (**B**) (A) distance〔ˈdɪstəns〕*n.* 距離

(B) ***mass***〔mæs〕*n.* 重量

(C) temperature〔ˈtɛmpərətʃə〕*n.* 溫度

(D) volume〔ˈvɑljəm〕*n.* 體積

第 16 至 20 題為題組

Every year Catemaco, a small town in the south of Mexico, hosts the Annual Witch Gathering. Healers and witch doctors converge on this beautiful lakeside town in March to make their yearly trade.

每年在墨西哥南部的一個小鎮──卡特馬可，都會舉辦年度女巫聚會。治療師和巫醫會在三月時，聚集到這個美麗的湖邊小鎮，來從事一年一度的交易。

host〔host〕*v.* 主辦　　　annual〔'ænjʊəl〕*adj.* 年度的
witch〔wɪtʃ〕*n.* 女巫　　　gathering〔'gæðrɪŋ〕*n.* 集會
healer〔'hilɚ〕*n.* 治療師　　converge〔kən'vɝdʒ〕*v.* 聚集
lakeside〔'lek,saɪd〕*n.* 湖邊　　trade〔tred〕*n.* 交易

<u>Ever</u> since pre-Hispanic times, Lake Catemaco has been a centre for
　16
alternative medicine and strange treatments. <u>In fact</u>, the area's association
　　　　　　　　　　　　　　　　　　　　　　　　17
with witchcraft dates back to Olmec times more than 2,000 years ago.

在西班牙統治時期以前，卡特馬可湖就一直是另類醫療和奇特療法的中心。
事實上，這個區域和巫術的關聯，要回溯到兩千多年前的奧爾梅克時期。

pre- 表示「以前的」字首。
Hispanic〔hɪs'pænɪk〕*adj.* 西班牙的
pre-Hispanic times 西班牙統治時期以前【指 1533 年以前】
centre〔'sɛntɚ〕*n.* 中心（= *center*）
alternative〔ɔl'tɝnətɪv〕*adj.* 另類的
association〔ə,soʃɪ'eʃən〕*n.* 關聯
witchcraft〔'wɪtʃ,kræft〕*n.* 巫術
date back to 追溯到
Olmec〔'olmek〕*adj.* 奧爾梅克的【1000-300 B.C.，印第安族奧爾梅克人，分布於墨西哥韋拉克魯斯州和塔瓦斯科州】

16. (**A**) *ever since* 自從…以來（= *since*）

17. (**C**) (A) in advance　事先　　　　(B) in all　總計
　　　　　　(C) *in fact*　事實上　　　　(D) in sum　總之

If you've ever seen the Sean Connery movie *Medicine Man*, then the
                                                              18
annual convention of wizards and witches will be familiar to you. If not,
                                                                      19
get prepared for the overwhelming attack of wizards and witches here.
如果你曾經看過史恩康納萊的電影——燃燒的天堂，那麼你就會對男巫和女巫
的年度會議感到熟悉。如果你沒看過那部電影，那你就要準備好，這裡的男巫
和女巫，會對你產生壓倒性的衝擊。

> convention〔kən'vɛnʃən〕 *n.* 會議　　wizard〔'wɪzəd〕 *n.* 男巫
> familiar〔fə'mɪljə〕 *adj.* 熟悉的
> overwhelming〔͵ovə'hwɛlmɪŋ〕 *adj.* 壓倒性的
> attack〔ə'tæk〕 *n.* 攻擊

18. (**C**) 本句已有連接詞 If，因此選副詞 (C) *then*「那麼」。

19. (**B**) 依句意，「如果」你「沒」看過那部電影，選 (B) *If not*。

Most witch doctors are guaranteed to be charlatans, not real doctors, who
go after some quick money from tourists. Yet, don't be surprised if the
    20
occasional remedy offered is effective.
我保證大部份的巫醫都是江湖郎中，不是真的醫生，他們只想從遊客身上迅速
賺到錢。但是，如果偶爾他們的治療有效，也不要太驚訝。

> guarantee〔͵gærən'ti〕 *v.* 保證
> charlatan〔'ʃɑrlətn̩〕 *n.* 江湖郎中；騙子
> occasional〔ə'keʒənl̩〕 *adj.* 偶爾的　　remedy〔'rɛmədɪ〕 *n.* 治療
> offer〔'ɔfə〕 *v.* 提供　　effective〔ə'fɛktɪv〕 *adj.* 有效的

20. (**A**)　(A) *go after* 尋求　　　　(B) turn down 拒絕；關小聲
　　　　　　　　(C) give away 贈送　　　(D) complain about 抱怨

第 21 至 25 題為題組

　　Young visitors to museums often complain about having museum
feet, the tired feeling one gets after spending too much time in a museum.
A case of museum feet makes one feel like saying: "This is boring. I could
                                                                       21
have done the painting myself. When can we sit down? What time is it?"

　　到博物館去參觀的年輕人，常會抱怨他們有 "museum feet"，也就是當一個人花太多時間待在一座博物館內，就會開始有的疲倦感。"museum feet" 的症狀會使一個人想說：「這真是無聊。我也可以畫出這樣的畫。我們什麼時候可以坐下？現在幾點了？」

　　　　museum〔mju'ziəm〕*n.* 博物館
　　　　complain〔kəm'plen〕*v.* 抱怨　　case〔kes〕*n.* 症狀
　　　　feel like 想要　　painting〔'pentɪŋ〕*n.* 畫

21.（**A**）依句意，選 (A) ***boring***「無聊的」。而 (B) 困難的，(C) 很酷的，(D) 刺激的，則不合句意。

　　Studies of museum behavior show that the average visitor spends about four seconds looking at one object. For young visitors, the time span can be <u>even</u> shorter. Children are more interested in smells, sounds, and
　　　　　　　　22
the "feel" of a place than looking at a work of art. If they stay in a museum too long, a feeling of boredom and monotony will build up, leading <u>eventually</u> to impatience and fatigue.
　　23
　　博物館行為的研究顯示，一般的參訪者會花四秒鐘左右，來看一個東西。而年紀小的參訪者，花的時間更短。兒童對氣味、聲音，以及一個地方的「感覺」，比看藝術品的興趣還濃厚。如果他們在博物館裡待太久，他們就會開始愈來愈覺得無聊和枯燥，最後就導致不耐煩和疲倦。

　　　　average〔'ævərɪdʒ〕*adj.* 一般的　　object〔'ɑbdʒɪkt〕*n.* 物體
　　　　span〔spæn〕*n.* 期間　　smell〔smɛl〕*n.* 氣味
　　　　sound〔saund〕*n.* 聲音　　work〔wɝk〕*n.* 作品
　　　　boredom〔'bɔrdəm〕*n.* 無聊　　monotony〔mə'nɑtn̩ɪ〕*n.* 枯燥無味
　　　　build up 增加　　***lead to*** 導致
　　　　impatience〔ɪm'peʃəns〕*n.* 不耐煩　　fatigue〔fə'tig〕*n.* 疲倦

22.（**C**）much、even、still、far 可修飾比較級，故選 (C)。

23.（**B**）(A) efficiently〔ə'fɪʃəntlɪ〕*adv.* 有效率地
　　　　(B) ***eventually***〔ɪ'vɛntʃuəlɪ〕*adv.* 最後
　　　　(C) fortunately〔'fɔrtʃənɪtlɪ〕*adv.* 幸運地
　　　　(D) permanently〔'pɝmənəntlɪ〕*adv.* 永遠

To avoid museum feet, try not to have children look at too many things
    24
in one visit. It is reported that young visitors get more out of a visit if
they focus on no more than nine objects. One and a half hours is the ideal
                        25
time to keep their eyes and minds sharp, and their feet happy!

要避免出現 "museum feet" 的症狀，就要試著別讓兒童一次看太多東西。研究報告指出，年輕的參訪者如果把注意力只集中在九件作品上，那麼這趟參訪會得到更多東西。讓他們的眼睛和頭腦保持敏銳最理想的時間，是一個半小時，而且他們的腳也會很輕鬆！

> report〔rɪ'port〕v. 報導；報告　　*get ~ out of* 從…中獲得~
> focus〔'fokəs〕v. 集中　　ideal〔aɪ'diəl〕*adj.* 理想的
> sharp〔ʃɑrp〕*adj.* 敏銳的

24. (**D**) (A) affect〔ə'fɛkt〕v. 影響　　(B) approach〔ə'protʃ〕v. 接近
　　　　　　 (C) assure〔ə'ʃur〕v. 向…保證　　(D) *avoid*〔ə'vɔɪd〕v. 避免

25. (**C**) (A) no better than　簡直是
　　　　　　 (B) no less than　不少於；與…一樣多
　　　　　　 (C) *no more than*　只；僅
　　　　　　 (D) no sooner than ~　沒有比~快

第 26 至 30 題為題組

In the desert of southwest Peru, enormous shapes, complex patterns,
and thousands of perfectly straight lines are cut into the desert's surface.
They are known as the Nazca lines and they cover 500 square kilometers.
                                              26
There are about fifty animal figures up to 275 meters long, including a
                                     27
monkey, a spider, and an "owl man."

祕魯西南的沙漠表面，被形狀巨大、圖案複雜，且數目成千的完美直線所切割。它們是著名的納斯卡線，覆蓋在五百平方公里的沙漠上。大約有五十個動物圖案是長達二百七十五公尺的，包括一隻猴子、蜘蛛，還有一個「貓頭鷹人」。

desert〔'dɛzət〕 n. 沙漠　　Peru〔pə'ru〕 n. 祕魯
enormous〔ɪ'nɔrməs〕 adj. 巨大的　　shape〔ʃep〕 n. 形狀
complex〔'kɑmplɛks〕 adj. 複雜的
pattern〔'pætən〕 n. 圖案；花樣
perfectly〔'pɝfɪktlɪ〕 adv. 完美無缺地　　straight〔stret〕 adj. 直的
surface〔'sɝfɪs〕 n. 表面　　 **be known as** 以…聞名
square〔skwɛr〕 adj. 平方的
kilometer〔'kɪlə,mitə〕 n. 公里　　figure〔'fɪgjə〕 n. 圖案
include〔ɪn'klud〕 v. 包括　　spider〔'spaɪdə〕 n. 蜘蛛
owl〔aʊl〕 n. 貓頭鷹

26. (**C**) (A) circle〔'sɝkl̩〕 v. 圈出；圍著　　(B) contain〔kən'ten〕 v. 包含
　　　　 (C) *cover*〔'kʌvə〕 v. 覆蓋　　(D) wrap〔ræp〕 v. 包；裹

27. (**C**) (A) far from 遠離　　(B) such as 像是
　　　　 (C) *up to* 高達　　(D) as much as 和…一樣多

The last of these lines were drawn about 1,000 years ago. More <u>amazing</u>
　　　　　　　　　　　　　　　　　　　　　　　　　　　　　28
is the fact that they can be viewed only from the air. Some people believe
the Nazca Indians were <u>somehow</u> able to fly, perhaps in balloons. Others
　　　　　　　　　　　　　　29
say the lines were landing areas for alien spaceships.

在這些線條當中，最後一條是在一千前左右畫的。更令人驚訝的是，我們只能從空中看見這些線條。有些人認為納斯卡印地安人可能有辦法飛行，也許是乘氣球飛行。其他人認為，這些線條是外星人太空船的降落區域。

view〔vju〕 v. 看　　Indian〔'ɪndɪən〕 n. 印地安人
balloon〔bə'lun〕 n. 氣球　　landing〔'lændɪŋ〕 n. 降落
area〔'ɛrɪə〕 n. 區域　　alien〔'eljən〕 adj. 外星人的
spaceship〔'spes,ʃɪp〕 n. 太空船

28. (**A**) (A) *amazing*〔ə'mezɪŋ〕 adj. 令人驚訝的
　　　　 (B) hesitating〔'hɛzə,tetɪŋ〕 adj. 猶豫不決的
　　　　 (C) interacting〔,ɪntə'æktɪŋ〕 adj. 互動的
　　　　 (D) satisfying〔'sætɪs,faɪɪŋ〕 adj. 令人滿意的

29. (**B**) (A) someday〔'sʌm,de〕adv. 將來有一天

　　(B) ***somehow***〔'sʌm,haʊ〕adv. 以某種方法

　　(C) sometime〔'sʌm,taɪm〕adv. 有一天；某時

　　(D) somewhere〔'sʌm,hwɛr〕adv. 在某處

Maybe the lines were to carry water for farming, or were used as a calendar. The only thing certain is that the Nazca lines remain one of the world's most fascinating <u>unsolved</u> mysteries.
　　　　　　　　　　30

也許這些線條是運送農業用水，或是當作日曆使用。唯一可以確定的是，納斯卡線仍是世界上最迷人的未解的謎。

　　　　carry〔'kærɪ〕v. 運送　　farming〔'farmɪŋ〕n. 農耕

　　　　calendar〔'kæləndɚ〕n. 日曆；月曆　　certain〔'sɝtn̩〕adj. 確定的

　　　　remain〔rɪ'men〕v. 仍然　　fascinating〔'fæsn̩,etɪŋ〕adj. 迷人的

　　　　mystery〔'mɪstrɪ〕n. 謎

30. (**D**) (A) unchanged〔ʌn'tʃendʒd〕adj. 未改變的

　　(B) undetermined〔,ʌndɪ't3mɪnd〕adj. 未決定的

　　(C) unfolded〔ʌn'foldɪd〕adj. 展開的

　　(D) ***unsolved***〔ʌn'salvd〕adj. 未解決的

三、文意選填：

<u>第 31 至 40 題為題組</u>

　　With one out of every two American marriages ending in divorce, custody of children has become an issue in the American society. Up until the late 1970s, it had been common practice in the United States to automatically <u>award</u> custody to the mother when a divorce occurred.
　　　　　　31

　　由於美國人每兩個婚姻中，就有一個是以離婚收場，所以孩子的監護權，就變成美國社會的重要議題。直到一九七〇年代末期，在美國離婚，一般的做法，都是將監護權自動判給母親。

　　　　marriage〔'mærɪdʒ〕n. 婚姻　　***end in*** 以…作為結束

　　　　divorce〔də'vors〕n. 離婚　　custody〔'kʌstədɪ〕n. 監護權

　　　　issue〔'ɪʃju〕n. 議題；問題；爭論點　　late〔let〕adj. 末期的

　　　　common〔'kamən〕adj. 一般的　　practice〔'præktɪs〕n. 慣例；做法

　　　　automatically〔,ɔtə'mætɪkl̩ɪ〕adv. 自動地　　occur〔ə'kɝ〕v. 發生

31. (**A**) 依句意，將監護權自動「判給」母親，選 (A) *award* 〔ə'wɔrd〕*v.* 將…
判歸（某人）。

However, since the 1970s, this practice has been <u>challenged</u>. Most
32
custody battles today are decided, in theory, on the basis of who is the
more fit parent for the child. The reality, nevertheless, is that most women
still win custody of their children in a <u>divorce</u>.
33

不過，自從一九七〇年代起，這項做法就受到質疑。現在大部份監護權的
戰爭，在理論上，是根據父親或母親，誰比較適合照顧孩子來判定。然而，實
際上，離婚的時候，大多還是女性會贏得孩子的監護權。

> battle〔'bætḷ〕*n.* 戰爭；爭鬥　　theory〔'θiərɪ〕*n.* 理論
> *in theory* 理論上　　　*on the basis of* 以…為基礎
> fit〔fɪt〕*adj.* 適合的　　reality〔rɪ'ælətɪ〕*n.* 事實
> nevertheless〔,nɛvəðə'lɛs〕*adv.* 然而
> win〔wɪn〕*v.* 贏得；獲得

32. (**B**) 依句意，選 (B) *challenged*。
challenge〔'tʃælɪndʒ〕*v.* 懷疑；對…提出異議；向…挑戰

33. (**E**) 依句意，選 (E) *divorce*〔də'vors〕*n.* 離婚。

This legal change was the result of the social changes that <u>took place</u>
34
in the United States during the 1960s and 1970s. These changes challenged
many of the <u>traditional</u> roles men and women were expected to play. As a
35
<u>consequence</u>, it is not uncommon nowadays to find women working outside
36
their homes and being very <u>concerned</u> about their careers and personal
37
lives. It is also not <u>unusual</u> to see men accepting roles that were once
38
considered the exclusive domain of women, such as shopping for groceries,
driving their children to and from school, or cleaning their homes.

　　這項法律上的轉變，是美國在一九六○至一九七○年間，所發生的社會變遷的結果。這些改變，挑戰了許多男人和女人，在傳統上被預期扮演的角色。因此，現在常會看到婦女出外工作，而且非常關心自己的事業與個人生活。也常會看到男人，接受以前被認爲是婦女專屬的領域的角色，像是購買雜貨、開車接送小孩上下學，或是打掃房子。

legal〔ˈligl̩〕*adj.* 法律的　　result〔rɪˈzʌlt〕*n.* 結果

role〔rol〕*n.* 角色　　expect〔ɪkˈspɛkt〕*v.* 預期；期待

play〔ple〕*v.* 扮演　　uncommon〔ʌnˈkɑmən〕*adj.* 異常的；少見的

career〔kəˈrɪr〕*n.* 事業　　personal〔ˈpɝsn̩l̩〕*adj.* 個人的

accept〔əkˈsɛpt〕*v.* 接受　　consider〔kənˈsɪdɚ〕*v.* 認爲

exclusive〔ɪkˈsklusɪv〕*adj.* 獨佔性的；佔有性的

domain〔doˈmen〕*n.* 領域；範圍　　***shop for*** 購買

grocery〔ˈgrosərɪ〕*n.* 雜貨　　drive〔draɪv〕*v.* 開車載（某人）

34.（**H**）依句意，選（H）***took place***「發生」。

35.（**I**）　依句意，選（I）***traditional***〔trəˈdɪʃənl̩〕*adj.* 傳統的。

36.（**D**）***as a consequence*** 因此

37.（**C**）***be concerned about*** 關心

38.（**J**）依句意，選（J）***unusual***〔ʌnˈjuʒʊəl〕*adj.* 罕見的；不尋常的。

Because of the <u>increase</u> in the divorce rate, the change in the roles
　　　　　　　　　　39
that men and women are expected to play, and the changing attitude of the
judicial system toward child custody, more men have started to <u>fight</u> for
　　　　　　　　　　　　　　　　　　　　　　　　　　　　　40
and win custody of their children when divorce occurs.

　　因爲離婚率增加，人們認爲男人與女人應扮演的角色已有所經改變，還有司法制度對於孩子監護權的態度改變，使得有更多男人，在離婚時，開始爭取並贏得孩子的監護權。

rate〔ret〕*n.* 比率　　attitude〔ˈætə,tjud〕*n.* 態度

judicial〔dʒuˈdɪʃəl〕*adj.* 司法的

system〔ˈsɪstəm〕*n.* 系統；制度

toward〔tord〕*prep.* 對於；關於

39.(**G**) 依句意，因為離婚率「增加」，故選 (G) *increase*〔ˋɪnkrɪs〕*n.* 增加。

40.(**F**) 有更多男人，在離婚時，開始「爭取」並贏得孩子的監護權，選 (F)*fight*
〔faɪt〕*v.* 戰鬥；奮鬥；爭鬥。　　　*fight for* 為⋯而戰；為⋯而爭鬥

四、篇章結構：

第 41 至 45 題為題組

　　Many people say that e-mail is just a faster way to deliver letters. The fact is that letter writing and e-mail are completely different processes. Handwritten or typed, letters travel in envelopes through actual space and take time getting from one place to another. ⁴¹(**C**) <u>The time and distance, as a matter of fact, influence the letter-writer.</u> If I am writing on paper to my brother in Kenya, I will be less likely to complain about the breakfast I had this morning. I will probably write about my relationships and some things that I've been thinking about. ⁴²(**E**) <u>I will also take more care with my style, trying to write in a way that is interesting and worth reading.</u> People tend to regard letters as important. My brother might save my letter; he might read it back to me years from now.

　　許多人說，電子郵件只是一種更快的送信方式。事實上，寫信和電子郵件是完全不同的過程。不論是手寫或打字的，信件在信封內，經由實際的空間旅行，花費時間從甲地到乙地。實際上，時間和距離影響寫信的人。如果我正在紙上寫信給在肯亞的哥哥，就比較不可能去抱怨我今天早上所吃的早餐。我可能會寫我和家人的關係，以及我一直在想的某些事。我也會更注意我的文體，試著用一種有趣，和值得閱讀的方式來寫信。人們往往認為信件很重要，我哥哥可能會把我的信存起來，可能幾年後，把這封信讀給我聽。

deliver〔dɪˋlɪvɚ〕*v.* 遞送(信件)　　process〔ˋprɑsɛs〕*n.* 過程
type〔taɪp〕*v.* 打字　　envelope〔ˋɛnvə͵lop〕*n.* 信封
actual〔ˋæktʃʊəl〕*adj.* 實際的　　*as a matter of fact* 實際上
influence〔ˋɪnflʊəns〕*v.* 影響
Kenya〔ˋkɛnjə〕*n.* 肯亞共和國【在非洲東部】
likely〔ˋlaɪklɪ〕*adj.* 有可能的　　relationship〔rɪˋleʃən͵ʃɪp〕*n.* 親戚關係
take care 小心；注意　　style〔staɪl〕*n.* 文體；風格

[43] **(A) E-mail is different.** It is instant, traveling from point to point. If you don't print it out, the message doesn't physically exist. With e-mail, geography is no obstacle and time is not important. [44] **(D) I can zap a message to Kenya whenever I want to, and it gets there almost in a second.** The ease of this kind of writing and sending probably makes for a different kind of communication. I can complain about the breakfast I had this morning or rattle on about friends and movies. That is because I am not so focused on style and profundity. [45] **(B) The downside is, I might be less likely to say something deeper.** My brother might glance at my mail, have a laugh, and then delete it.

電子郵件就不同了。它是即時的,從一個地方傳送到另一個地方。如果你不把它印出來,訊息實質上不存在。有了電子郵件,地理不是障礙,時間也不重要。我可以隨時快速地傳送訊息到肯亞,而且幾乎在一秒鐘內到達。這種寫信和寄信方式很輕鬆,所以或許有助於形成另一種溝通方式。我可以抱怨今天早上所吃的早餐,或喋喋不休地談論朋友和電影。那是因為我不是很專注在文體和深度。負面效應是,我可能比較不會去談更深入的事。我哥哥可能匆匆看一下我的信,笑一笑,然後刪了它。

instant〔'ɪnstənt〕*adj.* 即時的

point〔pɔɪnt〕*n.* 某一個地點　　***print out*** 把…印出來

physically〔'fɪzɪkl̩ɪ〕*adv.* 在物質上;實質上

exist〔ɪg'zɪst〕*v.* 存在

geography〔dʒi'agrəfɪ〕*n.* 地理

obstacle〔'abstəkl̩〕*n.* 障礙　　zap〔zæp〕*v.* 快速地做

ease〔iz〕*n.* 輕鬆　　***make for*** 有助於

rattle〔'rætl̩〕*v.* 喋喋不休地說　　***be focused on*** 專注於

profundity〔prə'fʌndətɪ〕*n.* 深度

downside〔'daʊn'saɪd〕*n.*（圖表等的）下降趨勢;負面效應

glance〔glæns〕*v.* 匆匆地一看

deep〔dip〕*adj.* 深入的　　laugh〔læf〕*n.* 笑

delete〔dɪ'lit〕*v.* 刪去

五、閱讀測驗：

第 46 至 48 題為題組

Rice balls with folded plastic wrappers separating the rice from the seaweed; a dozen kinds of cold tea in a dozen different bottles—enter any convenience store in Japan, and you're immediately struck by the great variety and quality of the packaging!

為了把米飯和海苔隔開，飯糰用摺好的塑膠封套包起來；各式各樣的冷飲茶裝在許多不同的瓶子裡——進入日本任何一家便利商店，你會立刻被許多包裝種類和品質所吸引！

rice ball 飯糰　　fold〔fold〕v. 摺
plastic〔'plæstɪk〕adj. 塑膠的　　wrapper〔'ræpɚ〕n. 包裝紙；封套
separate〔'sɛpə,ret〕v. 分開；隔開　　seaweed〔'si,wid〕n. 海苔
a dozen of 很多　　convenience〔kən'vinjəns〕n. 方便；便利
convenience store 便利商店　　immediately〔ɪ'midɪɪtlɪ〕adv. 立刻
strike〔straɪk〕v. 給予…印象（動詞三態：strike-struck-struck）
variety〔və'raɪətɪ〕n. 種類；多樣性　　quality〔'kwɑlətɪ〕n. 品質

Japanese companies have been accused of over-packaging; but within the Japanese cultural context, that's not really true. The Japanese tend to use more packaging because of a cultural emphasis on freshness and a lack of storage space at home. Moreover, they believe nice packaging adds value because it's a strong signal of quality. What's more, compared with Westerners, the Japanese are more connected with packaging as a symbol of appreciation, love and care. Packaging has, therefore, attained an important place in Japan's economy. The packaging market is worth over ¥7.4 trillion.

一直都有人譴責日本公司過度包裝；但是基於日本的文化背景，這未必是正確的。日本人傾向於使用較多包裝，是因為他們的文化對新鮮度很重視，而且家中缺乏儲存的空間。此外，他們相信良好的包裝可以增加價值感，因為這是品質的強烈表徵。還有，和西方人相較之下，日本人比較會將包裝和感謝、愛、以及關心的象徵連結在一起。因此，包裝在日本經濟上，佔有一個重要的地位。包裝市場的價值就超過七兆四千億日圓。

accuse〔ə'kjuz〕v. 控訴；譴責
context〔'kɑntɛkst〕n. 上下文；背景

tend to + *V*. 傾向於… 　　emphasis〔ˋɛmfəsɪs〕*n.* 重視；強調
freshness〔ˋfrɛʃnɪs〕*n.* 新鮮　　lack〔læk〕*n.* 缺乏
storage〔ˋstorɪdʒ〕*n.* 儲存　　signal〔ˋsɪgnḷ〕*n.* 象徵；表徵
compare〔kəmˋpɛr〕*v.* 比較
connected〔kəˋnɛktɪd〕*adj.* 有關連的；連結的
symbol〔ˋsɪmbḷ〕*n.* 象徵
appreciation〔ə͵priʃɪˋeʃən〕*n.* 感激；重視　　attain〔əˋten〕*v.* 達到
economy〔ɪˋkɑnəmɪ〕*n.* 經濟　　trillion〔ˋtrɪljən〕*n.* 一兆

New packaging is introduced to Japanese store shelves at a rate of 20 percent
per year, the highest rate in the world. In such an environment, a product has
to have more than just a nice graphic design to differentiate it from its
shelf-mates. The product has to speak to the consumer's needs with both
personality and practical value. In this changing industry, nothing is really
certain except one thing. You can be sure that the goods out there on display
on the shelves of the convenience store will soon be looking rather different.
新的包裝以每年百分之二十的比率，被引進到日本的商店貨架上，那是世界上
最高的比率。在這樣的環境中，一個產品為了要和架上其他產品有所區別，光
是有良好的平面設計是不夠的。產品必須要用特色和實際價值，來吸引消費者
的需求。在這個多變的產業裡，除了一件事之外，沒有什麼是確定的。你可以
確定的是，在便利商店的貨架上所展示出來的產品，很快就會看起來非常不一
樣了。

introduce〔͵ɪntrəˋdjus〕*v.* 引進　　shelf〔ʃɛlf〕*n.* 架子
rate〔ret〕*n.* 比率　　environment〔ɪnˋvaɪrənmənt〕*n.* 環境
graphic〔ˋgræfɪk〕*adj.* 平面藝術的　　***graphic design*** 平面設計
differentiate〔͵dɪfəˋrɛnʃɪ͵et〕*v.* 區分；區別（= *distinguish*）
speak to 對…有吸引力　　consumer〔kənˋsumɚ〕*n.* 消費者
personality〔͵pɝsṇˋælətɪ〕*n.* 特質；特性
practical〔ˋpræktɪkḷ〕*adj.* 實際的
industry〔ˋɪndəstrɪ〕*n.* 工業；產業　　certain〔ˋsɝtṇ〕*adj.* 確定的
display〔dɪˋsple〕*n.* 陳列；展示　　***on display*** 陳列中；展示中

46.(**C**) 這篇文章最有可能取自於＿＿＿＿＿＿。
　　(A) 食譜　　　　　　　　(B) 使用手冊
　　(C) 消費者報導　　　　　(D) 流行雜誌
　　cookbook〔ˋkʊk͵bʊk〕*n.* 食譜　　manual〔ˋmænjʊəl〕*n.* 手冊

47. (**D**) 下列何者不是日本人使用較多包裝的理由？

　　(A) 包裝有助於保持食物新鮮。

　　(B) 包裝有助於日本人表達感激。

　　(C) 日本人認為包裝是品質的表徵。

　　(D) 包裝是一種在經濟上和西方人競爭的方法。

　　compete〔kəm'pit〕v. 競爭

48. (**B**) 第二段中的 **shelf-mates** 最有可能表示＿＿＿＿＿＿。

　　(A) 工作上的同事。　　　　　　(B) 商店裡的其他產品。

　　(C) 顧客對其他產品的需求。　　(D) 包裝上其他的平面設計。

第 49 至 52 題為題組

　　Native Americans could not understand the white man's war on the wolf. The Lakota, Blackfeet, and Shoshone, among other tribes, considered the wolf their spiritual brother. They respected the animals' endurance and hunting ability, and warriors prayed to hunt like them. They draped themselves in wolf skins and paws, hoping they could acquire the wolf's hunting skills of stealth, courage, and stamina. Plains Indians wore wolf-skin disguises on raiding parties. Elite Comanche warriors were called wolves.

　　美國原住民無法理解白人對抗狼的戰爭。拉科他族、黑足族、休休尼族和其他部落等等，都認為狼是他們的心靈上的弟兄。他們敬重狼的耐力和狩獵能力，戰士們會祈禱，自己能像牠們一樣狩獵。他們披上狼皮和狼爪，希望自己能獲得狼那有著隱密、勇氣和耐力的狩獵技巧。平原印地安人在組成突擊隊伍時，會穿上狼皮來偽裝。最優秀的科曼奇族戰士被稱為狼。

　　　　Lakota〔lə'kotə〕n. 拉科他族（北美印地安人的一族）
　　　　Blackfeet〔'blæk'fit〕n. 黑足族（北美印地安人的一族）
　　　　Shoshone〔ʃo'ʃonɪ〕n. 美國休休尼族印地安人
　　　　tribe〔traɪb〕n. 部落
　　　　among other things 等等（= *among others* ; *and so on*）
　　　　spiritual〔'spɪrɪtʃuəl〕adj. 心靈的

endurance〔ɪn'dʊrəns〕n. 耐力　　warrior〔'wɔrɪɚ〕n. 戰士

drape〔drep〕v. 覆蓋；披上　　paw〔pɔ〕n. 爪子

acquire〔ə'kwaɪr〕v. 獲得　　stealth〔stɛlθ〕n. 隱密

courage〔'kɝɪdʒ〕n. 勇氣　　stamina〔'stæmənə〕n. 耐力

Plains Indians 平原印地安人　　disguise〔dɪs'gaɪz〕n., v. 偽裝

raid〔red〕v. 突擊；襲擊　　party〔'pɑrtɪ〕n. 隊伍

elite〔ɪ'lit〕adj. 最優秀的；精英的

Comanche〔ko'mæntʃi〕n. 科曼奇族（北美印地安人的一族）

The white settlers' war on the wolf raged on. Western ranchers continued to claim that thousands of cattle were killed every year by wolves. In 1884, Montana created its first wolf bounty—one dollar for every dead wolf, which increased to eight dollars in 1893. Over a period of thirty-five years, more than eighty thousand wolf carcasses were submitted for bounty payments in Montana. Moreover, the government even provided free poison. Finally, in 1914, ranchers persuaded the United States Congress to provide funds to exterminate wolves on public lands.

　　白人殖民者與狼的戰爭激烈地進行著。西部農牧場經營者們不斷地宣稱，每年有數以千計的牛被狼殺死。在一八八四年時，蒙大拿州創設了第一個獵狼賞金——每殺死一隻狼可領一美元，到了一八九三年賞金已增加到八美元。在三十五年的期間，蒙大拿州有八萬多隻狼屍體，被提報要求支付賞金。此外，政府甚至提供免費毒藥。最後，在一九一四年時，農牧場經營者說服了美國國會提供資金，將公有土地上的狼群全部消滅。

settler〔'sɛtlɚ〕n. 殖民者；移民者　　rage〔redʒ〕v. 激烈進行

rancher〔'ræntʃɚ〕n. 農（牧）場經營者　　cattle〔'kætl〕n. 牛

Montana〔mɑn'tænə〕n. 蒙大拿州（美國西北部之一州）

bounty〔'baʊntɪ〕n. 賞金　　period〔'pɪrɪəd〕n. 期間

carcass〔'kɑrkəs〕n.（動物）屍體

submit〔səb'mɪt〕v. 提出；繳交

payment〔'pemənt〕n. 支付金額

persuade〔pɚ'swed〕v. 說服　　Congress〔'kɑŋgrəs〕n. 國會

exterminate〔ɪk'stɝmə͵net〕v. 滅絕；把…全部消滅

The last wolves in the American West died hard. No place was safe, not even the nation's first national park, Yellowstone. The park was created in 1872, and from its very beginning, poisoned carcasses were set out to kill wolves. Nearly 140 wolves were killed by park rangers in Yellowstone from 1914 to 1926. In October 1926, two wolf cubs were trapped near a bison carcass. They were the last animals killed in the park's wolf control programs.

在美國西部僅存的狼群死得很慘。沒有一個地方是安全的，即使是在美國第一座國家公園——黃石公園。這座國家公園創建於一八七二年，從一開始，下了毒藥的屍體就被放在外面來毒死狼。從一九一四年到一九二六年，黃石國家公園警察殺死了將近一百四十隻狼。一九二六年十月，有兩隻小狼被美洲野牛屍體附近的陷阱抓住。牠們是公園狼隻控制計畫中最後被殺掉的動物。

Yellowstone National Park 黃石國家公園（自美國懷俄明州西北部
　　至愛達荷、蒙大拿兩州的一部分）　　***set out*** 擺出
ranger〔ˋrendʒɚ〕*n.*（國家公園、森林的）警察
cub〔kʌb〕*n.*（熊、獅、虎、狼等肉食動物的）幼獸
trap〔træp〕*v.* 使困住　　bison〔ˋbaɪsn̩〕*n.* 北美野牛

Ranchers had won the war against the wolf. Only in the northern woods of Wisconsin, Minnesota, and Michigan could the howl of native gray wolves be heard. The vast lands of the American West fell silent. The country had lost its greatest predator.

農牧場經營者在對抗狼的戰爭中獲得勝利。只有在威斯康辛州、明尼蘇達州和密西根州等地的北方森林裡，才聽得到土生土長的灰狼的嗥叫聲。美國西部的廣大土地是一片寂靜。這片土地已經失去它最偉大的掠食者了。

Wisconsin〔wɪsˋkɑnsn̩〕*n.* 威斯康辛州（美國中北部的一州）
Minnesota〔͵mɪnɪˋsotə〕*n.* 明尼蘇達州（美國中北部的一州）
Michigan〔ˋmɪʃəgən〕*n.* 密西根州（美國中北部的一州）
howl〔haʊl〕*n.* 嗥叫聲　　vast〔væst〕*adj.* 廣大的
silent〔ˋsaɪlənt〕*adj.* 寂靜的　　country〔ˋkʌntrɪ〕*n.* 土地
predator〔ˋprɛdətɚ〕*n.* 掠食者

49. (**D**) 白人想要殺掉灰狼是因為＿＿＿＿＿＿。

(A) 牠會攻擊人類　　　　　　(B) 牠會損壞農作物
(C) 印地安人很崇拜牠　　　　(D) 牠威脅到家畜的生命

attack〔ə'tæk〕v. 攻擊　　　damage〔'dæmɪdʒ〕v. 損壞
adore〔ə'dor〕v. 崇拜　　　threaten〔'θrɛtn̩〕v. 威脅
livestock〔'laɪv,stɑk〕n.（牛、馬、羊等）家畜

50. (**C**) 這篇文章最有可能是＿＿＿＿＿＿的人所寫的。

(A) 喜歡狩獵野生動物　　　　(B) 立法對抗灰狼
(C) 提倡保護灰狼　　　　　　(D) 欣賞灰狼狩獵技巧

make laws 立法　　　advocate〔'ædvə,ket〕v. 提倡
protection〔prə'tɛkʃən〕n. 保護　　　appreciate〔ə'priʃɪ,et〕v. 欣賞

51. (**D**) 狼快速消失的主要原因是什麼？

(A) 狼無法將牛隻當作食物。　　(B) 印地安人為了狼皮殺掉狼。
(C) 國家公園警察殺掉大多數的狼。
(D) 政府鼓勵殺狼行為。

52. (**A**) 印地安人敬重狼是因為狼＿＿＿＿＿＿。

(A) 擅長狩獵。　　　　　　　(B) 擅長偽裝。
(C) 擁有漂亮的皮和爪子。　　(D) 是白人的敵人。

第 53 至 56 題為題組

　　Recently, Dr. Stuart Campbell of a private health center in London published some ultrasound images of unborn babies between 26 and 34 weeks. The smiles of the babies in the pictures greatly shocked the public and were widely circulated on the Internet.

　　近來，在倫敦一家私人保健中心服務的史都・坎貝爾醫師，發表了幾張二十六週到三十四週之間，未出生嬰兒的超音波影像。在這些影像中的嬰兒微笑，使社會大眾大為震驚，這些照片在網路上廣泛地流傳。

recently〔'risn̩tlɪ〕adv. 近來　　　*health center* 保健中心
ultrasound〔'ʌltrə,saund〕n. 超音波　　　image〔'ɪmɪdʒ〕n. 影像
unborn〔ʌn'bɔrn〕adj. 未出生的　　　shock〔ʃɑk〕v. 震撼；震驚
widely〔'waɪdlɪ〕adv. 廣泛地　　　circulate〔'sɝkjə,let〕v. 流傳；散佈

For the past two years, the doctor has used the medical facility in the center and has offered state-of-the-art 3-D/4-D scanning services to expectant parents. He performs an average of 30 scans a week. His outspoken enthusiasm for this blessed technology is refreshing. "Parents love them," he said. "I hear so many couples laughing when they see the pictures—it's wonderful."

過去兩年來，該名醫師運用保健中心的醫療設施，為準爸媽們提供最先進的 3-D 及 4-D 的掃描服務。他平均一個禮拜做三十次掃描。對於這項值得慶幸的科技而言，他毫無保留的熱誠令人振奮。他表示：「父母親們愛死這些照片了。我聽到很多夫婦在看到照片時開懷大笑。這真是太棒了。」

medical〔'mɛdɪk!〕adj. 醫學的；醫療的
facility〔fə'sɪlətɪ〕n. 設施　　state-of-the-art adj. 最先進的
scanning〔'skænɪŋ〕n. 掃描　　service〔'sɝvɪs〕n. 設施；服務
expectant〔ɪk'spɛktənt〕adj. 期待的；等待的
perform〔pɚ'fɔrm〕v. 做；執行　　scan〔skæn〕n. 掃描
outspoken〔'aʊt'spokən〕adj. 坦率的；毫無保留地表示的
enthusiasm〔ɪn'θjuzɪˌæzəm〕n. 熱忱；狂熱
blessed〔'blɛsɪd〕adj. 值得慶幸的；令人喜悅的
refreshing〔rɪ'frɛʃɪŋ〕adj. 令人振奮的；有趣的

How have pro-abortion activists reacted after seeing the happy, grinning photos of these unborn babies?

看到這些未出生嬰兒快樂、微笑的照片之後，贊成墮胎人士的反應又是如何呢？

pro〔pro〕表「支持、贊成」之意　　abortion〔ə'bɔrʃən〕n. 墮胎
activist〔'æktɪvɪst〕n. 行動主義者；激進分子
grinning〔'grɪnɪŋ〕adj. 露齒而笑的

Anne Carp, a commentator for the *Guardian* who bills herself as a "medical sociologist," says the photos are simply misleading, and ridicules the anti-abortion lobby for being "intoxicated with evidence of a fetus' humanity." Australian Birth Control Services medical director Geoff Brodie complained that the photos "will be picked up by those groups that use anything and everything to stop abortions but ignore the fact that women have a right to choice."

英國衛報一位評論家，同時也自許為「醫療社會學家」的安妮・卡普說：「這些照片只是在誤導，她還嘲笑反對墮胎的遊說團體，因為他們『陶醉於這些胎兒具有人性的證據』。」澳洲生育管制局醫療主任，傑夫・布洛蒂抱怨說：這些照片「會被那些用盡各種手段，要阻止墮胎的團體拿去使用，但他們忽略了一個事實：婦女有選擇的權利。」

commentator〔ˈkɑmənˌtetə〕n. 評論家
guardian〔ˈgɑrdɪən〕n. 守護者　　***the Guardian***　（英國）衛報
bill A as B　把 A 描述成 B（= describe A as B）
misleading〔mɪsˈlidɪŋ〕adj. 誤導的　　ridicule〔ˈrɪdɪˌkjul〕v. 嘲笑
anti-abortion〔ˌæntɪ əˈbɔrʃən〕adj. 反墮胎的
lobby〔ˈlɑbɪ〕n. 遊說團體
intoxicated〔ɪnˈtɑksəˌketɪd〕adj. 陶醉的；興奮的
fetus〔ˈfitəs〕n.（受孕約三個月以上的）胎兒
humanity〔hjuˈmænətɪ〕n. 人性；人類
Australian Birth Control Services　澳洲生育管制局
director〔dəˈrɛktə〕n. 局長；主任　　***pick up***　取得

In America, the pro-abortion lobby is having the same hostile reaction. It was bad enough when conventional 2-D sonograms revealed unborn hearts beating and blurry hands waving, but the abortionists are absolutely aghast over rapidly spreading access to 3-D/4-D ultrasound technology. A writer for the liberal *American Prospect* said that the new technology "blurred the distinction between a fetus and a newborn infant."

在美國，贊成墮胎的遊說人士也有相同的反對情形。傳統 2-D 超音波顯示出未出生嬰兒的心跳，還有模糊的手在揮動，就已經夠糟了，不過替人施行墮胎手術的人，對於 3-D 及 4-D 超音波科技的快速普遍使用，則是完全被嚇得目瞪口呆。自由開明的「美國展望」雜誌的一位作家說：「這項新科技模糊了胎兒與新生兒之間的區別。」

hostile〔ˈhɑstl̩〕adj. 敵對的；有敵意的
conventional〔kənˈvɛnʃənl̩〕adj. 傳統的；老套的
sonogram〔ˈsonəˌgræm〕n. 超音波掃描圖
reveal〔rɪˈvil〕v. 透露；顯示　　blurry〔ˈblɜɪ〕adj. 模糊的
abortionist〔əˈbɔrʃənɪst〕n. 施行墮胎手術者
absolutely〔ˈæbsəˌlutlɪ〕adv. 絕對地；完全地
aghast〔əˈgæst〕adj. 嚇呆的　　access〔ˈæksɛs〕n. 接近；使用權
liberal〔ˈlɪbərəl〕adj. 自由的；開明的

prospect〔'prɑspɛkt〕*n.* 前景；展望
the American Prospect 美國展望（政論雜誌）
blur〔blɝ〕*v.* 使模糊　　distinction〔dɪ'stɪŋkʃən〕*n.* 區別

　　Despite these strong reactions from the pro-abortionists, the right of life takes precedence over a woman's right to choice. After all, nothing can be more persuasive than an unborn child's beaming face.

　　儘管贊成墮胎人士的反應強烈，生命權仍大過於婦女的選擇權。畢竟，沒有什麼比未出生嬰兒愉悅的笑容更有說服力了。

despite〔dɪ'spaɪt〕*prep.* 儘管
precedence〔prɪ'sidn̩s , 'prɛsədəns〕*n.* 優先權
take precedence over ～ 優於～；在～之上
persuasive〔pə'swesɪv〕*adj.* 有說服力的
beaming〔'bimɪŋ〕*adj.* 愉快的

53.(**B**) 作者對於墮胎的態度為何？
　　(A) 贊成。　　　(B) 反對。　　　(C) 中立。　　　(D) 漠不關心。
　　neutral〔'njutrəl〕*adj.* 中立的
　　indifferent〔ɪn'dɪfərənt〕*adj.* 漠不關心的

54.(**A**) 贊成墮胎人士對於未出生嬰兒微笑的照片作何反應？
　　(A) 全都不相信，並且不屑。　　(B) 全部稱讚，並且表示感激。
　　(C) 有些人尊重，有些人不屑。　　(D) 有些人稱讚，有些人失望。
　　disbelief〔,dɪsbə'lif〕*n.* 不相信；懷疑
　　scorn〔skɔrn〕*n.* 輕視；不屑　　applause〔ə'plɔz〕*n.* 鼓掌；稱讚
　　disappointment〔,dɪsə'pɔɪntmənt〕*n.* 失望

55.(**C**) 以下哪一個人最有可能是反對墮胎者？
　　(A) 安妮・卡普。　　　　　　(B) 傑夫・布洛帝。
　　(C) 史都・坎貝爾。　　　　　(D) 美國展望的一位作家。

56.(**D**) 我們可以從本文推論出下列哪一項敘述？
　　(A) 醫師發表未出生嬰兒的照片是錯誤的。
　　(B) 對於反對墮胎者而言，胎兒不等同於人類。
　　(C) 每個人都同意婦女可以自行決定要不要墮胎。
　　(D) 未出生嬰兒的超音波照片使反對墮胎人士感到高興。

第貳部分：非選擇題

一、英文翻譯：

1. 為提供一個無煙的用餐環境，許多餐廳不允許室內抽煙。

To provide a $\left\{\begin{array}{l}\text{no-smoking}\\\text{nonsmoking}\\\text{smoke-free}\end{array}\right\}$ dining environment,

$\left\{\begin{array}{l}\text{smoking indoors} \left\{\begin{array}{l}\text{is not allowed}\\\text{is banned}\\\text{is prohibited}\end{array}\right\} \text{in many restaurants.}\\\\\text{many restaurants} \left\{\begin{array}{l}\text{don't allow}\\\text{ban}\\\text{prohibit}\end{array}\right\} \text{smoking indoors.}\end{array}\right.$

2. 雖然遭到許多癮君子的反對，這對不抽煙的人的確是一大福音。

$\left.\begin{array}{l}\text{Although it is opposed by many smokers,}\\\\\text{Although many smokers} \left\{\begin{array}{l}\text{oppose}\\\text{object to}\end{array}\right\} \text{it,}\\\\\left.\begin{array}{l}\text{Despite}\\\text{In spite of}\\\text{Regardless of}\end{array}\right\} \text{the objections} \left\{\begin{array}{l}\text{by}\\\text{from}\end{array}\right\} \text{many smokers,}\end{array}\right\}$

it is indeed good news to $\left\{\begin{array}{l}\text{those who don't smoke.}\\\text{nonsmokers.}\end{array}\right.$

二、英文作文：(作文範例)

On Being Misunderstood

　　It seems that no matter how hard we try, we are not always understood. Misunderstandings can cause confusion or mistakes. Sometimes they are funny, but sometimes they can cause hurt feelings. This once happened to me.

Last year my teacher asked us to do some research and make a presentation to our class. This was a difficult challenge for me. One of my classmates had the same problem. I knew that she needed help, but I thought my advice would only make her more confused and worried. I even said to one of my friends that I hoped she wouldn't ask me for help. Unfortunately, she heard about this. She misunderstood my meaning and thought I was too selfish to help her. She even refused to speak to me after this.

Luckily, I found out why my classmate was upset and I was able to talk to her about it. When she understood my reason for not helping her, she forgave me. From this experience I learned that the only way to resolve a misunderstanding is to communicate.

misunderstand〔͵mɪsʌndɚˈstænd〕v. 誤會

no matter how 無論怎麼樣

misunderstanding〔͵mɪsʌndɚˈstændɪŋ〕n. 誤會

confusion〔kənˈfjuʒən〕n. 困惑

mistake〔məˈstek〕n. 錯誤；誤會　　hurt〔hɝt〕adj. 受傷的

once〔wʌns〕adv. 曾經　　research〔rɪˈsɝtʃ〕n. 研究

presentation〔͵prɛznˈteʃən〕n. 發表；描述

difficult〔ˈdɪfə͵kʌlt〕adj. 困難的

challenge〔ˈtʃælɪndʒ〕n. 挑戰　　advice〔ədˈvaɪs〕n. 建議

confused〔kənˈfjuzd〕adj. 困惑的

unfortunately〔ʌnˈfɔrtʃənɪtlɪ〕adv. 不幸地

meaning〔ˈminɪŋ〕n. 意思

selfish〔ˈsɛlfɪʃ〕adj. 自私的　　refuse〔rɪˈfjuz〕v. 拒絕

forgive〔fɚˈgɪv〕v. 原諒　　experience〔ɪkˈspɪrɪəns〕n. 經驗

resolve〔rɪˈzɑlv〕v. 解決

communicate〔kəˈmjunə͵ket〕v. 溝通

95 年指定科目考試英文科試題勘誤表

※ 這次指考的題目，合乎命題原則，兼具知識性、趣味性與教育性，錯誤又少，
　是近年來題目出得最好的一次。

題　號	修　正　意　見
詞彙 第 8 題	... *to their last relics.* → ... *to the last relics of their foundations*. 或 ... *to the ruins of their foundations*. * 如不改，句意較不清楚。
綜合測驗 第 11 至 15 題 倒數第 3、4 行	... *the International System of measures*.... → ... *the international system of measures*.... 或 ... *the International Systems of Units*（國際單位制）.... * 用錯專有名詞，前面是大寫，後面就要大寫。
閱讀測驗 第 49 題	(D) it threatened the *life* of his livestock → *it threatened his livestock*【避免重覆】 或 *it threatened the lives of his livestock* * life 該用複數 lives。
第 52 題	(B) *was good at disguising* → *was good at disguising itself* * 因為 disguise 是及物動詞。 (C) had beautiful *skins* and paws → had beautiful *skin* and paws * 由於 wolf 為單數，指牠的皮膚，應改為單數的 skin。

九十五學年度指定科目考試（英文）

大考中心公佈答案

題號	答案	題號	答案	題號	答案
1	D	21	A	41	C
2	B	22	C	42	E
3	B	23	B	43	A
4	D	24	D	44	D
5	B	25	C	45	B
6	A	26	C	46	C
7	A	27	C	47	D
8	B	28	A	48	B
9	C	29	B	49	D
10	A	30	D	50	C
11	C	31	A	51	D
12	B	32	B	52	A
13	A	33	E	53	B
14	D	34	H	54	A
15	B	35	I	55	C
16	A	36	D	56	D
17	C	37	C		
18	C	38	J		
19	B	39	G		
20	A	40	F		

九十五學年度指定科目考試
各科成績標準一覽表

科　目	頂　標	前　標	均　標	後　標	底　標
國　文	67	61	52	43	35
英　文	67	51	28	13	7
數學甲	62	50	35	20	12
數學乙	88	78	56	32	19
化　學	71	59	41	25	16
物　理	54	39	22	12	6
生　物	71	60	44	30	22
歷　史	56	49	40	29	20
地　理	60	52	40	29	20

※ 以上五項標準係依各該科全體到考考生成績計算，且均取整數（小數只捨不入），各標準計算方式如下：

頂標：成績位於第 88 百分位數之考生成績。
前標：成績位於第 75 百分位數之考生成績。
均標：成績位於第 50 百分位數之考生成績。
後標：成績位於第 25 百分位數之考生成績。
底標：成績位於第 12 百分位數之考生成績。

九十四年大學入學指定科目考試試題
英文考科

第壹部份：選擇題（佔72分）

一、詞彙（10％）

說明：　第1至10題，每題選出一個最適當的選項，標示在答案卡之「選擇題答案區」。每題答對得1分，答錯或劃記多於一個選項者倒扣1/3分，倒扣到本大題之實得分數為零為止，未作答者，不給分亦不扣分。

1. We have had plenty of rain so far this year, so there should be an _____ supply of fresh water this summer.
   (A) intense　　(B) ultimate　　(C) abundant　　(D) epidemic

2. I don't know for sure what I am going to do this weekend, but _____ I plan to visit an old friend of mine in southern Taiwan.
   (A) tentatively　(B) inevitably　(C) unknowingly　(D) numerously

3. Our chemistry teacher was on a one-month sick leave, so the principal had to find a teacher to _____ for her.
   (A) recover　　(B) navigate　　(C) rehearse　　(D) substitute

4. The gym is closed on Monday for routine _____ work. The facilities are kept in good condition by the regular checking and repairing.
   (A) disturbance　(B) eloquence　(C) maintenance　(D) alliance

5. If you exercise regularly, your blood _____ will be improved, and you will feel more energetic.
   (A) fatigue　　(B) tranquility　(C) fragrance　　(D) circulation

6. Nowadays people have to pass various tests for professional _____ so that they can be qualified for a well-paying job.
   (A) mechanics　(B) permission　(C) certificates　(D) perseverance

7. Though Dr. Wang has been away from his hometown for over ten years, he can still _____ his old house clearly.
   (A) nominate　(B) visualize　(C) prolong　(D) sprinkle

8. The speaker spent twenty minutes on one simple question. The explanation was so _____ that we could not see the point clearly.
   (A) coherent　(B) crucial　(C) various　(D) lengthy

9. The new tax policy proposed for the next fiscal year has been severely criticized by the _____ party leaders.
   (A) interaction　(B) exposition　(C) opposition　(D) occupation

10. Thousands of people flooded into the city to join the demonstration; as a result, the city's transportation system was almost _____.
    (A) testified　(B) paralyzed　(C) stabilized　(D) dissatisfied

二、綜合測驗（20％）

說明：　第11至30題，每題一個空格。請依文意選出一個最適當的選項，標示在答案卡之「選擇題答案區」。每題答對得1分，答錯或劃記多於一個選項者倒扣1/3分，倒扣到本大題之實得分數為零為止，未作答者，不給分亦不扣分。

第11至15題為題組

　　After a long day working in the office, Alexander hailed a taxi to take him home. Squeezing his body into the taxi, he noticed the shiny interior and the smell of brand new leather. After informing the driver of his ___11___, Alexander resorted to his reading of Dan Brown's intelligent thriller, *The Da Vinci Code*. Five minutes into the journey, he was on page 120: "…his Mona Lisa is neither male nor female…" Suddenly, Alexander ___12___ and noticed that the driver had detoured from the familiar route. To redirect the driver, Alexander tapped him on the shoulder. Out of the blue, the driver screamed, lost control of

the car, and almost hit a bus. The cab went up on the footpath and
____13____ stopped centimeters away from a shop window. For a second,
everything went quiet in the cab. Then the driver said, "Look, mate!
Don't ever do that again. You scared the living daylights out of me!"
Alexander apologized and said, "I didn't ____14____ that a little tap would
scare you so much." The driver replied, "Sorry, sir. It's not really your
____15____. Today is my first day as a cab driver. I've been driving a
funeral van for the last 25 years."

11. (A) motivation   (B) destination   (C) expectation   (D) solution
12. (A) looked up   (B) took off   (C) turned in   (D) got on
13. (A) hardly   (B) likely   (C) finally   (D) mainly
14. (A) find   (B) realize   (C) wonder   (D) admit
15. (A) matter   (B) decision   (C) trouble   (D) fault

第 16 至 20 題為題組

　　Today, with a couple of clicks, you can go anywhere in the world
without leaving your computer. So it should come as little ____16____ that
the Internet has headlined the top 25 innovations of the past quarter
century, according to a panel of technology leaders assembled to promote
inventiveness.

　　In creating the list, the group ____17____ twenty-five non-medically
related technological innovations that have become widely used since
1980. These innovations are readily recognizable by most Americans,
have had a direct impact on our everyday lives, and may also
dramatically affect our lives ____18____.

　　The top innovation, the Web, was created by British software
consultant Tim Berners-Lee. ____19____ by the multitude of information
systems requiring complicated access, Berners-Lee fashioned a universal

one that made information readily ___20___. He created HTML (hypertext markup language) and its rule of usage (HTTP, hypertext transfer protocol). In 1991 he unveiled the World Wide Web. Today, this No. 1 invention has become so commonplace that it is almost taken for granted.

16. (A) agreement　(B) surprise　(C) belief　(D) concern
17. (A) gives in　(B) takes over　(C) singles out　(D) turns down
18. (A) for a moment　　(B) at that time
　　(C) from then on　　(D) in the future
19. (A) Having frustrated　　(B) Frustrated
　　(C) To be frustrated　　(D) Been frustrated
20. (A) available　　(B) consistent
　　(C) important　　(D) unforgettable

第 21 至 25 題為題組

　　The world's largest collection of Khmer sculpture resides at Angkor, the former royal capital of Cambodia. The 7,000 pieces—full statues, heads and carved inscriptions—are breathtaking not only for their individual beauty, but also for ___21___ they represent: a road map to the origins of much of Southeast Asian culture. But the collection is not in a museum, and it is not open ___22___ visitors. It is held in unknown, guarded warehouses ___23___ only a few people can see it. These people assembled it by removing figures from the ruins of Cambodia's world-famous temples and replacing them with hollow, concrete ___24___. For the most part, these are hard to distinguish from the originals. Clever art thieves? No, these "art thieves" work for the Angkor Conservancy. ___25___ very large pieces too heavy to move, virtually all surviving Angkorian statues, wood carvings and artifacts have been replaced with copies.

21. (A) what   (B) which   (C) that   (D) when
22. (A) with   (B) by   (C) to   (D) among
23. (A) which   (B) where   (C) until   (D) unless
24. (A) strategies (B) courses   (C) ways   (D) fakes
25. (A) Except for (B) In spite of (C) Owing to   (D) In addition to

第 26 至 30 題為題組

Jean Piaget, a psychologist and pioneer in the study of child intelligence, was born in Switzerland in 1896. At age 10, he managed his first ___26___, a description of a partly albino sparrow he observed in a public park. At age 15, he ___27___ to devote his life to developing a biological explanation of knowledge.

He began his career as a zoologist, ___28___ mollusks and their adaptations to their environment. ___29___ age 21, he had already published 25 professional papers on that topic. Later, after working with Alfred Binet in Paris, he became interested in levels of logic used by children taking standardized tests on intelligence. Piaget ___30___ to establish a body of psychology all his life and became a very influential figure in educational psychology. His works were all written originally in French and were later translated into English.

26. (A) subscription (B) publication (C) obligation (D) transaction
27. (A) put down   (B) passed on   (C) ended up   (D) set out
28. (A) study   (B) studied   (C) studying   (D) being studied
29. (A) By   (B) In   (C) With   (D) On
30. (A) forgot   (B) afforded   (C) sought   (D) tended

三、文意選填（10％）

說明： 第 31 至 40 題，每題一個空格。請依文意在文章後所提供的 (A) 到 (J) 選項中分別選出最適當者，並將其字母代號標示在答案卡之「選擇題答案區」。每題答對得 1 分，答錯或劃記多於一個選項者倒扣 1/9 分，倒扣到本大題之實得分數為零為止，未作答者，不給分亦不扣分。

第 31 至 40 題為題組

　　Like pearls scattered in the East Sea, the Penghu archipelago is situated in the southwest of the Taiwan Strait. It consists of ___31___ one hundred islands, of which many are famous for their pure white-sand beaches. The broad beaches and beautiful underwater scenery are the major ___32___ of Penghu islands.

　　Among the one hundred or so islands, only 20 are inhabited. The ___33___ islands of Penghu have been kept intact without human intervention. The primitive conditions on these islands, their unique basalt rock formations and rich ecology bring ___34___ more surprises for visitors. These islands are designated as natural reservations, ___35___ they are endowed with remarkable and rare resources. For instance, Gupo (Grand Aunt) Island is the largest uninhabited island in the North Sea area and the main ___36___ of seaweed production. Like Gupo Island, Baisha (White Sand) Island is also uninhabited and has ___37___ the primitive, unspoiled character. The island features well-developed columnar basalt formations, which on the southern coastline are ___38___ spectacular. This is also one of the best areas of the Penghu Islands for bird watching. In addition, there are also pillar-shaped rock formations that are Mother Nature's ___39___ sculptures.

　　Like gifts from God, the yellow flowers that bloom ___40___ the basalt rock cracks and the beautiful songs of little singing birds on the meadows turn these islands into a paradise.

(A) attractions　　　(B) between　　(C) for　　　　　(D) location
(E) masterpiece　　　(F) nearly　　(G) particularly　(H) preserved
(I) even　　　　　　　(J) uninhabited

四、篇章結構（10％）

說明：　第 41 至 45 題，每題一個空格。請依文意在文章後所提供的 (A) 到 (E) 選項中分別選出最適當者，填入空格中，使篇章結構清晰有條理，並 其英文字母代號標示在答案卡之「選擇題答案區」。每題答對得 2 分， 答錯或劃記多於一個選項者倒扣 1/2 分，倒扣到本大題之實得分數為 零為止，未作答者，不給分亦不扣分。

第 41 至 45 題為題組

　　Many researchers have been interested in whether or not an individual's birth order has an effect on intelligence.　One of the first studies was carried out in the Netherlands during the early 1970s. ___41___ The test was called the "Raven," which is similar to the I.Q. test. The researchers found a strong relationship between the birth order of the test takers and their scores on the Raven test. ___42___

　　In 1975, Zajonc and Markus developed the confluence theory to explain the negative effect of birth order on intelligence involving the data from the Dutch. ___43___ However, Rutherford and Sewell in 1991 tested the theory and found no support for it.　They concluded that birth order effects did not exist.

　　___44___ On one side there are Zajonc and Markus, who state that birth order effects may be explained solely by family size and the spacing of births.　With short birth intervals, increasing order of birth will be associated with lower intelligence levels.　But with long birth intervals, this pattern may be reversed. ___45___ They show that the confluence model does not explain any relationship between birth order and intelligence that may exist in the American data.　Up to date, there is no agreement between these opposing views.　And such a debate may continue for years to come.

(A) There are definitely two sides to this issue.

(B) Scores decreased as the family size increased and also with birth order.

(C) An intelligence test was administered to over 350,000 Dutch males when they turned 19 years of age.

(D) On the other side are Rutherford and Sewell, who studied more than 10,000 American high school graduates.

(E) Since then, the theory has been elaborated and even extended to explain the positive effect of birth order on intelligence.

五、閱讀測驗（22％）

說明： 第 46 至 56 題，每題請分別根據各篇文章的文意選出一個最適當的選項，標示在答案卡之「選擇題答案區」。每題答對得 2 分，答錯或劃記多於一個選項者倒扣 2/3 分，倒扣到本大題之實得分數爲零爲止，未作答者，不給分亦不扣分。

第 46 至 49 題爲題組

In recent years, a craze for height has hit hard in industrializing Asian countries like Taiwan, Hong Kong and China, which boast seven of the world's 10 tallest buildings. The current tallest, at 101 floors, is the Taipei 101 in Taiwan, though Toronto's CN Tower is 180 feet higher, largely because of its huge antenna. Yet, in the Persian Gulf city of Dubai, the world's tallest building-to-be is already well under construction. Its pilings are already in place, plunging 160 feet into the earth. When it's finished, visitors will swoon over this city from 123 stories high, if not more. Currently, however, its exact height is still kept a secret to potential competitors in the world's race for the title of the tallest skyscraper.

While New York built skyscrapers because land was scarce, Dubai is doing it to get on the world map. "It's image, clearly," said Richard Rosan, president of its construction firm. "There's no practical reason for having a building this tall. You can't be scared of heights if you want to work on the top floor."

On paper, the Dubai Tower looks something like a giant space shuttle about to be launched into the clouds. Designers say the silvery steel-and-glass building will restore to the Arab world the honor of hosting the earth's tallest structure—a title lost in 1889 when the Eiffel Tower **upset** the 43-century reign of Egypt's Great Pyramid of Giza.

46. According to the passage, how tall will the Dubai Tower be?
    (A) At least 43 stories higher than Toronto's CN Tower.
    (B) 180 feet higher than Toronto's CN Tower.
    (C) At least 22 stories higher than the Taipei 101.
    (D) 160 feet higher than the Taipei 101.

47. The main purpose for building the Dubai Tower is _____.
    (A) for people who are not scared of heights to work on the top floor
    (B) for the construction company to maintain its business
    (C) for the Arab world to honor its industrialization
    (D) for the city of Dubai to gain world fame

48. Which of the following is true of the Dubai Tower?
    (A) It will include a 160-feet huge antenna.
    (B) It may be built in the shape of a space shuttle.
    (C) It uses silver as the major construction material.
    (D) It has already been built up to 180 feet above the ground.

49. The word **upset** in the last paragraph means _____.
    (A) distorted an important fact
    (B) knocked something over accidentally
    (C) defeated a strong competitor
    (D) made someone feel sad, worried, or angry

第 50 至 53 題爲題組

Dr. Thompson was pleased. Just three months after moving to the small Midwestern town, he had been invited to address an evening meeting of the Chamber of Commerce. Here was the perfect opportunity to show his knowledge of modern medicine and to get his practice off to a flourishing start. With this in mind, the doctor prepared carefully.

On the night of his speech, Dr. Thompson was delighted to see that the meeting hall was full. After being introduced, he strode confidently to the lectern and announced his topic: "Recent Advances in Medicine." He began with a detailed discussion of Creutzfeldt-Jakob disease, a rare brain disorder that had recently been covered in the *New England Journal of Medicine*. Next he outlined the progress that had been made in studying immune system disorders.

Just about this time, halfway through his speech, Dr. Thompson began to notice a certain restlessness in his audience. People were murmuring and shuffling their feet. Someone in the fourth row seemed to be glancing at a newspaper. Nevertheless, Dr. Thompson plowed on. He had saved the best for last. He quoted extensively from an article in *the Lancet* about genetic research, feeling sure his audience would be impressed by his familiarity with this prestigious British medical journal.

Then the speech was over. Dr. Thompson had expected to be surrounded by enthusiastic people, congratulating him and asking questions. Instead he found himself standing alone. Finally the president of the Chamber of Commerce came up to him. "Something tells me," said Dr. Thompson, "that my speech was not very successful. I can't understand it. I worked so hard to make it interesting." "Oh, it was a fine speech," replied the president. "But maybe it would have gone over better with a different audience. Creutzfeldt-Jakob disease is not exactly a factor in these people's everyday experience. You know, here we are in January. If you'd talked about ways to avoid getting the flu, you'd have **had them on the edge of their seats!**"

50. What is the main message of the passage?
   (A) A good speaker has to be fully prepared regardless of the audience.
   (B) A good speaker should display his learning to the audience in an enthusiastic way.
   (C) The more a speaker wants to please the audience, the more likely he will succeed.
   (D) The key to a successful speech is to make it meaningful and relevant to the audience.

51. What was the reaction of the audience to Dr. Thompson's speech?
   (A) They were bored because the medical topics were not their daily concern.
   (B) They did not understand him so they could only discuss among themselves.
   (C) They were impressed by his familiarity with advanced research in medicine.
   (D) They congratulated him on the success of the speech and asked him questions.

52. Which topic was **NOT** mentioned in the doctor's speech?
    (A) Genetic research.   (B) Flu.
    (C) Immune system disorder.   (D) Creutzfeldt-Jakob disease.

53. What does "**had them on the edge of their seats**" mean in the last sentence of the passage?
    (A) Had them stand up.   (B) Took them by surprise.
    (C) Caught their full attention. (D) Aroused their suspicion.

第 54 至 56 題為題組

When a company ventures into new markets, it will need to face various problems. These problems can be broadly classified into several categories, including (1) cultural factors, (2) economic issues, (3) geographical factors, (4) political/legal issues, (5) religious factors, and (6) technological issues. Find an appropriate category for the problems discussed in each of the following paragraphs.

A company will face problems of this kind, as it is an alien when compared to the business climate of the country. Coca-Cola, for instance, was faced with such a problem in India, when it was given a choice of either to reveal its secret formula or leave the country. Coke chose to leave. But when it was welcomed back after several years, it was subjected to harassment and constant interference from the political activists.

54. The most appropriate category for the above paragraph is _____.
    (A) religious factors   (B) economic issues
    (C) geographical factors   (D) political/legal issues

Problems of this kind can make an impact on the properties of a product. This impact forces a company to adapt its products in order to meet the needs of the local market. To solve the problems, the level of economic development in a market should be assessed, for example, by the level of revenue, buying power of local consumers, and by the state of infrastructure in the foreign market. These indicators can provide vital information to the company regarding its marketing strategy.

55. The most appropriate category for the above paragraph is _____.
    (A) cultural factors
    (B) economic issues
    (C) geographical factors
    (D) technological issues

These problems are perhaps the biggest issue a researcher can come across while studying new markets. This is because markets that can be classified as similar on various grounds tend to be dissimilar when it comes to this particular aspect. There are differences even within the same country. Accordingly, travel advertising in Canada is divided between the English audience and the French audience. While pictures of travel advertisements show a wife alone for the English audience, a man and wife are shown for the French audience. This is done because the French are more bound by family ties.

56. The most appropriate category for the above paragraph is _____.
    (A) cultural factors
    (B) economic issues
    (C) geographical factors
    (D) political/legal issues

第貳部份：非選擇題（佔 28％）

一、英文翻譯（8％）

說明： 1. 將下列兩句中文翻譯成適當之英文，並將答案寫在「答案卷」上。
　　　 2. 未按題意翻譯者，不予計分。

1. 身為地球村的成員，我們不應把自己侷限在這個小島上。

2. 我們不但應該參與國際性的活動，並且應該展現我們自己的文化特色。

二、英文作文（20％）

說明： 1. 依提示在「答案卷」上寫一篇英文作文。
　　　 2. 文長至少 120 個單詞。

提示： 指定科目考試完畢後，高中同學決定召開畢業後的第一次同學會，你
　　　 被公推負責主辦。請將你打算籌辦的活動寫成一篇短文。文分兩段，
　　　 第一段詳細介紹同學會的時間、地點及活動內容，第二段則說明採取
　　　 這種活動方式的理由。

九十四年度指定科目考試英文科試題詳解

第壹部分：選擇題

一、詞彙：

1. (**C**) We have had plenty of rain so far this year, so there should be an
   <u>abundant</u> supply of fresh water this summer.
   我們今年到目前為止，已經下了很多雨，所以這個夏天應該可以供
   應充足的淡水。
   (A) intense〔 ɪn'tɛns 〕*adj.* 強烈的
   (B) ultimate〔'ʌltəmɪt 〕*adj.* 最終的
   (C) ***abundant***〔 ə'bʌndənt 〕*adj.* 豐富的；充足的
   (D) epidemic〔ˌɛpə'dɛmɪk 〕*adj.* 流行的
   plenty of 很多　　***so far*** 到目前為止　　supply〔 sə'plaɪ 〕*n.* 供應
   fresh〔 frɛʃ 〕*adj.* 新鮮的；淡的　　***fresh water*** 淡水

2. (**A**) I don't know for sure what I am going to do this weekend, but
   <u>tentatively</u> I plan to visit an old friend of mine in southern Taiwan.
   我無法確知我這個週末要做什麼，但我暫時是打算要去南台灣，拜
   訪一位老朋友。
   (A) ***tentatively***〔'tɛntətɪvlɪ 〕*adv.* 暫時地；試驗性地
   (B) inevitably〔 ɪn'ɛvətəblɪ 〕*adv.* 不可避免地
   (C) unknowingly〔 ʌn'noɪŋlɪ 〕*adv.* 不知不覺地
   (D) numerously〔'njumərəslɪ 〕*adv.* 很多地
   for sure 確定地　　southern〔'sʌðən 〕*adj.* 南部的

3. (**D**) Our chemistry teacher was on a one-month sick leave, so the
   principal had to find a teacher to <u>substitute</u> for her.
   我們的化學老師請了一個月的病假，所以校長必須找一位老師來
   代替她。
   (A) recover〔 rɪ'kʌvə 〕*v.* 恢復
   (B) navigate〔'nævəˌget 〕*v.* 航行；領航
   (C) rehearse〔 rɪ'hɜs 〕*v.* 預演；排演
   (D) ***substitute***〔'sʌbstəˌtjut 〕*v.* 代替
   chemistry〔'kɛmɪstrɪ 〕*n.* 化學　　***sick leave*** 病假
   principal〔'prɪnsəpḷ 〕*n.* 校長

4. (**C**) The gym is closed on Monday for routine <u>maintenance</u> work. The facilities are kept in good condition by the regular checking and repairing.

體育館星期一沒開放，因為要做例行的<u>維修</u>工作。藉由定期的檢查和修理，那些設備才能保持在良好的狀態。

(A) disturbance〔dɪˈstɝbəns〕*n.* 擾亂
(B) eloquence〔ˈɛləkwəns〕*n.* 雄辯；口才
(C) ***maintenance***〔ˈmentənəns〕*n.* 維修
(D) alliance〔əˈlaɪəns〕*n.* 聯盟；同盟國

gym〔dʒɪm〕*n.* 體育館　　routine〔ruˈtin〕*adj.* 定期的；例行的
facilities〔fəˈsɪlətɪz〕*n. pl.* 設備　　condition〔kənˈdɪʃən〕*n.* 狀態
regular〔ˈrɛgjələ〕*adj.* 定期的；例行的　　repair〔rɪˈpɛr〕*v.* 修理

5. (**D**) If you exercise regularly, your blood <u>circulation</u> will be improved, and you will feel more energetic.

如果你規律地運動，你的血液<u>循環</u>就會改善，而且你會覺得更有活力。

(A) fatigue〔fəˈtig〕*n.* 疲倦
(B) tranquility〔trænˈkwɪlətɪ〕*n.* 平靜
(C) fragrance〔ˈfregrəns〕*n.* 香味；芳香
(D) ***circulation***〔ˌsɝkjəˈleʃən〕*n.* 循環

exercise〔ˈɛksəˌsaɪz〕*v.* 運動　　regularly〔ˈrɛgjələlɪ〕*adv.* 規律地
blood〔blʌd〕*n.* 血液　　improve〔ɪmˈpruv〕*v.* 改善
energetic〔ˌɛnəˈdʒɛtɪk〕*adj.* 充滿活力的

6. (**C**) Nowadays people have to pass various tests for professional <u>certificates</u> so that they can be qualified for a well-paying job.

現在，人們必須通過各種不同的專業<u>證照</u>考試，這樣一來，他們才有資格獲得高薪的工作。

(A) mechanics〔məˈkænɪks〕*n.* 力學；機械學
(B) permission〔pəˈmɪʃən〕*n.* 准許
(C) ***certificate***〔səˈtɪfəkɪt〕*n.* 證書；執照
(D) perseverance〔ˌpɝsəˈvɪrəns〕*n.* 毅力；不屈不撓

nowadays〔ˈnauəˌdez〕*adv.* 現在　　pass〔pæs〕*v.* 通過
various〔ˈvɛrɪəs〕*adj.* 各種不同的
professional〔prəˈfɛʃənḷ〕*adj.* 專業的
qualified〔ˈkwɑləˌfaɪd〕*adj.* 合格的
well-paying〔ˈwɛlˈpeɪŋ〕*adj.* 高薪的

7. (**B**) Though Dr. Wang has been away from his hometown for over ten years, he can still <u>visualize</u> his old house clearly.

雖然王醫師已經離開家鄉十年以上，他仍然可以<u>在心裡清楚地描繪出</u>老家的樣子。

 (A) nominate〔'nɑmə,net〕*v.* 提名
 (B) **visualize**〔'vɪʒʊəl,aɪz〕*v.* 清楚描繪在心裡；想像
 (C) prolong〔prə'lɔŋ〕*v.* 延長
 (D) sprinkle〔'sprɪŋkḷ〕*v.* 灑（液體、粉末）

8. (**D**) The speaker spent twenty minutes on one simple question. The explanation was so <u>lengthy</u> that we could not see the point clearly.

該名演講者花了二十分鐘在講一個簡單的問題。那段說明<u>冗長</u>到我們無法清楚了解重點所在。

 (A) coherent〔ko'hɪrənt〕*adj.* 有條理的
 (B) crucial〔'kruʃəl〕*adj.* 非常重要的
 (C) various〔'vɛrɪəs〕*adj.* 各種不同的
 (D) **lengthy**〔'lɛŋθɪ〕*adj.* 冗長的
 explanation〔,ɛksplə'neʃən〕*n.* 解釋；說明
 point〔pɔɪnt〕*n.* 重點

9. (**C**) The new tax policy proposed for the next fiscal year has been severely criticized by the <u>opposition</u> party leaders.

下個會計年度所提出的新租稅政策，遭到<u>反對</u>黨領袖的猛烈批評。

 (A) interaction〔,ɪntə'ækʃən〕*n.* 交互作用
 (B) exposition〔,ɛkspə'zɪʃən〕*n.* 解說；展覽會
 (C) **opposition**〔,ɑpə'zɪʃən〕*n.* 反對
 (D) occupation〔,ɑkjə'peʃən〕*n.* 職業；佔領
 tax〔tæks〕*n.* 稅　　policy〔'pɑləsɪ〕*n.* 政策
 propose〔prə'poz〕*v.* 提出；提議
 fiscal〔'fɪskḷ〕*adj.* 財政的
 fiscal year 會計年度
 severely〔sə'vɪrlɪ〕*adv.* 猛烈地；嚴格地
 criticize〔'krɪtə,saɪz〕*v.* 批評　　party〔'pɑrtɪ〕*n.* 政黨

10. (**B**) Thousands of people flooded into the city to join the demonstration; as a result, the city's transportation system was almost <u>paralyzed</u>.
數千人湧進這座城市參加示威遊行；結果導致這座城市的交通運輸系統幾乎癱瘓。

(A) testify〔'tɛstə,faɪ〕*v.* 證明；作證

(B) ***paralyze***〔'pærə,laɪz〕*v.* 使癱瘓

(C) stabilize〔'stebḷ,aɪz〕*v.* 使安定；使穩定

(D) dissatisfy〔dɪs'sætɪs,faɪ〕*v.* 使不滿

flood〔flʌd〕*v.* 湧到；大舉前往　　join〔dʒɔɪn〕*v.* 參加

demonstration〔,dɛmən'streʃən〕*n.* 示威遊行

as a result 結果；因此　　transportation〔,trænspɚ'teʃən〕*n.* 運輸

二、綜合測驗：

第 11 至 15 題為題組

After a long day working in the office, Alexander hailed a taxi to take him home. Squeezing his body into the taxi, he noticed the shiny interior and the smell of brand new leather. After informing the driver of his <u>destination</u>, Alexander resorted to his reading of Dan Brown's intelligent
　　11
thriller, *The Da Vinci Code*. Five minutes into the journey, he was on page 120: "…his Mona Lisa is neither male nor female…" Suddenly, Alexander <u>looked up</u> and noticed that the driver had detoured from the
　　　　　　12
familiar route.

在辦公室工作了漫長的一天之後，亞歷山大叫了部計程車載他回家。他把身體擠進計程車後，發現計程車的內部新得發亮，而且還有股新皮革的味道。在告知司機他的目的地之後，亞歷山大又開始讀丹・布朗的機智驚悚小說《達文西密碼》。上路後五分鐘，他讀到第 120 頁：「…他的蒙娜麗莎，既不是男的也不是女的…」突然間，亞歷山大抬頭看，注意到司機繞離了熟悉的路線。

hail〔hel〕*v.* 叫（計程車）　　squeeze〔skwiz〕*v.* 擠

shiny〔'ʃaɪnɪ〕*adj.* 閃亮的　　interior〔ɪn'tɪrɪɚ〕*n.* 內部

brand new 全新的（= *brand-new*）　　leather〔'lɛðɚ〕*n.* 皮革

inform〔ɪn'fɔrm〕*v.* 告知　　***resort to*** 訴諸（= *turn to*）

intelligent〔ɪn'tɛlədʒənt〕*adj.* 聰明的；機智的

thriller〔'θrɪlɚ〕*n.* 驚悚（恐怖）小說　　code〔kod〕*n.* 密碼

detour〔'ditʊr〕*v.* 繞行　　route〔rut〕*n.* 路線

11. (**B**) (A) motivation〔,motəˈveʃən〕*n.* 動機

　　　　　(B) ***destination***〔,dɛstəˈneʃən〕*n.* 目的地

　　　　　(C) expectation〔,ɛkspɛkˈteʃən〕*n.* 期待

　　　　　(D) solution〔 səˈluʃən〕*n.* 解決之道

12. (**A**) (A) ***look up*** 抬頭看　　　　(B) take off 起飛

　　　　　(C) turn in 繳交（= *hand in*）　(D) get on 上（車）

To redirect the driver, Alexander tapped him on the shoulder. Out of the
blue, the driver screamed, lost control of the car, and almost hit a bus.
The cab went up on the footpath and <u>finally</u> stopped centimeters away
　　　　　　　　　　　　　　　　　13
from a shop window.

為了使司機改變方向，亞歷山大拍拍他的肩膀。司機忽然尖叫，沒辦法控制車
子，而且幾乎撞上一台巴士。計程車開上了人行道，最後停在距離商店櫥窗幾
公分的地方。

　　　　　redirect〔,ridəˈrɛkt〕*v.* 使改方向　　tap〔 tæp〕*v.* 輕拍

　　　　　out of the blue 突然　　scream〔 skrim〕*v.* 尖叫

　　　　　lose control of … 失去對…的控制力　　cab〔 kæb〕*n.* 計程車

　　　　　footpath〔ˈfʊt,pæθ〕*n.* 人行道

　　　　　centimeter〔ˈsɛntə,mitɚ〕*n.* 公分

13. (**C**) (A) hardly〔ˈhɑrdlɪ〕*adv.* 幾乎不

　　　　　(B) likely〔ˈlaɪklɪ〕*adv.* 有可能

　　　　　(C) ***finally***〔ˈfaɪn̩lɪ〕*adv.* 最後；終於

　　　　　(D) mainly〔ˈmenlɪ〕*adv.* 主要地

For a second, everything went quiet in the cab. Then the driver said, "Look,
mate! Don't ever do that again. You scared the living daylights out of me!"
Alexander apologized and said, "I didn't' <u>realize</u> that a little tap would scare
　　　　　　　　　　　　　　　　　14
you so much." The driver replied, "Sorry, sir. It's not really your <u>fault</u>.
　　　　　　　　　　　　　　　　　15
Today is my first day as a cab driver. I've been driving a funeral van for
the last 25 years."

片刻間，計程車內一片沈寂。然後司機說：「喂，朋友！別再做這種事了。你快把我嚇死了。」亞歷山大一邊道歉一邊說：「我不知道輕輕拍你一下，會把你嚇成這樣。」司機回答說：「對不起，先生，其實也不是你的錯。今天是我第一天當計程車司機，我之前開了二十五年的靈車。」

look〔lʊk〕*interj.* 喂！
mate〔met〕*n.* 朋友；伙伴　　daylights〔ˈdeˌlaɪts〕*n.* 意識
scare the living daylights out of *sb.* 使某人嚇得幾乎要昏過去
apologize〔əˈpɑləˌdʒaɪz〕*v.* 道歉　　funeral〔ˈfjunərəl〕*n.* 葬禮
van〔væn〕*n.* 有蓋小貨車

14.（ **B** ）(A) find〔faɪnd〕*v.* 發現　　(B) ***realize***〔ˈriəˌlaɪz〕*v.* 了解
(C) wonder〔ˈwʌndɚ〕*v.* 想知道
(D) admit〔ədˈmɪt〕*v.* 承認

15.（ **D** ）(A) matter〔ˈmætɚ〕*n.* 問題；事情
(B) decision〔dɪˈsɪʒən〕*n.* 決定
(C) trouble〔ˈtrʌbḷ〕*n.* 煩惱　　(D) ***fault***〔fɔlt〕*n.* 過錯

第 16 至 20 題為題組

Today, with a couple of clicks, you can go anywhere in the world without leaving your computer. So it should come as little <u>surprise</u> that

16
the Internet has headlined the top 25 innovations of the past quarter century, according to a panel of technology leaders assembled to promote inventiveness.

現在你只要按兩下滑鼠，不用離開電腦，就可以到世界的每一個角落。所以你應該不會太訝異，根據為促進發明才能而召集的技術領袖研究小組表示，網際網路已成為過去二十五年來，二十五項革新中的主角。

a couple of 兩個；一對　　click〔klɪk〕*n.* 按滑鼠所發出的聲音
headline〔ˈhɛdˌlaɪn〕*v.* 成為主角　　innovation〔ˌɪnəˈveʃən〕*n.* 革新
panel〔ˈpænḷ〕*n.* 討論小組；研究小組
technology〔tɛkˈnɑlədʒɪ〕*n.* 技術
assemble〔əˈsɛmbḷ〕*v.* 聚集；召集
promote〔prəˈmot〕*v.* 增進；促進
inventiveness〔ɪnˈvɛntɪvnɪs〕*n.* 發明才能

16. (**B**) (A) agreement〔ə'grimənt〕*n.* 同意
　　　　 (B) ***surprise***〔sə'praɪz〕*n.* 驚訝
　　　　 (C) belief〔bə'lif〕*n.* 信念；信仰
　　　　 (D) concern〔kən'sɝn〕*n.* 關心的事

　　 In creating the list, the group <u>singles out</u> twenty-five non-medically
　　　　　　　　　　　　　　　　　　　17
related technological innovations that have become widely used since 1980.
These innovations are readily recognizable by most Americans, have had a
direct impact on our everyday lives, and may also dramatically affect our
lives <u>in the future</u>.
　　　18
　　　在編造這個名單時，該小組挑出了二十五個從一九八〇年起，就已經被廣
泛使用的技術革新，而它們都與醫學無關。很快地，大部分的美國人都知道了
這些革新，而且它們對我們的日常生活也有直接的影響，在未來，也有可能會
對我們的生活產生顯著的影響。

　　　　　 non-medically〔nɑn'mɛdɪkl̩ɪ〕*adv.* 非醫學上
　　　　　 technological〔ˌtɛknə'lɑdʒɪkl̩〕*adj.* 技術的
　　　　　 widely〔'waɪdlɪ〕*adv.* 廣泛地
　　　　　 readily〔'rɛdɪlɪ〕*adv.* 迅速地；輕易地
　　　　　 recognizable〔'rɛkəgˌnaɪzəbl̩〕*adj.* 認得的；可辨別的
　　　　　 impact〔'ɪmpækt〕*n.* 衝擊；強烈的影響
　　　　　 dramatically〔drə'mætɪkl̩ɪ〕*adv.* 顯著地
　　　　　 affect〔ə'fɛkt〕*v.* 影響

17. (**C**) (A) give in 放棄　　　　　　 (B) take over 接管
　　　　 (C) ***single out*** 挑選出　　　 (D) turn down 拒絕；關小聲

18. (**D**) 因句中有 may，是對未來的推測，且事情尚未發生，故應選
　　　　 (D) ***in the future***「在未來」，而 (A) for a moment「有一段
　　　　 時間」，(B) at that time「在那時候」，(C) from then on
　　　　 「從那時起」，均不合句意。

The top innovation, the Web, was created by British software consultant Tim Berners-Lee. <u>Frustrated</u> by the multitude of information systems
19
requiring complicated access, Berners-Lee fashioned a universal one that made information readily <u>available</u>. He created HTML (hypertext markup
20
language) and its rule of usage (HTTP, hypertext transfer protocol). In 1991 he unveiled the World Wide Web. Today, this No. 1 invention has become so commonplace that it is almost taken for granted.

最重要的革新——網際網路，是由英國的軟體顧問提姆・柏納李所創造的。柏納李覺得很挫折，因爲多數的資訊系統都需要複雜的存取，所以他就製造了一個通路，使得資訊的取得更容易。他創造了 HTML（超文字標記語言），以及它的使用規則（HTTP，超文字傳輸協定）。在一九九一年，他首度發表全球資訊網。如今，這個第一名的發明，已經變得如此普通，以致於幾乎被視爲理所當然。

today〔tə'de〕adv. 現在　　British〔'brɪtɪʃ〕adj. 英國的
software〔'sɔft,wɛr〕n. 軟體
consultant〔kən'sʌltṇt〕n. 顧問；諮詢者
multitude〔'mʌltə,tjud〕n. 多數
access〔'æksɛs〕n. 門徑；入口　　fashion〔'fæʃən〕v. 製造
universal〔,junə'vɜsḷ〕adj. 通用的；一般人都用的
HTML 超文字標記語言　　hypertext〔'haɪpə,tɛkst〕n. 超文字
markup〔'mɑrk,ʌp〕n. 標記　　usage〔'jusɪdʒ〕n. 用法
HTTP 超文字傳輸協定　　transfer〔træns'fɜ〕v. 轉移
protocol〔'protə,kɑl〕n. 電腦間資料傳輸的規則；協定
unveil〔ʌn'vel〕v. 首次發表　　**World Wide Web** 全球資訊網
invention〔ɪn'vɛnʃən〕n. 發明物
commonplace〔'kɑmən,ples〕adj. 普通的
be taken for granted 被視爲理所當然

19.（**B**）本句是由：Because he had been frustrated…轉化而來。副詞子句改爲分詞構句的步驟：① 去連接詞（Because）；② 去相同主詞（he）；③ 動詞改爲現在分詞（had been→having been）；④ being 或 having been 可省略，故選 (B) **Frustrated**〔'frʌstretɪd〕adj. 受挫的；沮喪的。

20. (**A**) (A) *available* ﹝ ə'veləbḷ ﹞*adj.* 可獲得的
　　　　 (B) consistent ﹝ kən'sɪstənt ﹞*adj.* 前後一致的
　　　　 (C) important ﹝ ɪm'pɔrtn̩t ﹞*adj.* 重要的
　　　　 (D) unforgettable ﹝ˌʌnfɚ'gɛtəbḷ ﹞*adj.* 難忘的

第 21 至 25 題為題組

　　 The world's largest collection of Khmer sculpture resides at Angkor, the former royal capital of Cambodia. The 7,000 pieces—full statues, heads and carved inscriptions—are breathtaking not only for their individual beauty, but also for <u>what</u> they represent: a road map to the origins of much
　　　　　　　　　　　　　　　　　　　　　21
of Southeast Asian culture. But the collection is not in a museum, and it is not open <u>to</u> visitors. It is held in unknown, guarded warehouses <u>where</u> only
　　　　 22　　　　　　　　　　　　　　　　　　　　　　　　 23
a few people can see it.

　　 世界上收藏最多高棉雕刻品的地方，就是吳哥窟，它是柬埔寨的古王城。這七千件雕刻—完整的雕像、頭像和雕刻的碑文—之所以令人驚嘆，不只是因為它們獨特的美，而且也因為它們所描繪的情景：這些雕刻說明了許多東南亞文化的起源。但是這些收藏沒有放在博物館裡，也沒有開放給觀光客參觀。它被存放在沒有人知道、且有人看守的倉庫，只有少數人能去參觀。

collection ﹝ kə'lɛkʃən ﹞*n.* 收藏　　　Khmer ﹝ kmɛr ﹞*n.* 高棉人
sculpture ﹝'skʌlptʃɚ ﹞*n.* 雕刻　　　reside ﹝ rɪ'zaɪd ﹞*v.* 存在
Angkor ﹝'æŋkɔr ﹞*n.* 吳哥窟　　　former ﹝'fɔrmɚ ﹞*adj.* 以前的
royal ﹝'rɔɪəl ﹞*adj.* 王室的　　　capital ﹝'kæpətḷ ﹞*n.* 首都；中心城市
Cambodia ﹝ kæm'bodɪə ﹞*n.* 高棉（柬埔寨）　　　piece ﹝ pis ﹞*n.* 件
statue ﹝'stætʃʊ ﹞*n.* 雕像　　　carve ﹝ kɑrv ﹞*v.* 雕刻
inscription ﹝ ɪn'skrɪpʃən ﹞*n.* 碑文
breathtaking ﹝'brɛθˌtekɪŋ ﹞*adj.* 令人驚嘆的
individual ﹝ˌɪndə'vɪdʒʊəl ﹞*adj.* 獨特的
represent ﹝ˌrɛprɪ'zɛnt ﹞*v.* 代表；描繪　　***road map*** 說明；指示
origin ﹝'ɔrədʒɪn ﹞*n.* 起源　　　Southeast ﹝ˌsaʊθ'ist ﹞*adj.* 東南的
Asian ﹝'eʃən ﹞*adj.* 亞洲的　　　hold ﹝ hold ﹞*v.* 儲存
unknown ﹝ ʌn'non ﹞*adj.* 無法得知的
guarded ﹝'gɑrdɪd ﹞*adj.* 被看守著的
warehouse ﹝'wɛrˌhaʊs ﹞*n.* 倉庫

21. (**A**) 前無先行詞，故空格應填複合關係代名詞，選 (A) *what* 相當於 the things that。

22. (**C**) *be open to sb.* 開放給某人

23. (**B**) 表「地點」，關係副詞須用 *where*，選 (B)。

These people assembled it by removing figures from the ruins of Cambodia's world-famous temples and replacing them with hollow, concrete <u>fakes</u>. For
24
the most part, these are hard to distinguish from the originals. Clever art thieves? No, these "art thieves" work for the Angkor Conservancy. <u>Except</u>
25
<u>for</u> very large pieces too heavy to move, virtually all surviving Angkorian statues, wood carvings and artifacts have been replaced with copies.

這些人為了要收集那些雕像，而從柬埔寨舉世聞名的寺廟廢墟把它們移走，並用空心的水泥仿製品來取代它們。大體上而言，很難分得出是仿製品還是原來的雕像。那些人是聰明的雅賊嗎？不，這些「雅賊」是替吳哥窟管理局工作。除了因為太重而無法移動的特大雕像之外，幾乎所有現存的吳哥窟雕像、木雕和文化遺物，都已被複製品取代了。

assemble〔əˋsɛmbḷ〕*v.* 收集
remove〔rɪˋmuv〕*v.* 移走　　figure〔ˋfɪgjɚ〕*n.* 雕像
ruins〔ˋruɪnz〕*n. pl.* 廢墟
world-famous〔ˋwɝldˋfeməs〕*adj.* 世界知名的
temple〔ˋtɛmpḷ〕*n.* 寺廟　　replace〔rɪˋples〕*v.* 取代
hollow〔ˋhɑlo〕*adj.* 空心的　　concrete〔kɑnˋkrit〕*adj.* 混凝土製的
for the most part 大體上　　distinguish〔dɪˋstɪŋgwɪʃ〕*v.* 分辨
original〔əˋrɪdʒənḷ〕*n.* 原作品
art thief 雅賊（專偷藝術作品的小偷）
conservancy〔kənˋsɝvənsɪ〕*n.* 管理局
virtually〔ˋvɝtʃʊəlɪ〕*adv.* 幾乎　　surviving〔sɚˋvaɪvɪŋ〕*adj.* 殘存的
artifact〔ˋɑrtɪˌfækt〕*n.* 文化遺物　　copy〔ˋkɑpɪ〕*n.* 複製品

24. (**D**) (A) strategy〔ˋstrætədʒɪ〕*n.* 策略
　　　　(B) course〔kors〕*n.* 課程；過程
　　　　(C) way〔we〕*n.* 道路；方法　　(D) *fake*〔fek〕*n.* 仿冒品

25. (**A**) 依句意，選 (A) *except for*「除了…（之外）」。而 (B) in spite of
　　　「儘管」，(C) owing to「由於」，(D) in addition to「除了…之外
　　　（還有）」，均不合句意。

第 26 至 30 題為題組

　　Jean Piaget, a psychologist and pioneer in the study of child
intelligence, was born in Switzerland in 1896. At age 10, he managed
his first <u>publication</u>, a description of a partly albino sparrow he observed
　　　　　　26
in a public park. At age 15, he <u>set out</u> to devote his life to developing a
　　　　　　　　　　　　　　27
biological explanation of knowledge.

　　　皮亞傑，是一位心理學家及研究兒童智能的先驅，於 1896 年出生瑞士。
他十歲時，設法發表了第一篇論文，描述他在公園觀察到，有隻麻雀患了部份
白化症。十五歲時，他開始將一生奉獻在闡述生物學對知識的解釋。

　　　　　psychologist〔saɪˋkɑlədʒɪst〕n. 心理學家
　　　　　pioneer〔͵paɪəˋnɪr〕n. 先驅
　　　　　intelligence〔ɪnˋtɛlədʒəns〕n. 智力
　　　　　Switzerland〔ˋswɪtsələnd〕n. 瑞士
　　　　　manage〔ˋmænɪdʒ〕v. 設法做到
　　　　　description〔dɪˋskrɪpʃən〕n. 描述；說明
　　　　　partly〔ˋpɑrtlɪ〕adv. 部份地
　　　　　albino〔ælˋbaɪno〕n. 白化症；白子　　　sparrow〔ˋspæro〕n. 麻雀
　　　　　observe〔əbˋzɝv〕v. 觀察　　observe〔dɪˋvot〕v. 奉獻；貢獻
　　　　　biological〔͵baɪəˋladʒɪkl̩〕adj. 生物學的
　　　　　explanation〔͵ɛkspləˋneʃən〕n. 說明；解釋

26. (**B**) (A) subscription〔səbˋskrɪpʃən〕n. 訂閱
　　　　　(B) *publication*〔͵pʌblɪˋkeʃən〕n. 出版品；發表
　　　　　(C) obligation〔͵ɑbləˋgeʃən〕n. 義務
　　　　　(D) transaction〔trænsˋækʃən〕n. 交易

27. (**D**) 依句意，選 (D) *set out*「開始；出發」。而 (A) put down「放下；寫下」，
　　　(B) pass on「傳遞」，(C) end up「結果」，均不合句意。

He began his career as a zoologist, <u>studying</u> mollusks and their
                                          28
adaptations to their environment. <u>By</u> age 21, he had already published 25
                                      29
professional papers on that topic. Later, after working with Alfred Binet
in Paris, he became interested in levels of logic used by children taking
standardized tests on intelligence. Piaget <u>sought</u> to establish a body of
                                              30
psychology all his life and became a very influential figure in educational
psychology. His works were all written originally in French and were
later translated into English.

　　他開始以動物學家為業，他研究軟體動物，以及牠們如何適應環境。到了二十一歲，他已經以這個主題發表了二十五篇專業論文。後來，和阿佛列‧比內在巴黎共事之後，他對孩童參加標準化的智力測驗時，所使用邏輯的程度變得很感興趣。皮亞傑一生都試圖要建立一套完整的心理學，後來他在教育心理學方面，變成相當具有影響力的人物。他的作品起初都是以法文書寫，之後再被翻成英文。

　　　　career〔kəˋrɪr〕n. 生涯　　zoologist〔zoˋɑlədʒɪst〕n. 動物學家
　　　　mollusk〔ˋmɑləsk〕n. 軟體動物（章魚、貝類等）
　　　　adaptation〔͵ædəpˋteʃən〕n. 適應　　publish〔ˋpʌblɪʃ〕v. 出版；發表
　　　　professional〔prəˋfɛʃənḷ〕adj. 專業的　　paper〔ˋpepɚ〕n. 論文
　　　　level〔ˋlɛvḷ〕n. 程度；水準　　logic〔ˋlɑdʒɪk〕n. 邏輯
　　　　standardize〔ˋstændəd͵aɪz〕v. 使標準化
　　　　establish〔əˋstæblɪʃ〕v. 建立　　*a body of* 全體的
　　　　psychology〔saɪˋkɑlədʒ〕n. 心理學
　　　　influential〔͵ɪnfluˋɛnʃəl〕adj. 有影響力的
　　　　figure〔ˋfɪgjɚ〕n.（重要的）人物
　　　　educational〔͵ɛdʒuˋkeʃənḷ〕adj. 教育的
　　　　originally〔əˋrɪdʒənḷɪ〕adv. 本來；起初
　　　　French〔frɛntʃ〕n. 法文　　translate〔trænsˋlet〕v. 翻譯

28. (**C**) 兩動詞間無連接詞，第二個動詞須改為現在分詞，故選 (C) *studying*。

29. (**A**) 依句意，「到了」二十一歲，選 (A) *By*。

30. (**C**) (B) afford〔əˋfɔrd〕v. 負擔得起
　　　　　(C) *seek*〔sik〕v. 試圖 < *to* >（過去式及過去分詞皆為 sought〔sɔt〕)
　　　　　(D) tend〔tɛnd〕v. 傾向於；易於 < *to* >

三、文意選填：

第 31 至 40 題為題組

Like pearls scattered in the East Sea, the Penghu archipelago is situated in the southwest of the Taiwan Strait. It consists of <u>nearly</u> one hundred
31
islands, of which many are famous for their pure white-sand beaches. The broad beaches and beautiful underwater scenery are the major <u>attractions</u>
32
of Penghu islands.

就像撒在東海的珍珠一樣，澎湖群島就位於台灣海峽的西南方。它是由將近一百座的島嶼所組成的，其中有很多座島是以純淨的白沙灘聞名。寬闊的海灘以及美麗的海底風光，都是澎湖群島主要的觀光勝地。

> pearl〔pɝl〕*n.* 珍珠　　　scatter〔'skætɚ〕*v.* 撒
> **the East Sea** 東海　　　archipelago〔ˌɑrkə'pɛləˌgo〕*n.* 群島
> **the Penghu archipelago** 澎湖群島
> **be situated in** 位於　　　**the Taiwan Strait** 台灣海峽
> consist〔kən'sɪst〕*v.* 由～組成　　　**be famous for** 以～著名
> pure〔pjʊr〕*adj.* 純淨的　　　broad〔brɔd〕*adj.* 寬闊的
> scenery〔'sinərɪ〕*n.* 景色　　　major〔'medʒɚ〕*adj.* 主要的

31. (**F**) 依句意，澎湖群島由「將近」一百座的島嶼所組成，選 (F) ***nearly***。
    nearly〔'nɪrlɪ〕*adv.* 將近

32. (**A**) 依句意，寬闊的海灘以及美麗的海底風光都是澎湖群島主要的「觀光勝地」，選 (A) ***attractions***。
    attraction〔ə'trækʃən〕*n.* 觀光勝地

Among the one hundred or so islands, only 20 are inhabited. The <u>uninhabited</u> islands of Penghu have been kept intact without human
33
intervention. The primitive conditions on these islands, their unique basalt rock formations and rich ecology bring <u>even</u> more surprises for visitors.
34
These islands are designated as natural reservations, <u>for</u> they are endowed
35
with remarkable and rare resources.

在大約一百座的島嶼當中，只有二十座是有人居住的。而那些無人居住的
澎湖島嶼則一直保持原狀，沒有人爲介入。這些島上的原始環境，它們獨特的
玄武岩地層以及豐富的生態，帶給遊客更多的驚喜。這些島被指定爲自然保育
區，因爲它們擁有驚人且稀有的資源。

> ***or so*** 大約　　**inhabited**〔 ɪnˈhæbɪtɪd 〕*adj.* 有人居住的
> **intact**〔 ɪnˈtækt 〕*adj.* 原封不動的
> **intervention**〔ˌɪntɚˈvɛnʃən 〕*n.* 介入
> **primitive**〔ˈprɪmətɪv 〕*adj.* 原始的　　**condition**〔 kənˈdɪʃən 〕*n.* 環境
> **unique**〔 juˈnɪk 〕*adj.* 獨特的　　**basalt**〔 bəˈsɔlt 〕*n.* 玄武岩
> **formation**〔 fɔrˈmeʃən 〕*n.* 地層　　**rich**〔 rɪtʃ 〕*adj.* 豐富的
> **ecology**〔 ɪˈkɑlədʒɪ 〕*n.* 生態　　**designate**〔ˈdɛzɪɡˌnet 〕*v.* 指定
> **reservation**〔ˌrɛzɚˈveʃən 〕*n.* 保育區
> **endow**〔 ɪnˈdau 〕*v.* 賦予；擁有
> **remarkable**〔 rɪˈmɑrkəbḷ 〕*adj.* 驚人的
> **rare**〔 rɛr 〕*adj.* 稀少的　　**resource**〔 rɪˈsors 〕*n.* 資源

33. (**J**) 依句意，「無人居住的」島嶼一直保持原狀，選 (J) ***uninhabited*** 。
    uninhabited〔ˌʌnɪnˈhæbɪtɪd 〕*adj.* 無人居住的

34. (**I**) 修飾比較級須用副詞 ***even***，選 (I)。

35. (**C**) 依句意，這些島被指定爲自然保育區，是「因爲」它們擁有驚人
    且稀有的資源，選 (C) ***for***。

For instance, Gupo (Grand Aunt) Island is the largest uninhabited island
in the North Sea area and the main <u>location</u> of seaweed production. Like
                                        36
Gupo Island, Baisha (White Sand) Island is also uninhabited and has
<u>preserved</u> the primitive, unspoiled character. The island features
 37
well-developed columnar basalt formations, which on the southern
coastline are <u>particularly</u> spectacular. This is also one of the best areas of
       38
the Penghu Islands for bird watching. In addition, there are also pillar-
shaped rock formations that are Mother Nature's <u>masterpiece</u> sculptures.
    39

舉例來說，姑婆嶼就是北海地區最大的無人島，也是主要的海藻產地。而白沙嶼就像姑婆嶼一樣，也是無人居住，它保存了原始且未經破壞的特色。這座島以發展良好的圓柱狀玄武岩地層為特色，而位於南方海岸線上的地層尤其壯觀。這裡同時也是澎湖群島最佳的賞鳥區之一。此外，這裡還有柱狀的岩層，這可是大自然的雕刻傑作。

> *for instance* 舉例來說　　　main〔 men 〕*adj.* 主要的
> seaweed〔'si‚wid 〕*n.* 海藻　　　production〔 prə'dʌkʃən 〕*n.* 生產
> unspoiled〔 ʌn'spɔɪld 〕*adj.* 未經破壞的
> character〔'kærɪktə 〕*n.* 特色　　　feature〔'fitʃə 〕*v.* 以～為特色
> well-developed〔'wɛldɪ'vɛləpt 〕*adj.* 發展良好的
> columnar〔 kə'lʌmnə 〕*adj.* 圓柱狀的　　　coastline〔'kost‚laɪn 〕*n.* 海岸
> spectacular〔 spɛk'tækjələ 〕*adj.* 壯觀的　　*in addition* 此外
> pillar-shaped〔'pɪlə'ʃept 〕*adj.* 柱狀的
> *Mother Nature* 大自然　　　sculpture〔'skʌlptʃə 〕*n.* 雕刻

36.（**D**）依句意，姑婆嶼是主要的海藻產「地」，選 (D) *location*。
　　　location〔 lo'keʃən 〕*n.* 地點

37.（**H**）依句意，白沙嶼就像姑婆嶼一樣，也是無人居住，它「保存」了原始且未經破壞的特色，故選 (H)。　　*preserve*〔 prɪ'zɝv 〕*v.* 保存

38.（**G**）修飾形容詞須用副詞，選 (G) *particularly*。
　　　particularly〔 pə'tɪkjələlɪ 〕*adv.* 特別地

39.（**E**）依句意，白沙嶼的柱狀岩層，是大自然的雕刻「傑作」，故選 (E)。
　　　masterpiece〔'mæstə‚pis 〕*n.* 傑作

Like gifts from God, the yellow flowers that bloom <u>between</u> the basalt
 40
rock cracks and the beautiful songs of little singing birds on the meadows
turn these islands into a paradise.

　　就像是上天所賜予的禮物一樣，綻放在玄武岩石縫間的黃花，以及在草地上歌唱的小鳥的優美歌聲，都讓這些島嶼蛻變成天堂。

> bloom〔 blum 〕*v.* 開花　　　crack〔 kræk 〕*n.* 裂縫
> meadow〔'mɛdo 〕*n.* 草地　　　*turn* A *into* B 把 A 轉變成 B
> paradise〔'pærə‚daɪs 〕*n.* 天堂

40.（**B**）依句意，綻放在玄武岩石縫「間」的黃花，選 (B) ***between***。

四、篇章結構：

第 41 至 45 題為題組

Many researchers have been interested in whether or not an individual's birth order has an effect on intelligence. One of the first studies was carried out in the Netherlands during the early 1970s. **[41] (C) An intelligence test was administered to over 350,000 Dutch males when they turned 19 years of age.** The test was called the "Raven," which is similar to the I.Q. test. The researchers found a strong relationship between the birth order of the test takers and their scores on the Raven test. **[42] (B) Scores decreased as the family size increased and also with birth order.**

　　許多研究人員一直對於個人的出生排行，是否會影響智力深感興趣。最早的研究之一，是一九七〇年代初期在荷蘭所進行的研究。有一項智力測驗，針對超過三十五萬名以上的男性來進行，當時他們的年齡均已超過十九歲。這項測驗叫做「瑞文氏測驗」，它和智力測驗很類似。研究人員發現受試者的出生排行，和他們在瑞文氏測驗中所得到的分數息息相關。分數會隨著家庭人數以及出生排行的增加而遞減。

researcher〔rɪ'sɜtʃɚ〕*n.* 研究人員　　***be interested in*** 對～有興趣
whether or not 是否　　individual〔͵ɪndə'vɪdʒʊəl〕*n.* 個人
birth〔bɝθ〕*n.* 出生　　order〔'ɔrdɚ〕*n.* 次序
have an effect on 對～有影響
intelligence〔ɪn'tɛlədʒəns〕*n.* 智力
study〔'stʌdɪ〕*n. v.* 研究　　***carry out*** 實施
Netherlands〔'nɛðɚləndz〕*n.* 荷蘭　　***intelligence test*** 智力測驗
administer〔əd'mɪnɪstɚ〕*v.* 施行＜*to*＞
Dutch〔dʌtʃ〕*adj.* 荷蘭的　*n.* 荷蘭　　male〔mel〕*n.* 男性
turn〔tɝn〕*v.* 到了（某年齡）
similar〔'sɪmələ〕*adj.* 類似的＜*to*＞　　***I.Q. test*** 智力測驗
strong〔strɔŋ〕*adj.* 極大的　　relationship〔rɪ'leʃən͵ʃɪp〕*n.* 關係
score〔skor〕*n.* 分數　　decrease〔dɪ'kris〕*v.* 減少
increase〔ɪn'kris〕*v.* 增加

In 1975, Zajonc and Markus developed the confluence theory to explain the negative effect of birth order on intelligence involving the data from the Dutch. ⁴³(E) <u>Since then, the theory has been elaborated and even extended to explain the positive effect of birth order on intelligence.</u> However, Rutherford and Sewell in 1991 tested the theory and found no support for it. They concluded that birth order effects did not exist.

在一九七五年時，Zajonc 和 Markus 發展出了一套合流理論，來解釋荷蘭的資料中，出生排行對於智力所造成的負面影響。從此以後，這個理論就被詳細說明，甚至於還延伸來說明出生排行對於智力所造成的正面影響。然而，Rutherford 和 Sewell 在一九九一年測試了這個理論，卻發現沒有一項證據支持這個理論。於是他們下結論說出生排行的影響根本不存在。

> develop〔dɪˋvɛləp〕v. 發展
> confluence〔ˋkɑnfluəns〕n.（思想）交匯　　theory〔ˋθiərɪ〕n. 理論
> negative〔ˋnɛgətɪv〕adj. 負面的　　involve〔ɪnˋvɑlv〕v. 有關
> data〔ˋdetə〕n. 數據；資料　　elaborate〔ɪˋlæbə͵ret〕v. 詳細說明
> extend〔ɪkˋstɛnd〕v. 延伸；擴展
> positive〔ˋpɑzətɪv〕adj. 正面的　　support〔səˋport〕n. 證據
> conclude〔kənˋklud〕v. 下結論　　exist〔ɪgˋzɪst〕v. 存在

⁴⁴(A) <u>There are definitely two sides to this issue.</u> On one side there are Zajonc and Markus, who state that birth order effects may be explained solely by family size and the spacing of births. With short birth intervals, increasing order of birth will be associated with lower intelligence levels. But with long birth intervals, this pattern may be reversed.

這個問題確實有種說法。一方面是 Zajonc 和 Markus，他們說出生排行的影響，只能用家庭人數多寡以及出生間隔來解釋。出生間隔短的話，遞增的出生排行就會和較低的智商有關。但是出生間隔長的話，這種模式就會逆轉。

> definitely〔ˋdɛfənɪtlɪ〕adv. 確實地
> side〔saɪd〕n.（事物）方面　　issue〔ˋɪʃju〕n. 問題
> state〔stet〕v. 提到　　solely〔ˋsolɪ〕adv. 只（＝ only）
> spacing〔ˋspesɪŋ〕n. 間隔　　interval〔ˋɪntə͵vḷ〕n. 間隔
> **be associated with** 和～有關聯　　level〔ˋlɛvḷ〕n. 程度
> pattern〔ˋpætən〕n. 模式　　reverse〔rɪˋvɝs〕v. 逆轉

45 **(D)** On the other side are Rutherford and Sewell, who studied more than 10,000 American high school graduates. They show that the confluence model does not explain any relationship between birth order and intelligence that may exist in the American data. Up to date, there is no agreement between these opposing views. And such a debate may continue for years to come.

另一方面是 Rutherford 和 Sewell，他們研究了超過一萬名的美國高中畢業生。他們表示合流模式並不能解釋那些可能存在於美國數據當中的現象，即出生排行和智力之間的關係。到目前為止，這些相反的觀點並未達成共識。而這樣的辯論也將在未來幾年繼續下去。

> graduate〔'grædʒʊɪt〕*n.* 畢業生　　model〔'mɑdḷ〕*n.* 模型
> agreement〔ə'grimənt〕*n.* 同意；一致
> opposing〔ə'pozɪŋ〕*adj.* 相反的　　view〔vju〕*n.* 觀點
> debate〔dɪ'bet〕*n.* 辯論　　continue〔kən'tɪnju〕*v.* 繼續

五、閱讀測驗：

第 46 至 49 題為題組

In recent years, a craze for height has hit hard in industrializing Asian countries like Taiwan, Hong Kong and China, which boast seven of the world's 10 tallest buildings. The current tallest, at 101 floors, is the Taipei 101 in Taiwan, though Toronto's CN Tower is 180 feet higher, largely because of its huge antenna. Yet, in the Persian Gulf city of Dubai, the world's tallest building-to-be is already well under construction. Its pilings are already in place, plunging 160 feet into the earth. When it's finished, visitors will swoon over this city from 123 stories high, if not more. Currently, however, its exact height is still kept a secret to potential competitors in the world's race for the title of the tallest skyscraper.

近年來，對於高度的狂熱，已經在工業化的亞洲國家，像是台灣、香港和中國，受到嚴重的衝擊，那些國家擁有全世界十大最高建築物中的七座。目前最高的建築物，是位於台灣的台北一〇一大樓，有一百一十層樓，雖然多倫多的西恩塔比它高一百八十英呎，但大多是因為它巨大的天線。然而，在波斯灣沿岸的城市杜拜，有棟即將成為世界最高的建築物，已經順利地在建造中。它的椿材都已經就定位，並且插入了地下一百六十英呎。當它完成時，觀光客會在一百二十三層樓，或者更高的地方，爲這座城市神魂顛倒。然而，目前它的正確高度仍然保密，不讓爭奪世界最高摩天樓頭銜的潛在競爭者知道。

in recent years 近年來　　craze〔krez〕*n.* 狂熱

industrialize〔ɪnˋdʌstrɪəl͵aɪz〕*v.* 使…工業化

boast〔bost〕*v.* 擁有　　current〔ˋkɝənt〕*adj.* 目前的；最近的

Toronto〔təˋranto〕*n.* 多倫多（加拿大安大略省首府）

CN Tower 西恩塔（＝ *Canada's National Tower* 加拿大國家紀念塔）

largely〔ˋlardʒlɪ〕*adv.* 主要地；大半地　　huge〔hjudʒ〕*adj.* 巨大的

antenna〔ænˋtɛnə〕*n.* 天線　　*Persian Gulf* 波斯灣

Dubai〔duˋbaɪ〕*n.* 杜拜（波斯灣南岸的一個酋長國）

building-to-be 即將成爲…的建築物

construction〔kənˋstrʌkʃən〕*n.* 建造

under construction 在建設中；工程進行中

piling〔ˋpaɪlɪŋ〕*n.* 打椿工程　　*in place* 在正確的位置

plunge〔plʌndʒ〕*v.* 插入　　swoon〔swun〕*v.* 陶醉；神魂顛倒

exact〔ɪgˋzækt〕*adj.* 正確的　　potential〔pəˋtɛnʃəl〕*adj.* 有潛力的

competitor〔kəmˋpɛtətɚ〕*n.* 競爭者　　race〔res〕*n.* 競爭

title〔ˋtaɪtl̩〕*n.* 頭銜　　skyscraper〔ˋskaɪ͵skrepɚ〕*n.* 摩天樓

While New York built skyscrapers because land was scarce, Dubai is doing it to get on the world map. "It's image, clearly," said Richard Rosan, president of its construction firm. "There's no practical reason for having a building this tall. You can't be scared of heights if you want to work on the top floor."

紐約建造摩天樓是因爲土地不足，然而杜拜卻是爲了登上世界地圖。它的建設公司總裁，理察・羅森說，「顯然地，它是一種形象。」「沒有任何實際的理由要蓋一座這麼高的建築物。如果你想要在頂樓工作，你就不能怕高。」

scarce〔skɛrs〕*adj.* 不足的　　*get on* 登上

image〔ˋɪmɪdʒ〕*n.* 形象　　clearly〔ˋklɪrlɪ〕*adv.* 顯然地

president〔ˋprɛzədənt〕*n.* 總裁　　firm〔fɝm〕*n.* 公司

practical〔ˋpræktɪkl̩〕*adj.* 實際的　　reason〔ˋrizn̩〕*n.* 理由

scared〔skɛrd〕*adj.* 害怕的　　*be scared of* 害怕

On paper, the Dubai Tower looks something like a giant space shuttle about to be launched into the clouds. Designers say the silvery steel-and-glass building will restore to the Arab world the honor of hosting the earth's tallest structure—a title lost in 1889 when the Eiffel Tower **upset** the 43-century reign of Egypt's Great Pyramid of Giza.

理論上，杜拜塔看起來像一艘即將發射到雲層裡的巨大太空梭。設計師說，這座銀白色的鋼鐵玻璃建築物，將會使阿拉伯世界恢復擁有世界上最高建築物的光榮——此頭銜在一八八九年喪失，當時是艾菲爾鐵塔推翻四十三世紀的埃及吉扎大金字塔的時代。

on paper 理論上　　 giant〔'dʒaɪənt〕*adj.* 巨大的
space shuttle 太空梭　　 launch〔lɔntʃ〕*v.* 發射
designer〔dɪ'zaɪnɚ〕*n.* 設計師　　 silvery〔'sɪlvərɪ〕*adj.* 銀白色的
restore〔rɪ'stor〕*v.* 恢復　　 honor〔'ɑnɚ〕*n.* 光榮
host〔host〕*v.* 擁有　　 structure〔'strʌktʃɚ〕*n.* 建築物
the Eiffel Tower 艾菲爾鐵塔　　 upset〔ʌp'sɛt〕*v.* 推翻
reign〔ren〕*n.* 統治時代；朝代　　 Egypt〔'idʒəpt〕*n.* 埃及
the Great Pyramid 大金字塔
Giza〔'gizə〕*n.* 吉扎（埃及開羅近郊的城市）

46.（**C**）根據本文，杜拜塔將會有多高？
　　(A) 至少比多倫多的西恩塔高四十三層樓。
　　(B) 比多倫多的西恩塔高一百八十英呎。
　　(C) <u>至少比台北一〇一大樓高二十二層樓。</u>
　　(D) 比台北一〇一大樓高一百六十英呎。

47.（**D**）建造杜拜塔的主要目的是＿＿＿＿＿＿。
　　(A) 爲了讓不怕高的人在頂樓工作
　　(B) 爲了讓建設公司維持它的生意
　　(C) 爲了讓阿拉伯世界紀念它的工業化
　　(D) <u>爲了讓杜拜這個城市聞名世界</u>

maintain〔men'ten〕*v.* 維持
industrialization〔ɪn,dʌstrɪəlaɪ'zeʃən〕*n.* 工業化
gain〔gen〕*v.* 獲得　　 fame〔fem〕*n.* 名聲

48. (**B**) 下列關於杜拜塔的敘述，何者爲眞？

(A) 它將包含一百六十英呎的巨大天線。

(B) 它可能會被蓋成太空梭的形狀。

(C) 它用銀來作爲主要的建材。

(D) 它已經被建到地面上一百八十英呎高了。

in the shape of 以⋯的形狀　　silver〔'sɪlvɚ〕*n.* 銀

material〔məˈtɪrɪəl〕*n.* 材料

49. (**C**) 最後一段的 **upset** 意思是＿＿＿＿＿。

(A) 曲解一個重要的事實。　(B) 不小心打翻某樣東西。

(C) 打敗強大的競爭著者。　(D) 使某人感到悲傷、擔心和生氣。

distort〔dɪsˈtɔrt〕*v.* 曲解；扭曲　　*knock over* 打翻

defeat〔dɪˈfit〕*v.* 打敗

第 50 至 53 題爲題組

　　Dr. Thompson was pleased. Just three months after moving to the small Midwestern town, he had been invited to address an evening meeting of the Chamber of Commerce. Here was the perfect opportunity to show his knowledge of modern medicine and to get his practice off to a flourishing start. With this in mind, the doctor prepared carefully.

　　湯普森醫生很高興。就在他搬到中西部小鎮三個月後，他就被邀請，在商會的夜間會議上發表演講。這是個絕佳的機會，能展現他對現代醫學的知識，使他執業當醫生，有一個很好的開始。這位醫生心裡一邊這樣想，一邊小心地準備著。

　　　　Dr.〔'dɑktɚ〕*n.* 醫生；博士（= *Doctor*）

　　　　pleased〔plizd〕*adj.* 高興的　　move〔muv〕*v.* 搬家

　　　　Midwestern〔mɪdˈwɛstɚn〕*adj.* 美國中西部的

　　　　address〔əˈdrɛs〕*v.* 向⋯講話　　meeting〔'mitɪŋ〕*n.* 會議

　　　　chamber〔'tʃembɚ〕*n.* 會館；會議廳

　　　　commerce〔'kɑmɚs〕*n.* 商業　　*the chamber of commerce* 商會

　　　　practice〔'præktɪs〕*n.*（醫生、律師等的）開業；業務

　　　　flourishing〔'flɝɪʃɪŋ〕*adj.* 興盛的；成功的

　　　　get off 使出發；起跑　　start〔stɑrt〕*n.* 開始

On the night of his speech, Dr. Thompson was delighted to see that the meeting hall was full. After being introduced, he strode confidently to the lectern and announced his topic: "Recent Advances in Medicine." He began with a detailed discussion of Creutzfeldt-Jakob disease, a rare brain disorder that had recently been covered in the *New England Journal of Medicine*. Next he outlined the progress that had been made in studying immune system disorders.

在湯普森博士演講當晚，他看到會議廳客滿，覺得很高興。在被介紹完之後，他充滿信心地大步走上講台，宣佈他的主題：「醫學最近的發展」。他從詳細地討論庫賈氏症開始，那是一種罕見的腦部疾病，最近在「新英格蘭醫學期刊」中有報導。接著他略述在研究免疫系統疾病方面的進展。

speech〔spitʃ〕*n.* 演講　delighted〔dɪˋlaɪtɪd〕*adj.* 高興的
hall〔hɔl〕*n.* 大廳　　full〔fʊl〕*adj.* 客滿的
introduce〔͵ɪntrəˋdjus〕*v.* 介紹　stride〔straɪd〕*v.* 跨大步走
confidently〔ˋkɑnfədəntlɪ〕*adj.* 充滿自信地
lectern〔ˋlɛktən〕*n.* 演講台　announce〔əˋnaʊns〕*v.* 宣佈
topic〔ˋtɑpɪk〕*n.* 主題　recent〔ˋrisn̩t〕*adj.* 最近的
advance〔ədˋvæns〕*n.* 進展；進步　detailed〔ˋditeld〕*adj.* 詳細的
Creutzfeldt-Jakob disease 克－雅二氏病；庫賈氏症（一種罕見、
　　致命的海綿狀病毒性腦部疾病）
rare〔rɛr〕*adj.* 罕見的　　brain〔bren〕*n.* 腦
disorder〔dɪsˋɔrdə〕*n.* 疾病　recently〔ˋrisn̩tlɪ〕*adv.* 最近
cover〔ˋkʌvə〕*v.* 報導　　***New England*** 新英格蘭（美國東北部六州）
journal〔ˋdʒɝn̩l〕*n.* 期刊　outline〔ˋaʊt͵laɪn〕*v.* 概述…的要點
progress〔ˋprɑgrɛs〕*n.* 進展　study〔ˋstʌdɪ〕*v.* 研究
immune〔ɪˋmjun〕*adj.* 免疫的

Just about this time, halfway through his speech, Dr. Thompson began to notice a certain restlessness in his audience. People were murmuring and shuffling their feet. Someone in the fourth row seemed to be glancing at a newspaper. Nevertheless, Dr. Thompson plowed on. He had saved the best for last. He quoted extensively from an article in *the Lancet* about genetic research, feeling sure his audience would be impressed by his familiarity with this prestigious British medical journal.

　　差不多在湯普森演講到一半時，他開始注意到，聽眾有點浮躁。有人在低聲說話，而且腳一直動來動去。坐在第四排的某個人，好像在看報紙。儘管如此，湯普森博士還是繼續賣力地演講。他把最好的留到最後。他大量引用 the Lancet 中，關於基因研究的文章，他有把握，他對這本英國權威醫學期刊如此熟悉，一定會使聽眾印象深刻。

just about 差不多　　halfway〔'hæf'we〕*adv.* 在中途
halfway through his speech 在他演講到一半時
notice〔'notɪs〕*v.* 注意到　　*a certain* 某種程度的；若干的
restlessness〔'rɛstlɪsnɪs〕*n.* 不安；浮躁
audience〔'ɔdɪəns〕*n.* 聽眾　　murmur〔'mɜmɚ〕*v.* 小聲說話
shuffle〔'ʃʌfl̩〕*v.* 把⋯四處移動　　row〔ro〕*n.* 排
seem〔sim〕*v.* 似乎　　glance〔glæns〕*v.* 看一眼；看一下
nevertheless〔ˌnɛvɚðə'lɛs〕*adv.* 儘管如此；然而
plow〔plaʊ〕*v.* 奮力從事　　*plow on* 繼續努力（講）下去
save〔sev〕*v.* 保存；保留　　quote〔kwot〕*v.* 引用
extensively〔ɪk'stɛnsɪvlɪ〕*adv.* 廣泛地；大規模地
article〔'ɑrtɪkl̩〕*n.* 文章
lancet〔'lænsɪt〕*n.*【外科】柳葉刀；雙刃小刀
genetic〔dʒə'nɛtɪk〕*adj.* 遺傳學的；基因的
research〔'risɜtʃ〕*n.* 研究　　impress〔ɪm'prɛs〕*v.* 使印象深刻
familiarity〔fəˌmɪlɪ'ærətɪ〕*n.* 熟悉
prestigious〔prɛs'tɪdʒɪəs〕*adj.* 有威信的；有聲望的
British〔'brɪtɪʃ〕*adj.* 英國的

　　Then the speech was over. Dr. Thompson had expected to be surrounded by enthusiastic people, congratulating him and asking questions. Instead he found himself standing alone. Finally the president of the Chamber of Commerce came up to him. "Something tells me," said Dr. Thompson, "that my speech was not very successful. I can't understand it. I worked so hard to make it interesting." "Oh, it was a fine speech," replied the president. "But maybe it would have gone over better with a different audience. Creutzfeldt-Jakob disease is not exactly a factor in these people's everyday experience. You know, here we are in January. If you'd talked about ways to avoid getting the flu, you'd have **had them on the edge of their seats!**"

　　然後，演講就結束了。湯普森醫生原本預期，大家會熱情地包圍他，向他祝賀，並且問他問題。相反地，他發現自己一個人站在那裡。最後，商會的主席走到他身邊。「有跡象顯示，」湯普森醫生說，「我的演講並不是很成功。我真是不明白。我很努力要讓演講有趣。」「喔，你講得不錯，」那位主席回答。「但是如果換不同的觀眾，應該會更受歡迎。這些人在日常生活中，不一定會體驗到庫賈氏症。你知道的，我們這裡現在是一月。如果你談論的是避免感染流行性感冒的方法，你早就讓他們覺得很興奮了！」

expect〔ɪk'spɛkt〕*v.* 預期；預料
surround〔sə'raʊnd〕*v.* 包圍
enthusiastic〔ɪn,θjuzɪ'æstɪk〕*adj.* 熱烈的；狂熱的
congratulate〔kən'grætʃə,let〕*v.* 恭喜；祝賀
instead〔ɪn'stɛd〕*adv.* 相反地；取而代之
alone〔ə'lon〕*adv.* 單獨地；獨自
president〔'prɛzədənt〕*n.* 主席
come up to 來到…身邊　　***go over*** 受（觀眾）歡迎
not exactly 不一定；未必　　factor〔'fæktɚ〕*n.* 因素；要素
flu〔flu〕*n.* 流行性感冒　　edge〔ɛdʒ〕*n.* 邊緣
on the edge of *one's seat* 對某事極為有興趣

50. (**D**) 本文的主旨為何？

(A) 好的演說者，不論聽眾是誰，都應該要充分準備。
(B) 好的演說者，應該要熱烈地向聽眾展示他的學問。
(C) 演說者愈想取悅觀眾，他就愈有可能成功。
(D) <u>成功演說的關鍵，就是要讓演說內容很有意義，而且與聽眾有</u>
　　<u>關聯。</u>

main〔men〕*adj.* 主要的　　message〔'mɛsɪdʒ〕*n.* 訊息；主旨
speaker〔'spikɚ〕*n.* 演說者　　***regardless of*** 不分；不管；不論
display〔dɪ'sple〕*v.* 展示　　learning〔'lɝnɪŋ〕*n.* 學問；知識
please〔pliz〕*v.* 取悅　　likely〔'laɪklɪ〕*adj.* 可能的
key〔ki〕*n.* 關鍵　　meaningful〔'minɪŋfḷ〕*adj.* 有意義的
relevant〔'rɛləvənt〕*adj.* 有關聯的

51. (**A**) 聽衆對於湯普森醫生的演講反應如何？

(A) 他們覺得無聊，因爲那些醫學上的主題，不是他們日常關心的事。

(B) 他們聽不懂他說的，所以只好彼此討論。

(C) 他十分熟悉醫學方面高深的研究，讓他們印象深刻。

(D) 他們恭喜他演講十分成功，並問他問題。

reaction〔rɪˋækʃən〕 *n.* 反應
daily〔ˋdelɪ〕 *adj.* 每天的；日常的
concern〔kənˋsɝn〕 *n.* 關心的事
advanced〔ədˋvænst〕 *adj.* 高深的；先進的

52. (**B**) 那位醫生的演講，**並未**提到什麼主題？

(A) 基因研究。 (B) 流行性感冒。

(C) 免疫系統的疾病。 (D) 庫賈氏症。

flu〔flu〕 *n.* 流行性感冒（ = *influenza*）

53. (**C**) 本文的最後一句中的 had them on the edge of their seats 是什麼意思？

(A) 要他們站起來。 (B) 使他們很驚訝。

(C) 吸引他們全部的注意力。 (D) 引起他們的懷疑。

take** sb. **by surprise 使某人很驚訝
catch〔kætʃ〕 *v.* 吸引（注意力）
arouse〔əˋrauz〕 *v.* 喚起 suspicion〔səˋspɪʃən〕 *n.* 懷疑

第 54 至 56 題爲題組

When a company ventures into new markets, it will need to face various problems. These problems can be broadly classified into several categories, including (1) cultural factors, (2) economic issues, (3) geographical factors, (4) political/legal issues, (5) religious factors, and (6) technological issues. Find an appropriate category for the problems discussed in each of the following paragraphs.

　　當一家公司要開發新市場的時候，需要面臨各種不同的問題。這些問題大體上可以區分成好幾種類別，包括 (1) 文化因素、(2) 經濟問題、(3) 地理因素、(4) 政治或法律問題、(5) 宗教因素，以及 (6) 技術問題。為下列每一段所探討的問題，找出適當的類別。

> venture〔'vɛntʃɚ〕v.（商業上）冒險投資；開發
> face〔fes〕v. 面臨（問題或困難）（= be faced with）
> various〔'vɛrɪəs〕adj. 各種不同的
> broadly〔'brɔdlɪ〕adv. 概括地；大體上
> classify〔'klæsə,faɪ〕v. 將…分類
> category〔'kætə,gorɪ〕n. 種類
> cultural〔'kʌltʃərəl〕adj. 文化的　　　factor〔'fæktɚ〕n. 因素
> economic〔,ikə'nɑmɪk〕adj. 經濟的　　　issue〔'ɪʃju〕n. 爭議；問題
> geographical〔,dʒiə'græfɪkḷ〕adj. 地理的
> political〔pə'lɪtɪkḷ〕adj. 政治的　　　legal〔'ligḷ〕adj. 有關法律的
> religious〔rɪ'lɪdʒəs〕adj. 宗教的
> technological〔,tɛknə'lɑdʒɪkḷ〕adj. 技術的；科技的
> appropriate〔ə'proprɪɪt〕adj. 合適的；相稱的

A company will face problems of this kind, as it is an alien when compared to the business climate of the country. Coca-Cola, for instance, was faced with such a problem in India, when it was given a choice of either to reveal its secret formula or leave the country. Coke chose to leave. But when it was welcomed back after several years, it was subjected to harassment and constant interference from the political activists.

　　　　公司一定會面臨這種問題，因為身處他國商業環境中，和其他公司比起來，就好像是個外國人。舉可口可樂公司為例，它們在印度就碰到這樣的問題，當時它們被迫做出選擇，要不就透露機密配方，不然就不要進入該國市場。可口可樂公司選擇離開。但是過了幾年後，印度又歡迎可口可樂公司重回該國市場，可是它們卻遭受到政治激進份子的騷擾和持續干預。

alien〔'eliən〕*n.* 外國人　　compare〔kəm'pɛr〕*v.* 比較＜ *to* ＞
Coca-Cola 可口可樂公司（ ＝ *Coke* ＝ *the Coca-Cola Company* ）
（ 在此以商標名代表公司名 ）
India〔'ɪndɪə〕*n.* 印度　　***either*** A ***or*** B 不是 A，就是 B
reveal〔rɪ'vil〕*v.* 揭露　　secret〔'sikrɪt〕*adj.* 機密的
formula〔'fɔrmjələ〕*n.* 配方
subject〔səb'dʒɛkt〕*n.* 使蒙受；使遭遇（ 常用被動語態 ）＜ *to* ＞
harassment〔'hærəsmənt〕*n.* 侵擾；騷擾
constant〔'kɑnstənt〕*adj.* 接連不斷的
interference〔,ɪntɚ'fɪrəns〕*n.* 干涉；干預
activist〔'æktəvɪst〕*n.* 激進分子

54. (**D**) 最適合上述段落的類別是 ＿＿＿＿＿＿。
　　(A) 宗教因素　　　　　　　(B) 經濟問題
　　(C) 地理因素　　　　　　　(D) <u>政治或法律問題</u>

Problems of this kind can make an impact on the properties of a product. This impact forces a company to adapt its products in order to meet the needs of the local market. To solve the problems, the level of economic development in a market should be assessed, for example, by the level of revenue, buying power of local consumers, and by the state of infrastructure in the foreign market. These indicators can provide vital information to the company regarding its marketing strategy.

這一類的問題可能會對產品性質造成影響。這種影響會迫使公司改造其產品，以符合當地市場的需求。為了解決這類問題，應該要評估該市場的經濟發展程度，例如了解該地的所得水準、當地消費者的購買力，以及了解外國市場的基礎建設情況。這些指標可以提供給企業在行銷策略方面的重要資訊。

impact〔'ɪmpækt〕*n.* 影響＜*on*＞

property〔'prɑpətɪ〕*n.* 特性；性質　　force〔fors〕*v.* 強迫；迫使

adapt〔ə'dæpt〕*v.* 改造（使適合）

in order to V. 爲了～（表目的）

meet〔mit〕*v.* 滿足；符合（要求）　　local〔'lokl̩〕*adj.* 當地的

level〔'lɛvl̩〕*n.* 水準；程度　　assess〔ə'sɛs〕*v.* 評估

revenue〔'rɛvə,nju〕*n.* 所得總額　　***buying power*** 購買力

consumer〔kən'sjumɚ〕*n.* 消費者　　state〔stet〕*n.* 情況

infrastructure〔'ɪnfrə,strʌktʃɚ〕*n.*（國家、社會等的經濟存續

　　所必需的）基礎建設（例如道路、交通設備等）

indicator〔'ɪndə,ketɚ〕*n.* 指標　　vital〔'vaɪtl̩〕*adj.* 極其重要的

regarding〔rɪ'gɑrdɪŋ〕*prep.* 關於

marketing〔'mɑrkɪtɪŋ〕*n.* 行銷　　strategy〔'strætədʒɪ〕*n.* 策略

55.（**B**）最適合上述段落的類別是＿＿＿＿＿＿。

　　(A) 文化因素　　　　　　　　(B) 經濟問題

　　(C) 地理因素　　　　　　　　(D) 技術問題

These problems are perhaps the biggest issue a researcher can
come across while studying new markets. This is because
markets that can be classified as similar on various grounds tend
to be dissimilar when it comes to this particular aspect. There
are differences even within the same country. Accordingly, travel
advertising in Canada is divided between the English audience
and the French audience. While pictures of travel advertisements
show a wife alone for the English audience, a man and wife are
shown for the French audience. This is done because the French
are more bound by family ties.

　　這些問題或許是研究人員在研究新市場時，可能會遇到的最大問題。因爲依據各種不同因素而被分到同一類的市場，往往在談到此一特殊層面時，就會產生差異。甚至在同一個國家內也會有差異存在。因此，加拿大的旅遊廣告將消費者區分爲英語區和法語區的觀眾。英語區觀眾看到的旅遊廣告圖片是婦女單獨一個人，但是給法語區觀眾看的是以夫妻檔爲主的廣告圖片。會這樣做是因爲法語區居民比較重視家庭關係。

researcher〔rɪˈsɝtʃɚ〕*n.* 研究員；調查者　　***come across*** 遇到
study〔ˈstʌdɪ〕*v.* 研究；調查　　ground〔graʊnd〕*n.* 根據；理由
on ~ ground 以～的根據　　***tend to V.*** 傾向～
dissimilar〔dɪˈsɪmələ〕*adj.* 不同的　　***when it comes to*** 說到；提到
particular〔pəˈtɪkjələ〕*adj.* 特別的　　aspect〔ˈæspɛkt〕*n.* 方面
accordingly〔əˈkɔrdɪŋlɪ〕*adv.* 因此
advertising〔ˈædvɚˌtaɪzɪŋ〕*n.* 廣告（總稱）
divide〔dəˈvaɪd〕*v.*（在～之間）分配 *< between >*
bind〔baɪnd〕*v.* 束縛；約束（過去式及過去分詞爲：bound〔baʊnd〕）
ties〔taɪz〕*n. pl.* 關係

56. (**A**) 最適合上述段落的類別是 _____ 。
(A) 文化因素　　　　　　(B) 經濟問題
(C) 地理因素　　　　　　(D) 政治或法律問題

第貳部分：非選擇題

一、英文翻譯：

1. 身爲地球村的成員，我們不應把自己侷限在這個小島上。

As $\left\{ \begin{array}{c} \text{a member} \\ \text{members} \end{array} \right\}$ of the global village, we should not $\left\{ \begin{array}{c} \text{confine} \\ \text{limit} \end{array} \right\}$

ourselves to $\left\{ \begin{array}{c} \text{this} \\ \text{our} \\ \text{the} \end{array} \right\}$ $\left\{ \begin{array}{c} \text{little} \\ \text{small} \end{array} \right\}$ island.

2. 我們不但應該參與國際性的活動，並且應該展現我們自己的文化特色。

We not only should $\begin{cases} \text{join in} \\ \text{participate in} \\ \text{take part in} \end{cases}$ international activities but

also should $\begin{cases} \text{represent} \\ \text{show} \\ \text{present} \\ \text{demonstrate} \\ \text{exhibit} \\ \text{display} \end{cases}$ our own cultural $\begin{cases} \text{characteristics.} \\ \text{features.} \end{cases}$

* 也可以寫成：should not only...but also represent....

二、英文作文：（作文範例）

An Activity for Graduates

　　Now that the Joint College Entrance Exam is over, we are about to begin a brand-new and exciting stage in our lives. However, it is important to remember the past and keep in touch with those who have made our high school years special. Therefore, we have organized a picnic for all the graduates. In addition to a barbecue, there will be games and a singing contest. The event will take place on Sunday, July 17, at Yangmingshan Park. Buses will leave the school at 11:00 am and return at 5:00 pm.

　　I hope that all of our graduates will attend, for this may be our last chance to spend some time together. During the activity we may share our memories of high school and our plans for the future. Most importantly, it is a chance for us to end our high school careers on a positive note by relaxing and having fun after enduring the stress of the JCEE.

94 年指定科目考試英文科試題勘誤表

※ 這次指考題目可看出命題教授的用心，題目出得不錯，但是，錯誤的地方，我們一定要告訴同學，以免學錯。

題　　號	修　　正　　意　　見
文意選填 第 31 至 40 題 第一段第 5 行	*Penghu islands* → *the Penghu islands* * 群島名稱應加定冠詞。（詳見「文法寶典」p.218）
第二段第 10 行	*the primitive* → *its primitive* 或 *a primitive* * 不定冠詞 a 和 an，常放在形容詞前。（詳見「文法寶典」p.215）
篇章結構 第 41 至 45 題 倒數第 3 行	*Up to date* → *To date* 或 *Up to now* 或 *So far* 表「到目前為止」。 * up to date 的意思「新式的；現代化的」，是形容詞片語。
閱讀測驗 第 46 至 49 題 第 4 行	*higher* → *taller* * 人和大樓的「高」，用 tall。
48 題　選項(A)	*a 160-feet huge antenna* → *a huge, 160-foot antenna* * 名詞做形容詞表單位，用單數。（詳見「文法寶典」p.87）
51 題　選項(A)	*their daily concern* → *one of their daily concerns* * 根據句意，每天關心的事情很多，應該是其中之一。
選項(B)	*discuss* → *talk* * discuss 是及物動詞。
52 題　選項(C)	*Immune system disorder* → *Immune system disorders* * disorder（疾病）是可數名詞，文章中第二段也出現過 disorders。
第 54 至 56 題 第一個框框 第 1-2 行	*... as it is an alien when compared to the business climate of the country.* → *... when it is an alien in the business environment of the country.* 或 *... as it is an alien when compared to other companies in the business environment of the country.* * when compared to 後須接比較對象，故應加入 other companies，如果不用 other companies，應直接把 when compared to 去掉。指一個國家的經濟「環境」，不用 business climate，而用 business environment。
第 4 行	*to reveal* → *revealing* *leave* → *leaving* * 因為做介系詞 of 的受詞。
第 6-7 行	*the political activists* → *political activists* * 因為為不指定，不須加定冠詞。
第二個框框 第 5 行	*...revenue, buying power...* → *...revenue, by the buying power* ... * 因為 and 連接 by the level ...，by the buying power ... 和 by the state of ...。 或 *... by the state of ...* → *... state of ...* * 把 by the state of 中的 by the 去掉，變成 and 連接三個名詞。

九十四學年度指定科目考試（英文）

大考中心公佈答案

題號	答案	題號	答案	題號	答案
1	C	21	A	41	C
2	A	22	C	42	B
3	D	23	B	43	E
4	C	24	D	44	A
5	D	25	A	45	D
6	C	26	B	46	C
7	B	27	D	47	D
8	D	28	C	48	B
9	C	29	A	49	C
10	B	30	C	50	D
11	B	31	F	51	A
12	A	32	A	52	B
13	C	33	J	53	C
14	B	34	I	54	D
15	D	35	C	55	B
16	B	36	D	56	A
17	C	37	H		
18	D	38	G		
19	B	39	E		
20	A	40	B		

九十四學年度指定科目考試

各科成績標準一覽表

科　目	頂　標	前　標	均　標	後　標	底　標
國　文	60	53	44	34	27
英　文	69	55	34	16	8
數學甲	59	47	32	19	11
數學乙	61	46	25	10	4
化　學	76	59	34	15	8
物　理	57	41	23	12	6
生　物	71	59	44	31	22
歷　史	56	48	35	22	13
地　理	55	47	36	25	18

※ 以上五項標準係依各該科全體到考考生成績計算，且均取整數（小數只捨不入），各標準計算方式如下：

頂標：成績位於第 88 百分位數之考生成績。

前標：成績位於第 75 百分位數之考生成績。

均標：成績位於第 50 百分位數之考生成績。

後標：成績位於第 25 百分位數之考生成績。

底標：成績位於第 12 百分位數之考生成績。

心得筆記欄

九十三年大學入學指定科目考試試題
英文考科

第壹部份：單一選擇題

一、詞彙與慣用語（15％）

說明：　第 1 至 15 題，每題選出最適當的一個選項，標示在答案卡之「選擇題答案區」。每題答對得 1 分，答錯倒扣 1/3 分，倒扣到本大題之實得分數為零為止。未答者，不給分亦不扣分。

1. The temple stages performances of Taiwanese opera every year as an expression of _____ to the Goddess of Mercy.
   (A) caution　　(B) gratitude　　(C) approval　　(D) dignity

2. All the students are required to attend the two-day _____ program so that they can have a complete understanding of the university they are admitted to.
   (A) orientation　　　　　　(B) accomplishment
   (C) enthusiasm　　　　　　(D) independence

3. The _____ of his new album has brought the pop singer a huge fortune as well as worldwide fame.
   (A) salary　　(B) release　　(C) bargain　　(D) harvest

4. One important purpose of the course is for the students to learn to make sound judgments so that they can _____ between fact and opinion without difficulty.
   (A) inform　　(B) undertake　　(C) manipulate　　(D) differentiate

5. In Taiwan, using electronic devices is prohibited on domestic flights because it _____ with the communication between the pilots and the control tower.
   (A) occupies　　(B) activates　　(C) interferes　　(D) eliminates

6. The famous actress decided to sue the magazine for purposely
   _____ what she actually said and did at the party.
   (A) assigning   (B) contributing   (C) foreseeing   (D) distorting

7. The little boy is very _____ : he is interested in a lot of different
   things and always wants to find out more about them.
   (A) accurate   (B) inquisitive   (C) manageable   (D) contemporary

8. The tourists enjoyed wholeheartedly the _____ scenery along the
   coast highway between Hualien and Ilan.
   (A) airtight   (B) breathtaking   (C) sentimental   (D) eccentric

9. The major theme in the _____ issue of the best-selling monthly
   magazine will be "Love and Peace."
   (A) forthcoming   (B) expensive
   (C) brilliant   (D) ambitious

10. Our English teacher always emphasizes the importance of learning
    new words in context rather than learning each of them _____.
    (A) individually   (B) exclusively
    (C) approximately   (D) supposedly

11. The old woman at the street corner must be lost. She is looking around
    _____ for someone to help her.
    (A) socially   (B) accidentally   (C) tremendously   (D) desperately

12. John is an experienced salesperson. Just observe closely how he
    interacts with customers and do _____. Then you will become
    an expert yourself.
    (A) edgewise   (B) likewise   (C) otherwise   (D) clockwise

13. A variety of preventive measures are now _____ in order to
    minimize the potential damage caused by the deadly disease.
    (A) by birth   (B) at will   (C) in place   (D) on call

14. With over fifty teams competing in the tournament, all the games will be played ＿＿＿＿＿＿＿.
    (A) eye to eye　(B) head to toe　(C) hand to mouth　(D) back to back

15. Did I say "a lot of dime"? Oh, I'm really sorry. I meant to say "a lot of time." It was a ＿＿＿＿＿＿＿.
    (A) slip of the tongue　　　　(B) thorn in my side
    (C) penny for your thoughts　　(D) leap in the dark

二、綜合測驗（15％）

說明：　第 16 至 30 題，每題一個空格。請依文意選出最適當的一個選項，標示在答案卡之「選擇題答案區」。每題答對得 1 分，答錯倒扣 1/3 分，倒扣到本大題之實得分數為零為止。未答者，不給分亦不扣分。

第 16 至 20 題為題組

　　If old newspapers are stacking up in your house, there are options other than tossing them out or selling them to a recycler. Some environmental scientists suggest turning newspapers ＿＿16＿＿ charcoal. This can be done by soaking sheets of newspaper in water for two hours and then ＿＿17＿＿ them into small pieces. These pieces are then compressed into balls. After the water is ＿＿18＿＿, the ball-shaped pieces are put under the sun to dry before they can be used as a firewood or charcoal substitute. ＿＿19＿＿ suggestion made by the experts is to dip newspaper sheets in vinegar and water, and use them to clean windows, mirrors, and tiles. Old papers can ＿＿20＿＿ be used to line rubbish bins and as packing material when mailing breakable goods.

16. (A) into　　　　(B) for　　　(C) off　　　　(D) upon
17. (A) tear　　　　(B) tore　　　(C) tearing　　(D) torn
18. (A) boiled down　(B) fired up　(C) kicked off　(D) squeezed out
19. (A) This　　　　(B) Another　(C) That　　　(D) Other
20. (A) soon　　　　(B) also　　　(C) thus　　　(D) rather

第 21 至 25 題為題組

Children's encounters with poetry should include three types of response —— enjoyment, exploration, and deepening understanding. These do not occur always as ___21___ steps but may happen simultaneously. Certainly, children must start with enjoyment ___22___ their interest in poetry dies. But if from the beginning they find delight in the poems they hear or read, they are ready and eager to ___23___ further —— more books and more poems of different sorts. Even the youngest children can learn to see implications ___24___ the obvious. To read for hidden meanings is to identify with the poet, to ask the poet's questions. This is reading for deeper understanding, ___25___ a thoughtful look at what lies beneath the surface. Enjoyment, exploration, and deeper understanding must all be part of children's experience with poetry if we are to help them to love it.

21. (A) childish　　(B) artistic　　(C) separate　　(D) innocent
22. (A) or　　　　　(B) and　　　　(C) so　　　　　(D) then
23. (A) escape　　　(B) explore　　(C) accustom　　(D) appear
24. (A) near　　　　(B) among　　　(C) beyond　　　(D) without
25. (A) take　　　　(B) takes　　　(C) to take　　　(D) taking

第 26 至 30 題為題組

Avian influenza, or "bird flu," is a contagious disease caused by viruses that normally infect only birds and, less commonly, pigs. ___26___ all bird species are thought to be susceptible to infection, domestic poultry flocks are especially vulnerable to infections that can rapidly reach epidemic proportions. Outbreaks of avian influenza ___27___ be devastating for the poultry industry and for farmers. For example, an outbreak of avian influenza in the USA in 1983–1984 resulted in the destruction of more than 17 million birds ___28___ nearly US$ 65 million. Economic consequences are often most serious in developing countries ___29___ poultry raising is an important source of income, and of food, for impoverished rural farmers and their families. When outbreaks become widespread within a country, control can be extremely difficult. ___30___, government authorities usually undertake aggressive emergency control measures as soon as an outbreak is detected.

26. (A) Not　　(B) While　　(C) Since　　(D) Unless
27. (A) can　　(B) shall　　(C) dare　　(D) need
28. (A) with a view to　　　　(B) in regard to
　　(C) at a cost of　　　　(D) on account of
29. (A) that　　(B) until　　(C) although　　(D) where
30. (A) Instead　　(B) Therefore　　(C) By no means　　(D) On the contrary

三、文意選填（10％）

說明：　第 31 至 40 題，每題一個空格。請依文意在文章後所提供的 (A) 到 (J)
　　　　選項中分別選出最適當者，並將其字母代號標示在答案卡之「選擇題答
　　　　案區」。每題答對得 1 分，答錯倒扣 1/9 分，倒扣到本大題之實得分數
　　　　爲零爲止。未答者，不給分亦不扣分。

第 31 至 40 題爲題組

　　Junior Achievement was started in Springfield, Massachusetts, in 1919 by Horace A. Moses. Mr. Moses, who had been a poor farm boy, had worked his way up to become one of the ___31___ industrialists in the United States. He was concerned that so many of the young people ___32___ for positions with his firm knew absolutely nothing about the way a corporation is run. As a solution to this problem, he ___33___ Junior Achievement, Inc.

　　In essence, Junior Achievement is an organization that gives high-school boys and girls a chance to become part of the operation of a ___34___ corporation while still in school. Every September, students are ___35___ the opportunity to join Junior Achievement through the co-operation of local school systems. Some students make products that range in size from earrings to quite ___36___ furniture for the home. Others produce weekly radio and television shows or operate banks, accounting ___37___, and advertising agencies.

　　Junior Achievement ___38___ range in size from those in the big cities, like New York and Los Angeles, to those in small towns with a ___39___ of a few thousand. Each program ___40___ with the size of the area and the amount of industrial and business activity in the city.

(A) miniature　　(B) elaborate　　(C) applying　　(D) programs
(E) founded　　　(F) firms　　　　(G) leading　　　(H) population
(I) varies　　　　(J) offered

四、篇章結構（10 ％）

說明：　第 41 至 45 題，每題一個空格。請依文意在文章後所提供的 (A) 到 (E) 選項中分別選出最適當者，填入空格中，使篇章結構清晰有條理，並將其英文字母代號標示在答案卡之「選擇題答案區」。每題答對得 2 分，答錯倒扣 1/2 分，倒扣到本大題之實得分數為零為止。未答者，不給分亦不扣分。

第 41 至 45 題為題組

　　Starting around 4,000 B.C., traditional Chinese brush painting has developed continuously over a period of more than six thousand years. ___41___

During the 1st century A.D., the art of painting religious murals gradually gained in prominence, with the introduction of Buddhism to China and the consequent building of temples. ___42___ For example, paintings of historical characters and stories of everyday life became extremely popular. Besides historical figures, landscape painting was also common in Chinese brush painting. By the 4th century, this particular type of painting had already established itself as an independent form of expression. ___43___ The blue-and-green landscape used bright blue, green and red pigments derived from minerals to create a richly decorative style; the ink-and-wash landscape relied on vivid brushwork and various intensity of ink to express the artist's conception of nature as well as his own emotions. ___44___ A great many artists in the 9th century painted in this genre and their subject matters included a rich variety of flowers, fruits, birds, insects, and fish.

Since the turn of the 20th century, painters have often mixed several colors on one brush or mixed their colors with black inks. ___45___ Such techniques have been widely adopted and further developed in the contemporary period.

(A) Another genre commonly found in Chinese brush painting was flower-and-bird painting.

(B) However, the subject matters later expanded beyond religious themes.

(C) As a result, they have obtained more natural and richly varied colors.

(D) Its growth has inevitably reflected the changes of time.

(E) It then gradually developed into two separate styles.

五、閱讀測驗（22％）

說明：　第 46 至 56 題，每題請分別根據各篇文章的文意選出最適當的一個選
項，標示在答案卡之「選擇題答案區」。每題答對得 2 分，答錯倒扣
2/3 分，倒扣到本大題之實得分數為零為止。未答者，不給分亦不扣分。

第 46 至 48 題為題組

These days, even a walk in the woods can be transformed into an "extreme" sport. Take "geocaching," for example. Hikers looking for something a little different on their treks created a global hunting game, hiding "caches"—— packs filled with goodies like CDs, photographs, and journals —— in obscure places throughout the world. They then post the coordinates at www.geocaching.com, where other hikers can use **them**, along with a global positioning system (GPS), to join the worldwide goose chase. Geocaching works on an honor system: When a geocacher takes something, he leaves a cache of his own behind. Vacationers can get in on this trend at resorts like Utah's Red Mountain Spa, where they can learn to use GPS and coordinates to find caches filled with spa products.

46. This passage was written mainly to inform its readers about
_____.
　(A) hunting practices
　(B) Utah's Red Mountain Spa
　(C) a global positioning system
　(D) a new form of outdoor activity

47. The pronoun **them** in line 7 refers to _____.
　(A) coordinates　　　　　(B) goodies
　(C) caches　　　　　　　(D) treks

48. It can be inferred from the passage that _____.
   (A) geocachers like to chase geese all over the world
   (B) one can learn to be a geocacher exclusively in Utah State
   (C) geocaching requires that items be exchanged among its participants
   (D) caches are spa products hidden in remote places throughout the world

第 49 至 52 題為題組

Even though she's just 5 years old, Cindy Smart speaks five languages. She's a good reader. She can tell time and do simple math, including multiplication and division. She's not a prodigy. She's just good programming. Cindy looks like an average doll, with long, blond hair, baby-blue eyes, and a button nose. But loaded with some devices, Cindy is the first doll that can see, think, and do as she's told.

The eagle-eyed Cindy follows in the path of other breakthrough toys like Sony's barking Robot Aibo, which was the first to popularize voice command in the late 1990s. Cindy takes Aibo's innovations one step beyond: she not only follows instructions but also recognizes shapes, colors, and words — and remembers. The effect is a doll that appears to be learning.

The toy company which produced Cindy Smart spent a decade trying to see how much human nature it could breathe into an inanimate object. Its engineers began researching basic and affordable artificial intelligence, creating minibots that sense light, sounds, and pressure. However, without the sense of sight, their toys seemed to be lacking one of the keenest abilities that life forms use to react to their environment.

So how do the engineers make a doll actually see? In Cindy's case, it's a multistep process. When presented a text like "I love you" and asked "Can you read this?" Cindy identifies **it** as one of 70 preprogrammed commands. Then the inbuilt digital camera scans a 15-degree radius in search of number-or letter-shaped objects. Buried in her belly, Cindy's 16-bit microprocessor compares the text with her database of 700 words. If it's a match, "I love you," she utters.

49. This passage most likely appears in a _____.
    (A) medical report   (B) classified ad
    (C) science journal   (D) music magazine

50. According to the passage, which of the following statements is true about Robot Aibo?
    (A) It could recognize shapes and colors.
    (B) It could respond to spoken commands.
    (C) It was put on the market no later than 1990.
    (D) It was created much later than Cindy Smart.

51. The pronoun **it** in the fourth paragraph most likely refers to _____.
    (A) the process   (B) the object
    (C) the radius   (D) the request

52. According to the passage, how can Cindy "see"?
    (A) She recognizes any text as "I love you."
    (B) She is equipped with a camera to search for text.
    (C) She is instructed by an engineer standing next to her.
    (D) She makes contact with the shapes of the text with her belly.

第 53 至 56 題爲題組

In June 1943, Frank Lloyd Wright received a letter from Hilla Rebay, the art adviser to Solomon R. Guggenheim, asking the architect to design a new building to house Guggenheim's four-year-old museum of Non-Objective Painting. The project evolved into a complex struggle pitting the architect against his clients, city officials, the art world, and public opinions. Both Guggenheim and Wright would die before the building's 1995 completion. The resultant achievement, the Solomon R. Guggenheim Museum, testifies not only to Wright's architectural genius, but also to the adventurous spirit that characterized its founders.

Wright made no secret of his disenchantment with Guggenheim's choice of New York for his museum: "I can think of several more desirable places in the world to build this great museum," Wright wrote in 1949 to his partner, "but we will have to try New York." To Wright, the city was overbuilt, overpopulated, and lacked architectural merit. Still, he proceeded with his client's wishes, considering locations on 36th Street, 54th Street, and Park Avenue (all in Manhattan), as well as in the Riverdale section of the Bronx, before settling on the present site on Fifth Avenue between 88th and 89th Streets. Its nearness to Central Park was key. As close to nature as one gets in New York, the park offered relief from the noise and congestion of the city.

Wright's design put his unique stamp on Modernist Architecture's rigid geometry. The building is a symphony of triangles, ovals, arcs, circles, and squares. The delicate vision took decades to be fulfilled. Some people, especially artists, criticized Wright for creating a museum environment that might overpower the art inside. "On the contrary," he wrote, "it was to make the building and the painting an uninterrupted, beautiful symphony such as never existed in the world of art before."

In conquering the regularity of geometric design and combining it with the plasticity of nature, Wright produced a vibrant building whose architecture is as refreshing now as it was 40 years ago. The Guggenheim is arguably Wright's most eloquent presentation and certainly the most important building of his late career.

53. The Guggenheim Museum was built _____.
    (A) in memory of Solomon Guggenheim
    (B) to keep Guggenheim's art collections
    (C) for a famous symphony orchestra
    (D) at the request of New York city officials

54. According to the passage, why was Wright **NOT** enthusiastic about building the Guggenheim Museum in New York City?
    (A) There were already too many people and buildings in New York City.
    (B) There were not enough enthusiastic architects to design the museum.
    (C) There was very little support from residents in New York City.
    (D) There was strong objection from Solomon R. Guggenheim.

55. We can learn from the passage that the Guggenheim Museum is located _____.
    (A) on the outskirts of New York City
    (B) within Central Park
    (C) in the area around 88th Street
    (D) in the Riverdale section of Bronx

56. According to the passage, what makes the Guggenheim Museum important in modern architecture?
   (A) The design of the museum is more powerful than the art works housed in it.
   (B) Both the architect and the owner of the museum died before its completion.
   (C) The building is a unique combination of many different geometric figures.
   (D) It was designed as a museum but could be used as a concert hall as well.

第貳部份：非選擇題

一、英文翻譯（8％）

說明： 1. 將下列兩句中文翻譯成適當之英文，並將答案寫在「答案卷」上。
　　　　2. 未按題意翻譯者，不予計分。

(a) 科技讓我們的生活更舒適，然而它也被利用來犯罪。

(b) 根據最近的新聞報導，最常見的例子是網際網路詐財（Internet scams）。

二、英文作文（20％）

說明： 1. 依提示在「答案卷」上寫一篇英文作文。
　　　　2. 文長至少 120 個單詞。

提示： 請以 “Travel Is the Best Teacher” 為主題，寫一篇至少 120 個字的英文作文。第一段針對文章主題，說明旅行的優點，並在第二段舉自己在國內或國外的旅行經驗，以印證第一段的說明。

九十三年度指定科目考試英文科試題詳解

第壹部分：單一選擇題

一、詞彙與慣用語：

1. (**B**) The temple stages performances of Taiwanese opera every year as an expression of <u>gratitude</u> to the Goddess of Mercy.
   台灣的廟會每年上演歌仔戲，表達對觀世音的<u>感謝</u>。
   (A) caution〔ˈkɔʃən〕n. 小心；謹慎
   (B) ***gratitude***〔ˈgrætəˌtjud〕n. 感激
   (C) approval〔əˈpruvḷ〕n. 贊成　　(D) dignity〔ˈdɪgnətɪ〕n. 尊嚴
   temple〔ˈtɛmpḷ〕n. 寺廟　　　stage〔stedʒ〕v. 上演
   performance〔pɚˈfɔrməns〕n. 表演　　***Taiwanese opera*** 歌仔戲
   expression〔ɪkˈsprɛʃən〕n. 表達　　***the Goddess of Mercy*** 觀世音

2. (**A**) All the students are required to attend the two-day <u>orientation</u> program so that they can have a complete understanding of the university they are admitted to. 所有的學生都必須參加為期兩天的<u>新生訓練</u>課程，以便他們能對即將要唸的大學有充分的瞭解。
   (A) ***orientation***〔ˌorɪɛnˈteʃən〕n. 新生訓練；定位
   (B) accomplishment〔əˈkamplɪʃmənt〕n. 完成
   (C) enthusiasm〔ɪnˈθjuzɪˌæzəm〕n. 熱忱
   (D) independence〔ˌɪndɪˈpɛndəns〕n. 獨立
   require〔rɪˈkwaɪr〕v. 要求　　***be admitted to*** 准許進入

3. (**B**) The <u>release</u> of his new album has brought the pop singer a huge fortune as well as worldwide fame.
   新專輯的<u>發行</u>，為這位流行歌手帶來了大量的財富及全球的知名度。
   (A) salary〔ˈsælərɪ〕n. 薪水　　(B) ***release***〔rɪˈlis〕n. 發行
   (C) bargain〔ˈbargɪn〕v. 討價還價　n. 便宜貨
   (D) harvest〔ˈharvɪst〕n. 收穫
   album〔ˈælbəm〕n. 專輯　　huge〔hjudʒ〕adj. 巨大的
   fortune〔ˈfɔrtʃən〕n. 財富　　***as well as*** 以及
   worldwide〔ˈwɜldˈwaɪd〕adj. 全世界的　　fame〔fem〕n. 名聲

4. (**D**) One important purpose of the course is for the students to learn to make sound judgments so that they can <u>differentiate</u> between fact and opinion without difficulty.

這門課的重要目的在於使學生學習做出正確的判斷，以便能毫無困難地<u>辨別</u>事實及意見。

(A) inform 〔 ɪnˈfɔrm 〕 v. 通知；告知 < of >
(B) undertake 〔 ˌʌndəˈtek 〕 v. 承擔
(C) manipulate 〔 məˈnɪpjəˌlet 〕 v. 操縱
(D) ***differentiate*** 〔 ˌdɪfəˈrɛnʃɪˌet 〕 v. 區別；辨別

purpose 〔ˈpɝpəs 〕 n. 目的　　sound 〔 saʊnd 〕 adj. 合理的；明智的
judgment 〔ˈdʒʌdʒmənt 〕 n. 判斷　　opinion 〔 əˈpɪnjən 〕 n. 意見

5. (**C**) In Taiwan, using electronic devices is prohibited on domestic flights because it <u>interferes</u> with the communication between the pilots and the control tower.

在台灣，國內的班機禁止使用電子器材，因為電子器材會<u>干擾</u>飛行員及塔台的通訊。

(A) occupy 〔ˈɑkjəˌpaɪ 〕 v. 佔據
(B) activate 〔ˈæktəˌvet 〕 v. 使活動；啟動
(C) ***interfere*** 〔 ˌɪntəˈfɪr 〕 v. 干預；（電波等互相）干擾 < with >
(D) eliminate 〔 ɪˈlɪməˌnet 〕 v. 消除

electronic 〔 ˌɪlɛkˈtrɑnɪk 〕 adj. 電子的　　device 〔 dɪˈvaɪs 〕 n. 裝置
prohibit 〔 proˈhɪbɪt 〕 v. 禁止　　domestic 〔 dəˈmɛstɪk 〕 adj. 國內的
flight 〔 flaɪt 〕 n. 班機　　communication 〔 kəˌmjunəˈkeʃən 〕 n. 通訊
pilot 〔ˈpaɪlət 〕 n. 飛行員　　***control tower*** 管制塔；塔台

6. (**D**) The famous actress decided to sue the magazine for purposely <u>distort</u> what she actually said and did at the party.

那位著名的女演員，決定要控告雜誌社，因為他們故意<u>扭曲</u>她在派對上的言行。

(A) assign 〔 əˈsaɪn 〕 v. 指派
(B) contribute 〔 kənˈtrɪbjʊt 〕 v. 貢獻
(C) foresee 〔 fɔrˈsi 〕 v. 預測；預知
(D) ***distort*** 〔 dɪsˈtɔrt 〕 v. 扭曲

sue 〔 su 〕 v. 控告　　purposely 〔ˈpɝpəslɪ 〕 adv. 故意地

7. (**B**) The little boy is very <u>inquisitive</u>: he is interested in a lot of different things and always wants to find out more about them.
那個小男孩非常<u>好問</u>：他對許多不同的事物感興趣，而且總是想要找出更多相關的內容。

    (A) accurate〔ˋækjərɪt〕*adj.* 準確的
    (B) *inquisitive*〔ɪnˋkwɪzətɪv〕*adj.* 好問的
    (C) manageable〔ˋmænɪdʒəbḷ〕*adj.* 可管理的；容易支配的
    (D) contemporary〔kənˋtɛmpə͵rɛrɪ〕*adj.* 當代的

8. (**B**) The tourists enjoyed wholeheartedly the <u>breathtaking</u> scenery along the coast highway between Hualien and Ilan.
觀光客盡情地享受從宜蘭到花蓮的海岸公路上那<u>令人讚嘆的</u>景致。

    (A) airtight〔ˋɛr͵taɪt〕*adj.* 密封的
    (B) *breathtaking*〔ˋbrɛθ͵tekɪŋ〕*adj.* 令人驚嘆的
    (C) sentimental〔͵sɛntəˋmɛntḷ〕*adj.* 多愁善感的
    (D) eccentric〔ɪkˋsɛntrɪk〕*adj.* 古怪的
    tourist〔ˋturɪst〕*n.* 觀光客　　scenery〔ˋsinərɪ〕*n.* 風景
    coast〔kost〕*n.* 海岸　　highway〔ˋhaɪ͵we〕*n.* 公路
    wholeheartedly〔ˋholˋhɑrtɪdlɪ〕*adv.* 全心全意地

9. (**A**) The major theme in the <u>forthcoming</u> issue of the best-selling monthly magazine will be "Love and Peace."
這本暢銷月刊<u>即將發行的</u>下一期當中，主要的主題是「愛與和平」。

    (A) *forthcoming*〔ˋforθˋkʌmɪŋ〕*adj.* 即將到來的；最近的
    (B) expensive〔ɪkˋspɛnsɪv〕*adj.* 昂貴的
    (C) brilliant〔ˋbrɪljənt〕*adj.* 燦爛的；有才能的
    (D) ambitious〔æmˋbɪʃəs〕*adj.* 有抱負的
    major〔ˋmedʒɚ〕*adj.* 主要的　　theme〔θim〕*n.* 主題
    issue〔ˋɪʃju〕*n.*（刊物發行的）期；號
    best-selling〔ˋbɛstˋsɛlɪŋ〕*adj.* 暢銷的

10. (**A**) Our English teacher always emphasizes the importance of learning new words in context rather than learning each of them <u>individually</u>. 我們的英文老師總是強調，由上下文學習單字，比<u>個別</u>學習單字還重要。

(A) *individually*〔ˌɪndəˈvɪdʒʊəlɪ〕*adv.* 個別地
(B) exclusively〔ɪkˈsklusɪvlɪ〕*adv.* 專門地；僅限於…
(C) approximately〔əˈprɑksəmɪtlɪ〕*adv.* 大約
(D) supposedly〔səˈpozɪdlɪ〕*adv.* 根據推測地

emphasize〔ˈɛmfəˌsaɪz〕*v.* 強調　　context〔ˈkɑntɛkst〕*n.* 上下文
rather than 而不是

11. (**D**) The old woman at the street corner must be lost. She is looking around <u>desperately</u> for someone to help her. 在街角的那位老太太一定是迷路了。她正<u>拼命地</u>環顧四週，想找人幫忙。

(A) socially〔ˈsoʃəlɪ〕*adv.* 社會上；社交上
(B) accidentally〔ˌæksəˈdɛntlɪ〕*adv.* 意外地
(C) tremendously〔trɪˈmɛndəslɪ〕*adv.* 巨大地
(D) *desperately*〔ˈdɛspərɪtlɪ〕*adv.* 拼命地

lost〔lɔst〕*adj.* 迷路的

12. (**B**) John is an experienced salesperson. Just observe closely how he interacts with customers and do <u>likewise</u>. Then you will become an expert yourself. 約翰是個非常有經驗的銷售員。你只要仔細地觀察他和顧客之間的互動，並且<u>同樣</u>照做。那麼你就可以變成一位專家。

(A) edgewise〔ˈɛdʒˌwaɪz〕*adv.* 刀刃朝外地
(B) *likewise*〔ˈlaɪkˌwaɪz〕*adv.* 同樣地
(C) otherwise〔ˈʌðəˌwaɪz〕*adv.* 否則
(D) clockwise〔ˈklɑkˌwaɪz〕*adv.* 順時鐘地

experienced〔ɪkˈspɪrɪənst〕*adj.* 有經驗的
observe〔əbˈzɝv〕*v.* 觀察　　closely〔ˈkloslɪ〕*adv.* 仔細地
interact〔ˌɪntəˈækt〕*v.* 互動＜*with*＞　　expert〔ˈɛkspɝt〕*n.* 專家

13. (**C**) A variety of preventive measures are now <u>in place</u> in order to minimize the potential damage caused by the deadly disease. 為了使致命的疾病所造成的傷害減到最小，現在各式各樣的防預措施都已<u>就緒</u>。

(A) by birth 天生　　　　　　(B) at will 隨意地
(C) *in place* 就緒；就定位　　(D) on call 隨叫隨到的

preventive〔prɪˈvɛntɪv〕*adj.* 預防的　　measure〔ˈmɛʒə〕*n.* 措施
potential〔pəˈtɛnʃəl〕*adj.* 可能的　　damage〔ˈdæmɪdʒ〕*n.* 損害
deadly〔ˈdɛdlɪ〕*adj.* 致命的　　disease〔dɪˈziz〕*n.* 疾病

14. (**D**) With over fifty teams competing in the tournament, all the games
will be played <u>back to back</u>.
這次的錦標賽有五十支隊伍參加，所有的比賽將會<u>連續地</u>舉行。

　　(A) see eye to eye 完全同意　　(B) from head to toe 從頭到腳
　　(C) live from hand to mouth 勉強糊口
　　(D) ***back to back*** （一個接著一個）連續地
　　compete〔kəm'pit〕*v.* 競爭　　　tournament〔'tɜnəmənt〕*n.* 錦標賽

15. (**A**) Did I say "a lot of dime"? Oh, I'm really sorry. I meant to say "a
lot of time." It was a <u>slip of the tongue</u>. 我剛才說的是"a lot of dime"
嗎？喔，我真的很抱歉。我打算說的是 "a lot of time"。是我<u>失言了</u>。

　　(A) ***a slip of the tongue*** 失言；說錯話　　tongue〔tʌŋ〕*n.* 舌頭
　　(B) a thorn in *one's* side 苦惱的原因；肉中刺（= *a thorn in one's flesh*）
　　　　thorn〔θɔrn〕*n.* 刺　　side〔saɪd〕*n.* 腹側
　　(C) A penny for your thoughts!【口語】你呆呆地在想什麼？
　　(D) a leap in the dark 魯莽的行為　　leap〔lip〕*n.* 跳躍
　　mean to + V. 打算～　　slip〔slɪp〕*n.*（偶然的）小過失

二、綜合測驗：

第 16 至 20 題為題組

　　If old newspapers are stacking up in your house, there are options other
than tossing them out or selling them to a recycler. Some environmental
scientists suggest turning newspapers <u>into</u> charcoal. This can be done by
　　　　　　　　　　　　　　　　　　　　　　　　16
soaking sheets of newspaper in water for two hours and then <u>tearing</u> them
　　　　　　　　　　　　　　　　　　　　　　　　　　　　　　　17
into small pieces. These pieces are then compressed into balls. After the
water is <u>squeezed out</u>, the ball-shaped pieces are put under the sun to dry
　　　　　　　18
before they can be used as a firewood or charcoal substitute.

　　如果你們家有成堆的舊報紙，那麼除了把它們丟掉，或賣給收破銅爛鐵的
人之外，還有別的選擇。有些環境科學家建議，可將報紙變成木炭。先把一張
張的報紙浸泡在水中兩小時後，再將它們撕成小碎片。接著將碎片壓成紙球。
把水擠壓出來之後，再將這些球形紙片放在太陽底下曬乾，之後就可以用來作
為柴薪或木炭的替代品了。

stack〔stæk〕*v.* 堆積＜*up*＞　　***stack up*** 堆積（＝*pile up*）

option〔'ɑpʃən〕*n.* 選擇（＝*choice*）　　***other than*** 除了～之外

toss〔tos〕*v.* 扔；丟

recycler〔ri'saɪklɚ〕*n.* 回收者；收破銅爛鐵的人

environmental〔ɪn,vaɪrən'mɛntḷ〕*adj.* 環境的

charcoal〔'tʃɑr,kol〕*n.* 木炭　　soak〔sok〕*v.* 使浸泡

sheet〔ʃit〕*n.*（紙的）一張　　compress〔kəm'prɛs〕*v.* 壓縮

ball-shaped〔,bɔl'ʃept〕*adj.* 球形的　　dry〔draɪ〕*v.* 變乾

firewood〔'faɪr,wud〕*n.* 柴薪

substitute〔'sʌbstə,tjut〕*n.* 替代物；代用品

16.(**A**) ***turn** A **into** B* 把 A 變成 B

17.(**C**) and 爲對等連接詞，須連接文法地位相同的單字、片語，或子句，前
面是動名詞 soaking，空格亦應填動名詞，故選 (C) ***tearing***。

tear〔tɛr〕*v.* 撕裂　　***tear*** ~ ***into pieces*** 把～撕成碎片

18.(**D**) (A) boil down 煮濃；濃縮　　boil〔bɔɪl〕*v.* 煮沸

(B) fire up 給（爐灶）添燃料；突然發怒

(C) kick off 踢開；【足球】開球；開始　　kick〔kɪk〕*v.* 踢

(D) ***squeeze out*** 擠出來　　squeeze〔skwiz〕*v.* 擠壓

Another suggestion made by the experts is to dip newspaper sheets in
19
vinegar and water, and use them to clean windows, mirrors, and tiles. Old

papers can also be used to line rubbish bins and as packing material when
20
mailing breakable goods.

專家的另一個建議就是，可將報紙浸泡在加了醋的水中，然後用來清理窗戶、
鏡子，和磁磚。舊報紙也可墊在垃圾箱底部，以及在郵寄易碎物品時，作爲包
裝材料。

expert〔'ɛkspɝt〕*n.* 專家　　dip〔dɪp〕*v.* 沾；浸泡（＝*soak*）

vinegar〔'vɪnɪgɚ〕*n.* 醋　　mirror〔'mɪrɚ〕*n.* 鏡子

tile〔taɪl〕*n.* 磁磚　　paper〔'pepɚ〕*n.* 報紙（＝*newspaper*）

line〔laɪn〕*v.* 作爲的…襯裡　　rubbish〔'rʌbɪʃ〕*n.* 垃圾

bin〔bɪn〕*n.*（有蓋的）大箱

rubbish bin 垃圾箱（＝*garbage can*）

　　packing〔'pækɪŋ〕*n.* 包裝；用品；包裝材料
　　material〔mə'tɪrɪəl〕*n.* 材料　　mail〔mel〕*v.* 郵寄
　　breakable〔'brekəbḷ〕*adj.* 易碎的；易破的
　　goods〔gʊdz〕*n.pl.* 商品；物品

19. (**B**) 依句意，專家所提供的「另一個」建議，選 (B) ***Another***。

20. (**B**) 依句意，舊報紙「也」可以用來墊在垃圾箱的底部，以及作爲郵寄
　　　易碎物品時的包裝材料，故選 (B) ***also***「也」。而 (A) soon「很快地」，
　　　(C) thus〔ðʌs〕*adv.* 因此，(D) rather〔'ræðɚ〕*adv.* 相當地 (= *very*)，
　　　均不合句意。

第 21 至 25 題爲題組

　　Children's encounters with poetry should include three types of response—enjoyment, exploration, and deepening understanding.　These do not occur always as <u>separate</u> steps but may happen simultaneously.
　　　　　　　　　　　　　　　　　　　21
Certainly, children must start with enjoyment <u>or</u> their interest in poetry
　　　　　　　　　　　　　　　　　　　　　　22
dies.　But if from the beginning they find delight in the poems they hear or read, they are ready and eager to <u>explore</u> further—more books and more
　　　　　　　　　　　　　　　　　　　23
poems of different sorts.

　　　兒童與詩的邂逅，應該包含三種反應——喜歡、探索，以及深入的了解。
這些反應的出現，未必是各不相關的步驟，而可能同時發生。當然，孩子們一
定得從喜歡開始，否則他們對詩的興趣就會消失了。不過，如果從一開始，他
們就很喜愛所讀或聽到的詩的話，他們就會願意並渴望更進一步探索——不同
種類的更多書和更多詩。

　　　　　encounter〔ɪn'kaʊntɚ〕*n.* 邂逅；遭遇
　　　　　poetry〔'po·ɪtrɪ〕*n.* 詩　　response〔rɪ'spɑns〕*n.* 反應
　　　　　enjoyment〔ɪn'dʒɔɪmənt〕*n.* 樂趣；喜好
　　　　　exploration〔ˌɛksplə'reʃən〕*n.* 探索
　　　　　deepening〔'dipənɪŋ〕*adj.* 逐漸加深的；深入的
　　　　　simultaneously〔ˌsaɪmḷ'tenɪəslɪ〕*adv.* 同時地 (= *at the same time*)
　　　　　delight〔dɪ'laɪt〕*n.* 愉快
　　　　　find delight in 喜愛 (= *take delight in = delight in*)
　　　　　ready〔'rɛdɪ〕*adj.* 願意的　　eager〔'igɚ〕*adj.* 渴望的
　　　　　further〔'fɝðɚ〕*adv.* 更進一步地　　sort〔sɔrt〕*n.* 種類

21. (**C**) 依句意，這些反應的發生未必是「各不相關的」，而可能是同時的，
選 (C) *separate* (ˊsɛpərɪt) *adj.* 個別的；不同的。而 (A) childish
(ˊtʃaɪldɪʃ) *adj.* 幼稚的，(B) artistic (ɑrˊtɪstɪk) *adj.* 藝術的，(D) innocent
(ˊɪnəsn̩t) *adj.* 無辜的；天眞的，均不合。

22. (**A**) 依句意，孩子們一定得從喜歡開始，「否則」他們對詩的興趣就會
消失了，選 (A) *or*。而 (B) 以及，(C) 所以，均不合句意，均不合句
意，(D) then「然後」，是副詞，而非連接詞，在此用法不合。

23. (**B**) (A) escape (əˊskep) *v.* 逃走
(B) *explore* (ɪkˊsplor) *v.* 探索
(C) accustom (əˊkʌstəm) *v.* 使習慣
(D) appear (əˊpɪr) *v.* 出現

Even the youngest children can learn to see implications <u>beyond</u> the
　　　　　　　　　　　　　　　　　　　　　　　　　　　　24
obvious. To read for hidden meanings is to identify with the poet, to ask
the poet's questions. This is reading for deeper understanding, <u>taking</u> a
　　　　　　　　　　　　　　　　　　　　　　　　　　　　　　　25
thoughtful look at what lies beneath the surface. Enjoyment, exploration,
and deeper understanding must all be part of children's experience with
poetry if we are to help them to love it.
即使是最年幼的小孩也可以學習，在明顯的事物以外，看出言外之意。想要讀
出詩中隱含的意義，就要將自己與詩人視爲一體，去詢問詩人想問的問題，這
就是閱讀以尋求更深入的了解，沉思隱藏在表面以下的深意。如果我們想要幫助
孩子們愛上詩，喜歡、探索，以及深入的了解，都必須是他們讀詩經驗的一部
分。

　　　implication (ˌɪmpləˊkeʃən) *n.* 暗示；言外之意
　　　obvious (ˊɑbvɪəs) *adj.* 明顯的　　hidden (ˊhɪdn̩) *adj.* 隱含的
　　　identify (aɪˊdɛntəˌfaɪ) *v.* 認同 < *with* >　　poet (ˊpo·ɪt) *n.* 詩人
　　　thoughtful (ˊθɔtfəl) *adj.* 沉思的；深思熟慮的　　lie (laɪ) *v.* 在
　　　beneath (bɪˊniθ) *prep.* 在～之下　　surface (ˊsɝfɪs) *n.* 表面
　　　be to V. 表示「責任、必要、意願、打算、可能性、命運、
　　　　預定、約定」等，在此作「想要」解。

24.（**C**）依句意，應是要在明顯的事物「之外」看出言外之意，故選
　　　　　(C) ***beyond*** 「在～之外」。而 (A) near 「接近」，(B) among
　　　　　「在～當中」，(D) without 「沒有」，均不合。

25.（**D**）空格原先引導形容詞子句，補充說明先行詞 reading for deeper
　　　　　understanding 意義為何，故須用 which takes，而關代可省略，
　　　　　動詞改為現在分詞，而用分詞，故選 (D) ***taking***。

第 26 至 30 題為題組

　　Avian influenza, or "bird flu," is a contagious disease caused by viruses
that normally infect only birds and, less commonly, pigs.　Underline{While} all bird
　　　　　　　　　　　　　　　　　　　　　　　　　　　　　　　　26
species are thought to be susceptible to infection, domestic poultry flocks
are especially vulnerable to infections that can rapidly reach epidemic
proportions.

　　鳥類的流行性感冒，也就是「禽流感」，是由一種病毒所引起，通常是鳥類，
有時候是豬，才會被感染的傳染性疾病。雖然一般認為，所有的鳥類都很容易
受到感染，但家禽尤其特別容易受感染，而且很快就會引發大規模的流行。

avian〔ˈevɪən〕*adj.* 鳥類的
influenza〔ˌɪnfluˈɛnzə〕*n.* 流行性感冒（= *flu*）　　***bird flu*** 禽流感
contagious〔kənˈtedʒəs〕*adj.* 藉由接觸而傳染的
　　cf. infectious〔ɪnˈfɛkʃəs〕*adj.*（藉由空氣、水而）傳染的
cause〔kɔz〕*v.* 導致；引起　　virus〔ˈvaɪrəs〕*n.* 病毒
normally〔ˈnɔrməlɪ〕*adv.* 通常　　infect〔ɪnˈfɛkt〕*v.* 感染
commonly〔ˈkɑmənlɪ〕*adv.* 普遍地；通常地　　pig〔pɪg〕*n.* 豬
species〔ˈspiʃɪz〕*n.* 種；種類【單複數同形】
susceptible〔səˈsɛptəbḷ〕*adj.* 易受影響的；易受感染的 < *to* >
infection〔ɪnˈfɛkʃən〕*n.* 感染；傳染病
domestic〔dəˈmɛstɪk〕*adj.* 家庭的；馴養的
poultry〔ˈpoltrɪ〕*n.* 家禽　　***domestic poultry*** 家禽
flock〔flɑk〕*n.*（羊、鵝、鴨、鳥等的）群
vulnerable〔ˈvʌlnərəbḷ〕*adj.* 易受傷害的；易受影響的 < *to* >
be vulnerable to 容易遭受（= *be susceptible to*）
rapidly〔ˈræpɪdlɪ〕*adv.* 快速地
epidemic〔ˌɛpəˈdɛmɪk〕*adj.* 流行性的；廣泛的
proportions〔prəˈporʃənz〕*n. pl.* 程度；範圍；規模
reach epidemic proportions 大規模流行

26. (**B**) 依句意，選 (B) *While*「雖然」。而 (A) not「不」，是副詞，不是連接詞，
　　　在此用法不合；(C) since「既然」，(D) unless「除非」，則不合句意。

Outbreaks of avian influenza <u>can</u> be devastating for the poultry industry
　　　　　　　　　　　　　　　27
and for farmers.　For example, an outbreak of avian influenza in the USA in
1983–1984 resulted in the destruction of more than 17 million birds <u>at a cost</u>
　　　　　　　　　　　　　　　　　　　　　　　　　　　　　　　28
<u>of</u> nearly US$ 65 million.
　　禽流感的爆發，對於家禽業者以及農夫而言，可能是很慘的事。舉例來說，
美國於 1983 至 1984 年間爆發的禽流感，造成超過一千七百萬隻家禽死亡，損
失將近六千五百萬美元。

　　　　　outbreak〔'aʊt,brek〕*n.* 爆發
　　　　　devastating〔'dɛvəs,tetɪŋ〕*adj.* 破壞性的；很慘的
　　　　　industry〔'ɪndəstrɪ〕*n.* …業　　***result in*** 導致；造成
　　　　　destruction〔dɪ'strʌkʃən〕*n.* 破壞；滅絕；死亡
　　　　　nearly〔'nɪrlɪ〕*adv.* 將近

27. (**A**) 依句意，選 (A) *can*「可能」。而 (B) shall〔ʃɔl〕*aux.* 將（= *will*），
　　　(C) dare「敢」，(D) need〔nid〕*v.* 必須，均不合句意。

28. (**C**) (A) with a view to　目的是為了　　(B) in regard to　關於
　　　(C) ***at a cost of***　以…為代價　　(D) on account of　因為；由於

Economic consequences are often most serious in developing countries
<u>where</u> poultry raising is an important source of income, and of food, for
　29
impoverished rural farmers and their families.　When outbreaks become
widespread within a country, control can be extremely difficult.　<u>Therefore</u>,
　　　　　　　　　　　　　　　　　　　　　　　　　　　　　　　30
government authorities usually undertake aggressive emergency control
measures as soon as an outbreak is detected.
禽流感對經濟所造成的影響，通常是在開發中國家最為嚴重，因為飼養家禽，
常是窮困的鄉下農夫及其家人重要的收入及食物來源。當禽流感在某個國家內
廣為流行時，想要控制疫情，可能是非常困難的。因此，當政府當局一發現禽
流感的疫情爆發時，通常就會採取積極的緊急管制措施。

economic〔͵ikə'nɑmɪk〕*adj.* 經濟（上）的
consequences〔'kɑnsə͵kwənsɪz〕*n. pl.* 後果；影響
developing countries 開發中國家　　raising〔'resɪŋ〕*n.* 飼養
source〔sors〕*n.* 來源　　income〔'ɪn͵kʌm〕*n.* 收入
impoverished〔ɪm'pɑvərɪʃt〕*adj.* 窮困的（＝*poor*）
rural〔'rʊrəl〕*adj.* 鄉村的　　widespread〔'waɪd'sprɛd〕*adj.* 普遍的
extremely〔ɪk'strimlɪ〕*adv.* 極度地；非常地
authorities〔ə'θɔrətɪz〕*n.pl.* 官方；當局
undertake〔͵ʌndə'tek〕*v.* 著手做；採取
aggressive〔ə'grɛsɪv〕*adj.* 侵略性的；積極的
emergency〔ɪ'mɝdʒənsɪ〕*adj.* 緊急的　　control〔kən'trol〕*n.* 管制
measure〔'mɛʒə〕*n.* 措施　　detect〔dɪ'tɛkt〕*v.* 發現

29.（**D**）表地點，關係副詞須用 ***where***，故選 (D)。

30.（**B**）依句意，選 (B) ***Therefore***「因此」。而 (A) instead「取而代之」, (C) by
　　no means「絕不」, (D) on the contrary「相反地」，均不合句意。

三、文意選填：

第 31 至 40 題為題組

　　Junior Achievement was started in Springfield, Massachusetts, in
1919 by Horace A. Moses. Mr. Moses, who had been a poor farm boy,
had worked his way up to become one of the <u>leading</u> industrialists in the
　　　　　　　　　　　　　　　　　　　　　　　　　　31
United States. He was concerned that so many of the young people
<u>applying</u> for positions with his firm knew absolutely nothing about the
　32
way a corporation is run. As a solution to this problem, he <u>founded</u> Junior
　　　　　　　　　　　　　　　　　　　　　　　　　　　　　33
Achievement, Inc.

　　「少年成就有限公司」於一九一九年，創立於麻塞諸塞州的春田市，創立
者是荷瑞斯‧模西斯先生。模西斯先生出身是貧苦的農家少年，他努力工作而
逐漸發跡，成為全美國最卓越的企業家之一。他很關心，有許多應徵他公司職
位的年輕人，完全不知道一家公司的經營方法，所以，他創立了「少年成就有
限公司」，來解決這個問題。

junior〔'dʒunjɚ〕 *adj.* 少年的　　achievement〔ə'tʃivmənt〕 *n.* 成就
work** one's **way up 逐漸發跡
industrialist〔ɪn'dʌstrɪəlɪst〕 *n.* 企業家
concerned〔kən's3nd〕 *adj.* 關心的；擔心的
position〔pə'zɪʃən〕 *n.* 職位　　firm〔f3m〕 *n.* 公司
absolutely〔'æbsə,lutlɪ〕 *adv.* 絕對地；完全地
corporation〔,kɔrpə'reʃən〕 *n.* 公司　　run〔rʌn〕 *v.* 經營；管理
solution〔sə'luʃən〕 *n.* 解決方法 < *to* >
***Inc**.* 股份有限公司（源自 incorporated〔ɪn'kɔrpə,retɪd〕 *adj.* 股份
　有限的）

31. (**G**) 依句意，他逐漸發跡，成為全美國「卓越的」企業家之一，
　　　選 (G) ***leading***。　　　***leading***〔'lidɪŋ〕 *adj.* 一流的；卓越的

32. (**C**) 依句意，許多年輕人去「應徵」他公司的職位，選 (C) ***applying***。
　　　apply for 申請；應徵

33. (**E**) 他「創立」了少年成就有限公司，選 (E) ***founded***。
　　　found〔faʊnd〕 *v.* 創立

　　In essence, Junior Achievement is an organization that gives high-
school boys and girls a chance to become part of the operation of a
<u>miniature</u> corporation while still in school. Every September, students
　　34
are <u>offered</u> the opportunity to join Junior Achievement through the co-
　　35
operation of local school systems. Some students make products that
range in size from earrings to quite <u>elaborate</u> furniture for the home.
　　　　　　　　　　　　　　　　　　36
Others produce weekly radio and television shows or operate banks,
accounting <u>firms</u>, and advertising agencies.
　　　37
　　在本質上，「少年成就有限公司」這個組織，給予高中男女學生在校期間，
有機會參與一個小型公司的運作。每年九月，學生們透過當地學校系統的合作，
得到機會加入「少年成就有限公司」。有些學生參與製作商品，小到從耳環，大
到可居家使用的相當精巧的家具都有。還有些學生製作每週的廣播及電視節
目，或是管理銀行、會計師事務所，以及廣告公司等等。

essence〔'ɛsn̩s〕n. 本質　　**in essence** 在本質上
organization〔ˌɔrgənə'zeʃən〕n. 組織
operation〔ˌɑpə'reʃən〕n. 經營；運作
co-operation〔koˌɑpə'reʃən〕n. 合作
range〔rændʒ〕v. 範圍有；涉及
range from A **to** B　（範圍）從 A 到 B 都有
earring〔'ɪrˌrɪŋ〕n. 耳環　　furniture〔'fɝnɪtʃə〕n. 家具
weekly〔'wiklɪ〕adj. 每週的　　show〔ʃo〕n. 節目
operate〔'ɑpəˌret〕v. 經營；管理
accounting〔ə'kauntɪŋ〕n. 會計學
advertising〔'ædvəˌtaɪzɪŋ〕adj. 廣告業的
agency〔'edʒənsɪ〕n. 代理商；公司

34.(**A**) **miniature**〔'mɪnɪətʃə〕adj. 小型的

35.(**J**) 依句意，學生們被「提供」工作機會，選 (J) **offered**。

36.(**B**) **elaborate**〔ɪ'læbərɪt〕adj. 精巧的；複雜的

37.(**F**) **firm**〔fɝm〕n. 公司　　**accounting firm** 會計師事務所

Junior Achievement <u>programs</u> range in size from those in the big
　　　　　　　　　　38
cities, like New York and Los Angeles, to those in small towns with a
<u>population</u> of a few thousand.　Each program <u>varies</u> with the size of the
39　　　　　　　　　　　　　　　　　　　　　40
area and the amount of industrial and business activity in the city.

「少年成就有限公司」所推出的計劃，其規模大小從大都市，如紐約、洛
杉磯，到人口只有數千人的小城鎮都有。每個計劃會隨著各個區域的大小，以
及該都市的工商業活動數量，而有所不同。

industrial〔ɪn'dʌstrɪəl〕adj. 工業的
business〔'bɪznɪs〕n. 商業　　activity〔æk'tɪvətɪ〕n. 活動

38.(**D**) 依句意，本段提到的是該公司的「計劃」，選 (D) **programs**。

39.(**H**) 小一點的城鎮「人口」可能只有數千人，選 (H) **population**。

40.(**I**) 依句意，每個計劃會隨著各區域的大小而「不同」，選 (I) **varied**。
vary〔'vɛrɪ〕v. 不同；變化　　**vary with** 隨著～而不同

四、篇章結構：

<u>第 41 至 45 題爲題組</u>

Starting around 4,000 B.C., traditional Chinese brush painting has developed continuously over a period of more than six thousand years. ⁴¹(D) <u>Its growth has inevitably reflected the changes of time.</u>

大約從西元前四千年開始，傳統中國國畫已經持續發展了六千多年。國畫的發展當然反映了時代的變遷。

around〔əˈraʊnd〕prep. 大約　　**B.C.** 西元前（= before Christ）
brush〔brʌʃ〕n. 毛筆　　**brush painting** 國畫
continuously〔kənˈtɪnjʊəslɪ〕adv. 連續不斷地
period〔ˈpɪrɪəd〕n. 時期
inevitably〔ɪnˈɛvətəblɪ〕adv. 不可避免地；必然地
reflect〔rɪˈflɛkt〕v. 反映

During the 1st century A.D., the art of painting religious murals gradually gained in prominence, with the introduction of Buddhism to China and the consequent building of temples. ⁴²(B) <u>However, the subject matters later expanded beyond religious themes.</u> For example, paintings of historical characters and stories of everyday life became extremely popular. Besides historical figures, landscape painting was also common in Chinese brush painting. By the 4th century, this particular type of painting had already established itself as an independent form of expression.

西元一世紀期間，隨著佛教引進中國，帶動寺廟的興建，宗教壁畫的繪畫藝術日趨顯赫。然而，題材後來擴展到宗教以外的主題。例如，歷史人物以及日常生活故事的繪畫，變得非常普遍。除了歷史人物之外，山水畫在中國國畫中也很常見。到了西元四世紀，此種獨特的繪畫類型已經建立了名聲，是一種獨立的表達形式。

A.D. 西元（= Anno Domini）　　religious〔rɪˈlɪdʒəs〕adj. 宗教的
mural〔ˈmjʊrəl〕n. 壁畫　　gradually〔ˈgrædʒʊəlɪ〕adv. 逐漸地
gain〔gen〕v. 獲得；增加
prominence〔ˈprɑmənəns〕n. 顯著；名聲
gain in prominence 日趨顯赫

introduction〔͵ɪntrə'dʌkʃən〕n. 引進
Buddhism〔'budɪzəm〕n. 佛教
consequent〔'kɑnsə͵kwɛnt〕adj. 隨之而來的
temple〔'tɛmpḷ〕n. 寺廟　　　***subject matter*** 題材；主題
expand〔ɪk'spænd〕v. 擴展　　　theme〔θim〕n. 主題
character〔'kærɪktɚ〕n. 人物（= figure〔'fɪg(j)ɚ〕）
everyday〔'ɛvrɪ'de〕adj. 日常的
extremely〔ɪk'strimlɪ〕adv. 非常
landscape〔'lænd͵skep〕n. 風景（畫）；山水畫
establish〔ə'stæblɪʃ〕v. 確立（名聲等）< *as* >
independent〔͵ɪndɪ'pɛndənt〕adj. 獨立的
form〔fɔrm〕n. 形式
expression〔ɪk'sprɛʃən〕n. 表達

43（E）It then gradually developed into two separate styles.　The blue-and-green landscape used bright blue, green and red pigments derived from minerals to create a richly decorative style; the ink-and-wash landscape relied on vivid brushwork and various intensity of ink to express the artist's conception of nature as well as his own emotions.　**44**（A）Another genre commonly found in Chinese brush painting was flower-and-bird painting. A great many artists in the 9th century painted in this genre and their subject matters included a rich variety of flowers, fruits, birds, insects, and fish.

國畫就此逐漸發展出兩種不同的風格。青綠山水技法運用取自礦物的顏料，有鮮豔的藍色、綠色和紅色，創造出極富裝飾效果的風格；潑墨山水畫憑藉著生動筆法和墨水濃度不同的變化，表達出畫家對自然的概念和自己的情感。在中國國畫中，另一個常見的類型是花鳥畫。西元九世紀，有非常多的畫家以這種類型作畫，題材包括非常多不同種類的花卉、水果、鳥類、昆蟲和魚類。

separate〔'sɛp(ə)rɪt〕adj. 個別的；不同的
blue-and-green 青綠（山水）畫的　　　pigment〔'pɪgmənt〕n. 顏料
derive〔dɪ'raɪv〕v. 起源 < *from* >　　　mineral〔'mɪnərəl〕n. 礦物
richly〔'rɪtʃlɪ〕adv. 豐富地

decorative〔ˋdɛkəˏretɪv〕*adj.* 裝飾性的　　ink〔ɪŋk〕*n.* 墨水
wash〔waʃ〕*n.* 淡水彩畫　　***ink-and-wash*** 潑墨（山水）畫的
rely on 依靠　　vivid〔ˋvɪvɪd〕*adj.* 生動的
brushwork〔ˋbrʌʃˏwɜk〕*n.* 筆法
various〔ˋvɛrɪəs〕*adj.* 各種不同的（= *a variety of* = *varied*）
intensity〔ɪnˋtɛnsətɪ〕*n.* 強度；濃度
conception〔kənˋsɛpʃən〕*n.* 概念；想法　　***as well as*** 以及
genre〔ˋʒɑnrə〕*n.*（尤指藝術作品的）類型
insect〔ˋɪnsɛkt〕*n.* 昆蟲

Since the turn of the 20th century, painters have often mixed several colors on one brush or mixed their colors with black inks. ⁴⁵(C) As a result, they have obtained more natural and richly varied colors. Such techniques have been widely adopted and further developed in the contemporary period.

自從十九世紀末，二十世紀交替之時，畫家已經經常用毛筆混合好幾種顏色，或是用黑色墨水加以混合。因此，畫作使用的色彩更加自然，並且具有豐富多樣性。這樣的技巧已經廣為運用，也在當代有了進一步的發展。

turn〔tɜn〕*n.* 轉換　　mix〔mɪks〕*v.* 混和
as a result 因此　　obtain〔əbˋten〕*v.* 獲得
technique〔tɛkˋnik〕*n.* 技巧　　widely〔ˋwaɪdlɪ〕*adv.* 廣泛地
adopt〔əˋdɑpt〕*v.* 採用　　further〔ˋfɝðə〕*adv.* 更進一步地
contemporary〔kənˋtɛmpəˏrɛrɪ〕*adj.* 當代的

五、閱讀測驗：

第 46 至 48 題為題組

These days, even a walk in the woods can be transformed into an "extreme" sport. Take "geocaching," for example. Hikers looking for something a little different on their treks created a global hunting game, hiding "caches"—packs filled with goodies like CDs, photographs, and journals—in obscure places throughout the world. They then post the coordinates at www.geocaching.com, where other hikers can use **them**, along with a global positioning system (GPS), to join the worldwide goose chase.

現在，即使是在森林裡漫步，也可以轉換成爲一種「極限」運動。以「尋寶遊戲」爲例。那些想要在旅途當中，尋找一點不同事物的健行者，就創立了一種全球尋寶遊戲，將「寶物」——也就是一包包裝滿吸引人的東西，例如 CD，照片以及雜誌——藏在全世界偏僻的地方。然後他們在 <u>www.geocaching.com</u> 上公布寶物的地理座標，其他的健行者可以使用這個網址上的<u>座標</u>，再加上全球（衛星）定位系統，一起加入這場全世界的搜索活動。

these days 最近；現在　　woods〔wʊdz〕*n. pl.* 森林
transform〔træns'fɔrm〕*v.* 使轉變
extreme〔ɪk'strim〕*adj.* 極度的
geocache〔'dʒiə'kæʃ〕*v.* 玩尋寶遊戲　　hiker〔'khaɪkə〕*n.* 健行者
trek〔trɛk〕*n.*（長而艱辛的）旅行　　create〔kri'et〕*v.* 創造
global〔'globl〕*adj.* 全球的　　*hunting game* 尋寶遊戲
cache〔kæʃ〕*n.* 隱藏起來的貴重物品
pack〔pæk〕*n.* 一包　　goodies〔'gʊdɪz〕*n. pl.* 特別吸引人的好東西
journal〔'dʒɜnl〕*n.* 雜誌；期刊　　obscure〔əb'skjʊr〕*adj.* 偏僻的
post〔post〕*v.* 公布　　coordinates〔ko'ɔrdnɪts〕*n. pl.* 座標
along with 連同　　position〔pə'zɪʃən〕*v.* 定位
GPS 全球衛星定位系統　　worldwide〔'wɜld'waɪd〕*adj.* 全世界的
goose chase （過程艱辛的）搜索活動；大海撈針

Geocaching works on an honor system: When a geocacher takes something, he leaves a cache of his own behind. Vacationers can get in on this trend at resorts like Utah's Red Mountain Spa, where they can learn to use GPS and coordinates to find caches filled with spa products.

尋寶遊戲是秉持著榮譽制度運作：當一個尋寶人拿走某樣東西時，他必須留下一樣他自己的寶物。渡假者也可以在旅遊勝地，像猶他州的紅山溫泉，加入這股風潮，他們可以在那裡學習使用全球（衛星）定位系統和座標，來找到裝滿溫泉產品的寶物。

honor〔'ɑnə〕*n.* 榮譽　　geocacher〔ˌdʒiə'kæʃə〕*n.* 玩尋寶遊戲的人
leave~behind 留下~
vacationer〔ve'keʃənə〕*n.* 渡假者（= *vacationist*）
get in on 加入　　trend〔trɛnd〕*n.* 趨勢
resort〔rɪ'zɔrt〕*n.* 度假勝地　　Utah〔'jutə〕*n.* 猶他州（在美國西部）
Red Mountain Spa 紅山溫泉　　*be filled with* 充滿了

46.(**D**) 本文主要是要告知讀者關於 ＿＿＿＿＿＿。

    (A) 打獵的慣例   (B) 猶他州的紅山溫泉

    (C) 一個全球衛星定位系統   (D) <u>一種新型的戶外活動</u>

    mainly〔ˈmenlɪ〕*adv.* 主要地   inform〔ɪnˈfɔrm〕*v.* 告知

    practice〔ˈpræktɪs〕*n.* 慣例；習慣的做法

47.(**A**) 第七行的代名詞 **them** 是指 ＿＿＿＿＿＿。

    (A) <u>座標</u>   (B) 吸引人的好東西

    (C) 寶物   (D) 旅行

    pronoun〔ˈpronaʊn〕*n.* 代名詞   ***refer to*** 是指

48.(**C**) 從本文我們可以推論出 ＿＿＿＿＿＿。

    (A) 尋寶人喜歡到全世界去追趕鵝

    (B) 只有在猶他州才可以學習當尋寶人

    (C) <u>尋寶遊戲要求參加者之間交換物品</u>

    (D) 寶物是藏在全世界偏遠地區的溫泉產品

    infer〔ɪnˈfɜ〕*v.* 推論   exclusively〔ɪkˈsklusɪvlɪ〕*adv.* 僅僅

    require〔rɪˈkwaɪr〕*v.* 要求   exchange〔ɪksˈtʃendʒ〕*v.* 交換

    participant〔pəˈtɪsəpənt〕*n.* 參加者   remote〔rɪˈmot〕*adj.* 偏僻的

<u>第 49 至 52 題為題組</u>

    Even though she's just 5 years old, Cindy Smart speaks five languages. She's a good reader. She can tell time and do simple math, including multiplication and division. She's not a prodigy. She's just good programming. Cindy looks like an average doll, with long, blond hair, baby-blue eyes, and a button nose. But loaded with some devices, Cindy is the first doll that can see, think, and do as she's told.

    即使辛蒂‧史瑪特只有五歲大,卻能夠說五種語言。她很會讀書。她看得懂時間,並能夠作簡單的數學計算,包括乘法及除法。她並不是個神童。她只是個很好的程式設計。辛蒂看起來就像是一般的洋娃娃,有長長的金色頭髮,一雙粉藍色的眼睛,以及像鈕扣般的鼻子。但由於配備有一些裝置,所以辛蒂是第一個能夠看東西、思考,還可以遵照指令做動作的洋娃娃。

tell time 懂得看時間　　multiplication〔͵mʌltəplə'keʃən〕*n.* 乘法
division〔də'vɪʒən〕*n.* 除法　　prodigy〔'prɑdədʒɪ〕*n.* 神童
programming〔'prɑgræmɪŋ〕*n.* 程式設計
average〔'ævərɪdʒ〕*adj.* 普通的；一般的
baby-blue〔'bebɪ͵blu〕*adj.* 粉藍色的
be loaded with 裝載有；裝配有　　device〔dɪ'vaɪs〕*n.* 裝置

The eagle-eyed Cindy follows in the path of other breakthrough toys like Sony's barking Robot Aibo, which was the first to popularize voice command in the late 1990s. Cindy takes Aibo's innovations one step beyond: she not only follows instructions but also recognizes shapes, colors, and words—and remembers. The effect is a doll that appears to be learning.

目光銳利的辛蒂跟隨著其他突破性的玩具的腳步，像是索尼在九〇年代末期推出的會叫的機器狗愛寶，它是第一個使聲控功能成爲潮流的玩具。辛蒂更超越了愛寶的創新：她不僅能夠聽從指令，還能夠辨識形狀、顏色，和文字 —— 並且都記得。這樣的結果使得辛蒂似乎具有學習能力。

eagle-eyed〔'igl͵aɪd〕*adj.* 目光銳利的；眼神炯炯的
follow in the path of 隨著～的腳步
breakthrough〔'brek͵θru〕*n.* 突破
popularize〔'pɑpjələ͵raɪz〕*v.* 使流行
voice command 聲控　　innovation〔͵ɪnə'veʃən〕*n.* 創新
take one step beyond 超越　　instruction〔ɪn'strʌkʃən〕*n.* 指示
recognize〔'rɛkəg͵naɪz〕*v.* 認出　　shape〔ʃep〕*n.* 形狀
effect〔ɪ'fɛkt〕*n.* 結果　　appear〔ə'pɪr〕*v.* 似乎

The toy company which produced Cindy Smart spent a decade trying to see how much human nature it could breathe into an inanimate object. Its engineers began researching basic and affordable artificial intelligence, creating minibots that sense light, sounds, and pressure. However, without the sense of sight, their toys seemed to be lacking one of the keenest abilities that life forms use to react to their environment.

　　生產辛蒂・史瑪特的玩具公司，花費十年的時間，設法想出該如何將人性注入無生命的物體裡。這家公司的工程師開始研究基本的，而且財力上也負擔得起的人工智慧，創造出可以感應光、聲音，以及壓力的迷你機械人。然而，缺少了視覺能力，他們的玩具似乎就缺少了一般生命體，用來和週遭環境互動的最敏銳的能力之一。

decade〔ˋdɛked〕n. 十年　　**human nature** 人性
breathe into 賦與（生命、氣息）
inanimate〔ɪnˋænəmɪt〕adj. 無生命的
affordable〔əˋfordəbl〕adj. 負擔得起的
artificial〔͵ɑrtəˋfɪʃəl〕adj. 人工的　　**artificial intelligence** 人工智慧
minibot〔ˋmɪnɪ͵bɑt〕n. 迷你機械人　　sense〔sɛns〕v. 感受
pressure〔ˋprɛʃɚ〕n. 壓力　　lack〔læk〕v. 缺乏
keen〔kin〕adj. 敏銳的　　**life form** 生命體
react〔rɪˋækt〕v. 反應；回應 < to >

　　So how do the engineers make a doll actually see? In Cindy's case, it's a multistep process. When presented a text like "I love you" and asked "Can you read this?" Cindy identifies **it** as one of 70 preprogrammed commands. Then the inbuilt digital camera scans a 15-degree radius in search of number-or letter-shaped objects. Buried in her belly, Cindy's 16-bit microprocessor compares the text with her database of 700 words. If it's a match, "I love you," she utters.

　　那麼，工程師是如何讓洋娃娃真的能夠看到東西呢？就辛蒂的例子而言，這是個多重步驟的過程。當我們對辛蒂說一段文字，像是「我愛你」，並問她：「妳能夠理解嗎？」辛蒂就會將它視為預先設定的七十種指令之一。接著，內建的數位相機會掃描十五度角範圍，來尋找有關數字或文字形狀的物體。隱藏於辛蒂腹部的十六位元微型處理器，會將這段文字，拿來與她資料庫裡的七百個文字作比對。一旦有相符的結果，她就會說出「我愛你」。

actually〔ˋæktʃʊəlɪ〕adv. 真正地
multistep〔ˋmʌltɪ͵stɛp〕n. 多重步驟
process〔ˋprɑsɛs〕n. 過程　　identify〔aɪˋdɛntə͵faɪ〕v. 辨認
preprogrammed〔priˋprogræmd〕adj. 預先設定的

command〔kə'mænd〕n. 指定　　inbuilt〔ɪn'bɪlt〕adj. 內建的
digital camera 數位相機　　scan〔skæn〕v. 掃描
radius〔'redɪəs〕n. 半徑；範圍　　***in search of*** 尋找
letter〔'lɛtɚ〕n. 字母　　bury〔'bɛrɪ〕v. 隱藏
belly〔'bɛlɪ〕n. 腹部　　bit〔bɪt〕n. 位元
microprocessor〔,maɪkro'prɑsɛsɚ〕n. 微型處理器
text〔tɛkst〕n. 原文；文字　　database〔'detə,bes〕n. 資料庫
match〔mætʃ〕n. 相配的人或事物　　utter〔'ʌtɚ〕v. 說出

49.(**C**) 本文最可能出現在 _____ 。

(A) 醫學報導　　　(B) 分類廣告　　　(C) 科學期刊　　　(D) 音樂雜誌

classified〔'klæsə,faɪd〕adj. 分類的
ad〔æd〕n. 廣告（= *advertisement*）

50.(**B**) 根據本文，下列關於機械狗愛寶的敘述何者是正確的？

(A) 它能夠辨識形狀和顏色。
(B) 它能夠對口說的指令作出反應。
(C) 它於一九九〇年之前上市。
(D) 它比辛蒂史瑪特更晚被創造出來。

respond〔rɪ'spɑnd〕v. 回應；反應　　spoken〔'spokən〕adj. 口說的
be put on the market 上市　　***no later than*** 不遲於

51.(**D**) 第四段裡的代名詞 it 最可能是指 _____ 。

(A) 過程　　　　(B) 物體　　　　(C) 範圍　　　　(D) 要求

request〔rɪ'kwst〕n. 要求

52.(**B**) 根據本文，辛蒂如何能夠「看到東西」呢？

(A) 她能辨認任何像「我愛你」這類的文字。
(B) 她配備有照相機，能搜尋文字。
(C) 有位工程師站在她旁邊來教導她。
(D) 她用肚子來接觸文字的形狀。

be equipped with 配備有　　instruct〔ɪn'strʌkt〕v. 教導
make contact with 和～接觸

第 53 至 56 題爲題組

In June 1943, Frank Lloyd Wright received a letter from Hilla Rebay, the art adviser to Solomon R. Guggenheim, asking the architect to design a new building to house Guggenheim's four-year-old museum of Non-Objective Painting. The project evolved into a complex struggle pitting the architect against his clients, city officials, the art world, and public opinions. Both Guggenheim and Wright would die before the building's 1995 completion. The resultant achievement, the Solomon R. Guggenheim Museum, testifies not only to Wright's architectural genius, but also to the adventurous spirit that characterized its founders.

在一九四三年六月，美國建築師法蘭克・洛伊・萊特收到了一封來自希拉・瑞貝的來信，她是所羅門・古根漢的美術顧問。信中她請求這位建築師設計一間能夠容納古根漢有四年歷史的博物館，該博物館專門展覽非物體的畫（即抽象畫）。但這項計劃卻演變成一場建築師與客戶、市政府官員、美術界、及輿論之間的複雜抗爭。在這棟建築物於一九九五年落成之前，古根漢和萊特均將已過世，但這隨之而來的成果，即古根漢博物館的完成，不僅證實了萊特在建築方面的天賦，也表現出了創立人特有的冒險精神。

adviser〔əd'vaɪzɚ〕n. 顧問　　architect〔'ɑrkə,tɛkt〕n. 建築師
design〔dɪ'zaɪn〕v. 設計　　house〔haʊz〕v. 容納
non-objective painting 非物體的畫；抽象畫
project〔'prɑdʒɛkt〕n. 計劃　　**evolve into** 發展成
complex〔'kɑmplɛks〕adj. 複雜的　　struggle〔'strʌgl̩〕n. 鬥爭；抗爭
pit A against B 使 A 與 B 競爭　　client〔'klaɪənt〕n. 客戶
official〔ə'fɪʃəl〕n. 官員　　world〔wɜld〕n. …界
public opinions 輿論　　completion〔kəm'pliʃən〕n. 完成
resultant〔rɪ'zʌltn̩t〕adj. 隨之而來的
achievement〔ə'tʃivmənt〕n. 成就；成果
testify〔'tɛstə,faɪ〕v. 成爲…的證據 < *to* >
architectural〔,ɑrkə'tɛktʃʊrəl〕adj. 建築上的
genius〔'dʒinjəs〕n. 天賦
adventurous〔əd'vɛntʃərəs〕adj. 愛冒險的
characterize〔'kærɪktə,raɪz〕v. 成爲…的特色
founder〔'faʊndɚ〕n. 創立人

Wright made no secret of his disenchantment with Guggenheim's choice of New York for his museum: "I can think of several more desirable places in the world to build this great museum," Wright wrote in 1949 to his partner, "but we will have to try New York." To Wright, the city was overbuilt, overpopulated, and lacked architectural merit. Still, he proceeded with his client's wishes, considering locations on 36th Street, 54th Street, and Park Avenue (all in Manhattan), as well as in the Riverdale section of the Bronx, before settling on the present site on Fifth Avenue between 88th and 89th Streets. Its nearness to Central Park was key. As close to nature as one gets in New York, the park offered relief from the noise and congestion of the city.

萊特充分表現出他對於選擇紐約蓋博物館的失望。「在世界各地，我可以想出好幾個建造這個大博物館更理想的地方，」他於一九四九年寫給夥伴的信中提到，「但是我們卻必須選擇紐約。」對萊特而言，紐約這個都市已經過度建設、人口太多，而且又缺乏建築價值。雖然如此，他還是著手去實現客戶的願望。他考慮了第三十六街、五十四街和公園大道（均位於曼哈頓），也考慮了布隆克斯區的里弗代耳區之後，才選定八十八和八十九街中間的第五大道的現址。由於這裡靠近中央公園，所以就成了做決定的重要關鍵。當人們到達紐約時，到中央公園就好像接近大自然一般，能使人們脫離城市中的喧囂及擁擠。

> disenchantment〔͵dɪsɪnˈtʃæntmənt〕n. 幻滅
> desirable〔dɪˈzaɪrəbḷ〕adj. 理想的
> overbuild〔ˈovəˈbɪld〕v. 在（土地）上建屋過多
> overpopulated〔͵ovəˈpɑpjə͵letɪd〕adj. 人口過多的
> merit〔ˈmɛrɪt〕n. 價值；優點
> proceed〔prəˈsid〕v. 著手＜with＞
> avenue〔ˈævə͵nju〕n. 大道　　section〔ˈsɛkʃən〕n. 區域
> settle〔ˈsɛtḷ〕v. 決定＜on＞　　site〔saɪt〕n. 地點
> key〔ki〕n. 關鍵　　*relief from* 解脫；脫離
> congestion〔kənˈdʒɛstʃən〕n. 擁擠；阻塞

Wright's design put his unique stamp on Modernist Architecture's rigid geometry. The building is a symphony of triangles, ovals, arcs, circles, and squares. The delicate vision took decades to be fulfilled. Some people, especially artists, criticized Wright for creating a museum environment that might overpower the art inside. "On the contrary," he wrote, "it was to make the building and the painting an uninterrupted, beautiful symphony such as never existed in the world of art before."

萊特的設計，是將他獨特的標記置於現代主義建築物的僵硬幾何學上。這棟建築物完美地融合了三角形、橢圓形、弧形、圓形、和四方形。他那精心雕琢的夢想，花了好幾十年才蓋完。有些人，特別是藝術家，批評萊特所創造出的美術館外觀環境，已經搶了其內部藝術品的光采。「相反地，」他寫道，「這就是要讓這棟建築物和繪畫之美一覽無遺，這種完美的融合是在藝術界中，前所未有的。」

unique〔ju'nik〕*adj.* 獨特的　　stamp〔stæmp〕*n.* 標記
modernist〔'mɑdənɪst〕*adj.* 現代主義的
architecture〔'ɑrkə,tɛktʃə〕*n.* 建築物；建築學
rigid〔'rɪdʒɪd〕*adj.* 僵硬的　　geometry〔dʒi'ɑmətrɪ〕*n.* 幾何學
symphony〔'sɪmfənɪ〕*n.* 交響曲；水乳交融；完美的融合
triangle〔'traɪ,æŋgl̩〕*n.* 三角形　　oval〔'ovl̩〕*n.* 橢圓形
arc〔ɑrk〕*n.* 弧形；拱形　　circle〔'sɝkl̩〕*n.* 圓形
square〔skwɛr〕*n.* 四方形；正方形　　delicate〔'dɛləkət〕*adj.* 精細的
vision〔'vɪʒən〕*n.* 夢想　　fulfill〔fʊl'fɪl〕*v.* 完成；實現
overpower〔'ovə'paʊə〕*v.* 勝過；搶光采　***on the contrary*** 相反地
uninterrupted〔ˌʌnɪntə'rʌptɪd〕*adj.* 不中斷的；一覽無遺的

In conquering the regularity of geometric design and combining it with the plasticity of nature, Wright produced a vibrant building whose architecture is as refreshing now as it was 40 years ago. The Guggenheim is arguably Wright's most eloquent presentation and certainly the most important building of his late career.

在征服了幾何圖形的規律，並與大自然的彈性相結合，萊特所創造出的，是一棟充滿活力的建築物，其中的建築就像是和四十年前剛完成時一樣的清新。這座古根漢博物館大概可稱得上是最能表現萊特特色的代表作，當然也是他晚期最重要的作品。

conquer〔'kɑŋkɚ〕v. 征服

regularity〔ˌrɛgjə'lærətɪ〕n. 規律　　combine〔kəm'baɪn〕v. 結合

plasticity〔plæs'tɪsətɪ〕n. 可塑性；適應性；彈性

vibrant〔'vaɪbrənt〕adj. 充滿活力的

refreshing〔rɪ'frɛʃɪŋ〕adj. 清新的

arguably〔'ɑrgjʊəblɪ〕adv. 大概

eloquent〔'ɛləkwənt〕adj. 口才好的；口若懸河的

presentation〔ˌprɛznˌ'teʃən〕n. 演說；表達

career〔kə'rɪr〕adj. 事業

53.(**B**) 建造古根漢博物館 _____。

　　(A) 是爲了紀念所羅門・古根漢

　　(B) 是爲了存放古根漢的藝術收藏品

　　(C) 是爲了有名的交響樂團

　　(D) 是應紐約市政府官員的要求

　　in memory of 紀念　　orchestra〔'ɔrkɪstrə〕n. 管絃樂團
　　at the request of 應…的要求

54.(**A**) 根據本文，爲什麼萊特對於在紐約市建造古根漢博物館並不熱中？

　　(A) 因爲在紐約市已有太多的人和建築物。

　　(B) 因爲沒有足夠有熱忱的建築師來設計這座博物館。

　　(C) 因爲幾乎得不到紐約市居民的支持。

　　(D) 因爲所羅門・古根漢強力反對。

　　enthusiastic〔ɪnˌθjuzɪ'æstɪk〕adj. 熱中的；熱心的
　　objection〔əb'dʒɛkʃən〕n. 反對

55.(**C**) 從本文我們可知，古根漢博物館位於 _____。

　　(A) 紐約市的郊區　　　　　　(B) 中央公園裡

　　(C) 八十八街附近　　　　　　(D) 布隆克斯區中的里弗代耳區

　　outskirts〔'aʊtˌskɝts〕n. pl. 郊區
　　on the outskirts of 在…的郊區（＝ *in the suburbs of*）

56. (**C**) 根據本文，是什麼讓古根漢博物館在現代建築中很重要？

　　(A) 博物館的設計比裡面收藏的美術品更有力。

　　(B) 建築師和博物館的擁有人皆在博物館完工之前過世。

　　(C) 博物館是很多不同的幾何圖案的獨特結合。

　　(D) 它被設計成博物館，但是也可以作爲音樂廳。

　　work〔wɜk〕*n.* 作品　　figure〔ˈfɪgjɚ〕*n.* 圖案

　　concert hall 音樂廳　　*as well* 也（＝*too*）

第貳部分：非選擇題

一、翻譯題：

1. Technology has made our lives (become) more comfortable

$$\left\{\begin{array}{l} \text{(,) but} \\ \text{; however,} \end{array}\right\}$$ it's also (being) used to commit crimes.

2. According to the latest news reports, the most common example is Internet scams.

二、英文作文：（作文範例）

Travel Is the Best Teacher

　　I believe that travel is the best teacher.　There are so many things you can learn from traveling that you may never experience in a classroom or from a book.　Traveling broadens your horizons.　It lets you meet new people and help you experience things in person instead of reading it.

　　I remember when I went to Greece for the first time.　I saw the ancient ruins of the Parthenon and the Acropolis.　They are amazing sights to behold.　You can feel the history vibrating from these buildings when you first lay eyes on them.　I also learned about Greek food and culture just by walking around the streets.　Another good thing about traveling is the people you get to meet.　I met many travelers in my hostel and we exchanged amazing stories that I still remember to this day.

　　These are things that you may read about in books or learn from teachers. But unless you experience them in person, you are just going to forget within a few years of time. Traveling has left a lasting impression on me, a feat not many of my teachers can claim to have accomplished.

experience〔ɪkˈspɪrɪəns〕v. 經歷；體驗
broaden〔ˈbrɔdn̩〕v. 增廣
horizons〔həˈraɪznz〕n. pl.（知識、經驗等的）範圍
broaden** one's **horizons 使某人增廣見聞　　***in person*** 親自
instead of 而不是　　　Greece〔gris〕n. 希臘
ancient〔ˈænʃənt〕adj. 古代的
ruins〔ˈruɪnz〕n. pl. 廢墟；遺跡
Parthenon〔ˈparθəˌnan〕n. 巴特農神殿（在希臘雅典衛城山崗上，
　為雅典娜女神的神殿）
Acropolis〔əˈkrapəlɪs〕n.（雅典的）衛城
amazing〔əˈmezɪŋ〕adj. 令人驚奇的
sights〔saɪts〕n. pl. 觀光名勝　　behold〔bɪˈhold〕v. 看
vibrate〔ˈvaɪbret〕v. 震動
lay eye on（第一次）看到（= *set eyes on*）
get to + V. 有機會去…　　hostel〔ˈhastl̩〕n. 青年旅舍
exchange〔ɪksˈtʃendʒ〕v. 交換　　***to this day*** 至今
lasting〔ˈlæstɪŋ〕adj. 持久的；永恆的
impression〔ɪmˈprɛʃən〕n. 印象 < on >
feat〔fit〕n. 功績　　claim〔klem〕v. 自稱
accomplish〔əˈkamplɪʃ〕v. 達成

九十三學年度指定科目考試（英文）

大考中心公佈答案

題號	答案	題號	答案	題號	答案
1	B	21	C	41	D
2	A	22	A	42	B
3	B	23	B	43	E
4	D	24	C	44	A
5	C	25	D	45	C
6	D	26	B	46	D
7	B	27	A	47	A
8	B	28	C	48	C
9	A	29	D	49	C
10	A	30	B	50	B
11	D	31	G	51	D
12	B	32	C	52	B
13	C	33	E	53	B
14	D	34	A	54	A
15	A	35	J	55	C
16	A	36	B	56	C
17	C	37	F		
18	D	38	D		
19	B	39	H		
20	B	40	I		

九十三學年度指定科目考試
各科成績標準一覽表

科　目	頂　標	前　標	均　標	後　標	底　標
國　文	73	67	58	47	39
英　文	58	44	27	15	9
數學甲	66	50	30	18	10
數學乙	65	50	32	19	12
化　學	66	51	30	15	7
物　理	75	59	35	19	12
生　物	80	71	57	43	33
歷　史	49	41	30	19	12
地　理	60	52	42	30	21

※ 以上五項標準係依各該科全體到考考生成績計算，且均取整數（小數只捨不入），各標準計算方式如下：

　頂標：成績位於第 88 百分位數之考生成績。

　前標：成績位於第 75 百分位數之考生成績。

　均標：成績位於第 50 百分位數之考生成績。

　後標：成績位於第 25 百分位數之考生成績。

　底標：成績位於第 12 百分位數之考生成績。

九十二年大學入學指定科目考試試題
英文考科

第壹部份：單一選擇題

一、詞彙與慣用語（15％）

說明：　第 1 至 15 題，每題選出最適當的一個選項，標示在答案卡之「選擇題答案區」。每題答對得 1 分，答錯倒扣 1/3 分，倒扣到本大題之實得分數為零為止。未答者，不給分亦不扣分。

1. Chinese parents are usually very _____ of their children. They want to make sure their children are safe and well taken care of all the time.
   (A) patient　　　(B) peculiar　　　(C) protective　　　(D) persuasive

2. On receiving my letter of complaint, the hotel manager sent me a written _____.
   (A) consent　　(B) scandal　　(C) lecture　　(D) apology

3. Jordan's performance _____ his teammates and they finally beat their opponents to win the championship.
   (A) signaled　　(B) promoted　　(C) opposed　　(D) inspired

4. Mr. Lin's comments were very difficult to follow because they were _____ related to the topic under discussion.
   (A) loosely　　(B) specifically　　(C) anxiously　　(D) typically

5. Jack came from a poor family, so his parents had to _____ many things to pay for his education.
   (A) inherit　　(B) qualify　　(C) sacrifice　　(D) purchase

6. The _____ of SARS has caused great inconvenience to many families in Taiwan.
   (A) destiny　　(B) contempt　　(C) outbreak　　(D) isolation

7. Victor's classmates are very _____ of him because he has just received a new cell phone for his birthday.
   (A) arrogant
   (B) envious
   (C) beloved
   (D) logical

8. Some people still believe, quite _____, that one can get AIDS by shaking hands with homosexuals.
   (A) hardly
   (B) consequently
   (C) mistakenly
   (D) generously

9. There are altogether 154 foreign students in this university, _____ a total of thirteen different countries.
   (A) constructing
   (B) representing
   (C) exploiting
   (D) participating

10. During a _____, many people become unemployed and very few new jobs are available.
   (A) recession
   (B) prediction
   (C) government
   (D) disappointment

11. Mr. and Mrs. Wang were worried about their baby girl because she _____ with the flu again.
   (A) put up
   (B) went forward
   (C) looked after
   (D) came down

12. Spider Man star Tobey Maguire may be forced to _____ the sequel because of his back injury.
   (A) back out of
   (B) set foot in
   (C) make use of
   (D) keep up with

13. Because many students were kept _____ about the lecture, the attendance was much smaller than expected.
   (A) out of order
   (B) on thin ice
   (C) without a doubt
   (D) in the dark

14. All his hard work in the past three years has _____ now that the student has graduated with top honors.
    (A) given in   (B) paid off
    (C) fallen apart   (D) come about

15. It's quite safe here in the city. You don't need to _____ when taking a walk —— even at night.
    (A) watch your back   (B) slip your mind
    (C) break your neck   (D) catch your breath

二、綜合測驗（15％）

說明： 第 16 至 30 題，每題一個空格。請依文意選出最適當的一個選項，標示在答案卡之「選擇題答案區」。每題答對得 1 分，答錯倒扣 1/3 分。倒扣到本大題之實得分數爲零爲止。未答者，不給分亦不扣分。

第 16 至 23 題爲題組

　　The Internet has replaced books as a major source of information for Taiwanese primary school students, according to a recent survey. The survey was conducted last December, and it ___16___ that 77 percent of the students considered the Internet to be the most convenient source of information. 14 percent of the respondents said they often ___17___ books for information instead of going online. Of all the students surveyed, 27 percent said they had never used the ___18___.

　　The survey randomly selected 4,200 students in 26 primary schools in ___19___ parts of Taiwan to investigate their reading habits. A total of 4,017 questionnaires were properly ___20___ by the respondents.

　　According to the survey, five percent of the school children indicated that they did not read any ___21___ reading materials. Of those who read such materials, 25 percent liked to read comics, 20 percent fables and stories, 15 percent books on natural sciences, and 12.3 percent books

on technology. The survey ___22___ indicated that 45 percent of the
school children read at least five books every month; ___23___ 45 percent
of them read less than three per month.

16. (A) took　　　(B) put　　　(C) knew　　　(D) found
17. (A) used up　(B) went off　(C) turned to　(D) made into
18. (A) Net　　　(B) survey　　(C) books　　　(D) respondents
19. (A) various　(B) convenient　(C) youthful　(D) routine
20. (A) taken in　(B) given off　(C) filled out　(D) picked on
21. (A) story　　(B) comic　　　(C) technology　(D) extracurricular
22. (A) thus　　　(B) further　　(C) otherwise　(D) for instance
23. (A) other　　(B) another　　(C) others'　　(D) the other's

第 24 至 30 題為題組

　　Science makes possible the use of new materials and new methods
of producing objects. For example, some 20th-century chairs are made
of steel and plastic. These materials, ___24___ , were undreamed of in
the 18th century.

　　As new materials develop, one invention often ___25___ another.
Steel, for instance, was developed by engineers in the 19th century.
___26___ its strength, steel soon became a useful building material.
___27___ steel construction, buildings could then have a great many
stories. But no one could be expected to walk up 8, 10, or 30 flights of
___28___ . Therefore, to make tall buildings more accessible to their
users, the elevator ___29___ . By providing much-needed space in a
world ___30___ people, tall buildings have solved a great problem of
the city and have completely changed our way of life.

24. (A) finally　　(B) however　　(C) in addition　　(D) as a result

25. (A) leads to　　(B) finds out　　(C) succeeds in　　(D) agrees with

26. (A) Prior to　　(B) Because of　　(C) In spite of　　(D) Not to mention

27. (A) In　　(B) For　　(C) With　　(D) Beside

28. (A) attendants　　(B) crews　　(C) planes　　(D) stairs

29. (A) invented　　　　　　(B) had invented
    (C) was invented　　　　(D) would have invented

30. (A) crowded with　　　　(B) jammed on
    (C) growing up　　　　　(D) increasing by

三、文意選填（10％）

說明：　第 31 至 40 題，每題一個空格。請依文意在文章後所提供的 (A) 到 (J)
　　　　選項中分別選出最適當者，並將其字母代號標示在答案卡之「選擇題答
　　　　案區」。每題答對得 1 分，答錯倒扣 1/9 分，倒扣到本大題之實得分數
　　　　為零為止。未答者，不給分亦不扣分。

第 31 至 40 題為題組

There are more than 50 different kinds of kangaroos in the world today. The smallest ones are only five centimeters tall but the biggest are more than two meters. Kangaroos cannot walk or run. They ___31___ jump. The best time to see kangaroos ___32___ is the evening and early morning. They spend the daytime ___33___ in the shade.

Straight after they are born, the joeys (baby kangaroos), which are only about two-and-a-half centimeters long, have to drag themselves to their mother's ___34___. They find their way there by ___35___ the pattern of their mother's hairs. They stay in the pouch ___36___ they are eight months old. After that, they leave home ___37___. Sometimes the joeys aren't too ___38___ on making their way in the big wide world. A 50 pound joey, for example, was once found still living in its mother's pouch.

Have you ever ___39___ why these animals are called "kangaroos"? Well, according to one story, when Captain Cook landed in Australia and heard the aborigines calling these ___40___ animals "Kangooroo," he wrote the name down as "kangaroo." That's how this animal got its name.

(A) keen   (B) following   (C) for good   (D) in action

(E) wondered   (F) just   (G) snoozing   (H) pouch

(I) amazing   (J) until

四、篇章結構（10％）

說明： 第 41 至 45 題，每題一個空格。請依文意在文章後所提供的 (A) 到 (E) 選項中分別選出最適當者，填入空格中，使篇章結構清晰有條理，並將其英文字母代號標示在答案卡之「選擇題答案區」。每題答對得 2 分，答錯倒扣 0.5 分，倒扣到本大題之實得分數為零為止。未答者，不給分亦不扣分。

第 41 至 45 題為題組

Two years ago, when we just moved into town, my daughter Amy came to ask me whether she could keep a pet puppy, because she needed to write a science report on that topic. ___41___ After several trips to pet shops, we finally decided on a Dalmatian and named him Derek.

The first two months were encouraging. ___42___ When I cooked dinner, he would take a walk with our daughter; a few times, Derek miraculously found his way home when Amy got lost. To reward him, we allowed him to eat at the table or to sleep with us.

But problems soon began after the science report. Many times, the spoiled puppy ruined our meals. And I started to feel irritated when Derek licked my cheek at dawn. ___43___ Finally, I thought it was time to get rid of the animal.

I remember it was a Friday afternoon. I drove around for 10 minutes and left Derek in a park. ____44____ The next day, with the help of a map, I left the doggie 30 minutes away, but Derek beat me home again. So, on Sunday, I took him on a long drive, arbitrarily turning left and right and making U-turns. I did everything I could to throw off his sense of direction.

____45____ She said, "Yes. Derek is having dinner with me. Where are you?" "I was about to ask myself the same question," I replied. "Put Derek on the phone. I need directions home."

(A) But when I pulled into the driveway, there was the puppy.
(B) Hours later I called my daughter and asked if she saw Derek.
(C) One time, I even shouted at Derek when he unplugged my computer.
(D) Derek became part of our life and seemed to fit into our family routine.
(E) Without any experience in raising pets, my husband and I first felt reluctant but later gave in.

五、閱讀測驗（30％）

說明：　第 46 至 60 題，每題請分別根據各篇文章的文意選出最適當的一個選項，標示在答案卡之「選擇題答案區」。每題答對得 2 分，答錯倒扣 2/3 分，倒扣到本大題之實得分數爲零爲止。未答者，不給分亦不扣分。

第 46 至 49 題爲題組

There is a lot to see and do in Bangkok if you can tolerate the traffic, noise, heat (in the hot season), floods (in the rainy season), and somewhat polluted air. The city is incredibly urbanized, but beneath its modern appearance lies an unmistakable Thai-ness. To say that Bangkok is not Thailand, as has been claimed by some, is like saying that New York is not America, Paris is not France, or London is not England. Bangkok caters to diverse interests: there are temples, museums and other historic sites for those interested in traditional Thai culture; an endless variety of good restaurants, clubs, international cultural and social events, as well as movies in several different languages and a modern art institute for those seeking contemporary Krung Thep, the Thai name for Bangkok. As William Warren, an American author now living in Thailand, has said, "The gift Bangkok offers me is the assurance I will never be bored."

46. What is the main idea of this passage?
    (A) The city of Bangkok is urbanized but it is also rich in traditional Thai culture.
    (B) Visitors to Bangkok might find the weather, the heat, and floods unbearable.
    (C) Bangkok is an international city, just like Paris, London, and New York.
    (D) There are a variety of restaurants and social events in Bangkok.

47. Which of the following is NOT mentioned in the passage as one of the problems that visitors might find in Bangkok?
    (A) Heavy traffic   (B) Dirty air
    (C) Hot weather   (D) Dense population

48. What can we infer from William Warren's comment on Bangkok at the end of the passage?
    (A) Bangkok is a place where visitors can buy many souvenirs.
    (B) Bangkok offers attractive travel insurance to visitors.
    (C) Bangkok is an exciting place to visit.
    (D) Bangkok reminds Warren of home.

49. According to the passage, which of the following places is the
    LAST CHOICE for a visitor who wishes to explore modern Krung
    Thep?
    (A) Temples　　　　　　　　(B) Restaurants
    (C) The art institute　　　　　(D) Movie theaters

第 50 至 53 題爲題組

　　Michael Jackson provoked new concerns for his children's welfare
after he took them to the zoo covered in strange, bright-colored veils "to
protect them from kidnappers."

　　The pop star was pictured walking through Berlin Zoo with his two
elder children, Prince Michael, five, and Paris, four.

　　Both youngsters had their faces completely covered in outlandish
see-through burgundy-colored veils —— a choice of dress which
Jackson's aides said was designed to disguise the youngsters to protect
them from being kidnapped.　But as they wandered through the zoo with
their famous father, it seemed an unlikely explanation.

　　The rare appearance came just 24 hours after the singer provoked
outrage by dangling his youngest child, baby Prince Michael II, from
the fourth-floor balcony of a hotel window.

　　The nine-month-old boy's face was covered with a white cloth,
which was again said to be a **precautionary measure** taken by the star
to protect his children from becoming kidnappers' targets.

　　As people across the world criticized Jackson as an unfit father, child
protection groups called on German police to take action against the pop
legend.　However, Berlin prosecutors said they were not investigating
the incident, and an inquiry could only be opened if a complaint was
filed against Jackson.

50. This passage is most likely taken from a _____.
    (A) personal letter   (B) travel brochure
    (C) research paper   (D) newspaper report

51. What did Michael Jackson do at Berlin Zoo that caught people's attention?
    (A) He was involved in the kidnapping of two children named Prince and Paris.
    (B) He covered his children in veils to prevent them from being kidnapped.
    (C) He tried to protect his children from kidnappers by hiding them in the zoo.
    (D) He wandered through the zoo with his face covered in a strange cloth.

52. What does "precautionary measure" mean in the passage?
    (A) A calculation done with great precision.
    (B) A plan carefully designed to achieve a goal.
    (C) A step taken to avoid some bad consequences.
    (D) A mathematical problem prepared with extreme care.

53. According to the passage, German police could take action against Michael Jackson only when _____.
    (A) Berlin prosecutors were investigated
    (B) more veils were used to cover the youngsters
    (C) an official complaint was made against him
    (D) child protection groups called the police again

第 54 至 60 題爲題組

　　Since the terrorist attack on America on September 11, hundreds of new security measures have been put in place to make Americans safer, or at least feel safer. Hotels and corporate offices now require guests to present a photo ID at check-ins and entrances. Airlines refuse to let passengers carry razor blades, scissors, or screwdrivers on flights.

At least one surefire way exists to improve security and protect personal privacy: positive passenger bag-matching. It would require that no checked bag be transported on a plane if its owner doesn't board the flight. Bag-matching became standard practice in Europe and Asia in the 1980s after suitcase bombs brought down Pan Am Flight 103 over Lockerbie, Air India Flight 182 en route to London, and UTA Flight 772 to Paris. In all three cases, the terrorists weren't on board.

Yet, in the U.S., where security is now top priority, authorities have chosen to ignore bag-matching. Instead, the Transportation Safety Administration (TSA) has embraced largely untested electronic-detection systems that screen bags for bombs and other explosives. Critics charge that the TSA has overlooked such an obvious, sensible security measure because U.S. airlines have opposed bag-matching for years. They fear it might delay flights and persuade short-haul travelers to take a train or drive instead.

After September 11, bag-matching was back on the agenda. Yet, struggling airlines complained that implementing it on all domestic flights would drive them into bankruptcy. Such claims have zero merit, says Arnold Barnett, a former chair of the Federal Aviation Administration's technical team. In 1996, the team was asked to investigate the feasibility of bag-matching. In a 1997 experiment, which tested 11 airlines, 50 pairs of cities, 8,000 flights, and 750,000 passengers, Barnett showed that domestic bag-matching would cause delays averaging seven minutes on only one in seven flights and would require no reduction in flight schedules.

Barnett argues that bag-matching would deter bombers far more than electronic-detection systems. It ensures that the terrorist will proceed to the gate to board his plane. If, while he's waiting, detection devices reveal a bomb, **he** could be quickly located and arrested. "The combination of bag-matching and explosives detection could be far more potent than either measure on its own," Barnett wrote in a Dec. 17 letter to TSA chief. He received a thank-you note that contained no indication that the TSA is contemplating action.

54. According to the passage, Pan Am Flight 103, Air India Flight 182, and UTA Flight 772 were similar in that _____.
    (A) they were brought down by terrorist attacks
    (B) they crashed because some terrorists were on board
    (C) they were the only international flights that crashed in 1980
    (D) they crashed because they didn't follow airline security measures

55. In which paragraph can the definition of bag-matching be found?
    (A) Paragraph 1   (B) Paragraph 2
    (C) Paragraph 3   (D) Paragraph 4

56. Which of the following is one of the reasons that airlines were unwilling to implement bag-matching on their flights?
    (A) Electronic-detection systems cost less than bag-matching.
    (B) Electronic-detection systems worked better in preventing hijacking.
    (C) Bag-matching would delay flights and discourage people from taking airplanes.
    (D) Bag-matching would invade passengers' privacy rather than ensure their security.

57. What is one important finding of Barnett's experiment on bag-matching and flight schedules?
    (A) Bag-matching on domestic flights resulted in seven-minute delays in only one-seventh of the flights.
    (B) Bag-matching forced airlines to reduce their schedules and to sacrifice the quality of their service.
    (C) Bag-matching, when tested on 11 airlines, proved to be ineffective and inconvenient for passengers.
    (D) Bag-matching caused domestic flights to change their schedules and to reduce their frequency of service.

58. The pronoun **he** (*he could be…*) in the last paragraph most likely refers to _____.
    (A) Arnold Barnett   (B) a potential terrorist
    (C) a security guard at the gate
    (D) an ordinary passenger boarding the plane

59. What can we infer from the last sentence in the passage (*He received a thank-you note that contained no indication that the TSA is contemplating action.*)?
    (A) The TSA appreciated Barnett's help and welcomed his suggestions.
    (B) The TSA took Barnett's advice seriously and put it into practice.
    (C) The TSA invited Barnett to come to work with them.
    (D) The TSA did not plan to implement Barnett's ideas.

60. The passage was written mainly to _____.
    (A) point out the necessary trade-offs between privacy and security
    (B) highlight the TSA's mission to improve airline security
    (C) argue for bag-matching as an effective security measure
    (D) advocate the use of electronic-detection systems

第貳部份：非選擇題

英文作文（20％）

說明： 1. 依提示在「答案卷」上寫一篇英文作文。

2. 文長約 120 至 150 個單詞左右。

3. 未依提示書寫各段主題句扣兩分。

提示： 小考、段考、複習考、畢業考、甚至校外其它各種大大小小的考試，已成為高中學生生活中不可或缺的一部份。請寫一篇 120 至 150 個單詞左右的英文作文，文分兩段，第一段以 Exams of all kinds have become a necessary part of my high school life. 為主題句；第二段則以 The most unforgettable exam I have ever taken is... 為開頭並加以發展。

❦ 九十二年度指定科目考試英文科試題詳解 ❦

第壹部分：單一選擇題

一、詞彙與慣用語：

1. (**C**) Chinese parents are usually very <u>protective</u> of their children.
   They want to make sure their children are safe and well taken
   care of all the time.
   中國的父母通常很<u>保護</u>他們的小孩。他們要確定自己的小孩是安全
   的，並且隨時受到良好的照顧。
   - (A) patient (ˈpeʃənt) *adj.* 有耐心的
   - (B) peculiar (pɪˈkjuljə) *adj.* 獨特的
   - (C) ***protective*** (prəˈtɛktɪv) *adj.* 保護的
   - (D) persuasive (pəˈswesɪv) *adj.* 有說服力的

   make sure 確定　　***take care of*** 照顧
   all the time 隨時；總是

2. (**D**) On receiving my letter of complaint, the hotel manager sent me a
   written <u>apology</u>.
   飯店的經理一收到我的抱怨信，就寄了一封<u>道歉</u>信給我。
   - (A) consent (kənˈsɛnt) *n.* 同意
   - (B) scandal (ˈskændḷ) *n.* 醜聞
   - (C) lecture (ˈlɛktʃə) *n.* 演講
   - (D) ***apology*** (əˈpɑlədʒɪ) *n.* 道歉

   complaint (kəmˈplent) *n.* 抱怨　　***a written apology*** 道歉信

3. (**D**) Jordan's performance <u>inspired</u> his teammates and they finally beat
   their opponents to win the championship.
   喬登的表現<u>激勵</u>了他的隊友，所以他們最後擊敗了對手，贏得冠軍。
   - (A) signal (ˈsɪgnḷ) *v.* 發信號
   - (B) promote (prəˈmot) *v.* 促進；升遷
   - (C) oppose (əˈpoz) *v.* 反對
   - (D) ***inspire*** (ɪnˈspaɪr) *v.* 激勵；鼓舞

   performance (pəˈfɔrməns) *n.* 表現
   teammate (ˈtimˌmet) *n.* 隊友　　beat (bit) *v.* 擊敗
   opponent (əˈponənt) *n.* 對手
   championship (ˈtʃæmpɪənˌʃɪp) *n.* 冠軍

4. (**A**) Mr. Lin's comments were very difficult to follow because they were <u>loosely</u> related to the topic under discussion.
林先生的評論很難了解，因爲它們和討論的主題<u>沒有多大</u>關聯。

 (A) *loosely* (ˋluslɪ) *adv.* 鬆散地；不嚴謹地
 (B) specifically (spɪˋsɪfɪk̩lɪ) *adv.* 明確地
 (C) anxiously (ˋæŋkʃəslɪ) *adv.* 焦慮地；不安地
 (D) typically (ˋtɪpɪk̩lɪ) *adv.* 典型地

 comment (ˋkɑmɛnt) *n.* 評論 follow (ˋfɑlo) *v.* 聽得懂；了解
 be related to～ 和～有關聯 topic (ˋtɑpɪk) *n.* 主題
 under discussion 討論中的

5. (**C**) Jack came from a poor family, so his parents had to <u>sacrifice</u> many things to pay for his education. 傑克來自貧窮的家庭，所以他的父母必須<u>犧牲</u>很多東西，來支付他的教育費。

 (A) inherit (ɪnˋhɛrɪt) *v.* 繼承
 (B) qualify (ˋkwɑlə͵faɪ) *v.* 使合格
 (C) *sacrifice* (ˋsækrə͵faɪs) *v.* 犧牲
 (D) purchase (ˋpɝtʃəs) *v.* 購買

6. (**C**) The <u>outbreak</u> of SARS has caused great inconvenience to many families in Taiwan. 嚴重急性呼吸道症候群的<u>爆發</u>，已經給台灣許多家庭帶來很大的不便。

 (A) destiny (ˋdɛstənɪ) *n.* 命運 (B) contempt (kənˋtɛmpt) *n.* 輕視
 (C) *outbreak* (ˋaʊt͵brek) *n.* 爆發 (D) isolation (͵aɪsḷˋeʃən) *n.* 孤立
 SARS 嚴重急性呼吸道症候群 (= *Severe Acute Respiratory Syndrome*)
 inconvenience (͵ɪnkənˋvinjəns) *n.* 不便；麻煩

7. (**B**) Victor's classmates are very <u>envious</u> of him because he has just received a new cell phone for his birthday.
威克特的同學非常<u>羨慕</u>他，因爲他剛收到新的手機，做爲生日禮物。

 (A) arrogant (ˋærəgənt) *adj.* 傲慢的
 (B) *envious* (ˋɛnvɪəs) *adj.* 羨慕的；嫉妒的
 (C) beloved (bɪˋlʌvɪd) *adj.* 深愛的；心愛的
 (D) logical (ˋlɑdʒɪk̩l) *adj.* 合邏輯的

8. (**C**) Some people still believe, quite <u>mistakenly</u>, that one can get AIDS
   by shaking hands with homosexuals.
   有些人仍然錯信，我們會因和同性戀者握手，而感染愛滋病。
   (A) hardly〔'hɑrdlɪ〕*adv.* 幾乎不
   (B) consequently〔'kɑnsə,kwɛntlɪ〕*adv.* 因此
   (C) *mistakenly*〔mə'stekənlɪ〕*adv.* 錯誤地
   (D) generously〔'dʒɛnərəslɪ〕*adv.* 慷慨地
   AIDS〔edz〕*n.* 後天免疫不全症候群；愛滋病
   shake hands 握手
   homosexual〔,homə'sɛkʃuəl〕*n.* 同性戀者

9. (**B**) There are altogether 154 foreign students in this university,
   <u>representing</u> a total of thirteen different countries.
   這所大學總計有一百五十四位外籍學生，一共代表了十三個不同
   的國家。
   (A) construct〔kən'strʌkt〕*v.* 建造
   (B) *represent*〔,rɛprɪ'zɛnt〕*v.* 代表
   (C) exploit〔ɪk'splɔɪt〕*v.* 開發
   (D) participate〔pɑr'tɪsə,pet〕*v.* 參加
   altogether〔,ɔltə'gɛðɚ〕*adv.* 總計　　　total〔'totl̩〕*n.* 總數

10. (**A**) During a <u>recession</u>, many people become unemployed and very
    few new jobs are available.
    在不景氣的時候，許多人失業，而且新工作很難找。
    (A) *recession*〔rɪ'sɛʃən〕*n.* 不景氣
    (B) prediction〔prɪ'dɪkʃən〕*n.* 預測
    (C) government〔'gʌvɚnmənt〕*n.* 政府
    (D) disappointment〔,dɪsə'pɔɪntmənt〕*n.* 失望
    unemployed〔,ʌnɪm'plɔɪd〕*adj.* 失業的
    available〔ə'veləbl̩〕*adj.* 可獲得的

11. (**D**) Mr. and Mrs. Wang were worried about their baby girl because she <u>came down with</u> the flu again.

王先生和王太太很擔心他們的小女嬰，因為她又<u>罹患</u>流行性感冒了。

    (A) put up with　忍受　 (B) go forward　前進；進步

    (C) look after　照顧　 (D) *come down with*　罹患（疾病）

be worried about　擔心　 flu〔flu〕*n.* 流行性感冒（= *influenza*）

12. (**A**) Spider Man star Tobey Maguire may be forced to <u>back out of</u> the sequel because of his back injury.

飾演蜘蛛人的明星陶比麥奎爾，可能會因為背部受傷，而被迫<u>退出</u>續集。

    (A) *back out of*　退出；放棄　(B) set foot in　踏進；<u>登陸</u>

    (C) make use of　利用　 (D) keep up with　趕上

spider〔'spaɪdɚ〕*n.* 蜘蛛　 force〔fors〕*v.* 強迫

sequel〔'sikwəl〕*n.* 續集　 injury〔'ɪndʒərɪ〕*n.* 傷

13. (**D**) Because many students were kept <u>in the dark</u> about the lecture, the attendance was much smaller than expected.

因為很多學生<u>不知道</u>有這場演講，所以出席的人數比預期少很多。

    (A) out of order　故障；順序混亂

    (B) on thin ice　如履薄冰；在危險的情況中

    (C) without a doubt　無疑地

    (D) *in the dark*　不知道　 *keep sb. in the dark*　隱瞞某人

attendance〔ə'tɛndəns〕*n.* 出席人數

expect〔ɪk'spɛkt〕*v.* 預期；期待

14. (**B**) All his hard work in the past three years has <u>paid off</u> now that the student has graduated with top honors.

這名學生過去三年一切的努力<u>有了成果</u>，因為他以最優等成績畢業。

    (A) give in　屈服　 (B) *pay off*　有了成果

    (C) fall apart　瓦解；失敗　(D) come about　發生（= *happen*）

now that　因為；既然　 graduate〔'grædʒʊ,et〕*v.* 畢業

honors〔'ɑnɚz〕*n.pl.* 優等成績（常用複數形）

15. (**A**) It's quite safe here in the city. You don't need to <u>watch your back</u>
　　when taking a walk——even at night.

　　在這個城市裡非常安全。即使在晚上散步的時候，也不必<u>小心背後</u>。

　　(A) ***watch one's back*** 小心背後　　(B) slip *one's* mind 被某人遺忘
　　(C) break *one's* neck 極度地努力；拼命
　　(D) catch *one's* breath 喘氣；鬆一口氣

　　take a walk 散步

二、綜合測驗：

<u>第 16 至 23 題為題組</u>

　　The Internet has replaced books as a major source of information for
Taiwanese primary school students, according to a recent survey. The
survey was conducted last December, and it <u>found</u> that 77 percent of the
　　　　　　　　　　　　　　　　　　　　　　16
students considered the Internet to be the most convenient source of
information. 14 percent of the respondents said they often <u>turned to</u> books
　　　　　　　　　　　　　　　　　　　　　　　　　　　17
for information instead of going online. Of all the students surveyed, 27
percent said they had never used the <u>Net</u>.
　　　　　　　　　　　　　　　　　18

　　根據一項最近的調查指出，網際網路已取代書本，成為台灣小學生取得資
訊的主要來源。這項調查是去年十二月進行的，調查中發現，百分之七十七的
學生認為，網際網路是最方便的資訊來源。百分之十四的回覆者說，他們找資
料還是經常查閱書本，而不會上網。在所有接受調查的學生當中，百分之二十
七的人說，他們從未使用過網際網路。

　　　　Internet〔'ɪntɚ͵nɛt〕*n.* 網際網路（ = *Net* = *Web*）
　　　　replace〔rɪ'ples〕*v.* 取代　　major〔'medʒɚ〕*adj.* 主要的
　　　　source〔sors〕*n.* 來源　　***primary school*** 小學
　　　　recent〔'risnt〕*adj.* 最近的　　survey〔'sɝve〕*n.*〔sɚ've〕*v.* 調查
　　　　conduct〔kən'dʌkt〕*v.* 進行；做
　　　　respondent〔rɪ'spɑndənt〕*n.* 回覆者　　***instead of*** 而不是

16. (**D**) 依句意，調查「發現」很多人使用網際網路，選 (D) ***found***。

17. (**C**) (A) use up 用完　(B) go off 爆炸；(鬧鐘)響
(C) ***turn to*** 求助(人)；查詢(書籍)
(D) make A into B 把 A 製成 B

18. (**A**) 依前後句意，應是百分之二十七的人未曾使用過「網際網路」，故選 (A) ***Net***，等於 Internet。

The survey randomly selected 4,200 students in 26 primary schools in various (19) parts of Taiwan to investigate their reading habits. A total of 4,017 questionnaires were properly filled out (20) by the respondents.

這項調查隨機挑選全台灣各地區，二十六所小學的四千兩百名學生，來調查他們的閱讀習慣。回覆者正確填寫的有效問卷，總共有四千零一十七件。

randomly〔ˈrændəmlɪ〕*adv.* 隨機地；任意地
investigate〔ɪnˈvɛstəˌget〕*v.* 調查　total〔ˈtotl〕*n.* 總數
questionnaire〔ˌkwɛstʃənˈɛr〕*n.* 問卷調查表
properly〔ˈprɑpɚlɪ〕*adv.* 適當地；正確地

19. (**A**) 做問卷調查，當然要挑選全台灣「各個」地區的學生，故選 (A) ***various***〔ˈvɛrɪəs〕*adj.* 各種不同的。而 (B) 方便的，(C) youthful〔ˈjuθfəl〕*adj.* 年輕的，(D) routine〔ruˈtin〕*adj.* 例行的，均不合句意。

20. (**C**) (A) take in 帶進；收容　(B) give off 發出(光、煙、味等)
(C) ***fill out*** 填寫　(D) pick on 選擇

According to the survey, five percent of the school children indicated that they did not read any extracurricular (21) reading materials. Of those who read such materials, 25 percent liked to read comics, 20 percent fables and stories, 15 percent books on natural sciences, and 12.3 percent books on technology. The survey further (22) indicated that 45 percent of the school children read at least five books every month; another (23) 45 percent of them read less than three per month.

　　根據此項調查，百分之五的學生指出，他們沒有閱讀任何的課外讀物。而在閱讀課外讀物的學生當中，百分之二十五喜歡看漫畫書，百分之二十喜歡閱讀寓言和故事，百分之十五喜歡閱讀有關自然科學的書，還有百分之十二點三喜歡閱讀有關科技類的書。這項調查進一步指出，有百分之四十五的學生，每個月至少讀五本書；另外有百分之四十五，每個月讀不到三本書。

indicate〔ˈɪndəˌket〕v. 指出　　material〔məˈtɪrɪəl〕n. 材料；資料
comics〔ˈkɑmɪks〕n. pl. 漫畫　　fable〔ˈfebḷ〕n. 寓言
natural science 自然科學　　technology〔tɛkˈnɑlədʒɪ〕n. 科技

21.（**D**）依句意，學生閱讀的材料，包括漫畫、寓言故事等，故應指「課外」讀物，選 (D) ***extracurricular***〔ˌɛkstrəkəˈrɪkjələ〕adj. 課外的。
　　而 (A) 故事，(B) 漫畫，(C) 科技，都只是課外讀物的一部分，故不合。

22.（**B**）(A) thus〔ðʌs〕adv. 因此
　　(B) ***further***〔ˈfɝðə〕adv. 更進一步地
　　(C) otherwise〔ˈʌðəˌwaɪz〕adv. 否則
　　(D) for instance　例如

23.（**B**）句子前面已提到百分之四十五，要再提到「另一個」百分之四十五，應用 ***another***，故選 (B)。

第 24 至 30 題為題組

　　Science makes possible the use of new materials and new methods of producing objects. For example, some 20th-century chairs are made of steel and plastic. These materials, <u>however</u>, were undreamed of in the 18th century.
　　　　　　　　　　　　　　　　　　　　24
　　As new materials develop, one invention often <u>leads to</u> another. Steel,
　　　　　　　　　　　　　　　　　　25
for instance, was developed by engineers in the 19th century. <u>Because of</u>
　　　　　　　　　　　　　　　　　　　　　　　　　26
its strength, steel soon became a useful building material. <u>With</u> steel
　　　　　　　　　　　　　　　　　　　　　　　27
construction, buildings could then have a great many stories. But no one could be expected to walk up 8, 10, or 30 flights of <u>stairs</u>. Therefore, to
　　　　　　　　　　　　　　　　　　　　　　28

make tall buildings more accessible to their users, the elevator <u>was invented</u>.
29

By providing much-needed space in a world <u>crowed with</u> people, tall
30

buildings have solved a great problem of the city and have completely
changed our way of life.

　　科學使人們得以使用新的材料，以及新的方法來製造東西。例如，某些二十世紀的椅子，是用鋼鐵和塑膠製成的。然而，這些材料在十八世紀，可是作夢都想不到的。

　　當新的材料發展出來時，常常是一個發明接著一個地出現。舉例來說，鋼鐵是由十九世紀的科學家發明出來的。因其強度甚高，鋼鐵很快就變成一種非常有用的建築材料。用鋼鐵結構，建築物可以有很多層樓。但是沒有人能爬八段、十段、或是三十段樓梯。因此，為了讓高樓更容易被人使用，電梯就被發明出來了。藉由提供這個擠滿人的世界所極度需要的空間，高樓解決了城市的一大問題，也完全改變了我們的生活方式。

material〔məˋtɪrɪəl〕n. 材料　　object〔ˋɑbdʒɪkt〕n. 東西；物品
undreamed of〔ʌnˋdrimd ɑv〕adj. 作夢都想不到的
develop〔dɪˋvɛləp〕v. 發展　　strength〔strɛŋθ〕n. 強度
construction〔kənˋstrʌkʃən〕n. 建造
a great many 很多的　　story〔ˋstorɪ〕n. 樓層
flight〔flaɪt〕n.（樓梯）一段
accessible〔ækˋsɛsəbḷ〕adj. 可利用的
elevator〔ˋɛlə͵vetɚ〕n. 電梯
completely〔kəmˋplitlɪ〕adv. 完全地

24.（**B**）依句意，選 (B) ***however***「然而」。而 (A) finally「最後」，(C) in addition「此外」，(D) as a result「因此」，均不合句意。

25.（**A**）(A) ***lead to*** 導致　　　　　　(B) find out　發現；找出
　　　　　(C) succeed in　成功地～　　　(D) agree with　同意

26.（**B**）(A) prior to　在～之前　　　　　(B) ***because of*** 因為
　　　　　(C) in spite of　儘管　　　　　(D) not to mention　更不用說

27.（**C**）依句意，選 (C) ***With***「用；以」。

28.（ **D** ）(A) attendant〔ə'tɛndənt〕*n.* 服務員；出席者

(B) crew〔kru〕*n.*（船、飛機、列車的）全體工作人員

(D) plane〔plen〕*n.* 飛機

(D) *stair*〔stɛr〕*n.* 樓梯

29.（ **C** ）依句意，樓梯是「被發明」的，故須用被動語態，選 (C) *was invented*。

30.（ **A** ）依句意，這個「擠滿」人的世界，故選 (A) *crowded with*。

(B) jam on　壓緊；用力踩

(C) grow up　長大

(D) increase by～　增加了～

三、文意選填：

<u>第 31 至 40 題為題組</u>

　　There are more than 50 different kinds of kangaroos in the world today.　The smallest ones are only five centimeters tall but the biggest are more than two meters.　Kangaroos cannot walk or run.　They <u>just</u> jump.
31

The best time to see kangaroos <u>in action</u> is the evening and early morning.
32

They spend the daytime <u>snoozing</u> in the shade.
33

　　現在全世界，有五十多種不同種類的袋鼠。最小的只有五公分高，但最大的卻超過兩公尺。袋鼠不會走路或跑步。牠們只會跳。要看袋鼠活動，最好的時間是傍晚或一大清早。牠們白天都躲在陰涼處打瞌睡。

　　　kangaroo〔ˌkæŋgə'ru〕*n.* 袋鼠　　　today〔tə'de〕*adv.* 現在
　　　centimeter〔'sɛntəˌmitə〕*n.* 公分
　　　meter〔'mitə〕*n.* 公尺　　　jump〔dʒʌmp〕*v.* 跳
　　　daytime〔'deˌtaɪm〕*n.* 白天　　　shade〔ʃed〕*n.* 陰暗處

31.（ **F** ）依句意，袋鼠「只」會跳，選 (F) *just*。

32.（ **D** ）*in action*　活動中

33. (**G**) 依句意，袋鼠會在陰涼處「打瞌睡」，選 (G) *snoozing*。
　　snooze〔snuz〕*v.* 打瞌睡

　　Straight after they are born, the joeys (baby kangaroos), which are only about two-and-a-half centimeters long, have to drag themselves to their mother's <u>pouch</u>.　They find their way there by <u>following</u> the pattern of their
　　　　　　 34　　　　　　　　　　　　　　　 35
mother's hairs.　They stay in the pouch <u>until</u> they are eight months old.
　　　　　　　　　　　　　　　　　 36
After that, they leave home <u>for good</u>.　Sometimes the joeys aren't too <u>keen</u>
　　　　　　　　　　 37　　　　　　　　　　　　　　　　　　　　 38
on making their way in the big wide world.　A 50 pound joey, for example, was once found still living in its mother's pouch.

　　小袋鼠出生之後，大約只有二點五公分長，必須費力緩慢地爬到媽媽的育兒袋中。牠們藉由跟隨著媽媽的毛髮紋路，而設法到達那裡。牠們會待在育兒袋裡，直到八個月大。之後，牠們就會永遠離開牠們的家。有時候，小袋鼠並不太熱衷於在廣大的世界裡前進。舉例來說，一隻五十磅的小袋鼠，就曾經被人發現，仍然住在媽媽的育兒袋裡。

　　　　straight〔stret〕*adv.* 馬上　　　joey〔'dʒɔɪ〕*n.* 小袋鼠
　　　　drag〔dræg〕*v.* 使費力緩慢地行進
　　　　find one's way 設法到達；找到路
　　　　pattern〔'pætən〕*n.* 圖案　　　*make one's way* （辛苦地）前進
　　　　wide〔waɪd〕*adj.* 寬廣的　　　pound〔paʊnd〕*n.* 磅
　　　　once〔wʌns〕*adv.* 曾經

34. (**H**) *pouch*〔paʊtʃ〕*n.* 育兒袋

35. (**B**) 小袋鼠藉由「跟隨」媽媽的毛髮紋路，可以找到路，選 (B) *following*。

36. (**J**) 小袋鼠會待在媽媽的育兒袋，「直到」八個月大，選 (J) *until*。

37. (**C**) *for good* 永遠地

38. (**A**) *be keen on* 熱衷於

Have you ever <u>wondered</u> why these animals are called "kangaroos"?
　　　　　　　39
Well, according to one story, when Captain Cook landed in Australia and
heard the aborigines calling these <u>amazing</u> animals "Kangaroo," he wrote
　　　　　　　　　　　　　　　　40
the name down as "kangaroo." That's how this animal got its name.

　　你曾經想要知道，爲什麼這些動物叫做 "kangaroo" 嗎？嗯，根據一個故
事的說法，當庫克船長在澳洲登陸時，他聽到當地的原住民，叫這些驚人的動
物 "Kangaroo"，於是他就把這個名字寫下來，變成 "kangaroo"。那就是這個
動物名字的由來。

　　　　land〔 lænd 〕v. 登陸
　　　　Australia〔 ɔ'streljə 〕n. 澳洲
　　　　aborigine〔,æbə'rɪdʒɪni 〕n. 原住民

39. (**E**)　依句意，你曾經「想知道」，爲什麼這些動物要叫做 "kangaroo"嗎，
　　　選 (E) ***wondered***。　　　***wonder***〔'wʌndɚ 〕v. 想知道

40. (**I**)　依句意，澳洲的原住民，叫這些「驚人的」動物 "Kangaroo"，選 (I)
　　　amazing〔 ə'mezɪŋ 〕adj. 驚人的。

四、篇章結構：

第 41 至 45 題爲題組

　　Two years ago, when we just moved into town, my daughter Amy came
to ask me whether she could keep a pet puppy, because she needed to write a
science report on that topic. <u>**41** (E) Without any experience in raising pets, my
husband and I first felt reluctant but later gave in.</u> After several trips to pet
shops, we finally decided on a Dalmatian and named him Derek.

　　兩年前，當我們剛搬到鎮上時，我女兒艾咪跑來問我，她是否可以養一隻
小狗當寵物，因爲她必須寫一篇關於那個主題的科學報告。由於沒有任何養寵
物的經驗，我和我先生一開始並不願意這麼做，但之後我們屈服了。在逛過幾
次寵物店之後，我們終於決定養一隻大麥町，並爲牠取名叫戴瑞克。

　　　　keep〔 kip 〕v. 飼養　　　pet〔 pɛt 〕adj.（當作）寵物的
　　　　puppy〔'pʌpɪ 〕n. 小狗　　raise〔 rez 〕v. 飼養

reluctant〔rɪˋlʌktənt〕*adj.* 不情願的　　***give in*** 屈服

trip〔trɪp〕*n.* 走一趟　　　　***pet shop*** 寵物店

Dalmatian〔dælˋmeʃən〕*n.* 大麥町　　name〔nem〕*v.* 給～命名

The first two months were encouraging. [42] **(D) Derek became part of our** **life and seemed to fit into our family routine.** When I cooked dinner, he would take a walk with our daughter; a few times, Derek miraculously found his way home when Amy got lost. To reward him, we allowed him to eat at the table or to sleep with us.

　　前兩個月非常順利。戴瑞克成為我們生活的一部份，並且似乎頗能適應我們家的日常生活。當我在煮飯時，牠會和我女兒去散步；有幾次，當艾咪迷路時，戴瑞克都能奇蹟似地找到回家的路。為了獎賞牠，我們允許牠在餐桌上和我們吃飯，或和我們一起睡覺。

encouraging〔ɪnˋkɝɪdʒɪŋ〕*adj.* 令人鼓舞的

fit into 符合；適應　　routine〔ruˋtin〕*n.* 日常的生活；例行公事

miraculously〔məˋrækjələslɪ〕*adv.* 奇蹟似地；不可思議地

get lost 迷路　　reward〔rɪˋwɔrd〕*v.* 獎賞；報酬

But problems soon began after the science report. Many times, the spoiled puppy ruined our meals. And I started to feel irritated when Derek licked my cheek at dawn. [43] **(C) One time, I even shouted at Derek when he** **unplugged my computer.** Finally, I thought it was time to get rid of the animal.

　　但在科學報告做完之後，問題很快就出現了。有好幾次，這隻被寵壞的小狗會破壞我們用餐。戴瑞克一大早就舔我的臉頰，讓我開始感到不高興。有一次，當戴瑞克拔掉我電腦的插頭時，我甚至對牠吼叫。到最後，我認為該是擺脫這隻狗的時候了。

spoiled〔spɔɪld〕*adj.* 被寵壞的　　ruin〔ˋruɪn〕*v.* 破壞

irritated〔ˋɪrəˏtetɪd〕*adj.* 不高興的　　lick〔lɪk〕*v.* 舔

cheek〔tʃik〕*n.* 臉頰　　***at dawn*** 黎明時；一大早

shout〔ʃaut〕*v.* 吼叫　　unplug〔ʌnˋplʌg〕*v.* 拔掉插頭

get rid of 擺脫；丟棄

I remember it was a Friday afternoon. I drove around for 10 minutes and left Derek in a park. **44 (A) But when I pulled into the driveway, there was the puppy.** The next day, with the help of a map, I left the doggie 30 minutes away, but Derek beat me home again. So, on Sunday, I took him on a long drive, arbitrarily turning left and right and making U-turns. I did everything I could to throw off his sense of direction.

　　我記得那是個星期五的下午。我開車開了大約十分鐘，然後把戴瑞克留在公園裡。但是當我駛進我們家的車道時，小狗就在那裡。隔天，我藉著地圖的輔助，把狗留在三十分鐘路程遠的地方，但是戴瑞克再度比我先到家。所以，在星期天，我帶著牠開了很長的一段路，我隨意地左轉、右轉，及迴轉。我盡可能使牠喪失方向感。

> *pull into* 把車子開靠近　　　driveway〔ˋdraɪˏwe〕*n.* 私人車道
> *with the help of* 藉由～的幫助　　doggie〔ˋdɔgɪ〕*n.* 小狗
> beat〔bit〕*v.* 搶在～之先；趕在～前面到達
> arbitrarily〔ˋɑrbəˏtrɛrəlɪ〕*adv.* 隨意地
> U-turn〔ˋjuˏtɝn〕*n.* U型轉彎；迴轉
> *throw off* 拋掉；擺脫掉　　*sense of direction* 方向感

45 (B) Hours later I called my daughter and asked if she saw Derek. She said, "Yes. Derek is having dinner with me. Where are you?" "I was about to ask myself the same question," I replied. "Put Derek on the phone. I need directions home."

　　幾小時後，我打電話問我女兒有沒有看見戴瑞克。她說：「有啊。牠和我正在吃晚餐。你在哪裡啊？」「我正想問我自己同樣的問題，」我回答。「叫戴瑞克聽電話。我需要知道回家的路。」

> *be about to V.* 將要；正要　　*put sb. on the phone* 叫某人聽電話
> directions〔dəˋrɛkʃəns〕*n.pl.* 指示方向（用複數形）

五、閱讀測驗：

第 46 至 49 題為題組

　　There is a lot to see and do in Bangkok if you can tolerate the traffic, noise, heat (in the hot season), floods (in the rainy season), and somewhat polluted air. The city is incredibly urbanized, but beneath its modern

appearance lies an unmistakable Thai-ness. To say that Bangkok is not
Thailand, as has been claimed by some, is like saying that New York is not
America, Paris is not France, or London is not England.

假如你可以忍受交通，噪音，炎熱（在炎熱的季節），水災（在雨季），和
有點污染的空氣，那麼在曼谷，你就有很多可以看和可以做的事。這個城市非
常都市化，但在它現代的外表下，仍保有明顯的泰國風。有些人一直宣稱，曼
谷不像泰國，這種說法就好比你宣稱紐約不像美國，巴黎不像法國，或是倫敦
不像英國一樣。

> tolerate〔ˋtɑləˏret〕v. 忍受　　heat〔hit〕n. 熱
> flood〔flʌd〕n. 水災　　somewhat〔ˋsʌmˏhwɑt〕adv. 有點
> polluted〔pəˋlutɪd〕adj. 污染的
> incredibly〔ɪnˋkrɛdəblɪ〕adv. 非常地；令人難以置信地
> urbanize〔ˋɝbənˏaɪz〕v. 使都市化　　beneath〔bɪˋniθ〕prep. 在…之下
> appearance〔əˋpɪrəns〕n. 外表　　lie〔laɪ〕v. 有
> unmistakable〔ˏʌnməˋstekəbḷ〕adj. 明顯的
> Thailand〔ˋtaɪlənd〕n. 泰國　　claim〔klem〕v. 宣稱

Bangkok caters to diverse interests: there are temples, museums and other
historic sites for those interested in traditional Thai culture; an endless
variety of good restaurants, clubs, international cultural and social events,
as well as movies in several different languages and a modern art institute
for those seeking contemporary Krung Thep, the Thai name for Bangkok.
As William Warren, an American author now living in Thailand, has said,
"The gift Bangkok offers me is the assurance I will never be bored."

曼谷有各種好玩的地方：有廟宇、博物館，和歷史古蹟，並提供給對泰國文化
感興趣的人，無限多種的好餐廳、俱樂部，和國際文化與社交的活動，以及好
幾種不同語言發音的電影，還有現代美術館，給那些想尋找現代 Krung Thep
（曼谷的泰文名字）的人士。就像一位現在居住於泰國的美國作家威廉・華倫
所說得，「曼谷提供給我最好的禮物，就是保證我絕不會覺得無聊。」

> ***cater to*** 提供；迎合　　diverse〔dəˋvɝs, daɪˋvɝs〕adj. 各種不同的
> interest〔ˋɪntrɪst〕n. 令人感興趣的事物或人
> temple〔ˋtɛmpḷ〕n. 廟宇　　historic〔hɪsˋtɔrɪk〕adj. 歷史的

site〔saɪt〕n. 地點　　***historic site*** 歷史古蹟
traditional〔trə'dɪʃənl〕*adj.* 傳統的
endless〔'ɛndlɪs〕*adj.* 無限的　　***a variety of*** 各式各樣的
institute〔'ɪnstə,tjut〕n. 會館；協會
contemporary〔kən'tɛmpə,rɛrɪ〕*adj.* 當代的
assurance〔ə'ʃʊrəns〕n. 保證

46.（**A**）本文的主旨爲何？

(A) 曼谷市具有都市風格，但是也有豐富的傳統泰國文化。
(B) 到曼谷的觀光客可能會覺得難以忍受它的天氣，熱度，和水災。
(C) 曼谷是國際性的都市，就像巴黎，倫敦，和紐約。
(D) 曼谷有各式各樣的餐廳和社交活動。

47.（**D**）下列何者不是本文所提到，觀光客可能會在曼谷遇到的問題？

(A) 擁擠的交通。　　　　　(B) 污濁的空氣。
(C) 炎熱的天氣。　　　　　(D) 密集的人口。

dense〔dɛns〕*adj.* 密集的　　population〔,pɑpjə'leʃən〕n. 人口

48.（**C**）在本文的結尾中，我們可以從威廉・華倫對於曼谷的評論推論出什麼？

(A) 曼谷是一個觀光客可以買到很多紀念品的地方。
(B) 曼谷提供觀光客具有吸引力的旅遊保險。
(C) 曼谷是一個引人入勝的觀光勝地。
(D) 曼谷讓華倫想起了家鄉。

infer〔ɪn'fɝ〕v. 推論　　comment〔'kɑmɛnt〕n. 評論
souvenir〔,suvə'nɪr〕n. 紀念品　　insurance〔ɪn'ʃʊrəns〕n. 保險
remind〔rɪ'maɪnd〕v. 使想起

49.（**A**）根據本文，下列何者是希望探索現代 Krung Thep 的觀光客，最不可能選擇的地方？

(A) 廟宇。　　　　　　　　(B) 餐廳。
(C) 美術館。　　　　　　　(D) 電影院。

explore〔ɪk'splor〕v. 探索

<u>第 50 至 53 題為題組</u>

Michael Jackson provoked new concerns for his children's welfare after he took them to the zoo covered in strange, bright-colored veils "to protect them from kidnappers."

The pop star was pictured walking through Berlin Zoo with his two elder children, Prince Michael, five, and Paris, four.

麥可傑克遜再度引發人們對他孩子權益的關切，這次是在他帶著小孩參觀動物園之後，因為他的孩子全都戴著奇怪的鮮豔面罩，這麼做的目的，據說是為了「保護他們免於綁架者的覬覦」。

這位流行巨星被人拍攝到，帶著兩個年齡較大的小孩參觀柏林動物園，一個是五歲的王子‧麥可，另一個是四歲的巴黎。

provoke〔prə'vok〕v. 引起　　concern〔kən'sɜn〕n. 關切
welfare〔'wɛl,fɛr〕n. 福利；權益　　cover〔'kʌvɚ〕v. 覆蓋
bright-colored〔'braɪt'kʌləd〕adj. 色彩鮮豔的
veil〔vel〕n. 面罩；面紗
protect sb. **from** sth. 保護某人免於…的傷害
kidnapper〔'kɪdnæpɚ〕n. 綁架者　　picture〔'pɪktʃɚ〕v. 拍照
Berlin〔bɜ'lɪn〕n. 柏林　　elder〔'ɛldɚ〕adj. 年長的

Both youngsters had their faces completely covered in outlandish see-through burgundy-colored veils—a choice of dress which Jackson's aides said was designed to disguise the youngsters to protect them from being kidnapped. But as they wandered through the zoo with their famous father, it seemed an unlikely explanation.

這兩個小孩的臉，整個都被怪異的透明酒紅色面罩蓋住——之所以選擇做這樣的打扮，根據麥可助理的說法，是為了不讓他的孩子曝光，保護他們不要被綁架。不過，由於這兩個小孩，和他們赫赫有名的父親在動物園四處走動，這種說法似乎難以成立。

youngster〔'jʌŋstɚ〕n. 小孩子
outlandish〔aut'lændɪʃ〕adj. 古怪的
see-through〔'si'θru〕adj. 透明的
burgundy〔'bɜgəndɪ〕n. 勃艮地紅葡萄酒
burgundy-colored〔'bɜgəndɪ'kʌləd〕adj. 酒紅色的

aide〔ed〕*n.* 助理　　***be designed to V.*** 目的是爲了～
disguise〔dɪsˋgaɪz〕*v.* 僞裝　　kidnap〔ˋkɪdnæp〕*v.* 綁架
wander〔ˋwɑndɚ〕*v.* 到處走　　unlikely〔ʌnˋlaɪklɪ〕*adj.* 不可能的
explanation〔͵ɛkspləˋneʃən〕*n.* 解釋；說明

The rare appearance came just 24 hours after the singer provoked
outrage by dangling his youngest child, baby Prince Michael II, from the
fourth-floor balcony of a hotel window.

The nine-month-old boy's face was covered with a white cloth, which
was again said to be a **precautionary measure** taken by the star to protect
his children from becoming kidnappers' targets.

　　這次罕見的公開露面，僅僅發生在這位流行歌手引發公憤的二十四小時之
後，當時他將他最小的小孩，也就是仍是嬰兒的巴黎‧麥可二世，在下榻旅館
四樓的窗戶陽台外晃來晃去。

　　而這位九個月大的男嬰臉上，蓋著一塊白布，據說這又是這位巨星所採取
的預防措施，目的是爲了不讓他的小孩成爲綁架者的目標。

rare〔rɛr〕*adj.* 罕見的　　appearance〔əˋpɪrəns〕*n.* 公開出現
outrage〔ˋaut͵redʒ〕*n.* 憤怒
dangle〔ˋdæŋgl̩〕*v.* (晃來晃去地) 吊著
balcony〔ˋbælkənɪ〕*n.* 陽台　　***be covered with*** 覆蓋著
cloth〔klɔθ〕*n.* 布　　***be said to V.*** 據說
precautionary〔prɪˋkɔʃən͵ɛrɪ〕*adj.* 預防的
measure〔ˋmɛʒɚ〕*n.* 措施　　target〔ˋtɑrgɪt〕*n.* 目標

As people across the world criticized Jackson as an unfit father, child
protection groups called on German police to take action against the pop
legend. However, Berlin prosecutors said they were not investigating the
incident, and an inquiry could only be opened if a complaint was filed
against Jackson.

　　由於全世界的人，都在批評麥可是個不稱職的父親，兒童保護團體要求德
國警方，對這位傳奇巨星採取行動。然而，柏林的檢察官卻表示，他們不會去
調查這起事件，除非有人對麥可提出控告，他們才會展開調查。

across the world 在全世界　　criticize〔ˋkrɪtə͵saɪz〕*v.* 批評
unfit〔ʌnˋfɪt〕*adj.* 不適任的

protection〔prə'tɛkʃən〕*n.* 保護　　***call on*** 向～要求；呼籲
take action 採取行動　　legend〔'lɛdʒənd〕*n.* 傳奇人物
prosecutor〔'prɑsɪˌkjutɚ〕*n.* 檢察官
investigate〔ɪn'vɛstəˌget〕*v.* 調查　　incident〔'ɪnsədənt〕*n.* 事件
inquiry〔ɪn'kwaɪrɪ,'ɪnkwərɪ〕*n.* 調查；審理
open〔'opən〕*v.* 展開；開始（行動）
complaint〔kəm'plent〕*n.* 控訴；控告；抱怨
file〔faɪl〕*v.* 提出（訴訟）< *against* >

50. (**D**) 本文最有可能是摘錄自 ＿＿＿＿＿＿。

　(A) 私人信函　　　　　(B) 旅遊手冊
　(C) 研究報告　　　　　(D) 報紙的報導

passage〔'pæsɪdʒ〕*n.*（一段）文章　　personal〔'pɝsn̩l〕*adj.* 私人的
brochure〔bro'ʃur〕*n.* 手冊　　research〔'risɝtʃ〕*n.* 研究

51. (**B**) 麥可在柏林動物園裏做了什麼事，引起人們的注意？

　(A) 他涉及綁架兩名叫做王子和巴黎的小孩。
　(B) 他讓他的小孩戴上面罩，以保護他們不被綁架。
　(C) 他把小孩藏匿在動物園，以保護他們不會被綁架。
　(D) 他在動物園裡走動，並用奇怪的面罩蓋住自己的臉。

catch* one's *attention 引起某人的注意
be involved in 涉及；捲入

52. (**C**) 文中「預防措施」的意思為何？

　(A) 非常精確的測量。　　(B) 詳細的計劃以達成目標。
　(C) 為了避免某些不好結果，所採取的行動。
　(D) 精心準備的數學難題。

calculation〔ˌkælkjə'leʃən〕*n.* 計算
precision〔prɪ'sɪʒən〕*n.* 精確
with great precision 非常精確地
achieve〔ə'tʃiv〕*v.* 達成　　step〔stɛp〕*n.* 行動
take steps 採取行動　　consequence〔'kɑnsəˌkwɛns〕*n.* 結果
mathematical〔ˌmæθə'mætɪkl̩〕*adj.* 數學的
extreme〔ɪk'strim〕*adj.* 非常的　　***with care*** 謹慎地；小心地

53.（ **C** ）根據本文，德國警方只有在 ＿＿＿＿＿＿ 時，才會對麥可傑克遜採取行動。

    (A) 柏林的檢察官被調查　　(B) 更多青少年用面罩蓋住自己的臉

    (C) <u>有人正式控告麥可</u>　　(D) 兒童保護團體再次報警

    official〔əˋfɪʃəl〕*adj.* 正式的

第 54 至 60 題為題組

    Since the terrorist attack on America on September 11, hundreds of new security measures have been put in place to make Americans safer, or at least feel safer. Hotels and corporate offices now require guests to present a photo ID at check-ins and entrances. Airlines refuse to let passengers carry razor blades, scissors, or screwdrivers on flights.

    自從美國於九月十一日遭受恐怖攻擊以來，已經執行了數百種新的安檢措施，以讓美國人更加安全，或者至少覺得比較心安。旅館和公司行號現在要求訪客，在投宿登記處和入口處，須出示附有照片的身分證明。航空公司不許乘客攜帶刮鬍刀、刀片、剪刀，或螺絲起子登機。

        terrorist〔ˋtɛrərɪst〕*adj.* 恐怖主義者的；恐怖分子的

        attack〔əˋtæk〕*n.* 攻擊　　　security〔sɪˋkjurətɪ〕*n.* 安全

        measure〔ˋmɛʒɚ〕*n.* 措施　　　***be put in place*** 使就定位

        corporate〔ˋkɔrpərɪt〕*adj.* 公司的　　　present〔prɪˋzɛnt〕*v.* 出示

        ID 身分證明（= identification〔aɪˏdɛntəfəˋkeʃən〕）

        check-in〔ˋtʃɛkˏɪn〕*n.* 登記投宿處；報到處

        airlines〔ˋɛrˏlaɪnz〕*n. pl.* 航空公司　　***razor blade*** 刮鬍刀刀片

        screwdriver〔ˋskruˏdraɪvɚ〕*n.* 螺絲起子

    At least one surefire way exists to improve security and protect personal privacy: positive passenger bag-matching. It would require that no checked bag be transported on a plane if its owner doesn't board the flight. Bag-matching became standard practice in Europe and Asia in the 1980s after suitcase bombs brought down Pan Am Flight 103 over Lockerbie, Air India Flight 182 en route to London, and UTA Flight 772 to Paris. In all three cases, the terrorists weren't on board.

　　至少有一種既能增進安全又能保護個人隱私，而且絕不會出錯的方法：確實核對乘客行李。這項規定要求行李的持有人，如果沒有登機，其託運的行李，就不能送上飛機。在一九八〇年代，泛美航空 103 號班機在洛克比、印度航空 182 號班機前往倫敦途中，以及法國聯合航空飛往巴黎的 772 號班機，接連發生手提箱炸彈爆炸事件後，行李核對在歐洲和亞洲已成爲慣例。而這三起事件中，恐怖份子都不在飛機上。

> surefire〔ˈʃʊrˌfaɪr〕*adj.* 一定會成功的　　privacy〔ˈpraɪvəsɪ〕*n.* 隱私
> positive〔ˈpɑzətɪv〕*adj.* 確實的
> bag-matching〔ˈbægˌmætʃɪŋ〕*n.* 行李核對（bag 在此指 baggage「行李」）
> check〔tʃɛk〕*v.* 託運　　board〔bord〕*v.* 登（機）
> suitcase〔ˈsutˌkes〕*n.* 手提箱　　bomb〔bɑm〕*n.* 炸彈
> ***bring down*** 擊落　　***en route***〔ɑnˈrut〕在途中（= *on the way*）
> ***on board*** 在飛機上

　　Yet, in the U.S., where security is now top priority, authorities have chosen to ignore bag-matching.　Instead, the Transportation Safety Administration (TSA) has embraced largely untested electronic-detection systems that screen bags for bombs and other explosives.　Critics charge that the TSA has overlooked such an obvious, sensible security measure because U.S. airlines have opposed bag-matching for years.　They fear it might delay flights and persuade short-haul travelers to take a train or drive instead.

　　然而，現今安全已成爲美國的最優先考量，當局卻選擇不採納行李核對的做法，反而是採用運輸安全局（TSA）未經測試過的電子偵測系統，來檢查行李是否藏有炸彈及其他爆裂物。批評者指責運輸安全局（TSA），因爲美國的航空公司數年來，都反對實施行李核對，所以才忽視這項明顯，而且很明智的安檢措施。他們怕這項檢查會延遲班機，使得短程旅客反而選擇搭火車或開車。

> top〔tɑp〕*adj.* 最重要的　　priority〔praɪˈɔrətɪ〕*n.* 優先的事物
> ***top priority*** 第一優先　　authorities〔əˈθɔrətɪz〕*n. pl.* 當局
> ignore〔ɪgˈnor〕*v.* 忽視（= *overlook*）
> transportation〔ˌtrænspəˈteʃən〕*n.* 運輸
> administration〔ədˌmɪnəˈstreʃən〕*n.* 管理部門；行政機構

embrace〔ɪmˈbres〕v. 採用
largely〔ˈlɑrdʒlɪ〕adv. 主要地（= mainly）
untested〔ʌnˈtɛstɪd〕adj. 未經試驗的
electronic-detection〔ˌɪlɛkˈtrɑnɪk dɪˈtɛkʃən〕n. 電子偵查
screen〔skrin〕v. 過濾；篩檢　　explosive〔ɪkˈsplosɪv〕n. 爆裂物
critic〔ˈkrɪtɪk〕n. 批評者　　charge〔tʃɑrdʒ〕v. 指責
sensible〔ˈsɛnsəbl̩〕adj. 明智的　　oppose〔əˈpoz〕v. 反對
short-haul〔ˈʃɔrtˈhɔl〕adj. 短程運輸的

After September 11, bag-matching was back on the agenda. Yet, struggling airlines complained that implementing it on all domestic flights would drive them into bankruptcy. Such claims have zero merit, says Arnold Barnett, a former chair of the Federal Aviation Administration's technical team. In 1996, the team was asked to investigate the feasibility of bag-matching. In a 1997 experiment, which tested 11 airlines, 50 pairs of cities, 8,000 flights, and 750,000 passengers, Barnett showed that domestic bag-matching would cause delays averaging seven minutes on only one in seven flights and would require no reduction in flight schedules.

　　911 之後，行李核對的措施又重新回到議程當中。然而，努力求生存的航空公司抱怨，如果所有國內航空班機都執行這項做法，會使他們破產。前聯邦航空局技術團隊主席，阿爾若得・巴內特表示，這種說法毫無價值。一九九六年，該團隊受委託調查行李核對的可行性。一九九七年的實驗，測試了十一家航空公司、五十組來回城市、八千班班次，和七十五萬名乘客，巴內特指出，國內航班實施行李核對，平均每七班飛機，只有一班延誤七分鐘，而且不會造成班次的減少。

agenda〔əˈdʒɛndə〕n. 議程
struggling〔ˈstrʌglɪŋ〕adj. 必須努力奮鬥才能求生存的
implement〔ˈɪmpləˌmɛnt〕v. 實施
domestic〔dəˈmɛstɪk〕adj. 國內的　　drive〔draɪv〕v. 迫使
bankruptcy〔ˈbæŋkrʌptsɪ〕n. 破產　　claim〔klem〕n. 主張
zero〔ˈzɪro〕adj. 零的；沒有的　　merit〔ˈmɛrɪt〕n. 價值
former〔ˈfɔrmə〕adj. 前任的　　chair〔tʃɛr〕n. 主席（= chairman）
federal〔ˈfɛdərəl〕adj.（美國）聯邦政府的

aviation〔͵evɪˋeʃən〕n. 航空　　technical〔ˋtɛknɪkḷ〕adj. 技術的
investigate〔ɪnˋvɛstə͵get〕v. 調查；研究
feasibility〔͵fizəˋbɪlətɪ〕n. 可行性　　average〔ˋævərɪdʒ〕v. 平均為～
reduction〔rɪˋdʌkʃən〕n. 減少　　schedule〔ˋskɛdʒul〕n. 時刻表

　　Barnett argues that bag-matching would deter bombers far more than
electronic-detection systems. It ensures that the terrorist will proceed to
the gate to board his plane. If, while he's waiting, detection devices reveal
a bomb, **he** could be quickly located and arrested. "The combination of
bag-matching and explosives detection could be far more potent than either
measure on its own," Barnett wrote in a Dec. 17 letter to TSA chief. He
received a thank-you note that contained no indication that the TSA is
contemplating action.

　　巴內特認為，行李核對會比電子偵測系統，更能有效遏止炸彈客的攻擊。
行李核對能夠確保，恐怖份子一定得走到登機門搭機。如果他在等候登機時，
偵測儀器發現有炸彈，他就會立刻被找到，並且被逮捕。「結合行李核對和爆炸
物偵測一起實施，比單獨實行任一種做法來得更加有效。」巴內特在十二月十
七日寫給 TSA 局長的信件中寫道。他收到一封感謝函，內容卻毫無 TSA 正考
慮這項措施的跡象。

argue〔ˋargju〕v. 主張；認為　　deter〔dɪˋtɝ〕v. 阻止
bomber〔ˋbamɚ〕n. 投擲或安置炸彈者（通常指恐怖份子）
ensure〔ɪnˋʃur〕v. 確保；保證
terrorist〔ˋtɛrərɪst〕n. 恐怖主義者；恐怖分子
proceed〔prəˋsid〕v.（沿特定路線）行進　　gate〔get〕n. 登機門
device〔dɪˋvaɪs〕n. 設備；儀器　　reveal〔rɪˋvil〕v. 顯示
locate〔loˋket〕v. 確定…的地點；找出　　arrest〔əˋrɛst〕v. 逮補
combination〔͵kambəˋneʃən〕n. 結合
explosives〔ɪkˋsplosɪvs〕adj. 爆裂物的
potent〔ˋpotṇt〕adj. 有效的　　*on one's own* 單獨地
a thank-you note 感謝函
indication〔͵ɪndəˋkeʃən〕n. 跡象；暗示
contemplate〔ˋkantɛm͵plet〕v. 仔細考慮
action〔ˋækʃən〕n. 措施

54.（**A**）根據本文，泛美航空 103 號班機、印度航空 182 號班機，以及法國
聯合航空 772 號班機，相似之處在於 ＿＿＿＿＿＿。
(A) 它們都遭恐怖攻擊活動擊落
(B) 它們都因爲班機上有些恐怖份子而墜毀
(C) 它們都唯一在一九八〇年墜機的國際班機
(D) 它們都因爲沒有遵守航空安全措施而墜機

crash〔 kræʃ〕 v.（飛機）墜毀

55.（**B**）哪一段有「行李核對」的定義？
(A) 第一段　　(B) 第二段　　(C) 第三段　　(D) 第四段

definition〔͵dɛfə'nɪʃən〕 n. 定義

56.（**C**）下列何者是航空公司不願讓他們的班機，實施行李核對的原因之一？
(A) 電子偵測系統的花費較行李核對要少。
(B) 電子偵測系統預防劫機的效果比較好。
(C) 行李核對會延誤班機，讓人們不想搭飛機。
(D) 行李核對會侵犯乘客的隱私，而不是確保他們的安全。

unwilling〔ʌn'wɪlɪŋ〕 adj. 不願意的　　prevent〔prɪ'vɛnt〕 v. 防止
hijacking〔'haɪ͵dʒækɪŋ〕 n. 劫機
discourage〔dɪs'kɝɪdʒ〕 v. 勸阻 < from >
invade〔ɪn'ved〕 v. 侵犯　　***rather than*** 而不是

57.（**A**）巴內特在行李核對和班次時刻表所做的實驗中，有何重要的發現？
(A) 國內航班執行行李核對時，造成七架班機當中，只有一架班機
延誤七分鐘。
(B) 行李核對迫使航空公司減少班次，並且犧牲服務品質。
(C) 針對十一家航空公司執行行李核對，結果證明，對乘客而言，
既無效又不方便。
(D) 行李核對會導致國內班機變更班次，並且降低服務的頻率。

finding〔'faɪndɪŋ〕 n. 發現　　sacrifice〔'sækrə͵faɪs〕 v. 犧牲
ineffective〔͵ɪnə'fɛktɪv〕 adj. 無效的
frequency〔'frikwənsɪ〕 n. 頻率

58. (**B**) 最後一段的代名詞 *he* (*he could be*...) 最有可能是指 ＿＿＿＿＿＿。

(A) 阿爾若得・巴內特

(B) 一個可能是恐怖份子的人

(C) 登機門附近的安全警衛

(D) 正在登機的普通旅客

pronoun〔ˈpronaʊn〕*n.* 代名詞　　　***refer to*** 是指

potential〔pəˈtɛnʃəl〕*adj.* 可能的　　　guard〔gɑrd〕*n.* 警衛

ordinary〔ˈɔrdṇ͵ɛrɪ〕*adj.* 普通的

59. (**D**) 從本文的最後一句話（他收到一封感謝函，裡面沒有任何跡象顯示，TSA 要考慮採納這項做法），我們可以推論出什麼？

(A) TSA 感謝巴內特的幫忙，並且欣然接受他的建議。

(B) TSA 認真看待巴內特的建議，並且加以執行。

(C) TSA 邀請巴內特和他們合作。

(D) TSA 不打算實施巴內特的構想。

infer〔ɪnˈfɝ〕*v.* 推論　　　appreciate〔əˈpriʃɪ͵et〕*v.* 感激

take～seriously 認真看待～　　　***put～into practice*** 實行～

60. (**C**) 本文主要是要 ＿＿＿＿＿＿。

(A) 在隱私和安全兩者之間權衡得失

(B) 強調 TSA 改善航空安全的任務

(C) 主張行李核對是有效的安檢措施

(D) 提倡使用電子偵測系統

point out 指出　　　trade-off〔ˈtred͵ɔf〕*n.* 權衡得失

highlight〔ˈhaɪ͵laɪt〕*v.* 強調　　　mission〔ˈmɪʃən〕*n.* 任務

advocate〔ˈædvə͵ket〕*v.* 提倡；主張

第貳部分：非選擇題

英文作文：（作文範例）

Exams of all kinds have become a necessary part of my high school life. This is an unavoidable reality that I have accepted. For the last year, I have been pressured and challenged by daily quizzes, weekly tests and exams. I sometimes feel like a test-taking machine. I'm not a big fan of exams; *however*, I realize they are an indispensable tool in measuring performance, knowledge and progress. I know exams are a positive challenge to help me improve. *Therefore*, I must face exams with courage and confidence.

The most unforgettable exam I have ever taken is the exam I'm taking right now! This College Entrance Exam is the most important exam of my life. The results will determine my future education and career path. The pressure is intense. My family expectations are very high! I am praying for a high score! *So*, here I sit, struggling and sweating over this composition. Of course this exam is the most unforgettable one!

unavoidable〔ˌʌnə'vɔɪdəbl̩〕*adj.* 無法避免的
reality〔rɪ'ælətɪ〕*n.* 事實　　pressure〔'prɛʃə〕*v.* 對～施加壓力
challenge〔'tʃælɪndʒ〕*v. n.* 挑戰　　daily〔'delɪ〕*adj.* 每天的
quiz〔kwɪz〕*n.* 小考　　weekly〔'wiklɪ〕*adj.* 每週的
test-taking machine 考試機器　　realize〔'rɪəˌlaɪz〕*v.* 了解
indispensable〔ˌɪndɪ'spɛnsəbl̩〕*adj.* 不可或缺的　　tool〔tul〕*n.* 工具
measure〔'mɛʒə〕*v.* 衡量　　performance〔pə'fɔrməns〕*n.* 表現
progress〔'pragrɛs〕*n.* 進步　　positive〔'pazətɪv〕*adj.* 正面的
confidence〔'kanfədəns〕*n.* 信心
unforgettable〔ˌʌnfə'gɛtəbl̩〕*adj.* 難忘的
college entrance exam 大學入學考試　　career〔kə'rɪr〕*n.* 事業
path〔pæθ〕*n.* 方向　　intense〔ɪn'tɛns〕*adj.* 強烈的
expectation〔ˌɛkspɛk'teʃən〕*n.* 期望　　pray〔pre〕*v.* 祈禱
score〔skor〕*n.* 分數　　struggle〔'strʌgl̩〕*v.* 掙扎；奮鬥
sweat〔swɛt〕*v.* 流汗　　composition〔ˌkampə'zɪʃən〕*n.* 作文

九十二學年度指定科目考試（英文）

大考中心公佈答案

題號	答案	題號	答案	題號	答案
1	C	21	D	41	E
2	D	22	B	42	D
3	D	23	B	43	C
4	A	24	B	44	B
5	C	25	A	45	B
6	C	26	B	46	A
7	B	27	C	47	D
8	C	28	D	48	C
9	B	29	C	49	A
10	A	30	A	50	D
11	D	31	F	51	B
12	A	32	D	52	C
13	D	33	G	53	C
14	B	34	H	54	A
15	A	35	B	55	B
16	D	36	J	56	C
17	C	37	C	57	A
18	A	38	A	58	B
19	A	39	E	59	D
20	C	40	I	60	C

九十二學年度指定科目考試
各科成績標準一覽表

科　　目	高　標	均　標	低　標
國　　文	63	50	38
英　　文	60	39	18
數　學　甲	60	43	25
數　學　乙	52	34	17
化　　學	48	32	16
物　　理	50	31	12
生　　物	63	46	29
歷　　史	51	36	22
地　　理	73	57	41

※ 以上三項標準係依各該科全體到考考生成績計算，且均取整數〔小數只捨不入〕，各標準計算方式如下：

高標：該科前百分之五十考生成績之平均。

均標：該科全體考生成績之平均。

低標：該科後百分之五十考生成績之平均。

心得筆記欄

九十一年大學入學指定科目考試試題
英文考科

第壹部份：單一選擇題

一、詞彙與慣用語（15％）

說明：　第 1 至 15 題，每題選出最適當的一個選項，標示在答案卡之「選擇題答案區」。每題答對得 1 分，答錯倒扣 1/3 分。未答者，不給分亦不扣分。

1. With her teachers' and parents' _____, Jane regained her confidence and has made great progress.
   (A) construction   (B) movement
   (C) association   (D) encouragement

2. One of Jane's finest qualities is that she takes the _____. She always takes the necessary action and does not wait for orders.
   (A) initiative   (B) charity   (C) vision   (D) advantage

3. Mr. Li is a senior _____ at a local bank. He keeps and examines financial records of people and companies.
   (A) volunteer   (B) traitor   (C) accountant   (D) economist

4. Jack doesn't look _____, but he is, in fact, excellent at sports, especially baseball.
   (A) athletic   (B) graceful   (C) enthusiastic   (D) conscientious

5. The jury spent over five hours trying to decide whether the defendant is _____ or guilty.
   (A) evident   (B) considerate   (C) mature   (D) innocent

6. Now that my computer is connected to the Internet, I can browse e-papers, send and receive e-mail, and _____ software.
   (A) upset   (B) overcharge   (C) undertake   (D) download

7. The traffic on Main Street was _____ for several hours due to a car accident in which six people were injured.
   (A) detected   (B) obstructed   (C) survived   (D) estimated

8. Hundreds of people _____ in the desert storm and many more were left homeless.
   (A) perished   (B) inspired   (C) mistreated   (D) dismissed

9. Mike arrived at the meeting _____ at ten o'clock—as it was scheduled—not a minute early or late.
   (A) flexibly   (B) punctually   (C) numerously   (D) approximately

10. A power failure _____ darkened the whole city, and it was not until two hours later that electricity was restored.
    (A) precisely   (B) roughly   (C) illogically   (D) temporarily

11. Sam couldn't _____ how to print out the document until the teacher showed him.
    (A) go through   (B) come up   (C) figure out   (D) get over

12. When they go for a walk, Johnny has to take long steps to _____ with his father.
    (A) break even   (B) keep pace
    (C) win pride   (D) take chance

13. The man is _____ a serious nervous breakdown because he is unable to deal with pressure from daily life.
    (A) on behalf of   (B) in the light of
    (C) on the verge of   (D) in front of

14. _____ treating the homeless man as a shame of the society, Mrs. Wang provided him with food and water.
    (A) Regardless of   (B) As a result of
    (C) In the event of   (D) Instead of

15. Mrs. Lin _____ her husband's complaints because, to her, facing
    the music is more constructive than complaining all day.
    (A) turned a deaf ear to   (B) took part in
    (C) showed him the way to   (D) took notice of

二、綜合測驗（15％）

說明： 第 16 至 30 題，每題一個空格。請依文意選出最適當的一個選項，標示
       在答案卡之「選擇題答案區」。每題答對得 1 分，答錯倒扣 1/3 分。未
       答者，不給分亦不扣分。

<u>第 16 至 20 題為題組</u>

More than 2.7 billion people will face severe shortages of fresh water
by 2025. There is, ___16___, only a limited amount of water on the planet.
Less than 3 percent of the world's water is fresh, and most of ___17___
is trapped in polar ice or buried underground in springs too deep to reach.
Freshwater lakes, rivers and reservoirs may seem ___18___ but provide
just a drop in the bucket. Even ___19___ supplies are sufficient or
plentiful, they are increasingly at risk due to various forms of pollution.
Fierce national competition ___20___ water resources has prompted fears
that water issues contain the seeds of violent conflict. International
cooperation is therefore by all means urgent.

16. (A) meanwhile   (B) besides   (C) in fact   (D) for example
17. (A) which   (B) it   (C) what   (D) them
18. (A) scarce   (B) empty   (C) numerous   (D) polluted
19. (A) how   (B) why   (C) what   (D) where
20. (A) for   (B) with   (C) to   (D) at

There are six international science Olympiads in the world. They are all organized with a simple intention—to ___21___ global understanding and mutual appreciation among young scientists in all countries. Each of the six science Olympiads ___22___ its specific aims. The aims of the International Mathematical Olympiad (IMO), for example, are three-fold. With arduous but interesting math problems, the first aim of the IMO is to discover, to encourage and, most important of all, to challenge ___23___ gifted young people all over the world. Secondly, it is by participating in any IMO contest that young mathematicians of all countries can foster friendly ___24___. Based upon its second aim, more international exchanges are encouraged and established. Any IMO contest brings not only young mathematicians together but also their instructors; ___25___, the IMO has as its final aim to create opportunities for the exchange of information on math teaching schedules and practices throughout the world.

21. (A) sponsor   (B) promote   (C) determine   (D) calculate

22. (A) has   (B) is   (C) have   (D) are

23. (A) destructively   (B) effectively
       (C) mutually   (D) mathematically

24. (A) behaviors   (B) messages   (C) relations   (D) guests

25. (A) whereas   (B) nevertheless   (C) therefore   (D) likewise

Many entertainment celebrities, on April 5, 2002, attended an anti-piracy demonstration in Taipei. The purpose of the rally was to ask fans to respect the copyright law and to stop buying ___26___ CDs.

Although the intellectual property right is to be protected by law, the fans may think otherwise. Obviously, it is the recording industry that wants to 　27　 piracy. Celebrities in the rally probably have no idea how much a CD of their music costs. After signing million-dollar contracts with recording companies, singers devote most of their time 　28　 their music perfect while companies are busy commercializing their products. It is the fans that support the kingdoms of the recording companies; 　29　, the industry never gives anything back to the fans—by lowering the prices of CDs. It is an easy arithmetic 　30　. When one can buy a CD of pop music for NT$50 anywhere on the streets, why does he or she want to spend NT$300 or more for the same one?

26.　(A) pirating　　(B) pirate　　(C) piracy　　(D) pirated
27.　(A) fight　　(B) kill　　(C) win　　(D) shut
28.　(A) in doing　　(B) for singing　　(C) to making　　(D) at playing
29.　(A) indeed　　(B) however　　(C) hence　　(D) furthermore
30.　(A) question　　(B) feedback　　(C) product　　(D) industry

三、文意選填（10％）

說明：　第 31 至 40 題，每題一個空格。請依文意在文章後所提供的(A) 到 (J) 選項中分別選出最適當者，並將其字母代號標示在答案卡之「選擇題答案區」。每題答對得 1 分，答錯倒扣 1/9 分。未答者，不給分亦不扣分。

第 31 至 40 題爲題組

　　Are you someone who practically lives in front of the computer—a *mouse potato*? Or are you nervous about new technology—a *technophobe*? 　31　, if you want to master the English language, you will need to be 　32　 those new computer words that seem to be popping up everywhere.

Luckily, most computer words are easy to learn. ___33___, many of these words probably already have similar forms in your own language. ___34___, the German word for computer is *Computer*, in South American Spanish it is *computador*, and in Japanese we ___35___ *konpyuta*.

Another reason why computer words are easy to learn is that many of them are so ___36___. They are words that often make us smile when we first hear them such as ___37___ (traditional mail rather than Internet-based mail) or *wysiwyg* (what-you-see-is-what-you-get).

To get a feeling for computer words, it helps to ___38___ the world that created them—*cyberculture*, as it is often called. The computer industry is ___39___ young people who think of themselves as very different from ___40___ business people in suits. It is a world that avoids heavy scientific-sounding language in favor of words that are simple, fresh and playful.

(A) For one thing　　(B) full of　　(C) understand　　(D) familiar with
(E) find　　　　　　(F) In either case　　　　　　　(G) For example
(H) traditional　　　(I) snail mail　　　　　　　　　(J) colorful

四、篇章結構（10％）

說明：　第41至50題，每題一個空格。請依文意在文章後所提供的(A)到(E)選
　　　　項中分別選出最適當者，填入空格中，使篇章結構清晰有條理，並將其
　　　　英文字母代號標示在答案卡之「選擇題答案區」。每題答對得1分，答
　　　　錯倒扣1/4分。未答者，不給分亦不扣分。

第41至45題為題組

Fiction is the name we use for stories that are make-believe, such as *Harry Potter* or *Alice in Wonderland*. ___41___ It can be so close to the truth that it seems as real as something that happened to you this morning. Or, fiction can be as fantastic as the most unbelievable fairy tale.

Not everything in a fictional story has to be made up. ___42___ *You*, of course, are real, and the *moon* is real, and many of the things that you could describe, such as the stars, the wind, and the pull of gravity, would be real. ___43___ It would be a trip you took in your imagination.

Nonfiction, on the other hand, is all about true things. ___44___ Someone's biography is nonfiction; so is your autobiography. So are articles in your local newspaper, and school reports on science. ___45___ Imagine writing history about the 1989 San Francisco earthquake, or a report about a high school sports team. An old proverb says, "Truth is stranger than fiction." Do you think that's true?

(A) Nothing is made up.

(B) History is nonfiction, too.

(C) But your trip through space would be fiction.

(D) You could write a story in which you fly to the moon.

(E) But fiction isn't always different from the way things usually are.

第 46 至 50 題為題組

Car windshield wipers were invented by Mary Anderson on a trip in New York City in 1903. While touring the city on a streetcar, Mary was not interested in the views on the streets. ___46___ Repeatedly, the motorman had to get out of the streetcar to wipe off the snow and ice collected on the windshield. New York streetcar motormen at that time had tried various ways to solve this problem. ___47___ Mary, sitting on her seat, quickly drew her device in her sketchbook. ___48___ Mary's device allowed the motorman to use a lever inside the streetcar to activate a swinging arm on the windshield to wipe off the snow and ice. Because the device was first designed for cold weather, it could be easily removed when warmer weather arrived. _____49_____ Even though her friends teased her about her awkward invention attached to a streetcar, Mary didn't give in to peer pressure. _____50_____ By 1913, her invention had become standard equipment on American cars. Windshield wipers save lives and make it easier to drive through storms.

(A) Her solution was simple.

(B) A year later, she received a patent for it.

(C) Its function of wiping rain was later considered and added.

(D) Instead, she paid much attention to the streetcar motorman.

(E) Wiping off the snow and ice by hand, however seemed to be the only solution.

五、閱讀測驗（30%）

說明：第 51 至 65 題，每題請分別根據各篇文章的文意選出最適當的一個選項，標示在答案卡之「選擇題答案區」。每題答對得 2 分，答錯倒扣 2/3 分。未答者，不給分亦不扣分。

第 51 至 53 題為題組

Both the Eskimos and the Plains Indians used open fires in their shelters for warmth but with very different consequences. The Eskimo house was an airtight igloo made of blocks of ice with a small tunnel-like entrance and a small chimney in the center for smoke from the fire. Temperatures inside this structure easily reached 70 to 80 degrees Fahrenheit although outside temperatures frequently dropped well below zero. Often, the igloo was so hot that the loss of body fluid through perspiration would force the Eskimos to drink cup after cup of ice water. The Plains Indians, on the other hand, placed their fire in a tepee made with long poles and animal skins with an entrance cut directly into one wall. In contrast to the Eskimo shelter, the tepee was far from airtight;

drafts came in around the door and through gaps between the skins. At night the Indians would crawl under their blankets, cover their heads, and shiver all night—so much that the blankets would shake! The difference between the Eskimo igloo and the Indian tepee was insulation: the igloo's walls were solid and airtight whereas those of the tepee permitted a great deal of air to enter.

51. This passage most likely occurs as part of _____.
    (A) a weather forecast
    (B) a book on fire prevention
    (C) a report on animal conservation
    (D) a magazine article on house construction

52. From the passage, it can be inferred that _____.
    (A) to enter an Eskimo house, one had to go through a long tunnel
    (B) the Eskimo igloo had better insulation than the Indian tepee
    (C) the Plains Indians enjoyed living in their shelters in winter days
    (D) there was a small chimney in every Indian tepee to release the smoke from the fire

53. This passage is written mainly to _____.
    (A) compare
    (B) tell a sad story
    (C) amuse the readers
    (D) report a scientific discovery

第 54 至 57 題為題組

Soapy's life was fine during spring, summer and autumn, but not so good in the winter. When November arrived, Soapy always found a way to stay indoors, away from the cold, and have three meals a day without paying one cent. The trick was simple: he broke the law.

Last autumn, when nights got too cold to sleep in the park, Soapy realized it was time to make arrangements for his annual winter trip. He walked over to Fifth Avenue around 10 a.m. one morning and sent a stone crashing through a glass window of a big department store. Then he stood calmly by the window, waiting. As he had expected, a policeman came running around the corner. Soapy confessed immediately that he was the one who had broken the window. Yet the policeman did not believe him. Soapy also failed in his second scheme: the woman he tried to harass verbally was, much to his surprise, overwhelmed and in fact thanked him for being the first man ever to say such sweet words to her.

It was about noon that Soapy came near a fancy restaurant. He decided to walk in for a big free lunch. When it was time for the bill, he told the manager he had no money and suggested that *he* have him arrested. The manager, realizing what was going on, asked Soapy to follow him into the kitchen, where a big pile of dirty dishes was waiting to be washed. Three hours later, the exhausted Soapy returned to the street.

Then the night came, and it was too cold for Soapy to sleep in Central Park. So he wandered about until he found himself standing in front of a church. The choir were practicing a song. "We often sang it in church. I showed great promise once, but look at me now. I've got to change. Yes, I'll take the job offered last week as a truck driver." At this moment, the policeman appeared again, arresting him on a charge of vandalism. Soapy was then taken to the night court, where the judge sentenced him to three months in jail.

54. What is the moral of this story?
    (A) You can do exactly what pleases you.
    (B) One has to pay for what he or she has done.
    (C) It's never too late to change into a better self.
    (D) We have to get well-prepared for the winters.

55. Soapy ＿＿＿＿＿.
    (A) broke a big pile of dishes while he was having lunch
    (B) was put in jail though he had decided to turn over a new leaf
    (C) was slapped on the face for saying inappropriate words to a woman
    (D) sang a song with the choir of the church and was greatly moved

56. Who does *he* in line 2, paragraph 3 refer to?
    (A) The policeman.　　　　(B) Soapy.
    (C) The manager.　　　　　(D) The judge.

57. Which of the following statements about the story is **TRUE**?
    (A) Soapy usually spent the cold winter in jail where he could have
        warmth and free meals.
    (B) Though Soapy had a job and a home, he enjoyed wandering
        on the streets, doing nothing.
    (C) The policeman did not believe what Soapy said because he
        dressed like a dignified gentleman.
    (D) The judge put Soapy in jail even though Soapy strongly
        protested that he had done nothing wrong.

第 58 至 61 題爲題組

　　Queen Victoria was monarch of Great Britain from 1837 until her
death in 1901. This period is often called the Victorian Age.

　　Queen Victoria was a stern and serious woman. One reason she was
so serious was that she had suffered a great loss. When she was twenty
years old, she married a German prince named Albert. Victoria and Albert
were deeply in love, and their marriage was extremely happy. In 1861,

after they had been married for twenty-one years, Albert died, leaving Queen Victoria heartbroken. For the rest of her life, the lonely Victoria **mourned** his loss. It was customary in those days for a widow to dress in black for a short time after the death of her husband. But Queen Victoria dressed in black for *forty years*. And for forty years, as another sign of her grief, she wrote her letters on white paper edged in black.

Even before Prince Albert died, Queen Victoria was known as a very serious woman. She had a strong sense of duty and worked very hard at all her tasks. In her diary she wrote, "I *love* to be employed; I *hate* to be idle." She never forgot that she was Britain's queen and always acted with great dignity. Victoria had high ideals and moral standards that sometimes made her seem stuffy. She was also very sure of herself. She always thought that she was right, and she expected everyone to agree with her.

58. Which of the following statements about Queen Victoria is **NOT** true according to the passage?
    (A) She had great confidence in herself.
    (B) She ruled Great Britain for sixty-four years.
    (C) She enjoyed her marriage to a German prince.
    (D) She became a serious woman after her beloved husband died.

59. Queen Victoria wrote her letters on white paper edged in black because _____.
    (A) she was a very stern woman
    (B) black was her favorite color
    (C) that was one way to show her feeling of sadness
    (D) it was a custom among monarchs of Great Britain

60. All of the following characteristics **EXCEPT** _____ can be used to properly describe Queen Victoria.
    (A) moral   (B) lonesome
    (C) workaholic   (D) compromising

61. The word **mourned** here means _____.
   (A) felt sad or sorrowful in a social situation
   (B) expressed publicly one's sadness because someone has died
   (C) checked regularly in order to find out what was happening
   (D) included in a group of numbers, ages, measurements with particular fixed limits

第 62 至 65 題為題組

Boll, a German scientist and the star of the Manhattan Project, was lecturing at a New York university on the 50th anniversary of the dropping of the atomic bomb on Japan. The speech had become part of his summer routine, justifying what had been done near the end of World War II. The scientific triumph of his career, in fact, had been paralyzing his life, silently troubling his conscience. He had been haunted with visions of the devastation of the Japanese city, Hiroshima. "Dreams have become nightmares," he conceded. Then his wife, an Austrian Jew whose parents were victims of the Nazi death camps, fell seriously ill, and designed a salvation journey for her husband, bringing together Boll and Amai, a woman from Hiroshima who lost her face to the world's first atomic blast.

Following his speech, Amai, wearing a face reconstructed by the skilled hands of an American surgeon, approached Boll. Now 56 and a documentary filmmaker, Amai wanted to interview him about his role in making the bomb. Boll looked to Amai to redeem himself for what he had done. And when Amai saw through Boll's façade to his inner depressed state, she recognized a shadowy reflection of the despair and exhaustion that possessed the Japanese after the war, and began to comprehend the price he had paid for victory.

62. Boll _____.
    (A) is a professor at the State University of New York
    (B) has been enjoying the triumph over the Japanese
    (C) was one of the scientists who made atomic bombs
    (D) has convinced himself that he did nothing wrong

63. Amai _____.
    (A) is a documentary filmmaker, who was not personally involved in World War II
    (B) lost her face in the world's first atomic bombing and is now wearing a new face
    (C) cannot forgive and forget those who have done so much harm to her and her country
    (D) sees the despair of the bomb-makers and enjoys the price they have paid for what they did

64. Boll's wife _____.
    (A) will not forgive the Nazis because her parents were killed in the Nazi concentration camps
    (B) fails to understand how troubled her husband feels after the destruction of Hiroshima
    (C) arranges the meeting for Boll to save him from the recurring nightmares about the atomic bombing
    (D) hopes that Amai will help Boll continue his life career as an atomic bomb-maker after her death

65. What is the author of the passage trying to tell the readers?
    (A) Killers hardly ever seek forgiveness from their victims.
    (B) People can always justify whatever they have done wrong.
    (C) Boll and his wife take great pride in the success of the Manhattan Project.
    (D) Victory in war will never be gained without paying the price.

第貳部份：非選擇題

英文作文（20％）

說明：　1. 依提示在「答案卷」上寫一篇英文作文。

　　　　2. 文長約 120 至 150 個單詞左右。

提示：　文章請以 "If I won two million dollars in the lottery, I would help…" 開始，敘述如果你或妳贏得台灣樂透彩新台幣兩百萬元之後，最想把全數金額拿去幫助的人、機構或組織，並寫出理由。

九十一年度指定科目考試英文科試題詳解

第壹部分：單一選擇題

一、詞彙與慣用語：

1. (**D**) With her teachers' and parents' <u>encouragement</u>, Jane regained her confidence and has made great progress.
   有了老師和父母的<u>鼓勵</u>，珍恢復信心，並有了很大的進步。
   (A) construction〔kən'strʌkʃən〕*n.* 建造
   (B) movement〔'muvmənt〕*n.* 動作
   (C) association〔ə,soʃı'eʃən〕*n.* 聯想；協會
   (D) ***encouragement***〔ın'kɝıdʒmənt〕*n.* 鼓勵

   regain〔rı'gen〕*v.* 恢復　　confidence〔'kɑnfədəns〕*n.* 信心
   progress〔'prɑgrɛs〕*n.* 進步

2. (**A**) One of Jane's finest qualities is that she takes the <u>initiative</u>. She always takes the necessary action and does not wait for orders. 珍最好的特質之一，就是她很<u>主動</u>。她總是會採取必要的行動，不用等別人命令。
   (A) ***initiative***〔ı'nıʃı,etıv〕*n.* 主動　　***take the initiative*** 採取主動
   (B) charity〔'tʃærətı〕*n.* 慈善　　(C) vision〔'vıʒən〕*n.* 視力
   (D) advantage〔əd'væntıdʒ〕*n.* 優點

   quality〔'kwɑlətı〕*n.* 特質　　order〔'ɔrdɚ〕*n.* 命令

3. (**C**) Mr. Li is a senior <u>accountant</u> at a local bank. He keeps and examines financial records of people and companies.
   李先生是當地一家銀行的高級<u>會計</u>。他記錄並檢查客戶和各公司的金融紀錄。
   (A) volunteer〔,vɑlən'tır〕*n.* 自願者
   (B) traitor〔'tretɚ〕*n.* 叛徒　　(C) ***accountant***〔ə'kauntənt〕*n.* 會計
   (D) economist〔ı'kɑnəmıst〕*n.* 經濟學家

   senior〔'sınjɚ〕*adj.* 高級的；資深的
   financial〔fə'nænʃəl〕*adj.* 財務的；金融的　　***keep records*** 做紀錄

4. (**A**) Jack doesn't look <u>athletic</u>, but he is, in fact, excellent at sports, especially baseball.

傑克看起來不太<u>會運動</u>，不過事實上，他運動方面表現傑出，特別是棒球。

　(A) *athletic*〔æθ'lɛtɪk〕*adj.* 會運動的
　(B) graceful〔'gresfəl〕*adj.* 優雅的
　(C) enthusiastic〔ɪn،θjuzɪ'æstɪk〕*adj.* 有熱誠的
　(D) conscientious〔،kɑnʃɪ'ɛnʃəs〕*adj.* 負責盡職的

excellent〔'ɛkslənt〕*adj.* 優秀的

5. (**D**) The jury spent over five hours trying to decide whether the defendant is <u>innocent</u> or guilty.

陪審團花了五個多小時的時間，試著做出被告是有罪還是<u>無罪</u>的決定。

　(A) evident〔'ɛvədənt〕*adj.* 明顯的
　(B) considerate〔kən'sɪdərɪt〕*adj.* 體貼的
　(C) mature〔mə'tʃʊr〕*adj.* 成熟的
　(D) *innocent*〔'ɪnəsn̩t〕*adj.* 無罪的；清白的

jury〔'dʒʊrɪ〕*n.* 陪審團　　defendant〔dɪ'fɛndənt〕*n.* 被告
guilty〔'gɪltɪ〕*adj.* 有罪的

6. (**D**) Now that my computer is connected to the Internet, I can browse e-papers, send and receive e-mail, and <u>download</u> software.

因為我的電腦和網際網路聯結，所以我可以瀏覽電子報、收發電子郵件，以及<u>下載</u>軟體。

　(A) upset〔ʌp'sɛt〕*v.* 使心煩
　(B) overcharge〔'ovɚ'tʃɑrdʒ〕*v.* 索價過高
　(C) undertake〔،ʌndɚ'tek〕*v.* 承擔
　(D) *download*〔'daʊn'lod〕*v.* 下載

now that 因為　　connect〔kə'nɛkt〕*v.* 聯結
Internet〔'ɪntɚ،nɛt〕*n.* 網際網路　　browse〔braʊz〕*v.* 瀏覽
e-paper〔'i،pepɚ〕*n.* 電子報　　e-mail〔'i،mel〕*n.* 電子郵件
software〔'sɔft،wɛr〕*n.* 軟體

7. (**B**) The traffic on Main Street was <u>obstructed</u> for several hours due to a car accident in which six people were injured.
因為一場有六人受傷的車禍，大街上的交通被<u>阻斷</u>了好幾個小時。
(A) detect〔dɪ'tɛkt〕*v.* 查出　　(B) ***obstruct***〔əb'strʌkt〕*v.* 阻斷
(C) survive〔sə'vaɪv〕*v.* 存活　(D) estimate〔'ɛstə,met〕*v.* 估計
due to 由於　　injure〔'ɪndʒɚ〕*v.* 使受傷

8. (**A**) Hundreds of people <u>perished</u> in the desert storm and many more were left homeless.
數以百計的人在沙漠風暴中<u>死亡</u>，還有更多人變得無家可歸。
(A) ***perish***〔'pɛrɪʃ〕*v.* 死亡　　(B) inspire〔ɪn'spaɪr〕*v.* 激勵
(C) mistreat〔mɪs'trit〕*v.* 虐待　(D) dismiss〔dɪs'mɪs〕*v.* 解散
desert〔'dɛzət〕*n.* 沙漠　　storm〔stɔrm〕*n.* 風暴
homeless〔'homlɪs〕*adj.* 無家可歸的

9. (**B**) Mike arrived at the meeting <u>punctually</u> at ten o'clock—as it was scheduled—not a minute early or late.
麥克如預定地<u>準時</u>到達會議——一分鐘不早，也一分鐘不晚。
(A) flexibly〔'flɛksəblɪ〕*adv.* 有彈性地
(B) ***punctually***〔'pʌŋktʃʊəlɪ〕*adv.* 準時地
(C) numerously〔'njumərəslɪ〕*adv.* 許多地
(D) approximately〔ə'praksəmɪtlɪ〕*adv.* 大約
schedule〔'skɛdʒʊl〕*v.* 預定

10. (**D**) A power failure <u>temporarily</u> darkened the whole city, and it was not until two hours later that electricity was restored.
一場停電<u>暫時</u>使整個城市陷入黑暗，直到兩小時後電力才恢復。
(A) precisely〔prɪ'saɪslɪ〕*adv.* 精確地
(B) roughly〔'rʌflɪ〕*adv.* 概略地；大約
(C) illogically〔ɪ'ladʒɪklɪ〕*adv.* 不合邏輯地
(D) ***temporarily***〔'tɛmpə,rɛrəlɪ〕*adv.* 暫時地
power failure 停電　　darken〔'darkən〕*v.* 使黑暗
electricity〔ɪ,lɛk'trɪsətɪ〕*n.* 電　　restore〔rɪ'stor〕*v.* 恢復

11. (**C**) Sam couldn't <u>figure out</u> how to print out the document until the teacher showed him.

直到老師跟山姆說明，他才<u>了解</u>如何列印出文件。

   (A) go through　通過　　　　　　(B) come up　接近；發生

   (C) ***figure out***　了解　　　　　(D) get over　克服；復原

print out 列印　　　document〔'dɑkjəmənt〕*n.* 文件

12. (**B**) When they go for a walk, Johnny has to take long steps to <u>keep pace</u> with his father.

當他們去散步的時候，強尼必須大步走才能<u>跟上</u>他爸爸。

   (A) break even　不分勝負　　　(B) ***keep pace***　跟上

   (C) win pride　贏得自尊　　　　(D) take a chance　冒險

take long steps 大步走

13. (**C**) The man is <u>on the verge of</u> a serious nervous breakdown because he is unable to deal with pressure from daily life.

這個人已經<u>瀕臨</u>神經崩潰的邊緣，因為他無法應付日常生活的壓力。

   (A) on behalf of　代表

   (B) in the light of　從～的觀點

   (C) ***on the verge of***　瀕臨；即將

   (D) in front of　在～前面

nervous〔'nɝvəs〕*adj.* 神經的　　　breakdown〔'brek,daʊn〕*n.* 崩潰

deal with 應付　　　pressure〔'prɛʃə〕*n.* 壓力

14. (**D**) <u>Instead of</u> treating the homeless man as a shame of the society, Mrs. Wang provided him with food and water.

王太太不把那遊民當作是社會裡的恥辱，<u>相反地</u>，她供應他食物和水。

   (A) regardless of　不顧

   (B) as a result of　由於

   (C) in the event of　萬一；倘若

   (D) ***instead of***　不…而～

treat～as… 把～視為…　　　shame〔ʃem〕*n.* 羞恥

provide sb. with sth. 供應某人某物

15. (**A**) Mrs. Lin <u>turned a deaf ear to</u> her husband's complaints because, to her, facing the music is more constructive than complaining all day.

林太太對她先生的抱怨<u>充耳不聞</u>，因為對她而言，面對現實比整天抱怨要有建設性多了。

(A) *turn a deaf ear to* 對～充耳不聞
(B) take part in 參加
(C) show *sb*. the way to 給某人帶路
(D) take notice of 注意到

complaint〔kəm'plent〕*n.* 抱怨　　***face the music*** 面對現實
constructive〔kən'strʌktɪv〕*adj.* 建設性的

二、綜合測驗：

<u>第 16 至 20 題為題組</u>

　　More than 2.7 billion people will face severe shortages of fresh water by 2025. There is, <u>in fact</u>, only a limited amount of water on the planet.
16

Less than 3 percent of the world's water is fresh, and most of <u>it</u> is trapped
17

in polar ice or buried underground in springs too deep to reach.

　　在西元二〇二五年前，有超過二十七億的人口，將會面臨淡水嚴重缺乏的問題。事實上，地球上的含水量非常有限。全世界不到百分之三的水是淡水，而且大部分都集中在極地的冰裡，或是埋在地底泉水中，太深了無法獲得。

billion〔'bɪljən〕*n.* 十億　　severe〔sə'vɪr〕*adj.* 嚴重的
shortage〔'ʃɔrtɪdʒ〕*n.* 缺乏　　***fresh water*** 淡水
limited〔'lɪmɪtɪd〕*adj.* 有限的　　planet〔'plænɪt〕*n.* 行星；地球
trap〔træp〕*v.* 困住；凝聚　　polar〔'polɚ〕*adj.* 極地的
bury〔'bɛrɪ〕*v.* 埋葬　　underground〔ˏʌndɚ'graund〕*adv.* 在地下
spring〔sprɪŋ〕*n.* 泉水

16. (**C**)　(A) meanwhile〔'minˏhwaɪl〕*adv.* 在此期間
　　　　　(B) besides〔bɪ'saɪdz〕*adv.* 此外
　　　　　(C) *in fact* 事實上
　　　　　(D) for example 例如

17. (**B**) 依句意，大部分的「淡水」集中在極地，在此需要代名詞，來代替已提過的名詞 water，故選 (B) *it*。

Freshwater lakes, rivers and reservoirs may seem <u>numerous</u> but provide
18
just a drop in the bucket.　Even <u>where</u> supplies are sufficient or plentiful,
19
they are increasingly at risk due to various forms of pollution.　Fierce
national competition <u>for</u> water resources has prompted fears that water
20
issues contain the seeds of violent conflict.　International cooperation is
therefore by all means urgent.

淡水的湖泊、河流和蓄水庫，看起來似乎很多，但只供應了滄海之一粟。甚至連那些供應量足夠或豐富的地方，也都由於各種污染，而逐漸受到危害。國際間水資源的競爭激烈，引起了恐懼，害怕水的問題會種下猛烈衝突的根源。因此，國際間的合作當然是非常迫切需要的。

> reservoir (ˈrɛzɚˌvɔr) *n.* 蓄水庫
> drop (drɑp) *n.* 水滴　　　bucket (ˈbʌkɪt) *n.* 水桶
> ***a drop in the bucket*** 滄海之一粟 (= *a drop in the ocean*)
> supply (səˈplaɪ) *n.* 供應量　　sufficient (səˈfɪʃənt) *adj.* 足夠的
> plentiful (ˈplɛntɪfəl) *adj.* 豐富的
> increasingly (ɪnˈkrisɪŋlɪ) *adv.* 逐漸地　　***at risk*** 處於危險中
> fierce (fɪrs) *adj.* 激烈的　　competition (ˌkɑmpəˈtɪʃən) *n.* 競爭
> resource (rɪˈsors) *n.* 資源　　prompt (prɑmpt) *v.* 促使
> issue (ˈɪʃju) *n.* 問題　　seed (sid) *n.* 種子；根源
> violent (ˈvaɪələnt) *adj.* 猛烈的　　conflict (ˈkɑnflɪkt) *n.* 衝突
> cooperation (koˌɑpəˈreʃən) *n.* 合作　　***by all means*** 務必；當然
> urgent (ˈɝdʒənt) *adj.* 迫切的；緊急的

18. (**C**)　(A) scarce (skɛrs) *adj.* 稀少的
　　　　　(B) empty (ˈɛmptɪ) *adj.* 空的
　　　　　(C) ***numerous*** (ˈnjumərəs) *adj.* 很多的
　　　　　(D) polluted (pəˈlutɪd) *adj.* 受到污染的

19. (**D**) 依句意，即使是「那些供應量足夠的地方」，選 (D) ***where***。

20. (**A**) 表示「為～」競爭，介系詞應用 ***for***，選 (A)。

第 21 至 25 題為題組

There are six international science Olympiads in the world. They are all organized with a simple intention — to <u>promote</u> global understanding
21

and mutual appreciation among young scientists in all countries. Each of the six science Olympiads <u>has</u> its specific aims. The aims of the
22

International Mathematical Olympiad (IMO), for example, are three-fold. With arduous but interesting math problems, the first aim of the IMO is to discover, to encourage and, most important of all, to challenge <u>mathematically</u> gifted young people all over the world.
23

全世界有六項國際奧林匹亞科學競賽，它們的組成都為了一個簡單的目的——促進全球之間的了解，及世界各國年輕科學家之間的相互賞識。這六項奧林匹亞科學競賽，都有其特定的目標。例如，國際奧林匹亞數學競賽，就有三重目標。利用困難、但有趣的數學問題，奧林匹亞數學競賽的首要目標為，發掘、鼓勵，最重要的是，挑戰全世界有數學天賦的年輕人。

Olympiad〔oˊlɪmpɪˌæd〕n. 國際奧林匹克競賽
organize〔ˊɔrgənˌaɪz〕v. 組織　　intention〔ɪnˊtɛnʃən〕n. 目的
global〔ˊglobḷ〕adj. 全球的　　mutual〔ˊmjutʃuəl〕adj. 相互的
appreciation〔əˌpriʃɪˊeʃən〕n. 欣賞；賞識
specific〔spɪˊsɪfɪk〕adj. 特定的　　aim〔em〕n. 目標
three-fold〔ˊθriˊfold〕adj. 三重的　　arduous〔ˊɑrdʒuəs〕adj. 困難的
challenge〔ˊtʃælɪndʒ〕v. 挑戰　　gifted〔ˊgɪftɪd〕adj. 有天賦的

21.(**B**) (A) sponsor〔ˊspɑnsɚ〕v. 贊助　　(B) ***promote***〔prəˊmot〕v. 促進
　　　　　　(C) determine〔dɪˊtɝmɪn〕v. 決定　　(D) calculate〔ˊkælkjəˌlet〕v. 計算

22.(**A**) 依句意，每一項活動都「有」其特定的目標，且主詞 each 為單數，故應用 ***has***，選 (A)。

23.(**D**) (A) destructively〔dɪˊstrʌktɪvlɪ〕adv. 破壞性地
　　　　　　(B) effectively〔ɪˊfɛktɪvlɪ〕adv. 有效地
　　　　　　(C) mutually〔ˊmjutʃuəlɪ〕adv. 相互地
　　　　　　(D) ***mathematically***〔ˌmæθəˊmætɪkəlɪ〕adv. 數學上

Secondly, it is by participating in any IMO contest that young
mathematicians of all countries can foster friendly <u>relations</u>. Based
24
upon its second aim, more international exchanges are encouraged and
established.　Any IMO contest brings not only young mathematicians
together but also their instructors; <u>therefore</u>, the IMO has as its final aim
25
to create opportunities for the exchange of information on math teaching
schedules and practices throughout the world.

其次，藉由參加任何奧林匹亞數學競賽，世界各國的年輕數學好手們，可以培
養友好的關係。基於此第二項目標，更多的國際交流可以受到鼓勵而建立。任
何一項奧林匹亞數學競賽，不僅可以讓年輕的數學好手齊聚一堂，也集合了他
們的指導老師；因此，奧林匹亞數學競賽的最後一項目標就是，為全世界的數
學教學活動和教學方式，創造更多機會，帶來更多資訊上的交流。

participate〔pəˈtɪsəˌpet〕*v.* 參加＜ *in* ＞
contest〔ˈkɑntɛst〕*n.* 比賽
mathematician〔ˌmæθəməˈtɪʃən〕*n.* 數學家
foster〔ˈfɑstɚ〕*v.* 促進；培養　　***based upon*** 基於
exchange〔ɪksˈtʃendʒ〕*n.* 交流　　establish〔əˈstæblɪʃ〕*v.* 建立
instructor〔ɪnˈstrʌktɚ〕*n.* 指導者　　create〔krɪˈet〕*v.* 創造
schedule〔ˈskɛdʒul〕*n.*（預定）活動
practice〔ˈpræktɪs〕*n.* 慣例；方法

24. (**C**)　(A) behavior〔bɪˈhevjɚ〕*n.* 行為
　　　(B) message〔ˈmɛsɪdʒ〕*n.* 訊息
　　　(C) ***relation***〔rɪˈleʃən〕*n.* 關係
　　　(D) guest〔gɛst〕*n.* 客人

25. (**C**)　依句意，前句敘述的是「原因」，而後句則說明「結果」，故本題應
　　　選 (C) ***therefore***「因此」。
　　　(A) whereas〔hwɛrˈæs〕*conj.* 然而
　　　(B) nevertheless〔ˌnɛvɚðəˈlɛs〕*adv.* 然而
　　　(D) likewise〔ˈlaɪkˌwaɪz〕*adv.* 同樣地

第 26 至 30 題為題組

　　Many entertainment celebrities, on April 5, 2002, attended an anti-piracy demonstration in Taipei. The purpose of the rally was to ask fans to respect the copyright law and to stop buying <u>pirated</u> CDs. Although
26
the intellectual property right is to be protected by law, the fans may think otherwise.

　　在二○○二年四月五日這一天，台北有許多娛樂圈的名人，參加一場反盜版的示威遊行。這次示威遊行的目的，是要呼籲歌迷尊重著作權法，並停止購買盜版 CD。雖然智慧財產權應受到法律的保護，但歌迷們可能並不那麼想。

　　　　entertainment〔͵ɛntɚˈtenmənt〕*n.* 娛樂
　　　　celebrity〔səˈlɛbrətɪ〕*n.* 名人　　attend〔əˈtɛnd〕*v.* 參加
　　　　anti-piracy〔͵æntɪˈpaɪrəsɪ〕*n.* 反盜版
　　　　demonstration〔͵dɛmənˈstreʃən〕*n.* 示威遊行
　　　　rally〔ˈrælɪ〕*n.* 集會；示威活動　　*be to + V.* 目的是為了；應該
　　　　fan〔fæn〕*n.* 歌迷　　copyright〔ˈkɑpɪ͵raɪt〕*n.* 著作權；版權
　　　　copyright law 著作權法　　***intellectual property right*** 智慧財產權
　　　　otherwise〔ˈʌðɚ͵waɪz〕*adv.* 不那樣

26. (**D**)　(A) pirating〔ˈpaɪrətɪŋ〕*n.* 盜版
　　　　　(B) pirate〔ˈpaɪrət〕*v.* 盜版　*n.* 海盜；盜版者
　　　　　(C) piracy〔ˈpaɪrəsɪ〕*n.* 盜版行為
　　　　　(D) ***pirated***〔ˈpaɪrətɪd〕*adj.* 盜版的

　　Obviously, it is the recording industry that wants to <u>fight</u> piracy. Celebrities
27
in the rally probably have no idea how much a CD of their music costs. After signing million-dollar contracts with recording companies, singers devote most of their time <u>to making</u> their music perfect while companies
28
are busy commercializing their products.

想要對抗盜版的，顯然是唱片業。參加這場示威遊行的名人，可能並不知道，他們專輯中的 CD，一張價值多少錢。在和唱片公司簽下百萬元的合約後，歌手大多數的時間，都在致力於製作出完美的音樂，而唱片公司則是忙著販售他們的產品。

obviously〔'ɑbvɪəslɪ〕*adv.* 顯然　　recording〔rɪ'kɔrdɪŋ〕*n.* 唱片
industry〔'ɪndəstrɪ〕*n.* 產業　　***recording industry*** 唱片業
sign〔saɪn〕*v.* 簽（約）　　contract〔'kɑntrækt〕*n.* 合約
devote〔dɪ'vot〕*v.* 奉獻　　***be busy + V-ing*** 忙於
commercialize〔kə'mɝʃəl,aɪz〕*v.* 使商品化；利用…賺錢
product〔'prɑdəkt,-dʌkt〕*n.* 產品

27.（**A**）(A) ***fight***〔faɪt〕*v.* 對抗　　(B) kill〔kɪl〕*v.* 殺死
　　　(C) win〔wɪn〕*v.* 贏　　(D) shut〔ʃʌt〕*v.* 關閉

28.（**C**）***devote* + 時間 + *to* + *V-ing*** 將時間用於…

It is the fans that support the kingdoms of the recording companies;
<u>however</u>, the industry never gives anything back to the fans — by lowering
　　29
the prices of CDs. It is an easy arithmetic <u>question</u>. When one can buy a
　　　　　　　　　　　　　　　　　　30
CD of pop music for NT$50 anywhere on the streets, why does he or she
want to spend NT$300 or more for the same one?
支持唱片界的人是歌迷：然而，唱片公司卻從未給歌迷任何回饋——降低 CD
的售價。這是個簡單的算術題。如果大家可以在街上隨處買到台幣 50 元的 CD，
那麼為什麼要花台幣 300 元或更多的錢，去買一張相同的 CD 呢？

kingdom〔'kɪŋdəm〕*n.* 界；領域　　feedback〔'fid,bæk〕*n.* 回饋
lower〔'loɚ〕*v.* 降低　　arithmetic〔ə'rɪθmə,tɪk〕*n.* 算術
pop music 流行音樂

29.（**B**）依句意，選 (B) ***however*** 「然而」。而 (A) indeed〔ɪn'did〕*adv.* 的確，
　　　(C) hence〔hɛns〕*adv.* 因此，(D) furthermore〔'fɝðɚ,mor〕*adv.* 此外，
　　　均不合句意。

30.（**A**）依句意，這是個簡單的算術「題」，選 (A) ***question***。而 (B) 回饋，
　　　(C) 產品，(D) 產業，均不合句意。

三、文意選填：

第 31 至 40 題為題組

Are you someone who practically lives in front of the computer — a *mouse potato*? Or are you nervous about new technology — a *technophobe*? <u>In either case</u>, if you want to master the English language, you will need
　　　　31
to be <u>familiar with</u> those new computer words that seem to be popping
　　　　　32
up everywhere.

你是不是實際生活在電腦前面的人——是個電腦族呢？或者你對於日新月異的科技感到不安——是個科技恐懼者？無論你是哪種情形，如果你想學好英文，你就必須熟悉這些幾乎是隨處可見的電腦新詞。

　　　practically〔'præktɪklɪ〕*adv.* 實際上
　　　mouse potato 電腦族；電腦迷（*本詞改編自* couch potato「*坐在沙發上不動的人*」）
　　　technology〔tɛk'nɑlədʒɪ〕*n.* 科技　　　～-phobe〔fob〕*n.* ～ 恐懼者
　　　technophobe〔'tɛkno,fob〕*n.* 科技恐懼者　　　***pop up*** 突然出現

31. (**F**) *in either case* 無論哪種情形

32. (**D**) *be familiar with* 對～熟悉

Luckily, most computer words are easy to learn. <u>For one thing</u>, many
　　　　　　　　　　　　　　　　　　　　　　　33
of these words probably already have similar forms in your own language.
<u>For example</u>, the German word for computer is *Computer*, in South American
　　34
Spanish it is *computador*, and in Japanese we <u>find</u> *konpyuta*.
　　　　　　　　　　　　　　　　　　　　　　35

　　還好，大部分的電腦詞彙都是簡單易學的。其一，這些字當中，有許多可能和你所使用的語言很類似。舉例來說，在德文中，電腦的寫法為 Computer，南美洲西班牙文的寫法為 computador，我們也可以發現日文中，電腦的寫法為 konpyuta。

　　　luckily〔'lʌkɪlɪ〕*adv.* 幸好；還好　　　form〔fɔrm〕*n.* 形狀

33. (**A**) *for one thing* 其一

34. (**G**) *for example* 舉例來說

35. (**E**) 依句意，我們可以「發現」日文的電腦叫做 konpyuta，選 (E) *find*。

Another reason why computer words are easy to learn is that many of them are so underline{colorful}. They are words that often make us smile when we
36
first hear them such as underline{snail mail} (traditional mail rather than Internet-based
37
mail) or *wysiwyg* (what-you-see-is-what-you-get).

　　電腦詞彙之所以這麼好學，另一個原因是，它們的用字大都相當有趣。當我們初次聽到這些字，像是「蝸牛信件」（非電子傳送的傳統郵件），或是 wysiwyg（你所看到的就是你所得到的），它們通常都能讓我們會心一笑。

　　snail〔snel〕*n.* 蝸牛　　traditional〔trəˈdɪʃənḷ〕*adj.* 傳統的
　　rather than 而不是　　-based〔best〕*adj.* 以～爲基礎的
　　Internet-based〔ˈɪntəˌnɛtˈbest〕*adj.* 用網路的

36. (**J**) *colorful*〔ˈkʌləfəl〕*adj.* 有趣的　由後面一句可知，這些字能讓人會
　　心一笑，因此它們應該很「有趣」，故選 (J)。

37. (**I**) *snail mail* 蝸牛信件（用來比喻傳統信件的遞送，像蝸牛一樣慢）

To get a feeling for computer words, it helps to underline{understand} the world
38
that created them — *cyberculture*, as it is often called. The computer industry is underline{full of} young people who think of themselves as very different from
39
underline{traditional} business people in suits. It is a world that avoids heavy
40
scientific-sounding language in favor of words that are simple, fresh and playful.

　　想要體會這些電腦詞彙，比較快的方法，就是先去了解創造出這些字的地方，也就是所謂的網路文化文化。電腦界裡大多是新新人類，他們都自認和那些穿西裝的企業家大不相同。在電腦世界裡，會避免使用聽起來難懂、又專業的科學術語，而偏好簡單、新鮮，而且有趣的用字。

　　cyber-〔ˈsaɪbə〕*adj.* 和網路有關的
　　cyberculture〔ˈsaɪbəˈkʌltʃə〕*n.* 網路文化　　***think of～as*** 認爲～是
　　suit〔sut〕*n.* 西裝　　heavy〔ˈhɛvɪ〕*adj.* 難懂的
　　scientific-sounding〔ˌsaɪənˈtɪfɪkˈsaʊndɪŋ〕*adj.* 聽起來很專業的
　　in favor of 偏好　　playful〔ˈplefəl〕*adj.* 有趣的

38. (**C**) 依句意，「了解」網路文化，能幫助人們體會電腦詞彙，故選 (C)
　　understand。

39. (**B**) *be full of* 充滿

40. (**H**) 依句意，從事電腦業的年輕人，都自認不同於「傳統的」的企業家，
故選 (H) *traditional*。

四、篇章結構：

第 41 至 45 題爲題組

　　Fiction is the name we use for stories that are make-believe, such as
Harry Potter or *Alice in Wonderland*.　<u>(**E**) But fiction isn't always different</u>
41

<u>from the way things usually are.</u>　It can be so close to the truth that it seems
as real as something that happened to you this morning.　Or, fiction can be
as fantastic as the most unbelievable fairy tale.

　　我們用小說這個名稱來稱呼虛構的故事，例如「**哈利波特**」或是「**愛麗絲
夢遊仙境**」。但是小說並不一定和平常的事物不同。它可能和今天早上發生在你
身上的事情一樣眞實。或者，小說可能和最令人難以置信的童話故事般那麼奇
妙。

　　　　fiction〔'fɪkʃən 〕*n.* 小說　　make-believe〔'mekbə‚liv 〕*adj.* 虛構的
　　　　fantastic〔 fæn'tæstɪk 〕*adj.* 奇妙的
　　　　unbelievable〔‚ʌnbɪ'livəbḷ 〕*adj.* 令人難以置信的
　　　　fairy tale 童話故事

　　Not everything in a fictional story has to be made up.　<u>(**D**) You could</u>
<u>write a story in which you fly to the moon.</u>　*You*, of course, are real,
42

and the *moon* is real, and many of the things that you could describe,
such as the stars, the wind, and the pull of gravity, would be real.
<u>(**C**) But your trip through space would be fiction.</u>　It would be a trip you
43

took in your imagination.

　　小說故事裡的事物並不一定都是虛構的。你可以寫一篇你飛向月亮的故
事。當然，**你**是眞的，**月亮**是眞的，還有許多你可以敘述的事情，例如星星、
風和重力加速度，都是眞的。但是你遨遊太空的旅程卻是虛構的。這是一段你
想像中的旅程。

fictional〔ˈfɪkʃənḷ〕*adj.* 虛構的　　***make up*** 編造

describe〔dɪˈskraɪb〕*v.* 描述　　　pull〔pʊl〕*n.* 拉力

gravity〔ˈɡrævətɪ〕*n.* 重力　　　space〔spes〕*n.* 太空

imagination〔ɪˌmædʒəˈneʃən〕*n.* 想像力

Nonfiction, on the other hand, is all about true things. <u>(A) Nothing is</u>
<u>made up.</u>　Someone's biography is nonfiction; so is your autobiography.
So are articles in your local newspaper, and school reports on science.
<u>(B) History is nonfiction, too.</u>　Imagine writing history about the 1989 San
Francisco earthquake, or a report about a high school sports team.　An old
proverb says, "Truth is stranger than fiction."　Do you think that's true?

　但是，非小說類的文學，則全都是關於眞實的事情，沒有任何事是虛構的。
某人的傳記是非小說類的文學；你的自傳也是。地方報紙的文章也是，以及學
校的科學報告也是。歷史也是非小說類。想像寫一篇關於一九八九年舊金山地
震的歷史，或是一篇關於高中球隊的報導。有一句諺語說：「事實比小說更離奇。」
你認爲是如此嗎？

nonfiction〔ˌnɑnˈfɪkʃən〕*n.* 非小說類的文學

on the other hand 但是；另一方面

biography〔baɪˈɑɡrəfɪ〕*n.* 傳記

autobiography〔ˌɔtəbaɪˈɑɡrəfɪ〕*n.* 自傳

article〔ˈɑrtɪkḷ〕*n.* 文章　　　local〔ˈlokḷ〕*adj.* 當地的

imagine〔ɪˈmædʒɪn〕*v.* 想像　　***San Francisco*** 舊金山

earthquake〔ˈɝθˌkwek〕*n.* 地震　　sports〔spɔrts〕*adj.* 運動的

proverb〔ˈprɑvɝb〕*n.* 諺語

第 46 至 50 題爲題組

　Car windshield wipers were invented by Mary Anderson on a trip in
New York City in 1903.　While touring the city on a streetcar, Mary was
not interested in the views on the streets.　<u>(D) Instead, she paid much</u>
<u>attention to the streetcar motorman.</u>　Repeatedly, the motorman had to get
out of the streetcar to wipe off the snow and ice collected on the windshield.

New York streetcar motormen at that time had tried various ways to solve the problem.　(E) Wiping off the snow and ice by hand, however, seemed

47
to be the only solution.

　　汽車雨刷是瑪麗・安德生在一九○三年，去紐約旅行的途中發明的。當瑪麗坐在電車上遊覽城市時，對街上的景色不感興趣。相反地，她很專心地看著電車司機。那位司機必須反覆地爬出電車，抹掉堆積在擋風玻璃上的雪和冰。那個時候的紐約電車司機，已經試過各種方法，想要解決這個問題。然而，用手把冰雪抹去，似乎是唯一的解決之道。

windshield〔ˋwɪndˏʃild〕n.（汽車）擋風玻璃
windshield wiper　（汽車）雨刷
streetcar〔ˋstritˏkɑr〕n. 電車
instead〔ɪnˋstɛd〕adv. 相反地　　***pay attention to*** 注意
motorman〔ˋmotəmən〕n. 電車司機　　***wipe off*** 抹去
collect〔kəˋlɛkt〕v. 積聚　　various〔ˋvɛrɪəs〕adj. 各式各樣的
seem〔sim〕v. 似乎　　solution〔səˋluʃən〕n. 解決之道

Mary, sitting on her seat, quickly drew her device in her sketchbook.
(A) Her solution was simple.　Mary's device allowed the motorman to use

48
a lever inside the streetcar to activate a swinging arm on the windshield to wipe off the snow and ice.　Because the device was first designed for cold weather, it could be easily removed when warmer weather arrived.
(C) Its function of wiping rain was later considered and added.

49
瑪麗坐在位子上，很快地在素描簿上畫出了一個裝置。她的解決方法很簡單。瑪麗所設計的裝置，可以讓電車司機，用一個車內的槓桿，啟動擋風玻璃上左右搖擺的臂狀物，來抹去冰雪。因為這個裝置最初是為了寒冷的天氣而設計，所以當天氣變暖時，很容易就可以取下。而把雨水抹去的功能，是後來經過考慮後而增加的。

device〔dɪˋvaɪs〕n. 裝置　　sketchbook〔ˋskɛtʃˏbʊk〕n. 素描簿
lever〔ˋlɛvə〕n.（機械之）手桿；任何似槓桿之物
activate〔ˋæktəˏvet〕v. 啟動　　swinging〔ˋswɪŋɪŋ〕adj. 搖擺的
remove〔rɪˋmuv〕v. 除去　　function〔ˋfʌŋkʃən〕n. 作用；功能

Even though her friends teased her about her awkward invention attached
to a streetcar, Mary didn't give in to peer pressure.　(**B**) A year later, she
received a patent for it.　By 1913, her invention had become standard
50
equipment on American cars.　Windshield wipers save lives and make it
easier to drive through storms.

即使朋友嘲笑她那個裝在電車上的笨拙發明，瑪麗並沒有因為同儕的壓力而放
棄。一年後，她獲得這項發明的專利權。到一九一三年的時候，她的發明已經
變成了美國汽車的標準配備。汽車雨刷能挽救生命，並且使汽車在暴風雨中行
進更為容易。

　　　　tease〔tiz〕*v.* 嘲弄　　　awkward〔'ɔkwəd〕*adj.* 笨拙的；不優美的
　　　　be attached to 安裝在　　　***give in to*** ~　向~屈服
　　　　peer pressure 同儕壓力　　　patent〔'petn̩t〕*n.* 專利權
　　　　equipment〔ɪ'kwɪpmənt〕*n.* 設備
　　　　standard equipment 標準配備

五、閱讀測驗：

第 51 至 53 題為題組

　　Both the Eskimos and the Plains Indians used open fires in their
shelters for warmth but with very different consequences.　The Eskimo
house was an airtight igloo made of blocks of ice with a small tunnel-like
entrance and a small chimney in the center for smoke from the fire.
Temperatures inside this structure easily reached 70 to 80 degrees
Fahrenheit although outside temperatures frequently dropped well below
zero.　Often, the igloo was so hot that the loss of body fluid through
perspiration would force the Eskimos to drink cup after cup of ice water.

　　愛斯基摩人和大平原印地安人，都在他們的房子裏用盆火取暖，但卻有非
常不一樣的結果。愛斯基摩人的房子是用雪塊蓋成的密閉圓頂小屋，有一個像
隧道般的入口，和在中間用來排煙的煙囪。雖然外面的溫度經常降到零度以下，
冰屋裏的溫度卻很容易就達到華氏七八十度。通常冰屋很熱，以致於因為排汗
而流失的體液，會迫使愛斯基摩人一杯接一杯地喝著冰水。

Eskimo〔ˈɛskəˌmo〕*n.* 愛斯基摩人
Plains Indian 大平原印地安人　　shelter〔ˈʃɛltɚ〕*n.* 住處
consequence〔ˈkɑnsəˌkwɛns〕*n.* 結果
airtight〔ˈɛrˈtaɪt〕*adj.* 不透氣的；密閉的
igloo〔ˈɪglu〕*n.*（愛斯基摩人用冰雪造的）圓頂住屋
block〔blɑk〕*n.* 一塊　　tunnel-like〔ˈtʌnḷˌlaɪk〕*adj.* 像隧道的
chimney〔ˈtʃɪmnɪ〕*n.* 煙囪　　temperature〔ˈtɛmprətʃɚ〕*n.* 溫度
structure〔ˈstrʌktʃɚ〕*n.* 建築物
Fahrenheit〔ˈfærənˌhaɪt〕*adj.* 華氏的　　fluid〔ˈfluɪd〕*n.* 液體
perspiration〔ˌpɝspəˈreʃən〕*n.* 流汗　　force〔fors〕*v.* 迫使

The Plains Indians, on the other hand, placed their fire in a tepee made with long poles and animal skins with an entrance cut directly into one wall. In contrast to the Eskimo shelter, the tepee was far from airtight; drafts came in around the door and through gaps between the skins. At night the Indians would crawl under their blankets, cover their heads, and shiver all night — so much that the blankets would shake! The difference between the Eskimo igloo and the Indian tepee was insulation: the igloo's walls were solid and airtight whereas those of the tepee permitted a great deal of air to enter.

另一方面，大平原印地安人會把火放在用長竿子和獸皮做成的帳棚裏，並直接在棚壁上開一個入口。和愛斯基摩人的住屋不同的是，帳棚絕不是密不通風的；風會從門邊，以及獸皮之間的縫隙吹進來。晚上的時候，印地安人會爬到毯子底下，蓋住頭，整晚發抖——抖得連毯子都在震動！愛斯基摩人的冰屋和印地安人的帳棚，其不同點在於對外隔離的程度：冰屋的牆壁堅固且密不透風，然而帳棚的棚壁卻會讓大量的空氣進入。

place〔ples〕*v.* 放置
tepee〔ˈtipi〕*n.*（印地安人的圓錐形）帳棚小屋
pole〔pol〕*n.* 竿子　　directly〔dəˈrɛktlɪ〕*adv.* 直接地
in contrast to 與…不同　　**far from** 絕非
draft〔dræft〕*n.*（穿過縫隙的）風　　gap〔gæp〕*n.* 縫隙
crawl〔krɔl〕*v.* 爬　　blanket〔ˈblæŋkɪt〕*n.* 毯子
shiver〔ˈʃɪvɚ〕*v.* 顫抖　　shake〔ʃek〕*v.* 震動
insulation〔ˌɪnsəˈleʃən〕*n.* 隔離　　solid〔ˈsɑlɪd〕*adj.* 堅固的
whereas〔hwɛrˈæz〕*conj.* 然而　　permit〔pɚˈmɪt〕*v.* 允許

51. (**D**) 本段文章最可能是 ＿＿＿＿＿＿ 中的一部分。

  (A) 一則天氣預報

  (B) 一本關於防火的書

  (C) 一篇關於動物保育的報導

  (D) <u>一本關於住屋建築雜誌的文章</u>

  likely〔'laɪklɪ〕*adj.* 可能的 occur〔ə'kɝ〕*v.* 發生；出現
  forecast〔'for,kæst〕*n.* 預報 prevention〔prɪ'vɛnʃən〕*n.* 預防
  conservation〔,kɑnsə'veʃən〕*n.* 保育
  construction〔kəns'trʌkʃən〕*n.* 建築

52. (**B**) 從本段文章可以推論出 ＿＿＿＿＿＿ 。

  (A) 要經過一個愛斯基摩人的房子，必須經過一條長長的隧道

  (B) <u>愛斯基摩人的冰屋比印地安人的帳棚有更好的對外隔離程度</u>

  (C) 大平原印地安人在冬天喜歡住在他們的帳棚裏

  (D) 每個印地安人的帳棚都有小煙囪用來排煙

  infer〔ɪn'fɝ〕*v.* 推論 release〔rɪ'lis〕*v.* 排放

53. (**A**) 本文主要是寫來 ＿＿＿＿＿＿ 。

  (A) <u>比較</u>   (B) 說傷心的故事

  (C) 娛樂讀者   (D) 報導一個科學發現

  compare〔kəm'pɛr〕*v.* 比較 amuse〔ə'mjuz〕*v.* 娛樂

第 54 至 57 題為題組

 Soapy's life was fine during spring, summer and autumn, but not so good in the winter. When November arrived, Soapy always found a way to stay indoors, away from the cold, and have three meals a day without paying one cent. The trick was simple: he broke the law.

 在春天、夏天和秋天時，索比的生活不成問題，但冬天就不怎麼好過了。當十一月來臨時，索比總是可以找到方法，待在室內以求避寒，並有三餐果腹而不付分文。方法很簡單：他犯法。

  cent〔sɛnt〕*n.* 一分錢
  trick〔trɪk〕*n.* 策略；方法 ***break the law*** 犯法

Last autumn, when nights got too cold to sleep in the park, Soapy realized it was time to make arrangements for his annual winter trip. He walked over to Fifth Avenue around 10 a.m. one morning and sent a stone crashing through a glass window of a big department store. Then he stood calmly by the window, waiting. As he had expected, a policeman came running around the corner. Soapy confessed immediately that he was the one who had broken the window. Yet the policeman did not believe him.

去年秋天，當天氣冷到夜晚無法讓他睡在公園裡時，索比知道，該是爲年度多季旅遊做準備的時候了。一天早上，大約十點左右，他走到第五大道，對著一家大型百貨公司的一扇玻璃窗，丟了一顆石頭，嘩啦一聲，玻璃破了。然後他鎮靜地站在玻璃窗旁等著。正如他所預料的，有個警察由街角跑來。索比立刻承認，他就是打破玻璃的人。但是，警察並不相信他。

> arrangement〔 ə'rendʒmənt 〕*n.* 安排　　annual〔'ænjuəl〕*adj.* 每年的
> avenue〔'ævəˌnju〕*n.* 大道　　send〔 sɛnd 〕*v.* 投擲
> crash〔 kræʃ 〕*v.* 嘩啦一聲破碎　　calmly〔'kɑmlɪ〕*adv.* 鎮靜地
> confess〔 kən'fɛs 〕*v.* 坦承

Soapy also failed in his second scheme: the woman he tried to harass verbally was, much to his surprise, overwhelmed and in fact thanked him for being the first man ever to say such sweet words to her.

索比第二個方法也失敗了：他試著用言語騷擾一位女士，讓他相當驚訝的是，這位女士雖然深受感動，但她竟然還向索比道謝，因爲他是第一個對她說這種甜言蜜語的人。

> scheme〔 skim 〕*n.* 計劃；方法　　harass〔 hə'ræs 〕*v.* 騷擾
> verbally〔'vɜblɪ〕*adv.* 口頭上；言語上
> *to one's surprise* 令某人驚訝的是
> overwhelmed〔ˌovə'hwɛlmd〕*adj.* 深受感動的

It was about noon that Soapy came near a fancy restaurant. He decided to walk in for a big free lunch. When it was time for the bill, he told the manager he had no money and suggested that *he* have him arrested. The manager, realizing what was going on, asked Soapy to follow him into the kitchen, where a big pile of dirty dishes was waiting to be washed. Three hours later, the exhausted Soapy returned to the street.

　　將近中午時，索比走到一家高級餐廳附近。他決定走進去白吃一頓豐盛的午餐。要付帳時，他告訴經理他沒錢，並建議這位經理報警逮捕他。經理明白他的目的，他叫索比跟著他走進廚房，那裡有一大堆的髒碗盤等著清洗。三個小時後，筋疲力盡的索比又回到街頭。

　　fancy（'fænsı）*adj.* 高級的　　　bill（bɪl）*n.* 帳單
　　arrest（ə'rɛst）*v.* 逮捕　　*a pile of* 一堆的
　　dish（dɪʃ）*n.* 盤子　　exhausted（ɪg'zɔstɪd）*adj.* 筋疲力盡的

　　Then the night came, and it was too cold for Soapy to sleep in Central Park. So he wandered about until he found himself standing in front of a church. The choir were practicing a song. "We often sang it in church. I showed great promise once, but look at me now. I've got to change. Yes, I'll take the job offered last week as a truck driver." At this moment, the policeman appeared again, arresting him on a charge of vandalism. Soapy was then taken to the night court, where the judge sentenced him to three months in jail.

　　接著夜晚來臨，天氣實在太冷了，索比無法睡在中央公園裡。所以他到處閒晃，直到他發現自己站在一間教堂前。裡頭的唱詩班正在練唱一首歌。「我們以前在教堂常唱這首歌。我也曾經是前途看起來一片光明的人，可是瞧瞧我現在這個樣子。我必須要改變！對了，上禮拜人家請我當卡車司機，我要去做這份工作。」就在這個時候，警察又出現了，以蓄意破壞的罪名逮捕他。索比於是被帶到夜間法庭，法官判他坐三個月的牢。

　　Central Park 紐約中央公園　　wander（'wɑndɚ）*v.* 到處走
　　choir（kwaɪr）*n.* 唱詩班　　promise（'prɑmɪs）*n.* 前途
　　charge（tʃɑrdʒ）*n.* 罪名　　vandalism（'vændl͵ɪzəm）*n.* 蓄意破壞
　　night court 夜間法院　　judge（dʒʌdʒ）*n.* 法官
　　sentence（'sɛntəns）*v.* 宣判　　jail（dʒel）*n.* 監牢

54.（**B**）本文的寓意為何？
　　(A) 你可以做任何你高興做的事。
　　(B) 人必須為自己的所作所為負責。
　　(C) 改過向善永遠不嫌晚。　　(D) 我們必須做好萬全準備以過冬。
　　moral（'mɔrəl）*n.* 寓意　　please（pliz）*v.* 使高興
　　self（sɛlf）*n.* 自我　　well-prepared（'wɛl.prɪ'pɛrd）*adj.* 準備充分的
　　（按：本文的寓意不明，(B) 雖然是大考中心公佈的參考答案，但不是最好的答案。）

55.（ **B** ）索比 ＿＿＿＿＿＿。
　　(A) 吃午餐時，打破一堆盤子
　　(B) <u>被關到牢裡，雖然他已經決定要改過自新</u>
　　(C) 被打了一巴掌，因爲他對一位女士說不禮貌的話
　　(D) 和教堂唱詩班合唱一首歌，並被深深感動

　　turn over a new leaf 改過自新　　　slap〔slæp〕*v.* 打耳光
　　slap sb. on the face 打某人一巴掌
　　inappropriate〔ˌɪnə'proprɪɪt〕*adj.* 不適當的；不禮貌的
　　move〔muv〕*v.* 感動

56.（ **C** ）第三段第二行的 he 指誰？
　　(A) 那位警察。　　　　　　(B) 索比。
　　(C) <u>那位經理。</u>　　　　　　(D) 那位法官。

　　refer to 是指～

57.（ **A** ）關於這個故事，下列哪個敘述爲「眞」？
　　(A) <u>索比常在監獄裡度過寒冬，那裡很溫暖，而且有免費的膳食。</u>
　　(B) 雖然索比有工作，還有個家，他還是喜歡在街上遊蕩，無所事事。
　　(C) 那位警察並不相信索比的話，因爲索比打扮得像一位高貴的紳士。
　　(D) 就算索比堅決辯稱他並沒有做錯事，法官仍然判他去坐牢。

　　warmth〔wɔrmθ〕*n.* 溫暖　　　dignified〔'dɪgnəˌfaɪd〕*adj.* 高貴的
　　protest〔prə'test〕*v.* 力辯

第 58 至 61 題爲題組

　　Queen Victoria was monarch of Great Britain from 1837 until her death in 1901. This period is often called the Victorian Age.

　　維多利亞是英國女王，她從一八三七年統治英國，直到一九〇一年她去世爲止。這段期間常被稱爲維多利亞時代。

　　monarch〔'mɑnək〕*n.* 君王
　　Great Britain 英國　　　period〔'pɪrɪəd〕*n.* 期間
　　age〔edʒ〕*n.* 時代

Queen Victoria was a stern and serious woman. One reason she was so serious was that she had suffered a great loss. When she was twenty years old, she married a German prince named Albert. Victoria and Albert were deeply in love, and their marriage was extremely happy. In 1861, after they had been married for twenty-one years, Albert died, leaving Queen Victoria heartbroken. For the rest of her life, the lonely Victoria **mourned** his loss. It was customary in those days for a widow to dress in black for a short time after the death of her husband. But Queen Victoria dressed in black for *forty years*. And for forty years, as another sign of her grief, she wrote her letters on white paper edged in black.

維多利亞女王是一位嚴厲且嚴肅的女人。她會如此嚴肅的原因是，她曾經遭受巨大的傷痛。當她二十歲時，她和一位名叫艾伯特的德國王子結婚。維多利亞和艾伯特彼此深愛，而且他們的婚姻非常美滿。在一八六一年，他們結婚二十一年之後，艾伯特去世了，徒留下心碎的維多利亞女王。在她的餘生，寂寞的維多利亞哀悼失去艾伯特。當時，寡婦在丈夫去世後的短時間內，穿著黑色衣服是一種習俗。但維多利亞女王卻穿了四十年之久。這四十年來，為了表示她的悲傷，她還用鑲黑邊的白紙寫信。

stern〔stɜn〕*adj.* 嚴厲的　　　suffer〔'sʌfɚ〕*v.* 遭受
loss〔lɔs〕*n.* 損失（本文指喪夫之痛）
named～ 名字叫做～　　　***be in love*** 戀愛
marriage〔'mærɪdʒ〕*n.* 婚姻　　extremely〔ɪk'strimlɪ〕*adv.* 非常
heartbroken〔'hɑrt,brokən〕*adj.* 心碎的
rest〔rɛst〕*n.* 剩下的部分　　mourn〔morn〕*v.* 哀悼
customary〔'kʌstəm,ɛrɪ〕*adj.* 風俗性的　　widow〔'wɪdo〕*n.* 寡婦
dress in black 穿黑色衣服　　sign〔saɪn〕*n.* 表示
grief〔grif〕*n.* 悲傷　　edge〔ɛdʒ〕*v.* 給～鑲邊

Even before Prince Albert died, Queen Victoria was known as a very serious woman. She had a strong sense of duty and worked very hard at all her tasks. In her diary she wrote, "I *love* to be employed; I *hate* to be idle." She never forgot that she was Britain's queen and always acted with great dignity. Victoria had high ideals and moral standards that sometimes made her seem stuffy. She was also very sure of herself. She always thought that she was right, and she expected everyone to agree with her.

　　即使在艾伯特王子去世之前，維多利亞女王就以身爲一位非常認眞的女人而聞名。她有強烈的責任感，而且非常努力於她所有的工作。在她的日記中，她寫著：「我喜愛忙碌；討厭偷懶。」她從未忘記她是英國的女王，而且舉止總是很有威嚴。維多利亞有崇高的理想以及道德標準，這有時候會讓她看起來有點沉悶無趣。她也總是非常有自信。她總是認爲她是對的，而且她期待每個人都和她意見一致。

> ***be known as*** 以～（身份）聞名　　***sense of duty*** 責任感
> task〔tæsk〕*n.* 工作　　diary〔'daɪərɪ〕*n.* 日記
> employed〔ɪm'plɔɪd〕*adj.* 忙碌的　　idle〔'aɪdl̩〕*adj.* 閒散的
> act〔ækt〕*v.* 行爲　　dignity〔'dɪgnətɪ〕*n.* 威嚴
> ideal〔aɪ'diəl〕*n.* 理想　　moral〔'mɔrəl〕*adj.* 道德的
> standard〔'stændəd〕*n.* 標準　　stuffy〔'stʌfɪ〕*adj.* 沉悶無趣的

58.（ **D** ）根據本文，以下關於維多利亞女王的敘述，何者不正確？
> (A) 她對自己很有信心。
> (B) 她統治英國六十四年。
> (C) 她和一位德國王子婚姻美滿。
> (D) 在她摯愛的丈夫去世之後，她變成一位嚴肅的女人。

> rule〔rul〕*v.* 統治　　beloved〔bɪ'lʌvɪd〕*adj.* 深愛的

59.（ **C** ）維多利亞女王在鑲黑邊的白紙上寫信是因爲 ＿＿＿＿＿＿。
> (A) 她是一個非常嚴格的女人
> (B) 黑色是她最喜歡的顏色
> (C) 那是表現她悲傷情緒的一種方式
> (D) 這是英國君王的習俗

> sadness〔'sædnɪs〕*n.* 悲傷　　custom〔'kʌstəm〕*n.* 習俗

60.（ **D** ）下列特徵都可以用來適當地描述維多利亞女王，除了 ＿＿＿＿＿＿。
> (A) moral〔'mɔrəl〕*adj.* 道德的
> (B) lonesome〔'lonsəm〕*adj.* 寂寞的
> (C) workaholic〔ˌwɝkə'halɪk〕*n.* 工作狂
> (D) ***compromising***〔'kamprəˌmaɪzɪŋ〕*adj.* 妥協的

> characteristic〔ˌkærɪktə'rɪstɪk〕*n.* 特徵
> properly〔'prapəlɪ〕*adv.* 適當地　　describe〔dɪ'skraɪb〕*v.* 描述

61.（ **B** ）"**mourned**" 這個字在這裡意思是 _____。

    (A) 在一個社交場合感到悲傷憂愁

    (B) <u>因為某人去世，公開地表達一個人的悲傷</u>

    (C) 定期檢查以便找出發生什麼事

    (D) 包括在一組限定範圍的數目、年齡和測量值當中

    sorrowful〔'sɑrofəl〕*adj.* 憂愁的   social〔'soʃəl〕*adj.* 社交的

    express〔ɪk'sprɛs〕*v.* 表達   publicly〔'pʌblɪklɪ〕*adv.* 公開地

    regularly〔'rɛgjələ‑lɪ〕*adv.* 定期地

    measurement〔'mɛʒə‑mənt〕*n.* 測量值   fixed〔fɪkst〕*adj.* 固定的

<u>第 62 至 65 題為題組</u>

    Boll, a German scientist and the star of the Manhattan Project, was lecturing at a New York university on the 50th anniversary of the dropping of the atomic bomb on Japan. The speech had become part of his summer routine, justifying what had been done near the end of World War II. The scientific triumph of his career, in fact, had been paralyzing his life, silently troubling his conscience. He had been haunted with visions of the devastation of the Japanese city, Hiroshima. "Dreams have become nightmares," he conceded.

    布爾，是一位德國科學家，也是曼哈頓計劃的名人，他正在紐約一間大學，為日本投下原子彈的五十週年紀念會上發表演說。這個演說已經成為他的夏季例行公事，為二次大戰末期發生的事辯護。事實上，他在科學上的成就，一直癱瘓他的生活，並默默地折磨他的良心。他一直被日本城市，廣島，遭受到破壞的景象困擾著。「夢想變成惡夢，」他承認說。

      star〔stɑr〕*n.* 明星；傑出人才   lecture〔'lɛktʃə‑〕*v.* 演講

      anniversary〔͵ænə'vɜsərɪ〕*n.* 週年紀念

      dropping〔'drɑpɪŋ〕*n.* 投下   ***atomic bomb*** 原子彈

      routine〔ru'tin〕*n.* 慣例；例行公事

      justify〔'dʒʌstə͵faɪ〕*v.* 使成為正當   triumph〔'traɪəmf〕*n.* 勝利

      paralyze〔'pærə͵laɪz〕*v.* 使停頓；使癱瘓

      silently〔'saɪləntlɪ〕*adv.* 默默地   conscience〔'kɑnʃəns〕*n.* 良心

      haunt〔hɔnt〕*v.* 縈繞心頭；困擾   vision〔'vɪʒən〕*n.* 景象

      devastation〔͵dɛvəs'teʃən〕*n.* 破壞

      Hiroshima〔'hiro'ʃima〕*n.*（日本）廣島市

      nightmare〔'naɪt͵mɛr〕*n.* 惡夢   concede〔kən'sid〕*v.* 承認

Then his wife, an Austrian Jew whose parents were victims of the Nazi death camps, fell seriously ill, and designed a salvation journey for her husband, bringing together Boll and Amai, a woman from Hiroshima who lost her face to the world's first atomic blast.

他太太是一位奧地利籍的猶太人，她的雙親是納粹死亡營裡的犧牲者，那時他太太病重，她爲他的先生安排一場救贖之旅，讓布爾和來自廣島的愛瑪見面，愛瑪在世界首度原子彈爆炸時容貌被毀。

Austrian〔'ɔstrɪən〕*adj.* 奧地利的　　Jew〔dʒu〕*n.* 猶太人
victim〔'vɪktɪm〕*n.* 受害者　　Nazi〔'natsɪ〕*n.* 納粹
fall〔fɔl〕*v.* 變成　　design〔dɪ'zaɪn〕*n.* 設計
salvation〔sæl've ʃən〕*n.* 拯救　　blast〔blæst〕*n.* 爆炸

Following his speech, Amai, wearing a face reconstructed by the skilled hands of an American surgeon, approached Boll. Now 56 and a documentary filmmaker, Amai wanted to interview him about his role in making the bomb. Boll looked to Amai to redeem himself for what he had done. And when Amai saw through Boll's façade to his inner depressed state, she recognized a shadowy reflection of the despair and exhaustion that possessed the Japanese after the war, and began to comprehend the price he had paid for victory.

他的演說過後，愛瑪，帶著美國外科醫生巧手重建的新臉孔去找布爾，愛瑪現年五十六歲，是紀錄片的製片人，她想要訪問布爾，了解他在製造原子彈的過程中所扮演的角色。布爾請愛瑪寬恕他所做過的事。但是當愛瑪從外表看透布爾內心的沮喪時，她看到他身上和戰後的日本人一樣，反映出一種疲憊和絕望的陰影，並開始了解他爲勝利所付出的代價。

reconstruct〔ˌrikən'strʌkt〕*v.* 重建　　skilled〔skɪld〕*adj.* 精巧的
surgeon〔'sɝdʒən〕*n.* 外科醫生　　approach〔ə'protʃ〕*v.* 接近
documentary〔ˌdɑkjə'mɛntərɪ〕*n.* 紀錄片
filmmaker〔'fɪlmˌmekɚ〕*n.* 製片人　　interview〔'ɪntɚˌvju〕*v.* 探訪
look to…for~ 指望　　redeem〔rɪ'dim〕*v.* 彌補
see through 看透　　façade〔fə'sad〕*n.* 外貌
depressed〔dɪ'prɛst〕*adj.* 沮喪的　　state〔stet〕*n.* 狀態
shadowy〔'ʃædəwɪ〕*adj.* 陰暗的　　reflection〔rɪ'flɛkʃən〕*n.* 反映
despair〔dɪ'spɛr〕*n.* 絕望　　exhaustion〔ɪg'zɔstʃən〕*n.* 疲憊
possess〔pə'zɛs〕*v.* 控制；擁有
comprehend〔ˌkɑmprɪ'hɛnd〕*v.* 了解

62.（ **C** ）布爾 ＿＿＿＿＿＿。
　　(A) 是紐約州立大學的教授
　　(B) 一直很享受戰勝日本人的感覺
　　(C) 是製造原子彈的其中一位科學家
　　(D) 確信他自己沒有做錯事

　　convince〔kən'vɪns〕v. 使確信

63.（ **B** ）愛瑪 ＿＿＿＿＿＿。
　　(A) 是紀錄片的製片家，並沒有親身參與二次大戰
　　(B) 在世界上第一次原子彈爆炸時失去她的臉，現在則擁有一張新臉孔
　　(C) 不能原諒和忘記那些曾經深深傷害過她和她國家的人
　　(D) 了解原子彈製造者的的絕望，並享受他們爲此所付出的代價

　　personally〔'pɝsnlɪ〕adv. 親身地
　　involve〔ɪn'vɑlv〕v. 使捲入；牽涉

64.（ **C** ）布爾的太太 ＿＿＿＿＿＿。
　　(A) 不會原諒納粹，因爲她的雙親在納粹的集中營裡被殺害
　　(B) 無法了解她先生在廣島的毀滅事件後所遭受的痛苦
　　(C) 爲布爾安排一個會面，使他不會一直做投原子彈轟炸的惡夢
　　(D) 希望愛瑪能在她死後，幫助布爾繼續從事製造原子彈的終生職業

　　concentration camp 集中營
　　destruction〔dɪ'strʌkʃən〕n. 破壞；毀滅
　　save sb. ***from V-ing*** 使某人免於～
　　recurring〔rɪ'kɝɪŋ〕adj. 反覆出現的

65.（ **D** ）本文的作者試著要告訴讀者什麼？
　　(A) 兇手幾乎不曾尋求受難者的寬恕。
　　(B) 人們總是能替自己所作錯的事辯解。
　　(C) 布爾和她的太太對於曼哈頓計劃的成功感到非常自豪。
　　(D) 戰爭的勝利沒有不用付出代價的。

　　forgiveness〔fɚ'gɪvnɪs〕n. 寬恕　　***take pride in*** 以～自豪

第貳部分：非選擇題

英文作文：(作文範例)

If I won two million dollars in the lottery, I would help the homeless people I see every day loitering around the train station. I don't know why those people are homeless, but I would bet there must be some sad stories there. It doesn't matter what those people have done or failed at in the past; no person deserves to live like that. I would not walk up to them and blatantly offer them money because it would rob them of their dignity. I would help them subtly.

I would contact the city Social Welfare Department and inform them of my intention and request them to set up a program to help the homeless. At the same time, I would volunteer some of my time to supervise the spending of the money and the distribution of the goods purchased with the money. We could also use the money to start a job training and placement program. Although two million dollars is not a big sum by any means, I do believe that this trivial amount could make a difference for the homeless. If everyone can chip in a little every day, then pretty soon homelessness will become a thing of the past.

loiter ('lɔɪtɚ) v. 閒混　　bet (bɛt) v. 打賭
deserve (dɪ'zɝv) v. 應得　　***walk up*** 走近
blatantly ('bletn̩tlɪ) adv. 公然地；突兀地　　rob (rɑb) v. 奪走
dignity ('dɪgnətɪ) n. 尊嚴　　subtly ('sʌtl̩ɪ) adv. 低調地
Social Welfare Department 社會福利局
inform (ɪn'fɔrm) v. 通知　　***set up*** 設立
program ('progræm) n. 計劃　　volunteer (,vɑlən'tɪr) v. 自願
supervise (,supɚ'vaɪz) v. 監督；管理
distribution (,dɪstrə'bjuʃən) n. 配給
placement ('plesmənt) n. 職業介紹
sum (sʌm) n. 總額；總數　　***by any times*** 無論如何
trivial ('trɪvɪəl) adj. 微不足道的　　***chip in*** 捐款

試評 91 年指考英文科試題

大考中心所命的試題，一向都具有很高的水準，今年指考的英文科試題卻有很多值得商榷的地方。

第一、指定科目考試（指考）與學科能力測驗（學測）須有更清楚的區分。

今年的試題閱讀量增多，難度也高於學科能力測驗。在 80 分鐘內要做完 65 個選擇題外加作文，考生的閱讀必須要快速才行。這樣的題量增多，難度加深，以及簡答與篇章結構兩題型與學測不同等三點，是否即為指考與學測的區分，大考中心似宜再說明清楚。

第二、閱讀測驗第 54 題斷章取義，答案有爭議。

閱讀測驗第 52 至 57 題的選文改寫自 O. Henry 的短篇小說 *The Cop and the Anthem*。故事主角 Soapy 是流浪漢，原先計畫以故意犯法被捕，以便在獄中白吃白住過冬。但在他被捕之前，Soapy 的想法已經改變，他不想再過漂泊的生活，而想接受卡車司機的工作。很諷刺地，他被警察以流浪的罪名逮捕而被判入獄(不是考題說的因 vandalism 被捕)，這樣一來，被捕入獄雖符合他原來的計畫，卻違反了後來的心願。故事的教訓應該是「不要輕易許願」(因為當願望實現時，你可能已經不需要它了)，而不是考卷上的「人要為自己的行為負責」。O. Henry 最擅長寫諷刺小說，*The Cop and the Anthem* 只是一個例子。根據以上討論，第 54 題沒有答案。

第三、閱讀測驗第 62 至 65 題的選文，時態錯誤太多，導致文章的脈絡不清。

選文用現在式敘述，使得事件發生次序錯亂。例如日本人 Amai 去見科學家 Boll 係在 Boll 的例行演講之後，但文中 Boll 的例行演講及 Amai 的訪問全用現在式，考生讀起來難免混淆。應如附表修正意見的建議，對文章做若干修改。

第四、作文題目有違常情。

由於限定所贏之 200 萬須全數捐出，考生恐得說一些謊話來完成這篇作文。最後，考卷用語有多處值得商榷。

指考是首考，命題者可能較沒經驗，所以試題有一些值得商榷的地方，我們把它們列在下面，供大考中心參考：

題號	原　　　　文	修　正　意　見
11	Sam couldn't figure out how to print out the document until the teacher **showed it to him**.	Sam couldn't figure out how to print out the document until the teacher **showed him**.
21-25	…the IMO **has its final aim** to create opportunities for the exchange of information on **math schedules and practice** throughout the world	…the IMO **has as its final aim the creation of** opportunities for the exchange of information on **math teaching schedules and practices** throughout the world
26-30	(a) …to ask fans to respect **the copyright** and to …	…to ask fans to respect **the copyright law (copyrights)** and　to …
	(b) Celebrities in the rally probably have **no idea about how much** a CD of their music albums costs.	Celebrities in the rally probably have **no idea how much** a CD of their music costs.
	(c) …the industry never **gives its feedback to** the fans	…the industry never **gives anything back to** the fans
41-45	**Alice** in the Wonderland	*Alice* **in** *Wonderland*
46-50 (E)	(a) By 1913, her invention **became** standard equipment on … (b) Wiping off…by **hands**…	(a) By 1913, her invention **had become** standard equipment on … (b) Wiping off…by **hand**…
51(D)	**a magazine** on house construction	**a magazine article** on house construction
54-57	Soapy always found **the way** to stay indoors, away from the cold, and **had** three meals a day …	Soapy always found **a way** to stay indoors, away from the cold, and (to) **have** three meals a day …

62-65	Boll, a German scientist **who was the star** of the Manhattan Project, **is lecturing** at a New York university on the 50th anniversary of the dropping of the atomic bomb on Japan. The speech **has become** part of his summer routine, **self-justifying** what was done near the end of World War II. The scientific triumph of his career, in fact, **has been** paralyzing his life, silently troubling his conscience. He **has been** haunted with visions of the devastation of the Japanese city, Hiroshima. "Dreams have become nightmares," **he concedes**. Then his wife, an Austrian Jew whose parents were victims of the Nazi death camps, **falls seriously ill, she designed** a salvation journey for her husband, bringing together Boll and Amai, a woman from Hiroshima who lost her face to the world's first atomic blast. Following his speech, Amai, wearing a face reconstructed by the skilled hands of an American surgeon, **approaches** Boll. Now 56 and a documentary filmmaker, **She wants** to interview him about his role in making the bomb. Boll looks to Amai to redeem himself for what **he has done**. And when Amai **sees** through Boll's façade to his inner depressed state, she **recognizes** a shadowy reflection of the despair and exhaustion that possessed the Japanese after the war, and **begins** to comprehend the price he has paid for victory.	Boll, a German scientist **and the star** of the Manhattan Project, **was lecturing** at a New York university on the 50th anniversary of the dropping of the atomic bomb on Japan. The speech **had became** part of his summer routine, **justifying** what had been done near the end of World War II. The scientific triumph of his career, in fact, **had been** paralyzing his life, silently troubling his conscience. He **had been** haunted with visions of the devastation of the Japanese city, Hiroshima. "Dreams have become nightmares," **he conceded**. Then his wife, an Austrian Jew whose parents were victims of the Nazi death camps, **fell seriously ill, and designed** a salvation journey for her husband, bringing together Boll and Amai, a woman from Hiroshima who lost her face to the world's first atomic blast. Following his speech, Amai, wearing a face reconstructed by the skilled hands of an American surgeon, **approached** Boll. Now 56 and a documentary filmmaker, **Amai wanted** to interview him about his role in making the bomb. Boll looked to Amai to redeem himself for what **he had done**. And when Amai **saw** through Boll's façade to his inner depressed state, she **recognized** a shadowy reflection of the despair and exhaustion that possessed the Japanese after the war, and **began** to comprehend the price he had paid for victory.
62 (D)	has convinced himself that he **had done** nothing wrong	has convinced himself that he **did** nothing wrong

九十一學年度指定科目考試（英文）
大考中心公佈答案

題號	答案	題號	答案	題號	答案	題號	答案
1	D	21	B	41	E	61	B
2	A	22	A	42	D	62	C
3	C	23	D	43	C	63	B
4	A	24	C	44	A	64	C
5	D	25	C	45	B	65	D
6	D	26	D	46	D		
7	B	27	A	47	E		
8	A	28	C	48	A		
9	C	29	B	49	C		
10	D	30	A	50	B		
11	C	31	F	51	D		
12	B	32	D	52	B		
13	C	33	A	53	A		
14	D	34	G	54	B		
15	A	35	E	55	B		
16	C	36	J	56	C		
17	B	37	I	57	A		
18	C	38	C	58	D		
19	D	39	B	59	C		
20	A	40	H	60	D		

九十一學年度指定科目考試
各科成績標準一覽表

科　　目	高　標	均　標	低　標
國　　文	52	43	33
英　　文	55	36	18
數　學　甲	62	45	27
數　學　乙	65	46	26
化　　學	55	35	16
物　　理	30	17	5
生　　物	58	42	26
歷　　史	61	47	33
地　　理	66	53	40

※ 以上三項標準係依各該科全體到考考生成績計算，且均取整數(小數只捨不入)，各標準計算方式如下：

高標：該科前百分之五十考生成績之平均。

均標：該科全體考生成績之平均。

低標：該科後百分之五十考生成績之平均。

★ 電腦統計歷屆指定科目考試單字 ★

2-D (95 年)
3-D (95 年)
4-D (95 年)

a.m. (91 年)
abbrevite (100 年)
abbreviated (99 年)
abbreviation (99 年)
abhor (96 年)
ability (93, 95, 97, 98, 99 年)
able (95, 96, 98, 100 年)
abolish (98 年)
aborigine (92 年)
abort (95 年)
abortion (95 年)
abortionist (95 年)
absolute (95 年)
absolutely (93, 95 年)
absorb (99 年)
abstract (99 年)
abundant (94 年)
academic (96, 98, 99, 100 年)
accept (95, 97 年)
acceptable (97, 98 年)
acceptance (96, 100 年)
access (94, 95, 96 年)
accessible (92, 97 年)
accessories (97 年)
accident (91, 98 年)
accidental (97 年)
accidentally (93, 94 年)
accommodations (96 年)
accomplish (97 年)

accomplishment (93 年)
accordance (96 年)
according (91, 92, 93, 94, 96, 98, 100 年)
accordingly (94, 99, 100 年)
account (93, 96 年)
accountant (91 年)
accounting (93 年)
accurate (93, 95 年)
accuse (95 年)
accustom (93 年)
achieve (92, 97 年)
achievement (93 年)
acknowledgment (97 年)
acquire (95, 100 年)
across (92 年)
act (91, 96 年)
action (91, 92, 98 年)
activate (91, 93 年)
active (99 年)
activism (99 年)
activist (94, 95 年)
activity (93, 95, 98 年)
actress (93 年)
actual (95 年)
actually (93, 97, 100 年)
ad (93, 99 年)
AD/HD (96 年)
adapt (94, 96, 98 年)
adaptation (94 年)
add (91, 95, 98, 99 年)
addict (96 年)
addicted (98 年)
addiction (98 年)
addition (92, 94, 99, 100 年)
additional (96, 97 年)

address (94, 98 年)
adjust (97 年)
adjustment (100 年)
administer (94 年)
administration (92 年)
administrative (96 年)
admission (99 年)
admit (93, 94 年)
adolescence (98 年)
adopt (93, 98, 100 年)
adoption (95 年)
adore (95 年)
adult (98, 100 年)
adulthood (98 年)
advance (94, 95, 96, 97, 100 年)
advanced (94 年)
advantage (91, 97 年)
adventure (100 年)
adventurous (93 年)
advertisement (94 年)
advertising (93, 94, 99 年)
advice (92 年)
adviser (93 年)
advocate (92, 95, 99 年)
affair (99 年)
affect (94, 95, 96, 97, 100 年)
affection (98 年)
afford (94 年)
affordable (93 年)
afraid (98, 100 年)
Africa (97 年)
African (97 年)
against (92, 95, 96 年)
aged (96, 99 年)
agency (93, 97 年)
agenda (92 年)

aggressive (93, 96 年)

aghast (95 年)

aging (96 年)

agree (95 年)

agreement (94 年)

agriculturally (98 年)

agriculture (96 年)

aid (98, 100 年)

aide (92 年)

AIDS (92 年)

aim (91, 98, 99 年)

air (91, 92, 95 年)

airline (92 年)

airtight (91, 93 年)

alarm (99 年)

albino (94 年)

album (93 年)

alcohol (97 年)

alien (94, 95 年)

alive (99 年)

allergic (98 年)

alliance (94 年)

all-male (97 年)

allow (91, 92, 98, 99, 100 年)

almost (91, 92, 93, 98, 99, 100 年)

alone (94, 98, 99, 100 年)

along (93 年)

already (93, 94, 97, 100 年)

alter (97, 98 年)

alternative (95, 98, 100 年)

although (93, 97, 100 年)

altogether (92, 99 年)

always (97 年)

amazing (92, 95 年)

Amazon (96 年)

ambitious (93 年)

America (95, 96, 98 年)

American (95, 98 年)

among (91, 93, 94, 95, 97, 98, 100 年)

amount (91, 93 年)

amuse (91 年)

amusing (97 年)

analysis (100 年)

anchor (100 年)

ancient (98 年)

Angkor (94 年)

Angkorian (94 年)

Angola (96 年)

angry (100 年)

anguish (100 年)

animal (100 年)

anniversary (91, 97 年)

announce (94, 97 年)

annoying (97 年)

annual (91, 95, 96, 98, 100 年)

annually (98 年)

anorexia nervosa (97 年)

another (95, 97, 98, 100 年)

ant (96 年)

antenna (94 年)

anti-abortion (95 年)

antioxidant (97 年)

anti-piracy (91 年)

anti-virus (96 年)

anxiety (96, 98 年)

anxiously (92, 96 年)

anywhere (94, 97 年)

apart (92, 97, 98 年)

apartment (98 年)

apologize (94, 97 年)

apology (92 年)

appeal (99 年)

appear (91, 93, 99, 100 年)

appearance (92, 98 年)

applause (95, 99 年)

appliance (98 年)

apply (93, 97 年)

appreciate (92, 95, 100 年)

appreciation (91, 95, 96, 98, 100 年)

appreciative (99 年)

approach (91, 95, 99 年)

appropriate (94, 95, 96 年)

approval (93, 97, 99 年)

approve (100 年)

approximately (91, 93, 99 年)

Arab (94 年)

arbitrarily (92 年)

arc (93 年)

archipelago (94 年)

architect (93 年)

architectural (93 年)

architecture (93, 100 年)

arduous (91 年)

area (97, 99, 100 年)

arguably (93 年)

argue (92 年)

argument (95 年)

arise (97, 99 年)

arithmetic (91 年)

around (91, 93, 96, 97, 100 年)

arouse (94 年)

arrange (91 年)

arrangement (91 年)

arrest (91, 92 年)

arrogant (92 年)

art (98 年)

article (91, 94 年)

artifact (94, 99 年)

artificial (93, 97 年)

artist (93, 97 年)

artistic (93, 96 年)

artistry (98 年)

ashamed (98年)
Asia (92, 99年)
Asian (94年)
aspect (94年)
assemble (94年)
assess (94年)
assign (93年)
assignment (98年)
associate (94年)
association (91, 95, 98, 99, 100年)
assurance (92年)
assure (95, 99年)
athlete (97年)
athletic (91, 97年)
athletics (97, 98年)
atomic (91年)
attach (91年)
attack (92, 95, 96年)
attain (95年)
attempt (97年)
attend (91, 93年)
attendance (92年)
attendant (92年)
attention (91, 92, 94, 96, 97, 98, 100年)
attentive (96年)
attitude (95, 96, 98, 99, 100年)
attract (97, 98, 99, 100年)
attraction (94年)
attractive (92年)
attribute (98年)
audience (94, 99年)
aunt (94年)
aurora (96年)
aurora borealis (96年)
Australia (92年)
Australian (95年)
Austrian (91年)

author (91, 92, 95, 96, 97年)
authority (100年)
authorities (91, 92, 93, 98年)
auto (100年)
autobiography (91年)
automatically (95年)
available (92, 94, 96, 97, 98年)
avenue (91, 93年)
average (92, 93, 95, 96, 97, 98, 99年)
avian (93年)
avian flu (95年)
aviation (92年)
avoid (91, 92, 94, 95, 98年)
await (96年)
award (95, 97, 100年)
aware (98年)
awkward (91年)

B.C. (93, 98年)
baby boomer (96年)
baby-blue (93年)
bachelor (100年)
background (98年)
bag (92年)
bag-matching (92年)
bake (96年)
balcony (92年)
balloon (95年)
ball-shaped (93年)
ban (100年)
Bangkok (92年)
bankrupt (96年)
bankruptcy (92年)
bargain (93年)
bark (93年)

basalt (94年)
base (100年)
baseball (97年)
based (91, 96年)
basic (93年)
basis (95, 99年)
basketball (97年)
battle (95年)
bay (96年)
beach (94年)
beaming (95年)
bean (99年)
bear (99年)
beat (92, 95, 96, 100年)
beauiful (100年)
beauty (94年)
because (94, 97, 98, 100年)
become (94, 97, 100年)
bee (96, 100年)
beforehand (97年)
begin (94, 97, 100年)
beginning (93, 95, 97, 98年)
behalf (91年)
behave (96年)
behavior (91, 95, 96, 98, 99, 100年)
behind (96年)
belief (94, 99年)
believe (91, 92, 95, 97年)
belly (93年)
beloved (91, 92年)
below (91年)
beneath (92, 93年)
benefactor (96年)
beret (97年)
Berlin (92年)
beside (92年)
besides (91, 93, 96年)
best-selling (93年)

betray (98年)

between (93, 94, 96, 97, 100年)

beware (98年)

beyond (93, 96, 97年)

Bhutan (96年)

Bible (98年)

bid (97年)

bill (91, 95, 99年)

billion (91, 97年)

bin (93年)

biography (91年)

biological (94, 96年)

biology (98年)

bird flu (93年)

birth (93, 94, 95年)

birth order (94年)

bison (95年)

bit (93, 97, 98年)

bitter (95年)

blade (92年)

blame (97年)

blanket (91年)

blast (91年)

blessed (95年)

blind (99, 100年)

blindfold (99年)

block (91, 97年)

blog (98, 99年)

blogger (99年)

blond (93年)

blood (94, 96年)

bloom (94年)

blueberry (97年)

blur (95年)

blurry (95年)

blurt (96年)

board (92年)

boast (94年)

boil (93年)

boiling (95年)

bomb (91, 92年)

bomber (92年)

border (97年)

borderline (97年)

bored (92, 94年)

boredom (95年)

boring (95年)

born (99年)

bottle (95年)

bounce (96年)

bound (94年)

bounty (95年)

bowling (97年)

brain (94, 97年)

brand new (94年)

break (97, 100年)

breakable (93年)

breakdown (91年)

breakthrough (93, 95年)

breath (92年)

breathe (93年)

breathtaking (93, 94年)

brevity (99年)

bribery (95年)

brick (97年)

bride (98, 100年)

bridge (96年)

bright (93, 97, 100年)

bright-colored (92年)

brilliant (93, 96年)

Britain (91年)

British (94, 96年)

broad (94年)

broadcast (97年)

broadly (94年)

brochure (92年)

broke (91年)

broken (91, 98年)

bronzed (97年)

browse (91年)

brush (93, 99年)

brush painting (93年)

brushwork (93年)

bucket (91年)

Buddhism (93年)

Buddhist (96年)

budget (97年)

build (100年)

building (92, 93, 94, 96, 97年)

building-to-be (94年)

bully (100年)

burden (96年)

burgundy-colored (92年)

burn (99年)

burst (95年)

Burundi (97年)

bury (91, 93年)

business (98, 100年)

button (93年)

buyer (98年)

bystander (100年)

cab (94年)

cache (93年)

café (97年)

calculate (91年)

calculation (92年)

calendar (95年)

California (98年)

calmly (91年)

Cambodia (94年)

camera (93, 100年)

camp (91年)

campaign (96, 99年)

campus (100年)
Canada (94, 96年)
capable (97年)
capital (94年)
captain (92年)
capture (100年)
caramel (99年)
carcass (95年)
care (92, 95, 96, 97, 98年)
career (91, 93, 94, 95, 98, 99年)
career-ending (97年)
carefully (97年)
caring (98年)
carpenter (97年)
carry (92, 94, 95年)
carve (94, 97, 99年)
carving (94年)
case (91, 92, 93, 95, 97, 98, 100年)
cash (96年)
catch (98, 100年)
category (94, 100年)
cater (92年)
cattle (95年)
cause (92, 93, 96, 97, 98, 99年)
caution (93年)
cautiously (98年)
celebrate (97年)
celebration (98年)
celebrity (91年)
cell (97, 99年)
cell phone (92年)
Celts (98年)
cent (98年)
center (91, 95, 97, 98, 100年)
centimeter (92, 94年)
central (91, 93, 97, 98, 99, 100年)
century (92, 93, 94, 96, 97, 100年)
CEO (98年)
certain (94, 95, 96, 98年)

certainly (93, 96年)
certificate (94年)
certification (96年)
Chad (97年)
chain (100年)
challenge (91, 95, 100年)
chamber (94年)
championship (92年)
chance (93, 95, 98年)
change (93, 95, 96, 97, 98, 99年)
changeable (99年)
channel (99年)
chaos (96年)
character (93, 94, 99年)
characteristic (91, 96年)
characterize (93, 96, 99, 100年)
charcoal (93年)
charge (91, 92年)
charitable (98年)
charity (91, 96, 98年)
charlatan (95年)
chase (93年)
Chatspeak (99年)
check-ins (92年)
cheek (92年)
chemical (97, 99, 100年)
chemistry (94年)
chief (92年)
child abuse (97年)
child care (98年)
childhood (96, 97, 98, 100年)
childish (93年)
childlike (97年)
chimney (91年)
China (93年)
chocolate (97年)
choice (93, 94, 95, 98, 99, 100年)
choir (91年)

choose (94, 96, 99年)
circle (93, 95, 100年)
circular (100年)
circulate (95, 98年)
circulation (94年)
circumstance (97, 98年)
citizen (96, 98, 99年)
civet (99年)
Civil War (96年)
civil War (97年)
claim (92, 95, 98, 100年)
clarify (100年)
classical (98年)
classified (93年)
classify (94年)
classmate (100年)
classroom (98年)
cleanup (98年)
clearly (94, 98, 99年)
clever (94年)
click (94年)
client (93年)
climate (94, 96年)
climb (96年)
cling (95年)
clockwise (93年)
close (100年)
closely (93, 99年)
cloth (92年)
cloud (94年)
club (92, 97年)
clue (99, 100年)
coach (97年)
coal (99年)
coast (93年)
coastal (96年)
coastline (94年)
Coca-Cola (94年)
cocaine (97年)

cockroach (99 年)
code (94 年)
co-exist (96 年)
coffee cherry (99 年)
coherent (94 年)
coin (99 年)
Coke (94 年)
colleague (96 年)
collect (91, 98, 100 年)
collection (93, 94, 99 年)
college (98 年)
collide (100 年)
colonization (97 年)
colony (97 年)
color (100 年)
colored (98 年)
colorful (91 97 年)
coloring (97 年)
columnar (94 年)
combination (92, 93, 97 年)
combine (93, 96, 98 年)
comfortable (100 年)
comic (92, 100 年)
comics (92 年)
command (93, 95 年)
comment (92, 95, 96 年)
commentator (95 年)
commerce (94 年)
commercialize (91 年)
commit (100 年)
commitment (95, 96, 99 年)
common (93, 95, 96, 97, 98, 99, 100 年)
commonly (93, 98, 99 年)
commonplace (94 年)
communicate (98, 99 年)
communication (93, 95, 98, 100 年)
communicator (96 年)

community (98 年)
commuter (99 年)
companionship (98 年)
company (91, 93, 94, 95, 96, 97, 99, 100 年)
comparable (99, 100 年)
comparatively (97 年)
compare (91, 93, 94, 95 年)
comparison (99 年)
compatible (97 年)
compensate (98 年)
compete (93, 95, 97 年)
competently (96 年)
competition (91, 97, 99 年)
competitive (97 年)
competitor (94, 96, 97 年)
complain (91, 92, 95 年)
complaint (91, 92 年)
complete (93, 96 年)
completely (92, 95, 98, 100 年)
completion (93, 99 年)
complex (93, 95, 97, 99 年)
complexity (99 年)
complicate (95 年)
complicated (94, 97 年)
composition (98 年)
comprehend (91 年)
comprehensive (100 年)
compress (93 年)
compromise (91 年)
compulsive (98 年)
computer (91, 92, 94, 96, 98, 100 年)
computer science (98, 100 年)
conceal (98 年)
concede (91 年)
concentration (91 年)
conception (93 年)

concern (92, 93, 94, 96, 100 年)
concerned (95, 98 年)
concert (93 年)
conclude (94, 99 年)
concrete (94, 99 年)
condense (95 年)
condition (94, 97, 100 年)
conduct (92, 99, 100 年)
confess (91 年)
confession (97 年)
confidence (91, 97, 98 年)
confidential (96, 98 年)
confidently (94 年)
confirm (96 年)
conflict (91, 96, 97, 99 年)
conflict-free (96 年)
confluence (94 年)
conform (96, 97 年)
confused (99 年)
congestion (93 年)
congratulate (94 年)
Congress (95 年)
connect (91, 95, 97, 100 年)
connection (96 年)
conquer (93 年)
conscience (91, 99 年)
conscientious (91 年)
consciously (95, 96, 97 年)
consent (92, 99 年)
consequence (91, 92, 93, 95, 98 年)
consequent (93 年)
consequently (92, 96, 98 年)
conservancy (94 年)
conservation (91, 99 年)
consider (91, 92, 93, 95, 97, 99, 100 年)
considerate (91 年)
consideration (97 年)

consist (94年)
consistent (94, 100年)
consonant (99年)
constant (94年)
constantly (96, 99年)
constitute (99年)
construction (91, 92, 94年)
constructive (91年)
consult (96年)
consultant (94年)
consume (97年)
consumer (94, 95, 96, 97年)
contact (93, 98年)
contagious (93年)
contain (91, 92, 95年)
contemplate (92年)
contemporary (92, 93, 97, 98年)
contempt (92年)
contentment (98年)
contest (91, 96, 97, 100年)
context (93, 95, 99年)
continue (91, 94, 95, 96, 98, 99, 100年)
continuously (93年)
contract (91, 100年)
contradict (100年)
contradictory (99年)
contrary (93, 97年)
contrast (91, 95, 99年)
contribute (93, 96, 98年)
contribution (99, 100年)
control (93, 94, 95, 96, 97年)
convenience store (95年)
convenient (92, 97年)
convention (95年)
conventional (95, 98年)
converge (95年)

conversation (96年)
conversion (95年)
convert (96, 99年)
convey (95, 99年)
convince (91, 98年)
cookbook (95年)
cool (95年)
cooperation (91, 99年)
co-operation (93年)
cooperative (97年)
coordinate (93年)
cope (96, 98年)
copy (94, 98年)
copyright (91, 98年)
copyrighted (98年)
corner (91, 93年)
corporate (92年)
corporation (93, 96年)
correct (98, 100年)
correctly (96, 99年)
correspond (97年)
costs (96年)
cotton (96, 100年)
count (96, 100年)
coutless (100年)
country (91, 92, 93, 94, 95, 96, 97, 99, 100年)
countryside (99年)
couple (94, 95年)
courage (95年)
course (94年)
court (91年)
courtesy (96年)
cover (91, 92, 94, 95, 99, 100年)
covergae (100年)
co-worker (95年)
crack (94, 98年)
craft (96, 98年)

crash (91, 92年)
crawl (91年)
craze (94年)
create (91, 93, 94, 95, 96, 97, 98, 99, 100年)
creation (99年)
creative (97, 99年)
creativity (99年)
creature (100年)
credit (98年)
crew (92年)
crime (100年)
crisis (95年)
critic (92, 95年)
critical (99年)
critically (100年)
criticize (92, 93, 94, 98, 99年)
critique (97年)
crop (95, 96年)
crowd (96, 100年)
crowded (91年)
crucial (94年)
cruelty (99年)
cub (95年)
cultural (92, 94, 95, 96年)
culture (92, 94, 96, 98, 100年)
curl (98年)
curly (98年)
current (94, 95, 97, 99年)
currently (94, 96, 99年)
curve (96年)
custody (95年)
custom (91, 98年)
customary (91年)
customer (93, 95, 96, 97, 99, 100年)
cut (96年)

Da Vinci (94年)
daily (91, 94, 99年)
Dalmatian (92年)
damage (93, 95, 97年)
dangling (92年)
Danish (97年)
dare (93年)
darken (91年)
data (94, 100年)
database (93年)
date (94, 95年)
daughter (98年)
dawn (92年)
daylight (94年)
daytime (92年)
dazzling (96年)
deadly (93年)
deaf (91年)
deal (91, 96, 98, 100年)
death camp (91年)
debate (94, 97年)
decade (93, 98, 99年)
deceased (99年)
decide (91, 92, 93, 95, 97, 98, 99, 100年)
decision (94, 97, 100年)
decision-making (98年)
decline (99, 100年)
decorative (93年)
decrease (94, 96, 100年)
deed (98年)
deepen (93年)
deeper (93年)
deeply (91年)
defeat (94, 98年)
defendant (91年)

deficit (96年)
definite (98年)
definitely (94年)
definition (92年)
degrade (96年)
degree (91, 93, 100年)
delay (92年)
delete (95年)
deliberately (95年)
delicate (93年)
delight (93年)
delighted (94年)
delinquency (98年)
deliver (95, 96, 97年)
demand (98, 99, 100年)
demanding (98年)
demonstration (91, 94, 95年)
Denmark (97年)
denounce (99年)
dense (92年)
deny (100年)
department (91, 97年)
depend (98, 99年)
dependent (96年)
depict (99年)
depiction (99年)
depressed (91, 98年)
depression (96年)
deprivation (98年)
deprive (95年)
derive (93年)
describe (91, 96, 97, 98年)
description (94年)
desert (91, 95年)
design (91, 92, 93, 95, 97, 98, 99年)
designate (94年)
designer (94年)
desirable (93年)
desire (96, 98, 99年)

despair (91年)
desperately (93年)
despite (95, 100年)
destination (94年)
destined (97年)
destiny (92年)
destroy (96, 97, 98, 99年)
destruction (91, 93年)
destructively (91年)
detail (98年)
detailed (94, 96, 99年)
detect (91, 93, 100年)
detection (92年)
deter (92年)
deteriorate (98年)
determine (91, 96年)
detour (94年)
devastating (93年)
devastation (91年)
develop (92, 93, 94, 95, 97, 98, 99, 100年)
developing (93, 96年)
development (94, 98年)
device (91, 92, 93, 97年)
devote (91, 94, 96, 97年)
devoted (99年)
diagnose (96年)
diagnosis (97年)
dialect (99年)
diamond (96年)
diary (91年)
dictator (100年)
diet (97年)
difference (91, 94, 99年)
different (91, 92, 93, 94, 95, 96, 97, 98, 99年)
differentiate (93, 95年)
differently (100年)
difficult (92, 93, 95, 96, 100年)

difficulty (93, 96, 98 年)

dig (100 年)

digest (99 年)

digestive (99 年)

digital (93, 98 年)

dignified (91 年)

dignity (91, 93 年)

diligent (99 年)

diligently (97 年)

dime (93 年)

dip (93 年)

direct (94 年)

direction (92, 99 年)

directly (91, 96, 97, 98, 99 年)

director (95, 98 年)

disability (96, 100 年)

disappear (96, 97 年)

disappearance (95 年)

disappoint (100 年)

disappointment (92, 95 年)

disapproval (98 年)

disapproving (96 年)

disbelief (95 年)

discharge (96 年)

discipline (99 年)

discount (96 年)

discourage (92 年)

discover (100 年)

discovery (91, 95, 100 年)

discrimination (96 年)

discuss (94, 99 年)

discussion (92, 94, 97 年)

disease (93, 94 年)

disenchantment (93 年)

disgraced (96 年)

disguise (92, 95 年)

disgust (100 年)

dish (99 年)

dishwasher (98 年)

dislike (97 年)

dismiss (91, 97 年)

disorder (94, 96 年)

display (94, 95 年)

dispute (99 年)

dissatisfied (94 年)

dissimilar (94 年)

distance (95, 97, 98 年)

distinction (95 年)

distinctive (97 年)

distinguish (94, 95 年)

distort (93, 94 年)

distress (100 年)

disturbance (94, 96 年)

diverse (92 年)

diversify (97 年)

divide (94 年)

division (93 年)

divorce (95 年)

doctor (100 年)

doctoral (100 年)

doctorate (100 年)

document (91, 96, 98, 99 年)

documentary (91 年)

doggie (92 年)

domain (95 年)

domestic (92, 93 年)

dominant (100 年)

donation (98 年)

double (100 年)

double check (95 年)

doubt (92 年)

download (91, 98 年)

downloader (98 年)

downloading (98 年)

downside (95 年)

dowry (98 年)

dozen (95 年)

draft (91 年)

drag (92 年)

drama (96 年)

dramatically (94 年)

drape (95 年)

draperies (96 年)

drastic (99 年)

draw (91, 95, 97 年)

dread (96 年)

dress (99 年)

drinker (97 年)

driveway (92 年)

drop (98 年)

dropping (99 年)

drug (97 年)

Dubai (94 年)

due (91, 95, 96, 98, 99 年)

durable (96 年)

during (91, 94, 97, 98 年)

Dutch (94 年)

duty (91 年)

DVD (100 年)

dwell (99 年)

dye (97, 98 年)

each (100 年)

eager (93 年)

eagle (99 年)

eagle-eyed (93 年)

earn (96 年)

earrings (93 年)

earth (94, 96, 99 年)

earthly (100 年)

earthquake (91, 100 年)

earthy (99 年)

ease (95 年)

easily (97 年)

east (94, 99 年)
eccentric (93 年)
ecological (96 年)
ecology (94 年)
economic (93, 94, 99 年)
economics (100 年)
economist (91 年)
economy (95, 96 年)
edge (91, 94, 99 年)
edgewise (93 年)
editor (99 年)
educated (98 年)
education (92, 98 年)
educational (94, 96 年)
effect (93, 94, 95, 99, 100 年)
effective (92, 95, 98 年)
effectively (91 年)
effectiveness (96 年)
efficiently (95, 97 年)
effort (96, 99 年)
Egypt (94, 98 年)
Egyptian (98 年)
Eiffel Tower (94 年)
either (92, 94, 98 年)
elaborate (93, 94, 100 年)
elder (92 年)
elderly (98 年)
electric (99 年)
electricity (91, 96 年)
electronic (92, 93 年)
element (97, 98, 99 年)
elevation (96 年)
elevator (92 年)
eliminate (93, 98 年)
elite (97 年)
eloquence (94 年)
eloquent (93 年)
elsewhere (99 年)
e-mail (91, 95, 99 年)

embed (97 年)
embrace (92 年)
emergence (99 年)
emergency (93 年)
emotion (93, 97, 98 年)
emotional (98, 100 年)
emotionally (97 年)
emperor (99 年)
emphasis (95 年)
emphasize (93 年)
employ (91 年)
employer (96 年)
emptiness (97 年)
en route (92 年)
enable (98 年)
enclose (100 年)
encounter (93 年)
encourage (91, 95, 96, 98, 100 年)
encouragement (91, 98 年)
encouraging (92 年)
endless (92 年)
endlessly (100 年)
endow (94 年)
endurance (95 年)
endure (98 年)
enemy (95, 97, 98 年)
energetic (94 年)
energy (95, 99 年)
enforce (100 年)
engine (100 年)
engineer (92, 93 年)
England (92 年)
enjoy (100 年)
enjoyable (100 年)
enjoyment (93 年)
enormous (95 年)
ensure (92, 99, 100 年)
enter (95, 98 年)
entertain (97 年)

entertainment (91 年)
enthusiasm (93, 95 年)
enthusiastic (91, 93, 94 年)
entire (96, 99 年)
entirely (98 年)
entrance (91, 92 年)
entry (100 年)
envelope (95 年)
envious (92 年)
environment (93, 94, 95, 96,
 98 年)
environmental (93, 99,
 100 年)
e-papers (91 年)
epidemic (93, 94 年)
equality (98 年)
equally (98 年)
equip (93, 95, 99 年)
equipment (91 年)
escape (93 年)
Eskimo (91 年)
especially (91, 93, 98, 99, 100 年)
essence (93 年)
essentially (99 年)
establish (91, 93, 94, 96, 97 年)
esteem (96 年)
estimate (98, 99 年)
estimated (91 年)
Ethiopia (97 年)
ethnic (97 年)
ethnic group (97 年)
Europe (92, 97, 98 年)
European (97 年)
evaluate (96 年)
even (98, 100 年)
event (91, 92, 97, 98 年)
eventually (95, 98, 100 年)
ever (91, 92, 95, 96 年)
everyday (93, 98 年)

evidence (95, 100 年)

evident (91 年)

evolve (93, 97 年)

exact (94 年)

exactly (91, 94, 96 年)

examine (91, 99, 100 年)

example (91, 92, 93, 94, 97, 98, 99, 100 年)

ex-boyfriend (97 年)

exceed (96, 97 年)

excellent (91, 96, 97 年)

except (91, 94, 95, 99 年)

exception (96 年)

exceptional (99 年)

exceptionally (96 年)

exchange (91, 93, 100 年)

excite (99, 100 年)

exciting (92, 95, 98 年)

exclude (95, 98 年)

exclusive (95 年)

exclusively (93, 96 年)

executive (98 年)

exercise (94 年)

exhausted (91 年)

exhaustion (91 年)

exhibit (99 年)

exist (92, 93, 94, 95, 100 年)

ex-lover (97 年)

expand (93, 97, 98, 100 年)

expect (91, 92, 94, 95, 96, 97, 100 年)

expectant (95 年)

expectation (94, 98 年)

expense (96, 100 年)

expensive (93, 100 年)

experience (92, 93, 94, 98 年)

experienced (93 年)

experiment (92, 99, 100 年)

experimentation (100 年)

expert (93, 97, 99, 100 年)

explain (94, 100 年)

explanation (92, 94, 99 年)

exploit (92, 96 年)

explore (100 年)

exploration (93 年)

explore (92, 93, 98, 99 年)

explosive (92 年)

export (96 年)

exporter (96 年)

expose (98 年)

exposition (94 年)

express (91, 93, 96, 97, 98, 99, 100 年)

expression (93, 98, 100 年)

expressive (96 年)

extend (94, 98 年)

extendable (100 年)

extension (97, 98 年)

extensively (94 年)

exterminate (95 年)

externally (98 年)

extinct (96 年)

cxtra (98 年)

extracurricular (92 年)

extraordinarily (99 年)

extraordinary (97, 98, 99 年)

extreme (92, 93, 96 年)

extremely (91, 93, 97 年)

eye level (96 年)

fable (92 年)

fabric (100 年)

façade (91 年)

face (91, 94, 96, 97, 99, 100 年)

facial (100 年)

facilities (94, 98 年)

facility (95 年)

fact (91, 93, 94, 95, 99, 100 年)

factor (94, 96 年)

factory (96 年)

faculty (99 年)

fade (100 年)

Fahrenheit (91 年)

fail (91, 100 年)

failure (91 年)

fair (98 年)

fairy tale (91 年)

faithful (96 年)

fake (94 年)

fall (95, 97 年)

fame (93, 94 年)

familiar (91, 94, 95, 100 年)

familiarity (94, 95 年)

famous (92, 93, 94, 99 年)

fan (91, 96, 97 年)

fancy (91 年)

fantastic (91, 100 年)

fare (100 年)

farewell (97 年)

farmer (93 年)

farming (95 年)

farther (96 年)

fascinated (97 年)

fascinating (95, 100 年)

fashion (94, 95, 97, 98 年)

fat (97 年)

fatigue (94, 95 年)

fault (94 年)

favor (91, 97 年)

favorite (91 年)

fear (91, 92, 100 年)

feasibility (92 年)

feature (94, 97, 98, 99 年)

federal (92 年)

feedback (91 年)

feeling (98, 100 年)

feelings (97, 98, 99 年)

female (94, 98, 100 年)

fertility (98 年)

fetus (95 年)

few (100 年)

fiber (100 年)

fiction (91 年)

fictional (91 年)

field (97, 98, 100 年)

fierce (91 年)

fiery (96 年)

fight (91, 95, 97, 99 年)

figure (91, 93, 94, 95, 96, 97, 100 年)

file (92, 98 年)

fill (93, 98 年)

film (100 年)

filmmaker (91 年)

final (91, 98 年)

finally (94, 95, 97 年)

financial (91, 100 年)

financially (96 年)

finding (92, 100 年)

fine (94, 98 年)

fine arts (99 年)

finish (94 年)

firewood (93 年)

firm (93, 94, 100 年)

first-hand (98 年)

fiscal (94 年)

fit (92, 95, 96, 97, 100 年)

fix (91, 99 年)

flame (96 年)

flash (96 年)

flashlight (97 年)

flavor (99, 100 年)

flexible (98 年)

flexibly (91 年)

flight (92, 93 年)

flock (93 年)

flood (92, 94, 95 年)

flooding (96 年)

floor (98 年)

flourish (94 年)

flu (92, 94 年)

fluent (98 年)

fluid (91 年)

fly (100 年)

focus (95, 96, 97, 98, 99 年)

fold (95, 96 年)

follow (91, 92, 93, 96, 98 年)

following (91, 92, 93, 94, 95, 96, 97, 98, 99, 100 年)

fond (96, 99 年)

foot (92 年)

footpath (94 年)

force (91, 92, 94, 96, 98, 99, 100 年)

forecast (91 年)

foreign (92, 94, 96, 97 年)

foresee (93 年)

forestry (96 年)

forever (98 年)

forget (91, 99 年)

forgive (91 年)

forgiveness (91 年)

form (91, 93, 96, 97, 98, 99, 100 年)

formation (94 年)

former (92, 94, 97, 99 年)

formula (94 年)

formulate (95 年)

forthcoming (93 年)

fortunately (95, 96 年)

fortune (93, 96, 100 年)

forward (92, 99 年)

fossil (99 年)

foster (91 年)

found (93 年)

foundation (98 年)

founder (93 年)

fragrance (94 年)

France (92, 97, 99 年)

free (95, 96, 98, 99 年)

freedom (98 年)

freezing (97 年)

French (94, 99 年)

frequency (92 年)

frequent (96 年)

frequently (91, 96, 100 年)

fresh (91, 94, 95, 100 年)

fresh water (91 年)

freshly (96 年)

freshness (95 年)

friendly (91 年)

friendship (98 年)

front (91, 98 年)

fruit (97, 100 年)

frustrated (94 年)

frustration (96 年)

fuel (99 年)

fulfill (93 年)

full (94, 97 年)

fully (94, 97, 99 年)

fun (98 年)

function (91, 96, 97, 100 年)

fund (95, 96 年)

fundamental (97 年)

funeral (94 年)

furious (98 年)

furniture (93 年)

further (92, 93, 96 年)

furthermore (91, 96 年)

future (94, 97, 98, 100 年)

gain (91, 93, 94, 96, 97, 98, 99, 100 年)

gallery (99 年)

Game Boy (97 年)

gamey (99 年)

gap (91, 98, 100 年)

garden (95 年)

gate (92 年)

gateway (97 年)

gather (97, 99 年)

gathering (95, 97 年)

GDP (96 年)

gear (100 年)

geese (93 年)

gender (98 年)

gene (95, 96 年)

generally (96, 97, 98 年)

generate (100 年)

generously (92 年)

genetic (94, 96 年)

genius (93 年)

genre (93 年)

gentleman (91 年)

geocacher (93 年)

geocaching (93 年)

geographical (94 年)

geography (95 年)

geometric (93 年)

geometry (93, 100 年)

German (91, 92, 99 年)

gesture (98 年)

giant (94, 96 年)

gift (100 年)

gifted (91 年)

given (99 年)

Giza (94 年)

glacier-covered (96 年)

glance (94, 95 年)

glass (99, 100 年)

global (91, 93, 96, 98, 99 年)

globe (98 年)

glorious (95 年)

glue (100 年)

goal (92, 96, 97, 98 年)

god (99 年)

Goddess (93 年)

gold (98 年)

gold-colored (99 年)

golf (97 年)

gone (98 年)

goodies (93 年)

goods (93, 95, 96, 98 年)

goose (93 年)

gossip (97 年)

gourmet (100 年)

govern (100 年)

government (92, 93, 95, 96, 99, 100 年)

GPS (93 年)

grab (98 年)

graceful (91 年)

grade (97, 98 年)

gradually (93 年)

graduate (94, 100 年)

graduated (92 年)

gratuation (100 年)

grammar (99 年)

grand (94, 99 年)

grandeur (97 年)

grandmother (98 年)

grant (94, 100 年)

graph (96 年)

graphic (95, 100 年)

grateful (98 年)

gravity (91 年)

gray (95 年)

great (97, 98, 100 年)

Great Britain (91, 96 年)

greatly (91, 95, 98, 100 年)

greatness (99 年)

greedy (98 年)

Greek (97, 98 年)

grief (91 年)

grin (95 年)

grocery (95 年)

groom (98 年)

ground (94, 100 年)

group (97, 100 年)

grow (96, 97, 98, 99, 100 年)

growing (99 年)

growth (93, 98 年)

guarantee (95 年)

guard (92, 94, 99 年)

guardian (95 年)

guest (91, 92 年)

guidance (96, 97 年)

guide (98 年)

guided (99 年)

guilty (91, 99 年)

gulf (94 年)

gym (94 年)

habit (92, 98, 99 年)

habitual (97 年)

hail (94 年)

haircut (98 年)

hairstyle (98 年)

half (98, 100 年)

halfway (94年)

hall (93, 94年)

hand (99年)

handgun (97年)

handle (96, 100年)

handwritten (95年)

hang (96年)

happen (91, 93, 97, 98, 100年)

harass (91年)

harassment (94年)

hard (97, 99年)

hard drive (98年)

hardly (91, 92, 94年)

harm (91, 99年)

harmful (97, 99, 100年)

harness (99年)

harvest (93, 99, 100年)

haste (100年)

hate (91年)

haunted (91年)

headline (94年)

heads side (99年)

healer (95年)

health (95, 96, 97, 98年)

healthy (97年)

heart (95, 96, 98年)

heart attack (98年)

heartbreaking (100年)

heartbroken (91年)

heat (92, 96, 99年)

heated (95年)

heat-related (96年)

heavily (96年)

heavy (91, 92, 94, 97, 98, 100年)

height (94年)

heights (96年)

helpless (97年)

hence (91年)

heroin (97年)

hesitate (95, 96年)

hidden (93年)

hide (93, 97, 98年)

high (100年)

high-end (99年)

highlight (92, 95年)

highly (97, 98, 100年)

high-quality (99年)

highway (93年)

hijack (92年)

hiker (93年)

Himalayan (96年)

hint (100年)

historic (92年)

historical (93年)

history (91, 97, 98, 99, 100年)

hit (94年)

hold (94, 96, 98, 100年)

hollow (94年)

homeless (91年)

homemaking (98年)

hometown (94, 96年)

homosexual (92年)

honest (96年)

Hong Kong (94年)

honor (92, 93, 94, 99年)

honorably (99年)

horror (100年)

host (94, 95年)

hostile (95, 96年)

hours (96, 97年)

house (93年)

housefly (99年)

hover (100年)

however (91, 92, 93, 94, 95, 96, 97, 98, 99, 100年)

howl (95年)

Hudson (96年)

huge (93, 94, 97年)

human (93, 94, 96, 99, 100年)

human being (95年)

humanity (95, 98, 100年)

humble (97年)

hundred (98年)

hungry (100年)

hunt (93, 95年)

hunting (93年)

hurt (96年)

husband (98年)

husbandry (96年)

hydroelectricity (96年)

hyperactive (96年)

hyperactivity (96年)

hypertext (94年)

hypothesis (100年)

i.e. (96年)

I.Q. (94年)

idea (98年)

ideal (91, 95, 100年)

identical (95年)

identify (93, 100年)

identity (98年)

idle (91年)

igloo (91年)

ignorance (99年)

ignore (92, 95, 100年)

illegal (96, 98年)

illegally (98年)

illness (96, 97年)

illogically (91年)

image (94, 95年)

imagination (91, 100年)
imagine (91, 96, 97年)
immediate (96年)
immediately (91, 95, 100年)
immense (97年)
immigrant (97年)
immune (94年)
impact (94, 100年)
impair (99年)
impatience (95年)
implement (92年)
implication (93年)
importance (93, 98年)
important (91, 92, 93, 94, 95, 96, 97, 98, 99, 100年)
impossible (97, 98年)
impoverished (93年)
impress (94年)
improve (92, 94, 97, 99, 100年)
impulsive (96年)
impulsivity (96年)
inability (97年)
inactivity (100年)
inanimate (93年)
inappropriate (91, 96年)
inattention (96年)
inattentive (96年)
inbuilt (93年)
Inc. (93年)
incentive (99年)
incident (92年)
include (91, 93, 94, 97, 98, 100年)
including (93, 94, 95, 98, 99年)
income (93年)
inconvenience (92, 100年)
inconvenient (92年)
increase (92, 94, 95, 96, 97, 98年)
increasing (94, 98, 100年)
increasingly (91, 96, 100年)

incredibly (92年)
indeed (91, 100年)
independence (93年)
independent (93, 97年)
India (92, 94, 96, 98年)
Indian (91, 95年)
indicate (92, 98, 100年)
indication (92年)
indicator (94年)
indifferent (95, 96, 99, 100年)
indirectly (96年)
individual (94, 97, 100年)
individually (93, 100年)
Indonesian (99年)
indoors (91年)
industrial (93, 96年)
industrialist (93年)
industrialization (94年)
industrialize (94年)
industry (91, 93, 95, 96, 98年)
ineffective (92年)
inevitably (93, 94年)
infant (95年)
infect (93年)
infection (93年)
infer (91, 92, 93, 95, 96, 98, 99, 100年)
inferior (97年)
inferiority (95年)
infinitive (97年)
influence (95, 96年)
influential (94年)
influentially (98年)
influenza (93年)
inform (93, 94, 99年)
information (91, 92, 94, 95, 96, 99, 100年)
informed (96年)
infrastructure (94年)

ingenuity (95年)
inhabit (94年)
inherit (92年)
initiative (91, 95年)
injure (91年)
injury (92, 97年)
ink (93年)
ink-and-wash (93年)
inner (91年)
innocent (91, 93年)
innovation (93, 94年)
innovative (96年)
inquiry (92年)
inquisitive (93年)
inscription (94, 99年)
insect (93, 99, 100年)
insecure (97年)
inside (91, 93, 99年)
inspect (99年)
inspiration (98年)
inspire (91, 92, 99年)
instance (92, 94, 95, 96, 99年)
instant (95年)
instant messaging (99年)
instantly (95年)
instead (91, 92, 93, 94, 96, 97, 98, 99年)
intention (98年)
instinct (99年)
institute (92年)
institution (96年)
instruct (93年)
instruction (96年)
instructions (93年)
instructor (91, 97年)
insulation (91年)
insurance (92年)
intact (94, 99年)
integrity (95年)

landlocked (96年)

landscape (93年)

language (91, 92, 93, 94, 95, 99年)

large (100年)

largely (92, 94, 99年)

last (96, 100年)

late (93, 99年)

later (91, 92, 93, 94, 96, 97, 99, 100年)

latest (99年)

Latin (97年)

laugh (98年)

launch (94, 99年)

law (95, 96, 98, 100年)

lawsuit (98年)

layer (99年)

layoff (96年)

lazy (96, 99年)

Le Procope (97年)

lead (96, 97, 98, 99, 100年)

leader (94, 98年)

leading (97, 97年)

leaf (91年)

leak (100年)

leap (93年)

least (94, 96, 97, 100年)

leather (94年)

leave (93, 94, 98, 99年)

lectern (94年)

lecture (91, 92年)

left (96年)

legal (94, 95年)

legally (100年)

legend (92年)

legendary (99年)

legitimate (96, 100年)

Lego (97年)

leisure (96年)

length (95, 100年)

lengthy (94年)

less (100年)

letter (93, 99年)

level (94, 96, 97年)

lever (91年)

liberal (95年)

liberation (98年)

Liberia (96年)

liberty (99年)

library (96, 97年)

license (98年)

lick (92年)

lie (92, 93, 97年)

lifestyle (98年)

light (91, 93, 96, 97, 99, 100年)

lightweight (100年)

like (100年)

likely (91, 92, 93, 94, 95, 96, 97, 98, 99, 100年)

like-minded (96年)

likewise (91, 93年)

limit (91, 97年)

limited (91, 99, 100年)

line (93, 97年)

linger (97年)

lingering (97年)

link (98, 100年)

liquid (95年)

list (100年)

literacy (99, 100年)

literary (97, 99, 100年)

literature (99年)

live (97年)

livestock (95年)

living (94, 95, 96年)

load (93年)

lobby (95年)

local (91, 93, 94, 96年)

locate (92, 93年)

location (93, 94, 97年)

lock (97, 98年)

locking (97年)

logic (94年)

logical (92, 98年)

London (92, 95年)

loneliness (98年)

lonely (91年)

lonesome (91年)

loosely (92年)

Los Angeles (93年)

lose (97, 100年)

loss (91, 96年)

lost (91, 92, 93, 94年)

lottery (91年)

loud (99年)

lousy (97年)

Louvre (99年)

lower (91, 94, 98年)

loyalty (99年)

luckily (91年)

machine (97年)

magazine (91, 93, 95, 99年)

mail (91, 93, 95年)

main (91, 92, 94, 96, 97, 98, 99, 100年)

mainly (91, 92, 93, 94, 97, 99年)

mainstream (96年)

maintain (94, 97年)

maintenance (94年)

major (92, 93, 94, 96, 99, 100年)

make-believe (91年)

male (94, 98, 100年)

manage (94, 96, 99, 100年)

manageable (93 年)
manager (91, 92, 97 年)
managing director (97 年)
Manhattan (91, 93 年)
manipulate (93 年)
manual (95, 100 年)
manufacture (96, 97 年)
map (94 年)
march (100 年)
marijuana (97 年)
market (93, 94, 96, 97, 99, 100 年)
marketing (94 年)
markup (94 年)
marriage (91, 95, 97, 98 年)
married (91 年)
marry (98 年)
mask (100 年)
mass (95, 96, 98 年)
Massachusetts (93 年)
master (91, 99 年)
masterpiece (94 年)
mastery (95 年)
match (93 年)
mate (94 年)
material (92, 93, 94, 97, 98, 100 年)
math (98 年)
mathematical (91, 92 年)
mathematically (91 年)
mathematician (91 年)
matter (94, 95 年)
mature (91, 96, 100 年)
maybe (94, 95, 97 年)
meadow (94 年)
meal (91, 92 年)
mean (97, 98, 99, 100 年)
meaning (93, 98 年)
meaningful (94 年)
means (91, 93 年)

meanwhile (91, 95 年)
measure (92, 93, 95, 98, 100 年)
measurement (91 年)
measurements (95, 96 年)
mechanic (94 年)
media (99 年)
mediate (100 年)
medical (93, 94, 95, 98, 100 年)
medicine (94, 95, 98, 100 年)
medium (98, 100 年)
meet (98 年)
meeting (94, 99 年)
meeting hall (97 年)
melon (99 年)
member (96 年)
memorial (97 年)
memory (93, 97, 99 年)
mental (99 年)
mention (92, 94, 97, 98, 100 年)
menu (99 年)
merchandise (100 年)
merchant (100 年)
mercy (93 年)
merit (92, 93 年)
message (91, 94, 95, 96, 100 年)
messenger (96, 97 年)
metal (96 年)
metaphor (98 年)
meter (92, 95 年)
method (92 年)
Mexico (95 年)
Michigan (95, 98 年)
microprocessor (93 年)
middle-class (98 年)
Midwestern (94 年)
mile (98 年)
military (96 年)
million (91, 93, 96, 97, 98, 100 年)
mind (97 年)

mine (96, 99 年)
mineral (93 年)
miniature (93 年)
minimize (93, 100 年)
Minnesota (95 年)
minor (97 年)
mint (99 年)
minute (92, 97 年)
miraculously (92 年)
mirror (93, 98 年)
miserable (96 年)
mislead (95 年)
misleading (95, 100 年)
misplace (97 年)
mission (92 年)
mistake (97, 98 年)
mistakenly (92 年)
mistreat (91 年)
mix (100 年)
mixed (93 年)
mobile phone (99 年)
model (94, 96, 100 年)
modern (92, 93, 94, 96, 97, 100 年)
modernist (93 年)
modernization (98 年)
modify (98 年)
molecular (98 年)
mollusk (94 年)
moment (91, 94 年)
Mona Lisa (94 年)
monarch (91 年)
monetary (98 年)
monitor (97, 99 年)
monotony (95 年)
Montana (95 年)
monthly (93 年)
mood (97 年)
moon (91 年)
moral (91 年)

moreover (95 年)
mostly (95, 96, 100 年)
Mother Nature (94 年)
motivation (94 年)
motorman (91 年)
motto (99 年)
mountain (93 年)
mountainous (96 年)
mourn (91 年)
mouse (91, 100 年)
mouth (93 年)
move (92, 94, 96, 97, 99 年)
moved (91 年)
movement (91, 98, 99 年)
moving (96 年)
MRT station (97 年)
much-needed (92 年)
multiplication (93 年)
multistep (93 年)
multitude (94 年)
mural (93 年)
murmur (94 年)
muscle (97 年)
museum (92, 93, 94, 95, 99 年)
museum feet (95 年)
mushroom (99 年)
musician (99 年)
mutual (91 年)
mutually (91 年)
mysterious (97 年)
mystery (95, 97 年)

nail (99 年)
naked (98 年)
name (92, 97, 98 年)
named (91, 92 年)

nation (95, 96, 97, 99 年)
national (91, 95, 98, 99, 100 年)
native (95, 98, 99 年)
natural (92, 94, 99, 100 年)
nature (93, 96 年)
navigate (94 年)
navy (97 年)
Nazca lines (95 年)
Nazi (91, 99 年)
nearly (93, 94, 95 年)
nearness (93 年)
necessarily (99 年)
necessary (91, 92, 98, 99, 100 年)
neck (92 年)
needed (98 年)
needs (95 年)
negative (94, 100 年)
neglect (98 年)
neighboring (96 年)
neither (94 年)
nervous (91, 97, 98 年)
Net (92, 96 年)
network (100 年)
neurological (96 年)
neutral (95 年)
nevertheless (91, 94, 95 年)
New England (94 年)
New York (94 年)
newborn (95 年)
news (95, 98, 100 年)
Nigeria (97 年)
nightmare (91 年)
Nobel Prize (99 年)
noise (92, 93 年)
nominate (94 年)
nonconsecutive (99 年)
nonfiction (91 年)
non-medically (94 年)
non-objective (93 年)

nonstop (99 年)
non-traditional (98 年)
nor (94 年)
normal (96, 100 年)
normally (93 年)
north (94, 96 年)
northern (95, 96, 98 年)
Norway (96 年)
note (96 年)
notice (91, 94, 100 年)
notify (97 年)
novel (97, 99, 100 年)
novelist (99 年)
nowadays (94, 95, 97, 100 年)
number (91, 93, 97, 99, 100 年)
numerous (91, 96, 100 年)
numerously (91, 94 年)

obey (97 年)
object (92, 93, 95, 99, 100 年)
objection (93, 98 年)
objective (97 年)
obligation (94 年)
obscure (93 年)
observe (93, 94, 97, 99, 100 年)
obstacle (95, 100 年)
obstruct (91 年)
obtain (93, 97 年)
obvious (92, 93 年)
obviously (91, 97 年)
occasion (100 年)
occasional (95 年)
occasionally (98 年)
occupation (94 年)
occupational (98 年)
occupy (93 年)

occur (91, 93, 95, 96, 98, 100 年)
odd (96 年)
odor (99, 100 年)
offer (91, 92, 93, 95, 96, 97, 98, 99, 100 年)
official (92, 93, 98, 100 年)
officiated (97 年)
oftentimes (97 年)
oil (99, 100 年)
Olympiad (91 年)
Olympiads (91 年)
once (92, 95, 96, 98, 100 年)
one-seventh (92 年)
ongoing (98 年)
Oniomania (98 年)
online (92, 96, 98 年)
opera (93 年)
operate (93 年)
operation (93, 96, 98 年)
opinion (93, 95 年)
opponent (92, 97 年)
opportunity (91, 93, 94, 98, 100 年)
oppose (92 年)
opposing (94, 99 年)
opposition (94, 96, 98 年)
optimistic (99, 100 年)
option (93, 99 年)
orb (100 年)
orbit (100 年)
orchestra (93 年)
order (91, 92, 93, 94, 96, 97, 98, 99, 100 年)
ordinary (92, 98 年)
organization (93, 96, 98 年)
organize (91, 98 年)
organized (997 年)
organizer (97 年)
orientation (93 年)

origin (94, 96 年)
original (94, 96, 100 年)
originally (94, 99 年)
originate (96, 100 年)
orphanage (98 年)
other (95, 96, 97, 98, 100 年)
others (95, 96, 97, 98 年)
otherwise (91, 92, 93, 99 年)
outbreak (92, 93 年)
outdoor (93 年)
outer (99, 100 年)
outgoing (96 年)
outlandish (92 年)
outlined (94 年)
output (100 年)
outrage (92 年)
outrageous (95 年)
outside (91, 95 年)
outskirts (93 年)
outspoken (95 年)
outstrip (100 年)
outward (98 年)
oval (93 年)
overbuilt (93 年)
over-cautiously (96 年)
overcharge (91 年)
overcome (97, 98, 100 年)
overflow (99 年)
overlook (92, 96 年)
over-packaging (95 年)
overpopulated (93 年)
overpower (93 年)
oversupply (100 年)
overtake (96 年)
overwhelm (96 年)
overwhelmed (91 年)
overwhelming (95 年)
owing (94 年)
owl (95 年)

own (97 年)
owner (92, 93 年)
ownership (98 年)

P

pace (91 年)
pack (93 年)
package (95 年)
packaging (95 年)
packing (93 年)
paid-for (99 年)
pain (98 年)
painful (100 年)
paint (93, 99 年)
paintbrush (98 年)
painter (93, 99 年)
painting (93, 95, 97, 99 年)
pair (92 年)
pale (97 年)
palm civet (99 年)
panel (94, 99 年)
pants (97 年)
paper (94 年)
paper-cutting (97 年)
paradise (94 年)
paragraph (92, 93, 94, 95, 96, 97, 98, 99, 100 年)
paralyze (91, 94 年)
parental (98 年)
Paris (97, 99 年)
Parisian (97 年)
participant (93 年)
participate (91, 92, 98 年)
participating (96 年)
particular (91, 93, 94, 96, 99 年)
particularly (94, 95, 98, 99 年)
partly (94, 97 年)

partner (93年)

party (94, 99年)

pass (94, 98年)

passage (91, 92, 93, 94, 95, 96, 97, 98, 99, 100年)

passenger (92年)

passer-by (100年)

passion (96年)

passively (95, 98年)

past (94, 96, 97, 100年)

pat (100年)

patent (91, 97年)

path (93年)

patient (92, 96, 97, 98年)

pattern (92, 94, 95, 100年)

paw (95年)

pay (92, 98年)

paying (98年)

payment (95, 96年)

payout (96年)

payroll (95年)

peace (93, 97, 99年)

peak (97, 99年)

pearl (94年)

peculiar (92年)

peer (91年)

peer-to-peer (98年)

penalize (96年)

penalty (96年)

penny (93年)

pension (96年)

people (93, 97, 100年)

peppermint (99年)

per (92, 95, 99, 100年)

perceive (96年)

percent (91, 92, 95, 98, 99年)

perfect (91, 94年)

perfectly (95年)

perform (95, 97, 100年)

performance (92, 93, 96, 97, 99年)

perhaps (94, 95, 98年)

period (91, 93, 95, 96, 98年)

perish (91年)

permanent (96, 100年)

permanently (95, 97年)

permission (94, 98年)

permit (91年)

perseverance (94年)

Persian (94年)

person (96, 98年)

personal (92, 95, 98, 99年)

personality (95年)

personally (91年)

personnel (96年)

perspiration (91年)

persuade (92, 95, 96年)

persuasive (92, 95年)

Peru (95年)

pet (92年)

pharmacists (98年)

pharmacy (98年)

phenomenon (96年)

philosophy (100年)

photo (95, 97年)

photo ID (92年)

photograph (93年)

phrase (99年)

physical (96, 97, 100年)

physically (95, 96年)

pianist (97, 100年)

pick (95, 98, 99年)

picking (100年)

picture (100年)

picture window (97年)

piece (97, 98, 100年)

pig (100年)

pigment (93年)

pile (91年)

pilings (94年)

pillar-shaped (94年)

pilot (93年)

pioneer (94年)

pipeline (99年)

piracy (91年)

pirate (91年)

Pittsburgh (96年)

place (96, 99, 100年)

plain (95, 96年)

plains (91年)

planet (91, 97, 100年)

plant (97, 98, 100年)

plastic (92, 95, 97年)

plasticity (93年)

play (97, 100年)

player (97, 98年)

playful (91年)

playwright (96, 97, 99年)

pleasant (98年)

please (94年)

pleased (94, 95年)

plentiful (91年)

plenty (94, 99年)

plow (94年)

plunge (94年)

poem (93, 99年)

poet (93, 99, 100年)

poetry (93年)

point (92, 94, 95, 96, 98, 99年)

poison (95年)

poisoned (95年)

poker (100年)

polar (91, 99年)

pole (91, 99年)

police (92, 98年)

police officer (98年)

policy (94, 96年)

polish (99, 100 年)

political (94, 96, 97, 98, 99 年)

politically (96 年)

politics (96, 98 年)

pollute (91, 92 年)

pollution (91, 97 年)

poor (97 年)

pop (91, 92, 93 年)

popular (93, 96, 97, 98, 99 年)

popularity (97, 98, 99 年)

popularize (93 年)

population (92, 93, 96, 97, 98 年)

pork (100 年)

portable (100 年)

portray (99 年)

position (93, 98 年)

positioning (93 年)

positive (91, 94 年)

possess (91 年)

possession (96 年)

possessor (97 年)

possibilities (96, 98 年)

possibility (97 年)

possible (97, 98 年)

post (93 年)

potato (91 年)

potent (92 年)

potential (92, 93, 94, 96, 97, 100 年)

potentially (97 年)

potted (98 年)

pouch (92 年)

poultry (93 年)

pound (92, 97, 99, 100 年)

powdered (98 年)

power (91, 94, 98, 99, 100 年)

powerful (93, 96, 99 年)

practical (94, 95 年)

practically (91 年)

practice (91, 92, 93, 94, 95, 97, 98, 99, 100 年)

praise (99 年)

pray (95 年)

precautionary (92 年)

precedence (95 年)

precisely (91 年)

precision (92 年)

precondition (97 年)

predator (95 年)

prediction (92 年)

prefer (99, 100 年)

pre-Hispanic (95 年)

premium (96 年)

prepare (92, 94, 95 年)

preprogrammed (93 年)

pre-Roman (98 年)

prescription (96 年)

present (92, 93, 95, 100 年)

presentation (93 年)

preserve (94, 96, 100 年)

president (94, 97, 99 年)

presidential (99 年)

press (99 年)

pressure (91, 93, 96, 97 年)

prestigious (94 年)

pretty (98 年)

prevent (92, 97, 98, 100 年)

prevention (91, 96 年)

preventive (93 年)

previously (96 年)

prey (100 年)

price (97, 99 年)

pride (91, 97 年)

primary (92, 97, 99 年)

primitive (94 年)

prince (91, 92 年)

principal (94, 97 年)

print (91, 95 年)

printed (99 年)

prior (92, 97 年)

priority (92 年)

privacy (92, 96, 100 年)

private (95 年)

privilege (100 年)

prize (99, 100 年)

pro-abortion (95 年)

pro-abortionist (95 年)

probable (96 年)

probably (95, 97, 98, 99, 100 年)

problem (92, 94, 96, 97, 98, 100 年)

procedure (97 年)

proceed (92, 93 年)

process (93, 95, 96, 98, 99 年)

prodigy (93 年)

produce (92, 93, 96, 97, 99 年)

product (91, 93, 94, 95, 96, 97, 100 年)

production (94, 100 年)

profession (96, 100 年)

professional (94, 96, 97, 98 年)

professionship (100 年)

professor (91 年)

profit (98, 99 年)

profundity (95 年)

program (93, 95, 97, 98, 99, 100 年)

programming (93 年)

progress (91, 94 年)

progressively (96 年)

prohibit (93 年)

project (91, 93, 98, 99 年)

prolong (94, 96 年)

prominence (93 年)

promise (91, 96 年)

promising (98 年)

promote (91, 92, 94, 96, 98, 99 年)

prompt (91, 98 年)
pronoun (92, 93 年)
proof (98 年)
proper (99 年)
properly (91, 92 年)
property (91, 94, 98, 100 年)
proportion (93 年)
propose (94, 98 年)
prosecutor (92 年)
prospect (95 年)
prosperously (99 年)
protect (91, 92, 97, 98, 99 年)
protection (92, 95, 98 年)
protective (92, 97 年)
protest (91, 97, 98 年)
protocol (94 年)
proud (97 年)
prove (92, 95, 96, 97 年)
proverb (91, 99 年)
provide (91, 92, 94, 95, 96, 97, 98, 99, 100 年)
provider (98 年)
provocative (98 年)
provoke (92, 100 年)
psychological (96 年)
psychologist (94, 100 年)
psychology (94, 96 年)
public (93, 94, 95, 96, 100 年)
publication (94, 100 年)
publicly (91 年)
publish (94, 95, 100 年)
pull (91, 92 年)
punctually (91 年)
punctuation (99 年)
punish (99 年)
punk (98 年)
puppy (92 年)
purchase (92, 98 年)
pure (94 年)

purpose (91, 93, 94, 97, 98 年)
purposely (93 年)
pursue (98 年)
pursuit (96 年)
push (97, 99 年)
puzzle (100 年)
pyramid (94 年)

qualifications (97 年)
qualified (94 年)
qualify (92, 98 年)
quality (91, 92, 95, 96, 98, 99 年)
quarter (94, 99 年)
queen (91 年)
quest (99 年)
questionnaire (92 年)
quickly (99 年)
quiet (94 年)
quite (97, 98 年)
quote (94 年)

raccoon (99 年)
race (94 年)
radiate (100 年)
radically (96 年)
radius (93, 100 年)
raged (95 年)
raiding (95 年)
railroad station (99 年)
rainforest (96 年)
raise (92, 93, 96, 98, 99 年)
rally (91 年)
rancher (95 年)

randomly (92, 98 年)
range (93, 95, 100 年)
ranger (95 年)
rapid (100 年)
rapidly (93, 95, 97 年)
rare (92, 99 年)
rarely (95, 97, 100 年)
rat (100 年)
rate (95, 98, 99 年)
rather (91, 92, 93, 95, 98, 99, 100 年)
rattle (95 年)
ray (96 年)
razor (92 年)
reach (93, 100 年)
react (93, 95 年)
reaction (94, 95, 98, 100 年)
readership (99 年)
readily (94 年)
reading (92, 93 年)
reality (95, 99 年)
realize (91, 94, 97, 100 年)
rear (98 年)
reason (91, 92, 94, 95, 96, 97, 98, 99, 100 年)
reasonable (97 年)
reasonably (95, 100 年)
rebel (96 年)
recall (100 年)
receipt (98 年)
receive (91, 92, 93, 96, 98, 99, 100 年)
receiver (100 年)
recent (92, 94, 96, 97, 100 年)
recently (94, 95, 99 年)
recession (92, 98, 9 年)
recklessly (98 年)
recognition (96 年)
recognizable (94 年)
recognize (91, 93, 99 年)

recommend (98, 99 年)
reconstruct (91, 97 年)
record (91, 95 年)
recorder (97 年)
recording (98 年)
recover (94, 97 年)
recovery (96 年)
recruit (100 年)
recur (91 年)
recycler (93 年)
recycling can (97 年)
redeem (91 年)
redirect (94 年)
reduce (92, 96, 99, 100 年)
reduction (92 年)
refer (91, 92, 93, 95, 97, 98, 99, 100 年)
reference (98 年)
refine (96 年)
refinement (96 年)
reflect (93, 97 年)
reflection (91 年)
reform (98, 100 年)
refresh (97 年)
refreshing (93, 95 年)
refrigerator (98, 100 年)
refuge (96 年)
refund (100 年)
refusal (100 年)
refuse (92, 100 年)
regain (91 年)
regard (93, 95, 97, 100 年)
regarding (94 年)
regardless (91, 94 年)
region (96, 97 年)
regional (99 年)
regretful (98 年)
regrettable (97 年)
regular (94, 99 年)

regularity (93 年)
regularly (91, 94, 97, 99 年)
regulate (95, 96 年)
regulation (97 年)
rehearse (94 年)
rehire (96 年)
reign (94, 99 年)
reinforce (95, 99 年)
reject (99 年)
relate (96, 97 年)
related (92, 94, 98, 99 年)
relation (91 年)
relationship (94, 95, 97 年)
relative (97 年)
relatively (97 年)
release (91, 93, 98, 99, 100 年)
relevant (94 年)
relics (95 年)
relief (93 年)
relieve (100 年)
religion (96 年)
religious (93, 94 年)
reluctant (92 年)
rely (93, 96 年)
remain (95, 97, 98 年)
remark (99 年)
remarkable (94 年)
remarkably (97 年)
remedy (95, 97 年)
remember (93, 99 年)
remind (92 年)
remote (93, 97 年)
remote control (97 年)
remotely (100 年)
remove (91, 94, 95, 99, 100 年)
renew (96 年)
renowned (99 年)
repair (94 年)
repeat (99 年)

repeatedly (91, 100 年)
repetitive (95 年)
replace (92, 94, 99, 100 年)
replacement (96, 97 年)
reply (92, 94 年)
report (92, 93, 95, 97, 99 年)
report card (97 年)
represent (92, 94, 96, 98, 99 年)
repress (98 年)
reproduction (99 年)
request (93, 99, 100 年)
require (92, 93, 94, 96, 97, 98, 100 年)
requirement (98 年)
research (92, 93, 94, 97, 98, 99, 100 年)
researcher (94, 96, 99, 100 年)
resemble (96 年)
reservation (94, 99 年)
reserved (98 年)
reservoir (91 年)
reside (94 年)
residence (97 年)
resident (93, 98 年)
resign (97 年)
resistance (96 年)
resistant (98 年)
resort (93, 94, 96 年)
resource (91, 94, 95, 96, 97 年)
respect (91, 95, 97, 100 年)
respond (93, 96, 98 年)
respondent (92 年)
response (93, 99 年)
responsible (97 年)
restaurant (91, 99 年)
restless (96 年)
restlessness (94 年)
restore (91, 94 年)
restrict (100 年)

restrictive (100 年)

result (91, 92, 93, 94, 95, 96, 97, 98, 99, 100 年)

resultant (93 年)

resulting (96 年)

retail (100 年)

retailer (96, 97 年)

retain (97, 100 年)

retire (96 年)

retirement (96 年)

retrieve (97, 99 年)

return (91, 97, 98 年)

reveal (92, 94, 95, 99, 100 年)

revenue (94 年)

reverse (94 年)

revolution (96 年)

reward (92, 98, 99 年)

rhythm (99 年)

rice (95 年)

rich (92, 93, 99 年)

richly (93 年)

richly colored (97 年)

rid (92 年)

ridicule (95 年)

right (95, 96, 100 年)

rigid (93 年)

ripen (99 年)

ripeness (99 年)

rise (96, 98 年)

risk (91, 97 年)

risky (100 年)

rob (98 年)

robot (93 年)

rock (94 年)

role (91, 95, 97, 98, 100 年)

role model (98 年)

romance (100 年)

room (98 年)

root (100 年)

rope (98 年)

rough (96 年)

roughly (91 年)

round (99, 100 年)

rout (94 年)

routine (91, 92, 94 年)

row (94, 96 年)

royal (94 年)

rubbish (93 年)

ruin (92 年)

ruins (94 年)

rule (91, 100 年)

run (93, 99 年)

rural (93, 97 年)

sacrifice (92 年)

sadness (91 年)

safety (92, 99 年)

sake (96 年)

salary (93, 98 年)

sales (96, 97 年)

salesperson (93 年)

salt (99 年)

salvation (91 年)

same (100 年)

San Francisco (91 年)

sanitation (97 年)

SARS (92 年)

satellite (99 年)

satisfaction (96 年)

satisfied (96 年)

satisfying (95 年)

save (94, 95, 98, 100 年)

scale (95 年)

scam (93 年)

scan (93, 95 年)

scandal (92, 95 年)

scarce (91, 94, 97, 99 年)

scarcely (95 年)

scare (94, 98 年)

scared (94 年)

scatter (94, 98 年)

scene (99 年)

scenery (93, 94 年)

schedule (91, 92, 99 年)

scheme (91, 96 年)

scholar (99 年)

schoolchildren (97 年)

schoolteacher (97 年)

science (92, 93, 96, 98, 100 年)

scientist (91, 93, 95, 96, 98, 99, 100 年)

scissors (92 年)

score (94 年)

scorn (95 年)

Scotland (96 年)

scream (94 年)

screen (92, 96 年)

screwdriver (92 年)

sculpted (99 年)

sculptor (99 年)

sculpture (94, 99 年)

sealed (96 年)

search (93, 99, 100 年)

searchlight (96 年)

season (92, 97 年)

seat (94 年)

seaweed (94, 95 年)

second (94, 95, 97, 100 年)

second-largest (99 年)

secondly (91 年)

secret (93, 94, 98, 100 年)

section (93 年)

secure (97 年)

security (92, 97, 98, 100 年)

seed (91年)

seek (91, 92, 94, 97年)

seem (91, 92, 93, 94, 96, 98年)

seemingly (99年)

see-through (92年)

select (92年)

self (97年)

self-esteem (98年)

send (95, 100年)

senior (91, 98年)

sense (91, 92, 93, 100年)

sensible (92年)

sensitive (100年)

sensitivity (100年)

sensual (99年)

sentence (91, 94年)

sentiment (98年)

sentimental (93年)

separate (93, 95年)

sequel (92年)

series (99年)

serious (91, 93, 96, 98, 100年)

seriously (91, 92, 96年)

serve (97, 98, 99年)

service (95, 98, 100年)

set (92, 94, 96, 97年)

setting (98年)

settle (93, 98年)

settler (95年)

several (92, 93, 96, 100年)

severe (91年)

severely (94, 99年)

shade (92年)

shadowy (91年)

shake (91, 92年)

Shakespeare (95年)

shall (93年)

shame (91年)

shape (93, 94, 95, 96年)

share (97, 98, 100年)

sharing (98年)

sharp (95年)

shave (98年)

sheet (93年)

shelf (95, 96年)

shelf-mate (95年)

shelter (91年)

shiny (94年)

shipment (97年)

shipper (96年)

shiver (91年)

shock (95, 98年)

shockingly (98年)

shop (98年)

shopkeeper (96年)

shopper (96年)

shopping (98年)

shopping center (97年)

shortage (91, 97, 99年)

short-cut (98年)

shortcut (99年)

short-haul (92年)

shortly (100年)

shoulder (94年)

show (92, 93, 94, 98, 100年)

shrine (100年)

shrinking (96年)

shuffle (94年)

shut (91年)

shy (98年)

side (94年)

sidewalk cafés (97年)

Sierra Leone (96年)

sight (93年)

sign (91, 96, 99年)

signal (92, 95年)

significance (97, 98年)

significant (96, 98年)

significantly (99年)

silence (98年)

silent (95, 98年)

silently (91年)

silk (100年)

silver (94年)

silvery (94年)

similar (91, 92, 94, 97, 98, 100年)

similarly (98, 100年)

simple (96, 98年)

simply (95年)

simultaneously (93, 97年)

since (100年)

singer (93年)

single (94, 98, 99年)

site (92, 93, 98, 100年)

situated (94, 96年)

situation (91, 97, 98年)

size (100年)

skeptical (99年)

sketchbook (91年)

skill (95, 96, 97, 99, 100年)

skilled (91年)

skin (91, 95年)

skinny (97年)

skyscraper (94年)

slang (99年)

slap (91年)

slight (100年)

slightly (96年)

slip (92, 93, 98年)

sloppy (99年)

smart (97, 98年)

smell (99, 100年)

smile-shaped (96年)

smoothly (98年)

smooth-shelled (98年)

smuggle (96年)

snail (91年)

snake (99年)

snooze (92年)

snowstorm (97年)

soak (93年)

soccer (97年)

sociable (99年)

social (91, 92, 95, 96, 100年)

socially (93, 97年)

society (91, 95, 97, 98, 100年)

sociologist (95年)

software (91, 94, 96, 100年)

solar (99, 100年)

solely (94, 97年)

solid (91年)

solution (91, 93, 94年)

solve (91, 92, 99年)

Somalia (97年)

Somalis (97年)

some (98年)

someday (95年)

somehow (95, 99年)

sometime (95年)

sometimes (91, 92, 96, 97, 100年)

somewhat (92年)

somewhere (95年)

sonogram (95年)

sophisticated (100年)

sorrow (97, 98年)

sorrowful (91年)

sort (93年)

sound (93年)

source (92, 93, 96, 98, 99年)

south (91, 95, 96年)

South African (96年)

southeast (99年)

Southeast Asian (94年)

Southeastern Asia (97年)

southern (94, 96年)

southwest (94, 95年)

souvenir (92年)

spa (93年)

space (91, 92, 95, 99年)

space shuttle (94年)

spaceship (95年)

spacing (94年)

Spain (98年)

span (95年)

Spanish (91, 98年)

sparrow (94年)

speaker (94年)

special (96, 98, 99年)

species (93, 96年)

specific (91, 100年)

specifically (92, 99年)

specimens (100年)

spectacle (96年)

spectacular (94年)

spectator (97年)

speculate (95年)

speech (91, 94, 95, 97, 98年)

speed (100年)

spelling (99年)

spider (92, 95, 100年)

spiral (100年)

spirit (93年)

spiritual (95年)

spite (94, 98年)

splendidly (100年)

split (97年)

spoiled (92年)

spoken (93年)

sponsor (91, 96年)

sport (100年)

sports (91, 97, 98年)

sports events (97年)

spotlight (99年)

spread (95, 96年)

sprinkle (94, 98年)

spy (98年)

square (93, 95年)

squeeze (93, 94年)

stability (95年)

stabilize (94年)

stack (93年)

stadium (97年)

staff (100年)

stage (93, 97年)

stair (92年)

stamina (95年)

stamp (93年)

standard (91, 92, 99年)

standardized (94年)

starring (96年)

start (98年)

starve (97年)

starving (97年)

state (91, 93, 94, 97, 98年)

statement (91, 93, 95, 97, 99, 100年)

state-of-the-art (95年)

statistical (97年)

statistics (96, 100年)

statue (94, 99年)

status (98, 100年)

stay (96, 100年)

stealth (95年)

steel (92, 96年)

steel-and-glass (94年)

steep (99年)

stem (96年)

step (91, 92, 93年)

stereotype (97年)

stereotyped (98年)

stern (91年)

sticky (100年)

stiff (100年)

still (93, 100 年)
stimulating (97 年)
stock (96, 99 年)
storage (95 年)
store (100 年)
story (94 年)
storyteller (100 年)
straight (92, 95, 98 年)
strain (96 年)
strait (94 年)
stranger (91 年)
strategy (94, 97 年)
streetcar (91 年)
strength (92, 97, 98, 100 年)
stress (96, 98, 99 年)
stressful (100 年)
stretch (98, 100 年)
strictly (97 年)
stride (94 年)
string (99 年)
strip (96 年)
strive (97 年)
strong (100 年)
strongly (91, 99 年)
struck (95 年)
structural (100 年)
structually (100 年)
structure (91, 94 年)
struggle (93 年)
struggling (92 年)
student (100 年)
student learner (98 年)
studies (95, 96, 97 年)
study (94, 96, 97, 98, 99, 100 年)
stuffy (91 年)
stumble (97 年)
style (93, 95 年)
subconscious (97 年)
subject (94, 98 年)

subject matter (93 年)
subjectively (95 年)
submit (95 年)
subscription (94, 99 年)
subsequent (100 年)
subsistence (96 年)
substance (97, 99 年)
substitute (93, 94, 98 年)
subtropical (96 年)
succeed (92, 94, 97 年)
success (94 年)
successful (94, 98, 100 年)
suddenly (94, 96 年)
such (97, 100 年)
sue (93, 98 年)
suffer (91, 96, 97, 98, 99, 100 年)
suffering (96 年)
sufficient (91 年)
sugar (99 年)
suggest (91, 93, 96, 97, 99, 100 年)
suggestion (92, 93 年)
suicide (100 年)
suit (91 年)
suitcase (92 年)
sum (95, 99 年)
summit (99 年)
sun (100 年)
sunlight (99 年)
superb (99 年)
superficially (97 年)
superhuman (98 年)
superior (99 年)
supermarket (96 年)
supplement (97 年)
supplier (99 年)
supply (91, 94, 96, 99, 100 年)
support (91, 93, 94, 96, 97, 98, 100 年)
supportive (100 年)

supposedly (93 年)
suppression (98 年)
surefire (92 年)
surface (93, 95, 100 年)
surgeon (91 年)
surpass (98, 100 年)
surprise (91, 94 年)
surprised (95 年)
surprising (99 年)
surround (94, 100 年)
survey (92, 98 年)
survive (91, 94, 96 年)
susceptible (93 年)
suspect (96 年)
suspend (97 年)
suspicion (94 年)
swarm (96 年)
sway (96 年)
Sweden (96 年)
sweep (96 年)
swing (91 年)
Switzerland (94 年)
swoon (94 年)
symbol (95, 98, 99 年)
symbolic (98 年)
symbolize (99 年)
sympathetic (96, 98, 100 年)
sympathy (99 年)
symphony (93 年)
symptom (96, 97 年)
system (92, 93, 94, 95, 96, 97, 98, 100 年)
systematically (96 年)

table (95 年)
tactic (98 年)

tactile (99年)

Taiwan (92, 93, 94, 97年)

Taiwanese (92, 93, 97年)

taker (94年)

talent (99年)

tap (94年)

tape (100年)

target (92, 99年)

task (91, 100年)

taste (99年)

tasteless (100年)

tax (94年)

teaching (97年)

team (91, 92, 93, 97, 100年)

teammate (92年)

teamwork (97年)

tear (93年)

tease (91年)

technical (92, 98年)

technique (93, 97年)

technological (94, 97年)

technology (91, 92, 94, 95, 96, 97, 98, 100年)

teenager (97, 98年)

teens (96年)

telegraph (96年)

temper (97年)

temperature (91, 95, 96, 97, 99年)

temple (92, 93, 94年)

temporarily (91, 96, 97年)

temporary (100年)

temptation (99年)

tempting (98年)

tend (94, 95, 98, 99年)

tendency (97, 100年)

tennis (97年)

tensile (100年)

tension (100年)

tentatively (94年)

tepee (91年)

term (98, 99年)

terminal (99年)

terms (96, 98年)

territorial (97年)

territory (97年)

terror (96年)

terrorist (92, 96年)

terrorize (96年)

testify (93, 94年)

text (93年)

text messaging (99年)

textbook (98年)

textese (99年)

texting language (99年)

Thai (92年)

Thailand (92年)

thank-you note (92年)

the Democratic
　Republic of Congo
　(96年)

the first place (96年)

the first prize (97年)

the Netherlands (94年)

the press (96年)

the U.S. (96年)

the United Kingdom
　(98年)

the United States (95, 96年)

theater (92, 96年)

theme (93, 97, 99年)

themselves (100年)

theory (94, 95年)

therefore (91, 92, 93, 95, 96, 97, 99, 100年)

thermometer (95年)

thief (94年)

thin (97年)

thorn (93年)

thoroughly (99, 100年)

though (93, 94, 95, 96, 97, 99年)

thought (93年)

thoughtful (93年)

thoughts (96年)

thousand (95, 98年)

thread (100年)

threat (98年)

threaten (95年)

threatening (96年)

three-fold (91年)

thriller (94年)

through (91, 92, 93, 94, 95, 96, 98, 99年)

throughout (91, 93, 96, 97, 98, 99, 100年)

throw (92, 97年)

thus (92, 93, 96, 97, 98, 99年)

Tibetan (96年)

ties (94年)

tile (93年)

till (100年)

times (95, 96, 98年)

Times Square (97年)

tiny (97年)

tiring (100年)

tissue (100年)

title (94, 97, 98年)

today (97, 98年)

toe (93年)

together (97, 98年)

tolerate (92年)

tongue (93年)

tool (95年)

top (92, 94, 98, 100年)

top floor (94年)

topic (92, 94, 98, 100年)

torment (99年)

torn (93年)

Toronto (94年)

torture (98年)

toss (93年)

total (92年)

totally (96年)

touch (100年)

tough (98年)

tour (99年)

tourism (96年)

tourist (93, 95年)

tournament (93年)

toward (95, 99, 100年)

towards (96, 98年)

tower (93, 94年)

toy (93, 97, 98年)

track (96年)

trade (95, 96, 99年)

trade-off (92年)

traditional (91, 92, 93, 95, 96, 99年)

traditionally (96年)

traffic (91, 92, 98年)

tragedy (100年)

train (97, 100年)

trainer (97年)

training (97年)

traitor (91年)

tranquility (94年)

transaction (94年)

transcript (96年)

transfer (94年)

transform (93, 99, 100年)

transformation (99年)

translate (94, 99年)

transport (92年)

transportation (92, 94年)

trap (91, 95年)

trash (98年)

treat (91, 98年)

treatment (95年)

trek (93年)

tremendously (93年)

trend (93年)

trial (98年)

triangle (93年)

tribe (95年)

trick (91年)

trigger (97年)

trillion (95年)

triumph (91年)

triumphant (100年)

tropical (96年)

trouble (94, 99年)

troubled (91, 99年)

troubling (91年)

try (93, 97, 100年)

tunnel (91年)

turn (93, 96, 97, 98, 100年)

turns (96年)

twice (98, 100年)

twins (95年)

twist (100年)

txt talk (99年)

type (93, 95, 98, 99, 100年)

typical (97年)

typically (92, 96, 97, 100年)

ultimate (94年)

ultrasound (95年)

ultra-thin (97年)

ultraviolet (97年)

unable (91, 98年)

unaware (98年)

unbearable (92年)

unbelievable (91年)

unborn (95年)

unchanged (95年)

uncommon (95年)

unconvincing (99年)

uncook (100年)

undergo (99年)

underground (91, 100年)

underline (98年)

underneath (100年)

underrepresented (98年)

understand (91, 94, 95, 97, 98年)

understanding (91, 93年)

undertake (91, 93年)

undertone (99年)

underwater (94年)

undetermined (95年)

undoubtedly (97年)

undream (92年)

uneasiness (96年)

unemployed (92年)

unexpected (98年)

unfailing (99年)

unfair (98年)

unfit (92年)

unfolded (95年)

unforgettable (92, 94年)

unfortunately (98, 100年)

unimaginable (96年)

uninhabited (94年)

uninterrupted (93年)

unique (93, 94, 98, 99年)

unit (95年)

universal (94年)

universe (97年)

university (91, 92, 93, 97, 98, 99, 100年)

unknowingly (94年)
unknown (94, 100年)
unlawful (96年)
unless (93, 94, 96, 97, 100年)
unlike (96, 99年)
unlikely (92年)
unmistakable (92年)
unpaid (97年)
unplug (92年)
unrelated (99, 100年)
unreliable (95年)
unsearched (100年)
unsolved (95年)
unspoiled (94年)
unspoken (100年)
unstable (97年)
unsuccessful (100年)
untested (92年)
until (95, 97, 100年)
unusual (95, 100年)
unveil (94年)
unwilling (92年)
update (96年)
upper class (97年)
upset (91, 94, 100年)
upward (96年)
urban (100年)
urbanized (92年)
urge (98年)
urgent (91, 95, 96年)
usable (99年)
usage (94年)
useful (92年)
user (92, 100年)
usual (100年)
usually (92, 93, 96, 98, 100年)
Utah (93年)
utensils (98年)

utter (93年)
U-turn (92年)
UV (97年)

 V

vacancy (97年)
vacationer (93年)
vaccine (95年)
vacuum (99年)
vacuum cleaner (98年)
vaguely (100年)
valuable (95, 97年)
value (95, 97, 99年)
van (94, 100年)
vandalism (91年)
vanilla (99年)
variation (95年)
varied (93年)
variety (92, 93, 95, 97, 99年)
various (91, 92, 93, 94, 98, 99年)
vary (93, 97, 100年)
vast (100年)
vastly (98年)
vegetable (97, 99年)
vegetation (100年)
veil (92年)
vendor (100年)
venture (94, 99年)
verb (97年)
verbal (100年)
verbally (91, 98年)
verge (91年)
versatile (97年)
vibrant (93年)
victim (91, 98, 100年)
victimize (99年)

Victoria (91年)
Victorian (91年)
victory (91年)
video (100年)
videotape (97年)
view (91, 93, 94, 95, 97, 98年)
vinegar (93年)
violate (98年)
violation (98年)
violator (96, 98年)
violence (100年)
violent (91年)
virtual (98年)
virtually (94年)
virus (93, 96年)
visible (96年)
vision (91, 93年)
visit (98年)
visitor (95, 98年)
visual (100年)
visualize (94年)
visually (99年)
vital (94年)
vitality (98年)
vivid (93, 100年)
voice (93, 97年)
volume (95年)
volunteer (91, 98年)
vowel (99年)
vulnerable (93年)

 W

wander (91, 92年)
war (96, 97, 100年)
wardrobe (100年)
warehouse (94年)

warfare (96 年)

warm (96, 97 年)

warming (98, 99 年)

warmth (91 年)

warn (99, 100 年)

warrior (95 年)

waste (99, 100 年)

watch (100 年)

watercolor (99 年)

wave (95 年)

way (93, 94, 97, 100 年)

weakness (97 年)

wear (94, 97, 100 年)

weather (91, 92, 99, 100 年)

weatherman (99 年)

weaver (96 年)

web (94, 100 年)

website (98, 99 年)

weekend (94, 99 年)

weekly (93 年)

weight (95, 97 年)

welfare (92)

well (99 年)

well-developed (94 年)

well-paying (94 年)

well-prepared (91 年)

west (95 年)

western (95 年)

Westerner (95 年)

whatever (91, 98 年)

whenever (95 年)

whereas (91 年)

whereby (98 年)

whether (91, 92, 94, 95, 100 年)

whichever (98 年)

while (91, 94, 96, 97, 99 年)

whoever (98 年)

whole (91, 96, 97, 98, 99, 100 年)

wholeheartedly (93 年)

wholly (96 年)

wide (92, 97, 100 年)

widely (93, 94, 95, 97 年)

widespread (93, 98 年)

widow (91 年)

wield (100 年)

wig (98 年)

wild (95 年)

willing (96, 99 年)

win (96, 97, 99, 100 年)

wind (91, 100 年)

winding (100 年)

windshield (91 年)

winner (99 年)

wipe (91 年)

wiper (91 年)

Wisconsin (95 年)

wish (93, 96 年)

wishes (97 年)

witch (95 年)

witchcraft (95 年)

within (93, 94, 95, 97 年)

without (96, 97 年)

wizard (95 年)

wolf (95 年)

wolf-skin (95 年)

wonder (92, 94, 97, 100 年)

wonderful (95 年)

wonderland (91 年)

wood (94 年)

wooden (96, 97 年)

woods (93, 95 年)

work force (96 年)

workaholic (91 年)

worker (96 年)

workforce (98 年)

works (93 年)

workshop (97 年)

world (93, 96, 97, 100 年)

World Wide Web (94 年)

world-famous (94 年)

worldwide (93, 100 年)

worried (94, 99, 100 年)

worst (94, 99, 100 年)

worth (95, 97, 100 年)

wound (100 年)

wrap (95 年)

wrapper (95 年)

wreck (99 年)

writer (95, 97, 98 年)

writing (91 年)

written (92 年)

year round (97 年)

year-long (99 年)

yearly (95 年)

Yellowstone (95 年)

yet (91, 92, 94, 96, 97, 99 年)

young (100 年)

youngster (92, 99 年)

youth (98 年)

youthful (92 年)

Zaire (97 年)

zap (95 年)

zero (91, 92 年)

zone (96 年)

zoologist (94 年)

★ 電腦統計歷屆指定科目考試成語 ★

19 years of age (94年)

a bit (97, 98年)

a body of (94年)

a couple of (94年)

a drop in the bucket
　(91年)

a flight of stairs (92年)

a great deal of (91年)

a great many (93年)

a lack of (95年)

a leap in the dark (93年)

a letter of complaint
　(92年)

a lot of (93, 97, 98年)

a penny for your
　thoughts (93年)

a pile of (91年)

a precautionary measure
　(92年)

a round of (99年)

a sense of duty (91年)

a slip of the tongue (93年)

a string of (99年)

a thank-you note (92年)

a thorn in my side (93年)

a variety of (92, 93, 99年)

a wide variety of (99年)

a work of art (95年)

above all (97年)

accept A as B (100年)

according to (91, 92, 93, 94,
　96, 98, 99年)

account for (96年)

achieve a goal (92年)

across the world (92年)

adapt to (96, 98年)

adjust to (97年)

after a while (97年)

after all (95年)

agree with (91, 92年)

aim to V. (98年)

all over (98年)

all over the world (91, 93,
　97年)

all the time (92, 95年)

all walks of life (98年)

along with (93年)

an old proverb says,
　(91年)

and so on (97年)

anorexia nervosa (97年)

apart from (98年)

a poker face (100年)

apologize for (97年)

appear to V. (93年)

apply for (93年)

apply to (97年)

arise from (99年)

around the globe (98年)

around the turn of the
　20th century (97年)

around the world (97年)

arouse *one's* suspicion
　(94年)

arrive at (91, 97年)

arrive in (96年)

as a child (96年)

as a consequence (95年)

as a matter of fact (95年)

as a part of (96年)

as a person (98年)

as a result (92, 93, 94, 98, 99年)

as a result of (91年)

as it is often called (91年)

as it turns out (96年)

as long ago as… (98年)

as long as (97年)

as many as (98年)

as much as (95年)

as soon as (93年)

as to (96年)

as usual (100年)

as well (93, 97年)

as well as (92, 93, 96, 99年)

as yet (97年)

as…as (91, 93, 97, 98年)

as…as possible (99年)

ask for (98年)

at a cost of (93年)

at a rate of (95年)

at all levels (97年)

at all times (96, 99年)

at an early age (98年)

at dawn (92年)

at eye level (96年)

at fault (100年)

at first (97年)

at least (92, 94, 96, 98年)

at most (97年)

at once (96年)

at one time (96年)

at *one's* best (96年)

at other times (96年)

at risk (91年)

at that time (91, 94年)

at the end of (92年)

at the expense of (100年)

at the request of (93年)

at the same rate (98年)

at the same time (96, 98, 100年)

at the time (97年)

at the time of (98年)

at this moment (91年)

at times (96年)

at will (93年)

at work (98年)

attempt to V. (97年)

avian flu (95年)

avian influenza (93年)

avoid + V-ing (94, 95年)

away from (91, 94, 98年)

baby boomer (96年)

back out of (92年)

back to back (93年)

based on (96年)

based upon (91年)

be a last resort (96年)

be able to V. (95, 96, 98年)

be about to V. (92, 94, 96年)

be accused of (95年)

be addicted to (96, 98年)

be admitted to (93年)

be afraid of (98年)

be against (98年)

be aghast over (95年)

be aimed at (99年)

be allergic to (98年)

be allowed to V. (98年)

be ashamed of (98年)

be associated with (94年)

be attached to (91年)

be available to (96年)

be aware of (98年)

be away from (94年)

be back on the agenda (92年)

be based on (96年)

be born to (96年)

be born with (99年)

be bound by (94年)

be busy V-ing (91, 98年)

be capable of (97年)

be classified as (94年)

be classified into (94年)

be close to (91年)

be closely related to (99年)

be compatible with (97年)

be connected to (91, 97年)

be connected with (95年)

be considered as (97年)

be covered with (99年)

be crowded with (92年)

be cut into (95, 97年)

be deeply in love (91年)

be dependent on (96年)

be derived from (93年)

be described as (96, 98年)

be designated as (94年)

be destined for (97年)

be diagnosed with (96年)

be different from (91, 96, 97年)

be dressed in black (91年)

be eager to V. (93年)

be edged in black (91年)

be endowed with (94年)

be enthusiastic about (93年)

be envious of (92年)

be equipped with (93, 99年)

be excellent at (91年)

be expected to V. (95, 96年)

be faced with (94年)

be faithful to (96年)

be familiar to (95年)

be familiar with (91年)

be famous for (94年)

be filled with (93年)

be focused on (95年)

be fond of (96, 99年)

be forced to V. (92, 98, 99年)

be free of (98年)

be full of (91, 97年)

be furious with (98年)

be going to V. (94, 98年)

be good at (95, 96年)

be guilty of (99年)

be haunted with (91年)

be home to (96, 97年)

be impressed by (94年)

be in the process of V-ing (98年)

be inferior to (97年)

be inferred from (95, 98年)

be interested in (91, 92, 93, 94, 95, 98 年)

be intoxicated with (95, 97年)

be introduced to (100年)

be involved in (91, 92, 95 年)

be jammed on (92年)

be just the same (97年)

be kept a secret (94年)

be kept in good condition (94年)

be known as (91, 95, 96, 99 年)

be left homeless (91 年)

be likely to V. (95, 98年)

be loaded with (93年)

be located (93年)

be lots of fun (98年)

be made into (92年)

be made of (91, 92 年)

be native to (99年)

be of high quality (96年)

be perceived as (96年)

be pleased with (95年)

be popular with (96年)

be praised as (99年)

be prompted to V. (98年)

be protective of (92年)

be proud of (97年)

be put in jail (91 年)

be put in place (92年)

be put on the market (93年)

be qualified for (94年)

be referred to as (98年)

be related to (92, 94, 97, 98, 99年)

be replaced with (94年)

be reported to V. (99年)

be required by (98年)

be required to V. (93, 96, 97, 98年)

be responsible for (97年)

be rich in (92, 99年)

be rooming with (98年)

be said to V. (92年)

be scared of (94年)

be scattered in (94年)

be set out to V. (95年)

be set to (96年)

be similar to (94年)

be situated in (94年)

be split apart (97年)

be sprinkled with (98年)

be struck by (95年)

be subject to (98年)

be subjected to (94年)

be substituted for (98 年)

be sure of (91 年)

be sure to V. (96年)

be surrounded by (94年)

be susceptible to (93年)

be suspected of (96年)

be taken for granted (94年)

be taken from (92, 95年)

be targeted at (99年)

be the same as (95年)

be thrown together (97年)

be to V. (95, 97年)

be transformed into (93年)

be translated as (99年)

be true about (97年)

be true of (94年)

be twice as likely to V. (98 年)

be unable to V. (91, 98 年)

be undreamed of (92年)

be unwilling to V. (92年)

be vulnerable to (93年)

be well know for (100年)

be willing to V. (96, 99年)

be worried about (92年)

be worth + V-ing (95, 97年)

beat *sb.* home (92年)

because of (92, 94, 95, 96, 98, 99年)

before long (99年)

begin with (94年)

believe in (95年)

beyond hope of (96年)

beyond recognition (96年)

bid farewell to (97年)

bill *oneself* as (95年)

bird flu (93年)

Birth Control (95年)

birth order (94年)

blurt out (96年)

boil down (93年)

both A and B (97年)

break even (91 年)

break into (98年)

break *one's* neck (92年)

break out (98 年)

break the law (91 年)

break up (97年)

bring down (92年)

bring together (91年)

brush painting (93年)

build up (95年)

by all means (91年)

by and large (96, 100年)

by birth (93年)

by contrast (95年)

by no means (93, 98年)

by now (99年)

by that time (96年)

by the end of (97, 99年)

by the time (96年)

by the way (97年)

call for (97年)

call on (92年)

call the police (92年)

cannot get anywhere (97年)

carry out (94年)

carve A into B (97年)

catch *one's* attention (92, 94年)

catch *one's* breath (92年)

catch up (100年)

cater to (92年)

cell phone (92年)

chain reaction (100年)

change into (91年)

child abuse (97年)

churn out (100年)

classified ads (93年)

cling to (95年)

close to (97年)

combine A with B (93, 98年)

come about (92年)

come across (94年)

come down with (92年)

come first (97年)

come from (97, 98年)

come in (97, 100年)

come near (91年)

come out (99年)

come to (98年)

come to realize (97年)

come up (91年)

come up to (94年)

commit suicide (100年)

compare A with B (93年)

compared to (94年)

compared with (95年)

compete with (95年)

complain about (95年)

concentration camp (91年)

conform to (96, 97年)

congratulate *sb.* on *sth.* (94年)

consider A (to be) B (92, 95年)

consist of (94, 100年)

construction company (94年)

contribute to (98年)

convert A into B (96年)

cope with (96, 98年)

copyright law (91年)

correspond to (97年)

count on (96年)

cut off (98年)

cut *one's* hair short (98年)

daily life (91年)

date back to (95年)

deal with (91, 96, 98年)

decide on (92年)

dense population (92年)

depend on (98, 99年)

detour from (94年)

develop into (93年)

devote *one's* life to V-ing (94年)

devote *one's* time to V-ing (91年)

devote *one's* whole self to (97年)

devote *oneself* to (96年)

die hard (95年)

die of (98年)

differentiate A from B (95年)

differentiate between A and B (93年)

dinner party (97年)

discourage *sb.* from V-ing (92年)

distinguish between A and B (95年)

distinguish from (94年)

do everything *one* can (92年)

do good deeds (98年)

do harm to (91年)

don't ever (94年)

double check (95年)

drag *oneself* to (92年)

drive *sb.* into bankruptcy (92年)

due to (91, 95, 96, 98, 99 年)

earn a fortune (96年)

either A or B (94, 98年)

emergency control
　measures (93年)

en route (92年)

enable *sb.* to V. (98年)

end in (95年)

end up (94, 96年)

enjoy V-ing (91 年)

equip *sb.* with (95年)

establish *oneself* as (93年)

even if (97年)

even though (91, 94 年)

everyday life (94年)

evolve into (93年)

except for (94年)

expose *sb.* to (98年)

eye to eye (93年)

fails to V. (91 年)

fall apart (92年)

fall ill (91 年)

fall out of favor (97年)

far from (91, 95 年)

fare well (100年)

feel like V-ing (95年)

fight for (95年)

fight over (99 年)

figure out (91, 96 年)

file a complaint against
　(92年)

files lawsuits against
　(98年)

fill A with B (96年)

fill in the gap (98年)

fill out (92年)

find out (91, 92, 93 年)

fire up (93年)

fiscal year (94年)

fit into (92, 97年)

fit *one's* needs (96年)

fix up (99年)

flood into (94年)

focus on (95, 96, 97, 98, 99年)

follow in the path of
　(93年)

follow instructions (93年)

follow *one's* heart (96年)

follow *one's* profession
　(96年)

for a moment (94年)

for a second (94年)

for example (91, 92, 93, 94,
　97, 98, 99, 100 年)

for good (92年)

for instance (92, 94, 95, 96,
　99年)

for one thing (91 年)

for *one's* sake (96年)

for some reason (98年)

for sure (94年)

for the first time (99年)

for the most part (94年)

for the rest of *one's* life
　(91 年)

for this purpose (98年)

for years (92年)

forgive and forget (91 年)

free of (96年)

fresh water (91 年)

from around the world
　(97年)

from its very beginning
　(95年)

from the air (95年)

from then on (94年)

function as (97年)

gain ground (100年)

gain popularity (98年)

gain world fame (94年)

gateway drug (97年)

gear up (100年)

get in on (93年)

get lost (92年)

get on (94年)

get out of (91 年)

get over (91, 97 年)

get prepared for (95年)

get rid of (92年)

get *sth.* off to a
　flourishing start (94年)

get well-prepared for
　(91 年)

give away (95, 96, 99年)

give back to (91年)

give in (92, 94年)

give in to (91 年)

give no consideration to
　(97年)

give off (92, 100年)

glance at (94, 95年)

go after (95年)

go away (96年)

go back (100年)

go back on *one's* own
　word (96年)

go bankrupt (96年)

go for a walk (91 年)

go forward (92年)

go off (92年)

go on (91, 96年)

go online (92年)

go over (94年)

go quiet (94年)

go through (91年)

go to college (98年)

go to university (97年)

go up (96年)

go up on (94年)

Great Britain (91, 96年)

grow long hair (98年)

grow to (97年)

grow up (92, 96, 97, 98年)

habitual drinker (97年)

had better (91年)

had *sb.* on the edge of
   sb.'s seats (94年)

hail a taxi (94年)

hand out (99年)

hand to mouth (93年)

hang from the sky (96年)

happen to (91, 97, 98年)

hardly ever (91年)

have a great many (92年)

have a laugh (95年)

have a lot to offer (99年)

have an effect on (94年)

have an impact on (94年)

have confidence in (91,
   97年)

have difficulty (in) +
   V-ing (96年)

have got to V. (91年)

have interest (99年)

have museum feet (95年)

have no idea (91, 98年)

have problems (in)
   + V-ing (97, 99年)

have to V. (94年)

have trouble V-ing (99年)

have…in common (95年)

head to toe (93年)

heavy traffic (92年)

here and now (96年)

here and there (96年)

historic sites (92年)

hit hard (94年)

hold out (98年)

hold the door open (96年)

hundreds of (91, 92, 98, 99年)

I.Q. test (94年)

identify with (93年)

if any (95年)

if ever (95年)

if not (95年)

if only (95, 96年)

in + V-ing (93, 94年)

in a second (95年)

in a…way (94, 95, 97年)

in accordance with (96年)

in action (92年)

in addition (92, 94, 98, 99年)

in addition to (94年)

in advance (95, 97年)

in all (95年)

in an effort to V. (99年)

in case (98年)

in case of (98年)

in comparison (99年)

in contrast (99年)

in contrast to (91年)

in control of (96年)

in decline (100年)

in early childhood (96年)

in either case (91年)

in essence (93年)

in fact (91, 95, 99年)

in favor of (91年)

in front of (91, 98年)

in large part (95年)

in memory of (93, 99年)

in *one's* case, (93年)

in order (98年)

in order to V. (91, 93, 96, 97,
   98年)

in other words (97年)

in peace (97年)

in place (93, 94, 100年)

in place of (100年)

in recent years (94年)

in regard to (93年)

in response to (99年)

in return (98年)

in search of (93年)

in short (95, 97年)

in silence (98年)

in some cases (100年)

in spite of (92, 94, 96, 98年)

in sum (95年)

in tears (100年)

in terms of (96, 98年)

in that (92年)

in the 1960s (98年)

in the dark (92年)

in the event of (91年)

in the future (94年)

in the late 1990s　(93年)

in the least　(96, 97年)

in the light of　(91年)

in the presence of　(100年)

in the shape of　(94, 96年)

in the world　(91, 92, 93, 94,
96, 97年)

in theory　(95年)

in this regard　(100年)

in this sense　(100年)

in this way　(99年)

in those days　(91年)

in town　(98年)

in turn　(95年)

inform *sb.* about *sth.*
(99年)

instead of　(91, 92, 96, 98年)

interact with　(97年)

invade *one's* privacy
(92年)

it is not until…that
(91年)

it is reported that　(95年)

it is…that　(91, 96年)

just as　(97年)

keep a pet　(92年)

keep *one's* eyes and
minds sharp　(95年)

keep *one's* head off
(99年)

keep pace　(91年)

keep *sth.* confidential
(96年)

keep *sth.* from V-*ing*
(96年)

keep up with　(92年)

kept a secret to *oneself*
(98年)

kick off　(93年)

knock off　(99年)

knock *sth.* over　(94年)

known as　(97年)

landscape painting　(93年)

large sums of　(99年)

laugh out loud　(99年)

lead *sb.* to V.　(96, 97, 99年)

lead to　(92, 95, 98, 100年)

learn about　(96年)

learn from　(98年)

leave *sb.* …　(91年)

leave *sth.* behind　(93年)

lend a hand to　(98年)

less than　(91, 92年)

link A to B　(98年)

listen to　(97, 99年)

live in　(92年)

live with　(97年)

lobby for　(95年)

look after　(92年)

look at　(91, 95, 99年)

look for　(93年)

look like　(96年)

look up　(94年)

lose control of　(94年)

lose *one's* face　(91年)

lose weight　(97年)

lots of　(99年)

make a commitment
(96年)

make a complaint
against *sb.*　(92年)

make a living　(96年)

make a move　(99年)

make accommodations
(96年)

make an impact on　(94年)

make arrangements
(91年)

make changes　(96年)

make contact with　(93年)

make for　(95年)

make friends　(98年)

make investments in
(96年)

make laws　(95年)

make money　(96, 98年)

make no secret of　(93年)

make *one's* diagnosis
(97年)

make *one's* way　(92年)

make progress　(91, 94年)

make *sth.* accessible to
sb.　(92年)

make sure　(92, 95年)

make up　(91, 96, 98年)

make up for　(98年)

make use of　(92年)

make U-turns　(92年)

manage to + V.　(100年)

meet a demand　(98年)

meet the needs of　(94年)

millions of　(98年)

mix A with B　(93年)

more and more　(96年)

more than　(91, 92, 93, 94, 95,
97, 98年)

most important of all
(91年)

Mother Nature (94年)
MRT station (97年)
much later than (93年)
much to *one's* surprise
(91年)
national park (95年)
need to V. (96年)
neither A nor B (94年)
nervous breakdown
(91年)
nervous system (97年)
newspaper report (92年)
next to (93年)
no better than (95年)
no later than (93年)
no less than (95年)
no longer (95, 97年)
no more than (95年)
no sooner than (95年)
not always (91年)
not only...but (also)
(91, 93, 94, 97, 98, 99年)
not to mention (92年)
not...until (91, 96, 99年)
nothing about (93年)
now that (91, 92, 96, 97, 98年)
of course (91年)
of the time (97年)
of this kind (94年)
offer *sth.* for *sb.* (98年)
off guard (98, 100年)
on a charge of (91年)
on a daily basis (99年)
on a one-month sick
leave (94年)
on a trip (91年)

on account of (93年)
on average (96, 97, 98年)
on behalf of (91年)
on board (92年)
on call (93, 100年)
on display (95年)
on one side (94年)
on *one's* own (92年)
on paper (94年)
on the basis of (95年)
on the contrary (93, 97年)
on the Internet (95, 96, 99年)
on the other hand (91, 96, 97, 98, 99年)
on the other side (94年)
on the outskirts (93年)
on the verge of (91年)
on the whole (96, 100年)
on thin ice (92年)
on top of (100年)
on various grounds (94年)
On V-ing (92年)
one time (92年)
open fire (91年)
or so (94, 97年)
originate in (96年)
other than (93年)
out of (95年)
out of order (92年)
out of the blue (94年)
out there (95年)
over a period of (95年)
over and over (100年)
over the Internet (98年)
owing to (94年)
participate in (98年)

pass a law (96年)
pass by (96年)
pass on (94年)
pay attention to (91, 96, 98年)
pay for (91, 92年)
pay off (92年)
pay the price (91年)
pick on (92年)
pick up (95, 97, 98年)
plan on (97年)
play a role (95年)
play an important part (97, 98年)
play sports (96年)
play the role of (97年)
play with (97年)
plenty of (94, 99年)
plow on (94年)
plunge into (94年)
point out (92年)
pop music (91年)
pop up (91年)
prefer A to B (99年)
preventive measures (93年)
primary school (92年)
print out (91, 95年)
prior to (92, 97年)
proceed to (92年)
proceed with (93年)
profit from (98年)
protect *sb.* from V-ing (92年)
protect...from (97年)
prove to be (92, 95, 97年)

provide *sb.* with *sth.*
(91, 96, 98 年)

provide *sth.* for *sth.* (98年)

public opinion (93年)

pull into (92年)

push *sb.* to the limit
(97年)

pushing forward (99年)

put down (94年)

put on a play (98年)

put *sb.* at risk of (97年)

put *sb.* on the phone
(92年)

put *sth.* into practice
(92年)

put together (97年)

put up with (92年)

rage on (95年)

raise money (98年)

randomly select (92年)

range from A to B (93年)

rather than (91, 92, 93, 99 年)

rattle on about (95年)

react to (95年)

recognize A as B (93年)

refer to (91, 92, 93, 95, 97, 99,
100 年)

reflect back (97年)

reflect on (97年)

regard A as B (95年)

regardless of (91, 94 年)

relate to (96, 97年)

rely on (93, 96年)

remind *sb.* of *sth.* (92年)

research paper (92年)

resort to (94年)

respond to (93年)

result from (96, 98年)

result in (92, 93, 96, 97, 99年)

rob *sb.* of *sth.* (98 年)

run dry (99年)

run out (99年)

run over (99 年)

save *sb.* from (91 年)

save the best for last
(94年)

scare the living
daylights out of *sb.*
(94年)

science journal (93年)

search for (93, 99年)

security measures (92年)

see the light (of day)
(100年)

seem to V. (91, 93, 94, 96, 98 年)

sells for (99年)

sense of direction (92年)

sense of sight (93年)

sense of smell (100年)

sentence *sb.* to... (91 年)

serve as (97年)

serve to V. (99年)

set foot in (92年)

set out (94年)

set out to V. (96年)

set up (97年)

settle on (93年)

shaking hands with (92年)

share with *sb.* (98年)

shave *one's* head (98年)

shop for (95, 96年)

shopping center (97年)

shortly after (100年)

shout at (92年)

show off (98年)

show *sb.* the way to
(91 年)

show up (96年)

since ancient times (98年)

since childhood (97年)

since then (94年)

single out (94年)

sit still (96年)

situated between A and
B (96年)

slip *one's* mind (92年)

slip out of (98年)

snail mail (91 年)

so as to V. (98年)

so far (94, 100年)

so that (93, 94, 96, 97年)

so...that (91, 94, 99 年)

Southeastern Asia (97年)

space shuttle (94年)

speak to *one's* needs
(95年)

speed up (100年)

split A into B (97年)

sports gathering (97年)

sports season (97年)

spy for (98年)

squeeze out (93年)

stack up (93年)

stand for (96年)

stand up (94年)

standard practice (92年)

start off (96年)

state of mind (97年)

stem from (96年)

stock up on (99年)

straight after (92年)

strictly controlled (97年)

strive to V. (97年)

stumble on (97年)

subject matter (93年)

substitute for (94年)

succeed in (92年)

such as (91, 93, 95, 96, 97, 98, 99年)

suffer from (97, 98年)

sweep the world (96年)

swoon over (94年)

take a job (96年)

take a step (92年)

take a test (94年)

take a trip (91年)

take a walk (92年)

take action (91, 92, 98年)

take an exam (92年)

take away (99年)

take care (95年)

take care of (92, 97, 98年)

take chance (91年)

take drugs (97年)

take in (92年)

take notice of (91年)

take off (94年)

take over (94, 100年)

take part in (91, 98年)

take place (95, 96年)

take precedence over (95年)

take pride in (91年)

take *sb.* by surprise (94年)

take steps to V. (91年)

take *sth.* for example (93年)

take *sth.* one step beyond (93年)

take the initiative (95年)

take time (95年)

take turns (96年)

take turns V-ing (98年)

taken measures (92年)

takes the initiative (91年)

talk about (94年)

talk with (98年)

tap *sb.* on the shoulder (94年)

tell time (93年)

tend to V. (94, 95, 98, 99年)

terrorist attack (92年)

test taker (94年)

thank *sb.* for *sth.* (91年)

that is (96年)

the aurora borealis (96年)

the Dutch (94年)

the first prize (97年)

the industrial revolution (96年)

the Internet (94年)

the key to (94年)

The more...the higher (98年)

The more...the more (94年)

the Nazca lines (95年)

the Netherlands (94年)

the next day (92年)

the next time (96年)

the press (96年)

the public (95, 100年)

the same as (98年)

the United States (95年)

the unknown (100年)

the upper class (97年)

the USA (93年)

the World Wide Web (94年)

there was a time when... (98年)

these days (93年)

think about (95年)

think of (93年)

think of A as B (91年)

think otherwise (91年)

thousands of (94, 95, 97, 98年)

three meals a day (91年)

throughout history (97, 98, 99, 100年)

throughout *one's* life (96年)

throughout the world (91, 93, 99年)

throw off (92年)

throw *sth.* together (97年)

to a point (98年)

to and fro (96年)

to and from (95年)

to be frank (100年)

to begin with (99年)

to name just a few (98年)

to this day (98年)

too...to V. (91, 94年)

took *one's* advice (92年)

toss out (93年)

trade in A for B (99年)

transform A into B (99年)

transportation system
　(94年)

travel brochure (92年)

travel insurance to
　visitors (92年)

try not to V. (95年)

try *one's* best (97年)

try to V. (91, 92, 93, 95, 96, 97, 98年)

turn a deaf ear to (91年)

turn A into B (94, 97, 99年)

turn down (94, 95年)

turn in (94年)

turn left (92年)

turn *one's* attention to
　(96年)

turn over a new leaf
　(91年)

turn *sb.* away (100年)

turn to (92, 98年)

turn to V. (97年)

ultraviolet (UV) light
　(97年)

under construction (94年)

under discussion (92年)

under the guidance of
　(97年)

urban center (100年)

up and down (96年)

up to (94, 95, 97, 99年)

up to date (94年)

up until (95年)

use up (92年)

vary from A to B (97年)

vary in (97年)

vary with (93年)

venture into (94年)

violate the law (98 年)

visual literacy (100年)

wait for (91, 95 年)

walk in (91 年)

walk over to (91 年)

walk through (92年)

wander about (91 年)

wander through (92年)

watch *one's* back (92年)

wear a new face (91 年)

wear *one's* hair long
　(98年)wear…hair (98年)

what's more (95, 96, 99年)

when it comes to (94年)

When it is time to V.
　(98 年)

whether A or B (91 年)

whether or not (94年)

whether…or not (95年)

while + V-ing (94年)

win the first place (96年)

wipe off (91 年)

wish to V. (92年)

with a view to (93年)

with care (92年)

with precision (92年)

with reference to (98年)

with the exception of
　(96年)

with the help of (96, 100年)

with the intention of
　V-ing (98年)

with top honors (92年)

within walking distance
　(97年)

without a doubt (92年)

work as (96, 98年)

work better (92年)

work for (94年)

work force (96年)

work hard (91, 94, 97 年)

work on (93, 97年)

work *one's* way up (93年)

work together (98年)

work with (94, 98年)

work with *sb.* (92年)

would like to V. (98年)

would rather V. (98年)

write about (95年)

write down (92年)

year round (97年)

years from now (95年)

years to come (94年)

zap a message (95年)

歷屆指考英文科試題詳解

主　　　編／劉　毅

發　行　所／學習出版有限公司　　☎ (02) 2704-5525

郵　撥帳　號／0512727-2　學習出版社帳戶

登　記　證／局版台業 2179 號

印　刷　所／裕強彩色印刷有限公司

台　北門　市／台北市許昌街 10 號 2 F　　☎ (02) 2331-4060

台灣總經銷／紅螞蟻圖書有限公司　　☎ (02) 2795-3656

美國總經銷／Evergreen Book Store　　☎ (818) 2813622

本公司網址　www.learnbook.com.tw

電　子郵　件　learnbook@learnbook.com.tw

售價：新台幣三百八十元正

2012 年 4 月 1 日初版